ELITE STUDENT EDITION

5 STEPS TO A 5

AP Calculus BC

2024

ELITE STUDENT EDITION

5 STEPS TO A 5

AP Calculus BC

2024

William Ma
Emily Pillar

Parts of Review Chapters by Carolyn Wheater

New York Chicago San Francisco Athens London Madrid
Mexico City Milan New Delhi Singapore Sydney Toronto

1 2 3 4 5 6 7 8 9   LHS   27 26 25 24 23
1 2 3 4 5 6 7 8 9   LHS   27 26 25 24 23   (Elite Student Edition)

ISBN   978-1-265-33978-4
MHID   1-265-33978-3

e-ISBN   978-1-265-34139-8
e-MHID   1-265-34139-7

ISBN   978-1-265-34183-1 (Elite Student Edition)
MHID   1-265-34183-4

e-ISBN   978-1-265-34357-6 (Elite Student Edition)
e-MHID   1-265-34357-8

McGraw Hill, the McGraw Hill logo, *5 Steps to a 5*, and related trade dress are trademarks or registered trademarks of McGraw Hill and/or its affiliates in the United States and other countries and may not be used without written permission. All other trademarks are the property of their respective owners. McGraw Hill is not associated with any product or vendor mentioned in this book.

AP, *Advanced Placement Program*, and *College Board* are registered trademarks of the College Board, which was not involved in the production of, and does not endorse, this product.

The series editor was Grace Freedson, and the project editor was Del Franz. Series design by Jane Tenenbaum.

McGraw Hill products are available at special quantity discounts to use as premiums and sales promotions or for use in corporate training programs. To contact a representative, please visit the Contact Us pages at www.mhprofessional.com.

McGraw Hill is committed to making our products accessible to all learners. To learn more about the available support and accommodations we offer, please contact us at accessibility@mheducation.com. We also participate in the Access Text Network (www.accesstext.org), and ATN members may submit requests through ATN.

CONTENTS

Dedication and Acknowledgments xii

Preface xiii

About the Authors xiv

Introduction: The Five-Step Program xv

STEP 1 **Set Up Your Study Plan**

1 **What You Need to Know About the AP Calculus BC Exam 3**

1.1 What Is Covered on the AP Calculus BC Exam? 4

1.2 What Is the Format of the AP Calculus BC Exam? 4

1.3 What Are the Advanced Placement Exam Grades? 5

How Is the AP Calculus BC Exam Grade Calculated? 5

1.4 Which Graphing Calculators Are Allowed for the Exam? 6

Calculators and Other Devices Not Allowed for the AP Calculus BC Exam 7

Other Restrictions on Calculators 7

2 **How to Plan Your Time 8**

2.1 Three Approaches to Preparing for the AP Calculus BC Exam 8

Overview of the Three Plans 8

2.2 Calendar for Each Plan 10

Summary of the Three Study Plans 13

STEP 2 **Determine Your Test Readiness**

3 **Take a Diagnostic Exam 17**

3.1 Getting Started! 21

3.2 Diagnostic Test 21

3.3 Answers to Diagnostic Test 27

3.4 Solutions to Diagnostic Test 28

3.5 Calculate Your Score 38

Short-Answer Questions 38

AP Calculus BC Diagnostic Exam 38

STEP 3 **Develop Strategies for Success**

4 **How to Approach Each Question Type 41**

4.1 The Multiple-Choice Questions 42

4.2 The Free-Response Questions 42

4.3 Using a Graphing Calculator 43

4.4 Taking the Exam 44

What Do I Need to Bring to the Exam? 44

Tips for Taking the Exam 45

STEP 4   **Review the Knowledge You Need to Score High**

Big Idea 1: Limits

5   Limits and Continuity 49

5.1   The Limit of a Function 50

Definition and Properties of Limits 50

Evaluating Limits 50

One-Sided Limits 52

Squeeze Theorem 55

5.2   Limits Involving Infinities 57

Infinite Limits (as $x \to a$) 57

Limits at Infinity (as $x \to \pm\infty$) 59

Horizontal and Vertical Asymptotes 61

5.3   Continuity of a Function 65

Continuity of a Function at a Number 65

Continuity of a Function over an Interval 65

Theorems on Continuity 65

5.4   Rapid Review 68

5.5   Practice Problems 69

5.6   Cumulative Review Problems 70

5.7   Solutions to Practice Problems 70

5.8   Solutions to Cumulative Review Problems 73

Big Idea 2: Derivatives

6   Differentiation 75

6.1   Derivatives of Algebraic Functions 76

Definition of the Derivative of a Function 76

Power Rule 79

The Sum, Difference, Product, and Quotient Rules 80

The Chain Rule 81

6.2   Derivatives of Trigonometric, Inverse Trigonometric, Exponential, and Logarithmic Functions 82

Derivatives of Trigonometric Functions 82

Derivatives of Inverse Trigonometric Functions 84

Derivatives of Exponential and Logarithmic Functions 85

6.3   Implicit Differentiation 87

Procedure for Implicit Differentiation 87

6.4   Approximating a Derivative 90

6.5   Derivatives of Inverse Functions 92

6.6   Higher Order Derivatives 94

L'Hôpital's Rule for Indeterminate Forms 95

6.7   Rapid Review 95

6.8   Practice Problems 97

6.9 Cumulative Review Problems 98

6.10 Solutions to Practice Problems 98

6.11 Solutions to Cumulative Review Problems 101

7 Graphs of Functions and Derivatives 103

7.1 Rolle's Theorem, Mean Value Theorem, and Extreme Value Theorem 103

Rolle's Theorem 104

Mean Value Theorem 104

Extreme Value Theorem 107

7.2 Determining the Behavior of Functions 108

Test for Increasing and Decreasing Functions 108

First Derivative Test and Second Derivative Test for Relative Extrema 111

Test for Concavity and Points of Inflection 114

7.3 Sketching the Graphs of Functions 120

Graphing without Calculators 120

Graphing with Calculators 121

7.4 Graphs of Derivatives 123

7.5 Parametric, Polar, and Vector Representations 128

Parametric Curves 128

Polar Equations 129

Types of Polar Graphs 129

Symmetry of Polar Graphs 130

Vectors 131

Vector Arithmetic 132

7.6 Rapid Review 133

7.7 Practice Problems 137

7.8 Cumulative Review Problems 139

7.9 Solutions to Practice Problems 140

7.10 Solutions to Cumulative Review Problems 147

8 Applications of Derivatives 149

8.1 Related Rate 149

General Procedure for Solving Related Rate Problems 149

Common Related Rate Problems 150

Inverted Cone (Water Tank) Problem 151

Shadow Problem 152

Angle of Elevation Problem 153

8.2 Applied Maximum and Minimum Problems 155

General Procedure for Solving Applied Maximum and Minimum Problems 155

Distance Problem 155

Area and Volume Problem 156

Business Problems 159

8.3 Rapid Review 160

8.4 Practice Problems 161

8.5 Cumulative Review Problems 163

8.6 Solutions to Practice Problems 164

8.7 Solutions to Cumulative Review Problems 171

9 More Applications of Derivatives 174

9.1 Tangent and Normal Lines 174

Tangent Lines 174

Normal Lines 180

9.2 Linear Approximations 183

Tangent Line Approximation (or Linear Approximation) 183

Estimating the nth Root of a Number 185

Estimating the Value of a Trigonometric Function of an Angle 185

9.3 Motion Along a Line 186

Instantaneous Velocity and Acceleration 186

Vertical Motion 188

Horizontal Motion 188

9.4 Parametric, Polar, and Vector Derivatives 190

Derivatives of Parametric Equations 190

Position, Speed, and Acceleration 191

Derivatives of Polar Equations 191

Velocity and Acceleration of Vector Functions 192

9.5 Rapid Review 195

9.6 Practice Problems 196

9.7 Cumulative Review Problems 198

9.8 Solutions to Practice Problems 199

9.9 Solutions to Cumulative Review Problems 204

Big Idea 3: Integrals and the Fundamental Theorems of Calculus

10 Integration 207

10.1 Evaluating Basic Integrals 208

Antiderivatives and Integration Formulas 208

Evaluating Integrals 210

10.2 Integration by U-Substitution 213

The U-Substitution Method 213

U-Substitution and Algebraic Functions 213

U-Substitution and Trigonometric Functions 215

U-Substitution and Inverse Trigonometric Functions 216

U-Substitution and Logarithmic and Exponential Functions 218

10.3 Techniques of Integration 221

Integration by Parts 221

Integration by Partial Fractions 222

10.4 Rapid Review 223

10.5   Practice Problems 224

10.6   Cumulative Review Problems 225

10.7   Solutions to Practice Problems 226

10.8   Solutions to Cumulative Review Problems 229

11 Definite Integrals 231

11.1   Riemann Sums and Definite Integrals 232

Sigma Notation or Summation Notation 232

Definition of a Riemann Sum 233

Definition of a Definite Integral 234

Properties of Definite Integrals 235

11.2   Fundamental Theorems of Calculus 237

First Fundamental Theorem of Calculus 237

Second Fundamental Theorem of Calculus 238

11.3   Evaluating Definite Integrals 241

Definite Integrals Involving Algebraic Functions 241

Definite Integrals Involving Absolute Value 242

Definite Integrals Involving Trigonometric, Logarithmic,
and Exponential Functions 243

Definite Integrals Involving Odd and Even Functions 245

11.4   Improper Integrals 246

Infinite Intervals of Integration 246

Infinite Discontinuities 247

11.5   Rapid Review 248

11.6   Practice Problems 249

11.7   Cumulative Review Problems 250

11.8   Solutions to Practice Problems 251

11.9   Solutions to Cumulative Review Problems 254

12 Areas, Volumes, and Arc Lengths 257

12.1   The Function $F(x) = \int_a^x f(t)dt$ 258

12.2   Approximating the Area Under a Curve 262

Rectangular Approximations 262

Trapezoidal Approximations 266

12.3   Area and Definite Integrals 267

Area Under a Curve 267

Area Between Two Curves 272

12.4   Volumes and Definite Integrals 276

Solids with Known Cross Sections 276

The Disc Method 280

The Washer Method 285

12.5 Integration of Parametric, Polar, and Vector Curves 289

Area, Arc Length, and Surface Area for Parametric Curves 289

Area and Arc Length for Polar Curves 290

Integration of a Vector-Valued Function 291

12.6 Rapid Review 292

12.7 Practice Problems 295

12.8 Cumulative Review Problems 296

12.9 Solutions to Practice Problems 297

12.10 Solutions to Cumulative Review Problems 305

13 More Applications of Definite Integrals 309

13.1 Average Value of a Function 310

Mean Value Theorem for Integrals 310

Average Value of a Function on [a, b] 311

13.2 Distance Traveled Problems 313

13.3 Definite Integral as Accumulated Change 316

Business Problems 316

Temperature Problem 317

Leakage Problem 318

Growth Problem 318

13.4 Differential Equations 319

Exponential Growth/Decay Problems 319

Separable Differential Equations 321

13.5 Slope Fields 324

13.6 Logistic Differential Equations 328

13.7 Euler's Method 330

Approximating Solutions of Differential Equations by Euler's Method 330

13.8 Rapid Review 332

13.9 Practice Problems 334

13.10 Cumulative Review Problems 336

13.11 Solutions to Practice Problems 337

13.12 Solutions to Cumulative Review Problems 343

Big Idea 4: Series

14 Series 346

14.1 Sequences and Series 347

Convergence 347

14.2 Types of Series 348

p-Series 348

Harmonic Series 348

Geometric Series 348

Decimal Expansion 349

14.3 Convergence Tests 350
   Divergence Test 350
   Integral Test 350
   Ratio Test 351
   Comparison Test 352
   Limit Comparison Test 352
   Informal Principle 353
14.4 Alternating Series 354
   Error Bound 354
   Absolute and Conditional Convergence 355
14.5 Power Series 357
   Radius and Interval of Convergence 357
14.6 Taylor Series 358
   Taylor Series and MacLaurin Series 358
   Common MacLaurin Series 359
14.7 Operations on Series 359
   Substitution 359
   Differentiation and Integration 360
   Error Bounds 361
14.8 Rapid Review 362
14.9 Practice Problems 364
14.10 Cumulative Review Problems 365
14.11 Solutions to Practice Problems 365
14.12 Solutions to Cumulative Review Problems 369

STEP 5

Build Your Test-Taking Confidence

AP Calculus BC Practice Exam 1 373
AP Calculus BC Practice Exam 2 403

ELITE
STUDENT
EDITION

5 Minutes to a 5

180 Activities and Questions in 5 Minutes a Day 433

Formulas and Theorems 687
Bibliography 695

DEDICATION AND ACKNOWLEDGMENTS

To
My wife, Mary
My daughters, Janet and Karen

I could not have written this book without the help of the following people:

My high school calculus teacher, *Michael Cantor*, who taught me calculus.

Professor *Leslie Beebe*, who taught me how to write.

David Pickman, who fixed my computer and taught me Equation Editor.

Jennifer Tobin, who tirelessly edited many parts of the manuscript and with whom I look forward to coauthor a math book in the future.

Robert Teseo and his calculus students who field-tested many of the problems.

Allison Litvack, *Rich Peck*, and *Liz Spiegel*, who proofread sections of the Practice Tests. And a special thanks to *Trisha Ho*, who edited Chapters 9 and 10.

Mark Reynolds, who proofread part of the manuscript.

Maxine Lifshitz, who offered many helpful comments and suggestions.

Grace Freedson, *Del Franz*, *Vasundhara Sawhney*, and *Charles Wall* for all their assistance.

Sam Lee and *Derek Ma*, who were on 24-hour call for technical support.

My older daughter, *Janet*, for not killing me for missing one of her concerts.

My younger daughter, *Karen*, who helped me with many of the computer graphics.

My wife, *Mary*, who gave me many ideas for the book and who often has more confidence in me than I have in myself.

PREFACE

Congratulations! You are an AP Calculus student. Not too shabby! As you know, AP Calculus is one of the most challenging subjects in high school. You are studying mathematical ideas that helped change the world. Not that long ago, calculus was taught at the graduate level. Today, smart young people like yourself study calculus in high school. Most colleges will give you credit if you score a 3 or more on the AP Calculus BC Exam.

So how do you do well on the AP Calculus BC Exam? How do you get a 5? Well, you've already taken the first step. You're reading this book. The next thing you need to do is to make sure that you understand the materials and do the practice problems. In recent years, the AP Calculus exams have gone through many changes. For example, today the questions no longer stress long and tedious algebraic manipulations. Instead, you are expected to be able to solve a broad range of problems including problems presented to you in the form of a graph, a chart, or a word problem. For many of the questions, you are also expected to use your calculator to find the solutions.

After having taught AP Calculus for many years and having spoken to students and other calculus teachers, we understand some of the difficulties that students might encounter with the AP Calculus exams. For example, some students have complained about not being able to visualize what the question was asking and other students said that even when the solution was given, they could not follow the steps. Under these circumstances, who wouldn't be frustrated? In this book, we have addressed these issues. Whenever possible, problems are accompanied by diagrams, and solutions are presented in a step-by-step manner. The graphing calculator is used extensively whenever it is permitted. The book also begins with a chapter on limits and continuity. These topics are normally taught in a pre-calculus course. If you're familiar with these concepts, you might skip this chapter and begin with Chapter 6.

So how do you get a 5 on the AP Calculus BC Exam?

Step 1: Set up your study program by selecting one of the three study plans in Chapter 2 of this book.
Step 2: Determine your test readiness by taking the Diagnostic Exam in Chapter 3.
Step 3: Develop strategies for success by learning the test-taking techniques offered in Chapter 4.
Step 4: Review the knowledge you need to score high by studying the subject materials in Chapter 5 through Chapter 14.
Step 5: Build your test-taking confidence by taking the Practice Exams provided in this book.

As an old martial artist once said, "First you must understand. Then you must practice." Have fun and good luck!

ABOUT THE AUTHORS

WILLIAM MA has taught calculus for many years. He received his BA and MA from Columbia University. He was the chairman of the Math Department at the Herricks School District on Long Island, New York, for many years before retiring. He also taught as adjunct instructor at Baruch College, Fordham University, and Columbia University. He is the author of several books, including test preparation books for the SAT, ACT, GMAT, and AP Calculus AB. He is currently a math consultant.

CAROLYN WHEATER teaches Middle School and Upper School Mathematics at The Nightingale-Bamford School in New York City. Educated at Marymount Manhattan College and the University of Massachusetts, Amherst, she has taught math and computer technology for thirty years to students from preschool through college.

EMILY PILLAR has taught calculus since 2014. She received her BS from Tulane University, earned a MS in Applied Mathematics and Engineering Sciences from Northwestern University and a MS in Mathematics Education from Fordham University. She taught at Schrieber High School in Port Washington and is currently teaching at Plainvew-Old Bethpage John F. Kennedy High School on Long Island.

INTRODUCTION: THE FIVE-STEP PROGRAM

How Is This Book Organized?

This book begins with an introduction to the Five-Step Program followed by 14 chapters reflecting the 5 steps.

- Step 1 provides an overview of the AP Calculus BC Exam, and offers three study plans for preparing for the Exam.
- Step 2 contains a diagnostic test with answers and explanations.
- Step 3 offers test-taking strategies for answering both multiple-choice and free-response questions, and for using a graphing calculator.
- Step 4 consists of 10 chapters providing a comprehensive review of all topics covered on the AP Calculus BC Exam. At the end of each chapter (beginning with Chapter 5), you will find a set of practice problems with solutions, a set of cumulative review problems with solutions, and a Rapid Review section giving you the highlights of the chapter.
- Step 5 provides three full practice AP Calculus BC Exams with answers, explanations, and worksheets to compute your score.

The book concludes with a summary of math formulas and theorems needed for the AP Calculus BC Exam. *(Please note that the exercises in this book are done with the TI-89 Graphing Calculator.)*

Introducing the Five-Step Preparation Program

This book is organized as a five-step program to prepare you to succeed in the AP Calculus BC Exam. These steps are designed to provide you with vital skills, strategies, and the practice that can lead you to that perfect 5. Here are the 5 steps.

Step 1: Set Up Your Study Plan

In this step you will read an overview of the AP Calculus BC Exam, including a summary of topics covered in the exam and a description of the format of the exam. You will also follow a process to help determine which of the following preparation programs is right for you:

- Full school year: September through May.
- One semester: January through May.
- Six weeks: Basic training for the exam.

Step 2: Determine Your Test Readiness

In this step you will take a diagnostic multiple-choice exam in calculus. This pre-test should give you an idea of how prepared you are to take the real exam before beginning to study for the actual AP Calculus BC Exam.

Step 3: Develop Strategies for Success

In this step you will learn strategies that will help you do your best on the exam. These strategies cover both the multiple-choice and free-response sections of the exam.

- Learn to read multiple-choice questions.
- Lean how to answer multiple-choice questions.
- Learn how to plan and write answers to the free-response questions.

Step 4: Review the Knowledge You Need to Score High

In this step you will learn or review the material you need to know for the test. This review section takes up the bulk of this book. It contains:

- A comprehensive review of AP Calculus BC.
- A set of practice problems.
- A set of cumulative review problems beginning with Chapter 5.
- A rapid review summarizing the highlights of the chapter.

Step 5: Build Your Test-Taking Confidence

In this step you will complete your preparation by testing yourself on practice exams. We have provided you with three complete practice exams in AP Calculus BC with solutions and scoring guides. Although these practice exams are not reproduced questions from the actual AP calculus exam, they mirror both the material tested by AP and the way in which it is tested.

Finally, at the back of this book you will find additional resources to aid your preparation. These include:

- A brief bibliography.
- A list of websites related to the AP Calculus BC exam.
- A summary of formulas and theorems related to the AP Calculus BC exam.

Introduction to the Graphics Used in This Book

To emphasize particular skills and strategies, we use several icons throughout this book. An icon in the margin will alert you that you should pay particular attention to the accompanying text. We use these icons:

This icon points out a very important concept or fact that you should not pass over.

This icon calls your attention to a strategy that you may want to try.

This icon indicates a tip that you might find useful.

ELITE STUDENT EDITION

5 STEPS TO A 5™

AP Calculus BC

2024

Set Up Your Study Plan

CHAPTER **1** What You Need to Know About the AP
          Calculus BC Exam

CHAPTER **2** How to Plan Your Time

CHAPTER 1

What You Need to Know About the AP Calculus BC Exam

IN THIS CHAPTER

Summary: Learn what topics are tested in the exam, what the format is, which calculators are allowed, and how the exam is graded.

Key Ideas

✪ The AP Calculus BC exam covers all of the topics in the AB exam as well as additional topics including Euler's Method, logistic differential equations, series, and more.

✪ The AP Calculus BC exam has 45 multiple-choice questions and 6 free-response questions. Each of the two types of questions makes up 50% of the grade.

✪ Many graphing calculators are permitted on the exam, including the TI-98.

✪ You may bring up to two approved calculators for the exam.

✪ You may store programs in your calculator and you are not required to clear the memories in your calculator for the exam.

1.1 What Is Covered on the AP Calculus BC Exam?

The AP Calculus AB and BC exams both cover the following topics:

- Functions, limits, and graphs of functions, continuity
- Definition and computation of derivatives, second derivatives, relationship between the graphs of functions and their derivatives, applications of derivatives, *L'Hôpital's* Rule
- Finding antiderivatives, definite integrals, applications of integrals, fundamental theorem of calculus, numerical approximations of definite integrals, separable differential equations, and slope fields

The BC exam covers all of these topics as well as parametric, polar, and vector functions, Euler's Method, antiderivatives by parts and by partial fractions, improper integrals, logistic differential equations, and series.

Students are expected to be able to solve problems that are expressed graphically, numerically, analytically, and verbally. For a more detailed description of the topics covered in the AP Calculus exams, visit the College Board AP website at: exploreap.org.

1.2 What Is the Format of the AP Calculus BC Exam?

The AP Calculus BC exam has 2 sections:

Section I contains 45 multiple-choice questions for which you are given 105 minutes to complete.

Section II contains 6 free-response questions for which you are given 90 minutes to complete.

The total time allotted for both sections is 3 hours and 15 minutes. Below is a summary of the different parts of each section.

Section I *Multiple-Choice*	Part A	30 questions	No Calculator	60 Minutes
	Part B	15 questions	Calculator	45 Minutes
Section II *Free-Response*	Part A	2 questions	Calculator	30 Minutes
	Part B	4 questions	No Calculator	60 Minutes

During the time allotted for Part B of Section II, students may continue to work on questions from Part A of Section II. However, they may not use a calculator at that time. Please note that you are not expected to be able to answer all the questions in order to receive a grade of 5. If you wish to see the specific instructions for each part of the test, visit the College Board website at: https://apstudent.collegeboard.org/apcourse/ap-calculus-bc/calculator-policy.

1.3 What Are the Advanced Placement Exam Grades?

Advanced Placement Exam grades are given on a 5-point scale with 5 being the highest grade. The grades are described below:

5 Extremely Well Qualified
4 Well Qualified
3 Qualified
2 Possibly Qualified
1 No Recommendation

How Is the AP Calculus BC Exam Grade Calculated?

- The exam has a total raw score of 108 points: 54 points for the multiple-choice questions in Section I and 54 points for the free-response questions for Section II.
- Each correct answer in Section I is worth 1.2 points; there is *no point deduction* for incorrect answers and no points are given for unanswered questions. For example, suppose your result in Section I is as follows:

Correct	Incorrect	Unanswered
40	5	0

Your raw score for Section I would be:

$40 \times 1.2 = 48$. Not a bad score!

- Each complete and correct solution for questions in Section II is worth 9 points.
- The total raw score for both Section I and II is converted to a 5-point scale. The cutoff points for each grade (1–5) vary from year to year. Visit the College Board website at: https://apstudent.collegeboard.org/exploreap/the-rewards/exam-scores for more information. Below is a rough estimate of the conversion scale:

Total Raw Score	Approximate AP Grade
80–108	5
65–79	4
50–64	3
36–49	2
0–35	1

Remember, these are approximate cutoff points.

1.4 Which Graphing Calculators Are Allowed for the Exam?

The following calculators are allowed:

CASIO	HEWLETT-PACKARD	TEXAS INSTRUMENTS
FX-6000 series	HP-9G	TI-73
FX-6200 series	HP-28 series	TI-80
FX-6300 series	HP-38G series	TI-81
FX-6500 series	HP-39 series	TI-82
FX-7000 series	HP-40G	TI-83
FX-7300 series	HP-48 series	TI-83 Plus
FX-7400 series	HP-49 series	TI-83 Plus Silver
FX-7500 series	HP-50 series	TI-84 Plus
FX-7700 series	HP Prime	TI-84 Plus SE
FX-7800 series		TI-84 Plus Silver
FX-8000 series	**RADIO SHACK**	TI-84 Plus C Silver
FX-8500 series	EC-4033	TI-84 Plus T
FX-8700 series	EC-4034	TI-84 Plus CE-T
FX-8800 series	EC-4037	TI-84 Plus CE Python
FX-9700 series		TI-84 Plus CE-T Python Ed.
FX-9750 series	**SHARP**	TI-85
FX-9860 series	EL-5200	TI-86
CFX-9800 series	EL-9200 series	TI-89
CFX-9850 series	EL-9300 series	TI-89 Titanium
CFX-9950 series	EL-9600 series (no stylus)	TI-Nspire
CFX-9970 series	EL-9900 series	TI-Nspire CX
FX 1.0 series		TI-Nspire CAS
Algebra FX 2.0 series	**OTHER**	TI-Nspire CX CAS
FX-CG-10 (PRIZM)	Datexx DS-883	TI-Nspire CM-C
FX-CG-20	Micronta	TI-Nspire CAS CX-C
FX-CG 500 (no stylus)	NumWorks	TI-Nspire CX-II CAS
FX-CG-50	Smart	TI-Nspire CX-T
Graph25 series		
Graph35 series		TI-Nspire CX-II
Graph75 series		TI-Nspire CX-T CAS
Graph85 series		TI-Nspire CX II-C CAS
Graph100 series		

For a more complete list, visit the College Board website at: https://apstudent.collegeboard
.org/apcourse/ap-calculus-bc/calculator-policy. If you wish to use a graphing calculator that
is not on the approved list, your teacher must obtain written permission from the ETS before
April 1 of the testing year.

Calculators and Other Devices Not Allowed for the AP Calculus BC Exam

- TI-92 Plus, Voyage 200, HP-95, and devices with QWERTY keyboards
- Non-graphing scientific calculators
- Laptop computers
- Pocket organizers, electronic writing pads, or pen-input devices
- Cellular phone calculators

Other Restrictions on Calculators

- You may bring up to 2 (but no more than 2) approved graphing calculators to the exam.
- You may not share calculators with another student.
- You may store programs in your calculator.
- You are not required to clear the memories in your calculator for the exam.
- You may not use the memories of your calculator to store secured questions and take them out of the testing room.

CHAPTER > 2

How to Plan Your Time

IN THIS CHAPTER

Summary: The right preparation plan for you depends on your study habits and the amount of time you have before the test.

Key Idea

✪ Choose the study plan that is right for you.

2.1 Three Approaches to Preparing for the AP Calculus BC Exam

Overview of the Three Plans

No one knows your study habits, likes, and dislikes better than you. So, you are the only one who can decide which approach you want and/or need to adopt to prepare for the Advanced Placement Calculus BC exam. Look at the brief profiles below. These may help you to place yourself in a particular prep mode.

   You are a full-year prep student (Plan A) if:

1. You are the kind of person who likes to plan for everything far in advance . . . and I mean far . . . ;
2. You arrive at the airport 2 hours before your flight because "you never know when these planes might leave early . . .";
3. You like detailed planning and everything in its place;
4. You feel you must be thoroughly prepared;
5. You hate surprises.

You are a one-semester prep student (Plan B) if:

1. You get to the airport 1 hour before your flight is scheduled to leave;
2. You are willing to plan ahead to feel comfortable in stressful situations, but are okay with skipping some details;
3. You feel more comfortable when you know what to expect, but a surprise or two is cool;
4. You're always on time for appointments.

You are a six-week prep student (Plan C) if:

1. You get to the airport just as your plane is announcing its final boarding;
2. You work best under pressure and tight deadlines;
3. You feel very confident with the skills and background you've learned in your AP Calculus class;
4. You decided late in the year to take the exam;
5. You like surprises;
6. You feel okay if you arrive 10–15 minutes late for an appointment.

2.2 Calendar for Each Plan

Plan A: You Have a Full School Year to Prepare

Although its primary purpose is to prepare you for the AP Calculus BC Exam you will take in May, this book can enrich your study of calculus, your analytical skills, and your problem-solving techniques.

SEPTEMBER–OCTOBER (Check off the activities as you complete them.)

_____ Determine into which student mode you would place yourself.

_____ Carefully read Steps 1 and 2.

_____ Get on the Web and take a look at the AP website(s).

_____ Skim the Comprehensive Review section. (These areas will be part of your year-long preparation.)

_____ Buy a few highlighters.

_____ Flip through the entire book. Break the book in. Write in it. Toss it around a little bit . . . highlight it.

_____ Get a clear picture of what your own school's AP Calculus curriculum is.

_____ Begin to use the book as a resource to supplement the classroom learning.

_____ Read and study Chapter 5—Limits and Continuity.

_____ Read and study Chapter 6—Differentiation.

_____ Read and study Chapter 7—Graphs of Functions and Derivatives.

NOVEMBER (The first 10 weeks have elapsed.)

_____ Read and study Chapter 8—Applications of Derivatives.

_____ Read and study Chapter 9—More Applications of Derivatives.

DECEMBER

_____ Read and study Chapter 10—Integration.

_____ Review Chapters 5–7.

JANUARY (20 weeks have now elapsed.)

_____ Read and study Chapter 11—Definite Integrals.

_____ Review Chapters 8–10.

FEBRUARY

_____ Read and study Chapter 12—Areas and Volumes.

_____ Read and study Chapter 13—More Applications of Definite Integrals.

_____ Take the Diagnostic Test.

_____ Evaluate your strengths and weaknesses.

_____ Study appropriate chapters to correct weaknesses.

MARCH (30 weeks have now elapsed.)

_____ Read and study Chapter 14—Series.

_____ Review Chapters 11–13.

APRIL

_____ Take Practice Exam 1 in first week of April.

_____ Evaluate your strengths and weaknesses.

_____ Study appropriate chapters to correct weaknesses.

_____ Review Chapters 5–14.

MAY—First Two Weeks (THIS IS IT!)

_____ Take Practice Exam 2.

_____ Score yourself.

_____ Study appropriate chapters to correct weaknesses.

_____ Get a good night's sleep the night before the exam. Fall asleep knowing you are well prepared.

GOOD LUCK ON THE TEST!

Plan B: You Have One Semester to Prepare

Working under the assumption that you've completed one semester of calculus studies, the following calendar will use those skills you've been practicing to prepare you for the May exam.

JANUARY

_____ Carefully read Steps 1 and 2.
_____ Read and study Chapter 5—Limits and Continuity.
_____ Read and study Chapter 6—Differentiation.
_____ Read and study Chapter 7—Graphs of Functions and Derivatives.
_____ Read and Study Chapter 8—Applications of Derivatives.

FEBRUARY

_____ Read and study Chapter 9—More Applications of Derivatives.
_____ Read and study Chapter 10—Integration.
_____ Read and study Chapter 11—Definite Integrals.
_____ Take the Diagnostic Test.
_____ Evaluate your strengths and weaknesses.
_____ Study appropriate chapters to correct weaknesses.
_____ Review Chapters 5–8.

MARCH (10 weeks to go.)

_____ Read and study Chapter 12—Areas and Volumes.

_____ Read and study Chapter 13—More Applications of Definite Integrals.
_____ Read and study Chapter 14—Series.
_____ Review Chapters 9–11.

APRIL

_____ Take Practice Exam 1 in first week of April.
_____ Evaluate your strengths and weaknesses.
_____ Study appropriate chapters to correct weaknesses.
_____ Review Chapters 5–14.

MAY—First Two Weeks (THIS IS IT!)

_____ Take Practice Exam 2.
_____ Score yourself.
_____ Study appropriate chapters to correct weaknesses.
_____ Get a good night's sleep the night before the exam. Fall asleep knowing you are well prepared.

GOOD LUCK ON THE TEST!

Plan C: You Have Six Weeks to Prepare

At this point, we are going to assume that you have been building your calculus knowledge base for more than six months. You will, therefore, use this book primarily as a specific guide to the AP Calculus BC Exam.

Given the time constraints, now is not the time to try to expand your AP Calculus curriculum. Rather, it is the time to limit and refine what you already do know.

APRIL 1st–15th

_____ Skim Steps 1 and 2.
_____ Skim Chapters 5–9.
_____ Carefully go over the "Rapid Review" sections of Chapters 5–9.
_____ Take the Diagnostic Test.
_____ Evaluate your strengths and weaknesses.
_____ Study appropriate chapters to correct weaknesses.

APRIL 16th–May 1st

_____ Skim Chapters 10–14.
_____ Carefully go over the "Rapid Review" sections of Chapters 10–14.

_____ Take Practice Exam 1.
_____ Score yourself and analyze your errors.
_____ Study appropriate chapters to correct weaknesses.

MAY—First Two Weeks (THIS IS IT!)

_____ Take Practice Exam 2.
_____ Score yourself and analyze your errors.
_____ Study appropriate chapters to correct weaknesses.
_____ Get a good night's sleep. Fall asleep knowing you are well prepared.

GOOD LUCK ON THE TEST!

Summary of the Three Study Plans

MONTH	PLAN A:	PLAN B:	PLAN C:
September–October	Chapters 5–7		
November	Chapters 8 & 9		
December	Chapter 10 Review Chapters 5–7		
January	Chapter 11 Review Chapters 8–10	Chapters 5–8	
February	Chapters 12 & 13 Diagnostic Test	Chapters 9–11 Diagnostic Test Review Chapters 5–8	
March	Chapter 14 Review Chapters 11–13	Chapters 12–14 Review Chapters 9–11	
April	Practice Exam 1 Review Chapters 5–14	Practice Exam 1 Review Chapters 5–14	Diagnostic Test Review Chapters 5–9 Practice Exam 1 Review Chapters 10–14
May	Practice Exam 2	Practice Exam 2	Practice Exam 2

STEP 2

Determine Your Test Readiness

CHAPTER 3 Take a Diagnostic Exam

CHAPTER 3

Take a Diagnostic Exam

IN THIS CHAPTER

Summary: Get started on your review by working out the problems in the diagnostic exam. Use the answer sheet to record your answers. After you have finished working the problems, check your answers with the answer key. The problems in the diagnostic exam are presented in small groups matching the order of the review chapters. Your results should give you a good idea of how well you are prepared for the AP Calculus BC exam at this time. Note those chapters that you need to study the most, and spend more time on them. Good luck. You can do it.

Key Ideas

✪ Work out the problems in the diagnostic exam carefully.
✪ Check your work against the given answers.
✪ Determine your areas of strength and weakness.
✪ Identify and mark the pages that you must give special attention.

DIAGNOSTIC TEST ANSWER SHEET

1. _____	21. _____	41. _____
2. _____	22. _____	42. _____
3. _____	23. _____	43. _____
4. _____	24. _____	44. _____
5. _____	25. _____	45. _____
6. _____	26. _____	46. _____
7. _____	27. _____	47. _____
8. _____	28. _____	48. _____
9. _____	29. _____	49. _____
10. _____	30. _____	50. _____
11. _____	31. _____	51. _____
12. _____	32. _____	52. _____
13. _____	33. _____	53. _____
14. _____	34. _____	54. _____
15. _____	35. _____	55. _____
16. _____	36. _____	56. _____
17. _____	37. _____	57. _____
18. _____	38. _____	58. _____
19. _____	39. _____	59. _____
20. _____	40. _____	60. _____

3.1 Getting Started!

Taking the Diagnostic Test helps you assess your strengths and weaknesses as you begin preparing for the AP Calculus BC exam. The questions in the Diagnostic Test contain both multiple-choice and open-ended questions. They are arranged by topic and designed to review concepts tested on the AP Calculus BC exam. All questions in the diagnostic test can be done without the use of a graphing calculator, except in a few cases where you need to find the numerical value of a logarithmic or exponential function.

3.2 Diagnostic Test

Chapter 5

1. A function f is continuous on $[-2, 0]$ and some of the values of f are shown below.

x	-2	-1	0
f	4	b	4

If $f(x) = 2$ has no solution on $[-2, 0]$, then b could be

(A) 3

(B) 2

(C) 0

(D) -2

2. Evaluate $\lim\limits_{x \to -\infty} \dfrac{\sqrt{x^2 - 4}}{2x}$.

3. If
$$h(x) = \begin{cases} \sqrt{x} & \text{if } x > 4 \\ x^2 - 12 & \text{if } x \le 4 \end{cases} \quad \text{find } \lim\limits_{x \to 4} h(x).$$

4. If $f(x) = |2xe^x|$, what is the value of $\lim\limits_{x \to 0^+} f'(x)$?

Chapter 6

5. If $f(x) = -2 \csc(5x)$, find $f'\left(\dfrac{\pi}{6}\right)$.

6. Given the equation $y = (x + 1)(x - 3)^2$, what is the instantaneous rate of change of y at $x = -1$?

7. What is $\lim\limits_{\Delta x \to 0} \dfrac{\tan\left(\dfrac{\pi}{4} + \Delta x\right) - \tan\left(\dfrac{\pi}{4}\right)}{\Delta x}$?

8. Evaluate $\lim\limits_{x \to \pi} \dfrac{e^x - e^\pi}{x^e - \pi^e}$.

Chapter 7

9. The graph of f is shown in Figure D-1. Draw a possible graph of f' on (a, b).

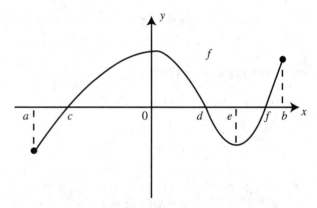

Figure D-1

10. The graph of the function g is shown in Figure D-2. Which of the following is true for g on (a, b)?

I. g is monotonic on (a, b).

II. g' is continuous on (a, b).

III. $g'' > 0$ on (a, b).

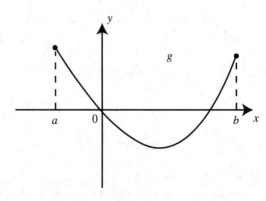

Figure D-2

11. The graph of f is shown in Figure D-3 and f is twice differentiable. Which of the following statements is true?

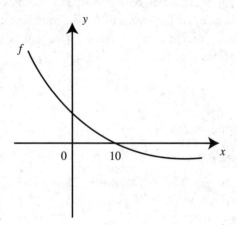

Figure D-3

(A) $f(10) < f'(10) < f''(10)$

(B) $f''(10) < f'(10) < f(10)$

(C) $f'(10) < f(10) < f''(10)$

(D) $f'(10) < f''(10) < f(10)$

12. The graph of f', the derivative of f, is shown in Figure D-4. At what value(s) of x is the graph of f concave up?

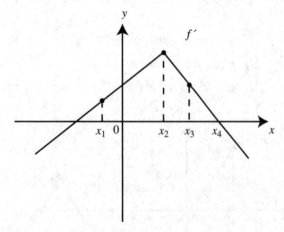

Figure D-4

13. How many points of inflection does the graph of $y = \sin(x^2)$ have on the interval $[-\pi,\ \pi]$?

14. If $g(x) = \int_a^x f(t)\,dt$ and the graph of f is shown in Figure D-5, which of the graphs in Figure D-6 on the next page is a possible graph of g?

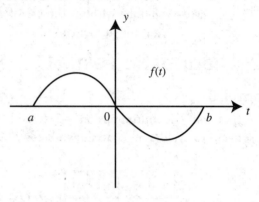

Figure D-5

15. The graphs of f', g', p', and q' are shown in Figure D-7 on the next page. Which of the functions f, g, p, or q have a point of inflection on (a, b)?

16. Find the rectangular equation of the curve defined by $x = 1 + e^{-t}$ and $y = 1 + e^t$.

Chapter 8

17. When the area of a square is increasing four times as fast as the diagonals, what is the length of a side of the square?

18. If $g(x) = |x^2 - 4x - 12|$, which of the following statements about g is/are true?

    I. g has a relative maximum at $x = 2$.

    II. g is differentiable at $x = 6$.

    III. g has a point of inflection at $x = -2$.

Chapter 9

19. Given the equation $y = \sqrt{x - 1}$, what is an equation of the normal line to the graph at $x = 5$?

20. What is the slope of the tangent to the curve $y = \cos(xy)$ at $x = 0$?

(A)

(B)

(C)

(D)

Figure D-6

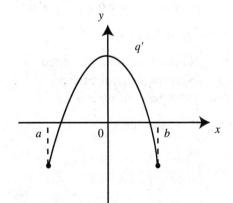

Figure D-7

21. The velocity function of a moving particle on the x-axis is given as $v(t) = t^2 - t$, $t \geq 0$. For what values of t is the particle's speed decreasing?

22. The velocity function of a moving particle is $v(t) = \dfrac{t^3}{3} - 2t^2 + 5$ for $0 \leq t \leq 6$. What is the maximum acceleration of the particle on the interval $0 \leq t \leq 6$?

23. Write an equation of the normal line to the graph of $f(x) = x^3$ for $x \geq 0$ at the point where $f'(x) = 12$.

24. At what value(s) of x do the graphs of $f(x) = \dfrac{\ln x}{x}$ and $y = -x^2$ have perpendicular tangent lines?

25. Given a differentiable function f with $f\left(\dfrac{\pi}{2}\right) = 3$ and $f'\left(\dfrac{\pi}{2}\right) = -1$. Using a tangent line to the graph at $x = \dfrac{\pi}{2}$, find an approximate value of $f\left(\dfrac{\pi}{2} + \dfrac{\pi}{180}\right)$.

26. An object moves in the plane on a path given by $x = 4t^2$ and $y = \sqrt{t}$. Find the acceleration vector when $t = 4$.

27. Find the equation of the tangent line to the curve defined by $x = 2t + 3$, $y = t^2 + 2t$ at $t = 1$.

Chapter 10

28. Evaluate $\displaystyle\int \dfrac{1 - x^2}{x^2}\, dx$.

29. If $f(x)$ is an antiderivative of $\dfrac{e^x}{e^x + 1}$ and $f(0) = \ln(2)$, find $f(\ln 2)$.

30. Find the volume of the solid generated by revolving about the x-axis the region bounded by the graph of $y = \sin 2x$ for $0 \leq x \leq \pi$ and the line $y = \dfrac{1}{2}$.

31. Evaluate $\displaystyle\int_2^5 \dfrac{1}{x^2 + 2x - 3}\, dx$.

32. Evaluate $\displaystyle\int x^2 \cos x\, dx$.

Chapter 11

33. Evaluate $\displaystyle\int_1^4 \dfrac{1}{\sqrt{x}}\, dx$.

34. If $\displaystyle\int_{-1}^k (2x - 3)\, dx = 6$, find k.

35. If $h(x) = \displaystyle\int_{\pi/2}^x \sqrt{\sin t}\, dt$, find $h'(\pi)$.

36. If $f'(x) = g(x)$ and g is a continuous function for all real values of x, then $\displaystyle\int_0^2 g(3x)\, dx$ is

    (A) $\dfrac{1}{3} f(6) - \dfrac{1}{3} f(0)$

    (B) $f(2) - f(0)$

    (C) $f(6) - f(0)$

    (D) $\dfrac{1}{3} f(0) - \dfrac{1}{3} f(6)$

37. Evaluate $\displaystyle\int_\pi^x \sin(2t)\, dt$.

38. If a function f is continuous for all values of x, which of the following statements is/are always true?

    I. $\displaystyle\int_a^c f(x)\,dx = \int_a^b f(x)\,dx + \int_b^c f(x)\,dx$

    II. $\displaystyle\int_a^b f(x)\,dx = \int_a^c f(x)\,dx - \int_c^b f(x)\,dx$

    III. $\displaystyle\int_b^c f(x)\,dx = \int_b^a f(x)\,dx - \int_c^a f(x)\,dx$

39. If $g(x) = \displaystyle\int_{\pi/2}^x 2\sin t\, dt$ on $\left[\dfrac{\pi}{2}, \dfrac{5\pi}{2}\right]$, find the value(s) of x, where g has a local minimum.

40. Evaluate $\int_0^\infty e^{-x}\,dx$.

Chapter 12

41. The graph of the velocity function of a moving particle is shown in Figure D-8. What is the total distance traveled by the particle during $0 \le t \le 6$?

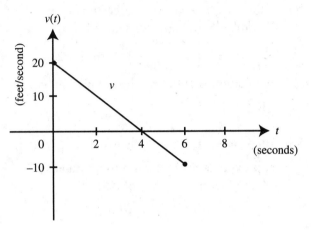

Figure D-8

42. The graph of f consists of four line segments, for $-1 \le x \le 5$ as shown in Figure D-9. What is the value of $\int_{-1}^{5} f(x)\,dx$?

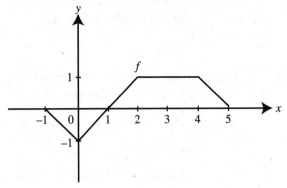

Figure D-9

43. Find the area of the region enclosed by the graph of $y = x^2 - x$ and the x-axis.

44. If $\int_{-k}^{k} f(x)\,dx = 0$ for all real values of k, then which of the graphs in Figure D-10 could be the graph of f?

(A)

(B)

(C)

(D)

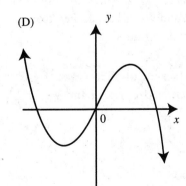

Figure D-10

45. The area under the curve $y = \sqrt{x}$ from $x = 1$ to $x = k$ is 8. Find the value of k.

46. For $0 \leq x \leq 3\pi$, find the area of the region bounded by the graphs of $y = \sin x$ and $y = \cos x$.

47. Let f be a continuous function on $[0, 6]$ that has selected values as shown below:

x	0	1	2	3	4	5	6
$f(x)$	1	2	5	10	17	26	37

Using three midpoint rectangles of equal widths, find an approximate value of

$$\int_0^6 f(x)\,dx.$$

48. Find the area of the region in the first quadrant bounded by the curves $r = 2\cos\theta$ and $r = 2\sin\theta$.

49. Determine the length of the curve defined by $x = 3t - t^3$ and $y = 3t^2$ from $t = 0$ to $t = 2$.

Chapter 13

50. If $\dfrac{dy}{dx} = 2\sin x$ and at $x = \pi$, $y = 2$, find a solution to the differential equation.

51. Water is leaking from a tank at the rate of $f(t) = 10\ln(t+1)$ gallons per hour for $0 \leq t \leq 10$, where t is measured in hours. How many gallons of water have leaked from the tank after exactly 5 hours?

52. Carbon-14 has a half-life of 5730 years. If y is the amount of Carbon-14 present and y

decays according to the equation $\dfrac{dy}{dt} = ky$, where k is a constant and t is measured in years, find the value of k.

53. What is the volume of the solid whose base is the region enclosed by the graphs of $y = x^2$ and $y = x + 2$ and whose cross sections are perpendicular to the x-axis are squares?

54. The growth of a colony of bacteria in a controlled environment is modeled by $\dfrac{dP}{dt} = .35P\left(1 - \dfrac{P}{4000}\right)$. If the initial population is 100, find the population when $t = 5$.

55. If $\dfrac{dy}{dx} = \dfrac{-y}{x^2}$ and $y = 3$ when $x = 2$, approximate y when $x = 3$ using Euler's Method with a step size of 0.5.

Chapter 14

56. If S is the sum of the series $\displaystyle\sum_{n=1}^{\infty} \dfrac{(-1)^n}{2n}$ and s_n, its nth partial sum, what is the maximum value of $|S - s_5|$?

57. Determine whether the series $\displaystyle\sum_{n=0}^{\infty} \dfrac{3}{(n+1)^4}$ converges or diverges.

58. For what values of x does the series
$$x - \frac{x^2}{2} + \frac{x^3}{3} - \frac{x^4}{4} + \cdots$$ converge absolutely?

59. Find the Taylor series expansion of $f(x) = \dfrac{1}{x}$ about the point $x = 2$.

60. Find the MacLaurin series for e^{-x^2}.

3.3 Answers to Diagnostic Test

1. A

2. $-\dfrac{1}{2}$

3. Does not exist

4. 2

5. $-20\sqrt{3}$

6. 16

7. 2

8. $\dfrac{e^{\pi-1}}{\pi^{e-1}}$

9. See Figure DS-2 in solution

10. II & III

11. C

12. $x < x_2$

13. 8

14. A

15. q

16. $y = \dfrac{x}{x-1}$

17. $2\sqrt{2}$

18. I

19. $y = -4x + 22$

20. 0

21. $\dfrac{1}{2} < t < 1$

22. 12

23. $y = \dfrac{-1}{12}x + \dfrac{49}{6}$

24. 1.370

25. 2.983

26. $\left\langle 8, -\dfrac{1}{32} \right\rangle$

27. $y = 2x - 7$

28. $\dfrac{-1}{x} - x + C$

29. $\ln 3$

30. 1.503

31. $\dfrac{1}{4}\ln\left(\dfrac{5}{2}\right)$

32. $x^2 \sin x + 2x \cos x - 2\sin x + C$

33. 2

34. $\{-2, 5\}$

35. 0

36. A

37. $\dfrac{-1}{2}\cos(2x) + \dfrac{1}{2}$

38. I & III

39. 2π

40. 1

41. 50 feet

42. 2

43. $\dfrac{1}{6}$

44. D

45. $13^{2/3}$

46. 5.657

47. 76

48. $\dfrac{\pi}{2} - 1$

49. 14

50. $y = -2\cos x$

51. 57.506

52. $\dfrac{-\ln 2}{5730}$

53. $\dfrac{81}{10}$

54. 514.325

55. 2.415

56. $\dfrac{1}{12}$

57. Converges

58. $-1 < x < 1$

59. $\displaystyle\sum_{n=0}^{\infty} \dfrac{(-1)^n}{2^{n+1}}(x-2)^n$

60. $\displaystyle\sum_{n=0}^{\infty} \dfrac{(-1)^n \left(x^{2n}\right)}{n!}$

3.4 Solutions to Diagnostic Test

Chapter 5

1. See Figure DS-1.
   If $b = 2$, then $x = -1$ would be a solution for $f(x) = 2$.
   If $b = 0$ or -2, $f(x) = 2$ would have two solutions.
   Thus, $b = 3$, choice (A).

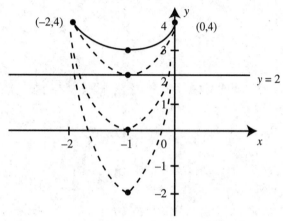

Figure DS-1

2. $\lim\limits_{x \to -\infty} \dfrac{\sqrt{x^2 - 4}}{2x} = \lim\limits_{x \to -\infty} \dfrac{\sqrt{x^2 - 4}/(-\sqrt{x^2})}{2x/(-\sqrt{x^2})}$

   (Note: as $x \to -\infty$, $x = -\sqrt{x^2}$.)

   $= \lim\limits_{x \to -\infty} \dfrac{-\sqrt{(x^2 - 4)/x^2}}{2}$

   $= \lim\limits_{x \to -\infty} \dfrac{-\sqrt{1 - (4/x^2)}}{2}$

   $= -\dfrac{\sqrt{1}}{2} = -\dfrac{1}{2}$

3. $h(x) = \begin{cases} \sqrt{x} & \text{if } x > 4 \\ x^2 - 12 & \text{if } x \le 4 \end{cases}$

   $\lim\limits_{x \to 4^+} h(x) = \lim\limits_{x \to 4^+} \sqrt{x} = \sqrt{4} = 2$

   $\lim\limits_{x \to 4^-} h(x) = \lim\limits_{x \to 4^-} (x^2 - 12) = (4^2 - 12) = 4$

   Since $\lim\limits_{x \to 4^+} h(x) \ne \lim\limits_{x \to 4^-} h(x)$, thus $\lim\limits_{x \to 4} h(x)$ does not exist.

4. $f(x) = |2xe^x| = \begin{cases} 2xe^x & \text{if } x \ge 0 \\ -2xe^x & \text{if } x < 0 \end{cases}$

   If $x \ge 0$, $f'(x) = 2e^x + e^x(2x) = 2e^x + 2xe^x$

$\lim\limits_{x \to 0^+} f'(x) = \lim\limits_{x \to 0^+} (2e^x + 2xe^x) = 2e^0 + 0 = 2$

Chapter 6

5. $f(x) = -2 \csc(5x)$
   $f'(x) = -2(-\csc 5x)\,[\cot(5x)]\,(5)$
   $\qquad = 10 \csc(5x) \cot(5x)$
   $f'\left(\dfrac{\pi}{6}\right) = 10 \csc\left(\dfrac{5\pi}{6}\right) \cot\left(\dfrac{5\pi}{6}\right)$
   $\qquad = 10(2)(-\sqrt{3}) = -20\sqrt{3}$

6. $y = (x + 1)(x - 3)^2;$
   $\dfrac{dy}{dx} = (1)(x - 3)^2 + 2(x - 3)(x + 1)$
   $\qquad = (x - 3)^2 + 2(x - 3)(x + 1)$
   $\dfrac{dy}{dx}\bigg|_{x=-1} = (-1 - 3)^2 + 2(-1 - 3)(-1 + 1)$
   $\qquad = (-4)^2 + 0 = 16$

7. $f'(x_1) = \lim\limits_{\Delta x \to 0} \dfrac{f(x_1 + \Delta x) - f(x_1)}{\Delta x}$

   Thus, $\lim\limits_{\Delta x \to 0} \dfrac{\tan\left(\dfrac{\pi}{4} + \Delta x\right) - \tan\left(\dfrac{\pi}{4}\right)}{\Delta x}$

   $= \dfrac{d}{dx}(\tan x)$ at $x = \dfrac{\pi}{4}$

   $= \sec^2\left(\dfrac{\pi}{4}\right) = (\sqrt{2})^2 = 2$

8. By *L'Hôpital's* Rule, $\lim\limits_{x \to \pi} \dfrac{e^x - e^\pi}{x^e - \pi^e} = \lim\limits_{x \to \pi} \dfrac{e^x}{e x^{e-1}}$

   $= \lim\limits_{x \to \pi} \dfrac{e^{x-1}}{x^{e-1}} = \dfrac{e^{\pi-1}}{\pi^{e-1}}.$

Chapter 7

9. See Figure DS-2 on the next page.

10. I. Since the graph of g is decreasing and then increasing, it is not monotonic.

    II. Since the graph of g is a smooth curve, g' is continuous.

    III. Since the graph of g is concave upward, $g'' > 0$.
    Thus, only statements II and III are true.

Based on the graph of f:

A possible graph of f'

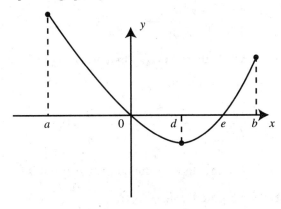

Figure DS-2

11. The graph indicates that (1) $f(10) = 0$,
(2) $f'(10) < 0$, since f is decreasing; and
(3) $f''(10) > 0$, since f is concave upward.
Thus, $f'(10) < f(10) < f''(10)$, choice (C).

12. See Figure DS-3.
The graph of f is concave upward for
$x < x_2$.

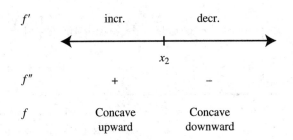

Figure DS-3

13. See Figure DS-4.
Enter $y^1 = \sin(x^2)$. Using the [*Inflection*]
function of your calculator, you obtain four
points of inflection on $[0, \pi]$. The points of
inflection occur at $x = 0.81, 1.81, 2.52$, and
3.07. Since $y_1 = \sin(x^2)$ is an even function,
there is a total of eight points of inflection on
$[-\pi, \pi]$. An alternate solution is to enter
$y^2 = \dfrac{d^2}{dx^2}(y_1(x), x, 2)$. The graph of y_2 crosses
the x-axis eight times, thus eight zeros on
$[-\pi, \pi]$.

Figure DS-4

14. Since $g(x) = \displaystyle\int_a^x f(t)dt$, $g'(x) = f(x)$.

See Figure DS-5.
The only graph that satisfies the behavior of g
is choice (A).

Figure DS-5

15. See Figure DS-6.
A change of concavity occurs at $x = 0$ for q.
Thus, q has a point of inflection at $x = 0$.
None of the other functions has a point of
inflection.

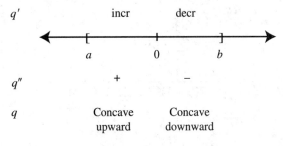

Figure DS-6

16. Solve $x = 1 + e^{-t}$ for t. $x - 1 = e^{-t} \Rightarrow$ $-\ln(x-1) = t$. Substitute in $y = 1 + e^t$.

$$y = 1 + e^{-\ln(x-1)} \Rightarrow y = 1 + \frac{1}{x-1}$$

$$\Rightarrow y = \frac{x}{x-1}$$

Chapter 8

17. Let z be the diagonal of a square. Area of a square $A = \dfrac{z^2}{2}$

$$\frac{dA}{dt} = \frac{2z}{2}\frac{dz}{dt} = z\frac{dz}{dt}.$$

Since $\dfrac{dA}{dt} = 4\dfrac{dz}{dt}$; $4\dfrac{dz}{dt} = z\dfrac{dz}{dt} \Rightarrow z = 4$.

Let s be a side of the square. Since the diagonal $z = 4$, $s^2 + s^2 = z^2$ or $2s^2 = 16$. Thus, $s^2 = 8$ or $s = 2\sqrt{2}$.

18. See Figure DS-7.
The graph of g indicates that a relative maximum occurs at $x = 2$; g is not differentiable at $x = 6$, since there is a *cusp* at $x = 6$; and g does not have a point of inflection at $x = -2$, since there is no tangent line at $x = -2$. Thus, only statement I is true.

Figure DS-7

Chapter 9

19.
$$y = \sqrt{x-1} = (x-1)^{1/2};$$
$$\frac{dy}{dx} = \frac{1}{2}(x-1)^{-1/2}$$
$$= \frac{1}{2(x-1)^{1/2}}$$
$$\left.\frac{dy}{dx}\right|_{x=5} = \frac{1}{2(5-1)^{1/2}} = \frac{1}{2(4)^{1/2}} = \frac{1}{4}$$

At $x = 5$, $y = \sqrt{x-1} = \sqrt{5-1}$
$= 2$; $(5, 2)$.

Slope of normal line = negative reciprocal of $\left(\dfrac{1}{4}\right) = -4$.

Equation of normal line:
$y - 2 = -4(x - 5) \Rightarrow y = -4(x - 5) + 2$ or
$\quad y = -4x + 22$.

20. $y = \cos(xy)$;

$$\frac{dy}{dx} = [-\sin(xy)]\left(1y + x\frac{dy}{dx}\right)$$

$$\frac{dy}{dx} = -y\sin(xy) - x\sin(xy)\frac{dy}{dx}$$

$$\frac{dy}{dx} + x\sin(xy)\frac{dy}{dx} = -y\sin(xy)$$

$$\frac{dy}{dx}[1 + x\sin(xy)] = -y\sin(xy)$$

$$\frac{dy}{dx} = \frac{-y\sin(xy)}{1 + x\sin(xy)}$$

At $x = 0$, $y = \cos(xy) = \cos(0)$
$\quad = 1$; $(0, 1)$

$$\left.\frac{dy}{dx}\right|_{x=0, y=1} = \frac{-(1)\sin(0)}{1 + 0\sin(0)} = \frac{0}{1} = 0.$$

Thus, the slope of the tangent at $x = 0$ is 0.

21. See Figure DS-8.
$$v(t) = t^2 - t$$

Set $v(t) = 0 \Rightarrow t(t-1) = 0$
$$\Rightarrow t = 0 \text{ or } t = 1$$

$a(t) = v'(t) = 2t - 1.$

Set $a(t) = 0 \Rightarrow 2t - 1 = 0$ or $t = \dfrac{1}{2}$.

Since $v(t) < 0$ and $a(t) > 0$ on $\left(\dfrac{1}{2}, 1\right)$, the speed of the particle is decreasing on $\left(\dfrac{1}{2}, 1\right)$.

V(t)	0 – – – – – – – – – – – – – – – – – 0 + + + + +		
t	0	$\frac{1}{2}$	1
$a(t)$	– – – – – – – – 0 + + + + + + + + + + + + + + + + + + +		

Figure DS-8

22. $v(t) = \dfrac{t^3}{3} - 2t^2 + 5$

$a(t) = v'(t) = t^2 - 4t$
See Figure DS-9.
The graph indicates that for $0 \le t \le 6$, the maximum acceleration occurs at the endpoint $t = 6$. $a(t) = t^2 - 4t$ and $a(6) = 6^2 - 4(6) = 12$.

Figure DS-9

23. $y = x^3, x \ge 0; \dfrac{dy}{dx} = 3x^2$

$f'(x) = 12 \Rightarrow \dfrac{dy}{dx} = 3x^2 = 12$

$\Rightarrow x^2 = 4 \Rightarrow x = 2$

Slope of normal = negative reciprocal of slope of tangent $= -\dfrac{1}{12}$.

At $x = 2$, $y = x^3 = 2^3 = 8$; $(2, 8)$

$$y - 8 = -\dfrac{1}{12}(x - 2).$$

Equation of normal line: $\Rightarrow y = -\dfrac{1}{12}(x - 2) + 8$

$$\text{or } y = -\dfrac{1}{12}x + \dfrac{49}{6}.$$

24. $f(x) = \dfrac{\ln x}{x}$; $f'(x) = \dfrac{(1/x)(x) - (1)\ln x}{x^2}$

$$= \dfrac{1}{x^2} - \dfrac{\ln x}{x^2}$$

$y = -x^2; \dfrac{dy}{dx} = -2x$
Perpendicular tangents

$\Rightarrow (f'(x))\left(\dfrac{dy}{dx}\right) = -1$

$\Rightarrow \left(\left(\dfrac{1}{x^2}\right) - \dfrac{\ln x}{x^2}\right)(-2x) = -1.$

Using the [*Solve*] function on your calculator, you obtain $x \approx 1.37015 \approx 1.370$.

25. $f\left(\dfrac{\pi}{2}\right) = 3 \Rightarrow \left(\dfrac{\pi}{2}, 3\right)$ is on the graph.

$f'\left(\dfrac{\pi}{2}\right) = -1 \Rightarrow$ slope of the tangent at $x = \dfrac{\pi}{2}$ is -1.

Equation of tangent line: $y - 3 =$

$-1\left(x - \dfrac{\pi}{2}\right)$ or $y = -x + \dfrac{\pi}{2} + 3$.

Thus, $f\left(\dfrac{\pi}{2} + \dfrac{\pi}{180}\right) \approx -\left(\dfrac{\pi}{2} + \dfrac{\pi}{180}\right)$

$$+ \dfrac{\pi}{2} + 3$$

$$\approx 3 - \dfrac{\pi}{180} \approx 2.98255$$

$$\approx 2.983.$$

26. Position is given by $x = 4t^2$ and $y = \sqrt{t}$, so velocity is $\dfrac{dx}{dt} = 8t$ and $\dfrac{dy}{dt} = \dfrac{1}{2\sqrt{t}}$. The acceleration will be $\dfrac{d^2x}{dt^2} = 8$, $\dfrac{d^2y}{dt^2} = -\dfrac{1}{4}t^{-3/2}$.

Evaluate $-\dfrac{1}{4}t^{-3/2}\Big]_{t=4} = -\dfrac{1}{4}\left(\dfrac{1}{8}\right) = -\dfrac{1}{32}$ to get

the acceleration vector $\left\langle 8, -\dfrac{1}{32}\right\rangle$.

27. The slope of the tangent line is $\dfrac{dy}{dx}\Big|_{t=1}$ and

$\dfrac{dx}{dt} = 2$, $\dfrac{dy}{dt} = 2t + 2$, so $\dfrac{dy}{dx}\Big|_{t=1}$

$$= \dfrac{2t + 2}{2}\Big|_{t=1} = t + 1\big|_{t=1} = 2. \text{ At } t = 1,$$

$x = 5, y = 3, \Rightarrow (5, 3)$,

So, the equation of the tangent line is

$y - 3 = 2(x - 5) \Rightarrow y = 2(x - 5) + 3 \Rightarrow y = 2x - 7$.

Chapter 10

28. $\int \dfrac{1-x^2}{x^2}\,dx = \int \left(\dfrac{1}{x^2}-\dfrac{x^2}{x^2}\right)dx$

$$= \int \left(\dfrac{1}{x^2}-1\right)dx$$

$$= \int (x^{-2}-1)dx = \dfrac{x^{-1}}{-1}-x+C$$

$$= -\dfrac{1}{x}-x+C$$

 KEY IDEA You can check the answer by differentiating your result.

29. Let $u = e^x + 1; \, du = e^x\,dx$.

$$f(x) = \int \dfrac{e^x}{e^x+1}\,dx = \int \dfrac{1}{u}\,du$$

$$= \ln|u| + C = \ln|e^x + 1| + C$$

$$f(0) = \ln|e^0 + 1| + C = \ln(2) + C$$

Since $f(0) = \ln 2 \Rightarrow \ln(2) + C$

$$= \ln 2 \Rightarrow C = 0.$$

Thus, $f(x) = \ln(e^x + 1)$ and $f(\ln 2)$

$$= \ln(e^{\ln 2} + 1) = \ln(2 + 1)$$

$$= \ln 3.$$

30. See Figure DS-10.
To find the points of intersection, set

$$\sin 2x = \dfrac{1}{2} \Rightarrow 2x = \sin^{-1}\left(\dfrac{1}{2}\right)$$

$$\Rightarrow 2x = \dfrac{\pi}{6} \text{ or } 2x = \dfrac{5\pi}{6} \Rightarrow x = \dfrac{\pi}{12} \text{ or } x = \dfrac{5\pi}{12}.$$

Volume of solid

$$= \pi \int_{\pi/12}^{5\pi/12} \left[(\sin 2x)^2 - \left(\dfrac{1}{2}\right)^2\right]dx.$$

Using your calculator, you obtain:
Volume of solid $\approx (0.478306)\pi$
$\approx 1.50264 \approx 1.503$.

Figure DS-10

31. $\displaystyle\int_2^5 \dfrac{1}{x^2+2x-3}\,dx = \int_2^5 \dfrac{1}{(x+3)(x-1)}\,dx$

Use a partial fraction decomposition with

$$\dfrac{A}{(x+3)} + \dfrac{B}{(x-1)} = \dfrac{1}{(x+3)(x-1)}, \text{ which}$$

gives $A = \dfrac{-1}{4}$ and $B = \dfrac{1}{4}$. Then the integral becomes

$$= \int_2^5 \dfrac{-1/4}{(x+3)}\,dx + \int_2^5 \dfrac{1/4}{(x-1)}\,dx$$

$$= \dfrac{-1}{4}\int_2^5 \dfrac{1}{(x+3)}\,dx + \dfrac{1}{4}\int_2^5 \dfrac{1}{(x-1)}\,dx$$

$$= \dfrac{-1}{4}\ln|x+3| + \dfrac{1}{4}\ln|x-1| \Big]_2^5$$

$$= \dfrac{1}{4}\left(\ln\left|\dfrac{x-1}{x+3}\right|\right)\Big]_2^5$$

$$= \dfrac{1}{4}\left[\left(\ln\left|\dfrac{4}{8}\right|\right) - \left(\ln\left|\dfrac{1}{5}\right|\right)\right]$$

$$= \dfrac{1}{4}\ln\left(\dfrac{5}{2}\right)$$

32. Integrate $\int x^2 \cos x\,dx$ by parts with $u = x^2$, $du = 2x\,dx$, $dv = \cos x\,dx$, and $v = \sin x$. The integral becomes
$$= x^2 \sin x - \int \sin x (2x)\,dx$$
$$= x^2 \sin x - 2\int x \sin x\,dx.$$
Use parts again for the remaining integral, letting $u = x$, $du = dx$, $dv = \sin x\,dx$, and $v = -\cos x$. The integral
$$= x^2 \sin x - 2\left[-x \cos x - \int (-\cos x)\,dx\right]$$

simplifies to

$$=x^2 \sin x + 2x \cos x - 2 \int \cos x \, dx,$$

and the final integration gives you
$$=x^2 \sin x + 2x \cos x - 2 \sin x + C.$$

Chapter 11

33. $\int_1^4 \dfrac{1}{\sqrt{x}} dx = \int_1^4 x^{-1/2} dx = \dfrac{x^{1/2}}{1/2} \Big]_1^4$

$$= 2x^{1/2} \Big]_1^4$$

$$= 2(4)^{1/2} - 2(1)^{1/2} = 4 - 2 = 2$$

34. $\int_{-1}^k (2x - 3) dx = x^2 - 3x \Big]_{-1}^k$

$$= k^2 - 3k - (1 + 3)$$

$$= k^2 - 3k - 4$$

Set $k^2 - 3k - 4 = 6 \Rightarrow k^2 - 3k - 10 = 0$

$\Rightarrow (k - 5)(k + 2) = 0 \Rightarrow k = 5$ or $k = -2$.

 KEY IDEA You can check your answer by evaluating $\int_{-1}^{-2} (2x - 3) dx$ and

$$\int_{-1}^5 (2x - 3) dx.$$

35. $h(x) = \int_{\pi/2}^x \sqrt{\sin t} \, dt \Rightarrow h'(x) = \sqrt{\sin x}$

$h'(\pi) = \sqrt{\sin \pi} = \sqrt{0} = 0$

36. Let $u = 3x; du = 3dx$ or $\dfrac{du}{3} = dx$.

$$\int g(3x) dx = \int g(u) \dfrac{du}{3} = \dfrac{1}{3} \int g(u) du$$

$$= \dfrac{1}{3} f(u) + c = \dfrac{1}{3} f(3x) + c$$

$$\int_0^2 g(3x) dx = \dfrac{1}{3} [f(3x)]_0^2$$

$$= \dfrac{1}{3} f(6) - \dfrac{1}{3} f(0)$$

Thus, the correct choice is (A).

37. $\int_\pi^x \sin(2t) dt = \left[\dfrac{-\cos(2t)}{2} \right]_\pi^x$

$$= \dfrac{-\cos(2x)}{2} - \left(-\dfrac{\cos(2\pi)}{2} \right)$$

$$= -\dfrac{1}{2} \cos(2x) + \dfrac{1}{2}$$

38. I. $\int_a^c f(x) dx = \int_a^b f(x) dx + \int_b^c f(x) dx$

The statement is true, since the upper and lower limits of the integrals are in sequence, i.e. $a \to c = a \to b \to c$.

II. $\int_a^b f(x) dx = \int_a^c f(x) dx - \int_c^b f(x) dx$

$$= \int_a^c f(x) dx + \int_b^c f(x) dx$$

The statement is not always true.

III. $\int_b^c f(x) dx = \int_b^a f(x) dx - \int_c^a f(x) dx$

$$= \int_b^a f(x) dx + \int_a^c f(x) dx$$

The statement is true.
Thus, only statements I and III are true.

39. Since $g(x) = \int_{\pi/2}^x 2 \sin t \, dt$, then

$g'(x) = 2 \sin x$.
Set $g'(x) = 0 \Rightarrow 2 \sin x = 0 \Rightarrow x = \pi$ or 2π
$g''(x) = 2 \cos x$ and $g''(\pi) = 2 \cos \pi = -2$ and $g''(2\pi) = 1$.
Thus g has a local minimum at $x = 2\pi$. You can also approach the problem geometrically by looking at the area under the curve. See Figure DS-11.

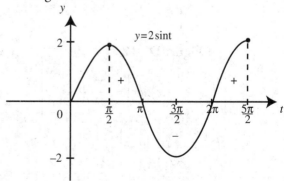

Figure DS-11

40. $\int_0^\infty e^{-x}\,dx = \lim_{k\to\infty} \int_0^k e^{-x}\,dx = \lim_{k\to\infty} \left[-e^{-x}\right]_0^k$

$= \lim_{k\to\infty} \left[-e^{-k} + e^0\right] = \lim_{k\to\infty} \left[-e^{-k} + 1\right] = 1$

Chapter 12

41. Total distance $= \int_0^4 v(t)\,dt + \left|\int_4^6 v(t)\,dt\right|$

$= \dfrac{1}{2}(4)(20) + \left|\dfrac{1}{2}(2)(-10)\right|$

$= 40 + 10 = 50$ feet

42. $\int_{-1}^5 f(x)\,dx = \int_{-1}^1 f(x)\,dx + \int_1^5 f(x)\,dx$

$= -\dfrac{1}{2}(2)(1) + \dfrac{1}{2}(2+4)(1)$

$= -1 + 3 = 2$

43. To find points of intersection, set
$y = x^2 - x = 0$
$\Rightarrow x(x-1) = 0 \Rightarrow x = 0$ or $x = 1$.
See Figure DS-12.

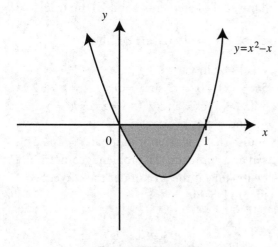

Figure DS-12

Area $= \left|\int_0^1 (x^2 - x)\,dx\right| = \left|\dfrac{x^3}{3} - \dfrac{x^2}{2}\right]_0^1$

$= \left|\left(\dfrac{1}{3} - \dfrac{1}{2}\right) - 0\right| = \left|-\dfrac{1}{6}\right|$

$= \dfrac{1}{6}$

44. $\int_{-k}^k f(x)\,dx = 0 \Rightarrow f(x)$ is an odd function, i.e., $f(x) = -f(-x)$. Thus the graph in choice (D) is the only odd function.

45. Area $= \int_1^k \sqrt{x}\,dx = \int_1^k x^{1/2}\,dx$

$= \left[\dfrac{x^{3/2}}{3/2}\right]_1^k$

$= \left[\dfrac{2}{3}x^{3/2}\right]_1^k = \dfrac{2}{3}k^{3/2} - \dfrac{2}{3}(1)^{3/2}$

$= \dfrac{2}{3}k^{3/2} - \dfrac{2}{3} = \dfrac{2}{3}\left(k^{3/2} - 1\right).$

Since A = 8, set $\dfrac{2}{3}\left(k^{3/2}-1\right)=8 \Rightarrow k^{3/2}-1$

$=12 \Rightarrow k^{3/2}=13$ or $k=13^{2/3}$.

46. See Figure DS-13.

Figure DS-13

Using the [*Intersection*] function of the calculator, you obtain the intersection points at $x = 0.785398,\ 3.92699$, and 7.06858.

Area $= \int_{0.785398}^{3.92699} (\sin x - \cos x)\,dx$

$+ \int_{3.92699}^{7.06858} (\cos x - \sin x)\,dx$

$= 2.82843 + 2.82843 \approx 5.65685 \approx 5.657$

You can also find the area by:

Area $= \int_{.785398}^{7.06858} |\sin x - \cos x|\,dx$

$\approx 5.65685 \approx 5.657.$

47. Width of a rectangle $= \dfrac{6-0}{3} = 2$.

Midpoints are $x = 1, 3,$ and 5 and $f(1) = 2$, $f(3) = 10$ and $f(5) = 26$.

$$\int_0^6 f(x)dx \approx 2(2 + 10 + 26) \approx 2(38) = 76$$

48. The intersection of the circles $r = 2\cos\theta$ and $r = 2\sin\theta$ can be found by adding the area swept out by $r = 2\sin\theta$ for $0 \le \theta \le \dfrac{\pi}{4}$ and the area swept by $r = 2\cos\theta$ for $\dfrac{\pi}{4} \le \theta \le \dfrac{\pi}{2}$.

$$A = \frac{1}{2}\int_0^{\pi/4} 4\sin^2\theta\,d\theta + \frac{1}{2}\int_{\pi/4}^{\pi/2} 4\cos^2\theta\,d\theta$$

$$= 2\int_0^{\pi/4}\sin^2\theta\,d\theta + 2\int_{\pi/4}^{\pi/2}\cos^2\theta\,d\theta$$

$$= \int_0^{\pi/4}(1 - \cos 2\theta)\,d\theta$$

$$+ \int_{\pi/4}^{\pi/2}(1 + \cos 2\theta)\,d\theta$$

$$= \left(\theta - \frac{1}{2}\sin 2\theta\right)\Big|_0^{\pi/4}$$

$$+ \left(\theta + \frac{1}{2}\sin 2\theta\right)\Big|_{\pi/4}^{\pi/2}$$

$$= \left[\frac{\pi}{4} - \frac{1}{2} - 0\right]$$

$$+ \left[\left(\frac{\pi}{2} + 0\right) - \left(\frac{\pi}{4} + \frac{1}{2}\right)\right]$$

$$= \frac{\pi}{2} - 1$$

49. Differentiate $x = 3t - t^3 \Rightarrow \dfrac{dx}{dt} = 3 - 3t^2$ and $y = 3t^2 \Rightarrow \dfrac{dy}{dt} = 6t$. The length of the curve from $t = 0$ to $t = 2$ is

$$L = \int_0^2 \sqrt{(3 - 3t^2)^2 + (6t)^2}\,dt$$

$$= \int_0^2 \sqrt{9 - 18t^2 + 9t^4 + 36t^2}\,dt$$

$$= \int_0^2 \sqrt{9 + 18t^2 + 9t^4}\,dt$$

$$= \int_0^2 3\sqrt{(1 + t^2)^2}\,dt = 3\int_0^2 (1 + t^2)\,dt$$

$$= 3\left(t + \frac{1}{3}t^3\right)\Big|_0^2 = 3t + t^3\Big|_0^2$$

$$= (6 + 8) - (0) = 14.$$

Chapter 13

50. $\dfrac{dy}{dx} = 2\sin x \Rightarrow dy = 2\sin x\,dx$

$$\int dy = \int 2\sin x\,dx \Rightarrow y = -2\cos x + C$$

At $x = \pi$, $y = 2 \Rightarrow 2 = -2\cos\pi + C$

$$\Rightarrow 2 = (-2)(-1) + C$$

$$\Rightarrow 2 = 2 + C = 0.$$

Thus, $y = -2\cos x$.

51. Amount of water leaked

$$= \int_0^5 10\ln(t + 1)\,dt.$$

Using your calculator, you obtain $10(6\ln 6 - 5)$, which is approximately 57.506 gallons.

52. $\dfrac{dy}{dx} = ky \Rightarrow y = y_0 e^{kt}$

Half-life $= 5730 \Rightarrow y = \dfrac{1}{2}y_0$

when $t = 5730$.

Thus, $\dfrac{1}{2}y_0 = y_0 e^{k(5730)} \Rightarrow \dfrac{1}{2} = e^{5730k}$.

$$\ln\left(\frac{1}{2}\right) = \ln\left(e^{5730k}\right) \Rightarrow \ln\left(\frac{1}{2}\right) = 5730k$$

$$\ln 1 - \ln 2 = 5730k \Rightarrow -\ln 2 = 5730k$$

$$k = \frac{-\ln 2}{5730}$$

53. See Figure DS-14.

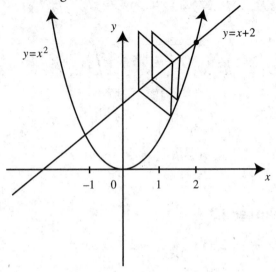

$y=x^2$

y

$y=x+2$

−1 0 1 2

x

Figure DS-14

To find points of intersection, set $x^2 = x + 2$
$\Rightarrow x^2 - x - 2 = 0 \Rightarrow x = 2$ or $x = -1$.
Area of cross section $= ((x + 2) - x^2)^2$.

Volume of solid, $V = \int_{-1}^{2} \left(x + 2 - x^2\right)^2 dx$.

Using your calculator, you obtain: $V = \dfrac{81}{10}$.

54. Separate and simplify

$$\frac{dP}{dt} = .35P \left(1 - \frac{P}{4000}\right).$$

$$\frac{1}{P\left(1 - \dfrac{P}{4000}\right)} dP = .35dt$$

$$\frac{4000}{P(4000 - P)} dP = .35dt$$

Integrate with a partial fraction decomposition.

$$\int \frac{4000}{P(4000 - P)} dP = \int .35dt$$

$$\int \frac{dP}{P} + \int \frac{dP}{4000 - P} = \int .35dt$$

$$\ln|P| - \ln|4000 - P| = .35t + C_1$$

$$\ln\left|\frac{P}{4000 - P}\right| = .35t + C_1$$

$$\frac{P}{4000 - P} = C_2 e^{.35t}$$

Population at $t = 0$ is 100, so

$$\frac{100}{4000 - 100} = \frac{100}{3900} = \frac{1}{39} = C_2.$$

The population model is $\dfrac{P}{4000 - P} = \dfrac{e^{.35t}}{39}$

$$\Rightarrow 39P = e^{.35t}(4000 - P)$$
$$\Rightarrow 39P + e^{.35t} P = 4000e^{.35t}$$
$$\Rightarrow P\left(39 + e^{.35t}\right) = 4000e^{.35t}$$
$$\Rightarrow P = \frac{4000e^{.35t}}{39 + e^{.35t}}$$
$$\Rightarrow P = \frac{4000}{39e^{-.35t} + 1}.$$

When $t = 5$, $P = \dfrac{4000}{39e^{-.35(5)} + 1}$

$$\Rightarrow P = \frac{4000}{39e^{-1.75} + 1}$$

$$\approx 514.325.$$

55. If $\dfrac{dy}{dx} = \dfrac{-y}{x^2}$ and $y = 3$ and $x = 2$, approximate y when $x = 3$. Use Euler's Method with an increment of 0.5.

$y(2) = 3$ and $\left(\dfrac{dy}{dx}\right)_{x=2,\ y=3} = \dfrac{-3}{4}$ so

$$y(2.5) = y(2) + 0.5\left(\frac{dy}{dx}\right)_{x=2,\ y=3}$$

$$= 3 + 0.5(-0.75) = 2.625$$

$$\left(\frac{dy}{dx}\right)_{x=2.5,\ y=2.625} = \frac{-2.625}{(2.5)^2}$$

$$= \frac{-21}{8(6.25)} = \frac{-21}{50}$$

$$= -0.42$$

$$y(3) = y(2.5) + 0.5\left(\frac{dy}{dx}\right)_{x=2.5,\ y=2.625}$$

$$= 2.625 + 0.5(-0.42)$$

$$= 2.625 - 0.21 = 2.415.$$

Chapter 14

56. Note that $\displaystyle\sum_{n=0}^{\infty} \frac{(-1)^n}{2n} = -\frac{1}{2} + \frac{1}{4} - \frac{1}{6} + \ldots$ is an

alternating series such that $a_1 > a_2 > a_3 \ldots$

i.e., $a_n > a_{n+1}$ and $\displaystyle\lim_{n\to\infty} a_n = \lim_{n\to\infty} \frac{1}{2n} = 0$.

Therefore $|S - s_n| \le a_{n+1}$ and, in this case,

$|S - s_5| \le a_6$, and $a_6 = \dfrac{1}{12}$. Thus

$|S - s_5| \le \dfrac{1}{12}$ is the maximum value.

57. The series $\displaystyle\sum_{n=0}^{\infty} \frac{3}{(n+1)^4}$ is a series with positive

terms, which can be compared to the series

$\displaystyle\sum_{n=0}^{\infty} \frac{3}{n^4}$. Also $\displaystyle\sum_{n=0}^{\infty} \frac{3}{n^4} = 3\sum_{n=0}^{\infty} \frac{1}{n^4}$ and $\displaystyle\sum_{n=0}^{\infty} \frac{1}{n^4}$

is a p-series with $p = 4$, and therefore

convergent. $\displaystyle\sum_{n=0}^{\infty} \frac{3}{(n+1)^4}$ is term by term

smaller than $\displaystyle\sum_{n=0}^{\infty} \frac{3}{n^4}$ and so $\displaystyle\sum_{n=0}^{\infty} \frac{3}{(n+1)^4}$

converges.

58. The series $x - \dfrac{x^2}{2} + \dfrac{x^3}{3} - \dfrac{x^4}{4} + \cdots$

is an alternating series with general term

$\dfrac{(-1)^{n-1} x^n}{n}$. Using the ratio test for absolute

convergence, we have $\displaystyle\lim_{n\to\infty} \left| \frac{x^{n+1}}{n+1} \cdot \frac{n}{x^n} \right| =$

$|x| \displaystyle\lim_{n\to\infty} \left(\frac{n}{n+1} \right) = |x|$. The series will

converge absolutely when $|x| < 1 \Rightarrow$
$-1 < x < 1$. We do not consider the end
points since the question asks for absolute
convergence.

59. Investigate the first few derivatives of

$f(x) = \dfrac{1}{x}$, $f'(x) = \dfrac{-1}{x^2}$, $f''(x) =$

$\dfrac{2}{x^3}$, $f'''(x) = \dfrac{-6}{x^4}$,

$f^{(4)}(x) = \dfrac{24}{x^5}$ and, in general, $f^{(n)}(x) = \dfrac{(-1)^n n!}{x^{n+1}}$.

Evaluate the derivatives at $x = 2$. $f(2) = \dfrac{1}{2}$,

$f'(2) = \dfrac{-1}{4}$, $f''(2) = \dfrac{2}{8}$,

$f'''(2) = \dfrac{-6}{16}$, $f^{(4)}(x) = \dfrac{24}{32}$

and, in general, $f^{(n)}(2) = \dfrac{(-1)^n n!}{2^{n+1}}$.

The Taylor series is $f(x) = \dfrac{1}{x}$

$= \displaystyle\sum_{n=0}^{\infty} \frac{\frac{(-1)^n n!}{2^{n+1}}}{n!} (x - 2)^n = \sum_{n=0}^{\infty} \frac{(-1)^n}{2^{n+1}} (x - 2)^n$

$= \dfrac{1/2}{0!} (x-2)^0 + \dfrac{-1/4}{1!} (x-2)^1 + \dfrac{2/8}{2!} (x-2)^2$

$+ \dfrac{-6/16}{3!} (x-2)^3 + \dfrac{24/32}{4!} (x-2)^4 + \cdots$

$= \dfrac{1}{2} - \dfrac{1}{4}(x-2) + \dfrac{1}{8}(x-2)^2 - \dfrac{1}{16}(x-2)^3$

$+ \dfrac{1}{32}(x-2)^4 - \cdots$

60. Begin with the MacLaurin series for e^x.
If $f(x) = e^x$, then $f'(x) = e^x$,
$f''(x) = e^x$, and $f^n(x) = e^x$.

Thus $e^x = 1 + x + \dfrac{x^2}{2!} + \dfrac{x^3}{3!} + \cdots$.

Replacing x by $-x^2$, we have

$e^{-x^2} = 1 - x^2 + \dfrac{x^4}{2!} - \dfrac{x^6}{3!} + \dfrac{x^8}{4!} - \cdots$.

Thus, $e^{-x^2} = \displaystyle\sum_{n=0}^{\infty} \frac{(-1)^n (x^{2n})}{n!}$.

3.5 Calculate Your Score

Short-Answer Questions

Questions 1–60 for AP Calculus BC

$$\text{Number of correct answers} = \underline{}$$
$$\text{raw score}$$

AP Calculus BC Diagnostic Exam

RAW SCORE	
AP CALCULUS BC	**APPROXIMATE AP GRADE**
47–60	5
37–46	4
29–36	3
21–28	2
0–20	1

STEP **3**

Develop Strategies
for Success

CHAPTER **4** How to Approach Each Question Type

CHAPTER 4

How to Approach Each Question Type

IN THIS CHAPTER

Summary: Knowing and applying question-answering strategies helps you succeed on tests. This chapter provides you with many test-taking tips to help you earn a 5 on the AP Calculus BC exam.

Key Ideas

✪ Read each question carefully.

✪ Do not linger on a question. Time yourself accordingly.

✪ For multiple-choice questions, sometimes it is easier to work backward by trying each of the given choices. You will be able to eliminate some of the choices quickly.

✪ For free-response questions, always show sufficient work so that your line of reasoning is clear.

✪ Write legibly.

✪ Always use calculus notations instead of calculator syntax.

✪ If the question involves decimals, round your final answer to 3 decimal places unless the question indicates otherwise.

✪ Trust your instincts. Your first approach to solving a problem is usually the correct one.

✪ Get a good night's sleep the night before.

4.1 The Multiple-Choice Questions

- There are 45 multiple-choice questions for the AP Calculus BC exam. These questions are divided into Section I–Part A, which consists of 30 questions for which the use of a calculator is not permitted; and Section I–Part B with 15 questions, for which the use of a graphing calculator is allowed. The multiple-choice questions account for 50% of the grade for the whole test.
- Do the easy questions first because all multiple-choice questions are worth the same amount of credit. You have 60 minutes for the 30 questions in Section I–Part A and 45 minutes for the 15 questions in Section I–Part B. Do not linger on any one question. Time yourself accordingly.
- There is no partial credit for multiple-choice questions, and you do not need to show work to receive credit for the correct answer.

- Read the question carefully. If there is a graph or a chart, look at it carefully. For example, be sure to know if the given graph is that of $f(x)$ or $f'(x)$. Pay attention to the scale of the x and y axes, and the unit of measurement.

- Never leave a question blank since there is **no penalty for incorrect answers.**
- If a question involves finding the derivative of a function, you must first find the derivative, and then see if you need to do additional work to get the final answer to the question. For example, if a question asks for an equation of the tangent line to a curve at a given point, you must first find the derivative, evaluate it at the given point (which gives you the slope of the line), and then proceed to find an equation of the tangent line. For some questions, finding the derivative of a given function (or sometimes, the antiderivative), is only the first step to solving the problem. It is not the final answer to the question. You might need to do more work to get the final answer.

- Sometimes, it is easier to work backward by trying each of the given choices as the final answer. Often, you will be able to eliminate some of the given choices quickly.
- If a question involves decimal numbers, do not round until the final answer, and at that point, the final answer is usually rounded to 3 decimal places. Look at the number of decimal places of the answers in the given choices.
- Trust your instincts. Usually your first approach to solving a problem is the correct one.
- Some multiple-choice questions require simplification such as factoring, reducing, or working with fractional exponents. When in doubt, plug a simple value (such as $x = 0$ or 1) into the answer choices to see which one is equivalent to your answer.

4.2 The Free-Response Questions

- There are 6 free-response questions in Section II–Part A consisting of 2 questions that allow the use of a calculator, and Part B with 4 questions that do not permit the use of a calculator. The 6 free-response questions account for 50% of the grade for the whole test.
- Read, Read, Read. Read the question carefully. Know what information is given, what quantity is being sought, and what additional information you need to find in order to answer the question.

- Always show a sufficient amount of work so that your line of reasoning is clear. This is particularly important in determining partial credit. In general, use complete sentences to explain your reasoning. Include all graphs, charts, relevant procedures, and theorems. Clearly indicate all the important steps that you have taken in solving the problem. A correct answer with insufficient work will receive minimal credit.

- When appropriate, represent the given information in calculus notations. For example, if it is given that the volume of a cone is decreasing at 2 cm^3 per second, write $\dfrac{dV}{dt} =$ −2 cm^3/sec. Similarly, represent the quantity being sought in calculus notations. For example, if the question asks for the rate of change of the radius of the cone at 5 seconds, write "Find $\dfrac{dr}{dt}$ at $t = 5$ sec."
- Do not forget to answer the question. Free-response questions tend to involve many computations. It is easy to forget to indicate the final answer. As a habit, always state the final answer as the last step in your solution, and if appropriate, include the unit of measurement in your final answer. For example, if a question asks for the area of a region, you may want to conclude your solution by stating that "The area of the region is 20 square units."
- Do the easy questions first. Each of the 6 free-response questions is worth the same amount of credit. There is no penalty for an incorrect solution.
- Pay attention to the scales of the x and y axes, the unit of measurement, and the labeling of given charts and graphs. For example, be sure to know whether a given graph is that of $f(x)$ or $f'(x)$.
- When finding relative extrema or points of inflection, you must show the behavior of the function that leads to your conclusion. Simply showing a sign chart is not sufficient.

- Often a question has several parts. Sometimes, in order to answer a question in one part of the question, you might need the answer to an earlier part of the question. For example, to answer the question in part (b), you might need the answer in part (a). If you are not sure how to answer part (a), make an educated guess for the best possible answer and then use this answer to solve the problem in part (b). If your solution in part (b) uses the correct approach but your final answer is incorrect, you could still receive full or almost full credit for your work.
- As with solving multiple-choice questions, trust your instincts. Your first approach to solving a problem is usually the correct one.
- Solve all parts of each problem; sometimes you can solve part (c), for example, without knowing how to solve (a) and (b).
- Do not waste time simplifying answers. All equivalent numeric or algebraic answers are accepted.

4.3 Using a Graphing Calculator

- The use of a graphing calculator is permitted in Section I–Part B multiple-choice questions and in Section II–Part A free-response questions.
- You are permitted to use the following 4 built-in capabilities of your graphing calculator to obtain an answer:

    1. plotting the graph of a function
    2. finding the zeros of a function
    3. calculating numerically the derivative of a function
    4. calculating numerically the value of a definite integral

For example, if you have to find the area of a region, you need to show a definite integral. You may then proceed to use the calculator to produce the numerical value of the definite integral without showing any supporting work. All other capabilities of your calculator can only be used to *check* your answer. For example, you may not use the built-in [*Inflection*] function of your calculator to find points of inflection. You must use calculus showing derivatives and indicating a change of concavity.

- You may *not* use calculator syntax to substitute for calculus notations. For example, you may *not* write "Volume = $\int (\pi (5x)^\wedge 2, x, 0, 3) = 225\,\pi$"; instead you need to write "Volume = $\pi \int_{0}^{3} (5x)^2 dx = 225\,\pi$."

- When using a graphing calculator to solve a problem, you are required to write the setup that leads to the answer. For example, if you are finding the volume of a solid, you must write the definite integral and then use the calculator to compute the numerical value, e.g., Volume = $\pi \int_{0}^{3} (5x)^2 dx = 22.5\,\pi$. Simply indicating the answer without writing the integral is considered an incomplete solution, for which you would receive minimal credit (possibly 1 point) instead of full credit for a complete solution.

- Set your calculator to radian mode, and change to degree mode only if necessary.

- If you are using a TI-89 graphing calculator, clear all previous entries for variables a through z before the AP Calculus BC exam.

- You are permitted to store computer programs in your calculator and use them in the AP Calculus BC Exam. Your calculator memories will not be cleared.

- Using the [*Trace*] function to find points on a graph may not produce the required accuracy. Most graphing calculators have other built-in functions that can produce more accurate results. For example, to find the x-intercepts of a graph, use the [*Zero*] function, and to find the intersection point of two curves, use the [*Intersection*] function.

- When decimal numbers are involved, do not round until the final answer. Unless otherwise stated, your final answer should be accurate to three places after the decimal point. You may also truncate your answer with four decimal places and eliminate the possibility of a rounding error.

- You may bring up to two calculators to the AP Calculus BC exam.

- Replace old batteries with new ones and make sure that the calculator is functioning properly before the exam.

4.4 Taking the Exam

What Do I Need to Bring to the Exam?

- Several Number 2 pencils.
- A good eraser and a pencil sharpener.
- Two black or blue pens.
- One or two approved graphing calculators with fresh batteries. (Be careful when you change batteries so that you don't lose your programs.)
- A watch.
- An admissions card or a photo I.D. card if your school or the test site requires it.
- Your Social Security number.
- Your school code number if the test site is not at your school.
- A simple snack *if the test site permits it*. (Don't try anything you haven't eaten before. You might have an allergic reaction.)
- A light jacket if you know that the test site has strong air conditioning.
- Do *not* bring Wite Out or scrap paper.

Tips for Taking the Exam

General Tips

- Write legibly.
- Label all diagrams.
- Organize your solution so that the reader can follow your line of reasoning.
- Use complete sentences whenever possible. Always indicate what the final answer is.

More Tips

- Do easy questions first.
- Write out formulas and indicate all major steps.
- Never leave a question blank, especially a multiple-choice question, since there is no penalty for incorrect answers.
- Be careful to bubble in the right grid, especially if you skip a question.
- Move on. Don't linger on a problem too long. Make an educated guess.
- Go with your first instinct if you are unsure.

Still More Tips

- Indicate units of measure.
- Simplify numeric or algebraic expressions only if the question asks you to do so.
- Carry all decimal places and round only at the end.
- Round to 3 decimal places unless the question indicates otherwise.
- Watch out for different units of measure, e.g., the radius, r, is 2 feet, find $\dfrac{dr}{dt}$ in inches per second.
- Use calculus notations and not calculator syntax, e.g., write $\int x^2 dx$ and not $\int (x^\wedge 2, \ x)$.
- Use only the four specified capabilities of your calculator to get your answer: plotting graphs, finding zeros, calculating numerical derivatives, and evaluating definite integrals. All other built-in capabilities can only be used to *check* your solution.
- Answer all parts of a question from Section II even if you think your answer to an earlier part of the question might not be correct.

Enough Already . . . Just 3 More Tips

- Be familiar with the instructions for the different parts of the exam. Review the practice exams in the back of this book. Visit the College Board website at: https://apstudent.collegeboard.org/apcourse/ap-calculus-bc for more information.
- Get a good night's sleep the night before.
- Have a light breakfast before the exam.

STEP 4

Review the Knowledge You Need to Score High

BIG IDEA **1: Limits**

    CHAPTER **5 Limits and Continuity**

BIG IDEA **2: Derivatives**

    CHAPTER **6 Differentiation**

    CHAPTER **7 Graphs of Functions and Derivatives**

    CHAPTER **8 Applications of Derivatives**

    CHAPTER **9 More Applications of Derivatives**

BIG IDEA **3: Integrals and the Fundamental Theorems of Calculus**

    CHAPTER **10 Integration**

    CHAPTER **11 Definite Integrals**

    CHAPTER **12 Areas, Volumes, and Arc Lengths**

    CHAPTER **13 More Applications of Definite Integrals**

BIG IDEA **4: Series**

    CHAPTER **14 Series**

CHAPTER 5

Big Idea 1: Limits
Limits and Continuity

IN THIS CHAPTER

Summary: On the AP Calculus BC exam, you will be tested on your ability to find the limit of a function. In this chapter, you will be shown how to solve several types of limit problems, which include finding the limit of a function as x approaches a specific value, finding the limit of a function as x approaches infinity, one-sided limits, infinite limits, and limits involving sine and cosine. You will also learn how to apply the concepts of limits to finding vertical and horizontal asymptotes as well as determining the continuity of a function.

Key Ideas

✪ Definition of the limit of a function
✪ Properties of limits
✪ Evaluating limits as x approaches a specific value
✪ Evaluating limits as x approaches $\pm$ infinity
✪ One-sided limits
✪ Limits involving infinities
✪ Limits involving sine and cosine
✪ Vertical and horizontal asymptotes
✪ Continuity

5.1 The Limit of a Function

Main Concepts: Definition and Properties of Limits, Evaluating Limits, One-Sided Limits, Squeeze Theorem

Definition and Properties of Limits

Definition of Limit

Let f be a function defined on an open interval containing a, except possibly at a itself. Then $\lim_{x \to a} f(x) = L$ (read as the limit of $f(x)$ as x approaches a is L) if for any $\varepsilon > 0$, there exists a $\delta > 0$ such that $|f(x) - L| < \varepsilon$ whenever $|x - a| < \delta$.

Properties of Limits

Given $\lim_{x \to a} f(x) = L$ and $\lim_{x \to a} g(x) = M$ and L, M, a, c, and n are real numbers, then:

1. $\lim_{x \to a} c = c$

2. $\lim_{x \to a} [c f(x)] = c \lim_{x \to a} f(x) = c L$

3. $\lim_{x \to a} [f(x) \pm g(x)] = \lim_{x \to a} f(x) \pm \lim_{x \to a} g(x) = L + M$

4. $\lim_{x \to a} [f(x) \cdot g(x)] = \lim_{x \to a} f(x) \cdot \lim_{x \to a} g(x) = L \cdot M$

5. $\lim_{x \to a} \dfrac{f(x)}{g(x)} = \dfrac{\lim_{x \to a} f(x)}{\lim_{x \to a} g(x)} = \dfrac{L}{M}, \ M \neq 0$

6. $\lim_{x \to a} [f(x)]^n = \left(\lim_{x \to a} f(x) \right)^n = L^n$

Evaluating Limits

If f is a continuous function on an open interval containing the number a, then $\lim_{x \to a} f(x) = f(a)$.

Common techniques in evaluating limits are:

1. Substituting directly
2. Factoring and simplifying
3. Multiplying the numerator and denominator of a rational function by the conjugate of either the numerator or denominator
4. Using a graph or a table of values of the given function

Example 1

Find the limit: $\lim_{x \to 5} \sqrt{3x + 1}$.

Substituting directly: $\lim_{x \to 5} \sqrt{3x + 1} = \sqrt{3(5) + 1} = 4$.

Example 2

Find the limit: $\lim\limits_{x \to \pi} 3x \sin x$.

Using the product rule, $\lim\limits_{x \to \pi} 3x \sin x = \left(\lim\limits_{x \to \pi} 3x \right) \left(\lim\limits_{x \to \pi} \sin x \right) = (3\pi)(\sin \pi) = (3\pi)(0) = 0$.

Example 3

Find the limit: $\lim\limits_{t \to 2} \dfrac{t^2 - 3t + 2}{t - 2}$.

Factoring and simplifying: $\lim\limits_{t \to 2} \dfrac{t^2 - 3t + 2}{t - 2} = \lim\limits_{t \to 2} \dfrac{(t - 1)(t - 2)}{(t - 2)}$

$$= \lim\limits_{t \to 2} (t - 1) = (2 - 1) = 1.$$

(Note that had you substituted $t = 2$ directly in the original expression, you would have obtained a zero in both the numerator and denominator.)

Example 4

Find the limit: $\lim\limits_{x \to b} \dfrac{x^5 - b^5}{x^{10} - b^{10}}$.

Factoring and simplifying: $\lim\limits_{x \to b} \dfrac{x^5 - b^5}{x^{10} - b^{10}} = \lim\limits_{x \to b} \dfrac{x^5 - b^5}{(x^5 - b^5)(x^5 + b^5)}$

$$= \lim\limits_{x \to b} \dfrac{1}{x^5 + b^5} = \dfrac{1}{b^5 + b^5} = \dfrac{1}{2b^5}.$$

Example 5

Find the limit: $\lim\limits_{t \to 0} \dfrac{\sqrt{t + 2} - \sqrt{2}}{t}$.

Multiplying both the numerator and the denominator by the conjugate of the numerator,

$\left(\sqrt{t + 2} + \sqrt{2} \right)$, yields $\lim\limits_{t \to 0} \dfrac{\sqrt{t + 2} - \sqrt{2}}{t} \left(\dfrac{\sqrt{t + 2} + \sqrt{2}}{\sqrt{t + 2} + \sqrt{2}} \right)$

$$= \lim\limits_{t \to 0} \dfrac{t + 2 - 2}{t \left(\sqrt{t + 2} + \sqrt{2} \right)}$$

$$= \lim\limits_{t \to 0} \dfrac{t}{t \left(\sqrt{t + 2} + \sqrt{2} \right)} = \lim\limits_{t \to 0} \dfrac{1}{\left(\sqrt{t + 2} + \sqrt{2} \right)} = \dfrac{1}{\sqrt{0 + 2} + \sqrt{2}} = \dfrac{1}{2\sqrt{2}}$$

$$= \dfrac{1}{2\sqrt{2}} \left(\dfrac{\sqrt{2}}{\sqrt{2}} \right) = \dfrac{\sqrt{2}}{4}.$$

(Note that substituting 0 directly into the original expression would have produced a 0 in both the numerator and denominator.)

Example 6

Find the limit: $\lim\limits_{x \to 0} \dfrac{3 \sin 2x}{2x}$.

Enter $y1 = \dfrac{3 \sin 2x}{2x}$ in the calculator. You see that the graph of $f(x)$ approaches 3 as x approaches 0. Thus, the $\lim\limits_{x \to 0} \dfrac{3 \sin 2x}{2x} = 3$. (Note that had you substituted $x = 0$ directly in the original expression, you would have obtained a zero in both the numerator and denominator.) (See Figure 5.1-1.)

[–10, 10] by [–4, 4]

Figure 5.1-1

Example 7

Find the limit: $\lim\limits_{x \to 3} \dfrac{1}{x - 3}$.

Enter $y1 = \dfrac{1}{x - 3}$ into your calculator. You notice that as x approaches 3 from the right, the graph of $f(x)$ goes higher and higher, and that as x approaches 3 from the left, the graph of $f(x)$ goes lower and lower. Therefore, $\lim\limits_{x \to 3} \dfrac{1}{x - 3}$ is undefined. (See Figure 5.1-2.)

[–2, 8] by [–4, 4]

Figure 5.1-2

> • Always indicate what the final answer is, e.g., "The maximum value of f is 5." Use complete sentences whenever possible.

One-Sided Limits

Let f be a function and let a be a real number. Then the right-hand limit: $\lim\limits_{x \to a^+} f(x)$ represents the limit of f as x approaches a from the right, and the left-hand limit: $\lim\limits_{x \to a^-} f(x)$ represents the limit of f as x approaches a from the left.

Existence of a Limit

Let f be a function and let a and L be real numbers. Then the two-sided limit: $\lim\limits_{x \to a} f(x) = L$ if and only if the one-sided limits exist and $\lim\limits_{x \to a^+} f(x) = \lim\limits_{x \to a^-} f(x) = L$.

Example 1

Given $f(x) = \dfrac{x^2 - 2x - 3}{x - 3}$, find the limits: (a) $\lim\limits_{x \to 3^+} f(x)$, (b) $\lim\limits_{x \to 3^-} f(x)$, and (c) $\lim\limits_{x \to 3} f(x)$.

Substituting $x = 3$ into $f(x)$ leads to a 0 in both the numerator and denominator. Factor $f(x)$ as $\dfrac{(x - 3)(x + 1)}{(x - 3)}$, which is equivalent to $(x + 1)$ where $x \neq 3$. Thus, (a) $\lim\limits_{x \to 3^+} f(x) = \lim\limits_{x \to 3^+} (x + 1) = 4$, (b) $\lim\limits_{x \to 3^-} f(x) = \lim\limits_{x \to 3^-} (x + 1) = 4$, and (c) since the one-sided limits exist and are equal, $\lim\limits_{x \to 3^+} f(x) = \lim\limits_{x \to 3^-} f(x) = 4$, therefore the two-sided limit $\lim\limits_{x \to 3} f(x)$ exists and $\lim\limits_{x \to 3} f(x) = 4$. (Note that $f(x)$ is undefined at $x = 3$, but the function gets arbitrarily close to 4 as x approaches 3. Therefore the limit exists.) (See Figure 5.1-3.)

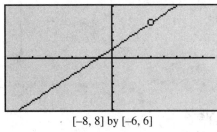

[−8, 8] by [−6, 6]

Figure 5.1-3

Example 2

Given $f(x)$ as illustrated in the accompanying diagram (Figure 5.1-4), find the limits: (a) $\lim\limits_{x \to 0^-} f(x)$, (b) $\lim\limits_{x \to 0^+} f(x)$, and (c) $\lim\limits_{x \to 0} f(x)$.

[−8,8] by [−10,10]

Figure 5.1-4

(a) As x approaches 0 from the left, $f(x)$ gets arbitrarily close to 0. Thus, $\lim\limits_{x \to 0^-} f(x) = 0$.

(b) As x approaches 0 from the right, $f(x)$ gets arbitrarily close to 2. Therefore, $\lim\limits_{x \to 0^+} f(x) = 2$. Note that $f(0) \neq 2$.

(c) Since $\lim\limits_{x \to 0^+} f(x) \neq \lim\limits_{x \to 0^-} f(x)$, $\lim\limits_{x \to 0} f(x)$ does not exist.

Example 3

Given the greatest integer function $f(x) = [x]$, find the limits: (a) $\lim\limits_{x \to 1^+} f(x)$, (b) $\lim\limits_{x \to 1^-} f(x)$, and (c) $\lim\limits_{x \to 1} f(x)$.

(a) Enter $y1 = \text{int}(x)$ in your calculator. You see that as x approaches 1 from the right, the function stays at 1. Thus, $\lim\limits_{x \to 1^+} [x] = 1$. Note that $f(1)$ is also equal to 1.

(b) As x approaches 1 from the left, the function stays at 0. Therefore, $\lim\limits_{x \to 1^-} [x] = 0$. Notice that $\lim\limits_{x \to 1^-} [x] \ne f(1)$.

(c) Since $\lim\limits_{x \to 1^-} [x] \ne \lim\limits_{x \to 1^+} [x]$, therefore, $\lim\limits_{x \to 1} [x]$ does not exist. (See Figure 5.1-5.)

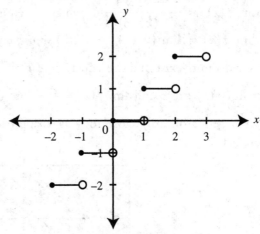

Figure 5.1-5

Example 4

Given $f(x) = \dfrac{|x|}{x}$, $x \ne 0$, find the limits: (a) $\lim\limits_{x \to 0^+} f(x)$, (b) $\lim\limits_{x \to 0^-} f(x)$, and (c) $\lim\limits_{x \to 0} f(x)$.

(a) From inspecting the graph, $\lim\limits_{x \to 0^+} = \dfrac{|x|}{x} = 1$, (b) $\lim\limits_{x \to 0^-} = \dfrac{|x|}{x} = -1$, and (c) since $\lim\limits_{x \to 0^+} \dfrac{|x|}{x} \ne$

$\lim\limits_{x \to 0^-} \dfrac{|x|}{x}$, therefore, $\lim\limits_{x \to 0} = \dfrac{|x|}{x}$ does not exist. (See Figure 5.1-6.)

[−4,4] by [−4,4]

Figure 5.1-6

Note that the general function $f(x) = \dfrac{|x - a|}{x - a}$ has a jump at $x = a$; that is, $\lim\limits_{x \to a} \dfrac{|x - a|}{x - a}$ does not exist.

Example 5

If $f(x) = \begin{cases} e^{2x} & \text{for } -4 \le x < 0 \\ xe^x & \text{for } 0 \le x \le 4 \end{cases}$, find $\lim\limits_{x \to 0} f(x)$.

$\lim\limits_{x \to 0^+} f(x) = \lim\limits_{x \to 0^+} xe^x = 0$ and $\lim\limits_{x \to 0^-} f(x) = \lim\limits_{x \to 0^-} e^{2x} = 1$.

Thus, $\lim\limits_{x \to 0} f(x)$ does not exist.

- Remember $\ln(e) = 1$ and $e^{\ln 3} = 3$ since $y = \ln x$ and $y = e^x$ are inverse functions.

Example 6

Evaluate the following limit: $\lim\limits_{x \to 2} f(g(x))$.

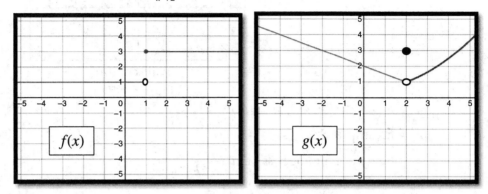

To evaluate this limit, you must evaluate the one-sided limits.

As x approaches 2 from the left, $\lim\limits_{x \to 2^-} g(x) = 1$, but it approaches it from above. Thus,

$$\lim_{x \to 2^-} f(g(x)) = \lim_{x \to 1^+} f(x) = 3.$$

As x approaches 2 from the right, $\lim\limits_{x \to 2^+} g(x) = 1$, but it approaches it from above. Thus,

$$\lim_{x \to 2^+} f(g(x)) = \lim_{x \to 1^+} f(x) = 3.$$

Since $\lim\limits_{x \to 2^-} f(g(x)) = \lim\limits_{x \to 2^+} f(g(x)) = 3$, then $\lim\limits_{x \to 2} f(g(x)) = 3$.

Squeeze Theorem

If f, g, and h are functions defined on some open interval containing a such that $g(x) \leq f(x) \leq h(x)$ for all x in the interval except possibly at a itself, and $\lim\limits_{x \to a} g(x) = \lim\limits_{x \to a} h(x) = L$, then $\lim\limits_{x \to a} f(x) = L$.

Example 1

Evaluate the following: $\lim\limits_{x \to 0} \left(x^2 \sin \left(\dfrac{\pi}{x} \right) \right)$.

Since $-1 \leq \sin \left(\dfrac{\pi}{x} \right) \leq 1, x^2(-1) \leq x^2 \sin \left(\dfrac{\pi}{x} \right) \leq x^2(1)$. If $\lim\limits_{x \to 0} -x^2 = 0$ and $\lim\limits_{x \to 0} x^2 = 0$, by the Squeeze Theorem, $\lim\limits_{x \to 0} \left(x^2 \sin \left(\dfrac{\pi}{x} \right) \right) = 0$.

Example 2

Find the limit if it exists: $\lim\limits_{x \to 0} \dfrac{\sin 3x}{x}$.

Substituting 0 into the expression would lead to 0/0. Rewrite $\dfrac{\sin 3x}{x}$ as $\dfrac{3}{3} \cdot \dfrac{\sin 3x}{x}$ and

thus, $\lim\limits_{x \to 0} \dfrac{\sin 3x}{x} = \lim\limits_{x \to 0} \dfrac{3 \sin 3x}{3x} = 3\lim\limits_{x \to 0} \dfrac{\sin 3x}{3x}$. As x approaches 0, so does $3x$. Therefore,

$3\lim\limits_{x \to 0} \dfrac{\sin 3x}{3x} = 3 \lim\limits_{3x \to 0} \dfrac{\sin 3x}{3x} = 3(1) = 3$. (Note that $\lim\limits_{3x \to 0} \dfrac{\sin 3x}{3x}$ is equivalent to $\lim\limits_{x \to 0} \dfrac{\sin x}{x}$ by

replacing $3x$ by x.) Verify your result with a calculator. (See Figure 5.1-7.)

[–10,10] by [–4,4]

Figure 5.1-7

Example 3

Find the limit if it exists: $\lim\limits_{h \to 0} \dfrac{\sin 3h}{\sin 2h}$.

Rewrite $\dfrac{\sin 3h}{\sin 2h}$ as $\dfrac{3\left(\dfrac{\sin 3h}{3h}\right)}{2\left(\dfrac{\sin 2h}{2h}\right)}$. As h approaches 0, so do $3h$ and $2h$. Therefore,

$$\lim_{h \to 0} \frac{\sin 3h}{\sin 2h} = \frac{3\lim\limits_{3h \to 0} \dfrac{\sin 3h}{3h}}{2\lim\limits_{2h \to 0} \dfrac{\sin 2h}{2h}} = \frac{3(1)}{2(1)} = \frac{3}{2}.$$ (Note that substituting $h = 0$ into the original

expression would have produced 0/0). Verify your result with a calculator. (See Figure 5.1-8.)

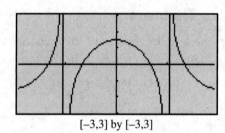

[–3,3] by [–3,3]

Figure 5.1-8

Example 4

Find the limit if it exists: $\lim\limits_{y \to 0} \dfrac{y^2}{1 - \cos y}$.

Substituting 0 in the expression would lead to 0/0. Multiplying both the numerator and denominator by the conjugate $(1 + \cos y)$ produces
$$\lim_{y \to 0} \frac{y^2}{1 - \cos y} \cdot \frac{(1 + \cos y)}{(1 + \cos y)} = \lim_{y \to 0} \frac{y^2(1 + \cos y)}{1 - \cos^2 y} = \lim_{y \to 0} \frac{y^2(1 + \cos y)}{\sin^2 y} = \lim_{y \to 0} \frac{y^2}{\sin^2 y} \cdot$$
$$\lim_{y \to 0}(1 + \cos^2 y) = \lim_{y \to 0}\left(\frac{y}{\sin y}\right)^2 \cdot \lim_{y \to 0}(1 + \cos^2 y) = \left(\lim_{y \to 0}\frac{y}{\sin y}\right)^2 \cdot \lim_{y \to 0}(1 + \cos^2 y) =$$
$$(1)^2(1 + 1) = 2. \text{ (Note that } \lim_{y \to 0}\frac{y}{\sin y} = \lim_{y \to 0}\frac{1}{\dfrac{\sin y}{y}} = \frac{\lim\limits_{y \to 0}(1)}{\lim\limits_{y \to 0}\dfrac{\sin y}{y}} = \frac{1}{1} = 1). \text{ Verify your result}$$

with a calculator. (See Figure 5.1-9.)

[–8,8] by [–2,10]

Figure 5.1-9

Example 5

Find the limit if it exists: $\lim\limits_{x \to 0} \dfrac{3x}{\cos x}$.

Using the quotient rule for limits, you have $\lim\limits_{x \to 0} \dfrac{3x}{\cos x} = \dfrac{\lim\limits_{x \to 0} (3x)}{\lim\limits_{x \to 0} (\cos x)} = \dfrac{0}{1} = 0$. Verify your result with a calculator. (See Figure 5.1-10.)

[–10,10] by [–30,30]

Figure 5.1-10

This can also be solved using *L'Hôpital's* Rule.

5.2 Limits Involving Infinities

Main Concepts: Infinite Limits (as $x \to a$), Limits at Infinity (as $x \to \infty$), Horizontal and Vertical Asymptotes

Infinite Limits (as x → a)

If f is a function defined at every number in some open interval containing a, except possibly at a itself, then

(1) $\lim\limits_{x \to a} f(x) = \infty$ means that $f(x)$ increases without bound as x approaches a.

(2) $\lim\limits_{x \to a} f(x) = -\infty$ means that $f(x)$ decreases without bound as x approaches a.

Limit Theorems

(1) If n is a positive integer, then

    (a) $\lim\limits_{x \to 0^+} \dfrac{1}{x^n} = \infty$

    (b) $\lim\limits_{x \to 0^-} \dfrac{1}{x^n} = \begin{cases} \infty & \text{if } n \text{ is even} \\ -\infty & \text{if } n \text{ is odd} \end{cases}$.

(2) If the $\lim\limits_{x \to a} f(x) = c$, $c > 0$, and $\lim\limits_{x \to a} g(x) = 0$, then

$$\lim_{x \to a} \frac{f(x)}{g(x)} = \begin{cases} \infty & \text{if } g(x) \text{ approaches 0 through positive values} \\ -\infty & \text{if } g(x) \text{ approaches 0 through negative values} \end{cases}.$$

(3) If the $\lim\limits_{x \to a} f(x) = c$, $c < 0$, and $\lim\limits_{x \to a} g(x) = 0$, then

$$\lim_{x \to a} \frac{f(x)}{g(x)} = \begin{cases} -\infty & \text{if } g(x) \text{ approaches 0 through positive values} \\ \infty & \text{if } g(x) \text{ approaches 0 through negative values} \end{cases}.$$

(Note that limit theorems 2 and 3 hold true for $x \to a^+$ and $x \to a^-$.)

Example 1

Evaluate the limit: (a) $\lim\limits_{x \to 2^+} \dfrac{3x - 1}{x - 2}$ and (b) $\lim\limits_{x \to 2^-} \dfrac{3x - 1}{x - 2}$.

The limit of the numerator is 5 and the limit of the denominator is 0 through positive values. Thus, $\lim\limits_{x \to 2^+} \dfrac{3x - 1}{x - 2} = \infty$. (b) The limit of the numerator is 5 and the limit of the denominator is 0 through negative values. Therefore, $\lim\limits_{x \to 2^-} \dfrac{3x - 1}{x - 2} = -\infty$. Verify your result with a calculator. (See Figure 5.2-1.)

[–5,7] by [–40,20]

Figure 5.2-1

Example 2

Find: $\lim\limits_{x \to 3^-} \dfrac{x^2}{x^2 - 9}$.

Factor the denominator obtaining $\lim\limits_{x \to 3^-} \dfrac{x^2}{x^2 - 9} = \lim\limits_{x \to 3^-} \dfrac{x^2}{(x - 3)(x + 3)}$. The limit of the numerator is 9 and the limit of the denominator is $(0)(6) = 0$ through negative values. Therefore, $\lim\limits_{x \to 3^-} \dfrac{x^2}{x^2 - 9} = -\infty$. Verify your result with a calculator. (See Figure 5.2-2.)

[–10,10] by [–10,10]

Figure 5.2-2

Example 3

Find: $\lim\limits_{x\to5^-}\dfrac{\sqrt{25-x^2}}{x-5}$.

Substituting 5 into the expression leads to 0/0. Factor the numerator $\sqrt{25-x^2}$ into $\sqrt{(5-x)(5+x)}$. As $x \to 5^-$, $(x-5) < 0$. Rewrite $(x-5)$ as $-(5-x)$ as $x \to 5^-$, $(5-x) > 0$ and thus, you may express $(5-x)$ as $\sqrt{(5-x)^2} = \sqrt{(5-x)(5-x)}$. Therefore, $(x-5) = -(5-x) = -\sqrt{(5-x)(5-x)}$. Substituting these equivalent expressions into the original problem, you have $\lim\limits_{x\to5^-}\dfrac{\sqrt{25-x^2}}{x-5} = -\lim\limits_{x\to5^-}\dfrac{\sqrt{(5-x)(5+x)}}{\sqrt{(5-x)(5-x)}} = $

$-\lim\limits_{x\to5^-}\sqrt{\dfrac{(5-x)(5+x)}{(5-x)(5-x)}} = -\lim\limits_{x\to5^-}\sqrt{\dfrac{(5+x)}{(5-x)}}$. The limit of the numerator is 10 and the limit of the denominator is 0 through positive values. Thus, the $\lim\limits_{x\to5^-}\dfrac{\sqrt{25-x^2}}{x-5} = -\infty$.

Example 4

Find: $\lim\limits_{x\to2^-}\dfrac{[x]-x}{2-x}$, where $[x]$ is the greatest integer value of x.

As $x \to 2^-$, $[x] = 1$. The limit of the numerator is $(1-2) = -1$. As $x \to 2^-$, $(2-x) = 0$ through positive values. Thus, $\lim\limits_{x\to2^-}\dfrac{[x]-x}{2-x} = -\infty$.

- Do easy questions first. The easy ones are worth the same number of points as the hard ones.

Limits at Infinity (as $x \to \pm\infty$)

If f is a function defined at every number in some interval (a, ∞), then $\lim\limits_{x\to\infty} f(x) = L$ means that L is the limit of $f(x)$ as x increases without bound.

If f is a function defined at every number in some interval $(-\infty, a)$, then $\lim\limits_{x\to-\infty} f(x) = L$ means that L is the limit of $f(x)$ as x decreases without bound.

Limit Theorem

If n is a positive integer, then

(a) $\lim\limits_{x\to\infty}\dfrac{1}{x^n} = 0$

(b) $\lim\limits_{x\to-\infty}\dfrac{1}{x^n} = 0$

Example 1

Evaluate the limit: $\lim\limits_{x\to\infty}\dfrac{6x-13}{2x+5}$.

Divide every term in the numerator and denominator by the highest power of x (in this case, it is x), and obtain:

$$\lim_{x \to \infty} \frac{6x - 13}{2x + 5} = \lim_{x \to \infty} \frac{6 - \dfrac{13}{x}}{2 + \dfrac{5}{x}} = \frac{\lim\limits_{x \to \infty}(6) - \lim\limits_{x \to \infty}\dfrac{13}{x}}{\lim\limits_{x \to \infty}(2) + \lim\limits_{x \to \infty}\left(\dfrac{5}{x}\right)} = \frac{\lim\limits_{x \to \infty}(6) - 13\lim\limits_{x \to \infty}\left(\dfrac{1}{x}\right)}{\lim\limits_{x \to \infty}(2) + 5\lim\limits_{x \to \infty}\left(\dfrac{1}{x}\right)}$$

$$= \frac{6 - 13(0)}{2 + 5(0)} = 3.$$

Verify your result with a calculator. (See Figure 5.2-3.)

[−10,30] by [−5,10]

Figure 5.2-3

Example 2

Evaluate the limit: $\lim\limits_{x \to -\infty} \dfrac{3x - 10}{4x^3 + 5}$.

Divide every term in the numerator and denominator by the highest power of x. In this

case, it is x^3. Thus, $\lim\limits_{x \to -\infty} \dfrac{3x - 10}{4x^3 + 5} = \lim\limits_{x \to -\infty} \dfrac{\dfrac{3}{x^2} - \dfrac{10}{x^3}}{4 + \dfrac{5}{x^3}} = \dfrac{0 - 0}{4 + 0} = 0.$

Verify your result with a calculator. (See Figure 5.2-4.)

[−4,4] by [−20,10]

Figure 5.2-4

Example 3

Evaluate the limit: $\lim\limits_{x \to \infty} \dfrac{1 - x^2}{10x + 7}$.

Divide every term in the numerator and denominator by the highest power of x. In this

case, it is x^2. Therefore, $\lim\limits_{x \to \infty} \dfrac{1 - x^2}{10x + 7} = \lim\limits_{x \to \infty} \dfrac{\dfrac{1}{x^2} - 1}{\dfrac{10}{x} + \dfrac{7}{x^2}} = \dfrac{\lim\limits_{x \to \infty}\left(\dfrac{1}{x^2}\right) - \lim\limits_{x \to \infty}(1)}{\lim\limits_{x \to \infty}\left(\dfrac{10}{x}\right) + \lim\limits_{x \to \infty}\dfrac{7}{x^2}}$. The limit

of the numerator is −1 and the limit of the denominator is 0. Thus, $\lim\limits_{x \to \infty} \dfrac{1 - x^2}{10x + 7} = -\infty.$

Verify your result with a calculator. (See Figure 5.2-5.)

[–10,30] by [–5,3]

Figure 5.2-5

Example 4

Evaluate the limit: $\lim\limits_{x \to -\infty} \dfrac{2x+1}{\sqrt{x^2+3}}$.

As $x \to -\infty$, $x < 0$ and thus, $x = -\sqrt{x^2}$. Divide the numerator and denominator by x (not x^2 since the denominator has a square root). Thus, you

have $\lim\limits_{x \to -\infty} \dfrac{2x+1}{\sqrt{x^2+3}} = \lim\limits_{x \to -\infty} \dfrac{\dfrac{2x+1}{x}}{\dfrac{\sqrt{x^2+3}}{x}}$. Replacing the x below $\sqrt{x^2+3}$ by $(-\sqrt{x^2})$,

you have $\lim\limits_{x \to -\infty} \dfrac{2x+1}{\sqrt{x^2+3}} = \lim\limits_{x \to -\infty} \dfrac{\dfrac{2x+1}{x}}{\dfrac{\sqrt{x^2+3}}{-\sqrt{x^2}}} \; \lim\limits_{x \to -\infty} \dfrac{2+\dfrac{1}{x}}{-\sqrt{1+\dfrac{3}{x^2}}} = \dfrac{\lim\limits_{x \to -\infty}(2) - \lim\limits_{x \to -\infty}\dfrac{1}{x}}{-\sqrt{\lim\limits_{x \to -\infty}(1) + \lim\limits_{x \to -\infty}\left(\dfrac{3}{x^2}\right)}} =$

$\dfrac{2}{-1} = -2$.

Verify your result with a calculator. (See Figure 5.2-6.)

[–4,10] by [–4,4]

Figure 5.2-6

• Remember that $\ln\left(\dfrac{1}{x}\right) = \ln(1) - \ln x = -\ln x$ and $y = e^{-x} = \dfrac{1}{e^x}$.

Horizontal and Vertical Asymptotes

A line $y = b$ is called a horizontal asymptote for the graph of a function f if either $\lim\limits_{x \to \infty} f(x) = b$ or $\lim\limits_{x \to -\infty} f(x) = b$.

A line $x = a$ is called a vertical asymptote for the graph of a function f if either $\lim\limits_{x \to a^+} f(x) = +\infty$ or $\lim\limits_{x \to a^-} f(x) = +\infty$.

Example 1

Find the horizontal and vertical asymptotes of the function $f(x) = \dfrac{3x + 5}{x - 2}$.

To find the horizontal asymptotes, examine the $\lim\limits_{x \to \infty} f(x)$ and the $\lim\limits_{x \to -\infty} f(x)$.

The $\lim\limits_{x \to \infty} f(x) = \lim\limits_{x \to \infty} \dfrac{3x + 5}{x - 2} = \lim\limits_{x \to \infty} \dfrac{3 + \dfrac{5}{x}}{1 - \dfrac{2}{x}} = \dfrac{3}{1} = 3$, and the $\lim\limits_{x \to -\infty} f(x) = \lim\limits_{x \to -\infty} \dfrac{3x + 5}{x - 2} =$

$\lim\limits_{x \to -\infty} \dfrac{3 + \dfrac{5}{x}}{1 - \dfrac{2}{x}} = \dfrac{3}{1} = 3$.

Thus, $y = 3$ is a horizontal asymptote.

To find the vertical asymptotes, look for x-values such that the denominator $(x - 2)$ would be 0, in this case, $x = 2$. Then examine:

(a) $\lim\limits_{x \to 2^+} f(x) = \lim\limits_{x \to 2^+} \dfrac{3x + 5}{x - 2} = \dfrac{\lim\limits_{x \to 2^+} (3x + 5)}{\lim\limits_{x \to 2^+} (x - 2)}$, the limit of the numerator is 11 and the limit

of the denominator is 0 through positive values, and thus, $\lim\limits_{x \to 2^+} \dfrac{3x + 5}{x - 2} = \infty$.

(b) $\lim\limits_{x \to 2^-} f(x) = \lim\limits_{x \to 2^-} \dfrac{3x + 5}{x - 2} = \dfrac{\lim\limits_{x \to 2^-} (3x + 5)}{\lim\limits_{x \to 2^-} (x - 2)}$, the limit of the numerator is 11 and the limit

of the denominator is 0 through negative values, and thus, $\lim\limits_{x \to 2^-} \dfrac{3x + 5}{x - 2} = -\infty$.

Therefore, $x = 2$ is a vertical asymptote.

Example 2

Find the horizontal and vertical asymptotes of the function $f(x) = \dfrac{2e^x - 1}{3 - 5e^x}$.

To find the horizontal asymptotes, examine the $\lim\limits_{x \to \infty} f(x)$ and the $\lim\limits_{x \to -\infty} f(x)$.

The $\lim\limits_{x \to \infty} f(x) = \lim\limits_{x \to \infty} \dfrac{2e^x - 1}{3 - 5e^x} = \lim\limits_{x \to \infty} \dfrac{2 - \frac{1}{e^x}}{\frac{3}{e^x} - 5} = -\dfrac{2}{5}$. To evaluate $\lim\limits_{x \to -\infty} f(x)$, since

$\lim\limits_{x \to -\infty} e^x = 0$, $\lim\limits_{x \to -\infty} \dfrac{2e^x - 1}{3 - 5e^x} = \lim\limits_{x \to -\infty} -\dfrac{1}{3} = -\dfrac{1}{3}$.

Thus, $y = -\dfrac{2}{5}$ and $y = -\dfrac{1}{3}$ are horizontal asymptotes.

To find the vertical asymptotes, look for x-values such that the denominator $(3 - 5e^x)$ would be 0. Solve $3 - 5e^x = 0 \to 3 = 5e^x \to \dfrac{3}{5} = e^x \to x = \ln \dfrac{3}{5}$. Then examine:

(a) $\displaystyle\lim_{x\to\ln\frac{3}{5}^+} f(x) = \lim_{x\to\ln\frac{3}{5}^+} \frac{2e^x-1}{3-5e^x} = \frac{\displaystyle\lim_{x\to\ln\frac{3}{5}^+} 2e^x-1}{\displaystyle\lim_{x\to\ln\frac{3}{5}^+} 3-5e^x}$, the limit of the numerator is $\dfrac{1}{5}$ and

the limit of the denominator is 0 through negative values, and thus, $\displaystyle\lim_{x\to\ln\frac{3}{5}^+} \frac{2e^x-1}{3-5e^x} = -\infty$.

(b) $\displaystyle\lim_{x\to\ln\frac{3}{5}^-} f(x) = \lim_{x\to\ln\frac{3}{5}^-} \frac{2e^x-1}{3-5e^x} = \frac{\displaystyle\lim_{x\to\ln\frac{3}{5}^-} 2e^x-1}{\displaystyle\lim_{x\to\ln\frac{3}{5}^-} 3-5e^x}$, the limit of the numerator is $\dfrac{1}{5}$ and

the limit of the denominator is 0 through positive values, and thus, $\displaystyle\lim_{x\to\ln\frac{3}{5}^-} \frac{2e^x-1}{3-5e^x} = \infty$.

Therefore, $x = \ln\dfrac{3}{5}$ is a vertical asymptote.

Example 3

Using your calculator, find the horizontal and vertical asymptotes of the function $f(x) = \dfrac{x}{x^2-4}$.

Enter $y1 = \dfrac{x}{x^2-4}$. The graph shows that as $x \to \pm\infty$, the function approaches 0, thus

$\displaystyle\lim_{x\to\infty} f(x) = \lim_{x\to-\infty} f(x) = 0$. Therefore, a horizontal asymptote is $y = 0$ (or the x-axis).

For vertical asymptotes, you notice that $\displaystyle\lim_{x\to 2^+} f(x) = \infty$, $\displaystyle\lim_{x\to 2^-} f(x) = -\infty$, and

$\displaystyle\lim_{x\to-2^+} f(x) = \infty$, $\displaystyle\lim_{x\to-2^-} f(x) = -\infty$. Thus, the vertical asymptotes are $x = -2$ and $x = 2$.
(See Figure 5.2-7.)

[–8,8] by [–4.4]

Figure 5.2-7

Example 4

Using your calculator, find the horizontal and vertical asymptotes of the function $f(x) = \dfrac{x^3+5}{x}$.

Enter $y1 = \dfrac{x^3+5}{x}$. The graph of $f(x)$ shows that as x increases in the first quadrant, $f(x)$ goes higher and higher without bound. As x moves to the left in the second quadrant, $f(x)$ again goes higher and higher without bound. Thus, you may conclude that $\displaystyle\lim_{x\to\infty} f(x) = \infty$

and $\displaystyle\lim_{x\to-\infty} f(x) = \infty$ and thus, $f(x)$ has no horizontal asymptote. For vertical asymptotes, you notice that $\lim\limits_{x \to 0^+} f(x) = \infty$, and $\lim\limits_{x \to 0^-} f(x) = -\infty$. Therefore, the line $x = 0$ (or the y-axis) is a vertical asymptote. (See Figure 5.2-8.)

[–5,5] by [–30,30]

Figure 5.2-8

Relationship between the limits of rational functions as $x \to \infty$ and horizontal asymptotes:

Given $f(x) = \dfrac{p(x)}{q(x)}$, then:

(1) If the degree of $p(x)$ is the same as the degree of $q(x)$, then $\lim\limits_{x \to \infty} f(x) = \lim\limits_{x \to -\infty} f(x) = \dfrac{a}{b}$, where a is the coefficient of the highest power of x in $p(x)$ and b is the coefficient of the highest power of x in $q(x)$. The line $y = \dfrac{a}{b}$ is a horizontal asymptote. See Example 1 on page 61.

(2) If the degree of $p(x)$ is smaller than the degree of $q(x)$, then $\lim\limits_{x \to \infty} f(x) = \lim\limits_{x \to -\infty} f(x) = 0$.

The line $y = 0$ (or x-axis) is a horizontal asymptote. See Example 2 on page 62.

(3) If the degree of $p(x)$ is greater than the degree of $q(x)$, then $\lim\limits_{x \to \infty} f(x) = \pm\infty$ and $\lim\limits_{x \to -\infty} f(x) = \pm\infty$. Thus, $f(x)$ has no horizontal asymptote. See Example 3 on page 62.

Example 5

Using your calculator, find the horizontal asymptotes of the function $f(x) = \dfrac{2\sin x}{x}$.

Enter $y1 = \dfrac{2\sin x}{x}$. The graph shows that $f(x)$ oscillates back and forth about the x-axis. As $x \to \pm\infty$, the graph gets closer and closer to the x-axis, which implies that $f(x)$ approaches 0. Thus, the line $y = 0$ (or the x-axis) is a horizontal asymptote. (See Figure 5.2-9.)

[–20,20] by [–3,3]

Figure 5.2-9

• When entering a rational function into a calculator, use parentheses for both the numerator and denominator, e.g., $(x - 2) + (x + 3)$.

5.3 Continuity of a Function

Main Concepts: Continuity of a Function at a Number, Continuity of a Function over an Interval, Theorems on Continuity

Continuity of a Function at a Number

A function f is said to be continuous at a number a if the following three conditions are satisfied:

1. $f(a)$ exists
2. $\lim_{x \to a} f(x)$ exists
3. $\lim_{x \to a} f(x) = f(a)$

The function f is said to be discontinuous at a if one or more of these three conditions are not satisfied and a is called the point of discontinuity.

Continuity of a Function over an Interval

A function is continuous over an interval if it is continuous at every point in the interval.

Theorems on Continuity

1. If the functions f and g are continuous at a, then the functions $f + g$, $f - g$, $f \cdot g$ and f/g, $g(a) \neq 0$, are also continuous at a.
2. A polynomial function is continuous everywhere.
3. A rational function is continuous everywhere, except at points where the denominator is zero.
4. Intermediate Value Theorem: If a function f is continuous on a closed interval $[a, b]$ and k is a number with $f(a) \leq k \leq f(b)$, then there exists a number c in $[a, b]$ such that $f(c) = k$.

Example 1

Find the points of discontinuity of the function $f(x) = \dfrac{x + 5}{x^2 - x - 2}$.

Since $f(x)$ is a rational function, it is continuous everywhere, except at points where the denominator is 0. Factor the denominator and set it equal to 0: $(x - 2)(x + 1) = 0$. Thus $x = 2$ or $x = -1$. The function $f(x)$ is undefined at $x = -1$ and at $x = 2$. Therefore, $f(x)$ is discontinuous at these points. Verify your result with a calculator. (See Figure 5.3-1.)

[−5,5] by [−10,10]

Figure 5.3-1

Example 2

Determine the intervals on which the given function is continuous:

$$f(x) = \begin{cases} \dfrac{x^2 + 3x - 10}{x - 2}, & x \neq 2 \\ 10, & x = 2 \end{cases}.$$

Check the three conditions of continuity at $x = 2$:

Condition 1: $f(2) = 10$.

Condition 2: $\lim\limits_{x \to 2} \dfrac{x^2 + 3x - 10}{x - 2} = \lim\limits_{x \to 2} \dfrac{(x + 5)(x - 2)}{x - 2} = \lim\limits_{x \to 2} (x + 5) = 7$.

Condition 3: $f(2) \neq \lim\limits_{x \to 2} f(x)$. Thus, $f(x)$ is discontinuous at $x = 2$.

The function is continuous on $(-\infty, 2)$ and $(2, \infty)$. Verify your result with a calculator. (See Figure 5.3-2.)

[−8,12] by [−3,17]

Figure 5.3-2

- Remember that $\dfrac{d}{dx}\left(\dfrac{1}{x}\right) = -\dfrac{1}{x^2}$ and $\displaystyle\int \dfrac{1}{x}\,dx = \ln |x| + C$.

Example 3

For what value of k is the function $f(x) = \begin{cases} x^2 - 2x, & x \leq 6 \\ 2x + k, & x > 6 \end{cases}$ continuous at $x = 6$?

For $f(x)$ to be continuous at $x = 6$, it must satisfy the three conditions of continuity.

Condition 1: $f(6) = 6^2 - 2(6) = 24$.

Condition 2: $\lim\limits_{x \to 6^-} (x^2 - 2x) = 24$; thus $\lim\limits_{x \to 6^-} (2x + k)$ must also be 24 in order for the $\lim\limits_{x \to 6} f(x)$ to equal 24. Thus, $\lim\limits_{x \to 6^-} (2x + k) = 24$, which implies $2(6) + k = 24$ and $k = 12$. Therefore, if $k = 12$,

Condition (3): $f(6) = \lim\limits_{x \to 6} f(x)$ is also satisfied.

Example 4

Given $f(x)$ as shown in Figure 5.3-3, (a) find $f(3)$ and $\lim\limits_{x \to 3} f(x)$, and (b) determine if $f(x)$ is continuous at $x = 3$. Explain your answer.

The graph of $f(x)$ shows that $f(3) = 5$ and the $\lim\limits_{x \to 3} f(x) = 1$. Since $f(3) \neq \lim\limits_{x \to 3} f(x)$, $f(x)$ is discontinuous at $x = 3$.

[−3,8] by [−4,8]

Figure 5.3-3

Example 5

If $g(x) = x^2 - 2x - 15$, using the Intermediate Value Theorem show that $g(x)$ has a root in the interval $[1, 7]$.

Begin by finding $g(1)$ and $g(7)$, and $g(1) = -16$ and $g(7) = 20$. If $g(x)$ has a root, then $g(x)$ crosses the x-axis, i.e., $g(x) = 0$. Since $-16 \leq 0 \leq 20$, by the Intermediate Value Theorem, there exists at least one number c in $[1, 7]$ such that $g(c) = 0$. The number c is a root of $g(x)$.

Example 6

A function f is continuous on $[0, 5]$, and some of the values of f are shown below.

x	0	3	5
f	−4	b	−4

If $f(x) = -2$ has no solution on $[0, 5]$, then b could be

(A) 1   (B) 0   (C) −2   (D) −5

If $b = -2$, then $x = 3$ would be a solution for $f(x) = -2$.

If $b = 0$, 1, or 3, $f(x) = -2$ would have two solutions for $f(x) = -2$.

Thus, $b = -5$, choice (D). (See Figure 5.3-4.)

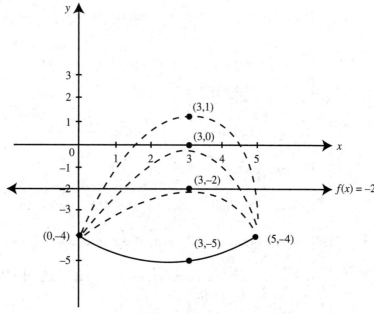

Figure 5.3-4

5.4 Rapid Review

1. Find $f(2)$ and $\lim\limits_{x \to 2} f(x)$ and determine if f is continuous at $x = 2$. (See Figure 5.4-1.)

   Answer: $f(2) = 2$, $\lim\limits_{x \to 2} f(x) = 4$, and f is discontinuous at $x = 2$.

Figure 5.4-1

2. Evaluate $\lim\limits_{x \to a} \dfrac{x^2 - a^2}{x - a}$.

   Answer: $\lim\limits_{x \to a} \dfrac{(x + a)(x - a)}{x - a} = 2a$.

3. Evaluate $\lim\limits_{x \to \infty} \dfrac{1 - 3x^2}{x^2 + 100x + 99}$.

   Answer: The limit is -3, since the polynomials in the numerator and denominator have the same degree.

4. Determine if $f(x) = \begin{cases} x + 6 & \text{for } x < 3 \\ x^2 & \text{for } x \geq 3 \end{cases}$ is continuous at $x = 3$.

   Answer: The function f is continuous, since $f(3) = 9$, $\lim\limits_{x \to 3^+} f(x) = \lim\limits_{x \to 3^-} f(x) = 9$, and $f(3) = \lim\limits_{x \to 3} f(x)$.

5. If $f(x) = \begin{cases} e^x & \text{for } x \neq 0 \\ 5 & \text{for } x = 0 \end{cases}$, find $\lim\limits_{x \to 0} f(x)$.

   Answer: $\lim\limits_{x \to 0} f(x) = 1$, since $\lim\limits_{x \to 0^+} f(x) = \lim\limits_{x \to 0^-} f(x) = 1$.

6. Evaluate $\lim\limits_{x \to 0} \dfrac{\sin 6x}{\sin 2x}$.

   Answer: The limit is $\dfrac{6}{2} = 3$, since $\lim\limits_{x \to 0} \dfrac{\sin x}{x} = 1$.

7. Evaluate $\lim\limits_{x \to 5^-} \dfrac{x^2}{x^2 - 25}$.

   Answer: The limit is $-\infty$, since $(x^2 - 25)$ approaches 0 through negative values.

8. Find the vertical and horizontal asymptotes of $f(x) = \dfrac{1}{x^2 - 25}$.

   Answer: The vertical asymptotes are $x = \pm 5$, and the horizontal asymptote is $y = 0$, since $\lim\limits_{x \to \pm\infty} f(x) = 0$.

5.5 Practice Problems

Part A—The use of a calculator is not allowed.

Find the limits of the following:

1. $\lim\limits_{x\to 0} (x-5)\cos x$

2. If $b \neq 0$, evaluate $\lim\limits_{x\to b} \dfrac{x^3 - b^3}{x^6 - b^6}$.

3. $\lim\limits_{x\to 0} \dfrac{2 - \sqrt{4-x}}{x}$

4. $\lim\limits_{x\to\infty} \dfrac{5-6x}{2x+11}$

5. $\lim\limits_{x\to-\infty} \dfrac{x^2 + 2x - 3}{x^3 + 2x^2}$

6. $\lim\limits_{x\to\infty} \dfrac{3x^2}{5x+8}$

7. $\lim\limits_{x\to-\infty} \dfrac{3x}{\sqrt{x^2-4}}$

8. If $f(x) = \begin{cases} e^x & \text{for } 0 \le x < 1 \\ x^2 e^x & \text{for } 1 \le x \le 5 \end{cases}$,
   find $\lim\limits_{x\to 1} f(x)$.

9. $\lim\limits_{x\to\infty} \dfrac{e^x}{1-x^3}$

10. $\lim\limits_{x\to 0} \dfrac{\sin 3x}{\sin 4x}$

11. $\lim\limits_{x\to 3^+} \dfrac{\sqrt{t^2-9}}{t-3}$

12. The graph of a function f is shown in Figure 5.5-1.
    Which of the following statements is/are true?

    I. $\lim\limits_{x\to 4^-} f(x) = 5$.

    II. $\lim\limits_{x\to 4} f(x) = 2$.

    III. $x = 4$ is not in the domain of f.

Part B—Calculators are allowed.

13. Find the horizontal and vertical asymptotes of the graph of the function
    $$f(x) = \frac{1}{x^2 + x - 2}.$$

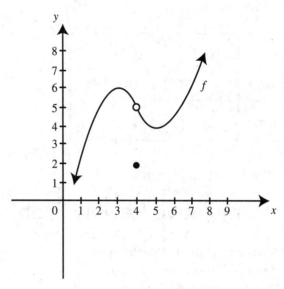

Figure 5.5-1

14. Find the limit: $\lim\limits_{x\to 5^+} \dfrac{5 + [x]}{5 - x}$ when $[x]$ is the greatest integer of x.

15. Find all x-values where the function
    $$f(x) = \frac{x+1}{x^2 + 4x - 12}$$
    is discontinuous.

16. For what value of k is the function
    $$g(x) = \begin{cases} x^2 + 5, & x \le 3 \\ 2x - k, & x > 3 \end{cases}$$
    continuous at $x = 3$?

17. Determine if
    $$f(x) = \begin{cases} \dfrac{x^2 + 5x - 14}{x - 2}, & \text{if } x \neq 2 \\ 12, & \text{if } x = 2 \end{cases}$$
    is continuous at $x = 2$. Explain why or why not.

18. Given $f(x)$ as shown in Figure 5.5-2, find

    (a) $f(3)$.

    (b) $\lim\limits_{x \to 3^+} f(x)$.

    (c) $\lim\limits_{x \to 3^-} f(x)$.

    (d) $\lim\limits_{x \to 3} f(x)$.

    (e) Is $f(x)$ continuous at $x = 3$? Explain why or why not.

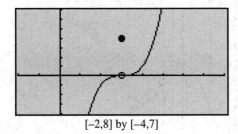

[−2,8] by [−4,7]

Figure 5.5-2

19. The function f is continuous on the closed interval $[-5, 5]$ and has values that are given in the table below. What is the minimum number of times that the function takes on the value $f(x) = -2$ on the interval $[-5, 5]$?

x	−5	−3	−1	1	3	5
$f(x)$	4	2	−3	1	−4	−5

(A) 1   (B) 2   (C) 3   (D) 4

20. Evaluate $\lim\limits_{x \to 0} \dfrac{1 - \cos x}{\sin^2 x}$.

5.6 Cumulative Review Problems

21. Write an equation of the line passing through the point $(2, -4)$ and perpendicular to the line $3x - 2y = 6$.

22. The graph of a function f is shown in Figure 5.6-1. Which of the following statements is/are true?

    I. $\lim\limits_{x \to 4^-} f(x) = 3$.

    II. $x = 4$ is not in the domain of f.

    III. $\lim\limits_{x \to 4} f(x)$ does not exist.

23. Evaluate $\lim\limits_{x \to 0} \dfrac{|3x - 4|}{x - 2}$.

24. Find $\lim\limits_{x \to 0} \dfrac{\tan x}{x}$.

25. Find the horizontal and vertical asymptotes of $f(x) = \dfrac{x}{\sqrt{x^2 + 4}}$.

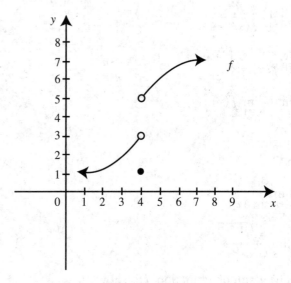

Figure 5.6-1

5.7 Solutions to Practice Problems

Part A—The use of a calculator is not allowed.

1. Using the product rule,
   $$\lim_{x \to 0} (x - 5)(\cos x) =$$

$$\left[\lim_{x \to 0} (x - 5)\right]\left[\lim_{x \to 0} (\cos x)\right]$$

$= (0 - 5)(\cos 0) = (-5)(1) = -5$.
(Note that $\cos 0 = 1$.)

2. Rewrite $\lim\limits_{x \to b} \dfrac{x^3 - b^3}{x^6 - b^6}$ as

$$\lim_{x \to b} \frac{x^3 - b^3}{(x^3 - b^3)(x^3 + b^3)} = \lim_{x \to b} \frac{1}{x^3 + b^3}.$$

Substitute $x = b$ and obtain

$$\frac{1}{b^3 + b^3} = \frac{1}{2b^3}.$$

3. Substituting $x = 0$ into the expression $\dfrac{2 - \sqrt{4 - x}}{x}$ leads to $0/0$, which is an indeterminate form. Thus, multiply both the numerator and denominator by the conjugate $\left(2 + \sqrt{4 - x}\right)$ and obtain

$$\lim_{x \to 0} \frac{2 - \sqrt{4 - x}}{x} \left(\frac{2 + \sqrt{4 - x}}{2 + \sqrt{4 - x}}\right)$$

$$= \lim_{x \to 0} \frac{4 - (4 - x)}{x\left(2 + \sqrt{4 - x}\right)}$$

$$= \lim_{x \to 0} \frac{x}{x\left(2 + \sqrt{4 - x}\right)}$$

$$= \lim_{x \to 0} \frac{1}{\left(2 + \sqrt{4 - x}\right)}$$

$$= \frac{1}{\left(2 + \sqrt{4 - (0)}\right)} = \frac{1}{4}.$$

4. Since the degree of the polynomial in the numerator is the same as the degree of the polynomial in the denominator,

$$\lim_{x \to \infty} \frac{5 - 6x}{2x + 11} = -\frac{6}{2} = -3.$$

5. Since the degree of the polynomial in the numerator is 2 and the degree of the polynomial in the denominator is 3,

$$\lim_{x \to -\infty} \frac{x^2 + 2x - 3}{x^3 + 2x^2} = 0.$$

6. The degree of the monomial in the numerator is 2 and the degree of the binomial in the denominator is 1. Thus,

$$\lim_{x \to \infty} \frac{3x^2}{5x + 8} = \infty.$$

7. Divide every term in both the numerator and denominator by the highest power of x. In this case, it is x. Thus, you have

$$\lim_{x \to -\infty} \frac{\dfrac{3x}{x}}{\dfrac{\sqrt{x^2 - 4}}{x}}. \text{ As } x \to -\infty, x = -\sqrt{x^2}.$$

Since the denominator involves a radical, rewrite the expression as

$$\lim_{x \to -\infty} \frac{\dfrac{3x}{x}}{\dfrac{\sqrt{x^2 - 4}}{-\sqrt{x^2}}} = \lim_{x \to -\infty} \frac{3}{-\sqrt{1 - \dfrac{4}{x^2}}}$$

$$= \frac{3}{-\sqrt{1 - 0}} = -3.$$

8. $\lim\limits_{x \to 1^+} f(x) = \lim\limits_{x \to 1^+} \left(x^2 e^x\right) = e$ and $\lim\limits_{x \to 1^-} f(x) = \lim\limits_{x \to 1^-} (e^x) = e$. Thus, $\lim\limits_{x \to 1} f(x) = e$.

9. $\lim\limits_{x \to \infty} e^x = \infty$ and $\lim\limits_{x \to \infty} \left(1 - x^3\right) = -\infty$. However, as $x \to \infty$, the rate of increase of e^x is much greater than the rate of decrease of $(1 - x^3)$. Thus,

$$\lim_{x \to \infty} \frac{e^x}{1 - x^3} = -\infty.$$

10. Divide both numerator and denominator by x and obtain $\lim\limits_{x \to 0} \dfrac{\dfrac{\sin 3x}{x}}{\dfrac{\sin 4x}{x}}$. Now rewrite the limit as $\lim\limits_{x \to 0} \dfrac{3\dfrac{\sin 3x}{3x}}{4\dfrac{\sin 4x}{4x}} = \dfrac{3}{4}\lim\limits_{x \to 0} \dfrac{\dfrac{\sin 3x}{3x}}{\dfrac{\sin 4x}{4x}}.$

As x approaches 0, so do $3x$ and $4x$. Thus, you have

$$\frac{3}{4} \frac{\lim\limits_{3x \to 0} \dfrac{\sin 3x}{3x}}{\lim\limits_{4x \to 0} \dfrac{\sin 4x}{4x}} = \frac{3(1)}{4(1)} = \frac{3}{4}.$$

11. As $t \to 3^+$, $(t - 3) > 0$, and thus $(t - 3) = \sqrt{(t - 3)^2}$. Rewrite the limit as

$$\lim_{t \to 3^+} \frac{\sqrt{(t - 3)(t + 3)}}{\sqrt{(t - 3)^2}} = \lim_{t \to 3^+} \frac{\sqrt{(t + 3)}}{\sqrt{(t - 3)}}.$$

The limit of the numerator is $\sqrt{6}$ and the denominator is approaching 0 through positive values. Thus, $\lim\limits_{t \to 3^+} \dfrac{\sqrt{t^2 - 9}}{t - 3} = \infty$.

12. The graph of f indicates that:

    I. $\lim\limits_{x \to 4^-} f(x) = 5$ is true.

    II. $\lim\limits_{x \to 4} f(x) = 2$ is false.

    (The $\lim\limits_{x \to 4} f(x) = 5$.)

    III. "$x = 4$ is not in the domain of f" is false since $f(4) = 2$.

Part B—Calculators are allowed

13. Examining the graph in your calculator, you notice that the function approaches the x-axis as $x \to \infty$ or as $x \to -\infty$. Thus, the line $y = 0$ (the x-axis) is a horizontal asymptote. As x approaches 1 from either side, the function increases or decreases without bound. Similarly, as x approaches -2 from either side, the function increases or decreases without bound. Therefore, $x = 1$ and $x = -2$ are vertical asymptotes. (See Figure 5.7-1.)

[−6,5] by [−3,3]

Figure 5.7-1

14. As $x \to 5^+$, the limit of the numerator $(5 + [5])$ is 10 and as $x \to 5^+$, the denominator approaches 0 through negative values. Thus, the

$$\lim_{x \to 5^+} \frac{5 + [x]}{5 - x} = -\infty.$$

15. Since $f(x)$ is a rational function, it is continuous everywhere except at values where the denominator is 0. Factoring and setting the denominator equal to 0, you have $(x + 6)\ (x - 2) = 0$. Thus, the the function is discontinuous at $x = -6$ and $x = 2$. Verify your result with a calculator. (See Figure 5.7-2.)

[−8,8] by [−4,4]

Figure 5.7-2

16. In order for $g(x)$ to be continuous at $x = 3$, it must satisfy the three conditions of continuity:

(1) $g(3) = 3^2 + 5 = 14$,

(2) $\lim\limits_{x \to 3^+} (x^2 + 5) = 14$, and

(3) $\lim\limits_{x \to 3^-} (2x - k) = 6 - k$, and the two one-sided limits must be equal in order for $\lim\limits_{x \to 3} g(x)$ to exist. Therefore,

$6 - k = 14$ and $k = -8$.

Now, $g(3) = \lim\limits_{x \to 3} g(x)$ and condition 3 is satisfied.

17. Checking with the three conditions of continuity:

(1) $f(2) = 12$,

(2) $\lim\limits_{x \to 2} \dfrac{x^2 + 5x - 14}{x - 2} =$

$\lim\limits_{x \to 2} \dfrac{(x + 7)(x - 2)}{x - 2} = \lim\limits_{x \to 2} (x + 7) = 9$, and

(3) $f(2) \neq \lim\limits_{x \to 2} (x + 7)$. Therefore, $f(x)$ is discontinuous at $x = 2$.

18. The graph indicates that (a) $f(3) = 4$, (b) $\lim\limits_{x \to 3^+} f(x) = 0$, (c) $\lim\limits_{x \to 3^-} f(x) = 0$, (d) $\lim\limits_{x \to 3} f(x) = 0$, and (e) therefore, $f(x)$ is not continuous at $x = 3$ since $f(3) \neq \lim\limits_{x \to 3} f(x)$.

19. In the intervals $[-3, -1]$, $[-1, 1]$, and $[1, 3]$, the function $f(x)$ attains values greater than and less than -2. Therefore, by the Intermediate Value Theorem (IVT) $f(x) = -2$ at least once in each of those intervals. Choice (C).

20. Substituting $x = 0$ would lead to 0/0. Substitute $(1 - \cos^2 x)$ in place of $\sin^2 x$ and obtain

$$\lim_{x \to 0} \frac{1 - \cos x}{\sin^2 x} = \lim_{x \to 0} \frac{1 - \cos x}{(1 - \cos^2 x)}$$

$$= \lim_{x \to 0} \frac{1 - \cos x}{(1 - \cos x)(1 + \cos x)}$$

$$= \lim_{x \to 0} \frac{1}{(1 + \cos x)}$$

$$= \frac{1}{1 + 1} = \frac{1}{2}.$$

Verify your result with a calculator. (See Figure 5.7-3)

[−10,10] by [−4,4]

Figure 5.7-3

5.8 Solutions to Cumulative Review Problems

21. Rewrite $3x - 2y = 6$ in $y = mx + b$ form, which is $y = \frac{3}{2}x - 3$. The slope of this line whose equation is $y = \frac{3}{2}x - 3$ is $m = \frac{3}{2}$. Thus, the slope of a line perpendicular to this line is $m = -\frac{2}{3}$. Since the perpendicular line passes through the point $(2, -4)$, therefore, an equation of the perpendicular line is
$y - (-4) = -\frac{2}{3}(x - 2)$, which is equivalent to $y + 4 = -\frac{2}{3}(x - 2)$.

22. The graph indicates that $\lim\limits_{x \to 4^-} f(x) = 3$, $f(4) = 1$, and $\lim\limits_{x \to 4} f(x)$ does not exist. Therefore, only statements I and III are true.

23. Substituting $x = 0$ into $\dfrac{|3x - 4|}{x - 2}$, you obtain $\dfrac{4}{-2} = -2$.

24. Rewrite $\lim\limits_{x \to 0} \dfrac{\tan x}{x}$ as $\lim\limits_{x \to 0} \dfrac{\sin x / \cos x}{x}$, which is equivalent to $\lim\limits_{x \to 0} \dfrac{\sin x}{x \cos x}$, which is equal to
$$\lim_{x \to 0} \frac{\sin x}{x} \cdot \lim_{x \to 0} \frac{1}{\cos x} = (1)(1) = 1.$$

25. To find horizontal asymptotes, examine the $\lim_{x \to \infty} f(x)$ and the $\lim_{x \to -\infty} f(x)$. The $\lim_{x \to \infty} f(x) = \lim_{x \to \infty} \dfrac{x}{\sqrt{x^2 + 4}}$. Dividing by the highest power of x (and in this case, it's x), you obtain $\lim_{x \to \infty} \dfrac{x/x}{\sqrt{x^2 + 4}/x}$. As $x \to \infty$, $x = \sqrt{x^2}$. Thus, you have $\lim_{x \to \infty} \dfrac{x/x}{\sqrt{x^2 + 4}/\sqrt{x^2}} = \lim_{x \to \infty} \dfrac{1}{\sqrt{\dfrac{x^2 + 4}{x^2}}}$ $= \lim_{x \to \infty} \dfrac{1}{\sqrt{1 + \dfrac{4}{x^2}}} = 1$. Thus, the line $y = 1$ is a horizontal asymptote.

The $\lim_{x \to -\infty} f(x) = \lim_{x \to -\infty} \dfrac{x}{\sqrt{x^2 + 4}}$. As $x \to -\infty$, $x = -\sqrt{x^2}$. Thus, $\lim_{x \to -\infty} \dfrac{x}{\sqrt{x^2 + 4}}$ $= \lim_{x \to -\infty} \dfrac{x/x}{\sqrt{x^2 + 4}/\left(-\sqrt{x^2}\right)} = \lim_{x \to -\infty} \dfrac{1}{-\sqrt{1 + \dfrac{4}{x^2}}} = -1$.

Therefore, the line $y = -1$ is a horizontal asymptote. As for vertical asymptotes, $f(x)$ is continuous and defined for all real numbers. Thus, there is no vertical asymptote.

CHAPTER 6

Big Idea 2: Derivatives
Differentiation

IN THIS CHAPTER

Summary: The derivative of a function is often used to find rates of change. It is also related to the slope of a tangent line. On the AP Calculus BC exam, many questions involve finding the derivative of a function. In this chapter, you will learn different techniques for finding a derivative, which include using the Power Rule, Product & Quotient Rules, Chain Rule, and Implicit Differentiation. You will also learn to find the derivatives of trigonometric, exponential, logarithmic, and inverse functions, as well as apply *L'Hôpital's* Rule.

Key Ideas

✪ Definition of the derivative of a function
✪ Power rule, product & quotient rules, and chain rule
✪ Derivatives of trigonometric, exponential, and logarithmic functions
✪ Derivatives of inverse functions
✪ Implicit differentiation
✪ Higher order derivatives
✪ Indeterminate forms and *L'Hôpital's* Rule

6.1 Derivatives of Algebraic Functions

Main Concepts: Definition of the Derivative of a Function; Power Rule; The Sum, Difference, Product, and Quotient Rules; The Chain Rule

Definition of the Derivative of a Function

The derivative of a function f, written as f', is defined as

$$f'(x) = \lim_{h \to 0} \frac{f(x+h) - f(x)}{h},$$

if this limit exists. (Note that $f'(x)$ is read as f prime of x.)
Other symbols of the derivative of a function are:

$$D_x f, \frac{d}{dx} f(x), \text{ and if } y = f(x), y', \frac{dy}{dx}, \text{ and } D_x y.$$

Let m_{tangent} be the slope of the tangent to a curve $y = f(x)$ at a point on the curve. Then,

$$m_{\text{tangent}} = f'(x) = \lim_{h \to 0} \frac{f(x+h) - f(x)}{h}$$

$$m_{\text{tangent}}(\text{at } x = a) = f'(a) = \lim_{h \to 0} \frac{f(a+h) - f(a)}{h} \text{ or } \lim_{x \to a} \frac{f(x) - f(a)}{x - a}.$$

(See Figure 6.1-1.)

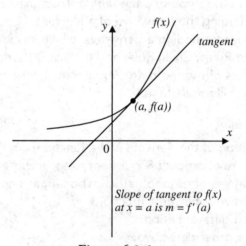

Slope of tangent to f(x)
at x = a is m = f'(a)

Figure 6.1-1

Given a function f, if $f'(x)$ exists at $x = a$, then the function f is said to be differentiable at $x = a$. If a function f is differentiable at $x = a$, then f is continuous at $x = a$. (Note that the converse of the statement is not necessarily true, i.e., if a function f is continuous at $x = a$, then f may or may not be differentiable at $x = a$.) Here are several examples of functions that are not differentiable at a given number $x = a$. (See Figures 6.1-2–6.1-5 on page 77.)

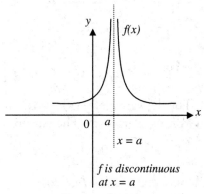

$x = a$

f is discontinuous
at $x = a$

Figure 6.1-2

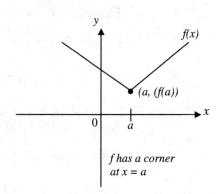

$(a, (f(a))$

f has a corner
at $x = a$

Figure 6.1-3

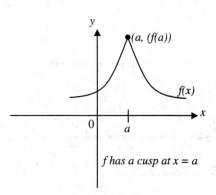

$(a, (f(a))$

$f(x)$

f has a cusp at $x = a$

Figure 6.1-4

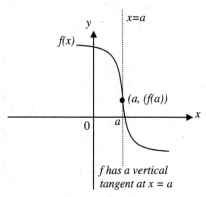

$x = a$

$f(x)$

$(a, (f(a))$

f has a vertical
tangent at $x = a$

Figure 6.1-5

Example 1

If $f(x) = x^2 - 2x - 3$, find (a) $f'(x)$ using the definition of derivative, (b) $f'(0)$, (c) $f'(1)$, and (d) $f'(3)$.

(a) Using the definition of derivative, $f'(x) = \lim\limits_{h \to 0} \dfrac{f(x + h) - f(x)}{h}$

$$= \lim_{h \to 0} \frac{[(x + h)^2 - 2(x + h) - 3] - [x^2 - 2x - 3]}{h}$$

$$= \lim_{h \to 0} \frac{[x^2 + 2xh + h^2 - 2x - 2h - 3] - [x^2 - 2x - 3]}{h}$$

$$= \lim_{h \to 0} \frac{2xh + h^2 - 2h}{h}$$

$$= \lim_{h \to 0} \frac{h(2x + h - 2)}{h}$$

$$= \lim_{h \to 0} (2x + h - 2) = 2x - 2.$$

(b) $f'(0) = 2(0) - 2 = -2$, (c) $f'(1) = 2(1) - 2 = 0$ and (d) $f'(3) = 2(3) - 2 = 4$.

Example 2

Evaluate $\lim\limits_{h \to 0} \dfrac{\cos(\pi + h) - \cos(\pi)}{h}$.

The expression $\lim\limits_{h \to 0} \dfrac{\cos(\pi + h) - \cos(\pi)}{h}$ is equivalent to the derivative of the function $f(x) = \cos x$ at $x = \pi$, i.e., $f'(\pi)$. The derivative of $f(x) = \cos x$ at $x = \pi$ is equivalent to the slope of the tangent to the curve of $\cos x$ at $x = \pi$. The tangent is parallel to the x-axis. Thus, the slope is 0 or $\lim\limits_{h \to 0} \dfrac{\cos(\pi + h) - \cos(\pi)}{h} = 0$.

Or, using an algebraic method, note that $\cos(a + b) = \cos(a)\cos(b) - \sin(a)\sin(b)$.

Then rewrite $\lim\limits_{h \to 0} \dfrac{\cos(\pi + h) - \cos(\pi)}{h} = \lim\limits_{h \to 0} \dfrac{\cos(\pi)\cos(h) - \sin(\pi)\sin(h) - \cos(\pi)}{h} =$

$\lim\limits_{h \to 0} \dfrac{-\cos(h) - (-1)}{h} = \lim\limits_{h \to 0} \dfrac{-\cos(h) + 1}{h} = \lim\limits_{h \to 0} \dfrac{-[\cos(h) - 1]}{h} = -\lim\limits_{h \to 0} \dfrac{[\cos(h) - 1]}{h} = 0.$

(See Figure 6.1-6.)

[−3.14,6.28] by [−3,3]

Figure 6.1-6

Example 3

If the function $f(x) = x^{2/3} + 1$, find all points where f is not differentiable.

The function $f(x)$ is continuous for all real numbers and the graph of $f(x)$ forms a "cusp" at the point $(0, 1)$. Thus, $f(x)$ is not differentiable at $x = 0$. (See Figure 6.1-7.)

[−5,5] by [−1,6]

Figure 6.1-7

Example 4

Using a calculator, find the derivative of $f(x) = x^2 + 4x$ at $x = 3$.

There are several ways to find $f'(3)$, using a calculator. One way is to use the [nDeriv] function of the calculator. From the main Home screen, select F3-Calc and then select [nDeriv]. Enter [nDeriv] $(x^2 + 4x,\ x)|x = 3$. The result is 10.

• Always write out all formulas in your solutions.

Power Rule

If $f(x) = c$ where c is a constant, then $f'(x) = 0$.
If $f(x) = x^n$ where n is a real number, then $f'(x) = nx^{n-1}$.
If $f(x) = cx^n$ where c is a constant and n is a real number, then $f'(x) = cnx^{n-1}$.

Summary of Derivatives of Algebraic Functions

$$\frac{d}{dx}(c) = 0, \quad \frac{d}{dx}(x^n) = nx^{n-1}, \quad \text{and} \quad \frac{d}{dx}(cx^n) = cnx^{n-1}$$

Example 1

If $f(x) = 2x^3$, find (a) $f'(x)$, (b) $f'(1)$, and (c) $f'(0)$.
Note that (a) $f'(x) = 6x^2$, (b) $f'(1) = 6(1)^2 = 6$, and (c) $f'(0) = 0$.

Example 2

If $y = \dfrac{1}{x^2}$, find (a) $\dfrac{dy}{dx}$ and (b) $\dfrac{dy}{dx}\big|_{x=0}$ (which represents $\dfrac{dy}{dx}$ at $x = 0$).

Note that (a) $y = \dfrac{1}{x^2} = x^{-2}$ and thus, $\dfrac{dy}{dx} = -2x^{-3} = \dfrac{-2}{x^3}$ and (b) $\dfrac{dy}{dx}\big|_{x=0}$ does not exist because the expression $\dfrac{-2}{0}$ is undefined.

Example 3

Here are several examples of algebraic functions and their derivatives:

FUNCTION	WRITTEN IN cx^n FORM	DERIVATIVE	DERIVATIVE WITH POSITIVE EXPONENTS
$3x$	$3x^1$	$3x^0 = 3$	3
$-5x^7$	$-5x^7$	$-35x^6$	$-35x^6$
$8\sqrt{x}$	$8x^{\frac{1}{2}}$	$4x^{-\frac{1}{2}}$	$\dfrac{4}{x^{\frac{1}{2}}}$ or $\dfrac{4}{\sqrt{x}}$
$\dfrac{1}{x^2}$	x^{-2}	$-2x^{-3}$	$\dfrac{-2}{x^3}$
$\dfrac{-2}{\sqrt{x}}$	$\dfrac{-2}{x^{\frac{1}{2}}} = -2x^{-\frac{1}{2}}$	$x^{-\frac{3}{2}}$	$\dfrac{1}{x^{\frac{3}{2}}}$ or $\dfrac{1}{\sqrt{x^3}}$
4	$4x^0$	0	0
π^2	$(\pi^2)x^0$	0	0

Example 4

Using a calculator, find $f'(x)$ and $f'(3)$ if $f(x) = \dfrac{1}{\sqrt{x}}$.

There are several ways of finding $f'(x)$ and $f'(9)$ using a calculator. One way to use the d [*Differentiate*] function. Go to the Home screen. Select *F3-Calc* and then select d [*Differentiate*]. Enter $d(1/\sqrt{(x)},\ x)$. The result is $f'(x) = \dfrac{-1}{2x^{\frac{3}{2}}}$. To find $f'(3)$, enter $d(1/\sqrt{(x)},\ x)|x = 3$. The result is $f'(3) = \dfrac{-1}{54}$.

The Sum, Difference, Product, and Quotient Rules

If u and v are two differentiable functions, then

$$\frac{d}{dx}(u \pm v) = \frac{du}{dx} \pm \frac{dv}{dx} \qquad \text{Sum \& Difference Rules}$$

$$\frac{d}{dx}(uv) = v\frac{du}{dx} + u\frac{dv}{dx} \qquad \text{Product Rule}$$

$$\frac{d}{dx}\left(\frac{u}{v}\right) = \frac{v\dfrac{du}{dx} - u\dfrac{dv}{dx}}{v^2},\ v \neq 0 \qquad \text{Quotient Rule}$$

Summary of Sum, Difference, Product, and Quotient Rules

$$(u \pm v)' = u' \pm v' \qquad (uv)' = u'v + v'u \qquad \left(\frac{u}{v}\right)' = \frac{u'v - v'u}{v^2}$$

Example 1

Find $f'(x)$ if $f(x) = x^3 - 10x + 5$.

Using the sum and difference rules, you can differentiate each term and obtain $f'(x) = 3x^2 - 10$. Or using your calculator, select the d [*Differentiate*] function and enter $d(x^3 - 10x + 5,\ x)$ and obtain $3x^2 - 10$.

Example 2

If $y = (3x - 5)(x^4 + 8x - 1)$, find $\dfrac{dy}{dx}$.

Using the product rule $\dfrac{d}{dx}(uv) = v\dfrac{du}{dx} + u\dfrac{dv}{dx}$, let $u = (3x - 5)$ and $v = (x^4 + 8x - 1)$.

Then $\dfrac{dy}{dx} = (3)(x^4 + 8x - 1) + (4x^3 + 8)(3x - 5) = (3x^4 + 24x - 3) + (12x^4 - 20x^3 + 24x - 40) = 15x^4 - 20x^3 + 48x - 43$. Or you can use your calculator and enter $d((3x - 5)(x^4 + 8x - 1),\ x)$ and obtain the same result.

Example 3

If $f(x) = \dfrac{2x - 1}{x + 5}$, find $f'(x)$.

Using the quotient rule $\left(\dfrac{u}{v}\right)' = \dfrac{u'v - v'u}{v^2}$, let $u = 2x - 1$ and $v = x + 5$. Then

$$f'(x) = \frac{(2)(x + 5) - (1)(2x - 1)}{(x + 5)^2} = \frac{2x + 10 - 2x + 1}{(x + 5)^2} = \frac{11}{(x + 5)^2},\ x \neq -5.\ \text{Or you can use}$$

your calculator and enter $d((2x - 1)/(x + 5),\ x)$ and obtain the same result.

Example 4

Using your calculator, find an equation of the tangent to the curve $f(x) = x^2 - 3x + 2$ at $x = 5$.

Find the slope of the tangent to the curve at $x = 5$ by entering $d(x^2 - 3x + 2, \ x)|x = 5$. The result is 7. Compute $f(5) = 12$. Thus, the point $(5, 12)$ is on the curve of $f(x)$. An equation of the line whose slope $m = 7$ and passing through the point $(5, 12)$ is $y - 12 = 7(x - 5)$.

> • Remember that $\dfrac{d}{dx} \ln x = \dfrac{1}{x}$ and $\displaystyle\int \ln x \ dx = x \ln x - x + c$. The integral formula is not usually tested in the BC exam.

The Chain Rule

If $y = f(u)$ and $u = g(x)$ are differentiable functions of u and x respectively, then $\dfrac{d}{dx}[f(g(x))] = f'(g(x)) \cdot g'(x)$ or $\dfrac{dy}{dx} = \dfrac{dy}{du} \cdot \dfrac{du}{dx}$.

Example 1

If $y = (3x - 5)^{10}$, find $\dfrac{dy}{dx}$.

Using the chain rule, let $u = 3x - 5$ and thus, $y = u^{10}$. Then, $\dfrac{dy}{du} = 10u^9$ and $\dfrac{du}{dx} = 3$.
Since $\dfrac{dy}{dx} = \dfrac{dy}{du} \cdot \dfrac{du}{dx}, \dfrac{dy}{dx} = (10u^9)(3) = 10(3x - 5)^9(3) = 30(3x - 5)^9$. Or you can use your calculator and enter $d((3x - 5)^{10}, \ x)$ and obtain the same result.

Example 2

If $f(x) = 5x\sqrt{25 - x^2}$, find $f'(x)$.

Rewrite $f(x) = 5x\sqrt{25 - x^2}$ as $f(x) = 5x(25 - x^2)^{\frac{1}{2}}$. Using the product rule, $f'(x) = (25 - x^2)^{\frac{1}{2}}\dfrac{d}{dx}(5x) + (5x)\dfrac{d}{dx}(25 - x^2)^{\frac{1}{2}} = 5(25 - x^2)^{\frac{1}{2}} + (5x)\dfrac{d}{dx}(25 - x^2)^{\frac{1}{2}}$.

To find $\dfrac{d}{dx}(25 - x^2)^{\frac{1}{2}}$, use the chain rule and let $u = 25 - x^2$.

Thus, $\dfrac{d}{dx}(25 - x^2)^{\frac{1}{2}} = \dfrac{1}{2}(25 - x^2)^{-\frac{1}{2}}(-2x) = \dfrac{-x}{(25 - x^2)^{\frac{1}{2}}}$. Substituting this quantity back

into $f'(x)$, you have $f'(x) = 5(25 - x^2)^{\frac{1}{2}} + (5x)\left(\dfrac{-x}{(25 - x^2)^{\frac{1}{2}}}\right) = \dfrac{5(25 - x^2) - 5x^2}{(25 - x^2)^{\frac{1}{2}}} =$

$\dfrac{125 - 10x^2}{(25 - x^2)^{\frac{1}{2}}}$. Or you can use your calculator and enter $d(5x\sqrt{25 - x^2}, \ x)$ and obtain the same result.

Example 3

If $y = \left(\dfrac{2x-1}{x^2}\right)^3$, find $\dfrac{dy}{dx}$.

Using the chain rule, let $u = \left(\dfrac{2x-1}{x^2}\right)$. Then $\dfrac{dy}{dx} = 3\left(\dfrac{2x-1}{x^2}\right)^2 \dfrac{d}{dx}\left(\dfrac{2x-1}{x^2}\right)$.

To find $\dfrac{d}{dx}\left(\dfrac{2x-1}{x^2}\right)$, use the quotient rule.

Thus, $\dfrac{d}{dx}\left(\dfrac{2x-1}{x^2}\right) = \dfrac{(2)(x^2)-(2x)(2x-1)}{(x^2)^2} = \dfrac{-2x^2+2x}{x^4}$. Substituting this

quantity back into $\dfrac{dy}{dx} = 3\left(\dfrac{2x-1}{x^2}\right)^2 \dfrac{d}{dx}\left(\dfrac{2x-1}{x^2}\right) = 3\left(\dfrac{2x-1}{x^2}\right)^2 \dfrac{-2x^2+2x}{x^4}$

$= \dfrac{-6(x-1)(2x-1)^2}{x^7}$.

An alternate solution is to use the product rule and rewrite $y = \left(\dfrac{2x-1}{x^2}\right)^3$ as $y = \dfrac{(2x-1)^3}{(x^2)^3} = \dfrac{(2x-1)^3}{x^6}$ and use the quotient rule. Another approach is to express $y = (2x-1)^3(x^{-6})$ and use the product rule. Of course, you can always use your calculator if you are permitted to do so.

6.2 Derivatives of Trigonometric, Inverse Trigonometric, Exponential, and Logarithmic Functions

Main Concepts: Derivatives of Trigonometric Functions, Derivatives of Inverse Trigonometric Functions, Derivatives of Exponential and Logarithmic Functions

Derivatives of Trigonometric Functions
Summary of Derivatives of Trigonometric Functions

$$\dfrac{d}{dx}(\sin x) = \cos x \qquad\qquad \dfrac{d}{dx}(\cos x) = -\sin x$$

$$\dfrac{d}{dx}(\tan x) = \sec^2 x \qquad\qquad \dfrac{d}{dx}(\cot x) = -\csc^2 x$$

$$\dfrac{d}{dx}(\sec x) = \sec x \tan x \qquad\qquad \dfrac{d}{dx}(\csc x) = -\csc x \cot x$$

Note that the derivatives of *cosine*, *cotangent*, and *cosecant* all have a negative sign.

Example 1

If $y = 6x^2 + 3\sec x$, find $\dfrac{dy}{dx}$.

$\dfrac{dy}{dx} = 12x + 3\sec x \tan x$.

Example 2

Find $f'(x)$ if $f(x) = \cot(4x - 6)$.

Using the chain rule, let $u = 4x - 6$. Then $f'(x) = [-\csc^2(4x - 6)][4] = -4\csc^2(4x - 6)$.

Or using your calculator, enter $d(1/\tan(4x - 6),\ x)$ and obtain $\dfrac{-4}{\sin^2(4x - 6)}$, which is an equivalent form.

Example 3

Find $f'(x)$ if $f(x) = 8\sin(x^2)$.

Using the chain rule, let $u = x^2$. Then $f'(x) = [8\cos(x^2)][2x] = 16x\cos(x^2)$.

Example 4

If $y = \sin x \cos(2x)$, find $\dfrac{dy}{dx}$.

Using the product rule, let $u = \sin x$ and $v = \cos(2x)$.

Then $\dfrac{dy}{dx} = \cos x \cos(2x) + [-\sin(2x)](2)(\sin x) = \cos x \cos(2x) - 2\sin x \sin(2x)$.

Example 5

If $y = \sin[\cos(2x)]$, find $\dfrac{dy}{dx}$.

Using the chain rule, let $u = \cos(2x)$. Then

$$\frac{dy}{dx} = \frac{dy}{du} \cdot \frac{du}{dx} = \cos[\cos(2x)]\frac{d}{dx}[\cos(2x)].$$

To evaluate $\dfrac{d}{dx}[\cos(2x)]$, use the chain rule again by making another u-substitution, this time for $2x$. Thus, $\dfrac{d}{dx}[\cos(2x)] = [-\sin(2x)]2 = -2\sin(2x)$. Therefore,

$\dfrac{dy}{dx} \cos[\cos(2x)](-2\sin(2x)) = -2\sin(2x)\cos[\cos(2x)]$.

Example 6

Find $f'(x)$ if $f(x) = 5x\csc x$.

Using the product rule, let $u = 5x$ and $v = \csc x$. Then $f'(x) = 5\csc x + (-\csc x \cot x)(5x) = 5\csc x - 5x(\csc x)(\cot x)$.

Example 7

If $y = \sqrt{\sin x}$, find $\dfrac{dy}{dx}$.

Rewrite $y = \sqrt{\sin x}$ as $y = (\sin x)^{1/2}$. Using the chain rule, let $u = \sin x$. Thus, $\dfrac{dy}{dx} = \dfrac{1}{2}(\sin x)^{-\frac{1}{2}}(\cos x) = \dfrac{\cos x}{2(\sin x)^{\frac{1}{2}}} = \dfrac{\cos x}{2\sqrt{\sin x}}$.

Example 8

If $y = \dfrac{\tan x}{1 + \tan x}$, find $\dfrac{dy}{dx}$.

Using the quotient rule, let $u = \tan x$ and $v = (1 + \tan x)$. Then,

$$\frac{dy}{dx} = \frac{(\sec^2 x)(1 + \tan x) - (\sec^2 x)(\tan x)}{(1 + \tan x)^2}$$

$$= \frac{\sec^2 x + (\sec^2 x)(\tan x) - (\sec^2 x)(\tan x)}{(1 + \tan x)^2}$$

$$= \frac{\sec^2 x}{(1 + \tan x)^2}, \text{ which is equivalent to } \frac{\dfrac{1}{(\cos x)^2}}{1 + \left(\dfrac{\sin x}{\cos x}\right)^2}$$

$$= \frac{\dfrac{1}{(\cos x)^2}}{\left(\dfrac{\cos x + \sin x}{\cos x}\right)^2} = \frac{1}{(\cos x + \sin x)^2}.$$

Note: For all of the above exercises, you can find the derivatives by using a calculator, provided that you are permitted to do so.

Derivatives of Inverse Trigonometric Functions
Summary of Derivatives of Inverse Trigonometric Functions

Let u be a differentiable function of x, then

$$\frac{d}{dx}\sin^{-1} u = \frac{1}{\sqrt{1 - u^2}}\frac{du}{dx}, \ |u| < 1 \qquad \frac{d}{dx}\cos^{-1} u = \frac{-1}{\sqrt{1 - u^2}}\frac{du}{dx}, \ |u| < 1$$

$$\frac{d}{dx}\tan^{-1} u = \frac{1}{1 + u^2}\frac{du}{dx} \qquad \frac{d}{dx}\cot^{-1} u = \frac{-1}{1 + u^2}\frac{du}{dx}$$

$$\frac{d}{dx}\sec^{-1} u = \frac{1}{|u|\sqrt{u^2 - 1}}\frac{du}{dx}, \ |u| > 1 \qquad \frac{d}{dx}\csc^{-1} u = \frac{-1}{|u|\sqrt{u^2 - 1}}\frac{du}{dx}, \ |u| > 1.$$

Note that the derivatives of $\cos^{-1} x$, $\cot^{-1} x$, and $\csc^{-1} x$ all have a "-1" in their numerators. Note that $\sin^{-1} x$ is equivalent to arcsin x, and so on.

Example 1

If $y = 5 \sin^{-1}(3x)$, find $\dfrac{dy}{dx}$.

Let $u = 3x$. Then $\dfrac{dy}{dx} = (5)\dfrac{1}{\sqrt{1 - (3x)^2}}\dfrac{du}{dx} = \dfrac{5}{\sqrt{1 - (3x)^2}}(3) = \dfrac{15}{\sqrt{1 - 9x^2}}$.

Or using a calculator, enter $d[5 \sin^{-1}(3x), \ x]$ and obtain the same result.

Example 2

Find $f'(x)$ if $f(x) = \tan^{-1}\sqrt{x}$.

Let $u = \sqrt{x}$. Then $f'(x) = \dfrac{1}{1 + (\sqrt{x})^2}\dfrac{du}{dx} = \dfrac{1}{1+x}\left(\dfrac{1}{2}x^{-\frac{1}{2}}\right) = \dfrac{1}{1+x}\left(\dfrac{1}{2\sqrt{x}}\right)$

$= \dfrac{1}{2\sqrt{x}(1+x)}$.

Example 3

If $y = \sec^{-1}(3x^2)$, find $\dfrac{dy}{dx}$.

Let $u = 3x^2$. Then $\dfrac{dy}{dx} = \dfrac{1}{|3x^2|\sqrt{(3x^2)^2 - 1}}\dfrac{du}{dx} = \dfrac{1}{3x^2\sqrt{9x^4 - 1}}(6x) = \dfrac{2}{x\sqrt{9x^4 - 1}}$.

Example 4

If $y = \cos^{-1}\left(\dfrac{1}{x}\right)$, find $\dfrac{dy}{dx}$.

Let $u = \left(\dfrac{1}{x}\right)$. Then $\dfrac{dy}{dx} = \dfrac{-1}{\sqrt{1 - \left(\dfrac{1}{x}\right)^2}}\dfrac{du}{dx}$.

Rewrite $u = \left(\dfrac{1}{x}\right)$ as $u = x^{-1}$. Then $\dfrac{du}{dx} = -1x^{-2} = \dfrac{-1}{x^2}$.

Therefore, $\dfrac{dy}{dx} = \dfrac{-1}{\sqrt{1 - \left(\dfrac{1}{x}\right)^2}}\dfrac{du}{dx} = \dfrac{-1}{\sqrt{1 - \left(\dfrac{1}{x}\right)^2}}\dfrac{-1}{x^2} = \dfrac{1}{\sqrt{\dfrac{x^2 - 1}{x^2}}(x^2)}$

$= \dfrac{1}{\dfrac{\sqrt{x^2 - 1}}{|x|}(x^2)} = \dfrac{1}{|x|\sqrt{x^2 - 1}}$.

Note: For all of the above exercises, you can find the derivatives by using a calculator, provided that you are permitted to do so.

Derivatives of Exponential and Logarithmic Functions
Summary of Derivatives of Exponential and Logarithmic Functions

Let u be a differentiable function of x, then

$$\frac{d}{dx}(e^u) = e^u\frac{du}{dx} \qquad\qquad \frac{d}{dx}(a^u) = a^u \ln a \frac{du}{dx},\ a > 0\ \&\ a \neq 1$$

$$\frac{d}{dx}(\ln u) = \frac{1}{u}\frac{du}{dx},\ u > 0 \qquad \frac{d}{dx}(\log_a u) = \frac{1}{u \ln a}\frac{du}{dx},\ a > 0\ \&\ a \neq 1.$$

For the following examples, find $\dfrac{dy}{dx}$ and verify your result with a calculator.

Example 1

$y = e^{3x} + 5xe^3 + e^3$

$\dfrac{dy}{dx} = (e^{3x})(3) + 5e^3 + 0 = 3e^{3x} + 5e^3$ (Note that e^3 is a constant.)

Example 2

$y = xe^x - x^2e^x$

Using the product rule for both terms, you have

$$\dfrac{dy}{dx} = (1)e^x + (e^x)x - \left[(2x)e^x + (e^x)x^2\right] = e^x + xe^x - 2xe^x - x^2e^x = e^x - xe^x - x^2e^x$$

$$= -x^2e^x - xe^x + e^x = e^x(-x^2 - x + 1).$$

Example 3

$y = 3^{\sin x}$

Let $u = \sin x$. Then, $\dfrac{dy}{dx} = (3^{\sin x})(\ln 3)\dfrac{du}{dx} = (3^{\sin x})(\ln 3)\cos x = (\ln 3)(3^{\sin x})\cos x.$

Example 4

$y = e^{(x^3)}$

Let $u = x^3$. Then, $\dfrac{dy}{dx} = \left[e^{(x^3)}\right]\dfrac{du}{dx} = \left[e^{(x^3)}\right]3x^2 = 3x^2e^{(x^3)}.$

Example 5

$y = (\ln x)^5$

Let $u = \ln x$. Then, $\dfrac{dy}{dx} = 5(\ln x)^4\dfrac{du}{dx} = 5(\ln x)^4\left(\dfrac{1}{x}\right) = \dfrac{5(\ln x)^4}{x}.$

Example 6

$y = \ln(x^2 + 2x - 3) + \ln 5$

Let $u = x^2 + 2x - 3$. Then, $\dfrac{dy}{dx} = \dfrac{1}{x^2 + 2x - 3}\dfrac{du}{dx} + 0 = \dfrac{1}{x^2 + 2x - 3}(2x + 2) = \dfrac{2x + 2}{x^2 + 2x - 3}.$

(Note that $\ln 5$ is a constant. Thus, the derivative of $\ln 5$ is 0.)

Example 7

$y = 2x \ln x + x$

Using the product rule for the first term,

you have $\dfrac{dy}{dx} = (2)\ln x + \left(\dfrac{1}{x}\right)(2x) + 1 = 2\ln x + 2 + 1 = 2\ln x + 3.$

Example 8

$y = \ln(\ln x)$

Let $u = \ln x$. Then $\dfrac{dy}{dx} = \dfrac{1}{\ln x}\dfrac{du}{dx} = \dfrac{1}{\ln x}\left(\dfrac{1}{x}\right) = \dfrac{1}{x \ln x}$.

Example 9

$y = \log_5(2x + 1)$

Let $u = 2x + 1$. Then $\dfrac{dy}{dx} = \dfrac{1}{(2x + 1)\ln 5}\dfrac{du}{dx} = \dfrac{1}{(2x + 1)\ln 5} \cdot (2) = \dfrac{2}{(2x + 1)\ln 5}$.

Example 10

Write an equation of the line tangent to the curve of $y = e^x$ at $x = 1$.

    The slope of the tangent to the curve $y = e^x$ at $x = 1$ is equivalent to the value of the derivative of $y = e^x$ evaluated at $x = 1$. Using your calculator, enter $d(e^\wedge(x),\ x)|x = 1$ and obtain e. Thus, $m = e$, the slope of the tangent to the curve at $x = 1$. At $x = 1$, $y = e^1 = e$, and thus the point on the curve is $(1, e)$. Therefore, the equation of the tangent is $y - e = e(x - 1)$ or $y = ex$. (See Figure 6.2-1.)

[−1,3] by [−2,8]

Figure 6.2-1

• Never leave a multiple-choice question blank. There is no penalty for incorrect answers.

6.3 Implicit Differentiation

Main Concept: Procedure for Implicit Differentiation

Procedure for Implicit Differentiation

Given an equation containing the variables x and y for which you cannot easily solve for y in terms of x, you can find $\dfrac{dy}{dx}$ by doing the following:

Steps 1: Differentiate each term of the equation with respect to x.

    2: Move all terms containing $\dfrac{dy}{dx}$ to the left side of the equation and all other terms to the right side.

    3: Factor out $\dfrac{dy}{dx}$ on the left side of the equation.

    4: Solve for $\dfrac{dy}{dx}$.

Example 1

Find $\dfrac{dy}{dx}$ if $y^2 - 7y + x^2 - 4x = 10$.

Step 1: Differentiate each term of the equation with respect to x. (Note that y is treated as a function of x.) $2y\dfrac{dy}{dx} - 7\dfrac{dy}{dx} + 2x - 4 = 0$

Step 2: Move all terms containing $\dfrac{dy}{dx}$ to the left side of the equation and all other terms to the right: $2y\dfrac{dy}{dx} - 7\dfrac{dy}{dx} = -2x + 4$.

Step 3: Factor out $\dfrac{dy}{dx}$: $\dfrac{dy}{dx}(2y - 7) = -2x + 4$.

Step 4: Solve for $\dfrac{dy}{dx}$: $\dfrac{dy}{dx} = \dfrac{-2x + 4}{(2y - 7)}$.

Example 2

Given $x^3 + y^3 = 6xy$, find $\dfrac{dy}{dx}$.

Step 1: Differentiate each term with respect to x: $3x^2 + 3y^2\dfrac{dy}{dx} = (6)y + \left(\dfrac{dy}{dx}\right)(6x)$.

Step 2: Move all $\dfrac{dy}{dx}$ terms to the left side: $3y^2\dfrac{dy}{dx} - 6x\dfrac{dy}{dx} = 6y - 3x^2$.

Step 3: Factor out $\dfrac{dy}{dx}$: $\dfrac{dy}{dx}(3y^2 - 6x) = 6y - 3x^2$.

Step 4: Solve for $\dfrac{dy}{dx}$: $\dfrac{dy}{dx} = \dfrac{6y - 3x^2}{3y^2 - 6x} = \dfrac{2y - x^2}{y^2 - 2x}$.

Example 3

Find $\dfrac{dy}{dx}$ if $(x + y)^2 - (x - y)^2 = x^5 + y^5$.

Step 1: Differentiate each term with respect to x:

$$2(x + y)\left(1 + \dfrac{dy}{dx}\right) - 2(x - y)\left(1 - \dfrac{dy}{dx}\right) = 5x^4 + 5y^4\dfrac{dy}{dx}.$$

Distributing $2(x + y)$ and $-2(x - y)$, you have

$$2(x + y) + 2(x + y)\dfrac{dy}{dx} - 2(x - y) + 2(x - y)\dfrac{dy}{dx} = 5x^4 + 5y^4\dfrac{dy}{dx}.$$

Step 2: Move all $\dfrac{dy}{dx}$ terms to the left side:

$$2(x + y)\dfrac{dy}{dx} + 2(x - y)\dfrac{dy}{dx} - 5y^4\dfrac{dy}{dx} = 5x^4 - 2(x + y) + 2(x - y).$$

Step 3:   Factor out $\dfrac{dy}{dx}$:

$$\frac{dy}{dx}[2(x+y)+2(x-y)-5y^4]=5x^4-2x-2y+2x-2y$$

$$\frac{dy}{dx}[2x+2y+2x-2y-5y^4]=5x^4-4y$$

$$\frac{dy}{dx}[4x-5y^4]=5x^4-4y.$$

Step 4:   Solve for $\dfrac{dy}{dx}$: $\dfrac{dy}{dx}=\dfrac{5x^4-4y}{4x-5y^4}$.

Example 4

Write an equation of the tangent to the curve $x^2+y^2+19=2x+12y$ at (4, 3).
The slope of the tangent to the curve at (4, 3) is equivalent to the derivative $\dfrac{dy}{dx}$ at (4, 3).

Using implicit differentiation, you have:

$$2x+2y\frac{dy}{dx}=2+12\frac{dy}{dx}$$

$$2y\frac{dy}{dx}-12\frac{dy}{dx}=2-2x$$

$$\frac{dy}{dx}(2y-12)=2-2x$$

$$\frac{dy}{dx}=\frac{2-2x}{2y-12}=\frac{1-x}{y-6}\text{ and }\frac{dy}{dx}\bigg|_{(4,3)}=\frac{1-4}{3-6}=1.$$

Thus, the equation of the tangent is $y-3=(1)(x-4)$ or $y-3=x-4$.

Example 5

Find $\dfrac{dy}{dx}$, if $\sin(x+y)=2x$.

$$\left[\cos(x+y)\left(1+\frac{dy}{dx}\right)\right]=2$$

$$1+\frac{dy}{dx}=\frac{2}{\cos(x+y)}$$

$$\frac{dy}{dx}=\frac{2}{\cos(x+y)}-1$$

6.4 Approximating a Derivative

Given a continuous and differentiable function, you can find the approximate value of a derivative at a given point numerically. Here are two examples.

Example 1

The graph of a function f on $[0, 5]$ is shown in Figure 6.4-1. Find the approximate value of $f'(3)$. (See Figure 6.4-1.)

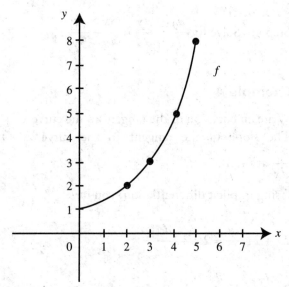

Figure 6.4-1

Since $f'(3)$ is equivalent to the slope of the tangent to $f(x)$ at $x = 3$, there are several ways you can find its approximate value.

Method 1: Using the slope of the line segment joining the points at $x = 3$ and $x = 4$.

$$f(3) = 3 \text{ and } f(4) = 5$$

$$m = \frac{f(4) - f(3)}{4 - 3} = \frac{5 - 3}{4 - 3} = 2$$

Method 2: Using the slope of the line segment joining the points at $x = 2$ and $x = 3$.

$$f(2) = 2 \text{ and } f(3) = 3$$

$$m = \frac{f(3) - f(2)}{3 - 2} = \frac{3 - 2}{3 - 2} = 1$$

Method 3: Using the slope of the line segment joining the points at $x = 2$ and $x = 4$.

$$f(2) = 2 \text{ and } f(4) = 5$$

$$m = \frac{f(4) - f(2)}{4 - 2} = \frac{5 - 2}{4 - 2} = \frac{3}{2}$$

Note that $\frac{3}{2}$ is the average of the results from methods 1 and 2.

Thus, $f'(3) \approx 1, 2,$ or $\frac{3}{2}$ depending on which line segment you use.

Example 2

Let f be a continuous and differentiable function. Selected values of f are shown below. Find the approximate value of f' at $x = 1$.

x	−2	−1	0	1	2	3
f	1	0	1	1.59	2.08	2.52

You can use the difference quotient $\dfrac{f(a + h) - f(a)}{h}$ to approximate $f'(a)$.

$$\text{Let } h = 1; \quad f'(1) \approx \frac{f(2) - f(1)}{2 - 1} \approx \frac{2.08 - 1.59}{1} \approx 0.49.$$

$$\text{Let } h = 2; \quad f'(1) \approx \frac{f(3) - f(1)}{3 - 1} \approx \frac{2.52 - 1.59}{2} \approx 0.465.$$

Or, you can use the symmetric difference quotient $\dfrac{f(a + h) - f(a - h)}{2h}$ to approximate $f'(a)$.

$$\text{Let } h = 1; \quad f'(1) \approx \frac{f(2) - f(0)}{2 - 0} \approx \frac{2.08 - 1}{2} \approx 0.54.$$

$$\text{Let } h = 2; \quad f'(1) \approx \frac{f(3) - f(-1)}{3 - (-1)} \approx \frac{2.52 - 0}{4} \approx 0.63.$$

Thus, $f'(3) \approx 0.49, 0.465, 0.54,$ or 0.63 depending on your method.

Note that f is decreasing on $(-2, -1)$ and increasing on $(-1, 3)$. Using the symmetric difference quotient with $h = 3$ would not be accurate. (See Figure 6.4-2.)

[−2,4] by [−2,4]

Figure 6.4-2

• Remember that the $\lim\limits_{x \to 0} \dfrac{\sin 6x}{\sin 2x} = \dfrac{6}{2} = 3$ because the $\lim\limits_{x \to 0} \dfrac{\sin x}{x} = 1$.

6.5 Derivatives of Inverse Functions

Let f be a one-to-one differentiable function with inverse function f^{-1}. If $f'(f^{-1}(a)) \neq 0$, then the inverse function f^{-1} is differentiable at a and $(f^{-1})'(a) = \dfrac{1}{f'(f^{-1}(a))}$. (See Figure 6.5-1.)

Figure 6.5-1

If $y = f^{-1}(x)$ so that $x = f(y)$, then $\dfrac{dy}{dx} = \dfrac{1}{dx/dy}$ with $\dfrac{dx}{dy} \neq 0$.

Example 1

If $f(x) = x^3 + 2x - 10$, find $(f^{-1})'(x)$.

Step 1: Check if $(f^{-1})'(x)$ exists. $f'(x) = 3x^2 + 2$ and $f'(x) > 0$ for all real values of x. Thus, $f(x)$ is strictly increasing, which implies that $f(x)$ is 1 − 1. Therefore, $(f^{-1})'(x)$ exists.

Step 2: Let $y = f(x)$ and thus $y = x^3 + 2x - 10$.

Step 3: Interchange x and y to obtain the inverse function $x = y^3 + 2y - 10$.

Step 4: Differentiate with respect to y: $\dfrac{dx}{dy} = 3y^2 + 2$.

Step 5: Apply formula $\dfrac{dy}{dx} = \dfrac{1}{dx/dy}$.

$\dfrac{dy}{dx} = \dfrac{1}{dx/dy} = \dfrac{1}{3y^2 + 2}$. Thus, $(f^{-1})'(x) = \dfrac{1}{3y^2 + 2}$.

Example 2

Example 1 could have been done by using implicit differentiation.

Step 1: Let $y = f(x)$, and thus $y = x^3 + 2x - 10$.

Step 2: Interchange x and y to obtain the inverse function $x = y^3 + 2y - 10$.

Step 3: Differentiate each term implicitly with respect to x.

$$\frac{d}{dx}(x) = \frac{d}{dx}(y^3) + \frac{d}{dx}(2y) - \frac{d}{dx}(-10)$$

$$1 = 3y^2\frac{dy}{dx} + 2\frac{dy}{dx} - 0$$

Step 4: Solve for $\frac{dy}{dx}$.

$$1 = \frac{dy}{dx}(3y^2 + 2)$$

$$\frac{dy}{dx} = \frac{1}{3y^2 + 2}. \text{ Thus, } (f^{-1})'(x) = \frac{1}{3y^2 + 2}.$$

Example 3

If $f(x) = 2x^5 + x^3 + 1$, find (a) $f(1)$ and $f'(1)$ and (b) $(f^{-1})(4)$ and $(f^{-1})'(4)$.
Enter $y1 = 2x^5 + x^3 + 1$. Since $y1$ is strictly increasing, thus $f(x)$ has an inverse.

(a) $f(1) = 2(1)^5 + (1)^3 + 1 = 4$
$f'(x) = 10x^4 + 3x^2$
$f'(1) = 10(1)^4 + 3(1)^2 = 13$

(b) Since $f(1) = 4$ implies the point $(1, 4)$ is on the curve $f(x) = 2x^5 + x^3 + 1$; Therefore, the point $(4, 1)$ (which is the reflection of $(1, 4)$ on $y = x$) is on the curve $(f^{-1})(x)$. Thus, $(f^{-1})(4) = 1$.

$$(f^{-1})'(4) = \frac{1}{f'(1)} = \frac{1}{13}$$

Example 4

If $f(x) = 5x^3 + x + 8$, find $(f^{-1})'(8)$.
Enter $y1 = 5x^3 + x + 8$. Since $y1$ is strictly increasing near $x = 8$, $f(x)$ has an inverse near $x = 8$.
Note that $f(0) = 5(0)^3 + 0 + 8 = 8$, which implies the point $(0, 8)$ is on the curve of $f(x)$. Thus, the point $(8, 0)$ is on the curve of $(f^{-1})(x)$.

$$f'(x) = 15x^2 + 1$$

$$f'(0) = 1$$

Therefore, $(f^{-1})'(8) = \frac{1}{f'(0)} = \frac{1}{1} = 1.$

- You do not have to answer every question correctly to get a 5 on the AP Calculus BC exam. But always select an answer to a multiple-choice question. There is no penalty for incorrect answers.

6.6 Higher Order Derivatives

If the derivative f' of a function f is differentiable, then the derivative of f' is the second derivative of f represented by f'' (reads as f double prime). You can continue to differentiate f as long as there is differentiability.

Some of the Symbols of Higher Order Derivatives

$$f'(x),\ f''(x),\ f'''(x),\ f^{(4)}(x)$$

$$\frac{dy}{dx},\ \frac{d^2y}{dx^2},\ \frac{d^3y}{dx^3},\ \frac{d^4y}{dx^4}$$

$$y',\ y'',\ y''',\ y^{(4)}$$

$$D_x(y),\ D_x^2(y),\ D_x^3(y),\ D_x^4(y)$$

Note that $\dfrac{d^2y}{dx^2} = \dfrac{d}{dx}\left(\dfrac{dy}{dx}\right)$ or $\dfrac{dy'}{dx}$.

Example 1

If $y = 5x^3 + 7x - 10$, find the first four derivatives.

$$\frac{dy}{dx} = 15x^2 + 7;\ \frac{d^2y}{dx^2} = 30x;\ \frac{d^3y}{dx^3} = 30;\ \frac{d^4y}{dx^4} = 0$$

Example 2

If $f(x) = \sqrt{x}$, find $f''(4)$.

Rewrite: $f(x) = \sqrt{x} = x^{1/2}$ and differentiate: $f'(x) = \dfrac{1}{2}x^{-1/2}$.

Differentiate again:

$$f''(x) = -\frac{1}{4}x^{-3/2} = \frac{-1}{4x^{3/2}} = \frac{-1}{4\sqrt{x^3}} \text{ and } f''(4) = \frac{-1}{4\sqrt{4^3}} = -\frac{1}{32}.$$

- When evaluating fractional exponents without a calculator, if possible, evaluate the root first to avoid working with larger numbers.

Example 3

If $y = x \cos x$, find y''.

Using the product rule, $y' = (1)(\cos x) + (x)(-\sin x) = \cos x - x \sin x$

$$y'' = -\sin x - [(1)(\sin x) + (x)(\cos x)]$$
$$= -\sin x - \sin x - x \cos x$$
$$= -2 \sin x - x \cos x.$$

Or, you can use a calculator and enter $d[x^* \cos x,\ x,\ 2]$ and obtain the same result.

L'Hôpital's Rule for Indeterminate Forms

Let *lim* represent one of the limits: $\lim\limits_{x \to c}$, $\lim\limits_{x \to c^+}$, $\lim\limits_{x \to c^-}$, $\lim\limits_{x \to \infty}$, *or* $\lim\limits_{x \to -\infty}$. Suppose $f(x)$ and $g(x)$ are differentiable, and $g'(x) \neq 0$ near c, except possibly at c, and suppose $\lim f(x) = 0$ and $\lim g(x) = 0$, then the $\lim \dfrac{f(x)}{g(x)}$ is an indeterminate form of the type $\dfrac{0}{0}$. Also, if $\lim f(x) = \pm\infty$ and $\lim g(x) = \pm\infty$, then the $\lim \dfrac{f(x)}{g(x)}$ is an indeterminate form of the type $\dfrac{\infty}{\infty}$. In both cases, $\dfrac{0}{0}$ and $\dfrac{\infty}{\infty}$, *L'Hôpital's* Rule states that $\lim \dfrac{f(x)}{g(x)} = \lim \dfrac{f'(x)}{g'(x)}$.

Example 4

Find $\lim\limits_{x \to 0} \dfrac{1 - \cos x}{x^2}$, if it exists.

Since $\lim\limits_{x \to 0} (1 - \cos x) = 0$ and $\lim\limits_{x \to 0} (x^2) = 0$, this limit is an inderminate form. Taking the derivatives, $\dfrac{d}{dx}(1 - \cos x) = \sin x$ and $\dfrac{d}{dx}(x^2) = 2x$. By *L'Hôpital's* Rule, $\lim\limits_{x \to 0} \dfrac{1 - \cos x}{x^2} = \lim\limits_{x \to 0} \dfrac{\sin x}{2x} = \dfrac{1}{2}\lim\limits_{x \to 0} \dfrac{\sin x}{x} = \dfrac{1}{2}$.

Example 5

Find $\lim\limits_{x \to \infty} x^3 e^{-x^2}$, if it exists.

Rewriting $\lim\limits_{x \to \infty} x^3 e^{-x^2}$ as $\lim\limits_{x \to \infty} \left(\dfrac{x^3}{e^{x^2}} \right)$ shows that the limit is an indeterminate form, since $\lim\limits_{x \to \infty} (x^3) = \infty$ and $\lim\limits_{x \to \infty} (e^{x^2}) = \infty$. Differentiating and applying *L'Hôpital's* Rule means that $\lim\limits_{x \to \infty} \left(\dfrac{x^3}{e^{x^2}} \right) = \lim\limits_{x \to \infty} \left(\dfrac{3x^2}{2xe^{x^2}} \right) = \dfrac{3}{2}\lim\limits_{x \to \infty} \left(\dfrac{x}{e^{x^2}} \right)$. Unfortunately, this new limit is also indeterminate. However, it is possible to apply *L'Hôpital's* Rule again, so $\dfrac{3}{2}\lim\limits_{x \to \infty} \left(\dfrac{x}{e^{x^2}} \right)$ equals to $\dfrac{3}{2}\lim\limits_{x \to \infty} \left(\dfrac{1}{2xe^{x^2}} \right)$. This expression approaches zero as x becomes large, so $\lim\limits_{x \to \infty} x^3 e^{-x^2} = 0$.

6.7 Rapid Review

1. If $y = e^{x^3}$, find $\dfrac{dy}{dx}$.

   Answer: Using the chain rule, $\dfrac{dy}{dx} = \left(e^{x^3} \right) (3x^2)$.

2. Evaluate $\lim\limits_{h \to 0} \dfrac{\cos\left(\dfrac{\pi}{6} + h \right) - \cos\left(\dfrac{\pi}{6} \right)}{h}$.

   Answer: The limit is equivalent to $\dfrac{d}{dx}\cos x \Big|_{x = \frac{\pi}{6}} = -\sin\left(\dfrac{\pi}{6} \right) = -\dfrac{1}{2}$.

3. Find $f'(x)$ if $f(x) = \ln(3x)$.

   Answer: $f'(x) = \dfrac{1}{3x}(3) = \dfrac{1}{x}$.

4. Find the approximate value of $f'(3)$. (See Figure 6.7-1.)

Figure 6.7-1

   Answer: Using the slope of the line segment joining $(2, 1)$ and $(4, 3)$,

   $f'(3) = \dfrac{3 - 1}{4 - 2} = 1$.

5. Find $\dfrac{dy}{dx}$ if $xy = 5x^2$.

   Answer: Using implicit differentiation, $1y + x\dfrac{dy}{dx} = 10x$. Thus, $\dfrac{dy}{dx} = \dfrac{10x - y}{x}$.

   Or simply solve for y leading to $y = 5x$ and thus, $\dfrac{dy}{dx} = 5$.

6. If $y = \dfrac{5}{x^2}$, find $\dfrac{d^2y}{dx^2}$.

   Answer: Rewrite $y = 5x^{-2}$. Then, $\dfrac{dy}{dx} = -10x^{-3}$ and $\dfrac{d^2y}{dx^2} = 30x^{-4} = \dfrac{30}{x^4}$.

7. Using a calculator, write an equation of the line tangent to the graph $f(x) = -2x^4$ at the point where $f'(x) = -1$.

   Answer: $f'(x) = -8x^3$. Using a calculator, enter [*Solve*] $(-8x^3 = -1, \ x)$ and obtain $x = \dfrac{1}{2} \Rightarrow f'\left(\dfrac{1}{2}\right) = -1$. Using the calculator $f\left(\dfrac{1}{2}\right) = -\dfrac{1}{8}$. Thus, tangent is $y + \dfrac{1}{8} = -1\left(x - \dfrac{1}{2}\right)$.

8. $\displaystyle\lim_{x \to 2} \dfrac{x^2 + x - 6}{x^2 - 4}$

   Answer: Since $\dfrac{x^2 + x - 6}{x^2 - 4} \to \dfrac{0}{0}$, consider $\displaystyle\lim_{x \to 2} \dfrac{2x + 1}{2x} = \dfrac{5}{4}$.

9. $\displaystyle\lim_{x \to \infty} \dfrac{\ln x}{x}$

   Answer: Since $\dfrac{\ln x}{x} \to \dfrac{\infty}{\infty}$, consider $\displaystyle\lim_{x \to \infty} \dfrac{1/x}{1} = \lim_{x \to \infty} \dfrac{1}{x} = 0$.

6.8 Practice Problems

Part A—The use of a calculator is not allowed.

Find the derivative of each of the following functions.

1. $y = 6x^5 - x + 10$

2. $f(x) = \dfrac{1}{x} + \dfrac{1}{\sqrt[3]{x^2}}$

3. $y = \dfrac{5x^6 - 1}{x^2}$

4. $y = \dfrac{x^2}{5x^6 - 1}$

5. $f(x) = (3x - 2)^5(x^2 - 1)$

6. $y = \sqrt{\dfrac{2x + 1}{2x - 1}}$

7. $y = 10 \cot(2x - 1)$

8. $y = 3x \sec(3x)$

9. $y = 10 \cos[\sin(x^2 - 4)]$

10. $y = 8 \cos^{-1}(2x)$

11. $y = 3e^5 + 4xe^x$

12. $y = \ln(x^2 + 3)$

Part B—Calculators are allowed.

13. Find $\dfrac{dy}{dx}$, if $x^2 + y^3 = 10 - 5xy$.

14. The graph of a function f on $[1, 5]$ is shown in Figure 6.8-1. Find the approximate value of $f'(4)$.

15. Let f be a continuous and differentiable function. Selected values of f are shown below. Find the approximate value of f' at $x = 2$.

x	−1	0	1	2	3
f	6	5	6	9	14

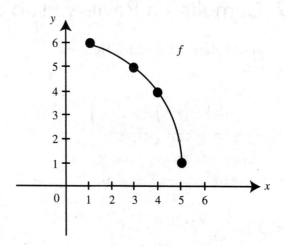

Figure 6.8-1

16. If $f(x) = x^5 + 3x - 8$, find $(f^{-1})'(-8)$.

17. Write an equation of the tangent to the curve $y = \ln x$ at $x = e$.

18. If $y = 2x \sin x$, find $\dfrac{d^2y}{dx^2}$ at $x = \dfrac{\pi}{2}$.

19. If the function $f(x) = (x - 1)^{2/3} + 2$, find all points where f is not differentiable.

20. Write an equation of the normal line to the curve $x \cos y = 1$ at $\left(2, \dfrac{\pi}{3}\right)$.

21. $\lim\limits_{x \to 3} \dfrac{x^2 - 3x}{x^2 - 9}$

22. $\lim\limits_{x \to 0^+} \dfrac{\ln(x + 1)}{\sqrt{x}}$

23. $\lim\limits_{x \to 0} \dfrac{e^x - 1}{\tan 2x}$

24. $\lim\limits_{x \to 0} \dfrac{\cos(x) - 1}{\cos(2x) - 1}$

25. $\lim\limits_{x \to \infty} \dfrac{5x + 2\ln x}{x + 3\ln x}$

6.9 Cumulative Review Problems

(Calculator) indicates that calculators are permitted.

26. Find $\lim\limits_{h \to 0} \dfrac{\sin\left(\dfrac{\pi}{2} + h\right) - \sin\left(\dfrac{\pi}{2}\right)}{h}$.

27. If $f(x) = \cos^2(\pi - x)$, find $f'(0)$.

28. Find $\lim\limits_{x \to \infty} \dfrac{x - 25}{10 + x - 2x^2}$.

29. (Calculator) Let f be a continuous and differentiable function. Selected values of

f are shown below. Find the approximate value of f' at $x = 2$.

x	0	1	2	3	4	5
f	3.9	4	4.8	6.5	8.9	11.8

30. (Calculator) If $f(x) = \begin{cases} \dfrac{x^2 - 9}{x - 3}, & x \neq 3, \\ 3, & x = 3 \end{cases}$

determine if $f(x)$ is continuous at $(x = 3)$. Explain why or why not.

6.10 Solutions to Practice Problems

Part A—The use of a calculator is not allowed.

1. Applying the power rule, $\dfrac{dy}{dx} = 30x^4 - 1$.

2. Rewrite $f(x) = \dfrac{1}{x} + \dfrac{1}{\sqrt[3]{x^2}}$ as
   $f(x) = x^{-1} + x^{-2/3}$. Differentiate:
   $f'(x) = -x^{-2} - \dfrac{2}{3}x^{-5/3} = -\dfrac{1}{x^2} - \dfrac{2}{3\sqrt[3]{x^5}}$.

3. Rewrite
   $y = \dfrac{5x^6 - 1}{x^2}$ as $y = \dfrac{5x^6}{x^2} - \dfrac{1}{x^2} = 5x^4 - x^{-2}$.
   Differentiate:
   $\dfrac{dy}{dx} = 20x^3 - (-2)x^{-3} = 20x^3 + \dfrac{2}{x^3}$.
   An alternate method is to differentiate
   $y = \dfrac{5x^6 - 1}{x^2}$ directly, using the quotient rule.

4. Applying the quotient rule,
   $$\dfrac{dy}{dx} = \dfrac{(2x)(5x^6 - 1) - (30x^5)(x^2)}{(5x^6 - 1)^2}$$
   $$= \dfrac{10x^7 - 2x - 30x^7}{(5x^6 - 1)^2}$$
   $$= \dfrac{-20x^7 - 2x}{(5x^6 - 1)^2} = \dfrac{-2x(10x^6 + 1)}{(5x^6 - 1)^2}.$$

5. Applying the product rule, $u = (3x - 2)^5$ and $v = (x^2 - 1)$, and then the chain rule,
   $$f'(x) = [5(3x - 2)^4(3)][x^2 - 1] + [2x]$$
   $$\times [(3x - 2)^5]$$
   $$= 15(x^2 - 1)(3x - 2)^4 + 2x(3x - 2)^5$$
   $$= (3x - 2)^4[15(x^2 - 1) + 2x(3x - 2)]$$
   $$= (3x - 2)^4[15x^2 - 15 + 6x^2 - 4x]$$
   $$= (3x - 2)^4(21x^2 - 4x - 15).$$

6. Rewrite $y = \sqrt{\dfrac{2x+1}{2x-1}}$ as

$y = \left(\dfrac{2x+1}{2x-1}\right)^{1/2}$. Applying first the chain rule and then the quotient rule,

$\dfrac{dy}{dx} = \dfrac{1}{2}\left(\dfrac{2x+1}{2x-1}\right)^{-1/2}$

$\times \left[\dfrac{(2)(2x-1)-(2)(2x+1)}{(2x-1)^2}\right]$

$= \dfrac{1}{2}\dfrac{1}{\left(\dfrac{2x+1}{2x-1}\right)^{1/2}}\left[\dfrac{-4}{(2x-1)^2}\right]$

$= \dfrac{1}{2}\dfrac{1}{\dfrac{(2x+1)^{1/2}}{(2x-1)^{1/2}}}\left[\dfrac{-4}{(2x-1)^2}\right]$

$= \dfrac{-2}{(2x+1)^{1/2}(2x-1)^{3/2}}.$

Note: $\left(\dfrac{2x+1}{2x-1}\right)^{1/2} = \dfrac{(2x+1)^{1/2}}{(2x-1)^{1/2}}$,

if $\dfrac{2x+1}{2x-1} > 0$, which implies $x < -\dfrac{1}{2}$

or $x > \dfrac{1}{2}$.

An alternate method of solution is to write

$y = \dfrac{\sqrt{2x+1}}{\sqrt{2x-1}}$ and use the quotient rule.

Another method is to write $y = (2x+1)^{1/2}(2x-1)^{1/2}$ and use the product rule.

7. Let $u = 2x - 1$,

$\dfrac{dy}{dx} = 10[-\csc^2(2x-1)](2)$

$= -20\csc^2(2x-1).$

8. Using the product rule,

$\dfrac{dy}{dx} = (3[\sec(3x)]) + [\sec(3x)\tan(3x)](3)[3x]$

$= 3\sec(3x) + 9x\sec(3x)\tan(3x)$

$= 3\sec(3x)[1 + 3x\tan(3x)].$

9. Using the chain rule, let $u = \sin(x^2 - 4)$.

$\dfrac{dy}{dx} = 10(-\sin[\sin(x^2-4)])[\cos(x^2-4)](2x)$

$= -20x\cos(x^2-4)\sin[\sin(x^2-4)]$

10. Using the chain rule, let $u = 2x$.

$\dfrac{dy}{dx} = 8\left(\dfrac{-1}{\sqrt{1-(2x)^2}}\right)(2) = \dfrac{-16}{\sqrt{1-4x^2}}$

11. Since $3e^5$ is a constant, its derivative is 0.

$\dfrac{dy}{dx} = 0 + (4)(e^x) + (e^x)(4x)$

$= 4e^x + 4xe^x = 4e^x(1+x)$

12. Let $u = (x^2 + 3)$, $\dfrac{dy}{dx} = \left(\dfrac{1}{x^2+3}\right)(2x)$

$= \dfrac{2x}{x^2+3}.$

Part B—Calculators are allowed.

13. Using implicit differentiation, differentiate each term with respect to x.

$2x + 3y^2\dfrac{dy}{dx} = 0 - \left[(5)(y) + \dfrac{dy}{dx}(5x)\right]$

$2x + 3y^2\dfrac{dy}{dx} = -5y - 5x\dfrac{dy}{dx}$

$3y^2\dfrac{dy}{dx} + 5x\dfrac{dy}{dx} = -5y - 2x$

$\dfrac{dy}{dx} = (3y^2 + 5x) = -5y - 2x$

$\dfrac{dy}{dx} = \dfrac{-5y - 2x}{3y^2 + 5x}$ or $\dfrac{dy}{dx} = \dfrac{-(2x+5y)}{5x+3y^2}$

14. Since $f'(4)$ is equivalent to the slope of the tangent to $f(x)$ at $x = 4$, there are several ways you can find its approximate value.

Method 1: Using the slope of the line segment joining the points at $x = 4$ and $x = 5$.

$f(5) = 1$ and $f(4) = 4$

$$m = \frac{f(5) - f(4)}{5 - 4}$$

$$= \frac{1 - 4}{1} = -3$$

Method 2: Using the slope of the line segment joining the points at $x = 3$ and $x = 4$.

$f(3) = 5$ and $f(4) = 4$

$$m = \frac{f(4) - f(3)}{4 - 3}$$

$$= \frac{4 - 5}{4 - 3} = -1$$

Method 3: Using the slope of the line segment joining the points at $x = 3$ and $x = 5$.

$f(3) = 5$ and $f(5) = 1$

$$m = \frac{f(5) - f(3)}{5 - 3}$$

$$= \frac{1 - 5}{5 - 3} = -2$$

Note that -2 is the average of the results from methods 1 and 2. Thus $f'(4) \approx -3$, -1, or -2 depending on which line segment you use.

15. You can use the difference quotient $\frac{f(a + h) - f(a)}{h}$ to approximate $f'(a)$.

Let $h = 1$; $f'(2) \approx \frac{f(3) - f(2)}{3 - 2} \approx$

$\frac{14 - 9}{3 - 2} \approx 5$.

Or, you can use the symmetric difference quotient $\frac{f(a + h) - f(a - h)}{2h}$ to approximate $f'(a)$.

Let $h = 1$; $f'(2) \approx \frac{f(3) - f(1)}{2 - 0} \approx$

$\frac{14 - 6}{2} \approx 4$.

Thus, $f'(2) \approx 4$ or 5 depending on your method.

16. Enter $y1 = x^5 + 3x - 8$. The graph of $y1$ is strictly increasing. Thus $f(x)$ has an inverse. Note that $f(0) = -8$. Thus the point $(0, -8)$ is on the graph of $f(x)$, which implies that the point $(-8, 0)$ is on the graph of $f^{-1}(x)$.
$f'(x) = 5x^4 + 3$ and $f'(0) = 3$.
Since $(f^{-1})'(-8) = \frac{1}{f'(0)}$, thus

$(f^{-1})'(-8) = \frac{1}{3}$.

17. $\frac{dy}{dx} = \frac{1}{x}$ and $\left.\frac{dy}{dx}\right|_{x=e} = \frac{1}{e}$

Thus, the slope of the tangent to $y = \ln x$ at $x = e$ is $\frac{1}{e}$. At $x = e$, $y = \ln x = \ln e = 1$, which means the point $(e, 1)$ is on the curve of $y = \ln x$. Therefore, an equation of the tangent is $y - 1 = \frac{1}{e}(x - e)$ or $y = \frac{x}{e}$. (See Figure 6.10-1.)

[−1.8] by [−3,3]

Figure 6.10-1

18. $\dfrac{dy}{dx} = (2)(\sin x) + (\cos x)(2x) =$

$2 \sin x + 2x \cos x$

$\dfrac{d^2y}{dx^2} = 2 \cos x + [(2)(\cos x) + (-\sin x)(2x)]$

$\qquad = 2 \cos x + 2 \cos x - 2x \sin x$

$\qquad = 4 \cos x - 2x \sin x$

$\dfrac{d^2y}{dx^2}\bigg|_{x=\pi/2} = 4 \cos\left(\dfrac{\pi}{2}\right) - 2\left(\dfrac{\pi}{2}\right)\left(\sin\left(\dfrac{\pi}{2}\right)\right)$

$\qquad = 0 - 2\left(\dfrac{\pi}{2}\right)(1) = -\pi$

Or, using a calculator, enter
$d(2x - \sin(x), x, 2)\; x = \dfrac{\pi}{2}$ and obtain $-\pi$.

19. Enter $y\,1 = (x-1)^{2/3} + 2$ in your calculator. The graph of $y\,1$ forms a cusp at $x = 1$. Therefore, f is not differentiable at $x = 1$.

20. Differentiate with respect to x:

$(1) \cos y + \left[(-\sin y)\dfrac{dy}{dx}\right](x) = 0$

$\cos y - x \sin y \dfrac{dy}{dx} = 0$

$\dfrac{dy}{dx} = \dfrac{\cos y}{x \sin y}$

$\dfrac{dy}{dx}\bigg|_{x=2,\,y=\pi/3} = \dfrac{\cos(\pi/3)}{(2)\sin(\pi/3)}$

$\qquad = \dfrac{1/2}{2\left(\sqrt{3}/2\right)} = \dfrac{1}{2\sqrt{3}}.$

Thus, the slope of the tangent to the curve at $(2, \pi/3)$ is $m = \dfrac{1}{2\sqrt{3}}.$

The slope of the normal line to the curve at $(2, \pi/3)$ is $m = -\dfrac{2\sqrt{3}}{1} = -2\sqrt{3}.$

Therefore, an equation of the normal line is $y - \pi/3 = -2\sqrt{3}(x-2).$

21. $\lim\limits_{x\to 3} \dfrac{x^2 - 3x}{x^2 - 9} = \lim\limits_{x\to 3} \dfrac{2x - 3}{2x} = \dfrac{1}{2}$

22. $\lim\limits_{x\to 0^+} \dfrac{\ln(x+1)}{\sqrt{x}} = \lim\limits_{x\to 0^+} \dfrac{1/(x+1)}{1/(2\sqrt{x})}$

$\qquad = \lim\limits_{x\to 0^+} \dfrac{2\sqrt{x}}{x+1} = 0$

23. $\lim\limits_{x\to 0} \dfrac{e^x - 1}{\tan 2x} = \lim\limits_{x\to 0} \dfrac{e^x}{2 \sec^2 2x} = \dfrac{1}{2}$

24. $\lim\limits_{x\to 0} \dfrac{\cos(x) - 1}{\cos(2x) - 1} = \lim\limits_{x\to 0} \dfrac{-\sin x}{-2 \sin(2x)}$

$\qquad = \lim\limits_{x\to 0} \dfrac{-\cos x}{-4 \cos(2x)} = \dfrac{1}{4}$

25. $\lim\limits_{x\to\infty} \dfrac{5x + 2\ln x}{x + 3\ln x} = \lim\limits_{x\to\infty} \dfrac{5 + (2/x)}{1 + (3/x)} = 5$

6.11 Solutions to Cumulative Review Problems

26. The expression
$\lim\limits_{h\to 0} \dfrac{\sin(\pi/2 + h) - \sin(\pi/2)}{h}$ is

the derivative of $\sin x$ at $x = \pi/2$, which is the slope of the tangent to $\sin x$ at $x = \pi/2$. The tangent to $\sin x$ at $x = \pi/2$ is parallel to the x-axis.

Therefore, the slope is 0, i.e.,

$\lim\limits_{h\to 0} \dfrac{\sin(\pi/2 + h) - \sin(\pi/2)}{h} = 0.$

An alternate method is to expand $\sin(\pi/2 + h)$ as
$\sin(\pi/2)\cos h + \cos(\pi/2)\sin h.$

Thus, $\lim\limits_{h\to 0}\dfrac{\sin(\pi/2 + h) - \sin(\pi/2)}{h} =$

$\lim\limits_{h\to 0}\dfrac{\sin(\pi/2)\cos h + \cos(\pi/2)\sin h - \sin(\pi/2)}{h}$

$= \lim\limits_{h\to 0}\dfrac{\sin(\pi/2)[\cos h - 1] + \cos(\pi/2)\sin h}{h}$

$= \lim\limits_{h\to 0}\sin\left(\dfrac{\pi}{2}\right)\left(\dfrac{\cos h - 1}{h}\right)$

$\quad - \lim\limits_{h\to 0}\cos\left(\dfrac{\pi}{2}\right)\left(\dfrac{\sin h}{h}\right)$

$= \sin\left(\dfrac{\pi}{2}\right)\lim\limits_{h\to 0}\left(\dfrac{\cos h - 1}{h}\right)$

$\quad - \cos\left(\dfrac{\pi}{2}\right)\lim\limits_{h\to 0}\left(\dfrac{\sin h}{h}\right)$

$= \left[\sin\left(\dfrac{\pi}{2}\right)\right]0 + \cos\left(\dfrac{\pi}{2}\right)(1)$

$= \cos\left(\dfrac{\pi}{2}\right) = 0.$

27. Using the chain rule, let $u = (\pi - x)$.
Then, $f'(x) = 2\cos(\pi - x)[-\sin(\pi - x)](-1)$

$\qquad\qquad = 2\cos(\pi - x)\sin(\pi - x)$

$\quad f'(0) = 2\cos\pi\sin\pi = 0.$

28. Since the degree of the polynomial in the denominator is greater than the degree of the polynomial in the numerator, the limit is 0.

29. You can use the difference quotient $\dfrac{f(a + h) - f(a)}{h}$ to approximate $f'(a)$.

Let $h = 1$; $f'(2) \approx \dfrac{f(3) - f(2)}{3 - 2}$

$\qquad\qquad \approx \dfrac{6.5 - 4.8}{1} \approx 1.7.$

Let $h = 2$; $f'(2) \approx \dfrac{f(4) - f(2)}{4 - 2}$

$\qquad\qquad \approx \dfrac{8.9 - 4.8}{2} \approx 2.05.$

Or, you can use the symmetric difference quotient $\dfrac{f(a + h) - f(a - h)}{2h}$ to approximate $f'(a)$.

Let $h = 1$; $f'(2) \approx \dfrac{f(3) - f(1)}{3 - 1}$

$\qquad\qquad \approx \dfrac{6.5 - 4}{2} \approx 1.25.$

Let $h = 2$; $f'(2) \approx \dfrac{f(4) - f(0)}{4 - 0}$

$\qquad\qquad \approx \dfrac{8.9 - 3.9}{4} \approx 1.25.$

Thus, $f'(2) = 1.7$, 2.05, or 1.25 depending on your method.

30. (See Figure 6.11-1.) Checking the three conditions of continuity:

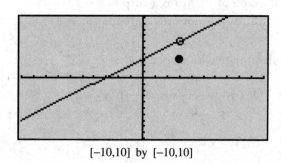

[−10,10] by [−10,10]

Figure 6.11-1

(1) $f(3) = 3$

(2) $\lim\limits_{x\to 3}\dfrac{x^2 - 9}{x - 3} = \lim\limits_{x\to 3}\left(\dfrac{(x + 3)(x - 3)}{(x - 3)}\right)$

$\qquad\qquad = \lim\limits_{x\to 3}(x + 3) = (3) + 3 = 6$

(3) Since $f(3) \neq \lim\limits_{x\to 3}f(x)$, $f(x)$ is discontinuous at $x = 3$.

CHAPTER **7**

Big Idea 2: Derivatives
Graphs of Functions and Derivatives

IN THIS CHAPTER

Summary: Many questions on the AP Calculus BC exam involve working with graphs of a function and its derivatives. In this chapter, you will learn how to use derivatives both algebraically and graphically to determine the behavior of a function. Applications of Rolle's Theorem, the Mean Value Theorem, and the Extreme Value Theorem are shown. You will also learn to sketch the graphs of parametric and polar equations.

Key Ideas

✪ Rolle's Theorem, Mean Value Theorem, and Extreme Value Theorem
✪ Test for Increasing and Decreasing Functions
✪ First and Second Derivative Tests for Relative Extrema
✪ Test for Concavity and Point of Inflection
✪ Curve Sketching
✪ Graphs of Derivatives
✪ Parametric and Polar Equations
✪ Vectors

7.1 Rolle's Theorem, Mean Value Theorem, and Extreme Value Theorem

Main Concepts: Rolle's Theorem, Mean Value Theorem, Extreme Value Theorem

- Set your calculator to Radians and change it to Degrees if/when you need to. Do not forget to change it back to Radians after you have finished using it in Degrees.

Rolle's Theorem

If f is a function that satisfies the following three conditions:

1. f is continuous on a closed interval $[a, b]$
2. f is differentiable on the open interval (a, b)
3. $f(a) = f(b) = 0$

then there exists a number c in (a, b) such that $f'(c) = 0$. (See Figure 7.1-1.)

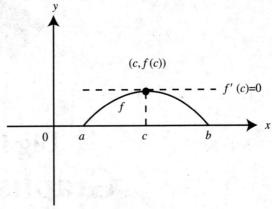

Figure 7.1-1

Note that if you change condition 3 from $f(a) = f(b) = 0$ to $f(a) = f(b)$, the conclusion of Rolle's Theorem is still valid.

Mean Value Theorem

If f is a function that satisfies the following conditions:

1. f is continuous on a closed interval $[a, b]$
2. f is differentiable on the open interval (a, b)

then there exists a number c in (a, b) such that $f'(c) = \dfrac{f(b) - f(a)}{b - a}$. (See Figure 7.1-2.)

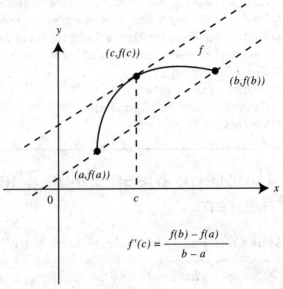

$$f'(c) = \frac{f(b) - f(a)}{b - a}$$

Figure 7.1-2

Example 1

If $f(x) = x^2 + 4x - 5$, show that the hypotheses of Rolle's Theorem are satisfied on the interval [−4, 0] and find all values of c that satisfy the conclusion of the theorem. Check the three conditions in the hypothesis of Rolle's Theorem:

(1) $f(x) = x^2 + 4x - 5$ is continuous everywhere since it is polynomial.
(2) The derivative $f'(x) = 2x + 4$ is defined for all numbers and thus is differentiable on (−4, 0).
(3) $f(0) = f(-4) = -5$. Therefore, there exists a c in (−4, 0) such that $f'(c) = 0$. To find c, set $f'(x) = 0$. Thus, $2x + 4 = 0 \Rightarrow x = -2$, i.e., $f'(-2) = 0$. (See Figure 7.1-3.)

[−5,3] by [−15,10]

Figure 7.1-3

Example 2

Let $f(x) = \dfrac{x^3}{3} - \dfrac{x^2}{2} - 2x + 2$. Using Rolle's Theorem, show that there exists a number c in the domain of f such that $f'(c) = 0$. Find all values of c.

Note $f(x)$ is a polynomial and thus $f(x)$ is continuous and differentiable everywhere. Enter $y1 = \dfrac{x^3}{3} - \dfrac{x^2}{2} - 2x + 2$. The zeros of $y1$ are approximately −2.3, 0.9, and 2.9 i.e., $f(-2.3) = f(0.9) = f(2.9) = 0$. Therefore, there exists at least one c in the interval (−2.3, 0.9) and at least one c in the interval (0.9, 2.9) such that $f'(c) = 0$. Use d [*Differentiate*] to find $f'(x)$: $f'(x) = x^2 - x - 2$. Set $f'(x) = 0 \Rightarrow x^2 - x - 2 = 0$ or $(x - 2)(x + 1) = 0$.

Thus, $x = 2$ or $x = -1$, which implies $f'(2) = 0$ and $f'(-1) = 0$. Therefore, the values of c are −1 and 2. (See Figure 7.1-4.)

[−8,8] by [−4,4]

Figure 7.1-4

Example 3

The points $P(1, 1)$ and $Q(3, 27)$ are on the curve $f(x) = x^3$. Using the Mean Value Theorem, find c in the interval $(1, 3)$ such that $f'(c)$ is equal to the slope of the secant $\overline{PQ}$.

The slope of secant $\overline{PQ}$ is $m = \dfrac{27 - 1}{3 - 1} = 13$. Since $f(x)$ is defined for all real numbers, $f(x)$ is continuous on $[1, 3]$. Also $f'(x) = 3x^2$ is defined for all real numbers. Thus, $f(x)$ is differentiable on $(1, 3)$. Therefore, there exists a number c in $(1, 3)$ such that $f'(c) = 13$.

Set $f'(c) = 13 \Rightarrow 3(c)^2 = 13$ or $c^2 = \dfrac{13}{3}$ $c = \pm\sqrt{\dfrac{13}{3}}$. Since only $\sqrt{\dfrac{13}{3}}$ is in the interval

$(1, 3)$, $c = \sqrt{\dfrac{13}{3}}$. (See Figure 7.1-5.)

[−4,4] by [−20,40]

Figure 7.1-5

Example 4

Let f be the function $f(x) = (x - 1)^{2/3}$. Determine if the hypotheses of the Mean Value Theorem are satisfied on the interval $[0, 2]$, and if so, find all values of c that satisfy the conclusion of the theorem.

Enter $y1 = (x - 1)^{2/3}$. The graph $y1$ shows that there is a cusp at $x = 1$. Thus, $f(x)$ is not differentiable on $(0, 2)$, which implies there may or may not exist a c in $(0, 2)$ such that $f'(c) = \dfrac{f(2) - f(0)}{2 - 0}$. The derivative $f'(x) = \dfrac{2}{3}(x - 1)^{-1/3}$ and $\dfrac{f(2) - f(0)}{2 - 0} = \dfrac{1 - 1}{2} = 0$. Set $\dfrac{2}{3}(x - 1)^{1/3} = 0 \Rightarrow x = 1$. Note that f is not differentiable $(a + x = 1)$. Therefore, c does not exist. (See Figure 7.1-6.)

[−8,8] by [−4,4]

Figure 7.1-6

- The formula for finding the area of an equilateral triangle is *area* = $\dfrac{s^2\sqrt{3}}{4}$ where s is the length of a side. You might need this to find the volume of a solid whose cross sections are equilateral triangles.

Extreme Value Theorem

If f is a continuous function on a closed interval $[a, b]$, then f has both a maximum and a minimum value on the interval.

Example 1

If $f(x) = x^3 + 3x^2 - 1$, find the maximum and minimum values of f on $[-2, 2]$. Since $f(x)$ is a polynomial, it is a continuous function everywhere. Enter $y1 = x^3 + 3x^2 - 1$. The graph of $y1$ indicates that f has a minimum of -1 at $x = 0$ and a maximum value of 19 at $x = 2$. (See Figure 7.1-7.)

[–3,3] by [–4,20]

Figure 7.1-7

Example 2

If $f(x) = \dfrac{1}{x^2}$, find any maximum and minimum values of f on $[0, 3]$. Since $f(x)$ is a rational function, it is continuous everywhere except at values where the denominator is 0. In this case, at $x = 0$, $f(x)$ is undefined. Since $f(x)$ is not continuous on $[0, 3]$, the Extreme Value Theorem may not be applicable. Enter $y1 = \dfrac{1}{x^2}$. The graph of $y1$ shows that as $x \rightarrow 0^+$, $f(x)$ increases without bound (i.e., $f(x)$ goes to infinity). Thus, f has no maximum value. The minimum value occurs at the endpoint $x = 3$ and the minimum value is $\dfrac{1}{9}$. (See Figure 7.1-8.)

[–1,4] by [–1,6]

Figure 7.1-8

7.2 Determining the Behavior of Functions

Main Concepts: Test for Increasing and Decreasing Functions, First Derivative Test and Second Derivative Test for Relative Extrema, Test for Concavity and Points of Inflection

Test for Increasing and Decreasing Functions

Let f be a continuous function on the closed interval $[a, b]$ and differentiable on the open interval (a, b).

1. If $f'(x) > 0$ on (a, b), then f is increasing on $[a, b]$.
2. If $f'(x) < 0$ on (a, b), then f is decreasing on $[a, b]$.
3. If $f'(x) = 0$ on (a, b), then f is constant on $[a, b]$.

Definition: Let f be a function defined at a number c. Then c is a critical number of f if either $f'(c) = 0$ or $f'(c)$ does not exist. (See Figure 7.2-1.)

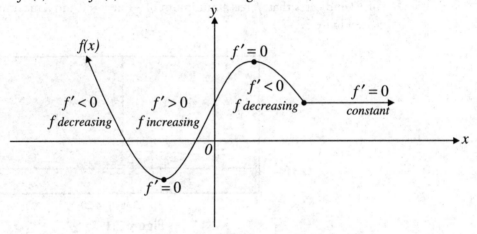

Figure 7.2-1

The following chart demonstrates the relationship between $f(x)$, $f'(x)$, and $f''(x)$.

$f(x)$	+ positive	– negative	↗ increasing	↘ decreasing	∪ concave up	∩ concave down
$f'(x)$			+ positive	– negative	↗ increasing	↘ decreasing
$f''(x)$					+ positive	– negative

Example 1

Find the critical numbers of $f(x) = 4x^3 + 2x^2$.

To find the critical numbers of $f(x)$, you have to determine where $f'(x) = 0$ and where $f'(x)$ does not exist. Note $f'(x) = 12x^2 + 4x$, and $f'(x)$ is defined for all real numbers. Let $f'(x) = 0$ and thus $12x^2 + 4x = 0$, which implies $4x(3x + 1) = 0 \Rightarrow x = -1/3$ or $x = 0$. Therefore, the critical numbers of f are 0 and $-1/3$. (See Figure 7.2-2.)

[−1,1] by [−1,1]

Figure 7.2-2

Example 2

Find the critical numbers of $f(x) = (x - 3)^{2/5}$.

$f'(x) = \dfrac{2}{5}(x - 3)^{-3/5} = \dfrac{2}{5(x - 3)^{3/5}}$. Note that $f'(x)$ is undefined at $x = 3$ and that $f'(x) \neq 0$. Therefore, 3 is the only critical number of f. (See Figure 7.2-3.)

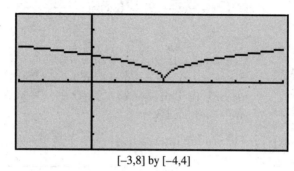

[–3,8] by [–4,4]

Figure 7.2-3

Example 3

The graph of f' on (1, 6) is shown in Figure 7.2-4. Find the intervals on which f is increasing or decreasing.

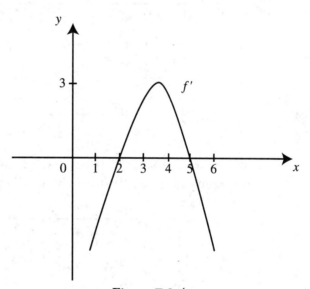

Figure 7.2-4

(See Figure 7.2-5.)

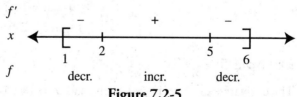

Figure 7.2-5

Thus, f is decreasing on [1, 2] and [5, 6] and increasing on [2, 5].

Example 4

Find the open intervals on which $f(x) = (x^2 - 9)^{2/3}$ is increasing or decreasing.

Step 1: Find the critical numbers of f.

$$f'(x) = \frac{2}{3}(x^2 - 9)^{-1/3}(2x) = \frac{4x}{3(x^2 - 9)^{1/3}}$$

Set $f'(x) = 0 \Rightarrow 4x = 0$ or $x = 0$.

Since $f'(x)$ is a rational function, $f'(x)$ is undefined at values where the denominator is 0. Thus, set $x^2 - 9 = 0 \Rightarrow x = 3$ or $x = -3$. Therefore, the critical numbers are -3, 0, and 3.

Step 2: Determine intervals.

Intervals are $(-\infty, -3)$, $(-3, 0)$, $(0, 3)$, and $(3, \infty)$.

Step 3: Set up a table.

INTERVALS	$(-\infty, -3)$	$(-3, 0)$	$(0, 3)$	$(3, \infty)$
Test Point	-5	-1	1	5
$f'(x)$	$-$	$+$	$-$	$+$
$f(x)$	decr	incr	decr	incr

Step 4: Write a conclusion. Therefore, $f(x)$ is increasing on $[-3, 0]$ and $[3, \infty)$ and decreasing on $(-\infty, -3]$ and $[0, 3]$. (See Figure 7.2-6.)

[−8,8] by [−1,5]

Figure 7.2-6

Example 5

The derivative of a function f is given as $f'(x) = \cos(x^2)$. Using a calculator, find the values of x on $\left[-\dfrac{\pi}{2}, \dfrac{\pi}{2}\right]$ such that f is increasing. (See Figure 7.2-7.)

[−π,π] by [−2,2]

Figure 7.2-7

Using the [*Zero*] function of the calculator, you obtain $x = 1.25331$ is a zero of f' on $\left[0, \dfrac{\pi}{2}\right]$. Since $f'(x) = \cos(x^2)$ is an even function, $x = -1.25331$ is also a zero on $\left[-\dfrac{\pi}{2}, 0\right]$. (See Figure 7.2-8.)

Figure 7.2-8

Thus, f is increasing on $[-1.2533, 1.2533]$.

- Bubble in the right grid. You have to be careful in filling in the bubbles especially when you skip a question.

First Derivative Test and Second Derivative Test for Relative Extrema

First Derivative Test for Relative Extrema

Let f be a continuous function and c be a critical number of f. (Figure 7.2-9.)

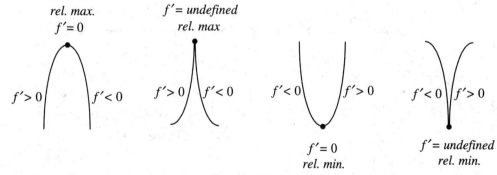

Figure 7.2-9

1. If $f'(x)$ changes from positive to negative at $x = c$ ($f' > 0$ for $x < c$ and $f' < 0$ for $x > c$), then f has a relative maximum at c.
2. If $f'(x)$ changes from negative to positive at $x = c$ ($f' < 0$ for $x < c$ and $f' > 0$ for $x > c$), then f has a relative minimum at c.

Second Derivative Test for Relative Extrema

Let f be a continuous function at a number c.

1. If $f'(c) = 0$ and $f''(c) < 0$, then $f(c)$ is a relative maximum.
2. If $f'(c) = 0$ and $f''(c) > 0$, then $f(c)$ is a relative minimum.
3. If $f'(c) = 0$ and $f''(c) = 0$, then the test is inconclusive. Use the First Derivative Test.

Example 1

The graph of f', the derivative of a function f, is shown in Figure 7.2-10. Find the relative extrema of f.

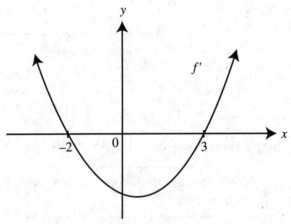

Figure 7.2-10

Solution: (See Figure 7.2-11.)

Figure 7.2-11

Thus, f has a relative maximum at $x = -2$, and a relative minimum at $x = 3$.

Example 2

Find the relative extrema for the function $f(x) = \dfrac{x^3}{3} - x^2 - 3x$.

Step 1: Find $f'(x)$.

$$f'(x) = x^2 - 2x - 3$$

Step 2: Find all critical numbers of $f(x)$.
Note that $f'(x)$ is defined for all real numbers.
Set $f'(x) = 0$: $x^2 - 2x - 3 = 0 \Rightarrow (x - 3)(x + 1) = 0 \Rightarrow x = 3$ or $x = -1$.

Step 3: Find $f''(x)$: $f''(x) = 2x - 2$.

Step 4: Apply the Second Derivative Test.
$f''(3) = 2(3) - 2 = 4 \Rightarrow f(3)$ is a relative minimum.
$f''(-1) = 2(-1) - 2 = -4 \Rightarrow f(-1)$ is a relative maximum.

$$f(3) = \frac{3^3}{3} - (3)^2 - 3(3) = -9 \text{ and } f(-1) = \frac{5}{3}.$$

Therefore, -9 is a relative minimum value of f and $\dfrac{5}{3}$ is a relative maximum value.

(See Figure 7.2-12.)

[–5,7] by [–10,10]

Figure 7.2-12

Example 3

Find the relative extrema for the function $f(x) = (x^2 - 1)^{2/3}$.

Using the First Derivative Test

Step 1: Find $f'(x)$.

$$f'(x) = \frac{2}{3}(x^2 - 1)^{-1/3}(2x) = \frac{4x}{3(x^2 - 1)^{1/3}}$$

Step 2: Find all critical numbers of f.
Set $f'(x) = 0$. Thus, $4x = 0$ or $x = 0$.
Set $x^2 - 1 = 0$. Thus, $f'(x)$ is undefined at $x = 1$ and $x = -1$. Therefore, the critical numbers are -1, 0 and 1.

Step 3: Determine intervals.

The intervals are $(-\infty, -1)$, $(-1, 0)$, $(0, 1)$, and $(1, \infty)$.

Step 4: Set up a table.

INTERVALS	$(-\infty, -1)$	$x = -1$	$(-1, 0)$	$x = 0$	$(0, 1)$	$x = 1$	$(1, \infty)$
Test Point	−2		−1/2		1/2		2
$f'(x)$	−	undefined	+	0	−	undefined	+
$f(x)$	decr	rel min	incr	rel max	decr	rel min	incr

Step 5: Write a conclusion.
Using the First Derivative Test, note that $f(x)$ has a relative maximum at $x = 0$ and relative minimums at $x = -1$ and $x = 1$.

Note that $f(-1) = 0$, $f(0) = 1$, and $f(1) = 0$. Therefore, 1 is a relative maximum value and 0 is a relative minimum value. (See Figure 7.2-13.)

[−3,3] by [−2,5]
Figure 7.2-13

- Do not forget the constant, C, when you write the antiderivative after evaluating an indefinite integral, e.g., $\int \cos x \, dx = \sin x + C$.

Test for Concavity and Points of Inflection
Test for Concavity

Let f be a differentiable function.

1. If $f'' > 0$ on an interval I, then f is concave upward on I.
2. If $f'' < 0$ on an interval I, then f is concave downward on I.

(See Figures 7.2-14 and 7.2-15.)

Figure 7.2-14

Figure 7.2-15

Points of Inflection

A point P on a curve is a point of inflection if:

1. the curve has a tangent line at P, and
2. the curve changes concavity at P (from concave upward to downward or from concave downward to upward).

(See Figures 7.2-16–7.2-18.)

Figure 7.2-16

Figure 7.2-17

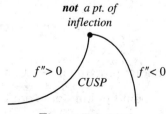

Figure 7.2-18

Note that if a point $(a, f(a))$ is a point of inflection, then $f''(c) = 0$ or $f''(c)$ does not exist. (The converse of the statement is not necessarily true.)

Note: There are some textbooks that define a point of inflection as a point where the concavity changes and do not require the existence of a tangent at the point of inflection. In that case, the point at the cusp in Figure 7.2-18 would be a point of inflection.

Example 1

The graph of f', the derivative of a function f, is shown in Figure 7.2-19. Find the points of inflection of f and determine where the function f is concave upward and where it is concave downward on $[-3, 5]$.

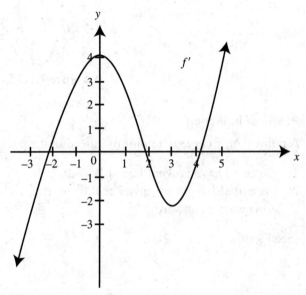

Figure 7.2-19

Solution: (See Figure 7.2-20.)

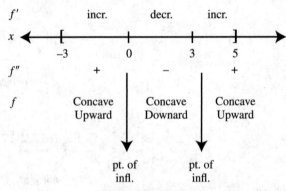

Figure 7.2-20

Thus, f is concave upward on $[-3, 0)$ and $(3, 5]$, and is concave downward on $(0, 3)$.

There are two points of inflection: one at $x = 0$ and the other at $x = 3$.

Example 2

Using a calculator, find the values of x at which the graph of $y = x^2 e^x$ changes concavity.

Enter $y1 = x\mathbin{\char`\^}2 * e\mathbin{\char`\^}x$ and $y2 = d(y1(x), x, 2)$. The graph of $y2$, the second derivative of y, is shown in Figure 7.2-21. Using the [*Zero*] function, you obtain $x = -3.41421$ and $x = -0.585786$. (See Figures 7.2-21 and 7.2-22.)

[–4,1] by [–2,5]

Figure 7.2-21

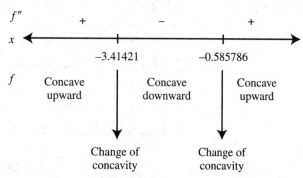

Figure 7.2-22

Thus, f changes concavity at $x = -3.41421$ and $x = -0.585786$.

Example 3

Find the points of inflection of $f(x) = x^3 - 6x^2 + 12x - 8$ and determine the intervals where the function f is concave upward and where it is concave downward.

Step 1: Find $f'(x)$ and $f''(x)$.
$f'(x) = 3x^2 - 12x + 12$
$f''(x) = 6x - 12$

Step 2: Set $f''(x) = 0$.
$6x - 12 = 0$
$x = 2$
Note that $f''(x)$ is defined for all real numbers.

Step 3: Determine intervals.

The intervals are $(-\infty, 2)$ and $(2, \infty)$.

Step 4:   Set up a table.

INTERVALS	$(-\infty, 2)$	$x = 2$	$(2, \infty)$
Test Point	0		5
$f''(x)$	–	0	+
$f(x)$	concave downward	point of inflection	concave upward

Since $f(x)$ has change of concavity at $x = 2$, the point $(2, f(2))$ is a point of inflection. $f(2) = (2)^3 - 6(2)^2 + 12(2) - 8 = 0$.

Step 5:   Write a conclusion.
Thus, $f(x)$ is concave downward on $(-\infty, 2)$, concave upward on $(2, \infty)$ and $f(x)$ has a point of inflection at $(2, 0)$. (See Figure 7.2-23.)

[–1,5] by [–5,5]

Figure 7.2-23

Example 4

Find the points of inflection of $f(x) = (x - 1)^{2/3}$ and determine the intervals where the function f is concave upward and where it is concave downward.

Step 1:   Find $f'(x)$ and $f''(x)$.

$$f'(x) = \frac{2}{3}(x - 1)^{-1/3} = \frac{2}{3(x - 1)^{1/3}}$$

$$f''(x) = -\frac{2}{9}(x - 1)^{-4/3} = \frac{-2}{9(x - 1)^{4/3}}$$

Step 2:   Find all values of x where $f''(x) = 0$ or $f''(x)$ is undefined.
Note that $f''(x) \neq 0$ and that $f''(1)$ is undefined.

Step 3:   Determine intervals.

The intervals are $(-\infty, 1)$, and $(1, \infty)$.

Step 4: Set up a table.

INTERVALS	$(-\infty, 1)$	$x = 1$	$(1, \infty)$
Test Point	0		2
$f''(x)$	–	undefined	–
$f(x)$	concave downward	no change of cancavity	concave downward

Note that since $f(x)$ has no change of concavity at $x = 1$, f does not have a point of inflection.

Step 5: Write a conclusion.
Therefore, $f(x)$ is concave downward on $(-\infty, \infty)$ and has no point of inflection. (See Figure 7.2-24.)

[–3,5] by [–1,4]

Figure 7.2-24

Example 5

The graph of f is shown in Figure 7.2-25 and f is twice differentiable. Which of the following statements is true?

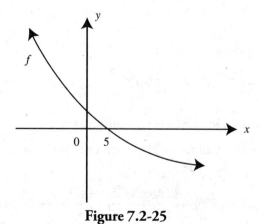

Figure 7.2-25

(A) $f(5) < f'(5) < f''(5)$

(B) $f''(5) < f'(5) < f(5)$

(C) $f'(5) < f(5) < f''(5)$

(D) $f'(5) < f''(5) < f(5)$

The graph indicates that (1) $f(5) = 0$, (2) $f'(5) < 0$, since f is decreasing; and (3) $f''(5) > 0$, since f is concave upward. Thus, $f'(5) < f(5) < f''(5)$, choice (C).

> • Move on. Do not linger on a problem too long. Make an educated guess. You can earn many more points from other problems.

7.3 Sketching the Graphs of Functions

Main Concepts: Graphing Without Calculators, Graphing with Calculators

Graphing Without Calculators

General Procedure for Sketching the Graph of a Function

Steps:

1. Determine the domain and if possible the range of the function $f(x)$.
2. Determine if the function has any symmetry, i.e., if the function is even ($f(x) = f(-x)$), odd ($f(x) = -f(-x)$), or periodic ($f(x + p) = f(x)$).
3. Find $f'(x)$ and $f''(x)$.
4. Find all critical numbers ($f'(x) = 0$ or $f'(x)$ is undefined) and possible points of inflection ($f''(x) = 0$ or $f''(x)$ is undefined).
5. Using the numbers in Step 4, determine the intervals on which to analyze $f(x)$.
6. Set up a table using the intervals, to
   (a) determine where $f(x)$ is increasing or decreasing.
   (b) find relative and absolute extrema.
   (c) find points of inflection.
   (d) determine the concavity of $f(x)$ on each interval.
7. Find any horizontal, vertical, or slant asymptotes.
8. If necessary, find the x-intercepts, the y-intercepts, and a few selected points.
9. Sketch the graph.

Example

Sketch the graph of $f(x) = \dfrac{x^2 - 4}{x^2 - 25}$.

Step 1: Domain: all real numbers $x \neq \pm 5$.

Step 2: Symmetry: $f(x)$ is an even function ($f(x) = f(-x)$); symmetrical with respect to the y-axis.

Step 3: $f'(x) = \dfrac{(2x)(x^2 - 25) - (2x)(x^2 - 4)}{(x^2 - 25)^2} = \dfrac{-42x}{(x^2 - 25)^2}$

$f''(x) = \dfrac{-42(x^2 - 25)^2 - 2(x^2 - 25)(2x)(-42x)}{(x^2 - 25)^4} = \dfrac{42(3x^2 + 25)}{(x^2 - 25)^3}$

Step 4: Critical numbers:

$f'(x) = 0 \Rightarrow -42x = 0$ or $x = 0$

$f'(x)$ is undefined at $x = \pm 5$, which are not in the domain.

Possible points of inflection:

$f''(x) \neq 0$ and $f''(x)$ is undefined at $x = \pm 5$, which are not in the domain.

Step 5: Determine intervals:

$$\longleftarrow \quad \overset{\mid}{-5} \quad \overset{\mid}{0} \quad \overset{\mid}{5} \quad \longrightarrow$$

Intervals are $(-\infty, -5)$, $(-5, 0)$, $(0, 5)$ and $(5, \infty)$.

Step 6: Set up a table:

INTERVALS	$(-\infty, -5)$	$x = -5$	$(-5, 0)$	$x = 0$	$(0, 5)$	$x = 5$	$(5, \infty)$
$f(x)$		undefined		4/25		undefined	
$f'(x)$	+	undefined	+	0	–	undefined	–
$f''(x)$	+	undefined	–	–	–	undefined	+
conclusion	incr concave upward		incr concave downward	rel max	decr concave downward		decr concave upward

Step 7: Vertical asymptote: $x = 5$ and $x = -5$

Horizontal asymptote: $y = 1$

Step 8: y-intercept: $\left(0, \dfrac{4}{25}\right)$

x-intercept: $(-2, 0)$ and $(2, 0)$

(See Figure 7.3-1.)

[–8,8] by [–4,4]

Figure 7.3-1

Graphing with Calculators
Example 1

Using a calculator, sketch the graph of $f(x) = -x^{5/3} + 3x^{2/3}$ indicating all relative extrema, points of inflection, horizontal and vertical asymptotes, intervals where $f(x)$ is increasing or decreasing, and intervals where $f(x)$ is concave upward or downward.

1. Domain: all real numbers; Range: all real numbers
2. No symmetry
3. Relative maximum: (1.2, 2.03)
   Relative minimum: (0, 0)
   Points of inflection: (−0.6, 2.56)
4. No asymptote
5. $f(x)$ is decreasing on $(-\infty, 0]$, $[1.2, \infty)$ and increasing on $(0, 1.2)$.
6. Evaluating $f''(x)$ on either side of the point of inflection (−0.6, 2.56)

$$d\left(-x \wedge \left(\frac{5}{3}\right) + 3 * x \wedge \left(\frac{2}{3}\right), x, 2\right) \quad x = -2 \rightarrow 0.19$$

$$d\left(-x \wedge \left(\frac{5}{3}\right) + 3 * x \wedge \left(\frac{2}{3}\right), x, 2\right) \quad x = -1 \rightarrow -4.66$$

$\Rightarrow f(x)$ is concave upward on $(-\infty, -0.6)$ and concave downward on $(-0.6, \infty)$. (See Figure 7.3-2.)

[−2,4] by [−4,4]

Figure 7.3-2

Example 2

Using a calculator, sketch the graph of $f(x) = e^{-x^2/2}$, indicating all relative minimum and maximum points, points of inflection, vertical and horizontal asymptotes, intervals on which $f(x)$ is increasing, decreasing, concave upward, or concave downward.

1. Domain: all real numbers; Range (0, 1]
2. Symmetry: $f(x)$ is an even function, and thus is symmetrical with respect to the y-axis.
3. Relative maximum: (0, 1)
   No relative minimum
   Points of inflection: (−1, 0.6) and (1, 0.6)
4. $y = 0$ is a horizontal asymptote; no vertical asymptote.
5. $f(x)$ is increasing on $(-\infty, 0]$ and decreasing on $[0, \infty)$.
6. $f(x)$ is concave upward on $(-\infty, -1)$ and $(1, \infty)$; and concave downward on $(-1, 1)$.

(See Figure 7.3-3.)

[−4,4] by [−1,2]

Figure 7.3-3

- When evaluating a definite integral, you do not have to write a constant C, e.g., $\int_1^3 2x\,dx = x^2\big|_1^3 = 8$. Notice, no C.

7.4 Graphs of Derivatives

The functions f, f', and f'' are interrelated, and so are their graphs. Therefore, you can usually infer from the graph of one of the three functions (f, f', or f'') and obtain information about the other two. Here are some examples.

Example 1

The graph of a function f is shown in Figure 7.4-1. Which of the following is true for f on (a, b)?

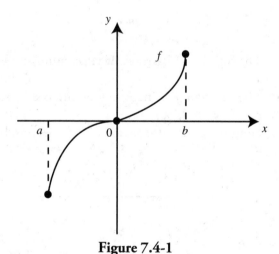

Figure 7.4-1

I. $f' \geq 0$ on (a, b)
II. $f'' > 0$ on (a, b)

Solution:

I. Since f is strictly increasing, $f' \geq 0$ on (a, b) is true.
II. The graph is concave downward on $(a, 0)$ and upward on $(0, b)$. Thus, $f'' > 0$ on $(0, b)$ only. Therefore, only statement I is true.

Example 2

Given the graph of f' in Figure 7.4-2, find where the function f: (a) has its relative maximum(s) or relative minimums, (b) is increasing or decreasing, (c) has its point(s) of inflection, (d) is concave upward or downward, and (e) if $f(-2) = f(2) = 1$ and $f(0) = -3$, draw a sketch of f.

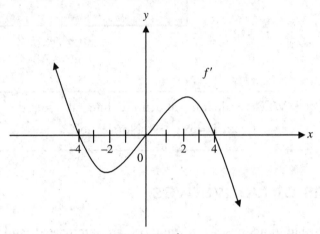

Figure 7.4-2

(a) Summarize the information of f' on a number line:

The function f has a relative maximum at $x = -4$ and at $x = 4$, and a relative minimum at $x = 0$.

(b) The function f is increasing on interval $(-\infty, -4]$ and $[0, 4]$, and f is decreasing on $[-4, 0]$ and $[4, \infty)$.

(c) Summarize the information of f'' on a number line:

A change of concavity occurs at $x = -2$ and at $x = 2$ and f' exists at $x = -2$ and at $x = 2$, which implies that there is a tangent line to the graph of f at $x = -2$ and at $x = 2$. Therefore, f has a point of inflection at $x = -2$ and at $x = 2$.

(d) The graph of f is concave upward on the interval $(-2, 2)$ and concave downward on $(-\infty, -2)$ and $(2, \infty)$.

(e) A sketch of the graph of f is shown in Figure 7.4-3.

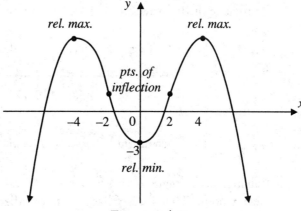

rel. max.   rel. max.

pts. of
inflection

-4   -2   0   2   4

-3

rel. min.

Figure 7.4-3

Example 3

Given the graph of f' in Figure 7.4-4, find where the function f (a) has a horizontal tangent, (b) has its relative extrema, (c) is increasing or decreasing, (d) has a point of inflection, and (e) is concave upward or downward.

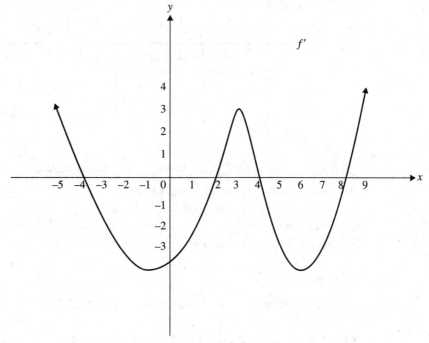

Figure 7.4-4

(a) $f'(x) = 0$ at $x = -4, 2, 4, 8$. Thus, f has a horizontal tangent at these values.
(b) Summarize the information of f' on a number line:

The First Derivative Test indicates that f has relative maximums at $x = -4$ and 4; and f has relative minimums at $x = 2$ and 8.

(c) The function f is increasing on $(-\infty, -4]$, $[2, 4]$, and $[8, \infty)$ and is decreasing on $[-4, 2]$ and $[4, 8]$.

(d) Summarize the information of f'' on a number line:

A change of concavity occurs at $x = -1$, 3, and 6. Since $f'(x)$ exists, f has a tangent at every point. Therefore, f has a point of inflection at $x = -1$, 3, and 6.

(e) The function f is concave upward on $(-1, 3)$ and $(6, \infty)$ and concave downward on $(-\infty, -1)$ and $(3, 6)$.

Example 4

A function f is continuous on the interval $[-4, 3]$ with $f(-4) = 6$ and $f(3) = 2$ and the following properties:

INTERVALS	(-4, -2)	x = -2	(-2, 1)	x = 1	(1, 3)
f'	–	0	–	undefined	+
f''	+	0	–	undefined	–

(a) Find the intervals on which f is increasing or decreasing.
(b) Find where f has its absolute extrema.
(c) Find where f has the points of inflection.
(d) Find the intervals where f is concave upward or downward.
(e) Sketch a possible graph of f.

Solution:

(a) The graph of f is increasing on $[1, 3]$ since $f' > 0$ and decreasing on $[-4, -2]$ and $[-2, 1]$ since $f' < 0$.

(b) At $x = -4$, $f(x) = 6$. The function decreases until $x = 1$ and increases back to 2 at $x = 3$. Thus, f has its absolute maximum at $x = -4$ and its absolute minimum at $x = 1$.

(c) A change of concavity occurs at $x = -2$, and since $f'(-2) = 0$, which implies a tangent line exists at $x = -2$, f has a point of inflection at $x = -2$.

(d) The graph of f is concave upward on $(-4, -2)$ and concave downward on $(-2, 1)$ and $(1, 3)$.

(e) A possible sketch of f is shown in Figure 7.4-5.

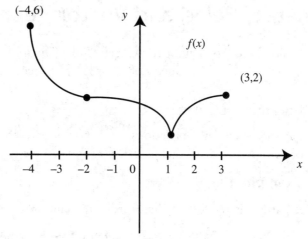

Figure 7.4-5

Example 5

If $f(x) = \left| \ln(x + 1) \right|$, find $\lim\limits_{x \to 0^-} f'(x)$. (See Figure 7.4-6.)

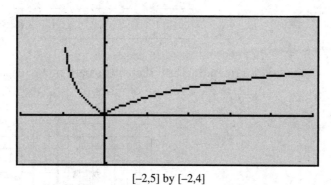

[–2,5] by [–2,4]

Figure 7.4-6

The domain of f is $(-1, \infty)$.

$$f(0) = \left| \ln(0 + 1) \right| = \left| \ln(1) \right| = 0$$

$$f(x) = \left| \ln(x + 1) \right| = \begin{cases} \ln(x + 1) & \text{if } x \geq 0 \\ -\ln(x + 1) & \text{if } x < 0 \end{cases}$$

Thus, $f'(x) = \begin{cases} \dfrac{1}{x + 1} & \text{if } x \geq 0 \\ -\dfrac{1}{x + 1} & \text{if } x < 0 \end{cases}$.

Therefore, $\lim\limits_{x \to 0^-} f'(x) = \lim\limits_{x \to 0^-} \left(-\dfrac{1}{x + 1} \right) = -1.$

7.5   Parametric, Polar, and Vector Representations

Main Concepts: Parametric Curves, Polar Equations, Types of Polar Graphs, Symmetry of Polar Graphs, Vectors, Vector Arithmetic

Parametric Curves

Parametric curves are relations $(x(t), y(t))$ for which both x and y are defined as functions of a third variable, t, that is, $x = f(t)$ and $y = g(t)$.

Example 1

A particle is moving in the coordinate plane in such a way that $x(t) = 2t - 5$ and $y(t) = 4 \sin\left(\dfrac{\pi}{t+1}\right)$ for $0 \le t \le 5$. Sketch the path of the particle and indicate the direction of motion.

Step 1:   Create a table of values.

t	0	1	2	3	4	5
$x(t)$	−5	−3	−1	1	3	5
$y(t)$	0	4	3.464	2.828	2.351	2

Step 2:   Plot the points and sketch the path of a particle as a smooth curve. Place arrows to indicate the direction of motion.

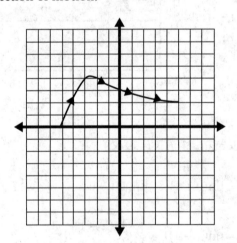

Example 2

A parametric curve is defined by $x = 2 + e^t$ and $y = e^{3t}$. Find the Cartesian equation of the curve.

Step 1:   Solve $x = 2 + e^t$ for t. $x - 2 = e^t$ so $t = \ln(x - 2)$.

Step 2:   Substitute $t = \ln(x - 2)$ into $y = e^{3t}$. $y = e^{3\ln(x-2)} = (x - 2)^3$.

Step 3:   Note that $t = \ln(x - 2)$ is defined only when $x > 2$. The equation of the curve is $y = (x - 2)^3$ with domain $(2, \infty)$.

Polar Equations

The polar coordinate system locates points by a distance from the origin or pole, and an angle of rotation. Points are represented by a coordinate pair (r, θ). If conversions between polar and Cartesian representations are necessary, make the appropriate substitutions and simplify.

$$x = r\cos\theta \qquad y = r\sin\theta \qquad r = \sqrt{x^2 + y^2} \qquad \theta = \tan^{-1}\left(\frac{y}{x}\right)$$

Example 1

Convert $r = 4\sin\theta$ to Cartesian coordinates.

Step 1: Substitute in $r = 4\sin\theta$ to get $\sqrt{x^2 + y^2} = 4\sin\left(\tan^{-1}\frac{y}{x}\right)$.

Step 2: Since $\sin\left(\tan^{-1}\frac{y}{x}\right) = \dfrac{y}{\sqrt{x^2 + y^2}}$, this becomes $\sqrt{x^2 + y^2} = 4\dfrac{y}{\sqrt{x^2 + y^2}}$.
Multiplying through by $\sqrt{x^2 + y^2}$, gives $x^2 + y^2 = 4y$.

Step 3: Complete the square on $x^2 + y^2 - 4y = 0$ to produce $x^2 + (y - 2)^2 = 4$.

Example 2

Find the polar representation of $\dfrac{x^2}{4} + \dfrac{y^2}{9} = 1$.

Step 1: Substitute in $\dfrac{x^2}{4} + \dfrac{y^2}{9} = 1$ to produce $\dfrac{(r\cos\theta)^2}{4} + \dfrac{(r\sin\theta)^2}{9} = 1$.

Step 2: Simplify and clear denominators to get $9r^2\cos^2\theta + 4r^2\sin^2\theta = 36$, then factor for $r^2(9\cos^2\theta + 4\sin^2\theta) = 36$.

Step 3: Divide to isolate $r^2 = \dfrac{36}{9\cos^2\theta + 4\sin^2\theta}$.

Step 4: Apply the Pythagorean identity to the denominator $r^2 = \dfrac{36}{5\cos^2\theta + 4}$.

Types of Polar Graphs

SHAPE	TYPICAL EQUATION	NOTES
Line	$\theta = k$	
Circle	$r = a$ $r = 2a\cos\theta$ $r = 2a\sin\theta$	Radius of the circle $= a$

(continued)

SHAPE	TYPICAL EQUATION	NOTES
Rose	$r = a \sin(n\theta)$ $r = a \cos(n\theta)$	Length of petal $=a$ If n is odd, n petals. If n is even, $2n$ petals.
Cardiod	$r = a \pm a \sin\theta$ $r = a \pm a \cos\theta$	
Limaçon	$r = a \pm b \sin\theta$ $r = a \pm b \cos\theta$	If $\dfrac{a}{b} < 1$, limaçon has an inner loop.
Spirals	$r = a\theta$ $r = a\sqrt{\theta}$ $r = \dfrac{a}{\theta}$ $r = \dfrac{a}{\sqrt{\theta}}$ $r = a e^{b\theta}$	

Example 1

Classify each of the following equations according to the shape of its graph. (a) $r = 5 + 7\cos\theta$, (b) $r = \dfrac{4}{\theta}$, (c) $r = 4 - 4\sin\theta$.

The equation in (a) is a limaçon, and since $\dfrac{5}{7} < 1$, it will have an inner loop. The equation in (b) is a spiral. Equation (c) appears at first glance to be a limaçon; however, since the coefficients are equal, it is a cardiod.

Example 2

Sketch the graph of $r = 3\cos(2\theta)$. The equation $r = 3\cos(2\theta)$ is a polar rose with four petals each 3 units long. Since $3\cos(0) = 3$, the tip of a petal sits at 3 on the polar axis.

Symmetry of Polar Graphs

A polar curve of the form $r = f(\theta)$ will be symmetric about the polar, or horizontal, axis if $f(\theta) = f(-\theta)$, symmetric about the line $\theta = \dfrac{\pi}{2}$ if $f(\theta) = f(\pi - \theta)$, and symmetric about the pole if $f(\theta) = f(\theta + \pi)$.

Example 1

Determine the symmetry, if any, of the graph of $r = 2 + 4\cos\theta$.

Step 1: Since $2 + 4\cos(-\theta) = 2 + 4\cos\theta$, the graph is symmetric about the polar axis.

Step 2: $2 + 4\cos(\pi - \theta) = 2 - 4\cos\theta$, so the graph is not symmetric about the line $\theta = \dfrac{\pi}{2}$.

Step 3: Since $2 + 4\cos(\theta + \pi) = 2 + 4[\cos\theta\cos\pi - \sin\theta\sin\pi] = 2 - 4\cos\theta$, the graph is not symmetric about the pole.

Example 2

Determine the symmetry, if any, of the graph $r = 3 - 3\sin\theta$.

Step 1: Since $3 - 3\sin(-\theta) = 3 + 3\sin\theta$ is not equal to $r = 3 - 3\sin\theta$, the graph is not symmetric about the polar axis.

Step 2: $3 - 3\sin(\pi - \theta) = 3 - 3\sin\theta$, so the graph is symmetric about the line $\theta = \pi/2$.

Step 3: Since $3 - 3\sin(\theta + \pi) = 3 - 3[\sin\theta\cos\pi + \sin\pi\cos\theta] = 3 + 3\sin\theta$, the graph is not symmetric about the pole.

Example 3

Determine the symmetry, if any, of the graph of $r = 5\cos(4\theta)$.

Step 1: Since $5\cos(4(-\theta)) = 5\cos 4\theta$, the graph is symmetric about the polar axis.

Step 2: $5\cos(4(\pi - \theta)) = 5\cos(4\pi - 4\theta)$ which, by identity, is equal to $5[\cos 4\pi \cos 4\theta + \sin 4\pi \sin\theta]$ or $5\cos 4\theta$, the graph is symmetric about the line $\theta = \pi/2$.

Step 3: Since $5\cos 4(\theta + \pi) = 5\cos(4\theta + 4\pi) = 5\cos(4\theta)$, the graph is symmetric about the pole.

Vectors

A vector represents a displacement of both magnitude and direction. The length, r, of the vector is its magnitude, and the angle, θ, it makes with the x-axis gives its direction. The vector can be resolved into a horizontal and a vertical component. $x = \|r\|\cos\theta$ and $y = \|r\|\sin\theta$.

A unit vector is a vector of magnitude 1. If $i = \langle 1, 0 \rangle$ is the unit vector parallel to the positive x-axis, that is, a unit vector with direction angle $\theta = 0$, and $j = \langle 0, 1 \rangle$ is the unit vector parallel to the y-axis, with an angle $\theta = \dfrac{\pi}{2}$, then any vector in the plane can be represented as $xi + yj$ or simply as the ordered pair $\langle x, y \rangle$. The magnitude of the vector is $\|r\| = \sqrt{x^2 + y^2}$, and the direction can be found from $\tan\theta = \dfrac{y}{x}$. Since $\tan^{-1}\left(\dfrac{y}{x}\right)$ will return values in quadrant I or quadrant IV, if the terminal point of the vector falls in quadrant II or quadrant III, the direction angle will be equal to $\tan^{-1}\left(\dfrac{y}{x}\right) + \pi$.

Example 1

Find the magnitude and direction of the vector represented by $\langle 6, -3 \rangle$.

Step 1: Calculate the magnitude $\|r\| = \sqrt{(6)^2 + (-3)^2} = \sqrt{45} = 3\sqrt{5}$.

Step 2: The terminal point of the vector is in the fourth quadrant. Calculate $\theta =$ $\tan^{-1}\left(\dfrac{-3}{6}\right) = \tan^{-1}\left(\dfrac{-1}{2}\right) \approx -.464$ radians. This angle falls in quadrant IV.

Example 2

Find the magnitude and direction of the vector represented by $\langle -5, -5 \rangle$.

Step 1: Calculate the magnitude $\|r\| = \sqrt{(-5)^2 + (-5)^2} = \sqrt{50} = 5\sqrt{2}$.

Step 2: The terminal point of the vector is in the third quadrant. Calculate $\tan^{-1}\left(\dfrac{-5}{-5}\right) = \tan^{-1}(1) = \dfrac{\pi}{4}$ radians. The direction angle is $\theta = \dfrac{\pi}{4} + \pi = \dfrac{5\pi}{4}$.

Example 3

Find the magnitude and direction of the vector represented by $\langle -1, \sqrt{3} \rangle$.

Step 1: Calculate the magnitude $\|r\| = \sqrt{(-1)^2 + (\sqrt{3})^2} = \sqrt{4} = 2$.

Step 2: The terminal point of the vector is in the second quadrant. Calculate $\tan^{-1}\left(\dfrac{\sqrt{3}}{-1}\right) = \tan^{-1}(-\sqrt{3}) = -\dfrac{\pi}{3}$ radians. The direction angle is $\theta = -\dfrac{\pi}{3} + \pi = \dfrac{2\pi}{3}$.

Example 4

Find the ordered pair representation of a vector of magnitude 12 and direction $\dfrac{-\pi}{4}$. $x = 12\cos\left(\dfrac{-\pi}{4}\right) = 6\sqrt{2}$ and $y = 12\sin\left(\dfrac{-\pi}{4}\right) = -6\sqrt{2}$ so the vector is $\left\langle 6\sqrt{2}, -6\sqrt{2} \right\rangle$.

Vector Arithmetic

If C is a constant, $r_1 = \langle x_1, y_1 \rangle$ and $r_2 = \langle x_2, y_2 \rangle$, then:

Addition: $r_1 + r_2 = \langle x_1 + x_2, y_1 + y_2 \rangle$

Subtraction: $r_1 - r_2 = \langle x_1 - x_2, y_1 - y_2 \rangle$

Scalar Multiplication: $Cr_1 = \langle Cx_1, Cy_1 \rangle$

Note: $\|Cr_1\| = \|C\| \cdot \|r_1\|$

Dot Product: The dot product of two vectors is $r_1 \cdot r_2 = \|r_1\| \cdot \|r_2\| \cdot \cos\theta$ or $r_1 \cdot r_2 = x_1 x_2 + y_1 y_2$.

Parallel and Perpendicular Vectors

If $r_2 = Cr_1$, then r_1 and r_2 are parallel.

If $r_1 \cdot r_2 = 0$, then r_1 and r_2 are perpendicular or orthogonal.

The angle between two vectors can be found by $\cos\theta = \dfrac{r_1 \cdot r_2}{\|r_1\| \cdot \|r_2\|}$.

Example 1

Given $r_1 = \langle 4, -7\rangle$, $r_2 = \langle -3, -2\rangle$ and $r_3 = \langle -1, 5\rangle$, find $3r_1 - 5r_2 + 2r_3$.

$3r_1 - 5r_2 + 2r_3 = 3\langle 4, -7\rangle - 5\langle -3, -2\rangle + 2\langle -1, 5\rangle = \langle 12, -21\rangle - \langle -15, -10\rangle + \langle -2, 10\rangle = \langle 27, -11\rangle + \langle -2, 10\rangle = \langle 25, -1\rangle.$

Example 2

Determine whether the vectors $r_1 = \langle 4, -7\rangle$ and $r_2 = \langle -3, -2\rangle$ are orthogonal. If the vectors are not orthogonal, approximate the angle between them.

Step 1: Find the dot product $r_1 \cdot r_2 = 4(-3) + (-7)(-2) = 2$. Since the dot product is not equal to zero, the vectors are not orthogonal.

Step 2: If θ is the angle between the vectors, then $\cos\theta = \dfrac{r_1 \cdot r_2}{\|r_1\| \cdot \|r_2\|}$. The dot product is

2, $\|r_1\| = \sqrt{65}$, and $\|r_2\| = \sqrt{13}$, so $\cos\theta = \dfrac{2}{\sqrt{65} \cdot \sqrt{13}} = \dfrac{2\sqrt{5}}{65} \approx 0.0688$ and

$\theta \approx 1.5019$ radians.

7.6 Rapid Review

1. If $f'(x) = x^2 - 4$, find the intervals where f is decreasing. (See Figure 7.6-1.)

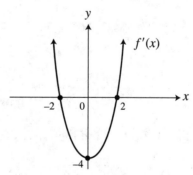

Figure 7.6-1

Answer: Since $f'(x) < 0$ if $-2 < x < 2$, f is decreasing on $(-2, 2)$.

2. If $f''(x) = 2x - 6$ and f' is continuous, find the values of x where f has a point of inflection. (See Figure 7.6-2.)

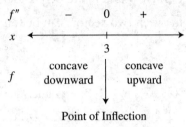

Figure 7.6-2

Answer: Thus, f has a point of inflection at $x = 3$.

3. (See Figure 7.6-3.) Find the values of x where f has change of concavity.

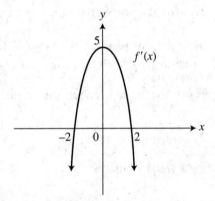

Figure 7.6-3

Answer: f has a change of concavity at $x = 0$. (See Figure 7.6-4.)

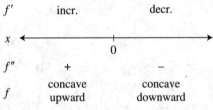

Figure 7.6-4

4. (See Figure 7.6-5.) Find the values of x where f has a relative minimum.

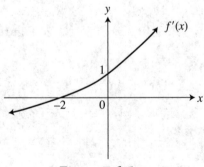

Figure 7.6-5

Answer: f has a relative minimum at $x = -2$. (See Figure 7.6-6.)

Figure 7.6-6

5. (See Figure 7.6-7.) Given f is twice differentiable, arrange $f(10)$, $f'(10)$, $f''(10)$ from smallest to largest.

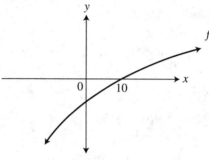

Figure 7.6-7

Answer: $f(10) = 0$, $f'(10) > 0$ since f is increasing, and $f''(10) < 0$ since f is concave downward. Thus, the order is $f''(10)$, $f(10)$, $f'(10)$.

6. (See Figure 7.6-8.) Find the values of x where f' is concave up.

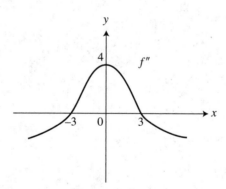

Figure 7.6-8

Answer: f' is concave upward on $(-\infty, 0)$. (See Figure 7.6-9.)

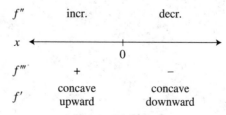

Figure 7.6-9

7. The path of an object is defined by $x = 2t$, $y = t + 1$. Find the location of the object when $t = 5$.

   Answer: When $t = 5$, $x = 2(5) = 10$ and $y = 5 + 1 = 6$ so the location is $(10, 6)$.

8. Identify the shape of each equation: (a) $r = \dfrac{\theta}{5}$; (b) $r = 6\cos 3\theta$

   Answers: (a) spiral, (b) rose

9. Find the magnitude of the vector $\left\langle 1, -\sqrt{3} \right\rangle$ and the angle it makes with the positive x-axis.

   Answers: Magnitude $= \sqrt{1^2 + (-\sqrt{3})^2} = \sqrt{1 + 3} = 2$.

   $$\text{Angle} = \tan^{-1}\left(\dfrac{-\sqrt{3}}{1}\right) = \dfrac{-\pi}{3}.$$

10. If $a = \langle 4, -2 \rangle$, $b = \langle -3, 1 \rangle$, and $c = \langle 0, 5 \rangle$, find $3a - 2b + c$.

   Answer: $3\langle 4, -2 \rangle - 2\langle -3, 1 \rangle + \langle 0, 5 \rangle = \langle 12, -6 \rangle + \langle 6, -2 \rangle + \langle 0, 5 \rangle = \langle 18, -8 \rangle + \langle 0, 5 \rangle = \langle 18, -3 \rangle$.

7.7 Practice Problems

Part A—The use of a calculator is not allowed.

1. If $f(x) = x^3 - x^2 - 2x$, show that the hypotheses of Rolle's Theorem are satisfied on the interval $[-1, 2]$ and find all values of c that satisfy the conclusion of the theorem.

2. Let $f(x) = e^x$. Show that the hypotheses of the Mean Value Theorem are satisfied on $[0, 1]$ and find all values of c that satisfy the conclusion of the theorem.

3. Determine the intervals in which the graph of $f(x) = \dfrac{x^2 + 9}{x^2 - 25}$ is concave upward or downward.

4. Given $f(x) = x + \sin x \; 0 \le x \le 2\pi$, find all points of inflection of f.

5. Show that the absolute minimum of $f(x) = \sqrt{25 - x^2}$ on $[-5, 5]$ is 0 and the absolute maximum is 5.

6. Given the function f in Figure 7.7-1, identify the points where:

    (a) $f' < 0$ and $f'' > 0$, (b) $f' < 0$ and $f'' < 0$,
    (c) $f' = 0$,   (d) f'' does not exist.

7. Given the graph of f'' in Figure 7.7-2, determine the values of x at which the function f has a point of inflection. (See Figure 7.7-2.)

8. If $f''(x) = x^2(x + 3)(x - 5)$, find the values of x at which the graph of f has a change of concavity.

9. The graph of f' on $[-3, 3]$ is shown in Figure 7.7-3. Find the values of x on $[-3, 3]$ such that (a) f is increasing and (b) f is concave downward.

Figure 7.7-1

Figure 7.7-2

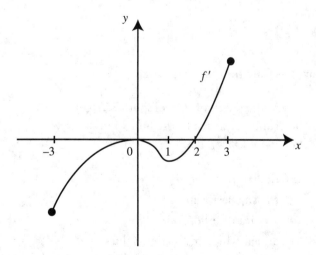

Figure 7.7-3

10. The graph of f is shown in Figure 7.7-4 and f is twice differentiable. Which of the following has the largest value:

    (A) $f(-1)$
    (B) $f'(-1)$
    (C) $f''(-1)$
    (D) $f(-1)$ and $f'(-1)$

Figure 7.7-5

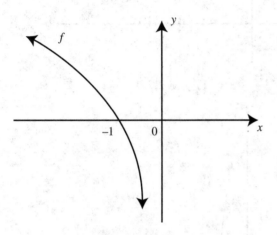

Figure 7.7-4

Sketch the graphs of the following functions indicating any relative and absolute extrema, points of inflection, intervals on which the function is increasing, decreasing, concave upward or concave downward.

11. $f(x) = x^4 - x^2$

12. $f(x) = \dfrac{x + 4}{x - 4}$

Part B—Calculators are allowed.

13. Given the graph of f' in Figure 7.7-5, determine at which of the four values of x (x_1, x_2, x_3, x_4) f has:

    (a) the largest value,
    (b) the smallest value,
    (c) a point of inflection,
    (d) and at which of the four values of x does f'' have the largest value.

14. Given the graph of f in Figure 7.7-6, determine at which values of x is

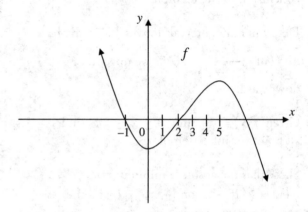

Figure 7.7-6

    (a) $f'(x) = 0$
    (b) $f''(x) = 0$
    (c) f' a decreasing function.

15. A function f is continuous on the interval $[-2, 5]$ with $f(-2) = 10$ and $f(5) = 6$ and the following properties:

INTERVALS	(−2, 1)	x = 1	(1, 3)	x = 3	(3, 5)
f'	+	0	−	undefined	+
f''	−	0	−	undefined	+

    (a) Find the intervals on which f is increasing or decreasing.
    (b) Find where f has its absolute extrema.
    (c) Find where f has points of inflection.
    (d) Find the intervals where f is concave upward or downward.
    (e) Sketch a possible graph of f.

16. Given the graph of f' in Figure 7.7-7, find where the function f

    (a) has its relative extrema.
    (b) is increasing or decreasing.
    (c) has its point(s) of inflection.
    (d) is concave upward or downward.
    (e) if $f(0) = 1$ and $f(6) = 5$, draw a sketch of f.

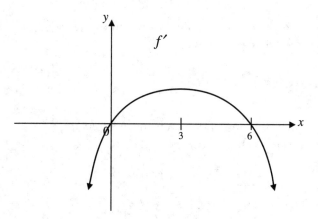

Figure 7.7-7

17. If $f(x) = |x^2 - 6x - 7|$, which of the following statements about f are true?

    I. f has a relative maximum at $x = 3$.
    II. f is differentiable at $x = 7$.
    III. f has a point of inflection at $x = -1$.

18. How many points of inflection does the graph of $y = \cos(x^2)$ have on the interval $[-\pi, \pi]$?

Sketch the graphs of the following functions indicating any relative extrema, points of inflection, asymptotes, and intervals where the function is increasing, decreasing, concave upward or concave downward.

19. $f(x) = 3e^{-x^2/2}$

20. $f(x) = \cos x \sin^2 x \ [0, 2\pi]$

21. Find the Cartesian equation of the curve defined by $x = \dfrac{t}{2}, y = t^2 - 4t + 1$.

22. Find the polar equation of the line with Cartesian equation $y = 3x - 5$.

23. Identify the type of graph defined by the equation $r = 2 - \sin\theta$ and determine its symmetry, if any.

24. Find the value of k so that the vectors $\langle 3, -2 \rangle$ and $\langle 1, k \rangle$ are orthogonal.

25. Determine whether the vectors $\langle 5, -3 \rangle$ and $\langle 5, 3 \rangle$ are orthogonal. If not, find the angle between the vectors.

7.8 Cumulative Review Problems

(Calculator) indicates that calculators are permitted.

26. Find $\dfrac{dy}{dx}$ if $(x^2 + y^2)^2 = 10xy$.

27. Evaluate $\displaystyle\lim_{x \to 0} \dfrac{\sqrt{x+9} - 3}{x}$.

28. Find $\dfrac{d^2y}{dx^2}$ if $y = \cos(2x) + 3x^2 - 1$.

29. (Calculator) Determine the value of k such that the function

$$f(x) = \begin{cases} x^2 - 1, & x \le 1 \\ 2x + k, & x > 1 \end{cases} \text{ is continuous}$$

for all real numbers.

30. A function f is continuous on the interval $[-1, 4]$ with $f(-1) = 0$ and $f(4) = 2$ and the following properties:

INTERVALS	(−1, 0)	x = 0	(0, 2)	x = 2	(2, 4)
f'	+	undefined	+	0	−
f''	+	undefined	−	0	−

(a) Find the intervals on which f is increasing or decreasing.

(b) Find where f has its absolute extrema.

(c) Find where f has points of inflection.

(d) Find intervals on which f is concave upward or downward.

(e) Sketch a possible graph of f.

31. Evaluate $\lim\limits_{x \to \pi} \dfrac{2x}{\sin x}$.

32. Evaluate $\lim\limits_{x \to \frac{1}{2}} \dfrac{3 - 6x}{4x^2 - 1}$.

33. Find the polar equation of the ellipse $x^2 + 4y^2 = 4$.

7.9 Solutions to Practice Problems

Part A—The use of a calculator is not allowed.

1. Condition 1: Since $f(x)$ is a polynomial, it is continuous on $[-1, 2]$.

   Condition 2: Also, $f(x)$ is differentiable on $(-1, 2)$ because $f'(x) = 3x^2 - 2x - 2$ is defined for all numbers in $[-1, 2]$.

   Condition 3: $f(-1) = f(2) = 0$. Thus, $f(x)$ satisfies the hypotheses of Rolle's Theorem, which means there exists a c in $[-1, 2]$ such that $f'(c) = 0$. Set $f'(x) = 3x^2 - 2x - 2 = 0$. Solve $3x^2 - 2x - 2 = 0$, using the quadratic formula and obtain $x = \dfrac{1 \pm \sqrt{7}}{3}$. Thus, $x \approx 1.215$ or -0.549 and both values are in the interval $(-1, 2)$. Therefore, $c = \dfrac{1 \pm \sqrt{7}}{3}$.

2. Condition 1: $f(x) = e^x$ is continuous on $[0, 1]$.

   Condition 2: $f(x)$ is differentiable on $(0, 1)$ since $f'(x) = e^x$ is defined for all numbers in $[0, 1]$.

   Thus, there exists a number c in $[0, 1]$ such that $f'(c) = \dfrac{e^1 - e^0}{1 - 0} = (e - 1)$.

   Set $f'(x) = e^x = (e - 1)$. Thus, $e^x = (e - 1)$. Take ln of both sides. $\ln(e^x) = \ln(e - 1) \Rightarrow x = \ln(e - 1)$.

Thus, $x \approx 0.541$, which is in the interval $(0, 1)$. Therefore, $c = \ln(e - 1)$.

3. $f(x) = \dfrac{x^2 + 9}{x^2 - 25}$,

   $f'(x) = \dfrac{2x(x^2 - 25) - (2x)(x^2 + 9)}{(x^2 - 25)^2}$

   $= \dfrac{-68x}{(x^2 - 25)^2}$, and

   $f''(x)$

   $= \dfrac{-68(x^2 - 25)^2 - 2(x^2 - 25)(2x)(-68x)}{(x^2 - 25)^4}$

   $= \dfrac{68(3x^2 + 25)}{(x^2 - 25)^3}$.

   Set $f'' > 0$. Since $(3x^2 + 25) > 0$, $\Rightarrow (x^2 - 25)^3 > 0 \Rightarrow x^2 - 25 > 0$, $x < -5$ or $x > 5$. Thus, $f(x)$ is concave upward on $(-\infty, -5)$ and $(5, \infty)$ and concave downward on $(-5, 5)$.

4. Step 1: $f(x) = x + \sin x$,
   $\qquad\quad f'(x) = 1 + \cos x$,
   $\qquad\quad f'' = -\sin x$.

   Step 2: Set $f''(x) = 0 \Rightarrow -\sin x = 0$ or $x = 0, \pi, 2\pi$.

Step 3: Check intervals.

f″   +   −

0   π   2π

f   concave   concave

upward   downward

Step 4: Check for tangent line: At $x = \pi$, $f'(x) = 1 + (-1) \Rightarrow 0$ there is a tangent line at $x = \pi$.

Step 5: Thus, (π, π) is a point of inflection.

5. Step 1: Rewrite $f(x)$ as $f(x) = (25 - x^2)^{1/2}$.

Step 2: $f'(x) = \dfrac{1}{2}(25 - x^2)^{-1/2}(-2x)$

$$= \frac{-x}{(25 - x^2)^{1/2}}$$

Step 3: Find critical numbers. $f'(x) = 0$; at $x = 0$; and $f'(x)$ is undefined at $x = \pm 5$.

Step 4:

$f''(x)$

$$= \frac{(-1)\sqrt{(25 - x^2)} - \dfrac{(-2x)(-x)}{2\sqrt{(25 - x^2)}}}{(25 - x^2)}$$

$$= \frac{-1}{(25 - x^2)^{1/2}} - \frac{x^2}{(25 - x^2)^{3/2}}$$

$f'(0) = 0$ and $f''(0) = \dfrac{1}{5}$ (and $f(0) = 5$) $\Rightarrow (0, 5)$ is a relative maximum. Since $f(x)$ is continuous on $[-5, 5]$, $f(x)$ has both a maximum and a minimum value on $[-5, 5]$ by the Extreme Value Theorem. And since the point $(0,5)$ is the only relative extremum, it is an absolute extramum. Thus, $(0,5)$ is an absolute maximum point and 5 is

the maximum value. Now we check the end points, $f(-5) = 0$ and $f(5) = 0$. Therefore, $(-5, 0)$ and $(5, 0)$ are the lowest points for f on $[-5, 5]$. Thus, 0 is the absolute minimum value.

6. (a) Point A $f' < 0 \Rightarrow$ decreasing and $f'' > 0 \Rightarrow$ concave upward.

(b) Point E $f' < 0 \Rightarrow$ decreasing and $f'' < 0 \Rightarrow$ concave downward.

(c) Points B and D $f' = 0 \Rightarrow$ horizontal tangent.

(d) Point C f'' does not exist $\Rightarrow$ vertical tangent.

7. A change in concavity $\Rightarrow$ a point of inflection. At $x = a$, there is a change of concavity; f'' goes from positive to negative $\Rightarrow$ concavity changes from upward to downward. At $x = c$, there is a change of concavity; f'' goes from negative to positive $\Rightarrow$ concavity changes from downward to upward. Therefore, f has two points of inflection, one at $x = a$ and the other at $x = c$.

8. Set $f''(x) = 0$. Thus, $x^2(x + 3)(x - 5) = 0 \Rightarrow x = 0$, $x = -3$, or $x = 5$. (See Figure 7.9-1.)

Thus, f has a change of concavity at $x = -3$ and at $x = 5$.

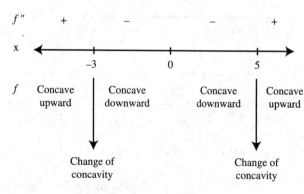

f″   +   −   −   +

x

          −3   0   5

f   Concave   Concave   Concave   Concave

upward   downward   downward   upward

          Change of   Change of

          concavity   concavity

Figure 7.9-1

9. (See Figure 7.9-2.)
   Thus, f is increasing on $[2, 3]$ and concave downward on $(0, 1)$.

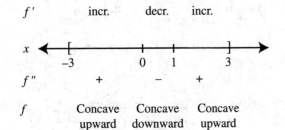

Figure 7.9-2

10. The correct answer is (A).
    $f(-1) = 0$; $f'(0) < 0$ since f is decreasing and $f''(-1) < 0$ since f is concave downward. Thus, $f(-1)$ has the largest value.

11. Step 1: Domain: all real numbers.

    Step 2: Symmetry: Even function ($f(x) = f(-x)$); symmetrical with respect to the y-axis.

Step 3: $f'(x) = 4x^3 - 2x$ and $f''(x) = 12x^2 - 2$.

Step 4: Critical numbers:
   $f'(x)$ is defined for all real numbers. Set $f'(x) = 4x^3 - 2x = 0 \Rightarrow 2x(2x^2 - 1) = 0 \Rightarrow x = 0$ or $x = \pm\sqrt{1/2}$.
   Possible points of inflection: $f''(x)$ is defined for all real numbers. Set $f''(x) = 12x^2 - 2 = 0 \Rightarrow 2(6x^2 - 1) = 0 \Rightarrow x = \pm\sqrt{1/6}$.

Step 5: Determine intervals:

$$\xleftarrow{\qquad}\underset{-\sqrt{1/2}}{|}\quad\underset{-\sqrt{1/6}}{|}\quad\underset{0}{|}\quad\underset{\sqrt{1/6}}{|}\quad\underset{\sqrt{1/2}}{|}\xrightarrow{\qquad}$$

Intervals are: $\left(-\infty, -\sqrt{1/2}\right)$, $\left(-\sqrt{1/2}, -\sqrt{1/6}\right)$, $\left(-\sqrt{1/6}, 0\right)$, $\left(0, \sqrt{1/6}\right)$, $\left(\sqrt{1/6}, \sqrt{1/2}\right)$, and $\left(\sqrt{1/2}, \infty\right)$.
Since $f'(x)$ is symmetrical with respect to the y-axis, you only need to examine half of the intervals.

Step 6: Set up a table (Table 7.9-1). The function has an absolute minimum value of $(-1/4)$ and no absolute maximum value.

Table 7.9-1

INTERVALS	$x = 0$	$(0, \sqrt{1/6})$	$x = \sqrt{1/6}$	$(\sqrt{1/6}, \sqrt{1/2})$	$x = \sqrt{1/2}$	$(\sqrt{1/2}, \infty)$
$f(x)$	0		$-5/36$		$-1/4$	
$f'(x)$	0	$-$	$-$	$-$	0	$+$
$f''(x)$	$-$	$-$	0	$+$	$+$	$+$
conclusion	rel max	decr concave downward	decr pt. of inflection	decr concave upward	rel min	incr concave upward

Step 7: Sketch the graph. (See Figure 7.9-3.)

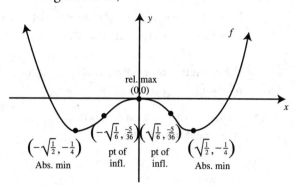

Figure 7.9-3

12. Step 1: Domain: all real numbers $x \neq 4$.

Step 2: Symmetry: none.

Step 3: Find f' and f''.

$$f'(x) = \frac{(1)(x-4) - (1)(x+4)}{(x-4)^2}$$

$$= \frac{-8}{(x-4)^2}, \quad f''(x) = \frac{16}{(x-4)^3}$$

Step 4: Critical numbers: $f'(x) \neq 0$ and $f'(x)$ is undefined at $x = 4$.

Step 5: Determine intervals.

Intervals are $(-\infty, 4)$ and $(4, \infty)$.

Step 6: Set up table as below:

INTERVALS	$(-\infty, 4)$	$(4, \infty)$
f'	–	–
f''	–	+
conclusion	decr concave downward	incr concave upward

Step 7: Horizontal asymptote:
$$\lim_{x \to \pm\infty} \frac{x+4}{x-4} = 1. \text{ Thus, } y = 1 \text{ is a}$$
horizontal asymptote.

Vertical asymptote:
$$\lim_{x \to 4^+} \frac{x+4}{x-4} = \infty \text{ and}$$
$$\lim_{x \to 4^-} \frac{x+4}{x-4} = -\infty. \text{ Thus, } x = 4 \text{ is a}$$
vertical asymptote.

Step 8: x-intercept: Set $f'(x) = 0$
$\Rightarrow x + 4 = 0$; $x = -4$.
y-intercept: Set $x = 0$
$\Rightarrow f(x) = -1$.

Step 9: Sketch the graph. (See Figure 7.9-4.)

Figure 7.9-4

13. (a)

The function f has the largest value (of the four choices) at $x = x_1$. (See Figure 7.9-5.)

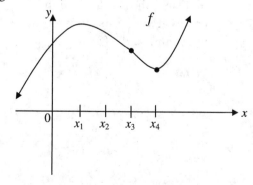

Figure 7.9-5

(b) And f has the smallest value at $x = x_4$.

(c)

A change of concavity occurs at $x = x_3$, and $f'(x_3)$ exists, which implies there is a tangent to f at $x = x_3$. Thus, at $x = x_3$, f has a point of inflection.

(d) The function f'' represents the slope of the tangent to f'. The slope of the tangent to f' is the largest at $x = x_4$.

14. (a) Since $f'(x)$ represents the slope of the tangent, $f'(x) = 0$ at $x = 0$, and $x = 5$.

(b) At $x = 2$, f has a point of inflection, which implies that if $f''(x)$ exists, $f''(x) = 0$. Since $f'(x)$ is differentiable for all numbers in the domain, $f''(x)$ exists, and $f''(x) = 0$ at $x = 2$.

(c) Since the function f is concave downward on $(2, \infty)$, $f'' < 0$ on $(2, \infty)$, which implies f' is decreasing on $(2, \infty)$.

15. (a) The function f is increasing on the intervals $(-2, 1)$ and $(3, 5)$ and decreasing on $(1, 3)$.

(b) The absolute maximum occurs at $x = 1$, since it is a relative maximum, $f(1) > f(-2)$ and $f(5) < f(-2)$. Similarly, the absolute minimum occurs at $x = 3$, since it is a relative minimum, and $f(3) < f(5) < f(-2)$.

(c) No point of inflection. (Note that at $x = 3$, f has a cusp.)

Note: Some textbooks define a point of inflection as a point where the concavity changes and do not require the existence of a tangent. In that case, at $x = 3$, f has a point of inflection.

(d) Concave upward on $(3, 5)$ and concave downward on $(-2, 3)$.

(e) A possible graph is shown in Figure 7.9-6.

Figure 7.9-6

16. (a)

The function f has its relative minimum at $x = 0$ and its relative maximum at $x = 6$.

(b) The function f is increasing on $[0, 6]$ and decreasing on $(-\infty, 0]$ and $[6, \infty)$.

(c)

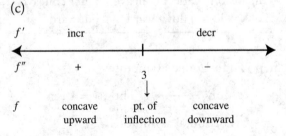

Since $f'(3)$ exists and a change of concavity occurs at $x = 3$, f has a point of inflection at $x = 3$.

(d) Concave upward on $(-\infty, 3)$ and downward on $(3, \infty)$.

(e) Sketch a graph. (See Figure 7.9-7.)

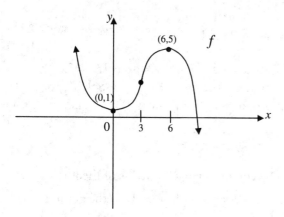

Figure 7.9-7

17. (See Figure 7.9-8.)

[–5,10] by [–5,20]

Figure 7.9-8

The graph of f indicates that a relative maximum occurs at $x = 3$, f is not differentiable at $x = 7$, since there is a cusp at $x = 7$, and f does not have a point of inflection at $x = -1$, since there is no tangent line at $x = -1$. Thus, only statement I is true.

18. (See Figure 7.9-9.)

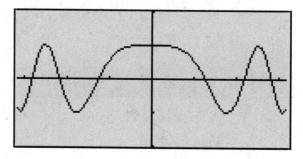

[–π,π] by [–2,2]

Figure 7.9-9

Enter $y1 = \cos(x^2)$
Using the [*Inflection*] function of your calculator, you obtain three points of inflection on $[0, \pi]$. The points of inflection occur at $x = 1.35521, 2.1945,$ and 2.81373. Since $y_1 = \cos(x^2)$ is an even function, there is a total of 6 points of inflection on $[-\pi, \pi]$. An alternate solution is to enter

$$y2 = \frac{d^2}{dx^2}\left(y_1(x), x, 2\right).$$ The graph of y_2 indicates that there are 6 zeros on $[-\pi, \pi]$.

19. Enter $y1 = 3 * e \wedge (-x \wedge 2/2)$. Note that the graph has a symmetry about the y-axis. Using the functions of the calculator, you will find:

(a) a relative maximum point at $(0, 3)$, which is also the absolute maximum point;

(b) points of inflection at $(-1, 1.819)$ and $(1, 1.819)$;

(c) $y = 0$ (the x-axis) a horizontal asymptote;

(d) y_1 increasing on $(-\infty, 0]$ and decreasing on $[0, \infty)$; and

(e) y_1 concave upward on $(-\infty, -1)$ and $(1, \infty)$ and concave downward on $(-1, 1)$. (See Figure 7.9-10.)

[−4,4] by [−1,4]

Figure 7.9-10

20. (See Figure 7.9-11.) Enter $y1 = \cos(x) *$ $(\sin(x)) \wedge 2$. A fundamental domain of y_1 is $[0, 2\pi]$. Using the functions of the calculator, you will find:

[−1,9.4] by [−1,1]

Figure 7.9-11

(a) relative maximum points at (0.955, 0.385), $(\pi, 0)$, and (5.328, 0.385), and relative minimum points at (2.186, −0.385) and (4.097, −0.385);

(b) points of inflection at (0.491, 0.196), $\left(\dfrac{\pi}{2}, 0\right)$, (2.651, −0.196), (3.632, −0.196), $\left(\dfrac{3\pi}{2}, 0\right)$, and (5.792, 0.196);

(c) no asymptote;

(d) function is increasing on intervals (0, 0.955), $(2.186, \pi)$, and (4.097, 5.328), and decreasing on intervals (0.955, 2.186), $(\pi, 4.097)$, and $(5.328, 2\pi)$;

(e) function is concave upward on intervals (0, 0.491), $\left(\dfrac{\pi}{2}, 2.651\right)$, $\left(3.632, \dfrac{3\pi}{2}\right)$, and $(5.792, 2\pi)$, and

concave downward on the intervals $\left(0.491, \dfrac{\pi}{2}\right)$, (2.651, 3.632), and $\left(\dfrac{3\pi}{2}, 5.792\right)$.

21. Solve $x = \dfrac{t}{2}$ for $t = 2x$ and substitute into $y = t^2 - 4t + 1$. $y = (2x)^2 - 4(2x) + 1 = 4x^2 - 8x + 1$.

22. Since $x = r\cos\theta$ and $y = r\sin\theta$, $y = 3x - 5$ becomes $r\sin\theta = 3r\cos\theta - 5$. Solving for r produces $r(\sin\theta - 3\cos\theta) = -5$ and $r = \dfrac{-5}{\sin\theta - 3\cos\theta}$.

23. The equation $r = 2 - \sin\theta$ is of the form $r = a - b\sin\theta$ with $\dfrac{a}{b} > 1$, so the graph is a limaçon with no inner loop. Since $r(-\theta) = 2 + \sin\theta \neq r(\theta)$, the graph is not symmetric about the polar axis. However, $r(\pi - \theta) = 2 - \sin(\pi - \theta)$ is equal to $2\sin\theta = r(\theta)$, so the graph is symmetric about the line $x = \dfrac{\pi}{2}$. Finally, $r(\theta + \pi) = 2 - \sin(\theta + \pi) = 2 + \sin\theta$ and so the graph is not symmetric about the pole.

24. The vectors $\langle 3, -2\rangle$ and $\langle 1, k\rangle$ will be orthogonal if the dot product is equal to zero. $\langle 3, -2\rangle \cdot \langle 1, k\rangle = 3.1 - 2k$ will be equal to zero when $2k = 3$ so $k = \dfrac{3}{2}$.

25. The dot product of $\langle 5, -3\rangle$ and $\langle 5, 3\rangle$ is $5 \cdot 5 + -3 \cdot 3 = 25 - 9 = 16$, so the vectors are not orthogonal. To find the angle between the vectors, begin by dividing the dot product by the product of the magnitudes of the two vectors. Both vectors have a magnitude of $\sqrt{34}$, so the quotient becomes $\dfrac{16}{34} = \dfrac{8}{17}$. The angle between the vectors is $\theta = \cos^{-1}\left(\dfrac{8}{17}\right) \approx 1.081$ radians.

7.10 Solutions to Cumulative Review Problems

26. $(x^2 + y^2)^2 = 10xy$

$$2\left(x^2 + y^2\right)\left(2x + 2y\frac{dy}{dx}\right)$$

$$= 10y + (10x)\frac{dy}{dx}$$

$$4x\left(x^2 + y^2\right) + 4y\left(x^2 + y^2\right)\frac{dy}{dx}$$

$$= 10y + (10x)\frac{dy}{dx}$$

$$4y\left(x^2 + y^2\right)\frac{dy}{dx} - (10x)\frac{dy}{dx}$$
$$= 10y - 4x\left(x^2 + y^2\right)$$

$$\frac{dy}{dx}\left(4y\left(x^2 + y^2\right) - 10x\right)$$
$$= 10y - 4x\left(x^2 + y^2\right)$$

$$\frac{dy}{dx} = \frac{10y - 4x\left(x^2 + y^2\right)}{4y\left(x^2 + y^2\right) - 10x}$$

$$= \frac{5y - 2x\left(x^2 + y^2\right)}{2y\left(x^2 + y^2\right) - 5x}$$

27. Substituting $x = 0$ in the expression $\dfrac{\sqrt{x + 9} - 3}{x}$ leads to $\dfrac{0}{0}$, an indeterminate form. Apply *L'Hôpital's* Rule and you

have $\displaystyle\lim_{x \to 0} \dfrac{\dfrac{1}{2}(x + 9)^{-\frac{1}{2}}(1)}{1}$ or $\dfrac{1}{2}(0 + 9)^{-\frac{1}{2}} = \dfrac{1}{6}$.

Alternatively,

$$\lim_{x \to 0} \frac{\sqrt{x + 9} - 3}{x}$$

$$= \lim_{x \to 0} \frac{\left(\sqrt{x + 9} - 3\right)}{x} \cdot \frac{\left(\sqrt{x + 9} + 3\right)}{\left(\sqrt{x + 9} + 3\right)}$$

$$= \lim_{x \to 0} \frac{(x + 9) - 9}{x\left(\sqrt{x + 9} + 3\right)}$$

$$= \lim_{x \to 0} \frac{x}{x\left(\sqrt{x + 9} + 3\right)}$$

$$= \lim_{x \to 0} \frac{1}{\sqrt{x + 9} + 3} = \frac{1}{\sqrt{0 + 9} + 3}$$

$$= \frac{1}{3 + 3} = \frac{1}{6}$$

28. $y = \cos(2x) + 3x^2 - 1$

$$\frac{dy}{dx} = [-\sin(2x)](2) + 6x =$$
$$-2\sin(2x) + 6x$$

$$\frac{d^2y}{dx^2} = -2(\cos(2x))(2) + 6 =$$
$$-4\cos(2x) + 6$$

29. (Calculator) The function f is continuous everywhere for all values of k except possibly at $x = 1$. Checking with the three conditions of continuity at $x = 1$:

(1) $f(1) = (1)^2 - 1 = 0$

(2) $\displaystyle\lim_{x \to 1^+}(2x + k) = 2 + k$, $\displaystyle\lim_{x \to 1^-}\left(x^2 - 1\right) = 0$;

thus, $2 + k = 0 \Rightarrow k = -2$. Since $\displaystyle\lim_{x \to 1^+} f(x) = \lim_{x \to 1^-} f(x) = 0$, therefore,
$\displaystyle\lim_{x \to 1} f(x) = 0$.

(3) $f(1) = \displaystyle\lim_{x \to 1} f(x) = 0$. Thus, $k = -2$.

30. (a) Since $f' > 0$ on $(-1, 0)$ and $(0, 2)$, the function f is increasing on the intervals $[-1, 0]$ and $[0, 2]$. Since $f' < 0$ on $(2, 4)$, f is decreasing on $[2, 4]$.

(b) The absolute maximum occurs at $x = 2$, since it is a relative maximum and it is the only relative extremum on $(-1, 4)$. The absolute minimum occurs at $x = -1$, since $f(-1) < f(4)$ and the function has no relative minimum on $[-1, 4]$.

(c) A change of concavity occurs at $x = 0$. However, $f'(0)$ is undefined, which implies f may or may not have a tangent at $x = 0$. Thus, f may or may not have a point of inflection at $x = 0$.

(d) Concave upward on $(-1, 0)$ and concave downward on $(0, 4)$.

(e) A possible graph is shown in Figure 7.10-1.

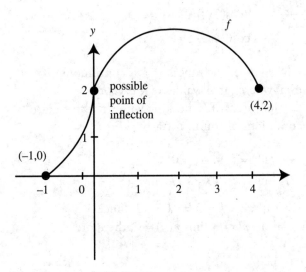

Figure 7.10-1

31. $\lim\limits_{x\to\pi} \dfrac{2x}{\sin x} \to \dfrac{2\pi}{\sin \pi} \to \dfrac{2\pi}{0}$. Note that *L'Hôpital's* Rule does not apply, since the form is not $\dfrac{0}{0}$. $\lim\limits_{x\to\pi^-} \dfrac{2x}{\sin x} = \infty$, but $\lim\limits_{x\to\pi^+} \dfrac{2x}{\sin x} = -\infty$; therefore, $\lim\limits_{x\to\pi} \dfrac{2x}{\sin x}$ does not exist.

32. $\lim\limits_{x\to\frac{1}{2}} \dfrac{3-6x}{4x^2-1} \to \dfrac{0}{0}$, but by *L'Hôpital's* Rule $\lim\limits_{x\to\frac{1}{2}} \dfrac{3-6x}{4x^2-1} = \lim\limits_{x\to\frac{1}{2}} \dfrac{-6}{8x} = \dfrac{-6}{4} = \dfrac{-3}{2}$

33. To convert $x^2 + 4y^2 = 4$ to a polar representation, recall that $x = r\cos\theta$ and $y = r\sin\theta$. Then, $(r\cos\theta)^2 + 4(r\sin\theta)^2 = 4$. Simplifying gives $r^2\cos^2\theta + 4r^2\sin^2\theta = 4$

$$r = \dfrac{2}{\sqrt{\cos^2\theta + 4\sin^2\theta}}$$

$$= \dfrac{2}{\sqrt{1 + 3\sin^2\theta}}$$

CHAPTER 8

Big Idea 2: Derivatives
Applications of Derivatives

IN THIS CHAPTER

Summary: Two of the most common applications of derivatives involve solving related rate problems and applied maximum and minimum problems. In this chapter, you will learn the general procedures for solving these two types of problems and to apply these procedures to examples. Both related rate and applied maximum and minimum problems appear often on the AP Calculus BC exam.

Key Ideas

◉ General Procedure for Solving Related Rate Problems
◉ Common Related Rate Problems
◉ Inverted Cone, Shadow, and Angle of Elevation Problems
◉ General Procedure for Solving Applied Maximum and Minimum Problems
◉ Distance, Area, Volume, and Business Problems

8.1 Related Rate

Main Concepts: General Procedure for Solving Related Rate Problems, Common Related Rate Problems, Inverted Cone (Water Tank) Problem, Shadow Problem, Angle of Elevation Problem

General Procedure for Solving Related Rate Problems

1. Read the problem and, if appropriate, draw a diagram.
2. Represent the given information and the unknowns by mathematical symbols.
3. Write an equation involving the rate of change to be determined. (If the equation contains more than one variable, it may be necessary to reduce the equation to one variable.)

4. Differentiate each term of the equation with respect to time.
5. Substitute all known values and known rates of change into the resulting equation.
6. Solve the resulting equation for the desired rate of change.
7. Write the answer and indicate the units of measure.

Common Related Rate Problems

Example 1

When the area of a square is increasing twice as fast as its diagonals, what is the length of a side of the square?

Let z represent the diagonal of the square. The area of a square is $A = \dfrac{z^2}{2}$.

$$\frac{dA}{dt} = 2z\frac{dz}{dt}\left(\frac{1}{2}\right) = z\frac{dz}{dt}$$

Since $\dfrac{dA}{dt} = 2\dfrac{dz}{dt}$, $2\dfrac{dz}{dt} = z\dfrac{dz}{dt} \Rightarrow z = 2$.

Let s be a side of the square. Since the diagonal $z = 2$, then $s^2 + s^2 = z^2$
$$\Rightarrow 2s^2 = 4 \Rightarrow s^2 = 4 \Rightarrow s^2 = 2 \text{ or } s = \sqrt{2}.$$

Example 2

Find the surface area of a sphere at the instant when the rate of increase of the volume of the sphere is nine times the rate of increase of the radius.

Volume of a sphere: $V = \dfrac{4}{3}\pi r^3$; Surface area of a sphere: $S = 4\pi r^2$.

$$V = \frac{4}{3}\pi r^3; \quad \frac{dV}{dt} = 4r^2\frac{dr}{dt}.$$

Since $\dfrac{dV}{dt} = 9\dfrac{dr}{dt}$, you have $9\dfrac{dr}{dt} = 4\pi r^2\dfrac{dr}{dt}$ or $9 = 4\pi r^2$.

Since $S = 4\pi r^2$, the surface area is $S = 9$ square units.

Note: At $9 = 4\pi r^2$, you could solve for r and obtain $r^2 = \dfrac{9}{4\pi}$ or $r = \dfrac{3}{2}\dfrac{1}{\sqrt{\pi}}$. You could then

substitute $r = \dfrac{3}{2}\dfrac{1}{\sqrt{\pi}}$ into the formula for surface area $S = 4\pi r^2$ and obtain 9. These steps
are of course correct but not necessary.

Example 3

The height of a right circular cone is always three times the radius. Find the volume of the cone at the instant when the rate of increase of the volume is twelve times the rate of increase of the radius.

Let r, h be the radius and height of the cone respectively.

Since $h = 3r$, the volume of the cone $V = \frac{1}{3}\pi r^2 h = \frac{1}{3}\pi r^2 (3r) = \pi r^3$.

$$V = \pi r^3; \quad \frac{dV}{dt} = 3\pi r^2 \frac{dr}{dt}.$$

When $\frac{dV}{dt} = 12\frac{dr}{dt}$, $12\frac{dr}{dt} = 3\pi r^2 \frac{dr}{dt} \Rightarrow 4 = \pi r^2 \Rightarrow r = \frac{2}{\sqrt{\pi}}$.

Thus, $V = \pi r^3 = \pi \left(\frac{2}{\sqrt{\pi}}\right)^3 = \pi \left(\frac{8}{\pi\sqrt{\pi}}\right) = \frac{8}{\sqrt{\pi}}$.

- Go with your first instinct if you are unsure. Usually that is the correct one.

Inverted Cone (Water Tank) Problem

A water tank is in the shape of an inverted cone. The height of the cone is 10 meters and the diameter of the base is 8 meters as shown in Figure 8.1-1. Water is being pumped into the tank at the rate of 2 m³/min. How fast is the water level rising when the water is 5 meters deep? (See Figure 8.1-1.)

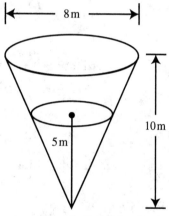

Figure 8.1-1

Solution:

Step 1: Define the variables. Let V be the volume of water in the tank; h be the height of the water level at t minutes; r be the radius of surface of the water at t minutes; and t be the time in minutes.

Step 2: Given: $\frac{dV}{dt} = 2$ m³/min. Height = 10 m, diameter = 8 m.

Find: $\frac{dh}{dt}$ at $h = 5$.

Step 3: Set up an equation: $V = \frac{1}{3}\pi r^2 h$.

Using similar triangles, you have $\frac{4}{10} = \frac{r}{h} \Rightarrow 4h = 10r$; or $r = \frac{2h}{5}$. (See Figure 8.1-2.)

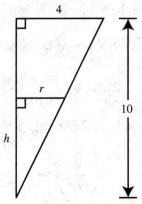

Figure 8.1-2

Thus, you can reduce the equation to one variable:

$$V = \frac{1}{3}\pi \left(\frac{2h}{5}\right)^2 h = \frac{4}{75}\pi h^3.$$

Step 4: Differentiate both sides of the equation with respect to t.

$$\frac{dV}{dt} = \frac{4}{75}\pi(3)h^2\frac{dh}{dt} = \frac{4}{25}\pi h^2\frac{dh}{dt}$$

Step 5: Substitute known values.

$$2 = \frac{4}{25}\pi h^2\frac{dh}{dt}; \frac{dh}{dt} = \left(\frac{25}{2}\right)\frac{1}{\pi h^2} \text{ m/min}$$

Evaluating $\frac{dh}{dt}$ at $h = 5$; $\left.\frac{dh}{dt}\right|_{h=5} = \left(\frac{25}{2}\right)\frac{1}{\pi(5)^2} \text{ m/min}$

$$= \frac{1}{2\pi} \text{ m/min.}$$

Step 6: Thus, the water level is rising at $\frac{1}{2\pi}$ m/min when the water is 5 m high.

Shadow Problem

A light on the ground 100 feet from a building is shining at a 6-foot tall man walking away from the light and toward the building at the rate of 4 ft/sec. How fast is his shadow on the building becoming shorter when he is 40 feet from the building? (See Figure 8.1-3.)

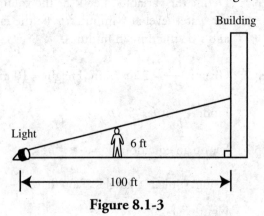

Figure 8.1-3

Solution:

Step 1: Let s be the height of the man's shadow; x be the distance between the man and the light; and t be the time in seconds.

Step 2: Given: $\dfrac{dx}{dt} = 4$ ft/sec; man is 6 ft tall; distance between light and building = 100 ft.

Find $\dfrac{ds}{dt}$ at $x = 60$.

Step 3: (See Figure 8.1-4.) Write an equation using similar triangles, you have:

Figure 8.1-4

$$\frac{6}{s} = \frac{x}{100}; \; s = \frac{600}{x} = 600x^{-1}$$

Step 4: Differentiate both sides of the equation with respect to t.

$$\frac{ds}{dt} = (-1)(600)x^{-2}\frac{dx}{dt} = \frac{-600}{x^2}\frac{dx}{dt} = \frac{-600}{x^2}(4) = \frac{-2400}{x^2} \text{ ft/sec}$$

Step 5: Evaluate $\dfrac{ds}{dt}$ at $x = 60$.

Note: When the man is 40 ft from the building, x (distance from the light) is 60 ft.

$$\left.\frac{ds}{dt}\right|_{x=60} = \frac{-2400}{(60)^2} \text{ ft/sec} = -\frac{2}{3} \text{ ft/sec}$$

Step 6: The height of the man's shadow on the building is changing at $-\dfrac{2}{3}$ ft/sec.

- Indicate units of measure, e.g., the velocity is 5 m/sec *or* the volume is 25 in³.

Angle of Elevation Problem

A camera on the ground 200 meters away from a hot air balloon, also on the ground, records the balloon rising into the sky at a constant rate of 10 m/sec. How fast is the camera's angle of elevation changing when the balloon is 150 m in the air? (See Figure 8.1-5.)

Figure 8.1-5

Step 1: Let x be the distance between the balloon and the ground; θ be the camera's angle of elevation; and t be the time in seconds.

Step 2: Given: $\dfrac{dx}{dt} = 10$ m/sec; distance between camera and the point on the ground where the balloon took off is 200 m, $\tan \theta = \dfrac{x}{200}$.

Step 3: Find $\dfrac{d\theta}{dt}$ at $x = 150$ m.

Step 4: Differentiate both sides with respect to t.

$$\sec^2 \theta \frac{d\theta}{dt} = \frac{1}{200} \frac{dx}{dt}; \quad \frac{d\theta}{dt} = \frac{1}{200} \left(\frac{1}{\sec^2 \theta} \right) (10) = \frac{1}{20 \sec^2 \theta}.$$

Step 5: $\sec \theta = \dfrac{y}{200}$ and at $x = 150$.

Using the Pythagorean Theorem: $y^2 = x^2 + (200)^2$

$$y^2 = (150)^2 + (200)^2$$

$$y = \pm 250.$$

Since $y > 0$, then $y = 250$. Thus, $\sec \theta = \dfrac{250}{200} = \dfrac{5}{4}$.

Evaluating $\dfrac{d\theta}{dt} \bigg|_{x=150} = \dfrac{1}{20 \sec^2 \theta} = \dfrac{1}{20 \left(\dfrac{5}{4} \right)^2}$ radian/sec

$$= \frac{1}{20 \left(\dfrac{5}{4} \right)^2} = \frac{1}{20 \left(\dfrac{25}{16} \right)} = \frac{1}{\dfrac{125}{4}} = \frac{4}{125} \text{ radian/sec}$$

or .032 radian/sec

$= 1.833$ deg/sec.

Step 6: The camera's angle of elevation changes at approximately 1.833 deg/sec when the balloon is 150 m in the air.

8.2 Applied Maximum and Minimum Problems

Main Concepts: General Procedure for Solving Applied Maximum and Minimum Problems, Distance Problem, Area and Volume Problem, Business Problems

General Procedure for Solving Applied Maximum and Minimum Problems

Steps:

1. Read the problem carefully, and if appropriate, draw a diagram.
2. Determine what is given and what is to be found and represent these quantities by mathematical symbols.
3. Write an equation that is a function of the variable representing the quantity to be maximized or minimized.
4. If the equation involves other variables, reduce the equation to a single variable that represents the quantity to be maximized or minimized.
5. Determine the appropriate interval for the equation (i.e., the appropriate domain for the function) based on the information given in the problem.
6. Differentiate to obtain the first derivative and to find critical numbers.
7. Apply the First Derivative Test or the Second Derivative Test by finding the second derivative.
8. Check the function values at the end points of the interval.
9. Write the answer(s) to the problem and, if given, indicate the units of measure.

Distance Problem

Find the shortest distance between the point A (19, 0) and the parabola $y = x^2 - 2x + 1$.

Solution:

Step 1: Draw a diagram. (See Figure 8.2-1.)

Figure 8.2-1

Step 2: Let $P(x, y)$ be the point on the parabola and let Z represent the distance between points $P(x, y)$ and $A(19, 0)$.

Step 3: Using the distance formula,

$$Z = \sqrt{(x-19)^2 + (y-0)^2} = \sqrt{(x-19)^2 + (x^2 - 2x + 1 - 0)^2}$$

$$= \sqrt{(x-19)^2 + \left((x-1)^2\right)^2} = \sqrt{(x-19)^2 + (x-1)^4}.$$

(Special case: In distance problems, the distance and the square of the distance have the same maximum and minimum points.) Thus, to simplify computations, let $L = Z^2 = (x-19)^2 + (x-1)^4$. The domain of L is $(-\infty, \infty)$.

Step 4: Differentiate: $\dfrac{dL}{dx} = 2(x-19)(1) + 4(x-1)^3(1)$

$$= 2x - 38 + 4x^3 - 12x^2 + 12x - 4 = 4x^3 - 12x^2 + 14x - 42$$

$$= 2(2x^3 - 6x^2 + 7x - 21).$$

$\dfrac{dL}{dx}$ is defined for all real numbers.

Set $\dfrac{dL}{dx} = 0$; $2x^3 - 6x^2 + 7x - 21 = 0$. The factors of 21 are $\pm 1, \pm 3, \pm 7$, and ± 21.

Using Synthetic Division, $2x^3 - 6x^2 + 7x - 21 = (x-3)(2x^2 + 7) = 0 \Rightarrow x = 3$. Thus, the only critical number is $x = 3$.

(Note: Step 4 could have been done using a graphing calculator.)

Step 5: Apply the First Derivative Test.

Step 6: Since $x = 3$ is the only relative minimum point in the interval, it is the absolute minimum.

Step 7: At $x = 3$, $Z = \sqrt{(3-19)^2 + (3^2 - 2(3) + 1)^2} = \sqrt{(-16)^2 + (4)^2}$

$$= \sqrt{272} = \sqrt{16}\sqrt{17} = 4\sqrt{17}.$$ Thus, the shortest distance is $4\sqrt{17}$.

- Simplify numeric or algebraic expressions only if the question asks you to do so.

Area and Volume Problem

Example—Area Problem

The graph of $y = -\dfrac{1}{2}x + 2$ encloses a region with the x-axis and y-axis in the first quadrant. A rectangle in the enclosed region has a vertex at the origin and the opposite vertex on the graph of $y = -\dfrac{1}{2}x + 2$. Find the dimensions of the rectangle so that its area is a maximum.

Solution:

Step 1:   Draw a diagram. (See Figure 8.2-2.)

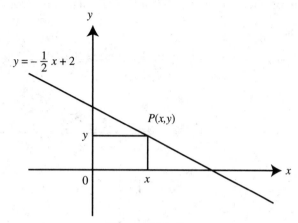

Figure 8.2-2

Step 2:   Let $P(x, y)$ be the vertex of the rectangle on the graph of $y = -\dfrac{1}{2}x + 2$.

Step 3:   Thus, the area of the rectangle is:

$$A = xy \text{ or } A = x\left(-\frac{1}{2}x + 2\right) = -\frac{1}{2}x^2 + 2x.$$

The domain of A is $[0, 4]$.

Step 4:   Differentiate:

$$\frac{dA}{dx} = -x + 2.$$

Step 5: $\dfrac{dA}{dx}$ is defined for all real numbers.

Set $\dfrac{dA}{dx} = 0 \Rightarrow -x + 2 = 0; \; x = 2.$

$A(x)$ has one critical number $x = 2$.

Step 6:   Apply Second Derivative Test:

$$\frac{d^2A}{dx^2} = -1 \Rightarrow A(x) \text{ has a relative maximum point at } x = 2; A(2) = 2.$$

Since $x = 2$ is the only relative maximum, it is the absolute maximum. (Note that at the endpoints: $A(0) = 0$ and $A(4) = 0$.)

Step 7:   At $x = 2$, $y = -\dfrac{1}{2}(2) + 2 = 1.$

Therefore, the length of the rectangle is 2, and its width is 1.

Example—Volume Problem (with calculator)

If an open box is to be made using a square sheet of tin, 20 inches by 20 inches, by cutting a square from each corner and folding the sides up, find the length of a side of the square being cut so that the box will have a maximum volume.

Solution:

Step 1: Draw a diagram. (See Figure 8.2-3.)

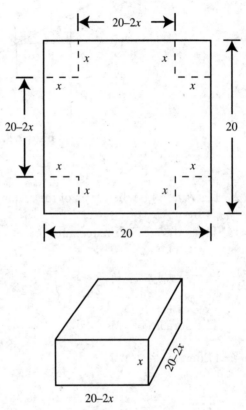

Figure 8.2-3

Step 2: Let x be the length of a side of the square to be cut from each corner.

Step 3: The volume of the box is $V(x) = x(20 - 2x)(20 - 2x)$.
The domain of V is $[0, 10]$.

Step 4: Differentiate $V(x)$.
Enter $d(x * (20 - 2x) * (20 - 2x), \, x)$ and we have $4(x - 10)(3x - 10)$.

Step 5: $V'(x)$ is defined for all real numbers:
Set $V'(x) = 0$ by entering: [*Solve*] $(4(x - 10)(3x - 10) = 0, \, x)$, and obtain $x = 10$

or $x = \dfrac{10}{3}$. The critical numbers of $V(x)$ are $x = 10$ and $x = \dfrac{10}{3}$. $V(10) = 0$ and

$V\left(\dfrac{10}{3}\right) = 592.59$. Since $V(10) = 0$, you need to test only $x = \dfrac{10}{3}$.

Step 6: Using the Second Derivative Test, enter $d(x * (20 - 2x) * (20 - 2x), x, 2)|x = \dfrac{10}{3}$

and obtain −80. Thus, $V\left(\dfrac{10}{3}\right)$ is a relative maximum. Since it is the only relative maximum on the interval, it is the absolute maximum. (Note at the other endpoint $x = 0$, $V(0) = 0$.)

Step 7: Therefore, the length of a side of the square to be cut is $x = \dfrac{10}{3}$.

> • The formula for the average value of a function f from $x = a$ to $x = b$ is
> $$\dfrac{1}{b-a} \int_a^b f(x)dx.$$

Business Problems
Summary of Formulas

1. $P = R - C$: Profit = Revenue − Cost

2. $R = xp$: Revenue = (Units Sold)(Price Per Unit)

3. $\overline{C} = \dfrac{C}{x}$: Average Cost = $\dfrac{\text{Total Cost}}{\text{Units produced/Sold}}$

4. $\dfrac{dR}{dx}$: Marginal Revenue ≈ Revenue from selling one more unit

5. $\dfrac{dP}{dx}$: Marginal Profit ≈ Profit from selling one more unit

6. $\dfrac{dC}{dx}$: Marginal Cost ≈ Cost of producing one more unit

Example 1

Given the cost function $C(x) = 100 + 8x + 0.1x^2$, (a) find the marginal cost when $x = 50$; and (b) find the marginal profit at $x = 50$, if the price per unit is $20.

Solution:

(a) Marginal cost is $C'(x)$. Enter $d(100 + 8x + 0.1x^2, x)|x = 50$ and obtain $18.

(b) Marginal profit is $P'(x)$
$P = R - C$
$P = 20x - (100 + 8x + 0.1x^2)$. Enter $d(20x - (100 + 8x + 0.1x\text{^}2, x)|x = 50$ and obtain 2.

> • Carry all decimal places and round only at the final answer. Round to 3 decimal places unless the question indicates otherwise.

Example 2

Given the cost function $C(x) = 500 + 3x + 0.01x^2$ and the demand function (the price function) $p(x) = 10$, find the number of units produced in order to have maximum profit.

Solution:

Step 1: Write an equation.
Profit = Revenue – Cost
$P = R - C$
Revenue = (Units Sold)(Price Per Unit)
$R = xp(x) = x(10) = 10x$
$P = 10x - (500 + 3x + 0.01x^2)$

Step 2: Differentiate.
Enter $d(10x - (500 + 3x + 0.01x^\wedge 2, x))$ and obtain $7 - 0.02x$.

Step 3: Find critical numbers.
Set $7 - 0.02x = 0 \Rightarrow x = 350$.
Critical number is $x = 350$.

Step 4: Apply Second Derivative Test.
Enter $d(10x - (500 + 3x + 0.01x^\wedge 2), x, 2)|x = 350$ and obtain -0.02.
Since $x = 350$ is the only relative maximum, it is the absolute maximum.

Step 5: Write a Solution.
Thus, producing 350 units will lead to maximum profit.

8.3 Rapid Review

1. Find the instantaneous rate of change at $x = 5$ of the function $f(x) = \sqrt{2x - 1}$.

   Answer: $f(x) = \sqrt{2x - 1} = (2x - 1)^{1/2}$
   $f'(x) = \frac{1}{2}(2x - 1)^{-1/2}(2) = (2x - 1)^{-1/2}$
   $f'(5) = \frac{1}{3}$

2. If h is the diameter of a circle and h is increasing at a constant rate of 0.1 cm/sec, find the rate of change of the area of the circle when the diameter is 4 cm.

   Answer: $A = \pi r^2 = \pi \left(\frac{h}{2}\right)^2 = \frac{1}{4}\pi h^2$
   $\frac{dA}{dt} = \frac{1}{2}\pi h \frac{dh}{dt} = \frac{1}{2}\pi(4)(0.1) = 0.2\pi$ cm²/sec.

3. The radius of a sphere is increasing at a constant rate of 2 inches per minute. In terms of the surface area, what is the rate of change of the volume of the sphere?

   Answer: $V = \frac{4}{3}\pi r^3$; $\frac{dV}{dt} = 4\pi r^2 \frac{dr}{dt}$, since $S = \pi r^2$, $\frac{dV}{dt} = 28$ in.³/min.

4. Using your calculator, find the shortest distance between the point (4, 0) and the line $y = x$. (See Figure 8.3-1.)

[–6.3,10] by [–2,6]
Figure 8.3-1

Answer:

$$S = \sqrt{(x-4)^2 + (y-0)^2} = \sqrt{(x-4)^2 + x^2}$$

Enter $y1 = ((x - 4)^\wedge 2 + x^\wedge 2)^\wedge(.5)$ and $y2 = d(y1(x), x)$.

Use the [*Zero*] function for $y2$ and obtain $x = 2$. Note that when $x < 2$, $y2 < 0$ and when $x > 2$, $y2 > 0$, which means at $x = 2$, $y1$ is a minimum. Use the [*Value*] function for $y1$ at $x = 2$ and obtain $y1 = 2.82843$. Thus, the shortest distance is approximately 2.828.

8.4 Practice Problems

Part A—The use of a calculator is not allowed.

1. A spherical balloon is being inflated. Find the volume of the balloon at the instant when the rate of increase of the surface area is eight times the rate of increase of the radius of the sphere.

2. A 13-foot ladder is leaning against a wall. If the top of the ladder is sliding down the wall at 2 ft/sec, how fast is the bottom of the ladder moving away from the wall when the top of the ladder is 5 feet from the ground? (See Figure 8.4-1.)

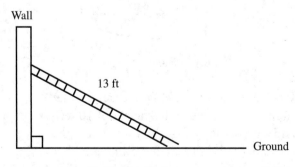

Figure 8.4-1

3. Air is being pumped into a spherical balloon at the rate of 100 cm³/sec. How fast is the diameter increasing when the radius is 5 cm?

4. A woman 5 feet tall is walking away from a streetlight hung 20 feet from the ground at the rate of 6 ft/sec. How fast is her shadow lengthening?

5. A water tank in the shape of an inverted cone has a height of 18 feet and a base radius of 12 feet. If the tank is full and the water is drained at the rate of 4 ft³/min, how fast is the water level dropping when the water level is 6 feet high?

6. Two cars leave an intersection at the same time. The first car is going due east at the rate of 40 mph and the second is going due south at the rate of 30 mph. How fast is the distance between the two cars increasing when the first car is 120 miles from the intersection?

7. If the perimeter of an isosceles triangle is 18 cm, find the maximum area of the triangle.

8. Find a number in the interval (0, 2) such that the sum of the number and its reciprocal is the absolute minimum.

9. An open box is to be made using a piece of cardboard 8 cm by 15 cm by cutting a square from each corner and folding the sides up. Find the length of a side of the square being cut so that the box will have a maximum volume.

10. What is the shortest distance between the point $\left(2, -\frac{1}{2}\right)$ and the parabola $y = -x^2$?

11. If the cost function is $C(x) = 3x^2 + 5x + 12$, find the value of x such that the average cost is a minimum.

12. A man with 200 meters of fence plans to enclose a rectangular piece of land using a river on one side and a fence on the other three sides. Find the maximum area that the man can obtain.

Part B—Calculators are allowed.

13. A trough is 10 meters long and 4 meters wide. (See Figure 8.4-2.) The two sides of the trough are equilateral triangles. Water is pumped into the trough at 1 m³/min. How fast is the water level rising when the water is 2 meters high?

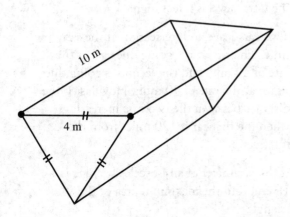

Figure 8.4-2

14. A rocket is sent vertically up in the air with the position function $s = 100t^2$ where s is measured in meters and t in seconds. A camera 3000 m away is recording the rocket. Find the rate of change of the angle of elevation of the camera 5 sec after the rocket went up.

15. A plane lifts off from a runway at an angle of 20°. If the speed of the plane is 300 mph, how fast is the plane gaining altitude?

16. Two water containers are being used. (See Figure 8.4-3.)

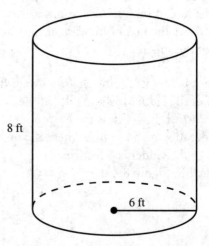

Figure 8.4-3

One container is in the form of an inverted right circular cone with a height of 10 feet and a radius at the base of 4 feet. The other container is a right circular cylinder with a radius of 6 feet and a height of 8 feet. If water is being drained from the conical container into the cylindrical container at the rate of 15 ft³/min, how fast is the water level falling in the conical tank when the water level in the conical tank is 5 feet high? How fast is the water level rising in the cylindrical container?

17. The wall of a building has a parallel fence that is 6 feet high and 8 feet from the wall. What is the length of the shortest ladder that passes over the fence and leans on the wall? (See Figure 8.4-4.)

18. Given the cost function $C(x) = 2500 + 0.02x + 0.004x^2$, find the product level such that the average cost per unit is a minimum.

19. Find the maximum area of a rectangle inscribed in an ellipse whose equation is $4x^2 + 25y^2 = 100$.

20. A right triangle is in the first quadrant with a vertex at the origin and the other two vertices on the x- and y-axes. If the hypotenuse passes through the point $(0.5, 4)$, find the vertices of the triangle so that the length of the hypotenuse is minimum.

Figure 8.4-4

8.5 Cumulative Review Problems

(Calculator) indicates that calculators are permitted.

21. If $y = \sin^2(\cos(6x - 1))$, find $\dfrac{dy}{dx}$.

22. Evaluate $\displaystyle\lim_{x\to\infty} \dfrac{100/x}{-4 + x + x^2}$.

23. The graph of f' is shown in Figure 8.5-1. Find where the function f: (a) has its relative extrema or absolute extrema; (b) is increasing or decreasing; (c) has its point(s) of inflection; (d) is concave upward or downward; and (e) if $f(3) = -2$, draw a possible sketch of f. (See Figure 8.5-1.)

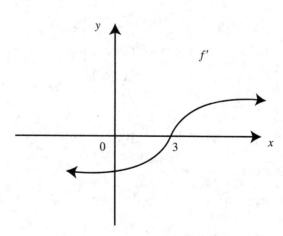

Figure 8.5-1

24. (Calculator) At what value(s) of x does the tangent to the curve $x^2 + y^2 = 36$ have a slope of -1.

25. (Calculator) Find the shortest distance between the point $(1, 0)$ and the curve $y = x^3$.

8.6 Solutions to Practice Problems

Part A—The use of a calculator is not allowed.

1. Volume: $V = \dfrac{4}{3}\pi r^3$;

   Surface Area: $S = 4\pi r^2$ $\dfrac{dS}{dt} = 8\pi r \dfrac{dr}{dt}$.

   Since $\dfrac{dS}{dt} = 8\dfrac{dr}{dt}$,

   $8\dfrac{dr}{dt} = 8\pi r \dfrac{dr}{dt} \Rightarrow 8 = 8\pi r$

   or $r = \dfrac{1}{\pi}$.

   At $r = \dfrac{1}{\pi}$, $V = \dfrac{4}{3}\pi \left(\dfrac{1}{\pi}\right)^3 = \dfrac{4}{3\pi^2}$ cubic units.

2. Pythagorean Theorem yields
   $x^2 + y^2 = (13)^2$.

   Differentiate: $2x\dfrac{dx}{dt} + 2y\dfrac{dy}{dt} = 0 \Rightarrow \dfrac{dy}{dt}$

   $= \dfrac{-x}{y}\dfrac{dx}{dt}$.

   At $x = 5$, $(5)^2 + y^2 = 13^2 \Rightarrow y = \pm 12$, since $y > 0$, $y = 12$.

   Therefore, $\dfrac{dy}{dt} = -\dfrac{5}{12}(-2)$ ft/sec $= \dfrac{5}{6}$ ft/sec.

   The ladder is moving away from the wall at $\dfrac{5}{6}$ ft/sec when the top of the ladder is 5 feet from the ground.

3. Volume of a sphere is $V = \dfrac{4}{3}\pi r^3$.

   Differentiate: $\dfrac{dV}{dt} = \left(\dfrac{4}{3}\right)(3)\pi r^2$

   $\dfrac{dr}{dt} = 4\pi r^2 \dfrac{dr}{dt}$.

   Substitute: $100 = 4\pi (5)^2$

   $\dfrac{dr}{dt} \Rightarrow \dfrac{dr}{dt} = \dfrac{1}{\pi}$ cm/sec.

   Let x be the diameter. Since

   $x = 2r$, $\dfrac{dx}{dt} = 2\dfrac{dr}{dt}$.

Thus, $\dfrac{dx}{dt}\bigg|_{r=5} = 2\left(\dfrac{1}{\pi}\right)$ cm/sec

$= \dfrac{2}{\pi}$ cm/sec. The diameter is increasing at $\dfrac{2}{\pi}$ cm/sec when the radius is 5 cm.

4. (See Figure 8.6-1.) Using similar triangles, with y the length of the shadow you have:

   $\dfrac{5}{20} = \dfrac{y}{y + x} \Rightarrow 20y = 5y + 5x \Rightarrow$

   $15y = 5x$ or $y = \dfrac{x}{3}$.

   Differentiate:

   $\dfrac{dy}{dt} = \dfrac{1}{3}\dfrac{dx}{dt} \Rightarrow \dfrac{dy}{dt} = \dfrac{1}{3}(6)$

   $= 2$ ft/sec.

Figure 8.6-1

5. (See Figure 8.6-2.) Volume of a cone

   $V = \dfrac{1}{3}\pi r^2 h$.

   Using similar triangles, you have

   $\dfrac{12}{18} = \dfrac{r}{h} \Rightarrow 2h = 3r$ or $r = \dfrac{2}{3}h$, thus

   reducing the equation to

   $V = \dfrac{1}{3}\pi \left(\dfrac{2}{3}h\right)^2 (h) = \dfrac{4\pi}{27}h^3$.

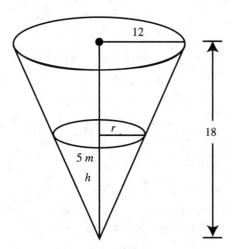

Figure 8.6-2

Differentiate: $\dfrac{dV}{dt} = \dfrac{4}{9}\pi h^2 \dfrac{dh}{dt}$.

Substituting known values:

$-4 = \dfrac{4\pi}{9}(6)^2 \dfrac{dh}{dt} \Rightarrow -4 = 16\pi \dfrac{dh}{dt}$ or

$\dfrac{dh}{dt} = -\dfrac{1}{4\pi}$ ft/min. The water level is

dropping at $\dfrac{1}{4\pi}$ ft/min when $h = 6$ ft.

6. (See Figure 8.6-3.)

Step 1: Using the Pythagorean Theorem, you have $x^2 + y^2 = z^2$. You also have $\dfrac{dx}{dt} = 40$ and $\dfrac{dy}{dt} = 30$.

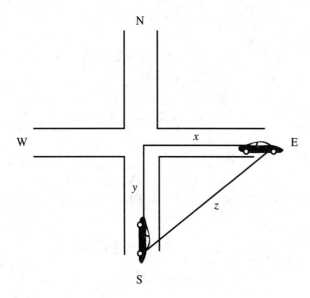

Figure 8.6-3

Step 2: Differentiate:
$$2x\frac{dx}{dt} + 2y\frac{dy}{dt} = 2z\frac{dz}{dt}.$$
At $x = 120$, both cars have traveled 3 hours and thus, $y = 3(30) = 90$. By the Pythagorean Theorem, $(120)^2 + (90)^2 = z^2 \Rightarrow z = 150$.

Step 3: Substitute all known values into the equation:
$$2(120)(40) + 2(90)(30) = 2(150)\frac{dz}{dt}.$$
Thus, $\dfrac{dz}{dt} = 50$ mph.

Step 4: The distance between the two cars is increasing at 50 mph at $x = 120$.

7. (See Figure 8.6-4.)

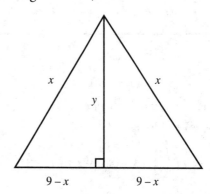

Figure 8.6-4

Step 1: Applying the Pythagorean Theorem, you have
$x^2 = y^2 + (9 - x)^2 \Rightarrow y^2 = x^2 - (9 - x)^2 = x^2 - \left(81 - 18x + x^2\right) = 18x - 81 = 9(2x - 9)$, or
$y = \pm\sqrt{9(2x - 9)} = \pm 3\sqrt{(2x - 9)}$ since $y > 0$,
$y = 3\sqrt{(2x - 9)}$.
The area of the triangle
$A = \dfrac{1}{2}\left(3\sqrt{2x - 9}\right)(18 - 2x) = \left(3\sqrt{2x - 9}\right)(9 - x) = 3(2x - 9)^{1/2}(9 - x)$.

Step 2: $\dfrac{dA}{dx} = \dfrac{3}{2}(2x-9)^{-1/2}(2)(9-x)$

$$+(-1)(3)(2x-9)^{1/2}.$$

$$= \dfrac{3(9-x)-3(2x-9)}{\sqrt{2x-9}}$$

$$= \dfrac{54-9x}{\sqrt{2x-9}}$$

Step 3: Set $\dfrac{dA}{dx} = 0 \Rightarrow 54-9x = 0$; $x = 6$.

$\dfrac{dA}{dx}$ is undefined at $x = \dfrac{9}{2}$. The

critical numbers are $\dfrac{9}{2}$ and 6.

Step 4: First Derivative Test:

Thus, at $x = 6$, the area A is a relative maximum.

$$A(6) = \left(\dfrac{1}{2}\right)(3)(\sqrt{2(6)-9})(9-6)$$

$$= 9\sqrt{3}$$

Step 5: Check endpoints. The domain of A is $[9/2, 9]$. $A(9/2) = 0$; and $A(9) = 0$. Therefore, the maximum area of an isosceles triangle with the perimeter of 18 cm is $9\sqrt{3}$ cm^2. (Note that at $x = 6$, the triangle is an equilateral triangle.)

8. Step 1: Let x be the number and $\dfrac{1}{x}$ be its reciprocal.

Step 2: $s = x + \dfrac{1}{x}$ with $0 < x < 2$.

Step 3: $\dfrac{ds}{dx} = 1 + (-1)x^{-2} = 1 - \dfrac{1}{x^2}$

Step 4: Set $\dfrac{ds}{dx} = 0 \Rightarrow 1 - \dfrac{1}{x^2} = 0$

$\Rightarrow x = \pm 1$, since the domain is $(0, 2)$, thus $x = 1$.

$\dfrac{ds}{dx}$ is defined for all x in $(0, 2)$.

Critical number is $x = 1$.

Step 5: Second Derivative Test:

$\dfrac{d^2s}{dx^2} = \dfrac{2}{x^3}$ and $\left.\dfrac{d^2s}{dx^2}\right|_{x=1} = 2.$

Thus, at $x = 1$, s is a relative minimum. Since it is the only relative extremum, at $x = 1$, it is the absolute minimum.

9. (See Figure 8.6-5.)

Figure 8.6-5

Step 1: Volume: $V = x(8-2x)(15-2x)$ with $0 \le x \le 4$.

Step 2: Differentiate: Rewrite as $V = 4x^3 - 46x^2 + 120x$

$$\dfrac{dV}{dx} = 12x^2 - 92x + 120.$$

Step 3: Set $V = 0 \Rightarrow 12x^2 - 92x + 120 = 0$ $\Rightarrow 3x^2 - 23x + 30 = 0$. Using the quadratic formula, you have $x = 6$ or $x = \dfrac{5}{3}$ and $\dfrac{dV}{dx}$ is defined for all real numbers.

Step 4: Second Derivative Test:

$$\frac{d^2V}{dx^2} = 24x - 92; \quad \left.\frac{d^2V}{dx^2}\right|_{x=6}$$

$$= 52 \text{ and } \left.\frac{d^2V}{dx^2}\right|_{x=\frac{5}{3}} = -52.$$

Thus, at $x = \dfrac{5}{3}$ is a relative maximum.

Step 5: Check endpoints.
At $x = 0$, $V = 0$ and at $x = 4$, $V = 0$. Therefore, at $x = \dfrac{5}{3}$, V is the absolute maximum.

10. (See Figure 8.6-6.)

Figure 8.6-6

Step 1: Distance formula:

$$Z = \sqrt{(x-2)^2 + \left(y - \left(-\frac{1}{2}\right)\right)^2}$$

$$= \sqrt{(x-2)^2 + \left(-x^2 + \frac{1}{2}\right)^2}$$

$$= \sqrt{x^2 - 4x + 4 + x^4 - x^2 + \frac{1}{4}}$$

$$= \sqrt{x^4 - 4x + \frac{17}{4}}$$

Step 2: Let $S = Z^2$, since S and Z have the same maximums and minimums.

$$S = x^4 - 4x + \frac{17}{4}; \quad \frac{dS}{dx} = 4x^3 - 4$$

Step 3: Set $\dfrac{dS}{dx} = 0$; $x = 1$ and $\dfrac{dS}{dx}$ is defined for all real numbers.

Step 4: Second Derivative Test:

$$\frac{d^2S}{dx^2} = 12x^2 \text{ and } \left.\frac{d^2S}{dx^2}\right|_{x=1} = 12.$$

Thus, at $x = 1$, Z has a minimum, and since it is the only relative extremum, it is the absolute minimum.

Step 5: At $x = 1$,

$$Z = \sqrt{(1)^4 - 4(1) + \frac{17}{4}}$$

$$= \sqrt{\frac{5}{4}}.$$

Therefore, the shortest distance is

$$\sqrt{\frac{5}{4}}.$$

11. Step 1: Average cost:

$$\overline{C} = \frac{C(x)}{x} = \frac{3x^2 + 5x + 12}{x}$$

$$= 3x + 5 + \frac{12}{x}.$$

Step 2: $\dfrac{d\overline{C}}{dx} = 3 - 12x^{-2} = 3 - \dfrac{12}{x^2}$

Step 3: Set $\dfrac{d\overline{C}}{dx} = 0 \Rightarrow 3 - \dfrac{12}{x^2} = 0 \Rightarrow$

$3 = \dfrac{12}{x^2} \Rightarrow x = \pm 2$. Since $x > 0$, $x = 2$

and $\overline{C}(2) = 17$. $\dfrac{d\overline{C}}{dx}$ is undefined at $x = 0$, which is not in the domain.

Step 4: Second Derivative Test:

$$\frac{d^2\overline{C}}{dx^2} = \frac{24}{x^3} \text{ and } \left.\frac{d^2\overline{C}}{dx^2}\right|_{x=2} = 3$$

Thus, at $x = 2$, the average cost is a minimum.

12. (See Figure 8.6-7.)

x x

$(200 - 2x)$

Figure 8.6-7

Step 1: Area:
$A = x(200 - 2x) = 200x - 2x^2$
with $0 \leq x \leq 100$.

Step 2: $A'(x) = 200 - 4x$

Step 3: Set $A'(x) = 0 \Rightarrow 200 - 4x = 0$;
$x = 50$.

Step 4: Second Derivative Test:
$A''(x) = -4$; thus at $x = 50$, the area is a relative maximum.
$A(50) = 5000 \text{ m}^2$.

Step 5: Check endpoints.
$A(0) = 0$ and $A(100) = 0$;
therefore at $x = 50$, the area is the absolute maximum and 5000 m^2 is the maximum area.

Part B—Calculators are allowed.

13. Step 1: Let h be the height of the trough and 4 be a side of one of the two equilateral triangles. Thus, in a 30–60 right triangle, $h = 2\sqrt{3}$.

Step 2: Volume:
$V = (\text{area of the triangle}) \cdot 10$
$= \left[\frac{1}{2}(h)\left(\frac{2}{\sqrt{3}}h\right)\right]10 = \frac{10}{\sqrt{3}}h^2$.

Step 3: Differentiate with respect to t.
$\frac{dV}{dt} = \left(\frac{10}{\sqrt{3}}\right)(2)h\frac{dh}{dt}$

Step 4: Substitute known values:
$1 = \frac{20}{\sqrt{3}}(2)\frac{dh}{dt}$;
$\frac{dh}{dt} = \frac{\sqrt{3}}{40}$ m/min.

The water level is raising $\frac{\sqrt{3}}{40}$ m/min when the water level is 2 m high.

14. (See Figure 8.6-8.)

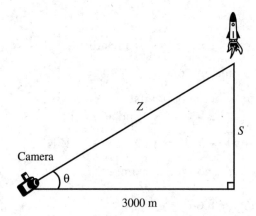

Figure 8.6-8

Step 1: $\tan\theta = S/3000$

Step 2: Differentiate with respect to t.

$\sec^2\theta\frac{d\theta}{dt} = \frac{1}{3000}\frac{dS}{dt}$;

$\frac{d\theta}{dt} = \frac{1}{3000}\left(\frac{1}{\sec^2\theta}\right)\frac{dS}{dt}$

$= \frac{1}{3000}\left(\frac{1}{\sec^2\theta}\right)(200t)$

Step 3: At $t = 5$; $S = 100(5)^2 = 2500$;
thus, $Z^2 = (3000)^2 + (2500)^2 = 15,250,000$. Therefore,
$Z = \pm 500\sqrt{61}$, since $Z > 0$,
$Z = 500\sqrt{61}$. Substitute known values into the equation:

$\frac{d\theta}{dt} =$

$\frac{1}{3000}\left(\dfrac{1}{\dfrac{500\sqrt{61}}{3000}}\right)^2(1000),$

since $\sec\theta = \dfrac{Z}{3000}$.

$\dfrac{d\theta}{dt} = 0.197$ radian/sec. The angle of elevation is changing at 0.197 radian/sec, 5 seconds after liftoff.

15. (See Figure 8.6-9.)

Figure 8.6-9

$\text{Sin } 20° = \dfrac{h}{300t}$

$h = (\sin 20°)300t;$

$\dfrac{dh}{dt} = (\sin 20°)(300) \approx 102.606$ mph. The plane is gaining altitude at 102.606 mph.

16. $V_{\text{cone}} = \dfrac{1}{3}\pi r^2 h$

Similar triangles: $\dfrac{4}{10} = \dfrac{r}{h} \Rightarrow 5r = 2h$ or

$r = \dfrac{2h}{5}.$

$V_{\text{cone}} = \dfrac{1}{3}\pi \left(\dfrac{2h}{5}\right)^2 h = \dfrac{4\pi}{75}h^3;$

$\dfrac{dV}{dt} = \dfrac{4\pi}{75}(3)h^2 \dfrac{dh}{dt}.$

Substitute known values:

$-15 = \dfrac{4\pi}{25}(5)^2 \dfrac{dh}{dt};$

$-15 = 4\pi \dfrac{dh}{dt}; \dfrac{dh}{dt} = \dfrac{-15}{4\pi} \approx -1.19$ ft/min.

The water level in the cone is falling at $\dfrac{-15}{4\pi}$ ft/min ≈ -1.19 ft/ min when the water level is 5 feet high.

$V_{\text{cylinder}} = \pi R^2 H = \pi(6)^2 H = 36\pi H.$

$\dfrac{dV}{dt} = 36\pi \dfrac{dH}{dt}; \dfrac{dH}{dt} = \dfrac{1}{36\pi}\dfrac{dV}{dt}; \dfrac{dH}{dt}$

$= \dfrac{1}{36\pi}(15) = \dfrac{5}{12\pi}$ ft/min

≈ 0.1326 ft/min or 1.592 in/min.

The water level in the cylinder is rising at $\dfrac{5}{12\pi}$ ft/min $= 0.133$ ft/min.

17. Step 1: Let x be the distance of the foot of the ladder from the higher wall. Let y be the height of the point where the ladder touches the higher wall. The slope of the ladder is $m = \dfrac{y-6}{0-8}$ or $m = \dfrac{6-0}{8-x}$.

Thus,

$\dfrac{y-6}{-8} = \dfrac{6}{8-x} \Rightarrow (y-6)(8-x)$

$= -48$

$\Rightarrow 8y - xy - 48 + 6x = -48$

$\Rightarrow y(8-x) = -6x \Rightarrow y = \dfrac{-6x}{8-x}.$

Step 2: Phythagorean Theorem:

$l^2 = x^2 + y^2 = x^2 + \left(\dfrac{-6x}{8-x}\right)^2$

Since $l > 0$, $l = \sqrt{x^2 + \left(\dfrac{-6x}{8-x}\right)^2}$,

$x > 8.$

Step 3: Enter $y1 = $

$\sqrt{\{x{\wedge}2 + [(-6 * x)/(8-x)]{\wedge}2\}}.$

The graph of y_1 is continuous on the interval $x > 8$. Use the [*Minimum*] function of the calculator and obtain $x = 14.604$; $y = 19.731$. Thus, the minimum value of l is 19.731, or the shortest ladder is approximately 19.731 feet.

18. Step 1: Average cost:

$\overline{C} = \dfrac{C}{x}$; thus, $\overline{C}(x)$

$= \dfrac{2500 + 0.02x + 0.004x^2}{x}$

$= \dfrac{2500}{x} + 0.02 + .004x.$

Step 2: Enter: $y1 = \dfrac{2500}{x} + .02 + .004 * x$

Step 3: Use the [*Minimum*] function in the calculator and obtain $x = 790.6$.

Step 4: Verify the result with the First Derivative Test. Enter $y2 = d(2500/x + .02 + .004x, x)$. Use the [*Zero*] function and obtain $x = 790.6$. Thus, $\dfrac{d\overline{C}}{dx} = 0$, at $x = 790.6$.
Apply the First Derivative Test:

Thus, the minimum average cost per unit occurs at $x = 790.6$. (The graph of the average cost function is shown in Figure 8.6-10.)

Figure 8.6-10

19. (See Figure 8.6-11.)

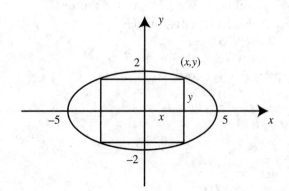

Figure 8.6-11

Step 1: Area $A = (2x)(2y); 0 \le x \le 5$ and $0 \le y \le 2$.

Step 2: $4x^2 + 25y^2 = 100$; $25y^2 = 100 - 4x^2$.

$$y^2 = \frac{100 - 4x^2}{25} \Rightarrow y = \pm\sqrt{\frac{100 - 4x^2}{25}}$$

Since $y \ge 0$,

$$y = \sqrt{\frac{100 - 4x^2}{25}} = \frac{\sqrt{100 - 4x^2}}{5}.$$

Step 3: $A = (2x)\left(\dfrac{2}{5}\right)\left(\sqrt{100 - 4x^2}\right)$

$$= \frac{4x}{5}\sqrt{100 - 4x^2}$$

Step 4: Enter $y1 = \dfrac{4x}{5}\sqrt{100 - 4x^2}$.
Use the [*Maximum*] function and obtain $x = 3.536$ and $y_1 = 20$.

Step 5: Verify the result with the First Derivative Test.
Enter

$$y2 = d\left(\frac{4x}{5}\sqrt{100 - 4x^2}, x\right).$$

Use the [*Zero*] function and obtain $x = 3.536$.
Note that:

The function f has only one relative extremum. Thus, it is the absolute extremum. Therefore, at $x = 3.536$, the area is 20 and the area is the absolute maxima.

20. (See Figure 8.6-12.)

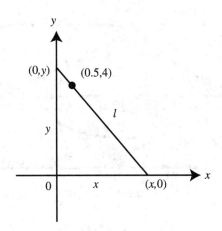

Figure 8.6-12

Step 1: Distance formula:
$l^2 = x^2 + y^2$; $x > 0.5$ and $y > 4$.

Step 2: The slope of the hypotenuse:
$$m = \frac{y-4}{0-0.5} = \frac{-4}{x-0.5}$$

$$\Rightarrow (y-4)(x-0.5) = 2$$

$$\Rightarrow xy - 0.5y - 4x + 2 = 2$$

$$y(x-0.5) = 4x$$

$$y = \frac{4x}{x-0.5}.$$

Step 3: $l^2 = x^2 + \left(\dfrac{4x}{x-0.5}\right)^2$;

$$l = \pm\sqrt{x^2 + \left(\frac{4x}{x-0.5}\right)^2}$$

Since $l > 0$, $l = \sqrt{x^2 + \left(\dfrac{4x}{x-0.5}\right)^2}$.

Step 4: Enter $y1 = \sqrt{x^2 + \left(\dfrac{4x}{x-0.5}\right)^2}$
and use the [*Minimum*] function of the calculator and obtain $x = 2.5$.

Step 5: Apply the First Derivative Test. Enter $y2 = d(y1(x), x)$ and use the [*Zero*] function and obtain $x = 2.5$.
Note that:

Since f has only one relative extremum, it is the absolute extremum.

Step 6: Thus, at $x = 2.5$, the length of the hypotenuse is the shortest. At $x = 2.5$, $y = \dfrac{4(2.5)}{2.5 - 0.5} = 5$. The vertices of the triangle are $(0, 0)$, $(2.5, 0)$, and $(0, 5)$.

8.7 Solutions to Cumulative Review Problems

21. Rewrite: $y = [\sin(\cos(6x - 1))]^2$
Thus, $\dfrac{dy}{dx} = 2 [\sin(\cos(6x - 1))]$

$\times [\cos(\cos(6x - 1))]$

$\times [-\sin(6x - 1)] (6)$

$= -12 \sin(6x - 1)$

$\times [\sin(\cos(6x - 1))]$

$\times [\cos(\cos(6x - 1))]$.

22. As $x \to \infty$, the numerator $\dfrac{100}{x}$ approaches 0 and the denominator increases without bound (i.e., ∞).

Thus, the $\displaystyle\lim_{x\to\infty} \dfrac{100/x}{-4 + x + x^2} = 0$.

23. (a) Summarize the information of f' on a number line.

Since f has only one relative extremum, it is the absolute extremum. Thus, at $x = 3$, it is an absolute minimum.

(b) The function f is decreasing on the interval $(-\infty, 3)$ and increasing on $(3, \infty)$.

(c)

No change of concavity $\Rightarrow$ No point of inflection.

(d) The function f is concave upward for the entire domain $(-\infty, \infty)$.

(e) Possible sketch of the graph for $f(x)$. (See Figure 8.7-1.)

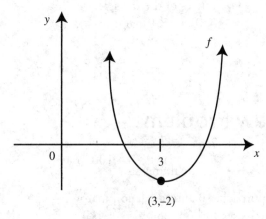

Figure 8.7-1

24. (Calculator) (See Figure 8.7-2.)

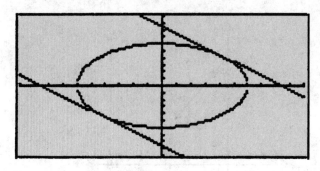

Figure 8.7-2

Step 1: Differentiate:
$$2x + 2y\frac{dy}{dx} = 0 \Rightarrow \frac{dy}{dx} = -\frac{x}{y}.$$

Step 2: Set $\frac{dy}{dx} = -1 \Rightarrow \frac{-x}{y} = -1 \Rightarrow$ $y = x$.

Step 3: Solve for y : $x^2 + y^2 = 36 \Rightarrow$ $y^2 = 36 - x^2$; $y = \pm\sqrt{36 - x^2}$.

Step 4: Thus, $y = x \Rightarrow \pm\sqrt{36 - x^2} = x \Rightarrow 36 - x^2 = x^2 \Rightarrow$ $36 = 2x^2$ or $x = \pm 3\sqrt{2}$.

25. (Calculator) (See Figure 8.7-3.)

Step 1: Distance formula:
$$z = \sqrt{(x - 1)^2 + (x^3)^2} = \sqrt{(x - 1)^2 + x^6}.$$

Figure 8.7-3

Step 2: Enter: $y1 = \sqrt{((x-1)^{\wedge}2 + x^{\wedge}6)}$.
Use the [*Minimum*] function of
the calculator and obtain
$x = .65052$ and $y1 = .44488$.
Verify the result with the First
Derivative Test. Enter
$y2 = d(y1(x), x)$ and use the
[*Zero*] function and obtain
$x = .65052$.

Thus, the shortest distance is
approximately 0.445.

CHAPTER 9

Big Idea 2: Derivatives
More Applications of Derivatives

IN THIS CHAPTER

Summary: Finding an equation of a tangent is one of the most common questions on the AP Calculus BC exam. In this chapter, you will learn how to use derivatives to find an equation of a tangent, and to use the tangent line to approximate the value of a function at a specific point. You will also learn to find derivatives of parametric, polar, and vector functions, and to apply derivatives to solve rectilinear motion problems.

Key Ideas

✪ Tangent and Normal Lines
✪ Linear Approximations
✪ Motion Along a Line
✪ Parametric, Polar, and Vector Derivatives

9.1 Tangent and Normal Lines

Main Concepts: Tangent Lines, Normal Lines

Tangent Lines
If the function y is differentiable at $x = a$, then the slope of the tangent line to the graph of y at $x = a$ is given as $m_{(\text{tangent at } x = a)} = \left. \dfrac{dy}{dx} \right|_{x=a}$.

Types of Tangent Lines

Horizontal Tangents: $\left(\dfrac{dy}{dx} = 0\right)$. (See Figure 9.1-1.)

Figure 9.1-1

Vertical Tangents: $\left(\dfrac{dy}{dx} \text{ does not exist, but } \dfrac{dx}{dy} = 0\right)$. (See Figure 9.1-2.)

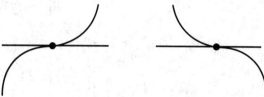

Figure 9.1-2

Parallel Tangents: $\left(\dfrac{dy}{dx}\bigg|_{x=a} = \dfrac{dy}{dx}\bigg|_{x=c}\right)$. (See Figure 9.1-3.)

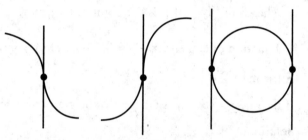

Figure 9.1-3

Example 1

Write an equation of the line tangent to the graph of $y = -3 \sin 2x$ at $x = \dfrac{\pi}{2}$. (See Figure 9.1-4.)

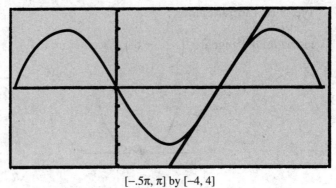

[$-.5\pi$, π] by [-4, 4]

Figure 9.1-4

$y = -3 \sin 2x$; $\dfrac{dy}{dx} = -3[\cos(2x)]2 = -6 \cos(2x)$

Slope of tangent at $\left(x = \dfrac{\pi}{2} \right)$: $\left. \dfrac{dy}{dx} \right|_{x=\pi/2} = -6 \cos [2(\pi/2)] = -6 \cos \pi = 6.$

Point of tangency at $x = \dfrac{\pi}{2}$, $y = -3 \sin(2x)$

$$= -3 \sin[2(\pi/2)] = -3 \sin(\pi) = 0.$$

Therefore, $\left(\dfrac{\pi}{2}, 0 \right)$ is the point of tangency.

Equation of tangent: $y - 0 = 6(x - \pi/2)$ or $y = 6x - 3\pi$.

Example 2

If the line $y = 6x + a$ is tangent to the graph of $y = 2x^3$, find the value(s) of a.

Solution:

$y = 2x^3$; $\dfrac{dy}{dx} = 6x^2$. (See Figure 9.1-5.)

[-2, 2] by [-6, 6]

Figure 9.1-5

The slope of the line $y = 6x + a$ is 6.

Since $y = 6x + a$ is tangent to the graph of $y = 2x^3$, thus $\dfrac{dy}{dx} = 6$ for some values of x.

Set $6x^2 = 6 \Rightarrow x^2 = 1$ or $x = \pm 1$.

At $x = -1$, $y = 2x^3 = 2(-1)^3 = -2$; $(-1, -2)$ is a tangent point. Thus, $y = 6x + a \Rightarrow$ $-2 = 6(-1) + a$ or $a = 4$.

At $x = 1$, $y = 2x^3 = 2(1)^3 = 2$; $(1, 2)$ is a tangent point. Thus, $y = 6x + a \Rightarrow 2 = 6(1) + a$ or $a = -4$.

Therefore, $a = \pm 4$.

Example 3

Find the coordinates of each point on the graph of $y^2 - x^2 - 6x + 7 = 0$ at which the tangent line is vertical. Write an equation of each vertical tangent. (See Figure 9.1-6.)

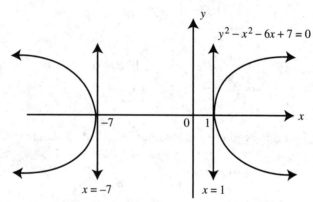

Figure 9.1-6

Step 1: Find $\dfrac{dy}{dx}$.

$$y^2 - x^2 - 6x + 7 = 0$$

$$2y\frac{dy}{dx} - 2x - 6 = 0$$

$$\frac{dy}{dx} = \frac{2x + 6}{2y} = \frac{x + 3}{y}$$

Step 2: Find $\dfrac{dx}{dy}$.

Vertical tangent $\Rightarrow \dfrac{dx}{dy} = 0$.

$$\frac{dx}{dy} = \frac{1}{dy/dx} = \frac{1}{(x + 3)/y} = \frac{y}{x + 3}$$

Set $\dfrac{dx}{dy} = 0 \Rightarrow y = 0$.

Step 3: Find points of tangency.

At $y = 0$, $y^2 - x^2 - 6x + 7 = 0$ becomes $-x^2 - 6x + 7 = 0 \Rightarrow x^2 + 6x - 7 = 0$
$\Rightarrow (x + 7)(x - 1) = 0 \Rightarrow x = -7$ or $x = 1$.

Thus, the points of tangency are $(-7, 0)$ and $(1, 0)$.

Step 4: Write equation for vertical tangents.

$x = -7$ and $x = 1$.

Example 4

Find all points on the graph of $y = |xe^x|$ at which the graph has a horizontal tangent.

Step 1: Find $\dfrac{dy}{dx}$.

$$y = |xe^x| = \begin{cases} xe^x & \text{if } x \geq 0 \\ -xe^x & \text{if } x < 0 \end{cases}$$

$$\frac{dy}{dx} = \begin{cases} e^x + xe^x & \text{if } x \geq 0 \\ -e^x - xe^x & \text{if } x < 0 \end{cases}$$

Step 2: Find the x-coordinate of points of tangency.

Horizontal tangent $\Rightarrow \dfrac{dy}{dx} = 0$.

If $x \geq 0$, set $e^x + xe^x = 0 \Rightarrow e^x(1 + x) = 0 \Rightarrow x = -1$ but $x \geq 0$, therefore, no solution.

If $x < 0$, set $-e^x - xe^x = 0 \Rightarrow -e^x(1 + x) = 0 \Rightarrow x = -1$.

Step 3: Find points of tangency.

At $x = -1$, $y = -xe^x = -(-1)e^{-1} = \dfrac{1}{e}$.

Thus at the point $(-1, 1/e)$, the graph has a horizontal tangent. (See Figure 9.1-7.)

[−3, 1] by [−0.5, 1.25]

Figure 9.1-7

Example 5

Using your calculator, find the value(s) of x to the nearest hundredth at which the slope of the line tangent to the graph of $y = 2 \ln (x^2 + 3)$ is equal to $-\dfrac{1}{2}$. (See Figures 9.1-8 and 9.1-9.)

[−5, 5] by [−1, 7]

Figure 9.1-8

y=-.499737x+4.41587

[−10, 3] by [−1, 10]

Figure 9.1-9

Step 1: Enter $y1 = 2 * \ln (x\char94 2 + 3)$.

Step 2: Enter $y2 = d(y_1(x), x)$ and enter $y_3 = -\dfrac{1}{2}$.

Step 3: Using the [*Intersection*] function of the calculator for y_2 and y_3, you obtain $x = -7.61$ or $x = -0.39$.

Example 6

Using your calculator, find the value(s) of x at which the graphs of $y = 2x^2$ and $y = e^x$ have parallel tangents.

Step 1: Find $\dfrac{dy}{dx}$ for both $y = 2x^2$ and $y = e^x$.

$$y = 2x^2; \frac{dy}{dx} = 4x$$

$$y = e^x; \frac{dy}{dx} = e^x$$

Step 2: Find the x-coordinate of the points of tangency. Parallel tangents $\Rightarrow$ slopes are equal.
Set $4x = e^x \Rightarrow 4x - e^x = 0$.
Using the [*Solve*] function of the calculator, enter [*Solve*] $(4x - e(x) = 0,\ x)$ and obtain $x = 2.15$ and $x = 0.36$.

- Watch out for different units of measure, e.g., the radius, r, is 2 feet, find $\dfrac{dr}{dt}$ in inches per second.

Normal Lines

The normal line to the graph of f at the point (x_1, y_1) is the line perpendicular to the tangent line at (x_1, y_1). (See Figure 9.1-10.)

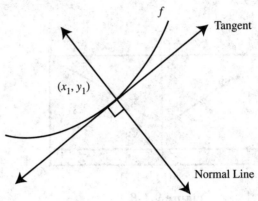

Figure 9.1-10

Note that the slope of the normal line and the slope of the tangent line at any point on the curve are negative reciprocals, provided that both slopes exist.

$$(m_{\text{normal line}})(m_{\text{tangent line}}) = -1.$$

Special Cases:
(See Figure 9.1-11.)
At these points, $m_{\text{tangent}} = 0$; but m_{normal} does not exist.

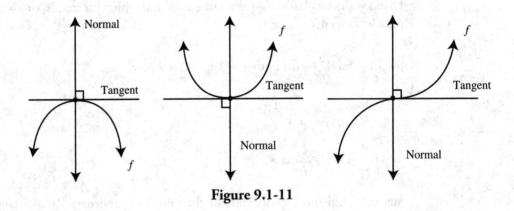

Figure 9.1-11

(See Figure 9.1-12.)
At these points, m_{tangent} does not exist; however $m_{\text{normal}} = 0$.

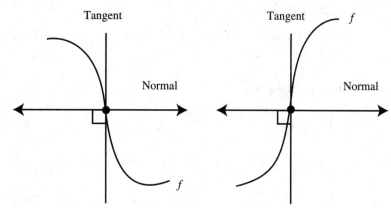

Figure 9.1-12

Example 1

Write an equation for each normal to the graph of $y = 2 \sin x$ for $0 \leq x \leq 2\pi$ that has a slope of $\frac{1}{2}$.

Step 1: Find m_{tangent}.

$$y = 2 \sin x; \quad \frac{dy}{dx} = 2 \cos x$$

Step 2: Find m_{normal}.

$$m_{\text{normal}} = -\frac{1}{m_{\text{tangent}}} = -\frac{1}{2 \cos x}$$

Set $m_{\text{normal}} = \frac{1}{2} \Rightarrow -\frac{1}{2 \cos x} = \frac{1}{2} \Rightarrow \cos x = -1$

$\Rightarrow x = \cos^{-1}(-1)$ or $x = \pi$. (See Figure 9.1-13.)

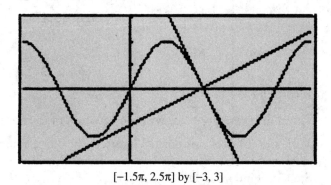

[-1.5π, 2.5π] by [-3, 3]

Figure 9.1-13

Step 3: Write equation of normal line.

At $x = \pi$, $y = 2 \sin x = 2(0) = 0$; $(\pi, 0)$.

Since $m = \frac{1}{2}$, equation of normal is:

$$y - 0 = \frac{1}{2}(x - \pi) \text{ or } y = \frac{1}{2}x - \frac{\pi}{2}.$$

Example 2

Find the point on the graph of $y = \ln x$ such that the normal line at this point is parallel to the line $y = -ex - 1$.

Step 1: Find $m_{tangent}$.

$$y = \ln x; \frac{dy}{dx} = \frac{1}{x}$$

Step 2: Find m_{normal}.

$$m_{normal} = \frac{-1}{m_{tangent}} = \frac{-1}{1/x} = -x$$

Slope of $y = -ex - 1$ is $-e$.
Since normal is parallel to the line $y = -ex - 1$, set $m_{normal} = -e \Rightarrow -x = -e$ or $x = e$.

Step 3: Find point on graph. At $x = e$, $y = \ln x = \ln e = l$. Thus the point of the graph of $y = \ln x$ at which the normal is parallel to $y = -ex - 1$ is $(e, 1)$. (See Figure 9.1-14.)

[−6.8, 9.8] by [−5, 3]

Figure 9.1-14

Example 3

Given the curve $y = \frac{1}{x}$: (a) write an equation of the normal to the curve $y = \frac{1}{x}$ at the point $(2, 1/2)$, and (b) does this normal intersect the curve at any other point? If yes, find the point.

Step 1: Find $m_{tangent}$.

$$y = \frac{1}{x}; \frac{dy}{dx} = (-1)(x^{-2}) = -\frac{1}{x^2}$$

Step 2: Find m_{normal}.

$$m_{normal} = \frac{-1}{m_{tangent}} = \frac{-1}{-1/x^2} = x^2$$

At $(2, 1/2)$, $m_{normal} = 2^2 = 4$.

Step 3: Write equation of normal.

$m_{\text{normal}} = 4; \ (2, 1/2)$

Equation of normal: $y - \dfrac{1}{2} = 4(x - 2)$, or $y = 4x - \dfrac{15}{2}$.

Step 4: Find other points of intersection.

$$y = \frac{1}{x}; \ y = 4x - \frac{15}{2}$$

Using the [*Intersection*] function of your calculator, enter $y1 = \dfrac{1}{x}$ and $y2 = 4x - \dfrac{15}{2}$ and obtain $x = -0.125$ and $y = -8$. Thus, the normal line intersects the graph of $y = \dfrac{1}{x}$ at the point $(-0.125, -8)$ as well.

• Remember that $\displaystyle\int 1 \, dx = x + C$ and $\dfrac{d}{dx}(1) = 0$.

9.2 Linear Approximations

Main Concepts: Tangent Line Approximation, Estimating the *n*th Root of a Number, Estimating the Value of a Trigonometric Function of an Angle

Tangent Line Approximation (or Linear Approximation)

An equation of the tangent line to a curve at the point $(a, f(a))$ is:
$y = f(a) + f'(a)(x - a)$, providing that f is differentiable at a. (See Figure 9.2-1.)
Since the curve of $f(x)$ and the tangent line are close to each other for points near $x = a$,
$f(x) \approx f(a) + f'(a)(x - a)$.

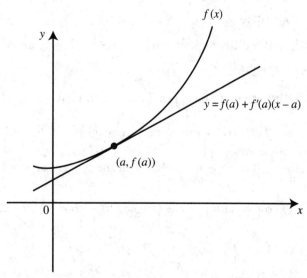

Figure 9.2-1

Example 1

Write an equation of the tangent line to $f(x) = x^3$ at $(2, 8)$. Use the tangent line to find the approximate values of $f(1.9)$ and $f(2.01)$.

Differentiate $f(x)$: $f'(x) = 3x^2$; $f'(2) = 3(2)^2 = 12$. Since f is differentiable at $x = 2$, an equation of the tangent at $x = 2$ is:

$$y = f(2) + f'(2)(x - 2)$$

$$y = (2)^3 + 12(x - 2) = 8 + 12x - 24 = 12x - 16$$

$$f(1.9) \approx 12(1.9) - 16 = 6.8$$

$$f(2.01) \approx 12(2.01) - 16 = 8.12. \text{ (See Figure 9.2-2.)}$$

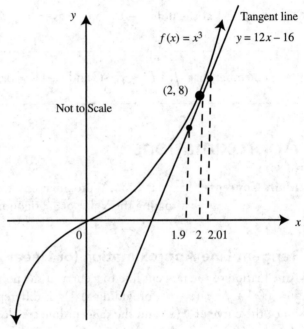

Figure 9.2-2

Example 2

If f is a differentiable function and $f(2) = 6$ and $f'(2) = -\dfrac{1}{2}$, find the approximate value of $f(2.1)$.

Using tangent line approximation, you have

(a) $f(2) = 6 \Rightarrow$ the point of tangency is $(2, 6)$;

(b) $f'(2) = -\dfrac{1}{2} \Rightarrow$ the slope of the tangent at $x = 2$ is $m = -\dfrac{1}{2}$;

(c) the equation of the tangent is $y - 6 = -\dfrac{1}{2}(x - 2)$ or $y = -\dfrac{1}{2}x + 7$;

(d) thus, $f(2.1) \approx -\dfrac{1}{2}(2.1) + 7 \approx 5.95$.

Example 3

The slope of a function at any point (x, y) is $-\dfrac{x+1}{y}$. The point $(3, 2)$ is on the graph of f. (a) Write an equation of the line tangent to the graph of f at $x = 3$. (b) Use the tangent line in part (a) to approximate $f(3.1)$.

(a) Let $y = f(x)$, then $\dfrac{dy}{dx} = -\dfrac{x+1}{y}$

$\left.\dfrac{dy}{dx}\right|_{x=3,\ y=2} = -\dfrac{3+1}{2} = -2.$

Equation of tangent: $y - 2 = -2(x - 3)$ or $y = -2x + 8$.

(b) $f(3.1) \approx -2(3.1) + 8 \approx 1.8$

Estimating the *n*th Root of a Number

Another way of expressing the tangent line approximation is:
$f(a + \Delta x) \approx f(a) + f'(a)\Delta x$, where Δx is a relatively small value.

Example 1

Find the approximation value of $\sqrt{50}$ using linear approximation.

Using $f(a + \Delta x) \approx f(a) + f'(a)\Delta x$, let $f(x) = \sqrt{x}$; $a = 49$ and $\Delta x = 1$.

Thus, $f(49 + 1) \approx f(49) + f'(49)(1) \approx \sqrt{49} + \dfrac{1}{2}(49)^{-1/2}(1) \approx 7 + \dfrac{1}{14} \approx 7.0714$.

Example 2

Find the approximate value of $\sqrt[3]{62}$ using linear approximation. Is the approximation an over- or underestimate of the actual value of the function?

Let $f(x) = x^{1/3}$, $a = 64$, $\Delta x = -2$. Since $f'(x) = \dfrac{1}{3}x^{-2/3} = \dfrac{1}{3x^{2/3}}$ and

$f'(64) = \dfrac{1}{3(64)^{2/3}} = \dfrac{1}{48}$, you can use $f(a + \Delta x) \approx f(a) + f'(a)\Delta x$. Thus, $f(62) =$

$f(64 - 2) \approx f(64) + f'(64)(-2) \approx 4 + \dfrac{1}{48}(-2) \approx 3.958$.

It can be determined if the tangent approximation is an over- or underestimate of the actual value based on the sign of $f''(x)$ (or the concavity of the function $f(x)$). Since $f''(x) = -\dfrac{2}{9}x^{-5/3}$ and $f''(64) = -\dfrac{2}{9}(64)^{-5/3} < 0$ ($f(x)$ is concave down), this approximation is an overestimate of the actual value.

- Use calculus notations and not calculator syntax, e.g., write $\displaystyle\int x^2 dx$ and not $\displaystyle\int (x^\wedge 2,\ x)$.

Estimating the Value of a Trigonometric Function of an Angle
Example

Approximate the value of $\sin 31°$.

Note: You must express the angle measurement in radians before applying linear approximations. $30° = \dfrac{\pi}{6}$ radians and $1° = \dfrac{\pi}{180}$ radians.

Let $f(x) = \sin x$, $a = \dfrac{\pi}{6}$ and $\Delta x = \dfrac{\pi}{180}$.

Since $f'(x) = \cos x$ and $f'\left(\dfrac{\pi}{6}\right) = \cos\left(\dfrac{\pi}{6}\right) = \dfrac{\sqrt{3}}{2}$, you can use linear approximations:

$$f\left(\frac{\pi}{6} + \frac{\pi}{180}\right) \approx f\left(\frac{\pi}{6}\right) + f'\left(\frac{\pi}{6}\right)\left(\frac{\pi}{180}\right)$$

$$\approx \sin\frac{\pi}{6} + \left[\cos\left(\frac{\pi}{6}\right)\right]\left(\frac{\pi}{180}\right)$$

$$\approx \frac{1}{2} + \frac{\sqrt{3}}{2}\left(\frac{\pi}{180}\right) = 0.515.$$

9.3 Motion Along a Line

Main Concepts: Instantaneous Velocity and Acceleration, Vertical Motion, Horizontal Motion

Instantaneous Velocity and Acceleration

Position Function: $s(t)$

Instantaneous Velocity: $v(t) = s'(t) = \dfrac{ds}{dt}$

If particle is moving to the right $\rightarrow$, then $v(t) > 0$.
If particle is moving to the left $\leftarrow$, then $v(t) < 0$.

Acceleration: $a(t) = v'(t) = \dfrac{dv}{dt}$ or $a(t) = s''(t) = \dfrac{d^2s}{dt^2}$

Instantaneous speed: $|v(t)|$

Example 1

The position function of a particle moving on a straight line is $s(t) = 2t^3 - 10t^2 + 5$. Find (a) the position, (b) instantaneous velocity, (c) acceleration, and (d) speed of the particle at $t = 1$.

Solution:

(a) $s(1) = 2(1)^3 - 10(1)^2 + 5 = -3$

(b) $v(t) = s'(t) = 6t^2 - 20t$

     $v(1) = 6(1)^2 - 20(1) = -14$

(c) $a(t) = v'(t) = 12t - 20$

     $a(1) = 12(1) - 20 = -8$

(d)   Speed $= |v(t)| = |v(1)| = 14$.

Example 2

The velocity function of a moving particle is $v(t) = \dfrac{t^3}{3} - 4t^2 + 16t - 64$ for $0 \le t \le 7$.

What is the minimum and maximum acceleration of the particle on $0 \le t \le 7$?

$$v(t) = \frac{t^3}{3} - 4t^2 + 16t - 64$$

$$a(t) = v'(t) = t^2 - 8t + 16$$

(See Figure 9.3-1.) The graph of $a(t)$ indicates that:

[−1, 7] by [−2.20]

Figure 9.3-1

(1) The minimum acceleration occurs at $t = 4$ and $a(4) = 0$.
(2) The maximum acceleration occurs at $t = 0$ and $a(0) = 16$.

Algebraically, $a'(t) = 2t - 8 = 2(t - 4) = 0$ when $t = 4$. Test this critical point and the end points to find $a(0) = 16$, $a(4) = 0$, and $a(7) = 9$. This confirms that the minimum occurs at $t = 4$ and the maximum at $t = 0$.

Example 3

The graph of the velocity function is shown in Figure 9.3-2.

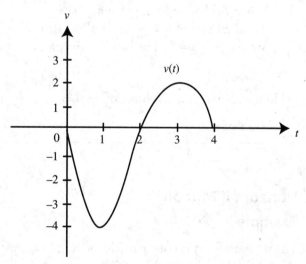

Figure 9.3-2

(a) When is the acceleration 0?
(b) When is the particle moving to the right?
(c) When is the speed the greatest?

Solution:

(a) $a(t) = v'(t)$ and $v'(t)$ is the slope of tangent to the graph of v. At $t = 1$ and $t = 3$, the slope of the tangent is 0.
(b) For $2 < t < 4$, $v(t) > 0$. Thus the particle is moving to the right during $2 < t < 4$.
(c) Speed $=|v(t)|$ at $t = 1$, $v(t) = -4$.
Thus, speed at $t = 1$ is $|-4| = 4$, which is the greatest speed for $0 \le t \le 4$.

• Use only the four specified capabilities of your calculator to get your answer: plotting graphs, finding zeros, calculating numerical derivatives, and evaluating definite integrals. All other built-in capabilities can only be used to *check* your solution.

Vertical Motion
Example

From a 400-foot tower, a bowling ball is dropped. The position function of the bowling ball $s(t) = -16t^2 + 400$, $t \ge 0$ is in seconds. Find:

(a) the instantaneous velocity of the ball at $t = 2$ seconds.
(b) the average velocity for the first 3 seconds.
(c) when the ball will hit the ground.

Solution:

(a) $v(t) = s'(t) = -32t$
$v(2) = 32(2) = -64$ ft/second
(b) Average velocity $= \dfrac{s(3) - s(0)}{3 - 0} = \dfrac{(-16(3)^2 + 400) - (0 + 400)}{3} = -48$ ft/second.
(c) When the ball hits the ground, $s(t) = 0$.
Thus, set $s(t) = 0 \Rightarrow -16t^2 + 400 = 0$; $16t^2 = 400$; $t = \pm 5$.
Since $t \ge 0$, $t = 5$. The ball hits the ground at $t = 5$ seconds.

• Remember that the volume of a sphere is $v = \dfrac{4}{3}\pi r^3$ and the surface area is $s = 4\pi r^2$.

Note that $v' = s$.

Horizontal Motion
Example

The position function of a particle moving in a straight line is $s(t) = t^3 - 6t^2 + 9t - 1$, $t \ge 0$. Describe the motion of the particle.

Step 1: Find $v(t)$ and $a(t)$.
$v(t) = 3t^2 - 12t + 9$

$a(t) = 6t - 12$

Step 2: Set $v(t)$ and $a(t) = 0$.

Set $v(t) = 0 \Rightarrow 3t^2 - 12t + 9 = 0 \Rightarrow 3(t^2 - 4t + 3) = 0$

$\Rightarrow 3(t - 1)(t - 3) = 0$ or $t = 1$ or $t = 3$.

Set $a(t) = 0 \Rightarrow 6t - 12 = 0 \Rightarrow 6(t - 2) = 0$ or $t = 2$.

Step 3: Determine the directions of motion. (See Figure 9.3-3.)

Figure 9.3-3

Step 4: Determine acceleration. (See Figure 9.3-4.)

Figure 9.3-4

Step 5: Draw the motion of the particle. (See Figure 9.3-5.)
$s(0) = -1$, $s(1) = 3$, $s(2) = 1$, and $s(3) = -1$

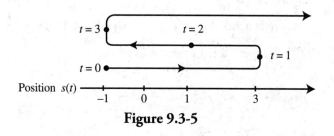

Figure 9.3-5

At $t = 0$, the particle is at -1 and moving to the right. It slows down and stops at $t = 1$ and at $t = 3$. It reverses direction (moving to the left) and speeds up until it reaches 1 at $t = 2$. It continues moving left but slows down and stops at -1 at $t = 3$. Then it reverses direction (moving to the right) again and speeds up indefinitely. (Note that "speeding up" is defined as when $|v(t)|$ increases; that is, $v(t)$ and $a(t)$ have the same sign. "Slowing down" is defined as when $|v(t)|$ decreases; that is, $v(t)$ and $a(t)$ have opposite signs.)

9.4 Parametric, Polar, and Vector Derivatives

Main Concepts: Derivatives of Parametric Equations; Position, Speed, and Acceleration; Derivatives of Polar Equations; Velocity and Acceleration of Vector Functions

Derivatives of Parametric Equations

If a function is defined parametrically, you can differentiate both $x(t)$ and $y(t)$ with respect to t, and then $\dfrac{dy}{dx} = \dfrac{dy}{dt} \div \dfrac{dx}{dt} = \dfrac{dy}{dt} \cdot \dfrac{dt}{dx}$.

Example 1

A curve is defined by $x(t) = t^2 - 3t$ and $y(t) = 5 \cos t$. Find $\dfrac{dy}{dx}$.

Step 1: Differentiate $x(t)$ and $y(t)$ with respect to t. $\dfrac{dx}{dt} = 2t - 3$ and $\dfrac{dy}{dt} = -5 \sin t$.

Step 2: $\dfrac{dy}{dx} = \dfrac{dy}{dt} \cdot \dfrac{dt}{dx} = \dfrac{-5 \sin t}{2t - 3}$

Example 2

A function is defined by $x(t) = 5t - 2$ and $y(t) = 9 - t^2$ when $-5 \le t \le 5$. Find the equation of any horizontal tangent lines to the curve.

Step 1: Differentiate $x(t)$ and $y(t)$ with respect to t. $\dfrac{dx}{dt} = 5$ and $\dfrac{dy}{dt} = -2t$.

Step 2: $\dfrac{dy}{dx} = \dfrac{dy}{dt} \cdot \dfrac{dt}{dx} = \dfrac{-2t}{5}$

Step 3: In order for the tangent line to be horizontal, $\dfrac{dy}{dx}$ must be equal to zero, therefore $t = 0$, $x = -2$, and $y = 9$.

Step 4: The equation of the horizontal tangent line at $(-2, 9)$ is $y = 9$.

Example 3

A curve is defined by $x(t) = t^2 - 5t + 2$ and $y(t) = \dfrac{1}{(t+2)^2}$ for $0 \le t \le 3$. Find the equation of the tangent line to the curve when $t = 1$.

Step 1: $\dfrac{dx}{dt} = 2t - 5$ and $\dfrac{dy}{dt} = \dfrac{-2}{(t+2)^3}$.

Step 2: $\dfrac{dy}{dx} = \dfrac{-2}{(t+2)^3} \cdot \dfrac{1}{(2t-5)}$

Step 3: At $t = 1$, $m = \dfrac{-2}{(3)^3} \cdot \dfrac{1}{(-3)} = \dfrac{2}{81}$, $x = 1 - 5 + 2 = -2$, and $y = \dfrac{1}{(3)^2} = \dfrac{1}{9}$.

Step 4: The equation of the tangent line is $y - \dfrac{1}{9} = \dfrac{2}{81}(x + 2)$ or $y = \dfrac{2}{81}x + \dfrac{13}{81}$.

Position, Speed, and Acceleration

When the motion of a particle is defined parametrically, its position is given by $(x(t), y(t))$.

The speed of the particle is $\sqrt{\left(\dfrac{dx}{dt}\right)^2 + \left(\dfrac{dy}{dt}\right)^2}$ and its acceleration is given by the vector $\left\langle \dfrac{d^2x}{dt^2}, \dfrac{d^2y}{dt^2} \right\rangle$.

Example 1

Find the speed and acceleration of a particle whose motion is defined by $x = 3t$ and $y = 9t - 3t^2$ when $t = 2$.

Step 1: Differentiate $\dfrac{dx}{dt} = 3$ and $\dfrac{dy}{dt} = 9 - 6t$. When $t = 2$, $\dfrac{dx}{dt} = 3$ and $\dfrac{dy}{dt} = -3$.

Step 2: Calculate the speed. $\sqrt{(3)^2 + (-3)^2} = \sqrt{18} = 3\sqrt{2}$

Step 3: Determine second derivatives. $\dfrac{d^2x}{dt^2} = 0$ and $\dfrac{d^2y}{dt^2} = -6$. The acceleration vector is $\langle 0, -6 \rangle$.

Example 2

A particle moves along the curve $y = \dfrac{1}{2}x^2 - \dfrac{1}{4}\ln x$ so that $x = \dfrac{1}{2}t^2$ and $t > 0$. Find the speed of the particle when $t = 1$.

Step 1: Substitute $x = \dfrac{1}{2}t^2$ in $y = \dfrac{1}{2}x^2 - \dfrac{1}{4}\ln x$ to find

$$y(t) = \frac{1}{2}\left(\frac{1}{2}t^2\right)^2 - \frac{1}{4}\ln\left(\frac{1}{2}t^2\right) = \frac{1}{8}t^4 - \frac{1}{4}\ln\left(\frac{1}{2}t^2\right)$$

$$= \frac{1}{8}t^4 - \frac{1}{4}(-\ln 2 + 2\ln t)$$

$$= \frac{t^4}{8} + \frac{\ln 2}{4} - \frac{\ln t}{2}.$$

Step 2: $\dfrac{dx}{dt} = t$ and $\dfrac{dy}{dt} = \dfrac{t^3}{2} - \dfrac{1}{2t}$. Evaluated at $t = 1$, $\dfrac{dx}{dt} = 1$ and $\dfrac{dy}{dt} = 0$.

Step 3: The speed of the particle is $\sqrt{(1)^2 + (0)^2} = 1$.

Derivatives of Polar Equations

For polar representations, remember that $r = f(\theta)$, so $x = r\cos\theta = f(\theta)\cos\theta$ and $y = r\sin\theta = f(\theta)\sin\theta$. Differentiating with respect to θ requires the product rule. $\dfrac{dx}{d\theta} = -r\sin\theta + \cos\theta\dfrac{dr}{d\theta}$ and $\dfrac{dy}{d\theta} = r\cos\theta + \sin\theta\dfrac{dr}{d\theta}$. Dividing $\dfrac{dy}{d\theta}$ by $\dfrac{dx}{d\theta}$ gives $\dfrac{dy}{dx} = \dfrac{r\cos\theta + \sin\theta\, dr/d\theta}{-r\sin\theta + \cos\theta\, dr/d\theta}$.

Example

Find the equation of the tangent line to the curve $r = 2 + 2\sin\theta$ when $\theta = \dfrac{\pi}{4}$.

Step 1: $\dfrac{dr}{d\theta} = 2\cos\theta$

Step 2:

$$\frac{dx}{d\theta} = -(2 + 2\sin\theta)\sin\theta + \cos\theta(2\cos\theta) = 2(\cos^2\theta - \sin^2\theta - \sin\theta)$$

By the Pythagorean identity,

$$2(\cos^2\theta - \sin^2\theta - \sin\theta) = 2(1 - \sin^2\theta - \sin^2\theta - \sin\theta)$$

$$= 2(1 - \sin\theta - 2\sin^2\theta) = 2(1 - 2\sin\theta)(1 + \sin\theta).$$

Also, $\dfrac{dy}{d\theta} = (2 + 2\sin\theta)\cos\theta + \sin\theta(2\cos\theta) = 2\cos\theta(1 + 2\sin\theta).$

Step 3: $\dfrac{dy}{dx} = \dfrac{2\cos\theta(1 + 2\sin\theta)}{2(1 - 2\sin\theta)(1 + \sin\theta)} = \dfrac{\cos\theta(1 + 2\sin\theta)}{(1 - 2\sin\theta)(1 + \sin\theta)}$

Step 4: When $\theta = \dfrac{\pi}{4}$, $\dfrac{dy}{dx} = \dfrac{\cos\dfrac{\pi}{4}\left(1 + 2\sin\dfrac{\pi}{4}\right)}{\left(1 - 2\sin\dfrac{\pi}{4}\right)\left(1 + \sin\dfrac{\pi}{4}\right)}.$

Evaluating, $\dfrac{dy}{dx} = \dfrac{\dfrac{\sqrt{2}}{2}(1 + \sqrt{2})}{(1 - \sqrt{2})\left(1 + \dfrac{\sqrt{2}}{2}\right)} = -1 - \sqrt{2}.$

Step 5: When $\theta = \dfrac{\pi}{4}$, $r = 2 + \sqrt{2}$, so $x = r\cos\theta = \left(2 + \sqrt{2}\right)\dfrac{\sqrt{2}}{2} = \sqrt{2} + 1$ and

$y = r\sin\theta = \left(2 + \sqrt{2}\right)\dfrac{\sqrt{2}}{2} = \sqrt{2} + 1.$

Step 6: The equation of the tangent line is $y - \left(\sqrt{2} + 1\right) = \left(-1 - \sqrt{2}\right)\left(x - \left(\sqrt{2} + 1\right)\right)$ or $y = \left(-1 - \sqrt{2}\right)x + 4 + 3\sqrt{2}.$

Velocity and Acceleration of Vector Functions

A vector-valued function assigns a vector to each element in a domain of real numbers. If $r = \langle x, y \rangle$ is a vector-valued function, $\lim r$ exists only if $\lim_{t \to c} x(t)$ and $\lim_{t \to c} y(t)$ exist. $\lim_{t \to c} r = \left\langle \lim_{t \to c} x(t), \lim_{t \to c} y(t) \right\rangle = \lim_{t \to c} x(t)i + \lim_{t \to c} y(t)j$. A vector-valued function is continuous at c if its component functions are continuous at c. The derivative of a vector-valued function is $\dfrac{dr}{dt} = \left\langle \dfrac{dx}{dt}, \dfrac{dy}{dt} \right\rangle = i\dfrac{dx}{dt} + j\dfrac{dy}{dt}.$

If $r = \langle x, y \rangle$ is a vector-valued function that represents the path of an object in the plane, and x and y are both functions of a variable t, $x = f(t)$ and $y = g(t)$, then the velocity of the object is $v = \dfrac{dr}{dt} = i\dfrac{dx}{dt} + j\dfrac{dy}{dt} = \left\langle \dfrac{dx}{dt}, \dfrac{dy}{dt} \right\rangle$. Speed is the magnitude of velocity, so $|v| = \sqrt{\left(\dfrac{dx}{dt}\right)^2 + \left(\dfrac{dy}{dt}\right)^2}$. The direction of v is along the tangent to the path. The acceleration vector is $\left\langle \dfrac{d^2x}{dt^2}, \dfrac{d^2y}{dt^2} \right\rangle$ and the magnitude of acceleration is

$|a| = \sqrt{\left(\dfrac{d^2x}{dt^2}\right)^2 + \left(\dfrac{d^2y}{dt^2}\right)^2}$. The vector T tangent to the path at t is $T(t) = \dfrac{r'(t)}{\|r'(t)\|}$ and

the normal vector at t is $N(t) = \dfrac{T'(t)}{\|T'(t)\|}$.

Example 1

The position function $r = \langle t^3, t^2 \rangle = t^3 i + t^2 j$ describes the path of an object moving in the plane. Find the velocity and acceleration of the object at the point $(8, 4)$.

Step 1: The velocity $v = \left\langle \dfrac{dx}{dt}, \dfrac{dy}{dt} \right\rangle = \langle 3t^2, 2t \rangle$. At the point $(8, 4)$, $t = 2$. Evaluated at
$t = 2$, the velocity $v = \langle 12, 4 \rangle$. The speed $|v| = \sqrt{144 + 16} \approx 12.649$.

Step 2: The acceleration vector $\left\langle \dfrac{d^2x}{dt^2}, \dfrac{d^2y}{dt^2} \right\rangle = \langle 6t, 2 \rangle$. Evaluated at $t = 2$, the acceleration
is $\langle 12, 2 \rangle$. The magnitude of the acceleration is $|a| = \sqrt{144 + 4} \approx 12.166$.

Example 2

The left field fence in Boston's Fenway Park, nicknamed the Green Monster, is 37 feet high and 310 feet from home plate. If a ball is hit 3 feet above the ground and leaves the bat at an angle of $\dfrac{\pi}{4}$, write a vector-valued function for the path of the ball and use the function to determine the minimum speed at which the ball must leave the bat to be a home run. At that speed, what is the maximum height the ball attains?

Step 1: The horizontal component of the ball's motion, the motion in the "x" direc-
tion, is $x = s \cdot \cos \dfrac{\pi}{4} \cdot t = \dfrac{s\sqrt{2}}{2} t$. The vertical component follows the parabolic
motion model $y = 3 + s \cdot \sin \dfrac{\pi}{4} t - \dfrac{1}{2} g t^2$, where g is the acceleration due to
gravity. The path of the ball can be represented by the vector-valued function
$r = \left\langle \dfrac{s \cdot \sqrt{2}}{2} t, 3 + \dfrac{s \cdot \sqrt{2}}{2} t - 16t^2 \right\rangle$.

Step 2: In order for the ball to clear the fence, its height must be greater than 37 feet when
its distance from the plate is 310 feet. $\dfrac{s \cdot \sqrt{2}}{2} t = 310$, solved for t, gives $t = \dfrac{620}{s \cdot \sqrt{2}}$
seconds. At this time, $3 + \dfrac{s \cdot \sqrt{2}}{2} t - 16t^2 = 3 + \dfrac{s\sqrt{2}}{2}\left(\dfrac{620}{s\sqrt{2}}\right) - 16\left(\dfrac{620}{s\sqrt{2}}\right)^2$, and

this value must exceed 37 feet. Setting $3 + \dfrac{s \cdot \sqrt{2}}{2}\left(\dfrac{620}{s \cdot \sqrt{2}}\right) - 16\left(\dfrac{620}{s \cdot \sqrt{2}}\right)^2 = 37$

and solving gives $s \approx 105.556$. The ball must leave the bat at 105.556 feet per second in order to clear the wall.

Step 3: Since $r = \left\langle \dfrac{s \cdot \sqrt{2}}{2}t, 3 + \dfrac{s \cdot \sqrt{2}}{2}t - 16t^2 \right\rangle$, the derivative is $r' = \left\langle \dfrac{s \cdot \sqrt{2}}{2}, 3 + \dfrac{s \cdot \sqrt{2}}{2} - 32t \right\rangle$, and the ball will attain its maximum height when the vertical component $3 + \dfrac{s \cdot \sqrt{2}}{2} - 32t$ is equal to zero. Since $s \approx 105.556$, $3 + \dfrac{105.556 \cdot \sqrt{2}}{2} - 32t = 0$ produces $t \approx 2.462$ seconds. For that value of t, $r = \left\langle \dfrac{105.556\sqrt{2}}{2}(2.462), 3 + \dfrac{105.556\sqrt{2}}{2}(2.462) - 16(2.462)^2 \right\rangle \approx$ $\langle 183.762, 89.779 \rangle$. The ball will reach a maximum height of 89.779 feet, when it is 183.762 feet from home plate.

Example 3

Find the velocity, acceleration, tangent, and normal vectors for an object on a path defined by the vector-valued function $r(t) = \left\langle e^t \cos t, e^t \sin t \right\rangle$ when $t = \dfrac{\pi}{2}$.

Step 1: $v(t) = r'(t) = \left\langle e^t(\cos t - \sin t), e^t(\sin t + \cos t) \right\rangle$. When evaluated at $t = \dfrac{\pi}{2}$, $v\left(\dfrac{\pi}{2}\right) = \left\langle -e^{\pi/2}, e^{\pi/2} \right\rangle \approx \langle -4.810, 4.810 \rangle$. The velocity vector is $\langle -4.810, 4.810 \rangle$.

Step 2: $a(t) = \left\langle -2e^t \sin t, 2e^t \cos t \right\rangle$. Evaluated at $t = \dfrac{\pi}{2}$, this is $a\left(\dfrac{\pi}{2}\right) = \left\langle -2e^{\pi/2}, 0 \right\rangle \approx \langle -9.621, 0 \rangle$.

Step 3: The tangent vector is given by $T(t) = \dfrac{r'(t)}{\|r'(t)\|}$. Since $r'(t) = \left\langle -e^t \sin t + e^t \cos t, e^t \sin t + e^t \cos t \right\rangle$, the tangent vector becomes $T(t) = \dfrac{\left\langle -e^t \sin t + e^t \cos t, e^t \sin t + e^t \cos t \right\rangle}{\sqrt{(-e^t \sin t + e^t \cos t)^2 + (e^t \sin t + e^t \cos t)^2}}$, which simplifies to $T(t) = \left\langle \dfrac{\cos t - \sin t}{\sqrt{2}}, \dfrac{\sin t + \cos t}{\sqrt{2}} \right\rangle$. When $t = \dfrac{\pi}{2}$, the tangent vector is $\left\langle \dfrac{-1}{\sqrt{2}}, \dfrac{1}{\sqrt{2}} \right\rangle = \left\langle \dfrac{-\sqrt{2}}{2}, \dfrac{\sqrt{2}}{2} \right\rangle$.

Step 4: The normal vector $N(t) = \dfrac{T'(t)}{\|T'(t)\|} = \dfrac{\left\langle \dfrac{\cos t - \sin t}{\sqrt{2}}, \dfrac{\sin t + \cos t}{\sqrt{2}} \right\rangle'}{\left\| \left\langle \dfrac{\cos t - \sin t}{\sqrt{2}}, \dfrac{\sin t + \cos t}{\sqrt{2}} \right\rangle' \right\|} = \left\langle \dfrac{-\cos t - \sin t}{\sqrt{2}}, \dfrac{\cos t - \sin t}{\sqrt{2}} \right\rangle$. At $t = \dfrac{\pi}{2}$, $N(t) = \left\langle \dfrac{-1}{\sqrt{2}}, \dfrac{1}{\sqrt{2}} \right\rangle = \left\langle \dfrac{-\sqrt{2}}{2}, \dfrac{\sqrt{2}}{2} \right\rangle$. Check $T\left(\dfrac{\pi}{2}\right) \cdot N\left(\dfrac{\pi}{2}\right) = \dfrac{-\sqrt{2}}{2} \cdot \dfrac{-\sqrt{2}}{2} + \dfrac{\sqrt{2}}{2} \cdot \dfrac{-\sqrt{2}}{2} = \dfrac{1}{2} - \dfrac{1}{2} = 0$ to be certain the tangent and normal vectors are orthogonal.

9.5 Rapid Review

1. Write an equation of the normal line to the graph $y = e^x$ at $x = 0$.

   Answer: $\left.\dfrac{dy}{dx}\right|_{x=0}$ $e^x = e^x\big|_{x=0} = e^0 = 1 \Rightarrow m_{\text{normal}} = -1$

   At $x = 0$, $y = e^0 = 1 \Rightarrow$ you have the point $(0, 1)$.
   Equation of normal: $y - 1 = -1(x - 0)$ or $y = -x + 1$.

2. Using your calculator, find the values of x at which the function $y = -x^2 + 3x$ and $y = \ln x$ have parallel tangents.

   Answer: $y = -x^2 + 3x \Rightarrow \dfrac{dy}{dx} = -2x + 3$

   $y = \ln x \Rightarrow \dfrac{dy}{dx} = \dfrac{1}{x}$

   Set $-2x + 3 = \dfrac{1}{x}$. Using the [*Solve*] function on your calculator, enter

   $[Solve]\left(-2x + 3 = \dfrac{1}{x}, x\right)$ and obtain $x = 1$ or $x = \dfrac{1}{2}$.

3. Find the linear approximation of $f(x) = x^3$ at $x = 1$ and use the equation to find $f(1.1)$.
   Answer: $f(1) = 1 \Rightarrow (1, 1)$ is on the tangent line and $f'(x) = 3x^2 \Rightarrow f'(1) = 3$.
   $y - 1 = 3(x - 1)$ or $y = 3x - 2$.
   $f(1.1) \approx 3(1.1) - 2 \approx 1.3$

4. (See Figure 9.5-1.)
   (a) When is the acceleration zero? (b) Is the particle moving to the right or left?

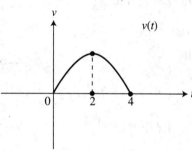

   Figure 9.5-1

   Answer: (a) $a(t) = v'(t)$ and $v'(t)$ is the slope of the tangent. Thus, $a(t) = 0$ at $t = 2$.
   (b) Since $v(t) \geq 0$, the particle is moving to the right.

5. Find the maximum acceleration of the particle whose velocity function is $v(t) = t^2 + 3$ on the interval $0 \leq t \leq 4$.
   Answer: $a(t) = v'(t) = 2(t)$ on the interval $0 \leq t \leq 4$, $a(t)$ has its maximum value at $t = 4$. Thus $a(t) = 8$. The maximum acceleration is 8.

6. Find the slope of the tangent to the curve defined by $x = 3t - 5$, $y = t^2 - 9$ when $t = 3$.

   Answer: $\dfrac{dx}{dt} = 3$ and $\dfrac{dy}{dt} = 2t\big|_{t=3} = 6$, so $\dfrac{dy}{dx} = \dfrac{dy}{dt} \div \dfrac{dx}{dt} = \dfrac{6}{3} = 2$.

7. Find the slope of the tangent line to the graph of $r = -3 \cos\theta$.

   Answer: $\dfrac{dr}{d\theta} = 3 \sin\theta$. Since $x = r\cos\theta$, $\dfrac{dx}{d\theta} = -r\sin\theta + \cos\theta\dfrac{dr}{d\theta} = 3\cos\theta\sin\theta$

   $+ 3\cos\theta\sin\theta = 6\sin\theta\cos\theta = 3\sin 2\theta$. Since $y = r\sin\theta$, $\dfrac{dy}{d\theta} = r\cos\theta$

   $+ \sin\theta\dfrac{dr}{d\theta} = -3\cos^2\theta + 3\sin^2\theta = -3(\cos^2\theta - \sin^2\theta) = -3\cos 2\theta$.

   $\dfrac{dy}{dx} = \dfrac{dy}{d\theta} \cdot \dfrac{d\theta}{dx} = \dfrac{-3\cos 2\theta}{3\sin 2\theta} = -\cot 2\theta$

8. Find $\dfrac{dr}{dt}$ for the vector function $r(t) = 3ti - 2tj = \langle 3t, -2t\rangle$.

   Answer: $\dfrac{dx}{dt} = 3$ and $\dfrac{dy}{dt} = -2$, so $\dfrac{dr}{dt} = \langle 3, -2\rangle$.

9.6 Practice Problems

Part A—The use of a calculator is not allowed.

1. Find the linear approximation of $f(x) = (1 + x)^{1/4}$ at $x = 0$ and use the equation to approximate $f(0.1)$.

2. Find the approximate value of $\sqrt[3]{28}$ using linear approximation.

3. Find the approximate value of $\cos 46°$ using linear approximation.

4. Find the point on the graph of $y = \left|x^3\right|$ such that the tangent at the point is parallel to the line $y - 12x = 3$.

5. Write an equation of the normal to the graph of $y = e^x$ at $x = \ln 2$.

6. If the line $y - 2x = b$ is tangent to the graph $y = -x^2 + 4$, find the value of b.

7. If the position function of a particle is $s(t) = \dfrac{t^3}{3} - 3t^2 + 4$, find the velocity and position of particle when its acceleration is 0.

8. The graph in Figure 9.6-1 represents the distance in feet covered by a moving particle in t seconds. Draw a sketch of the corresponding velocity function.

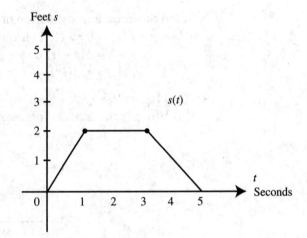

Figure 9.6-1

9. The position function of a moving particle is shown in Figure 9.6-2.

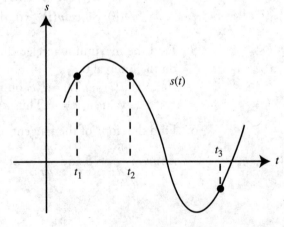

Figure 9.6-2

For which value(s) of t (t_1, t_2, t_3) is:

(a) the particle moving to the left?

(b) the acceleration negative?

(c) the particle moving to the right and slowing down?

10. The velocity function of a particle is shown in Figure 9.6-3.

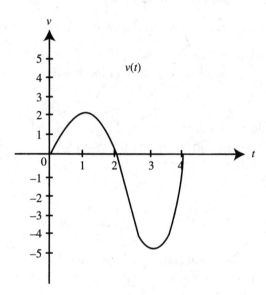

Figure 9.6-3

(a) When does the particle reverse direction?

(b) When is the acceleration 0?

(c) When is the speed the greatest?

11. A ball is dropped from the top of a 640-foot building. The position function of the ball is $s(t) = -16t^2 + 640$, where t is measured in seconds and $s(t)$ is in feet. Find:

(a) The position of the ball after 4 seconds.

(b) The instantaneous velocity of the ball at $t = 4$.

(c) The average velocity for the first 4 seconds.

(d) When the ball will hit the ground.

(e) The speed of the ball when it hits the ground.

12. The graph of the position function of a moving particle is shown in Figure 9.6-4.

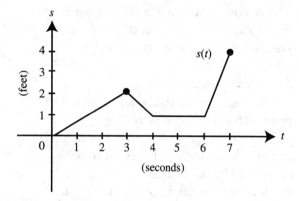

Figure 9.6-4

(a) What is the particle's position at $t = 5$?

(b) When is the particle moving to the left?

(c) When is the particle standing still?

(d) When does the particle have the greatest speed?

Part B—Calculators are allowed.

13. The position function of a particle moving on a line is $s(t) = t^3 - 3t^2 + 1$, $t \geq 0$, where t is measured in seconds and s in meters. Describe the motion of the particle.

14. Find the linear approximation of $f(x) = \sin x$ at $x = \pi$. Use the equation to find the approximate value of $f\left(\dfrac{181\pi}{180}\right)$.

15. Find the linear approximation of $f(x) = \ln(1 + x)$ at $x = 2$.

16. Find the coordinates of each point on the graph of $y^2 = 4 - 4x^2$ at which the tangent line is vertical. Write an equation of each vertical tangent.

17. Find the value(s) of x at which the graphs of $y = \ln x$ and $y = x^2 + 3$ have parallel tangents.

18. The position functions of two moving particles are $s_1(t) = \ln t$ and $s_2(t) = \sin t$ and the domain of both functions is $1 \leq t \leq 8$. Find the values of t such that the velocities of the two particles are the same.

19. The position function of a moving particle on a line is $s(t) = \sin(t)$ for $0 \le t \le 2\pi$. Describe the motion of the particle.

20. A coin is dropped from the top of a tower and hits the ground 10.2 seconds later. The position function is given as $s(t) = -16t^2 - v_0 t + s_0$, where s is measured in feet, t in seconds, and v_0 is the initial velocity and s_0 is the initial position. Find the approximate height of the building to the nearest foot.

21. Find the equation of the tangent line to the curve defined by $x = \cos t - 1$, $y = \sin t + t$ at the point where $x = \dfrac{-1}{2}$.

22. An object moves on a path defined by $x = e^{2t} + t$ and $y = 1 + e^t$. Find the speed of the object and its acceleration vector with $t = 2$.

23. Find the slope of the tangent line to the curve $r = 3 \sin 4\theta$ at $\theta = \dfrac{5\pi}{6}$.

24. The position of an object is given by $\left\langle 30t,\ 25 \sin \dfrac{t}{3} \right\rangle$. Find the velocity and acceleration vectors, and determine when the magnitude of the acceleration is equal to 2.

25. Find the tangent vector to the path defined by $r = \left\langle \ln t,\ \ln(t + 4) \right\rangle$ at the point where $t = 4$.

9.7 Cumulative Review Problems

(Calculator) indicates that calculators are permitted.

26. Find $\dfrac{dy}{dx}$ if $y = x \sin^{-1}(2x)$.

27. Given $f(x) = x^3 - 3x^2 + 3x - 1$ and the point $(1, 2)$ is on the graph of $f^{-1}(x)$. Find the slope of the tangent line to the graph of $f^{-1}(x)$ at $(1, 2)$.

28. Evaluate $\lim\limits_{x \to 100} \dfrac{x - 100}{\sqrt{x} - 10}$.

29. A function f is continuous on the interval $(-1, 8)$ with $f(0) = 0$, $f(2) = 3$, and $f(8) = 1/2$ and has the following properties:

(a) Find the intervals on which f is increasing or decreasing.
(b) Find where f has its absolute extrema.
(c) Find where f has the points of inflection.
(d) Find the intervals on which f is concave upward or downward.
(e) Sketch a possible graph of f.

30. The graph of the velocity function of a moving particle for $0 \le t \le 8$ is shown in Figure 9.7-1. Using the graph:

(a) Estimate the acceleration when $v(t) = 3$ ft/s.
(b) Find the time when the acceleration is a minimum.

INTERVALS	(−1, 2)	x = 2	(2, 5)	x = 5	(5, 8)
f'	+	0	−	−	−
f''	−	−	−	0	+

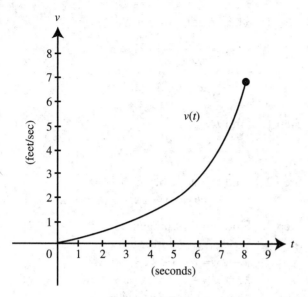

Figure 9.7-1

31. Find the Cartesian equation for the curve defined by $r = 4\cos\theta$.

32. The motion of an object is modeled by $x = 5\sin t$, $y = 1 - \cos t$. Find the y-coordinate of the object at the moment when its x-coordinate is 5.

33. Calculate $4u - 3v$ if $u = \langle 6, -1 \rangle$ and $v = \langle -4, 3 \rangle$.

34. Determine the symmetry, if any, of the graph of $r = 2\sin(4\theta)$.

35. Find the magnitude of the vector $3i + 4j$.

9.8 Solutions to Practice Problems

Part A—The use of a calculator is not allowed.

1. Equation of tangent line:

   $y = f(a) + f'(a)(x - a)$

   $f'(x) = \dfrac{1}{4}(1 + x)^{-3/4}(1) = \dfrac{1}{4}(1 + x)^{-3/4}$

   $f'(0) = \dfrac{1}{4}$ and $f(0) = 1$;

   thus, $y = 1 + \dfrac{1}{4}(x - 0) = 1 + \dfrac{1}{4}x$.

   $f(0.1) = 1 + \dfrac{1}{4}(0.1) = 1.025$

2. $f(a + \Delta x) \approx f(a) + f'(a)\Delta x$

   Let $f(x) = \sqrt[3]{x}$ and $f(28) = f(27 + 1)$.

   Then $f'(x) = \dfrac{1}{3}(x)^{-2/3}$,

   $f'(27) = \dfrac{1}{27}$, and $f(27) = 3$.

   $f(27 + 1) \approx f(27) + f'(27)(1) \approx$

   $3 + \left(\dfrac{1}{27}\right)(1) \approx 3.\overline{037}$

3. $f(a + \Delta x) \approx f(a) + f'(a)\Delta x$

   Convert to radians:

   $\dfrac{46}{180} = \dfrac{a}{\pi} \Rightarrow a = \dfrac{23\pi}{90}$ and $1° = \dfrac{\pi}{180}$;

   $45° = \dfrac{\pi}{4}$.

   Let $f(x) = \cos x$ and $f(45°) =$

   $f\left(\dfrac{\pi}{4}\right) = \cos\left(\dfrac{\pi}{4}\right) = \dfrac{\sqrt{2}}{2}$.

   Then $f'(x) = -\sin x$ and

   $f'(45°) = f'\left(\dfrac{\pi}{4}\right) = -\dfrac{\sqrt{2}}{2}$

   $f(46°) = f\left(\dfrac{23\pi}{90}\right) = f\left(\dfrac{\pi}{4} + \dfrac{\pi}{180}\right)$

   $f\left(\dfrac{\pi}{4} + \dfrac{\pi}{180}\right) \approx f\left(\dfrac{\pi}{4}\right) +$

   $f'\left(\dfrac{\pi}{4}\right)\left(\dfrac{\pi}{180}\right) \approx \dfrac{\sqrt{2}}{2} - \left(\dfrac{\sqrt{2}}{2}\right)\left(\dfrac{\pi}{180}\right)$

   $\approx \dfrac{\sqrt{2}}{2} - \dfrac{\pi\sqrt{2}}{360}$

4. Step 1: Find m_{tangent}.

$$y = |x^3| = \begin{cases} x^3 & \text{if } x \geq 0 \\ -x^3 & \text{if } x < 0 \end{cases}$$

$$\frac{dy}{dx} = \begin{cases} 3x^2 & \text{if } x > 0 \\ -3x^2 & \text{if } x < 0 \end{cases}$$

Step 2: Set m_{tangent} = slope of line $y - 12x = 3$.
Since $y - 12x = 3 \Rightarrow y = 12x + 3$, then $m = 12$.
Set $3x^2 = 12 \Rightarrow x = \pm 2$ since $x \geq 0, x = 2$.
Set $-3x^2 = 12 \Rightarrow x^2 = -4$. Thus $\varnothing$.

Step 3: Find the point on the curve. (See Figure 9.8-1.)

$$y = 12.x - 16.$$

[−3, 4] by [−5, 15]

Figure 9.8-1

At $x = 2$, $y = x^3 = 2^3 = 8$.
Thus, the point is (2, 8).

5. Step 1: Find m_{tangent}.

$$y = e^x; \frac{dy}{dx} = e^x$$

$$\left.\frac{dy}{dx}\right|_{x=\ln 2} = e^{\ln 2} = 2$$

Step 2: Find m_{normal}.
At $x = \ln 2$, $m_{\text{normal}} = \dfrac{-1}{m_{\text{tangent}}} = -\dfrac{1}{2}$.

Step 3: Write equation of normal.
At $x = \ln 2$, $y = e^x = e^{\ln 2} = 2$. Thus the point of tangency is (ln 2, 2).

The equation of normal:

$$y - 2 = -\frac{1}{2}(x - \ln 2) \text{ or }$$

$$y = -\frac{1}{2}(x - \ln 2) + 2.$$

6. Step 1: Find m_{tangent}.

$$y = -x^2 + 4; \frac{dy}{dx} = -2x.$$

Step 2: Find the slope of line $y - 2x = b$
$y - 2x = b \Rightarrow y = 2x + b$ or $m = 2$.

Step 3: Find point of tangency.
Set m_{tangent} = slope of line
$y - 2x = b \Rightarrow -2x = 2 \Rightarrow x = -1$.
At $x = -1$, $y = -x^2 + 4 = -(-1)^2 + 4 = 3$; (−1, 3).

Step 4: Find b.
Since the line $y - 2x = b$ passes through the point (−1, 3), thus $3 - 2(-1) = b$ or $b = 5$.

7. $v(t) = s'(t) = t^2 - 6t$;
$a(t) = v'(t) = s''(t) = 2t - 6$
Set $a(t) = 0 \Rightarrow 2t - 6 = 0$ or $t = 3$.
$v(3) = (3)^2 - 6(3) = -9$;
$s(3) = \dfrac{(3)^3}{3} - 3(3)^2 + 4 = -14$.

8. On the interval (0, 1), the slope of the line segment is 2. Thus the velocity $v(t) = 2$ ft/s. On (1, 3), $v(t) = 0$ and on (3, 5), $v(t) = -1$. (See Figure 9.8-2.)

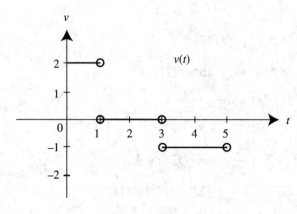

Figure 9.8-2

9. (a) At $t = t_2$, the slope of the tangent is negative. Thus, the particle is moving to the left.

   (b) At $t = t_1$, and at $t = t_2$, the curve is concave downward $\Rightarrow \dfrac{d^2s}{dt^2} =$ acceleration is negative.

   (c) At $t = t_1$, the slope > 0 and thus the particle is moving to the right. The curve is concave downward $\Rightarrow$ the particle is slowing down.

10. (a) At $t = 2$, $v(t)$ changes from positive to negative, and thus the particle reverses its direction.

    (b) At $t = 1$, and at $t = 3$, the slope of the tangent to the curve is 0. Thus, the acceleration is 0.

    (c) At $t = 3$, speed is equal to $|-5| = 5$ and 5 is the greatest speed.

11. (a) $s(4) = -16(4)^2 + 640 = 384$ ft

    (b) $v(t) = s'(t) = -32t$
        $v(4) = -32(4)$ ft/s $= -128$ ft/s

    (c) Average Velocity $= \dfrac{s(4) - s(0)}{4 - 0}$
        $= \dfrac{384 - 640}{4} = -64$ ft/s.

    (d) Set $s(t) = 0 \Rightarrow -16t^2 + 640 = 0 \Rightarrow$
        $16t^2 = 640$ or $t = \pm 2\sqrt{10}$.
        Since $t \geq 0$, $t = +2\sqrt{10}$ or $t \approx 6.32$ s.

    (e) $|v(2\sqrt{10})| = |-32(2\sqrt{10})| =$
        $|-64\sqrt{10}|$ ft/s or ≈ 202.39 ft/s

12. (a) At $t = 5$, $s(t) = 1$.

    (b) For $3 < t < 4$, $s(t)$ decreases. Thus, the particle moves to the left when $3 < t < 4$.

    (c) When $4 < t < 6$, the particle stays at 1.

    (d) When $6 < t < 7$, speed $= 2$ ft/s, the greatest speed, which occurs where s has the greatest slope.

Part B—Calculators are allowed.

13. Step 1: $v(t) = 3t^2 - 6t$
             $a(t) = 6t - 6$

    Step 2: Set $v(t) = 0 \Rightarrow 3t^2 - 6t = 0 \Rightarrow$
             $3t(t - 2) = 0$, or $t = 0$ or $t = 2$
             Set $a(t) = 0 \Rightarrow 6t - 6 = 0$ or $t = 1$.

    Step 3: Determine the directions of motion. (See Figure 9.8-3.)

Figure 9.8-3

    Step 4: Determine acceleration. (See Figure 9.8-4.)

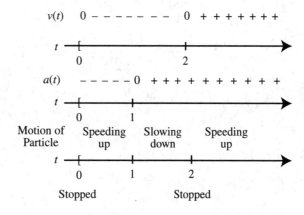

Figure 9.8-4

    Step 5: Draw the motion of the particle. (See Figure 9.8-5.) $s(0) = 1$, $s(1) = -1$, and $s(2) = -3$.

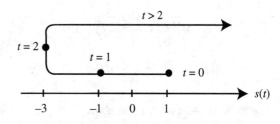

Figure 9.8-5

The particle is initially at 1 ($t = 0$). It moves to the left speeding up until $t = 1$, when it reaches −1. Then it continues moving to the left, but slowing down until $t = 2$ at −3. The particle reverses direction, moving to the right and speeding up indefinitely.

14. Linear approximation:
$y = f(a) + f'(a)(x - a)$ $a = \pi$
$f(x) = \sin x$ and $f(\pi) = \sin \pi = 0$
$f'(x) = \cos x$ and $f'(\pi) = \cos \pi = -1$.
Thus, $y = 0 + (-1)(x - \pi)$ or
$y = -x + \pi$.
$f\left(\dfrac{181\pi}{180}\right)$ is approximately:

$y = -\left(\dfrac{181\pi}{180}\right) + \pi = \dfrac{-\pi}{180}$ or $\approx$

-0.0175.

15. $y = f(a) + f'(a)(x - a)$
$f(x) = \ln(1 + x)$ and
$f(2) = \ln(1 + 2) = \ln 3$

$f'(x) = \dfrac{1}{1 + x}$ and $f'(2) = \dfrac{1}{1 + 2} = \dfrac{1}{3}$.

Thus, $y = \ln 3 + \dfrac{1}{3}(x - 2)$.

16. Step 1: Find $\dfrac{dy}{dx}$.

$y^2 = 4 - 4x^2$

$2y\dfrac{dy}{dx} = -8x \Rightarrow \dfrac{dy}{dx} = \dfrac{-4x}{y}$

Step 2: Find $\dfrac{dx}{dy}$.

$\dfrac{dx}{dy} = \dfrac{1}{dy/dx} = \dfrac{1}{-4x/y} = \dfrac{-y}{4x}$

Set $\dfrac{dx}{dy} = 0 \Rightarrow \dfrac{-y}{4x} = 0$ or $y = 0$.

Step 3: Find points of tangency.
At $y = 0$, $y^2 = 4 - 4x^2$ becomes
$0 = 4 - 4x^2$
$\Rightarrow x = \pm 1$.

Thus, points of tangency are
(1, 0) and (−1, 0).

Step 4: Write equations of vertical tangents $x = 1$ and $x = -1$.

17. Step 1: Find $\dfrac{dy}{dx}$ for $y = \ln x$ and $y = x^2 + 3$.

$y = \ln x$; $\dfrac{dy}{dx} = \dfrac{1}{x}$

$y = x^2 + 3$; $\dfrac{dy}{dx} = 2x$

Step 2: Find the x-coordinate of point(s) of tangency.
Parallel tangents $\Rightarrow$ slopes are equal. Set $\dfrac{1}{x} = 2x$.
Using the [Solve] function of your calculator, enter [Solve]
$\left(\dfrac{1}{x} = 2x, x\right)$ and obtain
$x = \dfrac{\sqrt{2}}{2}$ or $x = \dfrac{-\sqrt{2}}{2}$. Since for
$y = \ln x$, $x > 0$, $x = \dfrac{\sqrt{2}}{2}$.

18. $s_1(t) = \ln t$ and $s_1'(t) = \dfrac{1}{t}$; $1 \le t \le 8$.
$s_2(t) = \sin(t)$ and
$s_2'(t) = \cos(t)$; $1 \le t \le 8$.
Enter $y1 = \dfrac{1}{x}$ and $y2 = \cos(x)$. Use the [Intersection] function of the calculator and obtain $t = 4.917$ and $t = 7.724$.

19. Step 1: $s(t) = \sin t$
$v(t) = \cos t$
$a(t) = -\sin t$

Step 2: Set $v(t) = 0 \Rightarrow \cos t = 0$;
$t = \dfrac{\pi}{2}$ and $\dfrac{3\pi}{2}$.
Set $a(t) = 0 \Rightarrow -\sin t = 0$;
$t = \pi$ and 2π.

Step 3: Determine the directions of motion. (See Figure 9.8-6.)

Figure 9.8-6

Step 4: Determine acceleration. (See Figure 9.8-7.)

Figure 9.8-7

Step 5: Draw the motion of the particle. (See Figure 9.8-8.)

Figure 9.8-8

The particle is initially at 0, $s(0) = 0$. It moves to the right but slows down to a stop at 1 when $t = \dfrac{\pi}{2}$, $s\left(\dfrac{\pi}{2}\right) = 1$. It then turns and moves to the left speeding up until it reaches 0, when $t = \pi$, $s(\pi) = 0$ and continues to the left, but slowing down to a stop at -1 when $t = \dfrac{3\pi}{2}$, $s\left(\dfrac{3\pi}{2}\right) = -1$.

It then turns around again, moving to the right, speeding up to 0 when $t = 2\pi$, $s(2\pi) = 0$.

20. $s(t) = -16t^2 + v_0 t + s_0$
    s_0 = height of building and $v_0 = 0$.
    Thus, $s(t) = -16t^2 + s_0$.
    When the coin hits the ground, $s(t) = 0$,
    $t = 10.2$. Thus, set $s(t) = 0 \Rightarrow$
    $-16t^2 + s_0 = 0 \Rightarrow -16(10.2)^2 + s_0 = 0$
    $s_0 = 1664.64$ ft. The building is approximately 1665 ft tall.

21. When $x = \dfrac{-1}{2} = \cos t - 1$, $\cos t = \dfrac{1}{2}$,
    and $t = \dfrac{\pi}{3}$, and so $y = \sin\left(\dfrac{\pi}{3}\right) +$
    $\dfrac{\pi}{3} = \dfrac{\sqrt{3}}{2} + \dfrac{\pi}{3}$. Find $\dfrac{dx}{dt} = -\sin t$ and
    $\dfrac{dy}{dt} = \cos t + 1$, and divide to find
    $\dfrac{dy}{dx} = \dfrac{\cos t + 1}{-\sin t}$. Evaluate at $t = \dfrac{\pi}{3}$ to find
    the slope $m = \dfrac{\cos(\pi/3) + 1}{-\sin(\pi/3)}$
    $= \dfrac{3/2}{-\sqrt{3}/2} = -\sqrt{3}$. Therefore, the
    equation of the tangent line is
    $y - \left(\dfrac{\sqrt{3}}{2} + \dfrac{\pi}{3}\right) = -\sqrt{3}\left(x + \dfrac{1}{2}\right)$, or
    simplifying, $y = -\sqrt{3}x + \dfrac{\pi}{3}$.

22. Differentiate to find $\dfrac{dx}{dt} = 2e^{2t} + 1$ and
    $\dfrac{dy}{dt} = e^t$. The speed of the object is
    $\sqrt{(2e^{2t} + 1)^2 + (e^t)^2}$
    $= \sqrt{4e^{4t} + 5e^{2t} + 1}$. When $t = 2$,
    $\sqrt{4e^{4t} + 5e^{2t} + 1} \approx 110.444$. Find second
    derivatives $\dfrac{d^2x}{dt^2} = 4e^{2t}$ and $\dfrac{d^2y}{dt^2} = e^t$ and
    evaluate at $t = 2$ to find the acceleration
    vector $\langle 4e^{2t}, e^t \rangle \approx \langle 218.393, 7.389 \rangle$.

23. Since $x = r\cos\theta$ and $y = \sin\theta$,
    $\dfrac{dy}{dx} = \dfrac{dy}{d\theta} \div \dfrac{dx}{d\theta}$
    $= \dfrac{r\cos\theta + \sin\theta\,(dr/d\theta)}{-r\sin\theta + \cos\theta\,(dr/d\theta)}$.

Find $\dfrac{dr}{d\theta} = 12\cos 4\theta$ and substitute.

$$\frac{dy}{dx} = \frac{(3\sin 4\theta)\cos\theta + \sin\theta\,(12\cos 4\theta)}{-(3\sin 4\theta)\sin\theta + \cos\theta\,(12\cos 4\theta)}.$$

When $\theta = \dfrac{5\pi}{6}$, $4\theta = \dfrac{10\pi}{3} = \dfrac{4\pi}{3} + 2\pi$, so

the functions of $\dfrac{10\pi}{3}$ are equal to those of

$\dfrac{4\pi}{3}$. Evaluate $\dfrac{dy}{dx} =$

$$\frac{(3\sin(4\pi/3))\cos(5\pi/6) + \sin(5\pi/6)(12\cos(4\pi/3))}{-(3\sin(4\pi/3))\sin(5\pi/6) + \cos(5\pi/6)(12\cos(4\pi/3))}$$

at

$$= \frac{\left(3\left(-\sqrt{3}/2\right)\right)\left(-\sqrt{3}/2\right) + (1/2)(12(-1/2))}{-\left(3\left(-\sqrt{3}/2\right)\right)(1/2) + \left(-\sqrt{3}/2\right)(12(-1/2))}$$

$$= \frac{(9/4) - 3}{(3\sqrt{3}/4) + 3\sqrt{3}} = -\frac{\sqrt{3}}{15}.$$ The slope of

the tangent line is $\dfrac{-\sqrt{3}}{15}$.

24. If the position of the object is given by $\left\langle 30t,\ 25\sin\dfrac{t}{3}\right\rangle$, then the velocity vector

is $\left\langle \dfrac{dx}{dt}, \dfrac{dy}{dt}\right\rangle = \left\langle 30,\ \dfrac{25}{3}\cos\dfrac{t}{3}\right\rangle$, and

the acceleration vector is

$\left\langle \dfrac{d^2x}{dt^2}, \dfrac{d^2y}{dt^2}\right\rangle = \left\langle 0,\ \dfrac{-25}{9}\sin\dfrac{t}{3}\right\rangle$. The

magnitude of the acceleration is equal to

$\left|\dfrac{-25}{9}\sin\dfrac{t}{3}\right| = 2$ when $\sin\dfrac{t}{3} = \dfrac{18}{25}$. Solve to

find $t = 3\sin^{-1}\dfrac{18}{25} \approx 2.411$.

25. If $r = \langle \ln t,\ \ln(t+4)\rangle$, then
$\dfrac{dr}{dt} = \left\langle \dfrac{1}{t}, \dfrac{1}{t+4}\right\rangle$. Evaluate at $t = 4$ for
$\dfrac{dr}{dt} = \left\langle \dfrac{1}{4}, \dfrac{1}{8}\right\rangle$, then find

$\left\|\dfrac{dr}{dt}\right\| = \sqrt{\left(\dfrac{1}{t}\right)^2 + \left(\dfrac{1}{t+4}\right)^2}$, which, at

$t = 4$, is equal to

$\left\|\dfrac{dr}{dt}\right\| = \sqrt{\dfrac{1}{16} + \dfrac{1}{64}} = \dfrac{\sqrt{5}}{8}$. The tangent

vector is $T = \dfrac{\langle 1/t,\ 1/(t+4)\rangle}{\sqrt{5/8}}$

$= \left\langle \dfrac{8}{t\sqrt{5}}, \dfrac{8}{(t+4)\sqrt{5}}\right\rangle$. When $t = 4$,

$T = \left\langle \dfrac{2\sqrt{5}}{5}, \dfrac{\sqrt{5}}{5}\right\rangle$.

9.9 Solutions to Cumulative Review Problems

26. Using product rule, let $u = x$; $v = \sin^{-1}(2x)$.

$$\frac{dy}{dx} = (1)\sin^{-1}(2x) + \frac{1}{\sqrt{1-(2x)^2}}(2)(x)$$

$$= \sin^{-1}(2x) + \frac{2x}{\sqrt{1-4x^2}}$$

27. Let $y = f(x) \Rightarrow y = x^3 - 3x^2 + 3x - 1$. To find $f^{-1}(x)$, switch x and y: $x = y^3 - 3y^2 + 3y - 1$.

$$\frac{dx}{dy} = 3y^2 - 6y + 3$$

$$\frac{dy}{dx} = \frac{1}{dx/dy} = \frac{1}{3y^2 - 6y + 3}$$

$$\frac{dy}{dx}\bigg|_{y=2} = \frac{1}{3(2)^2 - 6(2) + 3} = \frac{1}{3}$$

28. Substituting $x = 100$ into the expression
$\dfrac{x - 100}{\sqrt{x} - 10}$ would lead to $\dfrac{0}{0}$. Apply
$L'H\hat{o}pital's$ Rule and you have $\displaystyle\lim_{x\to 100}\dfrac{1}{\frac{1}{2}x^{-\frac{1}{2}}}$

or $\dfrac{1}{\frac{1}{2}(100)^{-\frac{1}{2}}} = 20$.

Another approach to solve the problem is as follows: Multiply both numerator and denominator by the conjugate of the denominator ($\sqrt{x} + 10$):

$$\lim_{x \to 100} \frac{(x - 100)}{(\sqrt{x} - 10)} \cdot \frac{(\sqrt{x} + 10)}{(\sqrt{x} + 10)} =$$

$$\lim_{x \to 100} \frac{(x - 100)(\sqrt{x} + 10)}{(x - 100)}$$

$$\lim_{x \to 100} (\sqrt{x} + 10) = 10 + 10 = 20.$$

An alternative solution is to factor the numerator:

$$\lim_{x \to 10} \frac{(\sqrt{x} - 10)(\sqrt{x} + 10)}{(\sqrt{x} - 10)} = 20.$$

29. (a) $f' > 0$ on $(-1, 2)$, f is increasing on $(-1, 2)$ $f' < 0$ on $(2, 8)$, f is decreasing on $(2, 8)$.

   (b) At $x = 2$, $f' = 0$ and $f'' < 0$, thus at $x = 2$, f has a relative maximum. Since it is the only relative extremum on the interval, it is an absolute maximum. Since f is a continuous function on a closed interval and at its endpoints $f(-1) < 0$ and $f(8) = 1/2$, f has an absolute minimum at $x = -1$.

   (c) At $x = 5$, f has a change of concavity and f' exists at $x = 5$.

   (d) $f'' < 0$ on $(-1, 5)$, f is concave downward on $(-1, 5)$.
       $f'' > 0$ on $(5, 8)$, f is concave upward on $(5, 8)$.

   (e) A possible graph of f is given in Figure 9.9-1.

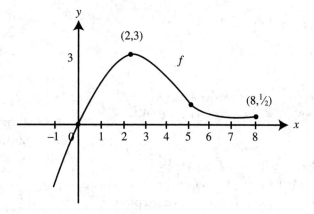

Figure 9.9-1

30. (a) $v(t) = 3$ ft/s at $t = 6$. The tangent line to the graph of $v(t)$ at $t = 6$ has a slope of approximately $m = 1$. (The tangent passes through the points $(8, 5)$ and $(6, 3)$; thus $m = 1$.) Therefore the acceleration is 1 ft/s^2.

   (b) The acceleration is a minimum at $t = 0$, since the slope of the tangent to the curve of $v(t)$ is the smallest at $t = 0$.

31. To convert $r = 4 \cos \theta$ to a Cartesian representation, recall that $r = \sqrt{x^2 + y^2}$ and $\tan \theta = \dfrac{y}{x}$. Then,

$$\sqrt{x^2 + y^2} = 4 \cos \left(\tan^{-1} \frac{y}{x} \right).$$ Since

$$\cos \left(\tan^{-1} \frac{y}{x} \right) = \frac{x}{\sqrt{x^2 + y^2}},$$ the equation

becomes $\sqrt{x^2 + y^2} = \dfrac{4x}{\sqrt{x^2 + y^2}}$. Multiply

through by $\sqrt{x^2 + y^2}$ to produce $x^2 + y^2 = 4x$. Completing the square produces $(x - 2)^2 + y^2 = 4$.

32. When $x = 5 \sin t = 5$, $t = \dfrac{\pi}{2}$, so

    $y = 1 - \cos \dfrac{\pi}{2} = 1$.

33. If $u = \langle 6, -1 \rangle$ and $v = \langle -4, 3 \rangle$, $4\langle 6, -1 \rangle$
    $- 3\langle -4, 3 \rangle = \langle 24, -4 \rangle + \langle 12, -9 \rangle =$
    $\langle 36, -13 \rangle$.

34. Replace θ with $-\theta$. $2 \sin(-4\theta) =$
    $-2 \sin(4\theta) \neq 2 \sin(4\theta)$, so the graph is not
    symmetric about the polar axis. Replace θ

    with $\pi - \theta$. $2 \sin(4(\pi - \theta)) = 2 \sin(4\pi - 4\theta)$
    $= 2 [\sin 4\pi \cos 4\theta - \sin 4\theta \cos 4\pi] =$
    $-2 \sin 4\theta \neq 2 \sin 4\theta$, so the graph is not
    symmetric about the line $x = \dfrac{\pi}{2}$. Replace

    θ with $\theta + \pi$.
    $2 \sin(4(\theta + \pi)) = 2 \sin(4\theta + 4\pi) =$
    $2 [\sin 4\theta \cos 4\pi + \cos 4\theta \sin 4\pi] = 2 \sin 4\theta$,
    so the graph is symmetric about the pole.

35. The magnitude of the vector $3i + 4j$ is
    $\left\| 3i + 4j \right\| = \sqrt{3^2 + 4^2} = 5$.

CHAPTER 10

Big Idea 3: Integrals and the Fundamental Theorems of Calculus
Integration

IN THIS CHAPTER

Summary: On the AP Calculus BC exam, you will be asked to evaluate integrals of various functions. In this chapter, you will learn several methods of evaluating integrals including U-Substitution, Integration by Parts, and Integration by Partial Fractions. Also, you will be given a list of common integration and differentiation formulas, and a comprehensive set of practice problems. It is important that you work out these problems and check your solutions with the given explanations.

Key Ideas
○ Evaluating Integrals of Algebraic Functions
○ Integration Formulas
○ U-Substitution Method Involving Algebraic Functions
○ U-Substitution Method Involving Trigonometric Functions
○ U-Substitution Method Involving Inverse Trigonometric Functions
○ U-Substitution Method Involving Logarithmic and Exponential Functions
○ Integration by Parts
○ Integration by Partial Fractions

10.1 Evaluating Basic Integrals

Main Concepts: Antiderivatives and Integration Formulas, Evaluating Integrals

- Answer all parts of a question from Section II even if you think your answer to an earlier part of the question might not be correct. Also, if you do not know the answer to part one of a question, and you need it to answer part two, just make it up and continue.

Antiderivatives and Integration Formulas

Definition: A function F is an antiderivative of another function f if $F'(x) = f(x)$ for all x in some open interval. Any two antiderivatives of f differ by an additive constant C. We denote the set of antiderivatives of f by $\int f(x)dx$, called the indefinite integral of f.

Integration Rules:

1. $\int f(x)dx = F(x) + C \Leftrightarrow F'(x) = f(x)$

2. $\int a\, f(x)dx = a \int f(x)dx$

3. $\int -f(x)dx = - \int f(x)dx$

4. $\int [f(x) \pm g(x)]\, dx = \int f(x)dx \pm \int g(x)dx$

Differentiation Formulas: Integration Formulas:

1. $\dfrac{d}{dx}(x) = 1$

2. $\dfrac{d}{dx}(ax) = a$

3. $\dfrac{d}{dx}(x^n) = nx^{n-1}$

4. $\dfrac{d}{dx}(\cos x) = -\sin x$

5. $\dfrac{d}{dx}(\sin x) = \cos x$

6. $\dfrac{d}{dx}(\tan x) = \sec^2 x$

7. $\dfrac{d}{dx}(\cot x) = -\csc^2 x$

8. $\dfrac{d}{dx}(\sec x) = \sec x\ \tan x$

9. $\dfrac{d}{dx}(\csc x) = -\csc x(\cot x)$

1. $\int 1 dx = x + C$

2. $\int a\, dx = ax + C$

3. $\int x^n dx = \dfrac{x^{n+1}}{n+1} + C,\ n \neq -1$

4. $\int \sin x\, dx = -\cos x + C$

5. $\int \cos x\, dx = \sin x + C$

6. $\int \sec^2 x\, dx = \tan x + C$

7. $\int \csc^2 x\, dx = -\cot x + C$

8. $\int \sec x(\tan x)\, dx = \sec x + C$

9. $\int \csc x(\cot x)\, dx = -\csc x + C$

Differentiation Formulas (cont.):

10. $\dfrac{d}{dx}(\ln x) = \dfrac{1}{x}$

11. $\dfrac{d}{dx}(e^x) = e^x$

12. $\dfrac{d}{dx}(a^x) = (\ln a)a^x$

13. $\dfrac{d}{dx}(\sin^{-1} x) = \dfrac{1}{\sqrt{1-x^2}}$

14. $\dfrac{d}{dx}(\tan^{-1} x) = \dfrac{1}{1+x^2}$

15. $\dfrac{d}{dx}(\sec^{-1} x) = \dfrac{1}{|x|\sqrt{x^2-1}}$

Integration Formulas (cont.):

10. $\displaystyle\int \dfrac{1}{x}\,dx = \ln|x| + C$

11. $\displaystyle\int e^x\,dx = e^x + C$

12. $\displaystyle\int a^x\,dx = \dfrac{a^x}{\ln a} + C\ a > 0, a \neq 1$

13. $\displaystyle\int \dfrac{1}{\sqrt{1-x^2}}\,dx = \sin^{-1} x + C$

14. $\displaystyle\int \dfrac{1}{1+x^2}\,dx = \tan^{-1} x + C$

15. $\displaystyle\int \dfrac{1}{|x|\sqrt{x^2-1}}\,dx = \sec^{-1} x + C$

More Integration Formulas:

16. $\displaystyle\int \tan x\,dx = \ln|\sec x| + C$ or $-\ln|\cos x| + C$

17. $\displaystyle\int \cot x\,dx = \ln|\sin x| + C$ or $-\ln|\csc x| + C$

18. $\displaystyle\int \sec x\,dx = \ln|\sec x + \tan x| + C$

19. $\displaystyle\int \csc x\,dx = \ln|\csc x - \cot x| + C$

20. $\displaystyle\int \ln x\,dx = x\ln|x| - x + C$

21. $\displaystyle\int \dfrac{1}{\sqrt{a^2-x^2}}\,dx = \sin^{-1}\left(\dfrac{x}{a}\right) + C$

22. $\displaystyle\int \dfrac{1}{a^2+x^2}\,dx = \dfrac{1}{a}\tan^{-1}\left(\dfrac{x}{a}\right) + C$

23. $\displaystyle\int \dfrac{1}{x\sqrt{x^2-a^2}}\,dx = \dfrac{1}{a}\sec^{-1}\left|\dfrac{x}{a}\right| + C$ or $\dfrac{1}{a}\cos^{-1}\left|\dfrac{a}{x}\right| + C$

24. $\displaystyle\int \sin^2 x\,dx = \dfrac{x}{2} - \dfrac{\sin(2x)}{4} + C$. Note: $\sin^2 x = \dfrac{1-\cos 2x}{2}$

Note: After evaluating an integral, always check the result by taking the derivative of the answer (i.e., taking the derivative of the antiderivative).

- Remember that the volume of a right-circular cone is $v = \dfrac{1}{3}\pi r^2 h$, where r is the radius of the base and h is the height of the cone.

Evaluating Integrals

INTEGRAL	REWRITE	ANTIDERIVATIVE
$\int x^3 dx$		$\dfrac{x^4}{4} + C$
$\int dx$	$\int 1 dx$	$x + C$
$\int 5 dx$		$5x + C$
$\int \sqrt{x}\, dx$	$\int x^{1/2} dx$	$\dfrac{x^{3/2}}{3/2} + C$ or $\dfrac{2x^{3/2}}{3} + C$
$\int x^{5/2} dx$		$\dfrac{x^{7/2}}{7/2} + C$ or $\dfrac{2x^{7/2}}{7} + C$
$\int \dfrac{1}{x^2} dx$	$\int x^{-2} dx$	$\dfrac{x^{-1}}{-1} + C$ or $\dfrac{-1}{x} + C$
$\int \dfrac{1}{\sqrt[3]{x^2}} dx$	$\int \dfrac{1}{x^{2/3}} dx = \int x^{-2/3} dx$	$\dfrac{x^{1/3}}{1/3} + C$ or $3\sqrt[3]{x} + C$
$\int \dfrac{x+1}{x} dx$	$\int \left(1 + \dfrac{1}{x}\right) dx$	$x + \ln|x| + C$
$\int x(x^5 + 1) dx$	$\int (x^6 + x) dx$	$\dfrac{x^7}{7} + \dfrac{x^2}{2} + C$

Example 1

Evaluate $\int (x^5 - 6x^2 + x - 1)\, dx$.

Applying the formula $\int x^n dx = \dfrac{x^{n+1}}{n+1} + C, \; n \neq -1$.

$\int (x^5 - 6x^2 + x - 1) dx = \dfrac{x^6}{6} - 2x^3 + \dfrac{x^2}{2} - x + C$

Example 2

Evaluate $\int \left(\sqrt{x} + \dfrac{1}{x^3}\right) dx$.

Rewrite $\int \left(\sqrt{x} + \dfrac{1}{x^3}\right) dx$ as $\int \left(x^{1/2} + x^{-3}\right) dx = \dfrac{x^{3/2}}{3/2} + \dfrac{x^{-2}}{-2} + C$

$= \dfrac{2}{3} x^{3/2} - \dfrac{1}{2x^2} + C$.

Example 3

If $\dfrac{dy}{dx} = 3x^2 + 2$, and the point $(0, -1)$ lies on the graph of y, find y.

Since $\dfrac{dy}{dx} = 3x^2 + 2$, then y is an antiderivative of $\dfrac{dy}{dx}$. Thus,

$y = \displaystyle\int \left(3x^2 + 2 \right) dx = x^3 + 2x + C$. The point $(0, -1)$ is on the graph of y.

Thus, $y = x^3 + 2x + C$ becomes $-1 = 0^3 + 2(0) + C$ or $C = -1$. Therefore, $y = x^3 + 2x - 1$.

Example 4

Evaluate $\displaystyle\int \left(1 - \dfrac{1}{\sqrt[3]{x^4}} \right) dx$.

Rewrite as $\displaystyle\int \left(1 - \dfrac{1}{x^{4/3}} \right) dx = \int \left(1 - x^{-4/3} \right) dx$

$$= x - \dfrac{x^{-1/3}}{-1/3} + C = x + \dfrac{3}{\sqrt[3]{x}} + C.$$

Example 5

Evaluate $\displaystyle\int \dfrac{3x^2 + x - 1}{x^2} dx$.

Rewrite as $\displaystyle\int \left(3 + \dfrac{1}{x} - \dfrac{1}{x^2} \right) dx = \int \left(3 + \dfrac{1}{x} - x^{-2} \right) dx$

$$= 3x + \ln|x| - \dfrac{x^{-1}}{-1} + C = 3x + \ln|x| + \dfrac{1}{x} + C.$$

Example 6

Evaluate $\displaystyle\int \sqrt{x} \left(x^2 - 3 \right) dx$.

Rewrite $\displaystyle\int x^{1/2} \left(x^2 - 3 \right) dx = \int \left(x^{5/2} - 3x^{1/2} \right) dx$

$$= \dfrac{x^{7/2}}{7/2} - \dfrac{3x^{3/2}}{3/2} + C = \dfrac{2}{7}x^{7/2} - 2\sqrt{x^3} + C.$$

Example 7

Evaluate $\displaystyle\int \left(x^3 - 4\sin x \right) dx$.

$$\int \left(x^3 - 4\sin x \right) dx = \dfrac{x^4}{4} + 4\cos x + C.$$

Example 8

Evaluate $\displaystyle\int \left(4\cos x - \cot x \right) dx$.

$$\int \left(4\cos x - \cot x \right) dx = 4\sin x - \ln\left|\sin x\right| + C.$$

Example 9

Evaluate $\int \dfrac{\sin x - 1}{\cos} dx.$

Rewrite $\int \left(\dfrac{\sin x}{\cos x} - \dfrac{1}{\cos x} \right) dx = \int (\tan x - \sec x) \, dx = \int \tan x \, dx - \int \sec x \, dx$

$$= \ln|\sec x| - \ln|\sec x + \tan x| + C = \ln\left|\dfrac{\sec x}{\sec x + \tan x}\right| + C$$

or $-\ln|\sin x + 1| + C.$

Example 10

Evaluate $\int \dfrac{e^{2x}}{e^x} dx.$

Rewrite the integral as $\int e^x dx = e^x + C.$

Example 11

Evaluate $\int \dfrac{3}{1 + x^2} dx.$

Rewrite as $3 \int \dfrac{1}{1 + x^2} dx = 3 \tan^{-1} x + C.$

Example 12

Evaluate $\int \dfrac{1}{\sqrt{9 - x^2}} dx.$

Rewrite as $\int \dfrac{1}{\sqrt{3^2 - x^2}} dx = \sin^{-1}\left(\dfrac{x}{3}\right) + C.$

Example 13

Evaluate $\int 7^x dx.$

$$\int 7^x \, dx = \dfrac{7^x}{\ln 7} + C$$

Reminder: You can always check the result by taking the derivative of the answer.

 KEY IDEA

 TIP

- Be familiar with the instructions for the different parts of the exam before the day of exam. Review the instructions in the practice tests provided at the end of this book.

10.2 Integration by U-Substitution

Main Concepts: The U-Substitution Method, U-Substitution and Algebraic Functions, U-Substitution and Trigonometric Functions, U-Substitution and Inverse Trigonometric Functions, U-Substitution and Logarithmic and Exponential Functions

The U-Substitution Method
The Chain Rule for Differentiation

$$\frac{d}{dx}F(g(x)) = f(g(x))g'(x), \quad \text{where } F' = f$$

The Integral of a Composite Function

If $f(g(x))$ and f' are continuous and $F' = f$, then

$$\int f(g(x))g'(x)dx = F(g(x)) + C.$$

Making a U-Substitution

Let $u = g(x)$, then $du = g'(x)dx$

$$\int f(g(x))g'(x)dx = \int f(u)du = F(u) + C = F(g(x)) + C.$$

STRATEGY

Procedure for Making a U-Substitution

Steps:
1. Given $f(g(x))$; let $u = g(x)$.
2. Differentiate: $du = g'(x)dx$.
3. Rewrite the integral in terms of u.
4. Evaluate the integral.
5. Replace u by $g(x)$.
6. Check your result by taking the derivative of the answer.

U-Substitution and Algebraic Functions
Another Form of the Integral of a Composite Function

If f is a differentiable function, then

$$\int (f(x))^n f'(x)dx = \frac{(f(x))^{n+1}}{n+1} + C, n \neq -1.$$

Making a U-Substitution

Let $u = f(x)$; then $du = f'(x)dx$.

$$\int (f(x))^n f'(x)dx = \int u^n du = \frac{u^{n+1}}{n+1} + C = \frac{(f(x))^{n+1}}{n+1} + C, n \neq -1$$

Example 1

Evaluate $\int x(x + 1)^{10} dx$.

Step 1. Let $u = x + 1$; then $x = u - 1$.

Step 2. Differentiate: $du = dx$.

Step 3. Rewrite: $\int (u - 1) u^{10} du = \int \left(u^{11} - u^{10} \right) du$.

Step 4. Integrate: $\dfrac{u^{12}}{12} - \dfrac{u^{11}}{11} + C$.

Step 5. Replace u: $\dfrac{(x + 1)^{12}}{12} - \dfrac{(x + 1)^{11}}{11} + C$.

Step 6. Differentiate and Check: $\dfrac{12 (x + 1)^{11}}{12} - \dfrac{11 (x + 1)^{10}}{11}$

$$= (x + 1)^{11} - (x + 1)^{10}$$
$$= (x + 1)^{10}(x + 1 - 1)$$
$$= (x + 1)^{10}x \text{ or } x(x + 1)^{10}.$$

Example 2

Evaluate $\int x \sqrt{x - 2}\, dx$.

Step 1. Let $u = x - 2$; then $x = u + 2$.

Step 2. Differentiate: $du = dx$.

Step 3. Rewrite: $\int (u + 2) \sqrt{u}\, du = \int (u + 2)u^{1/2} du = \int \left(u^{3/2} + 2u^{1/2} \right) du$.

Step 4. Integrate: $\dfrac{u^{5/2}}{5/2} + \dfrac{2u^{3/2}}{3/2} + C$.

Step 5. Replace: $\dfrac{2 (x - 2)^{5/2}}{5} + \dfrac{4 (x - 2)^{3/2}}{3} + C$.

Step 6. Differentiate and Check: $\left(\dfrac{5}{2}\right) \dfrac{2 (x - 2)^{3/2}}{5} + \left(\dfrac{3}{2}\right) \dfrac{4 (x - 2)^{1/2}}{3}$

$$= (x - 2)^{3/2} + 2 (x - 2)^{1/2}$$
$$= (x-2)^{1/2} [(x-2)+2]$$
$$= (x-2)^{1/2}\, x \text{ or } x \sqrt{x-2}.$$

Example 3

Evaluate $\int (2x - 5)^{2/3} dx$.

Step 1. Let $u = 2x - 5$.

Step 2. Differentiate: $du = 2dx \Rightarrow \dfrac{du}{2} = dx$.

Step 3. Rewrite: $\int u^{2/3}\dfrac{du}{2} = \dfrac{1}{2}\int u^{2/3}\,du.$

Step 4. Integrate: $\dfrac{1}{2}\left(\dfrac{u^{5/3}}{5/3}\right) + C = \dfrac{3u^{5/3}}{10} + C.$

Step 5. Replace u: $\dfrac{3(2x-5)^{5/3}}{10} + C.$

Step 6. Differentiate and Check: $\left(\dfrac{3}{10}\right)\left(\dfrac{5}{3}\right)(2x-5)^{2/3}\,(2) = (2x-5)^{2/3}.$

Example 4

Evaluate $\displaystyle\int \dfrac{x^2}{(x^3-8)^5}\,dx.$

Step 1. Let $u = x^3 - 8.$

Step 2. Differentiate: $du = 3x^2\,dx \Rightarrow \dfrac{du}{3} = x^2\,dx.$

Step 3. Rewrite: $\displaystyle\int \dfrac{1}{u^5}\dfrac{du}{3} = \dfrac{1}{3}\int \dfrac{1}{u^5}\,du = \dfrac{1}{3}\int u^{-5}\,du.$

Step 4. Integrate: $\dfrac{1}{3}\left(\dfrac{u^{-4}}{-4}\right) + C.$

Step 5. Replace u: $\dfrac{1}{-12}\left(x^3-8\right)^{-4} + C$ or $\dfrac{-1}{12\left(x^3-8\right)^4} + C.$

Step 6. Differentiate and Check: $\left(-\dfrac{1}{12}\right)(-4)\left(x^3-8\right)^{-5}\left(3x^2\right) = \dfrac{x^2}{(x^3-8)^5}.$

U-Substitution and Trigonometric Functions
Example 1

Evaluate $\displaystyle\int \sin 4x\,dx.$

Step 1. Let $u = 4x.$

Step 2. Differentiate: $du = 4\,dx$ or $\dfrac{du}{4} = dx.$

Step 3. Rewrite: $\displaystyle\int \sin u\dfrac{du}{4} = \dfrac{1}{4}\int \sin u\,du.$

Step 4. Integrate: $\dfrac{1}{4}(-\cos u) + C = -\dfrac{1}{4}\cos u + C.$

Step 5. Replace u: $-\dfrac{1}{4}\cos(4x) + C.$

Step 6. Differentiate and Check: $\left(-\dfrac{1}{4}\right)(-\sin 4x)(4) = \sin 4x.$

Example 2

Evaluate $\int 3\left(\sec^2 x\right)\sqrt{\tan x}\, dx$.

Step 1. Let $u = \tan x$.

Step 2. Differentiate: $du = \sec^2 x\, dx$.

Step 3. Rewrite: $3\int (\tan x)^{1/2}\sec^2 x\, dx = 3\int u^{1/2}\, du$.

Step 4. Integrate: $3\dfrac{u^{3/2}}{3/2} + C = 2u^{3/2} + C$.

Step 5. Replace u: $2(\tan x)^{3/2} + C$ or $2\tan^{3/2} x + C$.

Step 6. Differentiate and Check: $(2)\left(\dfrac{3}{2}\right)\left(\tan^{1/2} x\right)\left(\sec^2 x\right) = 3\left(\sec^2 x\right)\sqrt{\tan x}$.

Example 3

Evaluate $\int 2x^2\cos\left(x^3\right) dx$.

Step 1. Let $u = x^3$.

Step 2. Differentiate: $du = 3x^2 dx \Rightarrow \dfrac{du}{3} = x^2 dx$.

Step 3. Rewrite: $2\int \left[\cos\left(x^3\right)\right]x^2 dx = 2\int \cos u\,\dfrac{du}{3} = \dfrac{2}{3}\int \cos u\, du$.

Step 4. Integrate: $\dfrac{2}{3}\sin u + C$.

Step 5. Replace u: $\dfrac{2}{3}\sin\left(x^3\right) + C$.

Step 6. Differentiate and Check: $\dfrac{2}{3}\left[\cos\left(x^3\right)\right]3x^2 = 2x^2\cos\left(x^3\right)$.

- Remember that the area of a semicircle is $\dfrac{1}{2}\pi r^2$. Do not forget the $\dfrac{1}{2}$. If the cross sections of a solid are semicircles, the integral for the volume of the solid will involve $\left(\dfrac{1}{2}\right)^2$ which is $\dfrac{1}{4}$.

U-Substitution and Inverse Trigonometric Functions
Example 1

Evaluate $\int \dfrac{dx}{\sqrt{9 - 4x^2}}$.

Step 1. Let $u = 2x$.

Step 2. Differentiate: $du = 2dx$; $\dfrac{du}{2} = dx$.

Step 3. Rewrite: $\displaystyle\int \frac{1}{\sqrt{9-u^2}}\frac{du}{2} = \frac{1}{2}\int \frac{du}{\sqrt{3^2-u^2}}.$

Step 4. Integrate: $\displaystyle\frac{1}{2}\sin^{-1}\left(\frac{u}{3}\right) + C.$

Step 5. Replace u: $\displaystyle\frac{1}{2}\sin^{-1}\left(\frac{2x}{3}\right) + C.$

Step 6. Differentiate and Check: $\displaystyle\frac{1}{2}\frac{1}{\sqrt{1-(2x/3)^2}}\cdot\frac{2}{3} = \frac{1}{3}\frac{1}{\sqrt{1-4x^2/9}}$

$$= \frac{1}{\sqrt{9}}\frac{1}{\sqrt{1-4x^2/9}} = \frac{1}{\sqrt{9\,(1-4x^2/9)}}$$

$$= \frac{1}{\sqrt{9-4x^2}}.$$

Example 2

Evaluate $\displaystyle\int \frac{1}{x^2+2x+5}dx.$

Step 1. Rewrite: $\displaystyle\int \frac{1}{(x^2+2x+1)+4} = \int \frac{1}{(x+1)^2+2^2}dx$

$$= \int \frac{1}{2^2+(x+1)^2}dx.$$

Let $u = x + 1$.

Step 2. Differentiate: $du = dx.$

Step 3. Rewrite: $\displaystyle\int \frac{1}{2^2+u^2}du.$

Step 4. Integrate: $\displaystyle\frac{1}{2}\tan^{-1}\left(\frac{u}{2}\right) + C.$

Step 5. Replace u: $\displaystyle\frac{1}{2}\tan^{-1}\left(\frac{x+1}{2}\right) + C.$

Step 6. Differentiate and Check: $\displaystyle\left(\frac{1}{2}\right)\frac{1\,(1/2)}{1+[(x+1)/2]^2} = \left(\frac{1}{4}\right)\frac{1}{1+(x+1)^2/4}$

$$= \left(\frac{1}{4}\right)\frac{4}{4+(x+1)^2} = \frac{1}{x^2+2x+5}.$$

- If the problem gives you that the diameter of a sphere is 6 and you are using formulas such as $v = \dfrac{4}{3}\pi r^3$ or $s = 4\pi r^2$, do not forget that $r = 3$.

U-Substitution and Logarithmic and Exponential Functions

Example 1

Evaluate $\int \dfrac{x^3}{x^4 - 1} dx$.

Step 1. Let $u = x^4 - 1$.

Step 2. Differentiate: $du = 4x^3 dx \Rightarrow \dfrac{du}{4} = x^3 dx$.

Step 3. Rewrite: $\int \dfrac{1}{u} \dfrac{du}{4} = \dfrac{1}{4} \int \dfrac{1}{u} du$.

Step 4. Integrate: $\dfrac{1}{4} \ln |u| + C$.

Step 5. Replace u: $\dfrac{1}{4} \ln \left| x^4 - 1 \right| + C$.

Step 6. Differentiate and Check: $\left(\dfrac{1}{4} \right) \dfrac{1}{x^4 - 1} \left(4x^3 \right) = \dfrac{x^3}{x^4 - 1}$.

Example 2

Evaluate $\int \dfrac{\sin x}{\cos x + 1} dx$.

Step 1. Let $u = \cos x + 1$.

Step 2. Differentiate: $du = -\sin x \, dx \Rightarrow -du = \sin x \, dx$.

Step 3. Rewrite: $\int \dfrac{-du}{u} = -\int \dfrac{du}{u}$.

Step 4. Integrate: $-\ln |u| + C$.

Step 5. Replace u: $-\ln \left| \cos x + 1 \right| + C$.

Step 6. Differentiate and Check: $-\left(\dfrac{1}{\cos x + 1} \right) (-\sin x) = \dfrac{\sin x}{\cos x + 1}$.

Example 3

Evaluate $\int \dfrac{x^2 + 3}{x - 1} dx$.

Step 1. Rewrite: $\dfrac{x^2 + 3}{x - 1} = x + 1 + \dfrac{4}{x - 1}$ by dividing $(x^2 + 3)$ by $(x - 1)$.

$$\int \dfrac{x^2 + 3}{x - 1} dx = \int \left(x + 1 + \dfrac{4}{x - 1} \right) dx = \int (x + 1) \, dx + \int \dfrac{4}{x - 1} dx$$

$$= \dfrac{x^2}{2} + x + 4 \int \dfrac{1}{x - 1} dx$$

Let $u = x - 1$.

Step 2. Differentiate: $du = dx$.

Step 3.   Rewrite: $4 \int \dfrac{1}{u}\, du.$

Step 4.   Integrate: $4 \ln |u| + C.$

Step 5.   Replace u: $4 \ln |x - 1| + C.$

$$\int \dfrac{x^2 + 3}{x - 1}\, dx = \dfrac{x^2}{2} + x + 4 \ln |x - 1| + C.$$

Step 6.   Differentiate and Check:

$$\dfrac{2x}{2} + 1 + 4 \left(\dfrac{1}{x - 1} \right) + C = x + 1 + \dfrac{4}{x - 1} = \dfrac{x^2 + 3}{x - 1}.$$

Example 4

Evaluate $\displaystyle\int \dfrac{\ln x}{3x}\, dx.$

Step 1.   Let $u = \ln x.$

Step 2.   Differentiate: $du = \dfrac{1}{x}\, dx.$

Step 3.   Rewrite: $\dfrac{1}{3} \displaystyle\int u\, dx.$

Step 4.   Integrate: $\left(\dfrac{1}{3} \right) \dfrac{u^2}{2} + C = \dfrac{1}{6} u^2 + C.$

Step 5.   Replace u: $\dfrac{1}{6} (\ln x)^2 + C.$

Step 6.   Differentiate and Check: $\dfrac{1}{6} (2) (\ln x) \left(\dfrac{1}{x} \right) = \dfrac{\ln x}{3x}.$

Example 5

Evaluate $\displaystyle\int e^{(2x-5)}\, dx.$

Step 1.   Let $u = 2x - 5.$

Step 2.   Differentiate: $du = 2dx \Rightarrow \dfrac{du}{2} = dx.$

Step 3.   Rewrite: $\displaystyle\int e^u \left(\dfrac{du}{2} \right) = \dfrac{1}{2} \displaystyle\int e^u\, du.$

Step 4.   Integrate: $\dfrac{1}{2} e^u + C.$

Step 5.   Replace u: $\dfrac{1}{2} e^{(2x-5)} + C.$

Step 6.   Differentiate and Check: $\dfrac{1}{2} e^{2x-5} (2) = e^{2x-5}.$

Example 6

Evaluate $\displaystyle\int \frac{e^x}{e^x+1}dx$.

Step 1. Let $u = e^x + 1$.

Step 2. Differentiate: $du = e^x dx$.

Step 3. Rewrite: $\displaystyle\int \frac{1}{u}du$.

Step 4. Integrate: $\ln|u| + C$.

Step 5. Replace u: $\ln\left|e^x + 1\right| + C$.

Step 6. Differentiate and Check: $\dfrac{1}{e^x + 1} \cdot e^x = \dfrac{e^x}{e^x + 1}$.

Example 7

Evaluate $\displaystyle\int xe^{3x^2}dx$.

Step 1. Let $u = 3x^2$.

Step 2. Differentiate: $du = 6x\,dx \Rightarrow \dfrac{du}{6} = x\,dx$.

Step 3. Rewrite: $\displaystyle\int e^u \frac{du}{6} = \frac{1}{6}\int e^u du$.

Step 4. Integrate: $\dfrac{1}{6}e^u + C$.

Step 5. Replace u: $\dfrac{1}{6}e^{3x^2} + C$.

Step 6. Differentiate and Check: $\dfrac{1}{6}\left(e^{3x^2}\right)(6x) = xe^{3x^2}$.

Example 8

Evaluate $\displaystyle\int 5^{(2x)}dx$.

Step 1. Let $u = 2x$.

Step 2. Differentiate: $du = 2dx \Rightarrow \dfrac{du}{2} = dx$.

Step 3. Rewrite: $\displaystyle\int 5^u \frac{du}{2} = \frac{1}{2}\int 5^u du$.

Step 4. Integrate: $\dfrac{1}{2}(5^u)/\ln 5 + C = 5^u/(2\ln 5) + C$.

Step 5. Replace u: $\dfrac{5^{2x}}{2\ln 5} + C$.

Step 6. Differentiate and Check: $(5^{2x})(2)\ln 5/(2\ln 5) = 5^{2x}$.

Example 9

Evaluate $\int x^3 5^{x^4} dx$.

Step 1. Let $u = x^4$.

Step 2. Differentiate: $du = 4x^3 dx \Rightarrow \dfrac{du}{4} = x^3 dx$.

Step 3. Rewrite: $\int 5^u \dfrac{du}{4} = \dfrac{1}{4} \int 5^u du$.

Step 4. Integrate: $\dfrac{1}{4}(5^u)/\ln 5 + C$.

Step 5. Replace u: $\dfrac{5^{x^4}}{4 \ln 5} + C$.

Step 6. Differentiate and Check: $5^{x^4}\left(4x^3\right) \ln 5/(4 \ln 5) = x^3 5^{x^4}$.

Example 10

Evaluate $\int (\sin \pi x)\, e^{\cos \pi x} dx$.

Step 1. Let $u = \cos \pi x$.

Step 2. Differentiate: $du = -\pi \sin \pi x\, dx; -\dfrac{du}{\pi} = \sin \pi x\, dx$.

Step 3. Rewrite: $\int e^u \left(\dfrac{-du}{\pi}\right) = -\dfrac{1}{\pi} \int e^u du$.

Step 4. Integrate: $-\dfrac{1}{\pi} e^u + C$.

Step 5. Replace u: $-\dfrac{1}{\pi} e^{\cos \pi x} + C$.

Step 6. Differentiate and Check: $-\dfrac{1}{\pi}(e^{\cos \pi x})(-\sin \pi x)\pi = (\sin \pi x)e^{\cos \pi x}$.

10.3 Techniques of Integration

Main Concepts: Integration by Parts, Integration by Partial Fractions

Integration by Parts

According to the product rule for differentiation $\dfrac{d}{dx}(uv) = u\dfrac{dv}{dx} + v\dfrac{du}{dx}$. Integrating tells us that $uv = \int u\dfrac{dv}{dx} + \int v\dfrac{du}{dx}$, and therefore $\int u\dfrac{dv}{dx} = uv - \int v\dfrac{du}{dx}$. To integrate a product, careful identification of one factor as u and the other as $\dfrac{dv}{dx}$ allows the application of this rule for integration by parts. Choice of one factor to be u (and therefore the other to be dv) is simpler if you remember the mnemonic **LIPET**.

Each letter in the acronym represents a type of function: **L**ogarithmic, **I**nverse trigonometric, **P**olynomial, **E**xponential, and **T**rigonometric. As you consider integrating by parts, assign the factor that falls earlier in the **LIPET** list as u, and the other as dv.

Example 1

$$\int xe^{-x}dx$$

Step 1: Identify $u = x$ and $dv = e^{-x}dx$ since x is a **P**olynomial, which comes before **E**xponential in **LIPET**.

Step 2: Differentiate $du = dx$ and integrate $v = -e^{-x}$.

Step 3: $\int xe^{-x}dx = -xe^{-x} - \int -e^{-x}dx = -xe^{-x} - e^{-x} + C$

Example 2

$$\int x \sin 4x\, dx$$

Step 1: Identify $u = x$ and $dv = \sin 4x\, dx$ since x is a **P**olynomial, which comes before **T**rigonometric in **LIPET**.

Step 2: Differentiate $du = dx$ and integrate $v = \dfrac{-1}{4} \cos 4x$.

Step 3: $\int x \sin 4x\, dx = \dfrac{-x}{4} \cos 4x + \dfrac{1}{4} \int \cos 4x\, dx = \dfrac{-x}{4} \cos 4x + \dfrac{1}{16} \sin 4x + C$

Integration by Partial Fractions

A rational function with a factorable denominator can be integrated by decomposing the integrand into a sum of simpler fractions. Each linear factor of the denominator becomes the denominator of one of the partial fractions.

Example 1

$$\int \frac{dx}{x^2 + 3x - 4}$$

Step 1: Factor the denominator: $\int \dfrac{dx}{x^2 + 3x - 4} = \int \dfrac{dx}{(x+4)(x-1)}$

Step 2: Let A and B represent the numerators of the partial fractions
$$\frac{1}{(x+4)(x-1)} = \frac{A}{x+4} + \frac{B}{x-1}.$$

Step 3: The algorithm for adding fractions tells us that $A(x-1) + B(x+4) = 1$, so $Ax + Bx = 0$ and $-A + 4B = 1$. Solving gives us $A = -0.2$ and $B = 0.2$.

Step 4: $\int \dfrac{dx}{x^2 + 3x - 4} = \int \dfrac{-0.2}{x+4}dx + \int \dfrac{0.2}{x-1}dx = -0.2 \ln(x+4) + 0.2 \ln(x-1) + C$

Example 2

$$\int \frac{x^5 + 2x^2 + 1}{x^3 - x}\,dx$$

Step 1:   Use long division to rewrite $\displaystyle\int \frac{x^5 + 2x^2 + 1}{x^3 - x}\,dx = \int \left(x^2 + 1 + \frac{2x^2 + x + 1}{x^3 - x}\right) dx =$
$$\int (x^2 + 1)\,dx + \int \frac{2x^2 + x + 1}{x^3 - x}\,dx.$$

Step 2:   Factor the denominator: $\displaystyle\frac{2x^2 + x + 1}{x^3 - x} = \frac{2x^2 + x + 1}{x(x + 1)(x - 1)}$

Step 3:   Let A, B, and C represent the numerators of the partial fractions.
$$\frac{2x^2 + x + 1}{x(x + 1)(x - 1)} = \frac{A}{x} + \frac{B}{x + 1} + \frac{C}{x - 1}$$

Step 4: $2x^2 + x + 1 = A(x + 1)(x - 1) + Bx(x - 1) + Cx(x + 1)$, therefore, $Ax^2 + Bx^2 + Cx^2 = 2x^2$, $Cx - Bx = x$, and $-A = 1$. Solving gives $A = -1$, $B = 1$, and $C = 2$.

Step 5: $\displaystyle\int \frac{x^5 + 2x^2 + 1}{x^3 - x}\,dx = \int (x^2 + 1)\,dx + \int \frac{-1}{x}\,dx + \int \frac{1}{x + 1}\,dx + \int \frac{2}{x - 1}\,dx$
$$= \frac{x^3}{3} + x - \ln x + \ln (x + 1) + 2 \ln (x - 1) + C$$

10.4 Rapid Review

1.   Evaluate $\displaystyle\int \frac{1}{x^2}\,dx$.

   Answer: Rewrite as $\displaystyle\int x^{-2}\,dx = \frac{x^{-1}}{-1} + C = -\frac{1}{x} + C$.

2.   Evaluate $\displaystyle\int \frac{x^3 - 1}{x}\,dx$.

   Answer: Rewrite as $\displaystyle\int \left(x^2 - \frac{1}{x}\right) dx = \frac{x^3}{3} - \ln |x| + C$.

3.   Evaluate $\displaystyle\int x\sqrt{x^2 - 1}\,dx$.

   Answer: Rewrite as $\displaystyle\int x(x^2 - 1)^{1/2}\,dx$. Let $u = x^2 - 1$.

   Thus, $\displaystyle\frac{du}{2} = x\,dx \Rightarrow \frac{1}{2}\int u^{1/2}\,du = \frac{1u^{3/2}}{2^{3/2}} + C = \frac{1}{3}(x^2 - 1)^{3/2} + C$.

4.   Evaluate $\displaystyle\int \sin x\,dx$.

   Answer: $-\cos x + C$.

5. Evaluate $\int \cos(2x)dx$.

   Answer: Let $u = 2x$ and obtain $\dfrac{1}{2}\sin 2x + C$.

6. Evaluate $\int \dfrac{\ln x}{x}dx$.

   Answer: Let $u = \ln x; du = \dfrac{1}{x}dx$ and obtain $\dfrac{(\ln x)^2}{2} + C$.

7. Evaluate $\int xe^{x^2}dx$.

   Answer: Let $u = x^2; \dfrac{du}{2} = xdx$ and obtain $\dfrac{e^{x^2}}{2} + C$.

8. $\int x \cos x\, dx$

   Answer: Let $u = x$, $du = dx$, $dv = \cos x dx$, and $v = \sin x$,

   then $\int x \cos x\, dx = x \sin x - \int \sin x\, dx = x \sin x + \cos x + C$.

9. $\int \dfrac{5}{(x+3)(x-7)}dx$

   Answer: $\int \dfrac{5}{(x+3)(x-7)}dx = \int \left(\dfrac{-1/2}{x+3} + \dfrac{1/2}{x-7} \right)dx$

   $= -\dfrac{1}{2}\ln|x+3| + \dfrac{1}{2}\ln|x-7| + C = \dfrac{1}{2}\ln\left|\dfrac{x-7}{x+3}\right| + C$

10.5 Practice Problems

Evaluate the following integrals in problems 1 to 25. No calculators are allowed. (However, you may use calculators to check your results.)

1. $\int (x^5 + 3x^2 - x + 1)dx$

2. $\int \left(\sqrt{x} - \dfrac{1}{x^2} \right)dx$

3. $\int x^3(x^4 - 10)^5 dx$

4. $\int x^3\sqrt{x^2 + 1}\, dx$

5. $\int \dfrac{x^2 + 5}{\sqrt{x - 1}}dx$

6. $\int \tan\left(\dfrac{x}{2} \right)dx$

7. $\int x\csc^2(x^2)dx$

8. $\int \dfrac{\sin x}{\cos^3 x}dx$

9. $\int \dfrac{1}{x^2 + 2x + 10}dx$

10. $\int \dfrac{1}{x^2}\sec^2\left(\dfrac{1}{x} \right)dx$

11. $\int (e^{2x})(e^{4x})dx$

12. $\int \dfrac{1}{x\ln x}dx$

13. $\displaystyle\int \ln(e^{5x+1})dx$

14. $\displaystyle\int \frac{e^{4x}-1}{e^x}dx$

15. $\displaystyle\int (9-x^2)\sqrt{x}\,dx$

16. $\displaystyle\int \sqrt{x}\left(1+x^{3/2}\right)^4 dx$

17. If $\dfrac{dy}{dx}=e^x+2$ and the point $(0, 6)$ is on the graph of y, find y.

18. $\displaystyle\int -3e^x \sin(e^x)dx$

19. $\displaystyle\int \frac{e^x-e^{-x}}{e^x+e^{-x}}dx$

20. If $f(x)$ is the antiderivative of $\dfrac{1}{x}$ and $f(1)=5$, find $f(e)$.

21. $\displaystyle\int x^2\sqrt{1-x}\,dx$

22. $\displaystyle\int 3x^2 \sin x\,dx$

23. $\displaystyle\int \frac{x\,dx}{x^2-3x-4}$

24. $\displaystyle\int \frac{dx}{x^2+x}$

25. $\displaystyle\int \frac{\ln x}{(x+5)^2}dx$

10.6 Cumulative Review Problems

(Calculator) indicates that calculators are permitted.

26. The graph of the velocity function of a moving particle for $0 \le t \le 10$ is shown in Figure 10.6-1.

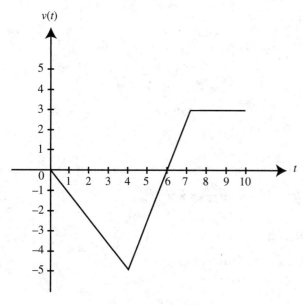

Figure 10.6-1

(a) At what value of t is the speed of the particle the greatest?

(b) At what time is the particle moving to the right?

27. Air is pumped into a spherical balloon, whose maximum radius is 10 meters. For what value of r is the rate of increase of the volume a hundred times that of the radius?

28. Evaluate $\displaystyle\int \frac{\ln^3(x)}{x}dx$.

29. (Calculator) The function f is continuous and differentiable on $(0, 2)$ with $f''(x) > 0$ for all x in the interval $(0, 2)$. Some of the points on the graph are shown below.

x	0	0.5	1	1.5	2
$f(x)$	1	1.25	2	3.25	5

Which of the following is the best approximation for $f'(1)$?

(a) $f'(1) < 2$
(b) $0.5 < f'(1) < 1$
(c) $1.5 < f'(1) < 2.5$
(d) $2.5 < f'(1) < 3.5$
(e) $f'(1) > 2$

30. The graph of the function f'' on the interval $[1, 8]$ is shown in Figure 10.6-2. At what value(s) of t on the open interval $(1, 8)$, if any, does the graph of the function f':

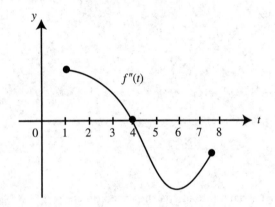

Figure 10.6-2

(a) have a point of inflection?
(b) have a relative maximum or minimum?
(c) become concave upward?

31. Evaluate $\lim\limits_{x \to -2} \dfrac{x^2 - x - 6}{x^2 - 4}$.

32. If the position of an object is given by $x = 4\sin(\pi t)$, $y = t^2 - 3t + 1$, find the position of the object at $t = 2$.

33. Find the slope of the tangent line to the curve $r = 3\cos\theta$ when $\theta = \dfrac{\pi}{4}$.

10.7 Solutions to Practice Problems

1. $\dfrac{x^6}{6} + x^3 - \dfrac{x^2}{2} + x + C$

2. Rewrite: $\displaystyle\int (x^{1/2} - x^{-2})dx$

$$= \dfrac{x^{3/2}}{3/2} - \dfrac{x^{-1}}{-1} + C$$

$$= \dfrac{2x^{3/2}}{3} + \dfrac{1}{x} + C.$$

3. Let $u = x^4 - 10$; $du = 4x^3 dx$ or

$$\dfrac{du}{4} = x^3 dx.$$

Rewrite: $\displaystyle\int u^5 \dfrac{du}{4} = \dfrac{1}{4}\int u^5 du$

$$= \left(\dfrac{1}{4}\right)\dfrac{u^6}{6} + C$$

$$= \dfrac{(x^4 - 10)^6}{24} + C.$$

4. Let $u = x^2 + 1 \Rightarrow (u - 1) = x^2$ and
$du = 2x\,dx$ or $\dfrac{du}{2} = x\,dx$.

Rewrite: $\displaystyle\int x^2\sqrt{x^2 + 1}(x\,dx)$

$$= \int (u - 1)\sqrt{u}\,\dfrac{du}{2}$$

$$= \frac{1}{2} \int (u-1)u^{1/2}\,du$$

$$= \frac{1}{2} \int (u^{3/2} - u^{1/2})\,du$$

$$= \frac{1}{2}\left(\frac{u^{5/2}}{5/2} - \frac{u^{3/2}}{3/2}\right) + C$$

$$= \frac{u^{5/2}}{5} - \frac{u^{3/2}}{3} + C$$

$$= \frac{(x^2+1)^{5/2}}{5} - \frac{(x^2+1)^{3/2}}{3} + C.$$

5. Let $u = x - 1; du = dx$ and $(u+1) = x$.

Rewrite: $\displaystyle \int \frac{(u+1)^2 + 5}{\sqrt{u}}\,du$

$$= \int \frac{u^2 + 2u + 6}{u^{1/2}}\,du$$

$$= \int \left(u^{3/2} + 2u^{1/2} + 6u^{-1/2}\right)\,du$$

$$= \frac{u^{5/2}}{5/2} + \frac{2u^{3/2}}{3/2} + \frac{6u^{1/2}}{1/2} + C$$

$$= \frac{2(x-1)^{5/2}}{5} + \frac{4(x-1)^{3/2}}{3}$$

$$+ 12(x-1)^{1/2} + C.$$

6. Let $u = \dfrac{x}{2}; du = \dfrac{1}{2}dx$ or $2\,du = dx$.

Rewrite: $\displaystyle \int \tan u (2\,du) = 2\int \tan u\,du$

$$= -2\ln|\cos u| + C$$

$$= -2\ln|\cos \frac{x}{2}| + C.$$

7. Let $u = x^2; du = 2x\,dx$ or $\dfrac{du}{2} = x\,dx$.

Rewrite: $\displaystyle \int \csc^2 u\,\frac{du}{2} = \frac{1}{2}\int \csc^2 u\,du$

$$= -\frac{1}{2}\cot u + C$$

$$= -\frac{1}{2}\cot(x^2) + C.$$

8. Let $u = \cos x; du = -\sin x\,dx$ or $-du = \sin x\,dx$.

Rewrite: $\displaystyle \int \frac{-du}{u^3} = -\int \frac{du}{u^3}$

$$= -\frac{u^{-2}}{-2} + C = \frac{1}{2\cos^2 x} + C.$$

9. Rewrite: $\displaystyle \int \frac{1}{(x^2+2x+1)+9}\,dx$

$$= \int \frac{1}{(x+1)^2 + 3^2}\,dx.$$

Let $u = x + 1; du = dx$.

Rewrite: $\displaystyle \int \frac{1}{u^2 + 3^2}\,du$

$$= \frac{1}{3}\tan^{-1}\left(\frac{u}{3}\right) + C$$

$$= \frac{1}{3}\tan^{-1}\left(\frac{x+1}{3}\right) + C.$$

10. Let $u = \dfrac{1}{x}; du = \dfrac{-1}{x^2}dx$ or $-du$

$$= \frac{1}{x^2}dx.$$

Rewrite: $\displaystyle \int \sec^2 u(-du) = -\int \sec^2 u\,du$

$$= -\tan u + C$$

$$= -\tan\left(\frac{1}{x}\right) + C.$$

11. Rewrite: $\displaystyle \int e^{(2x+4x)}\,dx = \int e^{6x}\,dx.$

Let $u = 6x; du = 6\,dx$ or $\dfrac{du}{6} = dx$.

Rewrite: $\displaystyle \int e^u \frac{du}{6} = \frac{1}{6}\int e^u\,du$

$$= \frac{1}{6}e^u + C = \frac{1}{6}e^{6x} + C.$$

12. Let $u = \ln x; du = \dfrac{1}{x}dx$.

Rewrite: $\displaystyle \int \frac{1}{u}\,du = \ln|u| + C$

$$= \ln|\ln x| + C.$$

13. Since e^x and $\ln x$ are inverse functions:

$$\int \ln\left(e^{5x+1}\right)\,dx = \int (5x+1)\,dx$$

$$= \frac{5x^2}{2} + x + C.$$

14. Rewrite: $\displaystyle\int \left(\frac{e^{4x}}{e^x} - \frac{1}{e^x}\right) dx$

$\displaystyle = \int \left(e^{3x} - e^{-x}\right) dx$

$\displaystyle = \int e^{3x} dx - \int e^{-x} dx.$

Let $u = 3x;\, du = 3dx;$

$\displaystyle\int e^{3x} dx = \int e^{u}\left(\frac{du}{3}\right) = \frac{1}{3}e^{u} + C_1$

$\displaystyle = \frac{1}{3}e^{3x} + C.$

Let $v = -x;\, dv = -dx;$

$\displaystyle\int e^{-x} dx = \int e^{v}(-dv) = e^{v} + C_2$

$\displaystyle = -e^{-x} + C_2$

Thus, $\displaystyle\int e^{3x} dx - \int e^{-x} dx$

$\displaystyle = \frac{1}{3}e^{3x} + e^{-x} + C.$

Note: C_1 and C_2 are arbitrary constants, and thus $C_1 + C_2 = C.$

15. Rewrite:

$\displaystyle\int (9 - x^2)x^{1/2} dx = \int \left(9x^{1/2} - x^{5/2}\right) dx$

$\displaystyle = \frac{9x^{3/2}}{3/2} - \frac{x^{7/2}}{7/2} + C$

$\displaystyle = 6x^{3/2} - \frac{2x^{7/2}}{7} + C.$

16. Let $u = 1 + x^{3/2};\, du = \frac{3}{2}x^{1/2} dx$ or

$\displaystyle\frac{2}{3} du = x^{1/2} dx = \sqrt{x}\, dx.$

Rewrite: $\displaystyle\int u^4 \left(\frac{2}{3} du\right) = \frac{2}{3}\int u^4 du$

$\displaystyle = \frac{2}{3}\left(\frac{u^5}{5}\right) + C = \frac{2\left(1 + x^{3/2}\right)^5}{15} + C.$

17. Since $\dfrac{dy}{dx} = e^x + 2$, then $y =$

$\displaystyle\int (e^x + 2) dx = e^x + 2x + C.$

The point $(0, 6)$ is on the graph of y.
Thus, $6 = e^0 + 2(0) + C \Rightarrow 6 = 1 + C$ or
$C = 5.$ Therefore, $y = e^x + 2x + 5.$

18. Let $u = e^x;\, du = e^x dx.$

Rewrite: $\displaystyle -3 \int \sin(u)du = -3(-\cos u) + C$

$= 3\cos(e^x) + C.$

19. Let $u = e^x + e^{-x};\, du = (e^x - e^{-x})\, dx.$

Rewrite: $\displaystyle\int \frac{1}{u} du = \ln|u| + C$

$= \ln|e^x + e^{-x}| + C$

or $= \ln\left|e^x + \dfrac{1}{e^x}\right| + C$

$= \ln\left|\dfrac{e^{2x} + 1}{e^x}\right| + C$

$= \ln|e^{2x} + 1| - \ln|e^x| + C$

$= \ln|e^{2x} + 1| - x + C.$

20. Since $f(x)$ is the antiderivative of $\dfrac{1}{x}$,

$\displaystyle f(x) = \int \frac{1}{x} d = \ln|x| + C.$

Given $f(1) = 5$; thus, $\ln(1) + C = 5$
$\Rightarrow 0 + C = 5$ or $C = 5.$

Thus, $f(x) = \ln|x| + 5$ and
$f(e) = \ln(e) + 5 = 1 + 5 = 6.$

21. Integrate $\displaystyle\int x^2 \sqrt{1 - x}\, dx$ by parts. Let

$u = x^2,\, du = 2x\, dx,$

$dv = \sqrt{1 - x}\, dx$, and $v = -\dfrac{2}{3}(1 - x)^{3/2}.$ Then

$\displaystyle\int x^2 \sqrt{1 - x}\, dx = -\frac{2}{3}x^2 (1 - x)^{3/2}$

$\displaystyle + \frac{4}{3}\int x(1 - x)^{3/2}\, dx.$ Use parts again with

$u = x,\, du = dx,\, dv = (1 - x)^{3/2} dx,$

and $v = -\dfrac{2}{5}(1 - x)^{5/2}$ so that

$\displaystyle\int x^2 \sqrt{1 - x}\, dx = -\frac{2}{3}x^2(1 - x)^{3/2}$

$\displaystyle + \frac{4}{3}\left[-\frac{2}{5}(1 - x)^{5/2} - \int -\frac{2}{5}(1 - x)^{5/2}\, dx\right].$

Integrate for $-\dfrac{2}{3}x^2 (1 - x)^{3/2} - \dfrac{8}{15}x$

$(1-x)^{5/2} - \frac{16}{105}x(1-x)^{7/2}$ and simplify to

$-\dfrac{2}{105}(1-x)^{3/2}\left[15x^2 + 12x + 8\right] + C.$

22. For $\displaystyle\int 3x^2 \sin x\, dx$, use integration by parts with $u = 3x^2$, $du = 6x\, dx$, $dv = \sin x\, dx$, and $v = -\cos x$.

$\displaystyle\int 3x^2 \sin x\, dx = -3x^2 \cos x +$

$\left[6x \sin x - \displaystyle\int 6 \sin x\, dx\right] = -3x^2 \cos x +$

$6x \sin x + 6 \cos x + C.$

23. Factor the denominator so that

$\displaystyle\int \dfrac{x\, dx}{x^2 - 3x - 4} = \int \dfrac{x\, dx}{(x-4)(x+1)}.$

Use a partial fraction decomposition,

$\dfrac{x}{(x-4)(x+1)} = \dfrac{A}{(x-4)} + \dfrac{B}{(x+1)}$, which

implies $Ax + A + Bx - 4B = x$. Solve

$A + B = 1$ and $A - 4B$ to find

$A = \dfrac{4}{5}$ and $B = \dfrac{1}{5}$. Integrate

$\displaystyle\int \dfrac{x\, dx}{x^2 - 3x - 4} = \int \dfrac{4/5}{x-4}\, dx +$

$\displaystyle\int \dfrac{1/5}{x+1}\, dx = \dfrac{4}{5} \ln|x-4|$

$+ \dfrac{1}{5} \ln|x+1| + C$

$= \dfrac{1}{5} \ln\left|(x-4)^4 (x+1)\right| + C.$

24. Factor $\displaystyle\int \dfrac{dx}{x^2 + x} = \int \dfrac{dx}{x(x+1)}$ and use

partial fractions. If $\dfrac{1}{x(x+1)}$

$= \dfrac{A}{x} + \dfrac{B}{(x+1)}$, $Ax + A + Bx = 1$ and

$A = -B = 1$.

$\displaystyle\int \dfrac{dx}{x^2 + x} = \int \dfrac{dx}{x} + \int \dfrac{-dx}{x+1}$

$= \ln|x| - \ln|x+1| + C$

$= \ln\left|\dfrac{x}{x+1}\right| + C.$

25. Begin with integration by parts, using

$u = \ln x$, $du = \dfrac{dx}{x}$, $dv = \dfrac{dx}{(x+5)^2}$,

and $v = \dfrac{-1}{x+5}$.

Then $\displaystyle\int \dfrac{\ln x}{(x+5)^2}\, dx$

$= \dfrac{-\ln|x|}{x+5} + \int \dfrac{dx}{x(x+5)}.$

Use partial fractions to decompose

$\dfrac{1}{x(x+5)} = \dfrac{A}{x} + \dfrac{B}{(x+5)}$. Solve to find

$A = -B = \dfrac{1}{5}$. Then $\displaystyle\int \dfrac{\ln x}{(x+5)^2}\, dx$

$= \dfrac{-\ln|x|}{x+5} + \dfrac{1}{5} \ln|x| - \dfrac{1}{5} \ln|x+5|$

$= \dfrac{-\ln|x|}{x+5} + \dfrac{1}{5} \ln\left|\dfrac{x}{x+5}\right| + C.$

10.8 Solutions to Cumulative Review Problems

26. (a) At $t = 4$, speed is 5, which is the greatest on $0 \le t \le 10$.

   (b) The particle is moving to the right when $6 < t < 10$.

27. $V = \dfrac{4}{3}\pi r^3$;

$\dfrac{dV}{dt} = \left(\dfrac{4}{3}\right)(3)\pi r^2 \dfrac{dr}{dt} = 4\pi r^2 \dfrac{dr}{dt}$

If $\dfrac{dV}{dt} = 100\dfrac{dr}{dt}$, then $100\dfrac{dr}{dt}$

$= 4\pi r^2 \dfrac{dr}{dt} \Rightarrow 100.$

$= 4\pi r^2$ or $r = \pm\sqrt{\dfrac{25}{\pi}} = \pm\dfrac{5}{\sqrt{\pi}}.$

Since $r \ge 0$, $r = \dfrac{5}{\sqrt{\pi}}$ meters.

28. Let $u = \ln x$; $du = \dfrac{1}{x}dx$.

Rewrite: $\displaystyle\int u^3 du = \dfrac{u^4}{4} + C = \dfrac{(\ln x)^4}{4} + C$

$= \dfrac{\ln^4(x)}{4} + C.$

29. Label given points as A, B, C, D, and E. Since $f''(x) > 0 \Rightarrow f$ is concave upward for all x in the interval $[0, 2]$.
Thus, $m_{\overline{BC}} < f'(x) < m_{\overline{CD}}$
$m_{\overline{BC}} = 1.5$ and $m_{\overline{CD}} = 2.5$.
Therefore, $1.5 < f'(1) < 2.5$, choice (c). (See Figure 10.8-1.)

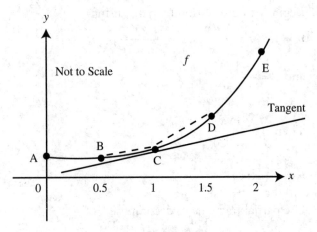

Figure 10.8-1

30. (a) f'' is decreasing on $[1, 6) \Rightarrow f''' < 0 \Rightarrow f'$ is concave downward on $[1, 6)$ and f'' is increasing on $(6, 8] \Rightarrow f'$ is concave upward on $(6, 8]$. Thus, at $x = 6$, f' has a change of concavity. Since f'' exists at $x = 6$ (which implies there is a tangent to the curve of f' at $x = 6$), f' has a point of inflection at $x = 6$.

(b) $f'' > 0$ on $[1, 4] \Rightarrow f'$ is increasing and $f'' < 0$ on $(4, 8] \Rightarrow f'$ is decreasing. Thus at $x = 4$, f' has a relative maximum at $x = 4$. There is no relative minimum.

(c) f'' is increasing on $[6, 8] \Rightarrow f' > 0 \Rightarrow f'$ is concave upward on $[6, 8]$.

31. $\displaystyle\lim_{x \to -2} \dfrac{x^2 - x - 6}{x^2 - 4} \to \dfrac{0}{0}$

$= \displaystyle\lim_{x \to -2} \dfrac{2x - 1}{2x} = \dfrac{5}{4}$

32. At $t = 2$, $x = 4\sin(2\pi) = 0$, and $y = 2^2 - 3 \cdot 2 + 1 = -1$, so the position of the object at $t = 2$ is $(0, -1)$.

33. To find the slope of the tangent line to the curve $r = 3\cos\theta$ when $\theta = \dfrac{\pi}{4}$, begin with $x = r\cos\theta$ and $y = r\sin\theta$, and find $\dfrac{dx}{d\theta}$ and $\dfrac{dy}{d\theta}$. $x = 3\cos^2\theta$ so $\dfrac{dx}{d\theta} = -6\cos\theta\sin\theta$. $y = 3\cos\theta\sin\theta$ so $\dfrac{dy}{d\theta} = 3\cos^2\theta - 3\sin^2\theta$. Then the slope of the tangent line is
$\dfrac{dy}{dx} = \dfrac{dy}{d\theta} \cdot \dfrac{d\theta}{dx} = \dfrac{3\cos^2\theta - 3\sin^2\theta}{-6\cos\theta\sin\theta} = \dfrac{\cos 2\theta}{-\sin 2\theta}.$
Evaluate at $\theta = \dfrac{\pi}{4}$ to get
$\dfrac{\cos\left(\pi/2\right)}{-\sin\left(\pi/2\right)} = \dfrac{0}{-1} = 0.$ The slope of the tangent line is zero, indicating that the tangent is horizontal.

CHAPTER 11

Big Idea 3: Integrals and the Fundamental Theorems of Calculus
Definite Integrals

IN THIS CHAPTER

Summary: In this chapter, you will be introduced to the summation notation, the concept of a Riemann Sum, the Fundamental Theorems of Calculus, and the properties of definite integrals. You will also be shown techniques for evaluating definite integrals involving algebraic, trigonometric, logarithmic, and exponential functions. In addition, you will learn how to work with improper integrals. The ability to evaluate integrals is a prerequisite to doing well on the AP Calculus BC exam.

Key Ideas
✪ Summation Notation
✪ Riemann Sums
✪ Properties of Definite Integrals
✪ The First Fundamental Theorem of Calculus
✪ The Second Fundamental Theorem of Calculus
✪ Evaluating Definite Integrals
✪ Improper Integrals

11.1 Riemann Sums and Definite Integrals

Main Concepts: Sigma Notation, Definition of a Riemann Sum, Definition of a Definite Integral, and Properties of Definite Integrals

Sigma Notation or Summation Notation

$$\sum_{i=1}^{n} a_1 + a_2 + a_3 + \cdots + a_n$$

where i is the index of summation, l is the lower limit, and n is the upper limit of summation. (Note: The lower limit may be any non-negative integer $\leq n$.)

Examples

$$\sum_{i=5}^{7} i^2 = 5^2 + 6^2 + 7^2$$

$$\sum_{k=0}^{3} 2k = 2(0) + 2(1) + 2(2) + 2(3)$$

$$\sum_{i=-1}^{3} (2i + 1) = -1 + 1 + 3 + 5 + 7$$

$$\sum_{k=1}^{4} (-1)^k (k) = -1 + 2 - 3 + 4$$

Summation Formulas

If n is a positive integer, then:

1. $\displaystyle\sum_{i=1}^{n} a = an$

2. $\displaystyle\sum_{i=1}^{n} i = \frac{n(n+1)}{2}$

3. $\displaystyle\sum_{i=1}^{n} i^2 = \frac{n(n+1)(2n+1)}{6}$

4. $\displaystyle\sum_{i=1}^{n} i^3 = \frac{n^2(n+1)^2}{4}$

5. $\displaystyle\sum_{i=1}^{n} i^4 = \frac{n(n+1)(6n^3 + 9n^2 + n - 1)}{30}$

Example

Evaluate $\displaystyle\sum_{i=1}^{n} \frac{i(i+1)}{n}$.

Rewrite: $\displaystyle\sum_{i=1}^{n} \frac{i(i+1)}{n}$ as $\displaystyle\frac{1}{n}\sum_{i=1}^{n}(i^2+i) = \frac{1}{n}\left(\sum_{i=1}^{n} i^2 + \sum_{i=1}^{n} i\right)$

$$= \frac{1}{n}\left(\frac{n(n+1)(2n+1)}{6} + \frac{n(n+1)}{2}\right)$$

$$= \frac{1}{n}\left[\frac{n(n+1)(2n+1) + 3n(n+1)}{6}\right] = \frac{(n+1)(2n+1) + 3(n+1)}{6}$$

$$= \frac{(n+1)\,[(2n+1)+3]}{6} = \frac{(n+1)(2n+4)}{6}$$

$$= \frac{(n+1)(n+2)}{3}.$$

> • Remember: In exponential growth/decay problems, the formulas are $\dfrac{dy}{dx} = ky$ and $y = y_0 e^{kt}$.

Definition of a Riemann Sum

Let f be defined on $[a, b]$ and x_i be points on $[a, b]$ such that $x_0 = a$, $x_n = b$, and $a < x_1 < x_2 < x_3 \cdots < x_{n-1} < b$. The points a, x_1, x_2, x_3, $\ldots x_{n+1}$, and b form a partition of f denoted as Δ on $[a, b]$. Let Δx_i be the length of the ith interval $[x_{i-1}, x_i]$ and c_i be any point in the ith interval. Then the Riemann sum of f for the partition is $\displaystyle\sum_{i=1}^{n} f(c_i)\Delta x_i$.

Example 1

Let f be a continuous function defined on $[0, 12]$ as shown below.

x	0	2	4	6	8	10	12
$f(x)$	3	7	19	39	67	103	147

Find the Riemann sum for $f(x)$ over $[0, 12]$ with 3 subdivisions of equal length and the midpoints of the intervals as c_i.

Length of an interval $\Delta x_i = \dfrac{12 - 0}{3} = 4.$ (See Figure 11.1-1.)

Figure 11.1-1

$$\text{Riemann sum} = \sum_{i=1}^{3} f(c_i)\Delta x_i = f(c_1)\Delta x_1 + f(c_2)\Delta x_2 + f(c_3)\Delta x_3$$

$$= 7(4) + 39(4) + 103(4) = 596$$

The Riemann sum is 596.

Example 2

Find the Riemann sum for $f(x) = x^3 + 1$ over the interval $[0, 4]$ using 4 subdivisions of equal length and the midpoints of the intervals as c_i. (See Figure 11.1-2.)

Figure 11.1-2

$$\text{Length of an interval } \Delta x_i = \frac{b-a}{n} = \frac{4-0}{4} = 1; \ c_i = 0.5 + (i-1) = i - 0.5.$$

$$\text{Riemann sum} = \sum_{i=1}^{4} f(c_i)\Delta x_i = \sum_{i=1}^{4} \left[(i-0.5)^3 + 1 \right] 1$$

$$= \sum_{i=1}^{4} (i-0.5)^3 + 1.$$

Enter $\sum \left((1-0.5)^3 + 1, i, 1, 4 \right) = 66.$

The Riemann sum is 66.

Definition of a Definite Integral

Let f be defined on $[a, b]$ with the Riemann sum for f over $[a, b]$ written as $\sum_{i=1}^{n} f(c_i)\Delta x_i$.

If $\max \Delta x_i$ is the length of the largest subinterval in the partition and the $\lim_{\max \Delta x_i \to 0} \sum_{i=1}^{n} f(c_i)\Delta x_i$ exists, then the limit is denoted by:

$$\lim_{\max \Delta x_i \to 0} \sum_{i=1}^{n} f(c_i)\Delta x_i = \int_a^b f(x)dx.$$

$\int_a^b f(x)dx$ is the definite integral of f from a to b.

Example 1

Use a midpoint Riemann sum with three subdivisions of equal length to find the approximate value of $\int_0^6 x^2 dx$.

$$\Delta x = \frac{6-0}{3} = 2, \ f(x) = x^2$$

midpoints are $x = 1, 3,$ and 5.

$$\int_0^6 x^2 dx \approx f(1)\Delta x + f(3)\Delta x + f(5)\Delta x = 1(2) + 9(2) + 25(2)$$

$$\approx 70$$

Example 2

Using the limit of the Riemann sum, find $\int_1^5 3x\, dx$.

Using n subintervals of equal lengths, the length of an interval

$$\Delta x_i = \frac{5-1}{n} = \frac{4}{n}; x_i = 1 + \left(\frac{4}{n}\right)i$$

$$\int_1^5 3x\, dx = \lim_{\max \Delta x_i \to 0} \sum_{i=1}^{n} f(c_i)\Delta x_i.$$

Let $c_i = x_i$; $\max \Delta x_i \to 0 \Rightarrow n \to \infty$.

$$\int_1^5 3x\, dx = \lim_{n \to \infty} \sum_{i=1}^{n} f\left(1 + \frac{4i}{n}\right)\left(\frac{4}{n}\right) = \lim_{n \to \infty} \sum_{i=1}^{n} 3\left(1 + \frac{4i}{n}\right)\left(\frac{4}{n}\right)$$

$$= \lim_{n \to \infty} \frac{12}{n} \sum_{i=1}^{n} \left(1 + \frac{4i}{n}\right) = \lim_{n \to \infty} \frac{12}{n}\left(n + \frac{4}{n}\left[n\left(\frac{n+1}{2}\right)\right]\right)$$

$$= \lim_{n \to \infty} \frac{12}{n}(n + 2(n + 1)) = \lim_{n \to \infty} \frac{12}{n}(3n + 2) = \lim_{n \to \infty} \left(36 + \frac{24}{n}\right) = 36$$

Thus, $\int_1^5 3x\, dx = 36$.

Properties of Definite Integrals

1. If f is defined on $[a, b]$, and the limit $\lim\limits_{\max \Delta x_i \to 0} \sum\limits_{i=1}^{n} f(x_i)\Delta x_i$ exists, then f is integrable on $[a, b]$.

2. If f is continuous on $[a, b]$, then f is integrable on $[a, b]$.

If $f(x), g(x),$ and $h(x)$ are integrable on $[a, b]$, then

3. $\displaystyle\int_a^a f(x)dx = 0$

4. $\displaystyle\int_a^b f(x)dx = -\int_b^a f(x)$

5. $\displaystyle\int_a^b Cf(x)dx = C\int_a^b f(x)dx$ when C is a constant.

6. $\displaystyle\int_a^b [f(x) \pm g(x)]\,dx = \int_a^b f(x)dx \pm \int_a^b g(x)dx$

7. $\displaystyle\int_a^b f(x)dx \geq 0$ provided $f(x) \geq 0$ on $[a, b]$.

8. $\displaystyle\int_a^b f(x)dx \geq \int_a^b g(x)dx$ provided $f(x) \geq g(x)$ on $[a, b]$.

9. $\displaystyle\left|\int_a^b f(x)dx\right| \leq \int_a^b |f(x)|\,dx$

10. $\displaystyle\int_a^b g(x)dx \leq \int_a^b f(x)dx \leq \int_a^b h(x)dx;$ provided $g(x) \leq f(x) \leq h(x)$ on $[a, b]$.

11. $m(b - a) \leq \displaystyle\int_a^b f(x)dx \leq M(b - a);$ provided $m \leq f(x) \leq M$ on $[a, b]$.

12. $\displaystyle\int_a^c f(x)dx = \int_a^b f(x)dx + \int_b^c f(x)dx;$ provided $f(x)$ is integrable on an interval containing a, b, c.

Examples

1. $\displaystyle\int_\pi^\pi \cos x\,dx = 0$

2. $\displaystyle\int_1^5 x^4 dx = -\int_5^1 x^4 dx$

3. $\displaystyle\int_{-2}^7 5x^2 dx = 5\int_{-2}^7 x^2 dx$

4. $\displaystyle\int_0^4 (x^3 - 2x + 1)\,dx = \int_0^4 x^3 dx - 2\int_0^4 x\,dx + \int_0^4 1dx$

5. $\displaystyle\int_1^5 \sqrt{x}dx = \int_1^3 \sqrt{x}dx + \int_3^5 \sqrt{x}dx$

Note: Or $\displaystyle\int_1^3 \sqrt{x}dx = \int_1^5 \sqrt{x}dx + \int_5^3 \sqrt{x}dx$

$\displaystyle\int_a^c = \int_a^b + \int_b^c$ a, b, c do not have to be arranged from smallest to largest.

The remaining properties are best illustrated in terms of the area under the curve of the function as discussed in the next section.

- Do not forget that $\int_{0}^{-3} f(x)dx = -\int_{-3}^{0} f(x)dx.$

11.2 Fundamental Theorems of Calculus

Main Concepts: First Fundamental Theorem of Calculus, Second Fundamental Theorem of Calculus

First Fundamental Theorem of Calculus

If f is continuous on $[a, b]$ and F is an antiderivative of f on $[a, b]$, then

$$\int_{a}^{b} f(x)dx = F(b) - F(a).$$

Note: $F(b) - F(a)$ is often denoted as $F(x)\big]_{a}^{b}$.

Example 1

Evaluate $\displaystyle\int_{0}^{2} \left(4x^3 + x - 1\right)dx.$

$$\int_{0}^{2} \left(4x^3 + x - 1\right)dx = \frac{4x^4}{4} + \frac{x^2}{2} - x \Big]_{0}^{2} = x^4 + \frac{x^2}{2} - x \Big]_{0}^{2}$$

$$= \left(2^4 + \frac{2^2}{2} - 2\right) - (0) = 16$$

Example 2

Evaluate $\displaystyle\int_{-\pi}^{\pi} \sin x\,dx.$

$$\int_{-\pi}^{\pi} \sin x\,dx = -\cos x \Big]_{-\pi}^{\pi} = [-\cos \pi] - [-\cos(-\pi)]$$

$$= [-(-1)] - [-(-1)] = (1) - (1) = 0$$

Example 3

If $\displaystyle\int_{-2}^{k} (4x + 1)dx = 30$, $k > 0$, find k.

$$\int_{-2}^{k} (4x + 1)dx = 2x^2 + x \Big]_{-2}^{k} = \left(2k^2 + k\right) - \left(2(-2)^2 - 2\right)$$

$$= 2k^2 + k - 6$$

Set $2k^2 + k - 6 = 30 \Rightarrow 2k^2 + k - 36 = 0$

$$\Rightarrow (2k + 9)(k - 4) = 0 \text{ or } k = -\frac{9}{2} \text{ or } k = 4.$$

Since $k > 0$, $k = 4$.

Example 4

If $f'(x) = g(x)$, and g is a continuous function for all real values of x, express $\int_2^5 g(3x)dx$ in terms of f.

Let $u = 3x$; $du = 3dx$ or $\dfrac{du}{3} = dx$.

$$\int g(3x)dx = \int g(u)\frac{du}{3} = \frac{1}{3}\int g(u)du = \frac{1}{3}f(u) + C$$

$$= \frac{1}{3}f(3x) + C$$

$$\int_2^5 g(3x)dx = \frac{1}{3}f(3x)\Big]_2^5 = \frac{1}{3}f(3(5)) - \frac{1}{3}f(3(2))$$

$$= \frac{1}{3}f(15) - \frac{1}{3}f(6)$$

Example 5

Evaluate $\int_0^4 \dfrac{1}{x-1}dx$.

Cannot evaluate using the First Fundamental Theorem of Calculus since $f(x) = \dfrac{1}{x-1}$ is discontinuous at $x = 1$.

Example 6

Using a graphing calculator, evaluate $\int_{-2}^2 \sqrt{4 - x^2}dx$.

Using a TI-89 graphing calculator, enter $\int \left(\sqrt{(4 - x\text{^}2)},\ x,\ -2,\ 2 \right)$ and obtain 2π.

Second Fundamental Theorem of Calculus

If f is continuous on $[a, b]$ and $F(x) = \displaystyle\int_a^x f(t)dt$, then $F'(x) = f(x)$ at every point x in $[a, b]$.

Example 1

Evaluate $\displaystyle\int_{\pi/4}^{x} \cos(2t)\, dt$.

Let $u = 2t$; $du = 2dt$ or $\dfrac{du}{2} = dt$.

$$\int \cos(2t)\,dt = \int \cos u \,\frac{du}{2} = \frac{1}{2}\int \cos u\, du$$

$$= \frac{1}{2}\sin u + C = \frac{1}{2}\sin(2t) + C$$

$$\int_{\pi/4}^{x} \cos(2t)\,dt = \frac{1}{2}\sin(2t)\Big]_{\pi/4}^{x}$$

$$= \frac{1}{2}\sin(2x) - \frac{1}{2}\sin\left(2\left(\frac{\pi}{4}\right)\right)$$

$$= \frac{1}{2}\sin(2x) - \frac{1}{2}\sin\left(\frac{\pi}{2}\right)$$

$$= \frac{1}{2}\sin(2x) - \frac{1}{2}$$

Example 2

If $h(x) = \displaystyle\int_{3}^{x} \sqrt{t+1}\, dt$ find $h'(8)$.

$$h'(x) = \sqrt{x+1}; \quad h'(8) = \sqrt{8+1} = 3$$

Example 3

Find $\dfrac{dy}{dx}$; if $y = \displaystyle\int_{1}^{2x} \frac{1}{t^3}\, dt$.

Let $u = 2x$; then $\dfrac{dy}{dx} = 2$.

Rewrite: $y = \displaystyle\int_{1}^{u} \frac{1}{t^3}\, dt$.

$$\frac{dy}{dx} = \frac{dy}{du}\cdot\frac{du}{dx} = \frac{1}{u^3}\cdot(2) = \frac{1}{(2x)^3}\cdot 2 = \frac{1}{4x^3}$$

Example 4

Find $\dfrac{dy}{dx}$; if $y = \displaystyle\int_{x^2}^{1} \sin t\, dt$.

Rewrite: $y = -\displaystyle\int_{1}^{x^2} \sin t\, dt$.

Let $u = x^2$; then $\dfrac{du}{dx} = 2x$.

Rewrite: $y = -\displaystyle\int_1^u \sin t \, dt$.

$$\frac{dy}{dx} = \frac{dy}{du} \cdot \frac{du}{dx} = (-\sin u)2x = (-\sin x^2)2x$$

$$= -2x \sin(x^2)$$

Example 5

Find $\dfrac{dy}{dx}$; if $y = \displaystyle\int_x^{x^2} \sqrt{e^t + 1} \, dt$.

$$y = \int_x^0 \sqrt{e^t + 1}\, dt + \int_0^{x^2} \sqrt{e^t + 1}\, dt = -\int_0^x \sqrt{e^t + 1}\, dt + \int_0^{x^2} \sqrt{e^t + 1}\, dt$$

$$= \int_0^{x^2} \sqrt{e^t + 1}\, dt - \int_0^x \sqrt{e^t + 1}\, dt$$

Since $y = \displaystyle\int_0^{x^2} \sqrt{e^t + 1}\, dt - \int_0^x \sqrt{e^t + 1}\, dt$

$$\frac{dy}{dx} = \left(\frac{d}{dx} \int_0^{x^2} \sqrt{e^t + 1}\, dt \right) - \left(\frac{d}{dx} \int_0^x \sqrt{e^t + 1}\, dt \right)$$

$$= \left(\sqrt{e^{x^2} + 1} \right) \frac{d}{dx}(x^2) - \left(\sqrt{e^x + 1} \right)$$

$$= 2x\sqrt{e^{x^2} + 1} - \sqrt{e^x + 1}.$$

Example 6

$F(x) = \displaystyle\int_1^x (t^2 - 4)dt$, integrate to find $F(x)$ and then differentiate to find $f'(x)$.

$$F(x) = \frac{t^3}{3} - 4t \Big]_1^x = \left(\frac{x^3}{3} - 4x \right) - \left(\frac{1^3}{3} - 4(1) \right)$$

$$= \frac{x^3}{3} - 4x + \frac{11}{3}$$

$$F'(x) = 3\left(\frac{x^2}{3} \right) - 4 = x^2 - 4$$

11.3 Evaluating Definite Integrals

Main Concepts: Definite Integrals Involving Algebraic Functions;
Definite Integrals Involving Absolute Value; Definite
Integrals Involving Trigonometric, Logarithmic, and
Exponential Functions; Definite Integrals Involving
Odd and Even Functions

- If the problem asks you to determine the concavity of f' (not f), you need to know if f'' is increasing or decreasing, or if f''' is positive or negative.

Definite Integrals Involving Algebraic Functions

Example 1

Evaluate $\int_1^4 \dfrac{x^3 - 8}{\sqrt{x}}\,dx$.

Rewrite: $\int_1^4 \dfrac{x^3 - 8}{\sqrt{x}}\,dx = \int_1^4 \left(x^{5/2} - 8x^{-1/2}\right)dx$

$$= \dfrac{x^{7/2}}{7/2} - \dfrac{8x^{1/2}}{1/2}\Bigg]_1^4 = \dfrac{2x^{7/2}}{7} - 16x^{1/2}\Bigg]_1^4$$

$$= \left(\dfrac{2(4)^{7/2}}{7} - 16(4)^{1/2}\right) - \left(\dfrac{2(1)^{7/2}}{7} - 16(1)^{1/2}\right) = \dfrac{142}{7}.$$

Verify your result with a calculator.

Example 2

Evaluate $\int_0^2 x(x^2 - 1)^7\,dx$.

Begin by evaluating the indefinite integral $\int x(x^2 - 1)^7\,dx$.

Let $u = x^2 - 1$; $du = 2x\,dx$ or $\dfrac{du}{2} = x\,dx$.

Rewrite: $\int \dfrac{u^7\,du}{2} = \dfrac{1}{2}\int u^7\,du = \dfrac{1}{2}\left(\dfrac{u^8}{8}\right) + C = \dfrac{u^8}{16} + C = \dfrac{(x^2 - 1)^8}{16} + C.$

Thus, the definite integral $\int_0^2 x(x^2 - 1)^7\,dx = \dfrac{(x^2 - 1)^8}{16}\Bigg]_0^2$

$$= \dfrac{(2^2 - 1)^8}{16} - \dfrac{(0^2 - 1)^8}{16} = \dfrac{3^8}{16} - \dfrac{(-1)^8}{16} = \dfrac{3^8 - 1}{16} = 410.$$

Verify your result with a calculator.

Example 3

Evaluate $\displaystyle\int_{-8}^{-1}\left(\sqrt[3]{y}+\frac{1}{\sqrt[3]{y}}\right)dy$.

Rewrite: $\displaystyle\int_{-8}^{-1}\left(y^{1/3}+\frac{1}{y^{1/3}}\right)dy=\int_{-8}^{-1}\left(y^{1/3}+y^{-1/3}\right)dy$

$$=\frac{y^{4/3}}{4/3}+\frac{y^{2/3}}{2/3}\Big]_{-8}^{-1}=\frac{3y^{4/3}}{4}+\frac{3y^{2/3}}{2}\Big]_{-8}^{-1}$$

$$=\left(\frac{3(-1)^{4/3}}{4}+\frac{3(-1)^{2/3}}{2}\right)$$

$$-\left(\frac{3(-8)^{4/3}}{4}+\frac{3(-8)^{2/3}}{2}\right)$$

$$=\left(\frac{3}{4}+\frac{3}{2}\right)-(12+6)=\frac{-63}{4}.$$

Verify your result with a calculator.

- You may bring up to 2 (but no more than 2) approved graphing calculators to the exam.

Definite Integrals Involving Absolute Value

Example 1

Evaluate $\displaystyle\int_{1}^{4}\left|3x-6\right|dx$.

Set $3x-6=0$; $x=2$; thus $\left|3x-6\right|=\begin{cases}3x-6 & \text{if } x\geq 2\\-(3x-6) & \text{if } x<2\end{cases}$.

Rewrite integral:

$$\int_{1}^{4}\left|3x-6\right|dx=\int_{1}^{2}-(3x-6)dx+\int_{2}^{4}(3x-6)dx$$

$$=\left[\frac{-3x^2}{2}+6x\right]_{1}^{2}+\left[\frac{3x^2}{2}-6x\right]_{2}^{4}$$

$$=\left(\frac{-3(2)^2}{2}-6(2)\right)-\left(\frac{-3(1)^2}{2}-6(1)\right)$$

$$+\left(\frac{3(4)^2}{2}-6(4)\right)-\left(\frac{3(2)^2}{2}-6(2)\right)$$

$$=(-6+12)-\left(-\frac{3}{2}+6\right)+(24-24)-(6-12)$$

$$=6-4\frac{1}{2}+0+6=\frac{15}{2}.$$

Verify your result with a calculator.

Example 2

Evaluate $\displaystyle\int_0^4 |x^2 - 4| \, dx$.

Set $x^2 - 4 = 0$; $x = \pm 2$.

Thus $|x^2 - 4| = \begin{cases} x^2 - 4 & \text{if } x \geq 2 \text{ or } x \leq -2 \\ -(x^2 - 4) & \text{if } -2 < x < 2 \end{cases}$.

Thus, $\displaystyle\int_0^4 |x^2 - 4| \, dx = \int_0^2 -(x^2 - 4) \, dx + \int_2^4 (x^2 - 4) \, dx$

$$= \left[\frac{-x^3}{3} + 4x \right]_0^2 + \left[\frac{x^3}{3} - 4x \right]_2^4$$

$$= \left(\frac{-2^3}{3} + 4(2) \right) - (0) + \left(\frac{4^3}{3} - 4(4) \right)$$

$$- \left(\frac{2^3}{3} - 4(2) \right)$$

$$= \left(\frac{-8}{3} + 8 \right) + \left(\frac{64}{3} - 16 \right) - \left(\frac{8}{3} - 8 \right) = 16.$$

Verify your result with a calculator.

- You are not required to clear the memories in your calculator for the exam.

Definite Integrals Involving Trigonometric, Logarithmic, and Exponential Functions

Example 1

Evaluate $\displaystyle\int_0^\pi (x + \sin x) \, dx$.

Rewrite: $\displaystyle\int_0^\pi (x + \sin x) \, dx = \frac{x^2}{2} - \cos x \Big]_0^\pi = \left(\frac{\pi^2}{2} - \cos \pi \right) - (0 - \cos 0)$

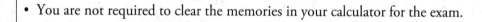

$$= \frac{\pi^2}{2} + 1 + 1 = \frac{\pi^2}{2} + 2.$$

Verify your result with a calculator.

Example 2

Evaluate $\displaystyle\int_{\pi/4}^{\pi/2} \csc^2(3t) \, dt$.

Let $u = 3t$; $du = 3dt$ or $\dfrac{du}{3} = dt$.

Rewrite the indefinite integral: $\displaystyle\int \csc^2 u \frac{du}{3} = -\frac{1}{3}\cot u + c$

$$= -\frac{1}{3}\cot(3t) + c$$

$$\int_{\pi/4}^{\pi/2} \csc^2(3t)dt = -\frac{1}{3}\cot(3t)\Big]_{\pi/4}^{\pi/2}$$

$$= -\frac{1}{3}\left[\cot\left(\frac{3\pi}{2}\right) - \cot\left(\frac{3\pi}{4}\right)\right]$$

$$= -\frac{1}{3}[0 - (-1)] = -\frac{1}{3}.$$

Verify your result with a calculator.

Example 3

Evaluate $\displaystyle\int_1^e \frac{\ln t}{t}dt.$

Let $u = \ln t$, $du = \dfrac{1}{t}dt.$

Rewrite: $\displaystyle\int \frac{\ln t}{t}dt = \int u\, du = \frac{u^2}{2} + C = \frac{(\ln t)^2}{2} + C$

$$\int_1^e \frac{\ln t}{t}dt = \frac{(\ln t)^2}{2}\Bigg]_1^e = \frac{(\ln e)^2}{2} - \frac{(\ln 1)^2}{2}$$

$$= \frac{1}{2} - 0 = \frac{1}{2}.$$

Verify your result with a calculator.

Example 4

Evaluate $\displaystyle\int_{-1}^2 xe^{(x^2+1)}dx.$

Let $u = x^2 + 1$; $du = 2x\, dx$ or $\dfrac{dx}{2} = x\, dx.$

$$\int xe^{(x^2+1)}dx = \int e^u \frac{du}{2} = \frac{1}{2}e^u + C = \frac{1}{2}e^{(x^2+2)} + C$$

Rewrite: $\displaystyle\int_{-1}^2 xe^{(x^2+1)}dx = \frac{1}{2}e^{(x^2+1)}\Bigg]_{-1}^2 = \frac{1}{2}e^5 - \frac{1}{2}e^2 = \frac{1}{2}e^2\left(e^3 - 1\right).$

Verify your result with a calculator.

Definite Integrals Involving Odd and Even Functions

If f is an even function, that is, $f(-x) = f(x)$, and is continuous on $[-a, a]$, then

$$\int_{-a}^{a} f(x)dx = 2 \int_{0}^{a} f(x)dx.$$

If f is an odd function, that is, $F(x) = -f(-x)$, and is continuous on $[-a, a]$, then

$$\int_{-a}^{a} f(x)dx = 0.$$

Example 1

Evaluate $\displaystyle\int_{-\pi/2}^{\pi/2} \cos x\, dx$.

Since $f(x) = \cos x$ is an even function,

$$\int_{-\pi/2}^{\pi/2} \cos x\, dx = 2 \int_{0}^{\pi/2} \cos x\, dx = 2\left[\sin x\right]_{0}^{\pi/2} = 2\left[\sin\left(\frac{\pi}{2}\right) - \sin(0)\right]$$

$$= 2(1 - 0) = 2.$$

Verify your result with a calculator.

Example 2

Evaluate $\displaystyle\int_{-3}^{3} \left(x^4 - x^2\right)dx$.

Since $f(x) = x^4 - x^2$ is an even function, i.e., $f(-x) = f(x)$, thus

$$\int_{-3}^{3} \left(x^4 - x^2\right)dx = 2 \int_{0}^{3} \left(x^4 - x^2\right)dx = 2\left[\frac{x^5}{5} - \frac{x^3}{3}\right]_{0}^{3}$$

$$= 2\left[\left(\frac{3^5}{5} - \frac{3^3}{3}\right) - 0\right] = \frac{396}{5}.$$

Verify your result with a calculator.

Example 3

Evaluate $\displaystyle\int_{-\pi}^{\pi} \sin x\, dx$.

Since $f(x) = \sin x$ is an odd function, i.e., $f(-x) = -f(x)$, thus

$$\int_{-\pi}^{\pi} \sin x\, dx = 0.$$

Verify your result algebraically.

$$\int_{-\pi}^{\pi} \sin x\, dx = -\cos x\Big]_{-\pi}^{\pi} = (-\cos \pi) - [-\cos(-\pi)]$$

$$= [-(-1)] - [-(1)] = (1) - (1) = 0$$

You can also verify the result with a calculator.

Example 4

If $\displaystyle\int_{-k}^{k} f(x)dx = 2 \int_{0}^{k} f(x)dx$ for all values of k, then which of the following could be the graph of f? (See Figure 11.3-1.)

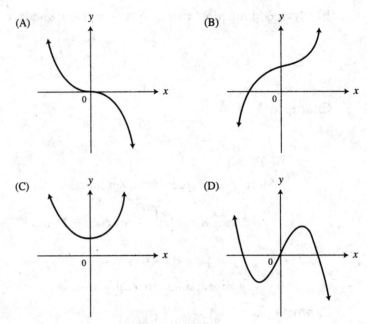

Figure 11.3-1

$$\int_{-k}^{k} f(x)dx = \int_{-k}^{0} f(x)dx + \int_{0}^{k} f(x)dx$$

Since $\displaystyle\int_{-k}^{k} f(x)dx = 2 \int_{0}^{k} f(x)dx$, then $\displaystyle\int_{0}^{k} f(x)dx = \int_{-k}^{0} f(x)dx$.

Thus, f is an even function. Choice (C).

11.4 Improper Integrals

Main Concepts: Infinite Intervals of Integration, Infinite Discontinuities

Infinite Intervals of Integration

Improper integrals are integrals with infinite intervals of integration or infinite discontinuities within the interval of integration. For infinite intervals of integration, $\displaystyle\int_{a}^{\infty} f(x)dx = \lim_{l \to \infty} \int_{a}^{l} f(x)dx$ and $\displaystyle\int_{-\infty}^{b} f(x)dx = \lim_{l \to -\infty} \int_{l}^{b} f(x)dx$. If the limit exists, the integral converges.

$$\int_{-\infty}^{\infty} f(x)dx = \int_{-\infty}^{c} f(x)dx + \int_{c}^{\infty} f(x)dx \text{ for some value } c.$$

Example 1

Evaluate $\displaystyle\int_1^\infty \frac{1}{x}dx$.

$$\int_1^\infty \frac{1}{x}dx = \lim_{k\to\infty}\int_1^k \frac{1}{x}dx = \lim_{k\to\infty}[\ln x]_1^k = \lim_{k\to\infty}(\ln k) = \infty \text{ so the integral diverges.}$$

Example 2

Evaluate $\displaystyle\int_{-\infty}^\infty xe^{-x^2}dx$.

Since both limits of integration are infinite, consider the sum of the improper integrals $\displaystyle\int_{-\infty}^\infty xe^{-x^2}dx = \int_{-\infty}^0 xe^{-x^2}dx + \int_0^\infty xe^{-x^2}dx$. This sum is the sum of the limits

$$\lim_{k\to-\infty}\int_k^0 xe^{-x^2}dx + \lim_{c\to\infty}\int_0^c xe^{-x^2}dx = \lim_{k\to-\infty}\left[-\frac{1}{2}e^{-x^2}\right]_k^0 + \lim_{c\to\infty}\left[-\frac{1}{2}e^{-x^2}\right]_0^c =$$

$$\lim_{k\to-\infty}\left[-\frac{1}{2}+\frac{1}{2}e^{-k^2}\right] + \lim_{c\to\infty}\left[-\frac{1}{2}e^{-c^2}+\frac{1}{2}\right] = -\frac{1}{2}+\frac{1}{2} = 0. \text{ Since the limit exists, the integral}$$

converges and $\displaystyle\int_{-\infty}^\infty xe^{-x^2}dx = 0$.

Infinite Discontinuities

If the function has an infinite discontinuity at one of the limits of integration, then $\displaystyle\int_a^b f(x)dx = \lim_{l\to b^-}\int_a^l f(x)dx$ or $\displaystyle\int_a^b f(x)dx = \lim_{l\to a^+}\int_l^b f(x)dx$. If an infinite discontinuity occurs at $x = c$ within the interval of integration (a, b), then the integral can be broken into sections at the discontinuity and the sum of the two improper integrals can be found.

$$\int_a^b f(x)dx = \int_a^c f(x)dx + \int_c^b f(x)dx = \lim_{k\to c^-}\int_a^k f(x)dx + \lim_{l\to c^+}\int_l^b f(x)dx$$

Example

Evaluate $\displaystyle\int_0^{\pi/2} \frac{\cos x}{\sqrt{1-\sin x}}dx$.

Since $f(x) = \dfrac{\cos x}{\sqrt{1-\sin x}}$ has an infinite discontinuity at $x = \dfrac{\pi}{2}$, the integral is improper.

Evaluate $\displaystyle\int_0^{\pi/2} \frac{\cos x}{\sqrt{1-\sin x}}dx = \lim_{k\to\pi/2^-}\int_0^k \frac{\cos x}{\sqrt{1-\sin x}}dx = \lim_{k\to\pi/2^-}\left[-2\sqrt{1-\sin x}\right]_0^k =$

$\displaystyle\lim_{k\to\pi/2^-}\left[-2\sqrt{1-\sin k}+2\right] = 2.$ Since the limit exists, $\displaystyle\int_0^{\pi/2}\frac{\cos x}{\sqrt{1-\sin x}}dx = 2.$

11.5 Rapid Review

1. Evaluate $\displaystyle\int_{\pi/2}^{x} \cos t\, dt$.

   Answer: $\left.\sin t\right]_{x/2}^{x} = \sin x - \sin\left(\dfrac{\pi}{2}\right) = \sin x - 1$.

2. Evaluate $\displaystyle\int_{0}^{1} \dfrac{1}{x+1}\,dx$.

   Answer: $\left.\ln(x+1)\right]_{0}^{1} = \ln 2 - \ln 1 = \ln 2$.

3. If $G(x) = \displaystyle\int_{0}^{x} (2t+1)^{3/2}\,dt$, find $G'(4)$.

   Answer: $G'(x) = (2x+1)^{3/2}$ and $G'(4) = 9^{3/2} = 27$.

4. If $\displaystyle\int_{1}^{k} 2x\,dx = 8$, find k.

   Answer: $\left.x^2\right]_{1}^{k} = 8 \Rightarrow k^2 - 1 = 8 \Rightarrow k = \pm 3$.

5. If $G(x)$ is an antiderivative of $(e^x + 1)$ and $G(0) = 0$, find $G(1)$.

   Answer: $G(x) = e^x + x + C$
   $G(0) = e^0 + 0 + C = 0 \Rightarrow C = -1$.
   $G(1) = e^1 + 1 - 1 = e$.

6. If $G'(x) = g(x)$, express $\displaystyle\int_{0}^{2} g(4x)\,dx$ in terms of $G(x)$.

   Answer: Let $u = 4x$; $\dfrac{du}{4} = dx$.

   $\displaystyle\int g(u)\dfrac{du}{4} = \dfrac{1}{4} G(u)$. Thus, $\displaystyle\int_{0}^{2} g(4x)\,dx = \dfrac{1}{4}\left.G(4x)\right]_{0}^{2} = \dfrac{1}{4}[G(8) - G(0)]$.

7. $\displaystyle\int_{1}^{\infty} \dfrac{dx}{x^2}$

   Answer: $\displaystyle\int_{1}^{\infty} \dfrac{dx}{x^2} = \lim_{n\to\infty} \int_{1}^{n} \dfrac{dx}{x^2} = \lim_{n\to\infty}\left[\dfrac{-1}{x}\right]_{1}^{n} = \lim_{n\to\infty}\left[\dfrac{-1}{n} + 1\right] = 1$.

8. $\displaystyle\int_{0}^{1} \dfrac{dx}{\sqrt{x}}$

   Answer: $\displaystyle\int_{0}^{1} \dfrac{dx}{\sqrt{x}} = \lim_{k\to 0^+} \int_{k}^{1} \dfrac{dx}{\sqrt{x}} = \lim_{k\to 0^+}\left[2\sqrt{x}\right]_{k}^{1} = \lim_{k\to 0^+}\left[2 - 2\sqrt{k}\right] = 2$.

11.6 Practice Problems

Part A—The use of a calculator is not allowed.

Evaluate the following definite integrals.

1. $\int_{-1}^{0} (1 + x - x^3)dx$

2. $\int_{6}^{11} (x - 2)^{1/2} dx$

3. $\int_{1}^{3} \frac{t}{t+1} dt$

4. $\int_{0}^{6} |x - 3| dx$

5. If $\int_{0}^{k} (6x - 1)dx = 4$, find k.

6. $\int_{0}^{\pi} \frac{\sin x}{\sqrt{1 + \cos x}} dx$

7. If $f'(x) = g(x)$ and g is a continuous function for all real values of x, express $\int_{1}^{2} g(4x)dx$ in terms of f.

8. $\int_{\ln 2}^{\ln 3} 10e^x dx$

9. $\int_{e}^{e^2} \frac{1}{t+3} dt$

10. If $f(x) = \int_{-\pi/4}^{x} \tan^2(t)dt$, find $f'\left(\frac{\pi}{6}\right)$.

11. $\int_{-1}^{1} 4xe^{x^2} dx$

12. $\int_{-\pi}^{\pi} (\cos x - x^2)dx$

Part B—Calculators are allowed.

13. Find k if $\int_{0}^{2} (x^3 + k)dx = 10$.

14. Evaluate $\int_{-1.2}^{3.1} 2\theta \cos\theta \, d\theta$ to the nearest 100th.

15. If $y = \int_{1}^{x^3} \sqrt{t^2 + 1} \, dt$, find $\frac{dy}{dx}$.

16. Use a midpoint Riemann sum with four subdivisions of equal length to find the approximate value of $\int_{0}^{8} (x^3 + 1)dx$.

17. Given $\int_{-2}^{2} g(x)dx = 8$ and $\int_{0}^{2} g(x)dx = 3$, find

(a) $\int_{-2}^{0} g(x)dx$

(b) $\int_{2}^{-2} g(x)dx$

(c) $\int_{0}^{-2} 5g(x)dx$

(d) $\int_{-2}^{2} 2g(x)dx$

18. Evaluate $\int_{0}^{1/2} \frac{dx}{\sqrt{1 - x^2}}$.

19. Find $\frac{dy}{dx}$ if $y = \int_{\cos x}^{\sin x} (2t + 1)dt$.

20. Let f be a continuous function defined on $[0, 30]$ with selected values as shown below:

x	0	5	10	15	20	25	30
$f(x)$	1.4	2.6	3.4	4.1	4.7	5.2	5.7

Use a midpoint Riemann sum with three subdivisions of equal length to find the approximate value of $\displaystyle\int_0^{30} f(x)\,dx$.

21. $\displaystyle\int_0^{\infty} e^{-x}\,dx$

22. $\displaystyle\int_{-\infty}^{0} \frac{dx}{(4-x)^2}$

23. $\displaystyle\int_0^{1} \ln x\,dx$

24. $\displaystyle\int_{-2}^{2} \frac{dx}{\sqrt{4-x^2}}$

25. $\displaystyle\int_{-1}^{8} \frac{dx}{\sqrt[3]{x}}$

11.7 Cumulative Review Problems

(Calculator) indicates that calculators are permitted.

26. Evaluate $\displaystyle\lim_{x\to-\infty} \frac{\sqrt{x^2-4}}{3x-9}$.

27. Find $\dfrac{dy}{dx}$ at $x=3$ if $y=\ln\left|x^2-4\right|$.

28. The graph of f', the derivative of f, $-6 \le x \le 8$ is shown in Figure 11.7-1.

Figure 11.7-1

(a) Find all values of x such that f attains a relative maximum or a relative minimum.
(b) Find all values of x such that f is concave upward.
(c) Find all values of x such that f has a change of concavity.

29. (Calculator) Given the equation
$9x^2 + 4y^2 - 18x + 16y = 11$,
find the points on the graph where the equation has a vertical or horizontal tangent.

30. (Calculator) Two corridors, one 6 feet wide and another 10 feet wide meet at a corner. (See Figure 11.7-2.) What is the maximum length of a pipe of negligible thickness that can be carried horizontally around the corner?

Figure 11.7-2

31. Evaluate $\displaystyle\lim_{x\to-1} \frac{1+\cos\pi x}{x^2-1}$.

32. Determine the speed of an object moving along the path described by $x=3-2t^2$, $y=t^2+1$ when $t=\dfrac{1}{2}$.

33. $\displaystyle\int 2x\sqrt{x+3}\,dx$

11.8 Solutions to Practice Problems

Part A—The use of a calculator is not allowed.

1. $\displaystyle\int_{-1}^{0}\left(1+x-x^{3}\right)dx$

$\displaystyle = x + \frac{x^{2}}{2} - \frac{x^{4}}{4}\Bigg]_{-1}^{0}$

$\displaystyle = 0 - \left[(-1) + \frac{(-1)^{2}}{2} - \frac{(-1)^{4}}{4}\right]$

$\displaystyle = \frac{3}{4}$

2. Let $u = x - 2$; $du = dx$.

$\displaystyle\int (x-2)^{1/2}dx = \int u^{1/2}du$

$\displaystyle = \frac{2u^{3/2}}{3} + C$

$\displaystyle = \frac{2}{3}(x-2)^{3/2} + C$

Thus, $\displaystyle\int_{6}^{11}(x-2)^{1/2}dx = \frac{2}{3}(x-2)^{3/2}\Big]_{6}^{11}$

$\displaystyle = \frac{2}{3}\left[(11-2)^{3/2}\right.$

$\displaystyle \left. -(6-2)^{3/2}\right]$

$\displaystyle = \frac{2}{3}(27-8) = \frac{38}{3}.$

3. Let $u = t + 1$; $du = dt$ and $t = u - 1$.

Rewrite: $\displaystyle\int \frac{t}{t+1}dt = \int \frac{u-1}{u}du$

$\displaystyle = \int\left(1 - \frac{1}{u}\right)du$

$\displaystyle = u - \ln|u| + C$

$\displaystyle = t + 1 - \ln|t+1| + C$

$\displaystyle\int_{1}^{3}\frac{t}{t+1}dt = \left[t+1-\ln|t+1|\right]_{1}^{3}$

$\displaystyle = \left[(3)+1-\ln|3+1|\right]$

$\displaystyle - \left((1)+1-\ln|1+1|\right)$

$= 4 - \ln 4 - 2 + \ln 2$

$= 2 - \ln 4 + \ln 2$

$= 2 - \ln(2)^{2} + \ln 2$

$= 2 - 2\ln 2 + \ln 2$

$= 2 - \ln 2.$

4. Set $x - 3 = 0$; $x = 3$.

$$|x-3| = \begin{cases} (x-3) & \text{if } x \geq 3 \\ -(x-3) & \text{if } x < 3 \end{cases}$$

$\displaystyle\int_{0}^{6}|x-3|\,dx = \int_{0}^{3}-(x-3)dx$

$\displaystyle \qquad\qquad + \int_{3}^{6}(x-3)dx$

$\displaystyle = \left[\frac{-x^{2}}{2} + 3x\right]_{0}^{3} + \left[\frac{x^{2}}{2} - 3x\right]_{3}^{6}$

$\displaystyle = \left(-\frac{(3)^{2}}{2} + 3(3)\right) - 0$

$\displaystyle \quad + \left(\frac{6^{2}}{2} - 3(6)\right) - \left(\frac{3^{2}}{2} - 3(3)\right)$

$\displaystyle = \frac{9}{2} + \frac{9}{2} = 9$

5. $\displaystyle\int_{0}^{k}(6x-1)dx = 3x^{2}-x\Big]_{0}^{k} = 3k^{2}-k$

Set $3k^{2} - k = 4 \Rightarrow 3k^{2} - k - 4 = 0$

$\Rightarrow (3k-4)(k+1) = 0$

$\displaystyle \Rightarrow k = \frac{4}{3}$ or $k = -1$.

Verify your results by evaluating

$\displaystyle\int_{0}^{4/3}(6x-1)dx$ and $\displaystyle\int_{0}^{-1}(6x-1)dx.$

6. Let $u = 1 + \cos x$; $du = -\sin x\, dx$ or $-du = \sin x\, dx$.

$$\int \frac{\sin x}{\sqrt{1 + \cos x}}\, dx = \int \frac{-1}{\sqrt{u}}(du)$$

$$= -\int \frac{1}{u^{1/2}}\, du$$

$$= -\int u^{-1/2}\, du$$

$$= -\frac{u^{1/2}}{1/2} + C$$

$$= -2u^{1/2} + C$$

$$= -2(1 + \cos x)^{1/2} + C$$

$$\int_0^\pi \frac{\sin x}{\sqrt{1 + \cos x}}\, dx = -2(1 + \cos x)^{1/2}\Big]_0^\pi$$

$$= -2\left[(1 + \cos \pi)^{1/2}\right.$$

$$\left. -(1 + \cos 0)^{1/2}\right]$$

$$= -2\left[0 - 2^{1/2}\right] = 2\sqrt{2}$$

7. Let $u = 4x$; $du = 4\, dx$ or $\dfrac{du}{4} = dx$.

$$\int g(4x)\, dx = \int g(u)\frac{du}{4} = \frac{1}{4}\int g(u)\, du$$

$$= \frac{1}{4} f(u) + C$$

$$= \frac{1}{4} f(4x) + C$$

$$\int_1^2 g(4x)\, dx = \frac{1}{4} f(4x)\Big]_1^2$$

$$= \frac{1}{4} f(4(2)) - \frac{1}{4}(f(4(1)))$$

$$= \frac{1}{4} f(8) - \frac{1}{4} f(4)$$

8. $$\int_{\ln 2}^{\ln 3} 10e^x\, dx = 10e^x\Big]_{\ln 2}^{\ln 3}$$

$$= 10\left[\left(e^{\ln 3}\right) - \left(e^{\ln 2}\right)\right]$$

$$= 10(3 - 2) = 10$$

9. Let $u = t + 3$; $du = dt$.

$$\int \frac{1}{t + 3}\, dt = \int \frac{1}{u}\, du = \ln|u| + C$$

$$= \ln|t + 3| + C$$

$$\int_e^{e^2} \frac{1}{t + 3}\, dt = \ln|t + 3|\,\Big]_e^{e^2}$$

$$= \ln(e^2 + 3) - \ln(e + 3)$$

$$= \ln\left(\frac{e^2 + 3}{e + 3}\right)$$

10. $f'(x) = \tan^2 x$;

$$f'\left(\frac{\pi}{6}\right) = \tan^2\left(\frac{\pi}{6}\right) = \left(\frac{1}{\sqrt{3}}\right)^2 = \frac{1}{3}$$

11. Let $u = x^2$; $du = 2x\, dx$ or $\dfrac{du}{2} = x\, dx$.

$$\int 4xe^{x^2}\, dx = 4\int e^u \left(\frac{du}{2}\right)$$

$$= 2\int e^u\, du = 2e^u + c = 2e^{x^2} + C$$

$$\int_{-1}^1 4xe^{x^2}\, dx = 2e^{x^2}\Big]_{-1}^1$$

$$= 2\left[e^{(1)^2} - e^{(-1)^2}\right] = 2(e - e) = 0$$

Note that $f(x) = 4xe^{x^2}$ is an odd function. Thus, $\displaystyle\int_{-a}^a f(x)\, dx = 0$.

12. $$\int_{-\pi}^\pi \left(\cos x - x^2\right) dx = \sin x - \frac{x^3}{3}\Bigg]_{-\pi}^\pi$$

$$= \left(\sin \pi - \frac{\pi^3}{3}\right)$$

$$- \left(\sin(-\pi) - \frac{(-\pi)^3}{3}\right)$$

$$= -\frac{\pi^3}{3} - \left(0 - \frac{-\pi^3}{3}\right)$$

$$= -\frac{2\pi^3}{3}$$

Note that $f(x) = \cos x - x^2$ is an even function. Thus, you could have written

$$\int_{-\pi}^{\pi} \left(\cos x - x^2\right)dx = 2\int_{0}^{\pi}\left(\cos x - x^2\right)dx$$

and obtained the same result.

Part B—Calculators are allowed.

13. $\displaystyle\int_{0}^{2}\left(x^3 + k\right)dx = \dfrac{x^4}{4} + kx\Big]_{0}^{2}$

$$= \left(\dfrac{2^4}{4} + k(2)\right) - 0$$

$$= 4 + 2k$$

Set $4 + 2k = 10$ and $k = 3$.

14. Enter $\displaystyle\int (2x * \cos(x), x, -1.2, 3.1)$ and obtain $-4.70208 \approx -4.702$.

15. $\dfrac{d}{dx}\left(\displaystyle\int_{1}^{x^3} \sqrt{t^2 + 1}\, dt\right)$

$$= \sqrt{(x^3)^2 + 1}\,\dfrac{d}{dx}\left(x^3\right)$$

$$= 3x^2\sqrt{x^6 + 1}$$

16. $\Delta x = \dfrac{8 - 0}{4} = 2$

Midpoints are $x = 1, 3, 5,$ and 7.

$\displaystyle\int_{0}^{8}\left(x^3 + 1\right)dx = \left(1^3 + 1\right)(2) + \left(3^3 + 1\right)(2)$

$$+ \left(5^3 + 1\right)(2) + \left(7^3 + 1\right)(2)$$

$$= (2)(2) + (28)(2) + (126)(2)$$

$$+ (344)(2) = 1000$$

17. (a) $\displaystyle\int_{-2}^{0} g(x)dx + \int_{0}^{2} g(x)dx$

$$= \int_{-2}^{2} g(x)dx; \int_{-2}^{0} g(x)dx + 3$$

$$= 8.\text{ Thus, } \int_{-2}^{0} g(x)dx = 5.$$

(b) $\displaystyle\int_{2}^{-2} g(x)dx = -\int_{-2}^{2} g(x)dx = -8$

(c) $\displaystyle\int_{0}^{-2} 5g(x)dx = 5\int_{0}^{-2} g(x)dx$

$$= 5\left(-\int_{-2}^{0} g(x)dx\right)$$

$$= 5(-5) = -25$$

(d) $\displaystyle\int_{-2}^{2} 2g(x)dx = 2\int_{-2}^{2} g(x)dx$

$$= 2(8) = 16$$

18. $\displaystyle\int_{0}^{1/2} \dfrac{dx}{\sqrt{1 - x^2}} = \sin^{-1}(x)\Big]_{0}^{1/2}$

$$= \sin^{-1}\left(\dfrac{1}{2}\right) - \sin^{-1}(0)$$

$$= \dfrac{\pi}{6} - 0 = \dfrac{\pi}{6}$$

19. $\displaystyle\int_{\cos x}^{\sin x}(2t + 1)dt = \int_{0}^{\sin x}(2t + 1)dt$

$$- \int_{0}^{\cos x}(2t + 1)dt$$

$\dfrac{dy}{dx} = \dfrac{d}{dx}\left(\displaystyle\int_{\cos x}^{\sin x}(2t + 1)dt\right) = (2\sin x + 1)\dfrac{d}{dx}$

$$(\sin x) - (2\cos x + 1)\dfrac{d}{dx}(\cos x)$$

$$= (2\sin x + 1)\cos x - (2\cos x + 1)(-\sin x)$$

$$= 2\sin x \cos x + \cos x + 2\sin x \cos x + \sin x$$

$$= 4\sin x \cos x + \cos x + \sin x$$

20. $\Delta x = \dfrac{30 - 0}{3} = 10$

Midpoints are $x = 5, 15,$ and 25.

$\displaystyle\int_{0}^{30} f(x)dx = [f(5)]10 + [f(15)]10 + [f(25)]10$

$$= (2.6)(10) + (4.1)(10) + (5.2)10$$

$$= 119$$

21. $\displaystyle\int_{0}^{\infty} e^{-x}dx = \lim_{k\to\infty}\int_{0}^{k} e^{-x}dx$

$$= \lim_{k\to\infty}\left(-e^{-x}\big|_{0}^{k}\right)$$

$$= \lim_{k\to\infty}\left(-e^{-k} + 1\right) = 1$$

22.
$$\int_{-\infty}^{0} \frac{dx}{(4-x)^2} = \lim_{k \to -\infty} \int_{k}^{0} \frac{dx}{(4-x)^2}$$

$$= \lim_{k \to -\infty} \left. \frac{-1}{4-x} \right|_{k}^{0}$$

$$= \lim_{k \to -\infty} \left(\frac{-1}{4-k} + \frac{1}{4} \right) = \frac{1}{4}$$

$$= 2\lim_{k \to 2} \left[\sin^{-1}\left(\frac{k}{2}\right) - \sin^{-1}(0) \right]$$

$$= 2\lim_{k \to 2^{-}} \left[\sin^{-1}\left(\frac{k}{2}\right) \right] = 2\left(\frac{\pi}{2}\right) = \pi$$

23.
$$\int_{0}^{1} \ln x \, dx = \lim_{k \to 0^{+}} \int_{k}^{1} \ln x \, dx$$

$$= \lim_{k \to 0^{+}} \left[x \ln x - x \right]_{k}^{1}$$

$$= \lim_{k \to 0^{+}} (-1 - k \ln k + k) = -1$$

25.
$$\int_{-1}^{8} \frac{dx}{\sqrt[3]{x}} = \int_{-1}^{0} \frac{dx}{\sqrt[3]{x}} + \int_{0}^{8} \frac{dx}{\sqrt[3]{x}}$$

$$= \lim_{k \to 0^{-}} \int_{-1}^{k} \frac{dx}{\sqrt[3]{x}} + \lim_{k \to 0^{+}} \int_{k}^{8} \frac{dx}{\sqrt[3]{x}}$$

$$= \lim_{k \to 0^{-}} \left[\frac{3}{2} x^{2/3} \right]_{-1}^{k} + \lim_{k \to 0^{-}} \left[\frac{3}{2} x^{2/3} \right]_{k}^{8}$$

$$= \lim_{k \to 0^{-}} \left[\frac{3}{2} k^{2/3} - \frac{3}{2} \right]$$

$$+ \lim_{k \to 0^{+}} \left[\frac{12}{2} - \frac{3}{2} k^{2/3} \right] = \frac{9}{2}$$

24.
$$\int_{-2}^{2} \frac{dx}{\sqrt{4-x^2}} = 2 \int_{0}^{2} \frac{dx}{\sqrt{4-x^2}}$$

$$= 2\lim_{k \to 2} \int_{0}^{k} \frac{dx}{\sqrt{4-x^2}}$$

$$= 2\lim_{k \to 2} \left[\sin^{-1}\left(\frac{x}{2}\right) \right]_{0}^{k}$$

11.9 Solutions to Cumulative Review Problems

26. As $x \to -\infty$, $x = -\sqrt{x^2}$.

$$\lim_{x \to -\infty} \frac{\sqrt{x^2 - 4}}{3x - 9} = \lim_{x \to -\infty} \frac{\sqrt{x^2 - 4}/-\sqrt{x^2}}{(3x - 9)/x}$$

$$= \lim_{x \to -\infty} \frac{-\sqrt{(x^2 - 4)/x^2}}{3 - (9/x)}$$

$$= \lim_{x \to -\infty} \frac{-\sqrt{1 - (4/x)^2}}{3 - 9/x}$$

$$= \frac{-\sqrt{1 - 0}}{3 - 0} = -\frac{1}{3}$$

27. $y = \ln|x^2 - 4|$, $\dfrac{dy}{dx} = \dfrac{1}{(x^2 - 4)}(2x)$

$$\left. \frac{dy}{dx} \right|_{x=3} = \frac{2(3)}{(3^2 - 4)} = \frac{6}{5}$$

28. (a) (See Figure 11.9-1.)

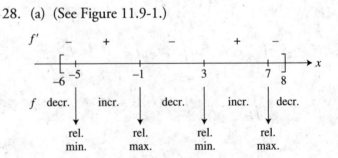

Figure 11.9-1

The function f has a relative minimum at $x = -5$ and $x = 3$, and f has a relative maximum at $x = -1$ and $x = 7$.

(b) (See Figure 11.9-2.)

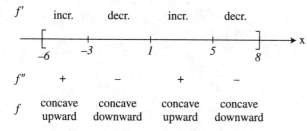

Figure 11.9-2

The function f is concave upward on intervals $(-6, -3)$ and $(1, 5)$.

(c) A change of concavity occurs at $x = -3$, $x = 1$, and $x = 5$.

29. (Calculator) Differentiate both sides of $9x^2 + 4y^2 - 18x + 16y = 11$.

$$18x + 8y\frac{dy}{dx} - 18 + 16\frac{dy}{dx} = 0$$

$$8y\frac{dy}{dx} + 16\frac{dy}{dx} = -18x + 18$$

$$\frac{dy}{dx}(8y + 16) = -18x + 18$$

$$\frac{dy}{dx} = \frac{-18x + 18}{8y + 16}$$

Horizontal tangent $\Rightarrow \dfrac{dy}{dx} = 0$.

Set $\dfrac{dy}{dx} = 0 \Rightarrow -18x + 18 = 0$ or $x = 1$.

At $x = 1$, $9 + 4y^2 - 18 + 16y = 11$
$$\Rightarrow 4y^2 + 16y - 20 = 0.$$

Using a calculator, enter [Solve] $(4y\verb|^|2 + 16y - 20 = 0, y)$; obtaining $y = -5$ or $y = 1$.

Thus, at each of the points at $(1, 1)$ and $(1, -5)$ the graph has a horizontal tangent.

Vertical tangent $\Rightarrow \dfrac{dy}{dx}$ is undefined.

Set $8y + 16 = 0 \Rightarrow y = -2$.

At $y = -2$, $9x^2 + 16 - 18x - 32 = 11$

$\Rightarrow 9x^2 - 18x - 27 = 0.$

Enter [Solve] $(9x^2 - 8x - 27 = 0, x)$ and obtain $x = 3$ or $x = -1$.

Thus, at each of the points $(3, -2)$ and $(-1, -2)$, the graph has a vertical tangent. (See Figure 11.9-3.)

Figure 11.9-3

30. (Calculator)

Step 1: (See Figure 11.9-4.) Let $P = x + y$ where P is the length of the pipe and x and y are as shown. The minimum value of P is the maximum length of the pipe to be able to turn in the corner. By similar triangles, $\dfrac{y}{10} = \dfrac{x}{\sqrt{x^2 - 36}}$

and thus, $y = \dfrac{10x}{\sqrt{x^2 - 36}}$, $x > 6$

$$P = x + y = x + \frac{10x}{\sqrt{x^2 - 36}}.$$

Figure 11.9-4

Step 2: Find the minimum value of P.
Enter
$y_t = x + 10 * x / \left(\sqrt{(x\char`^2 - 36)} \right)$.
Use the [*Minimum*] function of the calculator and obtain the minimum point (9.306, 22.388).

Step 3: Verify with the First Derivative Test.
Enter $y2 = (y1(x), x)$ and observe. (See Figure 11.9-5.)

Figure 11.9-5

Step 4: Check endpoints.
The domain of x is $(6, \infty)$.

Since $x = 9.306$ is the only relative extremum, it is the absolute minimum.
Thus, the maximum length of the pipe is 22.388 feet.

31. $\lim\limits_{x \to -1} \dfrac{1 + \cos \pi x}{x^2 - 1} = \lim\limits_{x \to -1} \dfrac{-\pi \sin \pi x}{2x}$

$= \dfrac{0}{-2} = 0$

32. $\dfrac{dx}{dt} = -4t$ $\dfrac{dy}{dt} = 2t$. The speed of the object

is $\sqrt{(-4t)^2 + (2t)^2} =$

$\sqrt{16t^2 + 4t^2} = \sqrt{20t^2} = 2t\sqrt{5}$. Evaluated

at $t = \dfrac{1}{2}$, the speed is $2\left(\dfrac{1}{2}\right)\sqrt{5} = \sqrt{5}$.

33. Integrate $\displaystyle\int 2x\sqrt{x+3}\,dx$ by parts with

$u = 2x, du = 2dx, dv = \sqrt{x+4}\,dx$, and

$v = \dfrac{2}{3}(x+4)^{3/2}$. Then

$\displaystyle\int 2x\sqrt{x+3}\,dx = \dfrac{4}{3}x(x+3)^{3/2} -$

$\dfrac{4}{3}\displaystyle\int (x+3)^{3/2}dx = \dfrac{4}{3}x(x+3)^{3/2} -$

$\dfrac{4}{3}\left(\dfrac{2}{5}(x+3)^{5/2}\right)$. Simplifying this

expression, we get $\displaystyle\int 2x\sqrt{x+3}\,dx$

$= \dfrac{4}{5}(x+3)^{3/2}(x-2)$.

CHAPTER 12

Big Idea 3: Integrals and the Fundamental Theorems of Calculus
Areas, Volumes, and Arc Lengths

IN THIS CHAPTER

Summary: In this chapter, you will be introduced to several important applications of the definite integral. You will learn how to find the length of a curve, the area under a curve, and the volume of a solid. Some of the techniques that you will be shown include finding the area under a curve by using rectangular and trapezoidal approximations, and finding the volume of a solid using cross sections, discs, and washers. These techniques involve working with algebraic expressions and lengthy computations. It is important that you work carefully through the practice problems provided in the chapter and check your solutions with the given explanations.

Key Ideas

✪ The function $F(x) = \int_a^x f(t)\,dt$
✪ Rectangular Approximations
✪ Trapezoidal Approximations
✪ Area Under a Curve
✪ Area Between Two Curves
✪ Solids with Known Cross Sections
✪ The Disc Method
✪ The Washer Method
✪ Area and Arc Length for Parametric and Polar Curves

12.1 The Function $F(x) = \int_a^x f(t)dt$

The Second Fundamental Theorem of Calculus defines

$$F(x) = \int_a^x f(t)dt$$

and states that if f is continuous on $[a, b]$, then $F'(x) = f(x)$ for every point x in $[a, b]$.

If $f \geq 0$, then $F \geq 0$. $F(x)$ can be interpreted geometrically as the area under the curve of f from $t = a$ to $t = x$. (See Figure 12.1-1.)

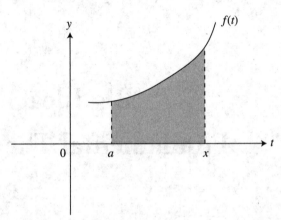

Figure 12.1-1

If $f < 0$, $F < 0$, $F(x)$ can be treated as the negative value of the area between the curve of f and the t-axis from $t = a$ to $t = x$. (See Figure 12.1-2.)

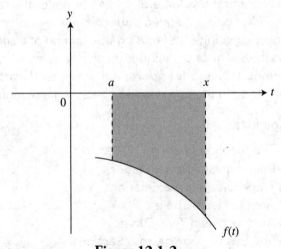

Figure 12.1-2

Example 1

If $F(x) = \int_0^x 2\cos t \; dt$ for $0 \le x \le 2\pi$, find the value(s) of x where f has a local minimum.

Method 1: Since $f(x) = \int_0^x 2\cos t \; dt$, $f'(x) = 2\cos x$.

Set $f'(x) = 0$; $2\cos x = 0$, $x = \dfrac{\pi}{2}$ or $\dfrac{3\pi}{2}$.

$f''(x) = -2\sin x$ and $f''\left(\dfrac{\pi}{2}\right) = -2$ and $f''\left(\dfrac{3\pi}{2}\right) = 2$.

Thus, at $x = \dfrac{3\pi}{2}$, f has a local minimum.

Method 2: You can solve this problem geometrically by using area. See Figure 12.1-3.

[0,2π] by [−3,3]

Figure 12.1-3

The area "under the curve" is above the t-axis on $[0,\ \pi/2]$ and below the x-axis on $[\pi/2,\ 3\pi/2]$. Thus the local minimum occurs at $3\pi/2$.

Example 2

Let $p(x) = \int_0^x f(t)dt$ and the graph of f is shown in Figure 12.1-4.

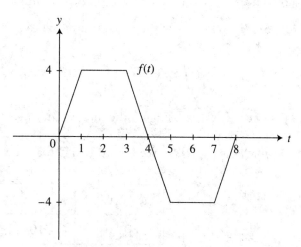

Figure 12.1-4

   (a) Evaluate: $p(0)$, $p(1)$, $p(4)$.
   (b) Evaluate: $p(5)$, $p(7)$, $p(8)$.
   (c) At what value of t does p have a maximum value?
   (d) On what interval(s) is p decreasing?
   (e) Draw a sketch of the graph of p.

Solution:

(a) $p(0) = \displaystyle\int_0^0 f(t)dt = 0$

$p(1) = \displaystyle\int_0^1 f(t)dt = \dfrac{(1)(4)}{2} = 2$

$p(4) = \displaystyle\int_0^4 f(t)dt = \dfrac{1}{2}(2+4)(4) = 12$

(Note: $f(t)$ forms a trapezoid from $t = 0$ to $t = 4$.)

(b) $p(5) = \displaystyle\int_0^5 f(t)dt = \int_0^4 f(t)dt + \int_4^5 f(t)dt$

$= 12 - \dfrac{(1)(4)}{2} = 10$

$p(7) = \displaystyle\int_0^7 f(t)dt = \int_0^4 f(t)dt + \int_4^5 f(t)dt + \int_5^7 f(t)dt$

$= 12 - 2 - (2)(4) = 2$

$p(8) = \displaystyle\int_0^8 f(t)dt = \int_0^4 f(t)dt + \int_4^8 f(t)dt$

$= 12 - 12 = 0$

(c) Since $f \geq 0$ on the interval $[0, 4]$, p attains a maximum at $t = 4$.

(d) Since $f(t)$ is below the x-axis from $t = 4$ to $t = 8$, if $x > 4$,

$$\int_0^x f(t)dt = \int_0^4 f(t)dt + \int_4^x f(t)dt \text{ where } \int_4^x f(t)dt < 0.$$

Thus, p is decreasing on the interval $(4, 8)$.

(e) $p(x) = \displaystyle\int_0^x f(t)dt$. See Figure 12.1-5 for a sketch.

x	0	1	2	3	4	5	6	7	8
$p(x)$	0	2	6	10	12	10	6	2	0

Figure 12.1-5

- Remember differentiability implies continuity, but the converse is not true, i.e., continuity does not imply differentiability, e.g., as in the case of a cusp or a corner.

Example 3

The position function of a moving particle on a coordinate axis is:

$$s = \int_0^t f(x)dx, \text{ where } t \text{ is in seconds and } s \text{ is in feet.}$$

The function f is a differentiable function and its graph is shown below in Figure 12.1-6.

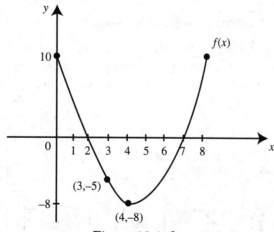

Figure 12.1-6

(a) What is the particle's velocity at $t = 4$?
(b) What is the particle's position at $t = 3$?
(c) When is the acceleration zero?
(d) When is the particle moving to the right?
(e) At $t = 8$, is the particle on the right side or left side of the origin?

Solution:

(a) Since $s = \int_0^t f(x)dx$, then $v(t) = s'(t) = f(t)$.

Thus, $v(4) = -8$ ft/sec.

(b) $s(3) = \int_0^3 f(x)dx = \int_0^2 f(x)dx + \int_2^3 f(x)dx = \frac{1}{2}(10)(2) - \frac{1}{2}(1)(5) = \frac{15}{2}$ ft.

(c) $a(t) = v'(t)$. Since $v'(t) = f'(t)$, $v'(t) = 0$ at $t = 4$. Thus, $a(4) = 0$ ft/sec^2.

(d) The particle is moving to the right when $v(t) > 0$. Thus, the particle is moving to the right on intervals $(0, 2)$ and $(7, 8)$.

(e) The area of f below the x-axis from $x = 2$ to $x = 7$ is larger than the area of f above the x-axis from $x = 0$ to $x = 2$ and $x = 7$ to $x = 8$. Thus, $\int_0^8 f(x)dx < 0$ and the particle is on the left side of the origin.

- Do not forget that $(fg)' = f'g + g'f$ and *not* $f'g'$. However, $\lim(fg) = (\lim f)(\lim g)$

12.2 Approximating the Area Under a Curve

Main Concepts: Rectangular Approximations, Trapezoidal Approximations

Rectangular Approximations

If $f \geq 0$, the area under the curve of f can be approximated using three common types of rectangles: left-endpoint rectangles, right-endpoint rectangles, or midpoint rectangles. (See Figure 12.2-1.)

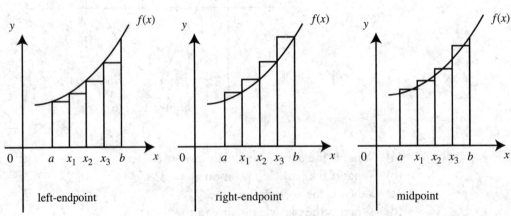

Figure 12.2-1

The area under the curve using n rectangles of equal length is approximately:

$$\sum_{i=1}^{n} (\text{area of rectangle}) = \begin{cases} \sum_{i=1}^{n} f(x_{i-1})\Delta x \text{ left-endpoint rectangles} \\ \sum_{i=1}^{n} f(x_i)\Delta x \text{ right-endpoint rectangles} \\ \sum_{i=1}^{n} f\left(\dfrac{x_i + x_{i-1}}{2}\right) \Delta x \text{ midpoint rectangles} \end{cases}$$

where $\Delta x = \dfrac{b-a}{n}$ and $a = x_0 < x_1 < x_2 < \cdots < x_n = b.$

If f is increasing on $[a, b]$, then left-endpoint rectangles are inscribed rectangles and the right-endpoint rectangles are circumscribed rectangles. If f is decreasing on $[a, b]$, then left-endpoint rectangles are circumscribed rectangles and the right-endpoint rectangles are inscribed. Furthermore,

$$\sum_{i=1}^{n} \text{inscribed rectangle} \leq \text{area under the curve} \leq \sum_{i=1}^{n} \text{circumscribed rectangle.}$$

Example 1

Find the approximate area under the curve of $f(x) = x^2 + 1$ from $x = 0$ to $x = 2$, using 4 left-endpoint rectangles of equal length. (See Figure 12.2-2.)

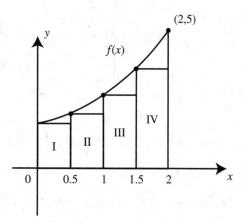

Figure 12.2-2

Let Δx_i be the length of ith rectangle. The length $\Delta x_i = \dfrac{2-0}{4} = \dfrac{1}{2}; x_{i-1} = \dfrac{1}{2}(i-1).$

Area under the curve $\approx \sum_{i=1}^{4} f(x_{i-1})\Delta x_i = \sum_{i=1}^{4} \left(\left(\dfrac{1}{2}(i-1)\right)^2 + 1\right)\left(\dfrac{1}{2}\right).$

Enter $\sum \left(\left(\left(0.5(x-1)\right)^2 + 1\right) * 0.5, x, 1, 4\right)$ and obtain 3.75.

Or, find the area of each rectangle:

$$\text{Area of Rect}_\text{I} = (f(0))\Delta x_1 = (1)\left(\frac{1}{2}\right) = \frac{1}{2}.$$

$$\text{Area of Rect}_\text{II} = f(0.5)\Delta x_2 = ((0.5)^2 + 1)\left(\frac{1}{2}\right) = 0.625.$$

$$\text{Area of Rect}_\text{III} = f(1)\Delta x_3 = (1^2 + 1)\left(\frac{1}{2}\right) = 1.$$

$$\text{Area of Rect}_\text{IV} = f(1.5)\Delta x_4 = (1.5^2 + 1)\left(\frac{1}{2}\right) = 1.625.$$

Area of $(\text{Rect}_\text{I} + \text{Rect}_\text{II} + \text{Rect}_\text{III} + \text{Rect}_\text{IV}) = 3.75$.

Thus, the approximate area under the curve of $f(x)$ is 3.75.

Example 2

Find the approximate area under the curve of $f(x) = \sqrt{x}$ from $x = 4$ to $x = 9$ using 5 right-endpoint rectangles. (See Figure 12.2-3.)

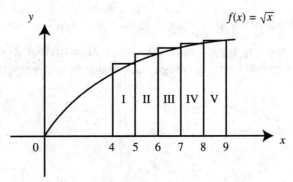

Figure 12.2-3

Let Δx_i be the length of ith rectangle. The length $\Delta x_i = \dfrac{9-4}{5} = 1$; $x_i = 4 + (1)i = 4 + i$.

$$\text{Area of Rect}_\text{I} = f(x_1)\Delta x_1 = f(5)(1) = \sqrt{5}.$$

$$\text{Area of Rect}_\text{II} = f(x_2)\Delta x_2 = f(6)(1) = \sqrt{6}.$$

$$\text{Area of Rect}_\text{III} = f(x_3)\Delta x_3 = f(7)(1) = \sqrt{7}.$$

$$\text{Area of Rect}_\text{IV} = f(x_4)\Delta x_4 = f(8)(1) = \sqrt{8}.$$

$$\text{Area of Rect}_\text{v} = f(x_5)\Delta x_5 = f(9)(1) = \sqrt{9} = 3.$$

$$\sum_{i=1}^{5} (\text{Area of Rect}_\text{I}) = \sqrt{5} + \sqrt{6} + \sqrt{7} + \sqrt{8} + 3 = 13.160.$$

Or, using $\sum$ notation:

$$\sum_{i=1}^{5} f(x_i)\,\Delta x_i = \sum_{i=1}^{5} f(4+i)(1) = \sum_{i=1}^{5} \sqrt{4+1}.$$

Enter $\sum\left(\sqrt{(4+x)}, x, 1, 5\right)$ and obtain 13.160.

Thus the area under the curve is approximately 13.160.

Example 3

The function f is continuous on $[1, 9]$ and $f > 0$. Selected values of f are given below:

x	1	2	3	4	5	6	7	8	9
$f(x)$	1	1.41	1.73	2	2.37	2.45	2.65	2.83	3

Using 4 midpoint rectangles, approximate the area under the curve of f for $x = 1$ to $x = 9$. (See Figure 12.2-4.)

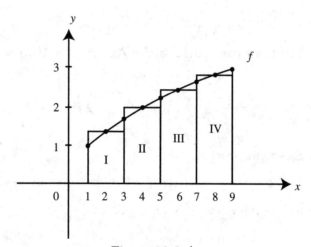

Figure 12.2-4

Let Δx_i be the length of ith rectangle. The length $\Delta x_i = \dfrac{9-1}{4} = 2$.

Area of $\text{Rect}_I = f(2)(2) = (1.41)2 = 2.82$.

Area of $\text{Rect}_{II} = f(4)(2) = (2)2 = 4$.

Area of $\text{Rect}_{III} = f(6)(2) = (2.45)2 = 4.90$.

Area of $\text{Rect}_{IV} = f(8)(2) = (2.83)2 = 5.66$.

Area of $(\text{Rect}_I + \text{Rect}_{II} + \text{Rect}_{III} + \text{Rect}_{IV}) = 2.82 + 4 + 4.90 + 5.66 = 17.38$.

Thus the area under the curve is approximately 17.38.

Trapezoidal Approximations

Another method of approximating the area under a curve is to use trapezoids. See Figure 12.2-5.

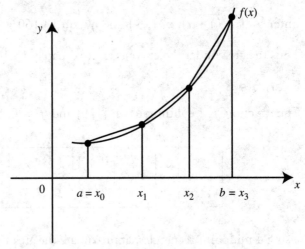

Figure 12.2-5

Formula for Trapezoidal Approximation

If f is continuous, the area under the curve of f from $x = a$ to $x = b$ is:

$$\text{Area} \approx \frac{b-a}{2n}\left[f(x_0) + 2f(x_1) + 2f(x_2) + \cdots + 2f(x_{n-1}) + f(x_n)\right].$$

Example

Find the approximate area under the curve of $f(x) = \cos\left(\dfrac{x}{2}\right)$ from $x = 0$ to $x = \pi$, using 4 trapezoids. (See Figure 12.2-6.)

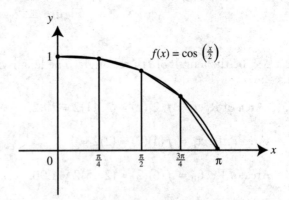

Figure 12.2-6

Since $n = 4$, $\Delta x = \dfrac{\pi - 0}{4} = \dfrac{\pi}{4}$.

Area under the curve:

$$\approx \frac{\pi}{4} \cdot \frac{1}{2} \left[\cos(0) + 2\cos\left(\frac{\pi/4}{2}\right) + 2\cos\left(\frac{\pi/2}{2}\right) + 2\cos\left(\frac{3\pi/4}{2}\right) + \cos\left(\frac{\pi}{2}\right) \right]$$

$$\approx \frac{\pi}{8} \left[\cos(0) + 2\cos\left(\frac{\pi}{8}\right) + 2\cos\left(\frac{\pi}{4}\right) + 2\cos\left(\frac{3\pi}{8}\right) + \cos\left(\frac{\pi}{2}\right) \right]$$

$$\approx \frac{\pi}{8} \left[1 + 2(.9239) + 2\left(\frac{\sqrt{2}}{2}\right) + 2(.3827) + 0 \right] \approx 1.9743.$$

- When using a graphing calculator in solving a problem, you are required to write the setup that leads to the answer. For example, if you are finding the volume of a solid, you must write the definite integral and then use the calculator to compute the numerical value, e.g., Volume $= \pi \int_0^3 (5x)^2 dx = 225\pi$. Simply indicating the answer without writing the integral would get you only one point for the answer. And you will not get full credit for the problem.

12.3 Area and Definite Integrals

Main Concepts: Area Under a Curve, Area Between Two Curves

Area Under a Curve

If $y = f(x)$ is continuous and non-negative on $[a, b]$, then the area under the curve of f from a to b is:

$$\text{Area} = \int_a^b f(x)dx.$$

If f is continuous and $f < 0$ on $[a, b]$, then the area under the curve from a to b is:

$$\text{Area} = -\int_a^b f(x)dx. \text{ See Figure 12.3-1.}$$

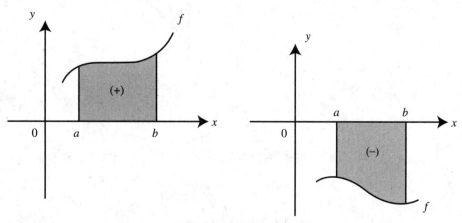

Figure 12.3-1

If $x = g(y)$ is continuous and non-negative on $[c, d]$, then the area under the curve of g from c to d is:

$$\text{Area} \int_c^d g(y)dy.$$ See Figure 12.3-2.

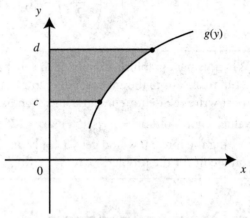

Figure 12.3-2

Example 1

Find the area under the curve of $f(x) = (x - 1)^3$ from $x = 0$ to $x = 2$.

Step 1. Sketch the graph of $f(x)$. See Figure 12.3-3.

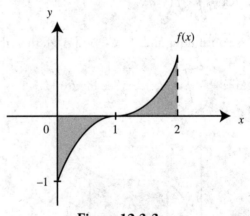

Figure 12.3-3

Step 2. Set up integrals.

$$\text{Area} = \left| \int_0^1 f(x)dx \right| + \int_1^2 f(x)dx.$$

Step 3. Evaluate the integrals.

$$\left| \int_0^1 (x-1)^3 dx \right| = \left| \frac{(x-1)^4}{4} \right]_0^1 \right| = \left| -\frac{1}{4} \right| = \frac{1}{4}$$

$$\int_1^2 (x-1)^3 dx = \frac{(x-1)^4}{4} \right]_1^2 = \frac{1}{4}$$

Thus, the total area is $\frac{1}{4} + \frac{1}{4} = \frac{1}{2}$.

Another solution is to find the area using a calculator.

Enter $\int \left(abs \left((x-1)^\wedge 3 \right), x, 0, 2 \right)$ and obtain $\frac{1}{2}$.

Example 2

Find the area of the region bounded by the graph of $f(x) = x^2 - 1$, the lines $x = -2$ and $x = 2$, and the x-axis.

Step 1. Sketch the graph of $f(x)$. See Figure 12.3-4.

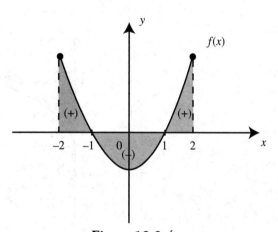

Figure 12.3-4

Step 2. Set up integrals.

$$\text{Area} = \int_{-2}^{-1} f(x)dx + \left| \int_{-1}^{1} f(x)dx \right| + \int_1^2 f(x)dx.$$

Step 3. Evaluate the integrals.

$$\int_{-2}^{-1} \left(x^2 - 1\right) dx = \frac{x^3}{3} - x \Big]_{-2}^{-1} = \frac{2}{3} - \left(-\frac{2}{3}\right) = \frac{4}{3}$$

$$\left|\int_{-1}^{1} \left(x^2 - 1\right) dx\right| = \left|\frac{x^3}{3} - x \right]_{-1}^{1}\right| = \left|-\frac{2}{3} - \left(\frac{2}{3}\right)\right| = \left|-\frac{4}{3}\right| = \frac{4}{3}$$

$$\int_{1}^{2} \left(x^2 - 1\right) dx = \frac{x^3}{3} - x \Big]_{1}^{2} = \frac{2}{3} - \left(-\frac{2}{3}\right) = \frac{4}{3}$$

Thus, the total area $= \frac{4}{3} + \frac{4}{3} + \frac{4}{3} = 4.$

Note: Since $f(x) = x^2 - 1$ is an even function, you can use the symmetry of the graph and set area $= 2\left(\left|\int_{0}^{1} f(x)dx\right| + \int_{1}^{2} f(x)dx\right).$

An alternate solution is to find the area using a calculator.

Enter $\int (abs\ (x^\wedge 2 - 1)\,,\ x,\ -2,\ 2)$ and obtain 4.

Example 3

Find the area of the region bounded by $x = y^2$, $y = -1$, and $y = 3$. See Figure 12.3-5.

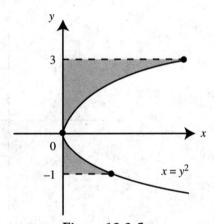

Figure 12.3-5

$$\text{Area} = \int_{-1}^{3} y^2 dy = \frac{y^3}{3} \Big]_{-1}^{3} = \frac{3^3}{3} - \frac{(-1)^3}{3} = \frac{28}{3}.$$

Example 4

Using a calculator, find the area bounded by $f(x) = x^3 + x^2 - 6x$ and the x-axis. See Figure 12.3-6.

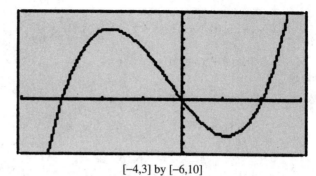

[−4,3] by [−6,10]

Figure 12.3-6

Step 1. Enter $y_1 = x\char`\^3 + x\char`\^2 - 6x$.

Step 2. Enter $\int (abs\ (x\char`\^3 + x\char`\^2 - 6*x)\, , x, -3, 2)$ and obtain 21.083.

Example 5

The area under the curve $y = e^x$ from $x = 0$ to $x = k$ is 1. Find the value of k.

Area $= \displaystyle\int_0^k e^x dx = e^x]_0^k = e^k - e^0 = e^k - 1 \Rightarrow e^k = 2$. Take ln of both sides:

$\ln(e^k) = \ln 2$; $k = \ln 2$.

Example 6

The region bounded by the x-axis and the graph of $y = \sin x$ between $x = 0$ and $x = \pi$ is divided into 2 regions by the line $x = k$. If the area of the region for $0 \le x \le k$ is twice the area of the region $k \le x \le \pi$, find k. (See Figure 12.3-7.)

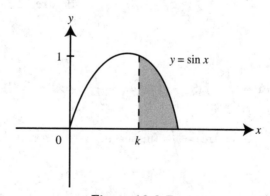

Figure 12.3-7

$$\int_0^k \sin x \, dx = 2 \int_k^\pi \sin x \, dx$$

$$-\cos x\big]_0^k = 2\left[-\cos x\right]_k^\pi$$

$$-\cos k - (-\cos(0)) = 2\left(-\cos \pi - (-\cos k)\right)$$

$$-\cos k + 1 = 2(1 + \cos k)$$

$$-\cos k + 1 = 2 + 2\cos k$$

$$-3\cos k = 1$$

$$\cos k = -\frac{1}{3}$$

$$k = \arccos\left(-\frac{1}{3}\right) = 1.91063$$

Area Between Two Curves

Area Bounded by Two Curves: See Figure 12.3-8.

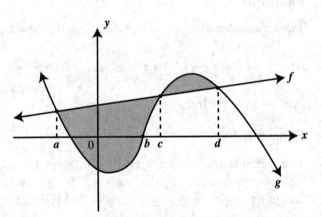

Figure 12.3-8

$$\text{Area} = \int_a^c \left[f(x) - g(x)\right] dx + \int_c^d \left[g(x) - f(x)\right] dx.$$

$$\text{Note: Area} = \int_a^d (\text{upper curve} - \text{lower curve}) \, dx.$$

Example 1

Find the area of the regions bounded by the graphs of $f(x) = x^3$ and $g(x) = x$. (See Figure 12.3-9.)

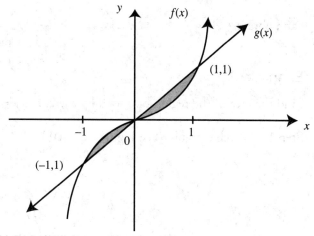

Figure 12.3-9

Step 1. Sketch the graphs of $f(x)$ and $g(x)$.

Step 2. Find the points of intersection.

Set $f(x) = g(x)$

$x^3 = x$

$\Rightarrow x(x^2 - 1) = 0$

$\Rightarrow x(x - 1)(x + 1) = 0$

$\Rightarrow x = 0,\ 1,\ \text{and} -1.$

Step 3. Set up integrals.

$$\text{Area} = \int_{-1}^{0} (f(x) - g(x))dx + \int_{0}^{1} (g(x) - f(x))dx$$

$$= \int_{-1}^{0} \left(x^3 - x\right)dx + \int_{0}^{1} \left(x - x^3\right)dx$$

$$= \left[\frac{x^4}{4} - \frac{x^2}{2}\right]_{-1}^{0} + \left[\frac{x^2}{2} - \frac{x^4}{4}\right]_{0}^{1}$$

$$= 0 - \left(\frac{(-1)^4}{4} - \frac{(-1)^2}{2}\right) + \left(\frac{1^2}{2} - \frac{1^4}{4}\right) - 0$$

$$= -\left(-\frac{1}{4}\right) + \frac{1}{4} = \frac{1}{2}.$$

Note: You can use the symmetry of the graphs and let area $= 2 \displaystyle\int_0^1 \left(x - x^3\right) dx$.

An alternate solution is to find the area using a calculator. Enter $\displaystyle\int (abs(x^{\wedge}3 - x), x, -1, 1)$

and obtain $\dfrac{1}{2}$.

Example 2

Find the area of the region bounded by the curve $y = e^x$, the y-axis and the line $y = e^2$.

Step 1. Sketch a graph. (See Figure 12.3-10.)

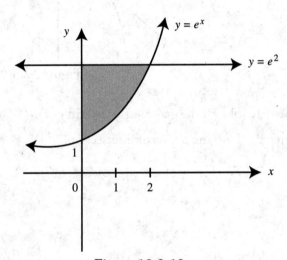

Figure 12.3-10

Step 2. Find the point of intersection. Set $e^2 = e^x \Rightarrow x = 2$.

Step 3. Set up an integral:

$$\text{Area} = \int_0^2 (e^2 - e^x) dx = (e^2)x - e^x \big]_0^2$$

$$= (2e^2 - e^2) - (0 - e^0)$$

$$= e^2 + 1.$$

Or using a calculator, enter $\displaystyle\int ((e^{\wedge}2 - e^{\wedge}x), x, 0, 2)$ and obtain $(e^2 + 1)$.

Example 3

Using a calculator, find the area of the region bounded by $y = \sin x$ and $y = \dfrac{x}{2}$ between $0 \leq x \leq \pi$.

Step 1. Sketch a graph. (See Figure 12.3-11.)

[–π,π] by [–1.5,1.5]

Figure 12.3-11

Step 2. Find the points of intersection.
Using the [*Intersection*] function of the calculator, the intersection points are $x = 0$ and $x = 1.89549$.

Step 3. Enter nInt(sin(x) – .5x, x, 0, 1.89549) and obtain $0.420798 \approx 0.421$.

(Note: You could also use the $\int$ function on your calculator and get the same result.)

Example 4

Find the area of the region bounded by the curve $xy = 1$ and the lines $y = -5$, $x = e$, and $x = e^3$.

Step 1. Sketch a graph. (See Figure 12.3-12.)

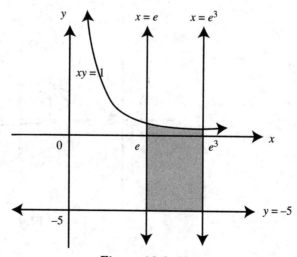

Figure 12.3-12

Step 2. Set up an integral.

$$\text{Area} = \int_{e}^{e^3} \left(\frac{1}{x} - (-5) \right) dx.$$

Step 3. Evaluate the integral.

$$\text{Area} = \int_{e}^{e^3} \left(\frac{1}{x} - (-5) \right) dx = \int_{e}^{e^3} \left(\frac{1}{x} + 5 \right) dx$$

$$= \ln |x| + 5x\Big]_{e}^{e^3} = \left[\ln(e^3) + 5(e^3) \right] - \left[\ln(e) + 5(e) \right]$$

$$= 3 + 5e^3 - 1 - 5e = 2 - 5e + 5e^3.$$

- Remember: if $f' > 0$, then f is increasing, and if $f'' > 0$ then the graph of f is concave upward.

12.4 Volumes and Definite Integrals

Main Concepts: Solids with Known Cross Sections, The Disc Method, The Washer Method

Solids with Known Cross Sections

If $A(x)$ is the area of a cross section of a solid and $A(x)$ is continuous on $[a, b]$, then the volume of the solid from $x = a$ to $x = b$ is:

$$V = \int_{a}^{b} A(x)\,dx.$$

(See Figure 12.4-1.)

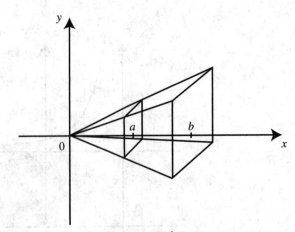

Figure 12.4-1

Note: A cross section of a solid is perpendicular to the height of the solid.

Example 1

The base of a solid is the region enclosed by the ellipse $\dfrac{x^2}{4} + \dfrac{y^2}{25} = 1$. The cross sections are perpendicular to the x-axis and are isosceles right triangles whose hypotenuses are on the ellipse. Find the volume of the solid. (See Figure 12.4-2.)

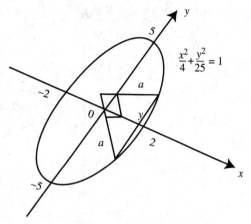

Figure 12.4-2

Step 1. Find the area of a cross section $A(x)$.

Pythagorean Theorem: $a^2 + a^2 = (2y)^2$

$$2a^2 = 4y^2$$

$$a = \sqrt{2}y, \ a > 0.$$

$$A(x) = \frac{1}{2}a^2 = \frac{1}{2}\left(\sqrt{2}y\right)^2 = y^2$$

Since $\dfrac{x^2}{4} + \dfrac{y^2}{25} = 1$, $\dfrac{y^2}{25} = 1 - \dfrac{x^2}{4}$ or $y^2 = 25 - \dfrac{25x^2}{4}$,

$$A(x) = 25 - \frac{25x^2}{4}.$$

Step 2. Set up an integral.

$$V = \int_{-2}^{2} \left(25 - \frac{25x^2}{4}\right) dx$$

Step 3. Evaluate the integral.

$$V = \int_{-2}^{2} \left(25 - \frac{25x^2}{4}\right) dx = 25x - \frac{25}{12}x^3 \Bigg]_{-2}^{2}$$

$$= \left(25(2) - \frac{25}{12}(2)^3\right) - \left(25(-2) - \frac{25}{12}(-2)^3\right)$$

$$= \frac{100}{3} - \left(-\frac{100}{3}\right) = \frac{200}{3}$$

The volume of the solid is $\dfrac{200}{3}$.

Verify your result with a graphing calculator.

Example 2

Find the volume of a pyramid whose base is a square with a side of 6 feet long and a height of 10 feet. (See Figure 12.4-3.)

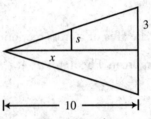

Figure 12.4-3

Step 1. Find the area of a cross section $A(x)$. Note each cross section is a square of side $2s$.

Similar triangles: $\dfrac{x}{s} = \dfrac{10}{3} \Rightarrow s = \dfrac{3x}{10}$.

$$A(x) = (2s)^2 = 4s^2 = 4\left(\frac{3x}{10}\right)^2 = \frac{9x^2}{25}$$

Step 2. Set up an integral.

$$V = \int_0^{10} \frac{9x^2}{25}\,dx$$

Step 3. Evaluate the integral.

$$V = \int_0^{10} \frac{9x^2}{25}\,dx = \left. \frac{3x^3}{25} \right]_0^{10} = \frac{3\,(10)^3}{25} - 0 = 120$$

The volume of the pyramid is 120 ft^3.

Example 3

The base of a solid is the region enclosed by a triangle whose vertices are (0, 0), (4, 0), and (0, 2). The cross sections are semicircles perpendicular to the x-axis. Using a calculator, find the volume of the solid. (See Figure 12.4-4.)

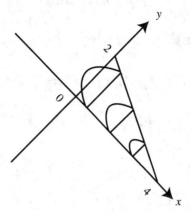

Figure 12.4-4

Step 1. Find the area of a cross section.
Equation of the line passing through (0, 2) and (4, 0):

$$y = mx + b; \ m = \frac{0-2}{4-0} = -\frac{1}{2}; \ b = 2$$

$$y = -\frac{1}{2}x + 2.$$

Area of semicircle $= \frac{1}{2}\pi r^2; \ r = \frac{1}{2}y = \frac{1}{2}\left(-\frac{1}{2}x + 2\right) = -\frac{1}{4}x + 1.$

$$A(x) = \frac{1}{2}\pi \left(\frac{y}{2}\right)^2 = \frac{\pi}{2}\left(-\frac{1}{4}x + 1\right)^2.$$

Step 2. Set up an integral.

$$V = \int_0^4 A(x)\,dx = \int_0^4 \frac{\pi}{2}\left(-\frac{1}{4}x + 1\right)^2 dx$$

Step 3. Evaluate the integral.

Enter $\int\left(\left(\frac{\pi}{2}\right) * (-.25x + 1)^{\wedge}2, \ x, \ 0, \ 4\right)$ and obtain 2.0944.

Thus the volume of the solid is 2.094.

- Remember: if $f' < 0$, then f is decreasing, and if $f'' < 0$ then the graph of f is concave downward.

The Disc Method

The volume of a solid of revolution using discs:

Revolving about the x-axis:

$$V = \pi \int_a^b (f(x))^2 \, dx, \quad \text{where} \quad f(x) = \text{radius}.$$

Revolving about the y-axis:

$$V = \pi \int_c^d (g(y))^2 \, dy, \quad \text{where} \quad g(y) = \text{radius}.$$

(See Figure 12.4-5.)

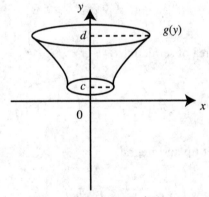

Figure 12.4-5

Revolving about a line $y = k$:

$$V = \pi \int_a^b (f(x) - k)^2 \, dx, \quad \text{where} \quad \left| f(x) - k \right| = \text{radius}.$$

Revolving about a line $x = h$:

$$V = \pi \int_c^d (g(y) - h)^2 \, dy, \quad \text{where} \quad \left| g(y) - h \right| = \text{radius}.$$

(See Figure 12.4-6.)

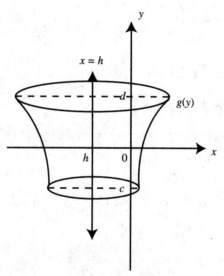

Figure 12.4-6

Example 1

Find the volume of the solid generated by revolving about the x-axis the region bounded by the graph of $f(x) = \sqrt{x-1}$, the x-axis, and the line $x = 5$.

Step 1. Draw a sketch. (See Figure 12.4-7.)

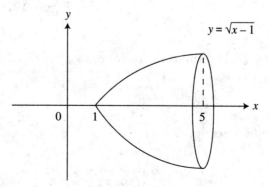

Figure 12.4-7

Step 2. Determine the radius of a disc from a cross section.

$$r = f(x) = \sqrt{x - 1}$$

Step 3. Set up an integral.

$$V = \pi \int_1^5 (f(x))^2 dx = \pi \int_1^5 \left(\sqrt{x - 1}\right)^2 dx$$

Step 4. Evaluate the integral.

$$V = \pi \int_1^5 \left(\sqrt{x - 1}\right)^2 dx = \pi \left[(x - 1)\right]_1^5 = \pi \left[\frac{x^2}{2} - x\right]_1^5$$

$$= \pi \left(\left(\frac{5^2}{2} - 5\right) - \left(\frac{1^2}{2} - 1\right)\right) = 8\pi$$

Verify your result with a calculator.

Example 2

Find the volume of the solid generated by revolving about the x-axis the region bounded by the graph of $y = \sqrt{\cos x}$ where $0 \le x \le \dfrac{\pi}{2}$, the x-axis, and the y-axis.

Step 1. Draw a sketch. (See Figure 12.4-8.)

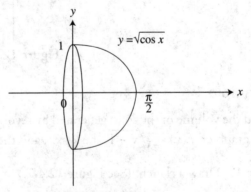

Figure 12.4-8

Step 2. Determine the radius from a cross section.

$$r = f(x) = \sqrt{\cos x}$$

Step 3. Set up an integral.

$$V = \pi \int_0^{\pi/2} \left(\sqrt{\cos x}\right)^2 dx = \pi \int_0^{\pi/2} \cos x \, dx$$

Step 4. Evaluate the integral.

$$V = \pi \int_0^{\pi/2} \cos x \, dx = \pi \left[\sin x \right]_0^{\pi/2} = \pi \left(\sin \left(\frac{\pi}{2} \right) - \sin 0 \right) = \pi$$

Thus, the volume of the solid is π.
Verify your result with a calculator.

Example 3

Find the volume of the solid generated by revolving about the y-axis the region in the first quadrant bounded by the graph of $y = x^2$, the y-axis, and the line $y = 6$.

Step 1. Draw a sketch. (See Figure 12.4-9.)

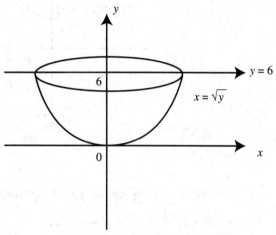

Figure 12.4-9

Step 2. Determine the radius from a cross section.

$$y = x^2 \Rightarrow x = \pm\sqrt{y}$$

$x = \sqrt{y}$ is the part of the curve involved in the region.

$$r = x = \sqrt{y}$$

Step 3. Set up an integral.

$$V = \pi \int_0^6 x^2 \, dy = \pi \int_0^6 \left(\sqrt{y} \right)^2 dy = \pi \int_0^6 y \, dy$$

Step 4. Evaluate the integral.

$$V = \pi \int_0^6 y \, dy = \pi \left[\frac{y^2}{2} \right]_0^6 = 18\pi$$

The volume of the solid is 18π.
Verify your result with a calculator.

Example 4

Using a calculator, find the volume of the solid generated by revolving about the line $y = 8$, the region bounded by the graph of $y = x^2 + 4$, and the line $y = 8$.

Step 1. Draw a sketch. (See Figure 12.4-10.)

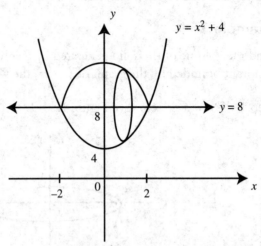

Figure 12.4-10

Step 2. Determine the radius from a cross section.

$$r = 8 - y = 8 - (x^2 + 4) = 4 - x^2$$

Step 3. Set up an integral.
To find the intersection points, set $8 = x^2 + 4 \Rightarrow x = \pm 2$.

$$V = \pi \int_{-2}^{2} \left(4 - x^2\right)^2 dx$$

Step 4. Evaluate the integral.

Enter $\displaystyle\int \left(\pi\, (4 - x\char`\^2)\char`\^\, 2,\ x,\ -2,\ 2\right)$ and obtain $\dfrac{512}{15}\pi$.

Thus, the volume of the solid is $\dfrac{512}{15}\pi$.

Verify your result with a calculator.

Example 5

Using a calculator, find the volume of the solid generated by revolving about the line $y = -3$, the region bounded by the graph of $y = e^x$, the y-axis, and the lines $x = \ln 2$ and $y = -3$.

Step 1. Draw a sketch. (See Figure 12.4-11.)

Figure 12.4-11

Step 2. Determine the radius from a cross section.

$$r = y - (-3) = y + 3 = e^x + 3$$

Step 3. Set up an integral.

$$V = \pi \int_0^{\ln 2} (e^x + 3)^2 \, dx$$

Step 4. Evaluate the integral.

Enter $\int \left(\pi \, (e^\wedge(x) + 3)^\wedge 2, \; x, \; 0 \; \ln(2) \right)$ and obtain $\pi \left(9 \ln 2 + \dfrac{15}{2} \right)$

$$= 13.7383\pi.$$

The volume of the solid is approximately 13.7383π.

- Remember: if f' is increasing, then $f'' > 0$ and the graph of f is concave upward.

The Washer Method

The volume of a solid (with a hole in the middle) generated by revolving a region bounded by 2 curves:

About the x-axis:

$$V = \pi \int_a^b \left[(f(x))^2 - (g(x))^2 \right] dx; \text{ where } f(x) = \text{outer radius and } g(x) = \text{inner radius.}$$

About the y-axis:

$$V = \pi \int_c^d \left[(p(y))^2 - (q(y))^2 \right] dy; \text{ where } p(y) = \text{outer radius and } q(y) = \text{inner radius.}$$

About a line $x = h$:

$$V = \pi \int_a^b \left[(f(x) - h)^2 - (g(x) - h)^2 \right] dx.$$

About a line $y = k$:

$$V = \pi \int_c^d \left[(p(y) - k)^2 - (q(y) - k)^2 \right] dy.$$

Example 1

Using the Washer Method, find the volume of the solid generated by revolving the region bounded by $y = x^3$ and $y = x$ in the first quadrant about the x-axis.

Step 1. Draw a sketch. (See Figure 12.4-12.)

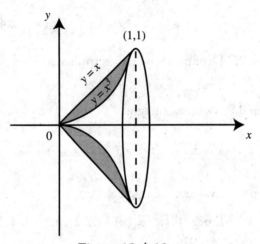

Figure 12.4-12

To find the points of intersection, set $x = x^3 \Rightarrow x^3 - x = 0$ or $x(x^2 - 1) = 0$, or $x = -1, 0, 1$. In the first quadrant $x = 0, 1$.

Step 2. Determine the outer and inner radii of a washer whose outer radius $= x$, and inner radius $= x^3$.

Step 3. Set up an integral.

$$V = \int_0^1 \left[x^2 - \left(x^3 \right)^2 \right] dx$$

Step 4. Evaluate the integral.

$$V = \int_0^1 \left(x^2 - x^6 \right) dx = \pi \left[\frac{x^3}{3} - \frac{x^7}{7} \right]_0^1$$

$$= \pi \left(\frac{1}{3} - \frac{1}{7} \right) = \frac{4\pi}{21}$$

Verify your result with a calculator.

Example 2

Using the Washer Method and a calculator, find the volume of the solid generated by revolving the region in Example 1 about the line $y = 2$.

Step 1. Draw a sketch. (See Figure 12.4-13.)

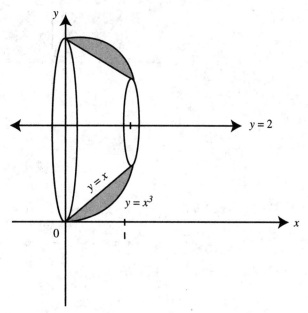

Figure 12.4-13

Step 2. Determine the outer and inner radii of a washer.
The outer radius $= (2 - x^3)$ and inner radius $= (2 - x)$.

Step 3. Set up an integral.

$$V = \pi \int_0^1 \left[\left(2 - x^3\right)^2 - \left(2 - x\right)^2 \right] dx$$

Step 4. Evaluate the integral.

Enter $\int \left(\pi * \left((2 - x^\wedge 3)^\wedge 2 - (2 - x)^\wedge 2\right), \ x, \ 0, \ 1 \right)$ and obtain $\dfrac{17\pi}{21}$.

The volume of the solid is $\dfrac{17\pi}{21}$.

Example 3

Using the Washer Method and a calculator, find the volume of the solid generated by revolving the region bounded by $y = x^2$ and $x = y^2$ about the y-axis.

Step 1. Draw a sketch. (See Figure 12.4-14.)

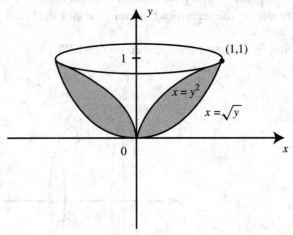

Figure 12.4-14

Intersection points: $y = x^2$; $x = y^2 \Rightarrow y = \pm\sqrt{x}$.

Set $x^2 = \sqrt{x} \Rightarrow x^4 = x \Rightarrow x^4 - x = 0 \Rightarrow x(x^3 - 1) = 0 \Rightarrow x = 0$ or $x = 1$

$x = 0$, $y = 0$ $(0, 0)$

$x = 1$, $y = 1$ $(1, 1)$.

Step 2. Determine the outer and inner radii of a washer, with outer radius: $x = \sqrt{y}$ and inner radius: $x = y^2$.

Step 3. Set up an integral.

$$V = \pi \int_0^1 \left(\left(\sqrt{y}\right)^2 - \left(y^2\right)^2 \right) dy$$

Step 4. Evaluate the integral.

Enter $\int \left(\pi * \left((\sqrt{y})^{\wedge}2 - (y^{\wedge}2)^{\wedge}2 \right), \ y, \ 0, \ 1 \right)$ and obtain $\dfrac{3\pi}{10}$.

The volume of the solid is $\dfrac{3\pi}{10}$.

12.5   Integration of Parametric, Polar, and Vector Curves

> **Main Concepts:** Area, Arc Length, and Surface Area for Parametric Curves; Area and Arc Length for Polar Curves; Integration of a Vector-Valued Function

Area, Arc Length, and Surface Area for Parametric Curves

Area for Parametric Curves

For a curve defined parametrically by $x = f(t)$ and $y = g(t)$, the area bounded by the portion of the curve between $t = \alpha$ and $t = \beta$ is $A = \displaystyle\int_{\alpha}^{\beta} g(t) f'(t)\, dt$.

Example 1

Find the area bounded by $x = 2 \sin t$, $y = 3 \sin^2 t$.

Step 1. Determine the limits of integration. The symmetry of the graph allows us to integrate from $t = 0$ to $t = \pi/2$ and multiply by 2.

Step 2. Differentiate $\dfrac{dx}{dt} = 2 \cos t$.

Step 3. $A = 2\displaystyle\int_{0}^{\pi/2} 3 \sin^2 t (2 \cos t)\, dt = 12 \int_{0}^{\pi/2} (\sin^2 t \cos t)\, dt = 4 \sin^3 t \Big|_{0}^{\pi/2} = 4$

Arc Length for Parametric Curves

The length of that arc is $L = \displaystyle\int_{\alpha}^{\beta} \sqrt{\left(\dfrac{dx}{dt}\right)^2 + \left(\dfrac{dy}{dt}\right)^2}\, dt$.

Example 2

Find the length of the arc defined by $x = e^t \cos t$ and $y = e^t \sin t$ from $t = 0$ to $t = 4$.

Step 1. Differentiate $\dfrac{dx}{dt} = e^t \cos t - e^t \sin t$ and $\dfrac{dy}{dt} = e^t \cos t + e^t \sin t$.

Step 2. $L = \displaystyle\int_{0}^{4} \sqrt{(e^t \cos t - e^t \sin t)^2 + (e^t \cos t + e^t \sin t)^2}\, dt$

$L = \displaystyle\int_{0}^{4} \sqrt{2e^{2t}(\cos^2 t + \sin^2 t)}\, dt = \int_{0}^{4} \sqrt{2e^{2t}}\, dt = \sqrt{2}\int_{0}^{4} e^t\, dt = \sqrt{2}\, e^t \Big|_{0}^{4}$

$= \sqrt{2}\, e^4 - \sqrt{2}$

Surface Area for Parametric Curves

The surface area created when that arc is revolved about the x-axis is

$$S = \int_{\alpha}^{\beta} 2\pi y \sqrt{\left(\dfrac{dx}{dt}\right)^2 + \left(\dfrac{dy}{dt}\right)^2}\, dt.$$

Example 3

Find the area of the surface generated by revolving about the x-axis the arc defined by $x = 3 - 2t$ and $y = \sqrt{20 - t^2}$ when $0 \le t \le 4$.

Step 1. Differentiate $\dfrac{dx}{dt} = -2$ and $\dfrac{dy}{dt} = \dfrac{-t}{\sqrt{20 - t^2}}$.

Step 2. $S = \displaystyle\int_0^4 2\pi \sqrt{20 - t^2} \sqrt{(-2)^2 + \left(\dfrac{-t}{\sqrt{20 - t^2}}\right)^2}\, dt$

$= 2\pi \displaystyle\int_0^4 \sqrt{20 - t^2} \sqrt{4 + \dfrac{t^2}{20 - t^2}}\, dt$

$= 2\pi \displaystyle\int_0^4 \sqrt{20 - t^2} \sqrt{\dfrac{80 - 3t^2}{20 - t^2}}\, dt$

$= 2\pi \displaystyle\int_0^4 \sqrt{80 - 3t^2}\, dt \approx 2\pi\,(31.7768) \approx 199.6595$

Area and Arc Length for Polar Curves

Area for Polar Curves

If $r = f(\theta)$ is a continuous polar curve on the interval $\alpha \le \theta \le \beta$ and $\alpha < \beta < \alpha + 2\pi$, then the area enclosed by the polar curve is $A = \dfrac{1}{2}\displaystyle\int_\alpha^\beta [f(\theta)]^2\, d\theta = \dfrac{1}{2}\displaystyle\int_\alpha^\beta r^2\, d\theta$.

Example 1

Find the area enclosed by $r = 2 + 2\cos\theta$ on the interval from $\theta = 0$ to $\theta = \pi$.

Step 1. Square $r^2 = 4 + 8\cos\theta + 4\cos^2\theta$.

Step 2. $A = \dfrac{1}{2}\displaystyle\int_0^\pi \left(4 + 8\cos\theta + 4\cos^2\theta\right) d\theta = 2\displaystyle\int_0^\pi \left(1 + 2\cos\theta + 2\cos^2\theta\right) d\theta$

$= 2\left[2\theta + 4\sin\theta + 2\left(\dfrac{\theta}{2} + \dfrac{1}{4}\sin 2\theta\right)\right]_0^\pi = 6\theta + 8\sin\theta + \sin 2\theta \Big|_0^\pi = 6\pi$

Arc Length for Polar Curves

For a polar graph defined on a interval (α, β), if the graph does not retrace itself in that interval and if $\dfrac{dr}{d\theta}$ is continuous, then the length of the arc from $\theta = \alpha$ to $\theta = \beta$ is $L = \displaystyle\int_\alpha^\beta \sqrt{r^2 + \left(\dfrac{dr}{d\theta}\right)^2}\, d\theta$.

Example 2

Find the length of the spiral $r = e^\theta$ from $\theta = 0$ to $\theta = \pi$.

Step 1. Differentiate $\dfrac{dr}{d\theta} = e^\theta$.

Step 2. Square $r^2 = e^{2\theta}$.

Step 3. $L = \displaystyle\int_0^\pi \sqrt{e^{2\theta} + e^{2\theta}}\, d\theta = \int_0^\pi \sqrt{2e^{2\theta}}\, d\theta = \sqrt{2} \int_0^\pi e^\theta\, d\theta = \sqrt{2}\, e^\theta \Big|_0^\pi$

$\qquad = \sqrt{2}\, e^\pi - \sqrt{2}$

Integration of a Vector-Valued Function

Integrating a Vector Function

For a vector-valued function $r(t) = \langle x(t), y(t) \rangle$, $\int r(t)\, dt = \int x(t)\, dt \cdot i + \int y(t)\, dt \cdot j$.

Example 1

The acceleration vector of a particle at any time $t \geq 0$ is $a(t) = \langle e^t, e^{2t} \rangle$. If at time $t = 0$, its velocity is $i + j$ and its displacement is 0, find the functions for the position and velocity at any time t.

Step 1. $a(t) = \langle e^t, e^{2t} \rangle$, so $v(t) = \displaystyle\int a(t)\, dt = \int x(t)\, dt \cdot i + \int y(t)\, dt \cdot j$

$v(t) = \displaystyle\int e^t\, dt \cdot i + \int e^{2t}\, dt \cdot j = e^t \cdot i + \dfrac{e^{2t}}{2} \cdot j + C$. Since velocity at $t = 0$ is known

to be $i + j$, $i + \dfrac{1}{2} \cdot j + C = i + j$, and $C = \dfrac{1}{2} \cdot j$; therefore, $v(t) = e^t \cdot i + \dfrac{e^{2t}}{2} \cdot j +$

$\dfrac{1}{2} \cdot j = \left\langle e^t, \dfrac{e^{2t} + 1}{2} \right\rangle$.

Step 2. The position function $s(t) = \displaystyle\int v(t)\, dt = \int e^t\, dt \cdot i + \int \dfrac{e^{2t} + 1}{2}\, dt \cdot j$.

$s(t) = \displaystyle\int v(t)\, dt = \int e^t\, dt \cdot i + \int \dfrac{e^{2t} + 1}{2}\, dt \cdot j = e^t \cdot i + \left(\dfrac{e^{2t} + 2t}{4} \right) \cdot j + C$.

Displacement is 0 at $t = 0$, so $i + \dfrac{1}{4} \cdot j + C = 0$ and $C = -i - \dfrac{1}{4} \cdot j$.

The position function $s(t) = e^t \cdot i + \left(\dfrac{e^{2t} + 2t}{4} \right) \cdot j - i - \dfrac{1}{4} \cdot j = (e^t - 1) i +$

$\left(\dfrac{e^{2t} + 2t - 1}{4} \right) j = \left\langle e^t - 1, \dfrac{e^{2t} + 2t - 1}{4} \right\rangle$.

Length of a Vector Curve

The length of a curve defined by the vector-valued function $r(t) = \langle x(t), y(t) \rangle$ traced from $t = a$ to $t = b$ is $s = \displaystyle\int_a^b \left\| r'(t) \right\| dt$.

Example 2

Find the length of the curve $r(t) = \langle 2\sin t, 5t \rangle$ from $t = 0$ to $t = \pi$.

Step 1. $r'(t) = \langle 2\cos t, 5 \rangle$

Step 2. $\|r'(t)\| = \sqrt{4\cos^2 t + 25}$

Step 3. With the aid of a graphing calculator, the arc length $s = \int_0^\pi \sqrt{4\cos^2 t + 25}\,dt$ can be found to be approximately equal to 16.319 units.

12.6 Rapid Review

1. If $f(x) = \int_0^x g(t)\,dt$ and the graph of g is shown in Figure 12.6-1. Find $f(3)$.

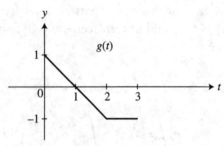

Figure 12.6-1

Answer: $f(3) = \int_0^3 g(t)\,dt = \int_0^1 g(t)\,dt + \int_1^3 g(t)\,dt$

$= 0.5 - 1.5 = -1$

2. The function f is continous on $[1, 5]$ and $f > 0$ and selected values of f are given below.

x	1	2	3	4	5
$f(x)$	2	4	6	8	10

Using 2 midpoint rectangles, approximate the area under the curve of f for $x = 1$ to $x = 5$.

Answer: Midpoints are $x = 2$ and $x = 4$ and the width of each rectangle

$= \dfrac{5 - 1}{2} = 2.$

Area $\approx$ Area of Rect$_1$ + Area of Rect$_2$ $\approx 4(2) + 8(2) \approx 24$.

3. Set up an integral to find the area of the regions bounded by the graphs of $y = x^3$ and $y = x$. Do not evaluate the integral.

Answer: Graphs intersect at $x = -1$, $x = 0$, and $x = 1$. (See Figure 12.6-2.)

$$\text{Area} = \int_{-1}^{0} \left(x^3 - x\right)dx + \int_{0}^{1} \left(x - x^3\right)dx.$$

Or, using symmetry, $\text{Area} = 2\int_{0}^{1} \left(x - x^3\right)dx.$

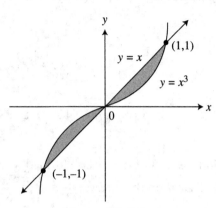

Figure 12.6-2

4. The base of a solid is the region bounded by the lines $y = x$, $x = 1$, and the x-axis. The cross sections are squares perpendicular to the x-axis. Set up an integral to find the volume of the solid. Do not evaluate the integral.

   Answer: Area of cross section $= x^2$.

   $$\text{Volume of solid} = \int_{0}^{1} x^2 dx.$$

5. Set up an integral to find the volume of a solid generated by revolving the region bounded by the graph of $y = \sin x$, where $0 \leq x \leq \pi$ and the x-axis, about the x-axis. Do not evaluate the integral.

   Answer: Volume $= \pi \int_{0}^{\pi} (\sin x)^2 dx.$

6. The area under the curve of $y = \dfrac{1}{x}$ from $x = a$ to $x = 5$ is approximately 0.916, where $1 \leq a < 5$. Using your calculator, find a.

   Answer: $\int_{a}^{5} \dfrac{1}{x}dx = \ln x\Big|_{a}^{5} = \ln 5 - \ln a = 0.916$

   $\ln a = \ln 5 - 0.916 \approx .693$

   $a \approx e^{0.693} \approx 2$

7. Find the length of the arc defined by $x = t^2$ and $y = 3t^2 - 1$ from $t = 2$ to $t = 5$.

Answer: $\dfrac{dx}{dt} = 2t$ and $\dfrac{dy}{dt} = 6t$. $L = \displaystyle\int_2^5 \sqrt{(2t)^2 + (6t)^2}\, dt = \int_2^5 \sqrt{40t^2}\, dt$

$= \displaystyle\int_2^5 2t\sqrt{10}\, dt = \left[t^2 \sqrt{10} \right]_2^5 = 25\sqrt{10} - 4\sqrt{10} = 21\sqrt{10}.$

8. Find the area bounded by the $r = 3 + \cos\theta$.

Answer: To trace out the graph completely, without retracing, we need $0 \le \theta \le 2\pi$. Then,

$$A = \frac{1}{2}\int_0^{2\pi} (3 + \cos\theta)^2\, d\theta = \frac{1}{2}\int_0^{2\pi}\left(9 + 6\cos\theta + \cos^2\theta \right) d\theta$$

$$= \frac{1}{2}\left[9\theta + 6\sin\theta + \frac{1}{2}\theta + \frac{1}{4}\sin 2\theta \right]_0^{2\pi} = \frac{1}{2}\left[(18\pi + \pi) - 0 \right] = \frac{19\pi}{2}.$$

9. Find the area of the surface formed when the curve defined by $x = \sin\theta$, and $y = 3\sin\theta$ on the interval $\dfrac{\pi}{3} \le \theta \le \dfrac{\pi}{6}$ is revolved about the x-axis.

Answer: $\dfrac{dx}{d\theta} = \cos\theta$ and $\dfrac{dy}{d\theta} = 3\cos\theta$, so

$$S = \int_{\pi/6}^{\pi/3} 2\pi(3\sin\theta)\sqrt{\cos^2\theta + 9\cos^2\theta}\, d\theta = 6\pi \int_{\pi/6}^{\pi/3} \sin\theta \sqrt{10\cos^2\theta}\, d\theta$$

$$= 3\pi\sqrt{10} \int_{\pi/6}^{\pi/3} 2\sin\theta\cos\theta\, d\theta = 3\pi\sqrt{10}\int_{\pi/6}^{\pi/3}\sin 2\theta\, d\theta$$

$$= -\frac{3}{2}\pi\sqrt{10}\cos 2\theta \bigg]_{\pi/6}^{\pi/3} = -\frac{3}{2}\pi\sqrt{10}\left[\left(\cos\frac{2\pi}{3}\right) - \left(\cos\frac{\pi}{3}\right) \right]$$

$$= -\frac{3}{2}\pi\sqrt{10}\left[\left(-\frac{1}{2}\right) - \left(-\frac{1}{2}\right) \right] = \frac{3}{2}\pi\sqrt{10}.$$

10. If $\left\langle \dfrac{dx}{dt}, \dfrac{dy}{dt} \right\rangle = \langle 5 - t^2, 4t - 3 \rangle$ and $\langle x_0, y_0 \rangle = \langle 0, 0 \rangle$, find $\langle x, y \rangle$.

Answer: $x = \displaystyle\int \left(5 - t^2 \right) dt = 5t - \frac{t^3}{3} + C_1$ and $y = \int (4t - 3)\, dt = 2t^2 - 3t + C_2.$

Since $\langle x_0, y_0 \rangle = \langle 0, 0 \rangle$, $C_1 = C_2 = 0$, so $\langle x, y \rangle = \left\langle 5t - \frac{1}{3}t^3,\ 2t^2 - 3t \right\rangle.$

12.7 Practice Problems

Part A—The use of a calculator is not allowed.

1. Let $F(x) = \displaystyle\int_0^x f(t)dt$, where the graph of

   f is given in Figure 12.7-1.

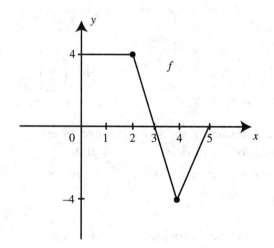

Figure 12.7-1

   (a) Evaluate $F(0)$, $F(3)$, and $F(5)$.
   (b) On what interval(s) is F decreasing?
   (c) At what value of t does F have a maximum value?
   (d) On what interval is F concave up?

2. Find the area of the region(s) enclosed by the curve $f(x) = x^3$, the x-axis, and the lines $x = -1$ and $x = 2$.

3. Find the area of the region(s) enclosed by the curve $y = |2x - 6|$, the x-axis, and the lines $x = 0$ and $x = 4$.

4. Find the approximate area under the curve

   $f(x) = \dfrac{1}{x}$ from $x = 1$ to $x = 5$, using four

   right-endpoint rectangles of equal lengths.

5. Find the approximate area under the curve $y = x^2 + 1$ from $x = 0$ to $x = 3$, using the Trapezoidal Rule with $n = 3$.

6. Find the area of the region bounded by the graphs $y = \sqrt{x}$, $y = -x$, and $x = 4$.

7. Find the area of the region bounded by the curves $x = y^2$ and $x = 4$.

8. Find the area of the region bounded by the graphs of all four equations:

   $f(x) = \sin\left(\dfrac{x}{2}\right)$; x-axis; and the lines,

   $x = \dfrac{\pi}{2}$ and $x = \pi$.

9. Find the volume of the solid obtained by revolving about the x-axis, the region bounded by the graphs of $y = x^2 + 4$, the x-axis, the y-axis, and the lines $x = 3$.

10. The area under the curve $y = \dfrac{1}{x}$ from $x = 1$ to $x = k$ is 1. Find the value of k.

11. Find the volume of the solid obtained by revolving about the y-axis the region bounded by $x = y^2 + 1$, $x = 0$, $y = -1$, and $y = 1$.

12. Let R be the region enclosed by the graph $y = 3x$, the x-axis, and the line $x = 4$. The line $x = a$ divides region R into two regions such that when the regions are revolved about the x-axis, the resulting solids have equal volume. Find a.

Part B—Calculators are allowed.

13. Find the volume of the solid obtained by revolving about the x-axis the region bounded by the graphs of $f(x) = x^3$ and $g(x) = x^2$.

14. The base of a solid is a region bounded by the circle $x^2 + y^2 = 4$. The cross sections of the solid perpendicular to the x-axis are equilateral triangles. Find the volume of the solid.

15. Find the volume of the solid obtained by revolving about the y-axis, the region bounded by the curves $x = y^2$, and $y = x - 2$.

For Problems 16 through 19, find the volume of the solid obtained by revolving the region as described below. (See Figure 12.7-2.)

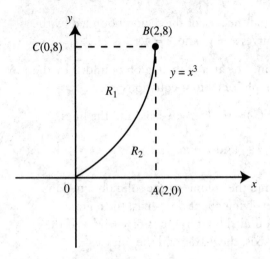

x	0	2	4	6	8	10	12
$f(x)$	1	2.24	3	3.61	4.12	4.58	5

Figure 12.7-2

16. R_1 about the x-axis.

17. R_2 about the y-axis.

18. R_1 about the line $\overleftrightarrow{BC}$.

19. R_2 about the line $\overleftrightarrow{AB}$.

20. The function $f(x)$ is continuous on $[0, 12]$ and the selected values of $f(x)$ are shown in the table.

Find the approximate area under the curve of f from 0 to 12 using three midpoint rectangles.

21. Find the area bounded by the curve defined by $x = 2 \cos t$ and $y = 3 \sin t$ from $t = 0$ to $t = \pi$.

22. Find the length of the arc of $r = \sin^2\left(\dfrac{\theta}{2}\right)$ from $\theta = 0$ to $\theta = \pi$.

23. Find the area of the surface formed when the curve defined by $x = e^t \sin t$ and $y = e^t \cos t$ from $t = 0$ to $t = \dfrac{\pi}{2}$ is revolved about the x-axis.

24. Find the area bounded by $r = 2 + 2 \sin \theta$.

25. The acceleration vector for an object is $\langle -e^t,\ e^t \rangle$. Find the position of the object at $t = 1$ if the initial velocity is $v_0 = \langle 3, 1 \rangle$ and the initial position of the object is at the origin.

12.8 Cumulative Review Problems

(Calculator) indicates that calculators are permitted.

26. If $\displaystyle\int_{-a}^{a} e^{x^1}\, dx = k$, find $\displaystyle\int_{0}^{a} e^{x^2}\, dx$ in terms of k.

27. A man wishes to pull a log over a 9 foot high garden wall as shown in Figure 12.8-1. He is pulling at a rate of 2 ft/sec. At what rate is the angle between the rope and the ground changing when there are 15 feet of rope between the top of the wall and the log?

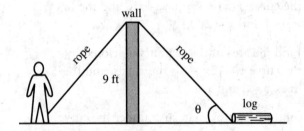

Figure 12.8-1

28. (Calculator) Find a point on the parabola $y = \dfrac{1}{2}x^2$ that is closest to the point (4, 1).

29. The velocity function of a particle moving along the x-axis is $v(t) = t \cos(t^2 + 1)$ for $t \geq 0$.

   (a) If at $t = 0$, the particle is at the origin, find the position of the particle at $t = 2$.

   (b) Is the particle moving to the right or left at $t = 2$?

   (c) Find the acceleration of the particle at $t = 2$ and determine if the velocity of the particle is increasing or decreasing. Explain why.

30. (Calculator) given $f(x) = xe^x$ and $g(x) = \cos x$, find:

   (a) the area of the region in the first quadrant bounded by the graphs $f(x), g(x),$ and $x = 0$.

   (b) The volume obtained by revolving the region in part (a) about the x-axis.

31. Find the slope of the tangent line to the curve defined by $r = 5 \cos 2\theta$ at the point where $\theta = \dfrac{3\pi}{2}$.

32. $\displaystyle\int \frac{2}{x^2 - 4x}\,dx$

33. $\displaystyle\int_e^\infty \frac{dx}{x}$

12.9 Solutions to Practice Problems

Part A—The use of a calculator is not allowed.

1. (a) $F(0) = \displaystyle\int_0^0 f(t)\,dt = 0$

   $F(3) = \displaystyle\int_0^3 f(t)\,dt$

   $\quad = \dfrac{1}{2}(3 + 2)(4) = 10$

   $F(5) = \displaystyle\int_0^5 f(t)\,dt$

   $\quad = \displaystyle\int_0^3 f(t)\,dt + \int_3^5 f(t)\,dt$

   $\quad = 10 + (-4) = 6$

   (b) Since $\displaystyle\int_3^5 f(t)\,dt \leq 0$, F is decreasing on the interval $[3, 5]$.

   (c) At $t = 3$, F has a maximum value.

   (d) $F'(x) = f(x)$, $F'(x)$ is increasing on $(4, 5)$, which implies $F''(x) > 0$. Thus F is concave upward on $(4, 5)$.

2. (See Figure 12.9-1.)

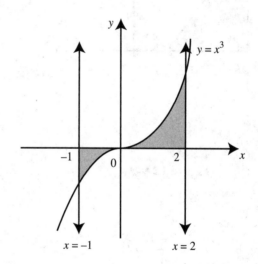

Figure 12.9-1

$A = \left| \displaystyle\int_{-1}^0 x^3\,dx \right| + \displaystyle\int_0^2 x^3\,dx$

$\quad = \left| \left[\dfrac{x^4}{4} \right]_{-1}^0 \right| + \left[\dfrac{x^4}{4} \right]_0^2$

$\quad = \left| 0 - \dfrac{(-1)^4}{4} \right| + \left(\dfrac{2^4}{4} - 0 \right)$

$\quad = \dfrac{1}{4} + 4 = \dfrac{17}{4}$

3. (See Figure 12.9-2.)
   Set $2x - 6 = 0$; $x = 3$ and

   $$f(x) = \begin{cases} 2x - 6 & \text{if } x \geq 3 \\ -(2x - 6) & \text{if } x < 3 \end{cases}.$$

   $$A = \int_0^3 -(2x - 6)\,dx + \int_3^4 (2x - 6)\,dx$$

   $$= \left[-x^2 + 6x\right]_0^3 + \left[x^2 - 6x\right]_3^4$$

   $$= \left[-(3)^2 + 6(3)\right]$$

   $$- 0 + \left[4^2 + 6(4)\right] - \left[3^2 - 6(3)\right]$$

   $$= 9 + 1 = 10$$

Figure 12.9-3

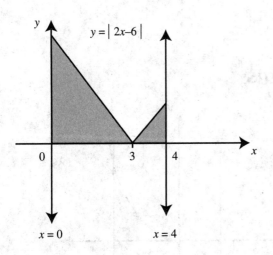

Figure 12.9-2

4. (See Figure 12.9-3.)
   Length of $\Delta x_1 = \dfrac{5 - 1}{4} = 1$.

   Area of $\text{Rect}_\text{I} = f(2)\Delta x_1 = \dfrac{1}{2}(1) = \dfrac{1}{2}$.

   Area of $\text{Rect}_\text{II} = f(3)\Delta x_2 = \dfrac{1}{3}(1) = \dfrac{1}{3}$.

   Area of $\text{Rect}_\text{III} = f(4)\Delta x_3 = \dfrac{1}{4}(1) = \dfrac{1}{4}$.

   Area of $\text{Rect}_\text{IV} = f(5)\Delta x_4 = \dfrac{1}{5}(1) = \dfrac{1}{5}$.

   Total Area $= \dfrac{1}{2} + \dfrac{1}{3} + \dfrac{1}{4} + \dfrac{1}{5} = \dfrac{77}{60}$.

5. (See Figure 12.9-4.)

   Trapezoid Rule $= \dfrac{b - a}{2n}\left(f(a) + 2f(x_1)\right.$

   $$\left. + 2f(x_2) + f(b)\right).$$

   $$A = \dfrac{3 - 0}{2(3)}\left(f(0) + 2f(1) + 2f(2) + f(3)\right)$$

   $$= \dfrac{1}{2}(1 + 4 + 10 + 10) = \dfrac{25}{2}$$

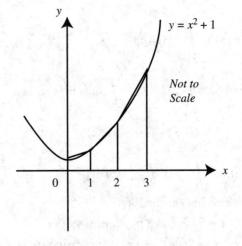

Figure 12.9-4

6. (See Figure 12.9-5.)

$$A = \int_0^4 \left(\sqrt{x} - (-x) \right) dx$$

$$= \int_0^4 \left(x^{1/2} + x \right) dx = \left[\frac{2x^{3/2}}{3} + \frac{x^2}{2} \right]_0^4$$

$$= \left(\frac{2(4)^{3/2}}{3} + \frac{4^2}{2} \right) - 0$$

$$= \frac{16}{3} + 8 = \frac{40}{3}$$

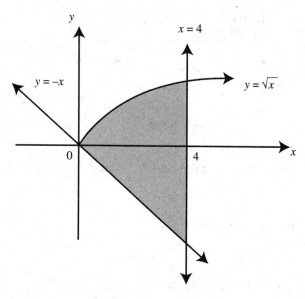

Figure 12.9-5

7. (See Figure 12.9-6.)
Intersection points: $4 = y^2 \Rightarrow y = \pm 2$.

$$A = \int_{-2}^2 \left(4 - y^2 \right) dy = \left[4y - \frac{y^3}{3} \right]_{-2}^2$$

$$= \left(4(2) - \frac{2^3}{3} \right) - \left(4(-2) - \frac{(-2)^3}{3} \right)$$

$$= \left(8 - \frac{8}{3} \right) - \left(-8 + \frac{8}{3} \right)$$

$$= \frac{16}{3} + \frac{16}{3} = \frac{32}{3}$$

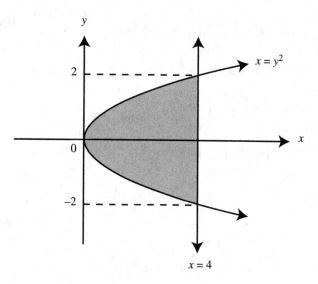

Figure 12.9-6

You can use the symmetry of the region and obtain the area $= 2 \int_0^2 (4 - y^2) dy$. An alternative method is to find the area by setting up an integral with respect to the x-axis and expressing $x = y^2$ as $y = \sqrt{x}$ and $y = -\sqrt{x}$.

8. (See Figure 12.9-7.)

$$A = \int_{\pi/2}^{\pi} \sin \left(\frac{x}{2} \right) dx$$

Let $u = \dfrac{x}{2}$ and $du = \dfrac{dx}{2}$ or $2\,du = dx$.

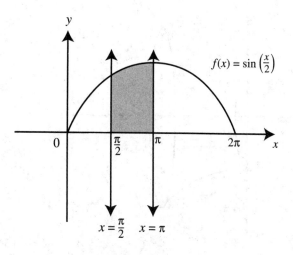

Figure 12.9-7

$$\int \sin\left(\frac{x}{2}\right) dx = \int \sin u (2du)$$

$$= 2 \int \sin u\, du = -2 \cos u + c$$

$$= -2 \cos\left(\frac{x}{2}\right) + c$$

$$A = \int_{\pi/2}^{\pi} \sin\left(\frac{x}{2}\right) dx = \left[-2 \cos\left(\frac{x}{2}\right)\right]_{\pi/2}^{\pi}$$

$$= -2 \left[\cos\left(\frac{\pi}{2}\right) - \cos\left(\frac{\pi/2}{2}\right) \right]$$

$$= -2 \left(\cos\left(\frac{\pi}{2}\right) - \cos\left(\frac{\pi}{4}\right) \right)$$

$$= -2 \left(0 - \frac{\sqrt{2}}{2} \right) = \sqrt{2}$$

9. (See Figure 12.9-8.)
    Using the Disc Method:

$$V = \pi \int_{0}^{3} \left(x^2 + 4\right)^2 dx$$

$$= \pi \int_{0}^{3} \left(x^4 + 8x^2 + 16\right) dx$$

$$= \pi \left[\frac{x^5}{5} + \frac{8x^3}{3} + 16x \right]_{0}^{3}$$

$$= \pi \left[\frac{3^5}{5} + \frac{8(3)^3}{3} + 16(3) \right] - 0 = \frac{843}{5}\pi$$

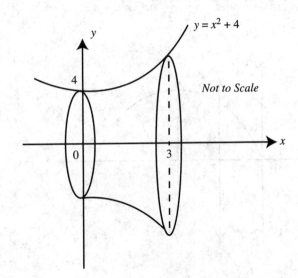

Figure 12.9-8

10. Area

$$= \int_{1}^{k} \frac{1}{x} dx = \ln x]_{1}^{k} = \ln k - \ln 1 = \ln k.$$

Set $\ln k = 1$. Thus $e^{\ln k} = e^1$ or $k = e$.

11. (See Figure 12.9-9.)

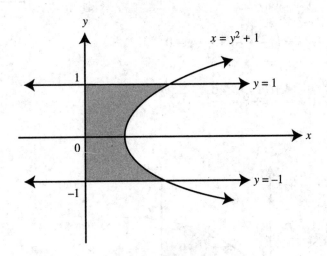

Figure 12.9-9

Using the Disc Method:

$$V = \pi \int_{-1}^{1} \left(y^2 + 1\right)^2 dy$$

$$= \pi \int_{-1}^{1} \left(y^4 + 2y^2 + 1\right) dy$$

$$= \pi \left[\frac{y^5}{5} + \frac{2y^3}{3} + y \right]_{-1}^{1}$$

$$= \pi \left[\left(\frac{1^5}{5} + \frac{2(1)^3}{3} + 1 \right) \right.$$

$$\left. - \left(\frac{(-1)^5}{5} + \frac{2(-1)^3}{3} + (-1) \right) \right]$$

$$= \pi \left(\frac{28}{15} + \frac{28}{15} \right) = \frac{56\pi}{15}$$

Note: You can use the symmetry of the region and find the volume by

$$2\pi \int_{0}^{1} \left(y^2 + 1\right)^2 dy.$$

12. Volume of solid by revolving R:

$$V_R = \int_0^4 \pi (3x)^2 dx = \pi \int_0^4 9x^2 dx$$

$$= \pi \left[3x^3 \right]_0^4 = 192\pi$$

Set $\int_0^a \pi (3x)^2 dx = \dfrac{192\pi}{2}$

$$\Rightarrow 3a^3\pi = 96\pi$$

$$a^3 = 32$$

$$a = (32)^{1/3} = 2\,(2)^{2/3}$$

You can verify your result by evaluating

$$\int_0^{2(2)^{2/3}} \pi (3x)^2 dx.$$ The result is 96π.

Part B—Calculators are allowed.

13. (See Figure 12.9-10.)

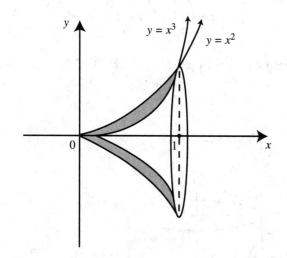

Figure 12.9-10

Step 1. Using the Washer Method:
Points of intersection: Set
$x^3 = x^2 \Rightarrow x^3 - x^2 = 0 \Rightarrow$
$x^2(x - 1) = 0$ or $x = 1$.
Outer radius $= x^2$;
Inner radius $= x^3$.

Step 2. $V = \pi \int_0^1 \left((x^2)^2 - (x^3)^2 \right) dx$

$$= \pi \int_0^1 (x^4 - x^6)dx$$

Step 3. Enter $\int (\pi(x\char94 4 - x\char94 6),\ x,\ 0,\ 1)$

and obtain $\dfrac{2\pi}{35}$.

14. (See Figure 12.9-11.)

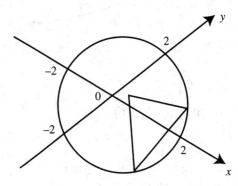

Figure 12.9-11

Step 1. $x^2 + y^2 = 4 \Rightarrow y^2 = 4 - x^2 \Rightarrow$
$y = \pm\sqrt{4 - x^2}$
Let $s =$ a side of an equilateral
triangle $s = 2\sqrt{4 - x^2}$.

Step 2. Area of a cross section:

$$A(x) = \frac{s^2\sqrt{3}}{4} = \frac{\left(2\sqrt{4 - x^2}\right)^2 \sqrt{3}}{4}.$$

Step 3. $V = \int_{-2}^2 \left(2\sqrt{4 - x^2}\right)^2 \dfrac{\sqrt{3}}{4} dx$

$$= \int_{-2}^2 \sqrt{3}(4 - x\char94 2)dx$$

Step 4. Enter $\int \left(\sqrt{(3)} * (4 - x^2),\ x,\ -2,\ 2\right)$

and obtain $\dfrac{32\sqrt{3}}{3}$.

15. (See Figure 12.9-12.)

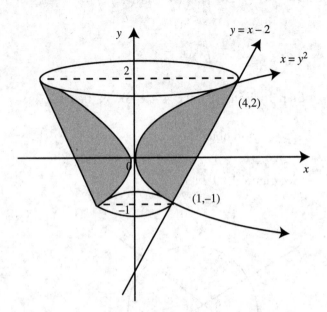

Figure 12.9-12

Step 1. Using the Washer Method:
Points of Intersection:
$y = x - 2 \Rightarrow x = y + 2$
Set $y^2 = y + 2$
$\Rightarrow y^2 - y - 2 = 0$
$\Rightarrow (y - 2)(y + 1) = 0$
or $y = -1$ or $y = 2$.

Outer radius $= y + 2$;
Inner radius $= y^2$.

Step 2. $V = \pi \int_{-1}^{2} \left((y + 2)^2 - (y^2)^2 \right) dy$

Step 3. Enter $\pi \int \left((y + 2)^2 \right.$

$\left. -y^4, \ -1, \ 2 \right)$ and obtain $\dfrac{72}{5}\pi$.

16. (See Figure 12.9-13.)

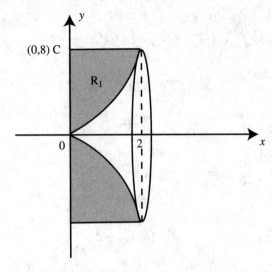

Figure 12.9-13

Step 1. Using the Washer Method:
$y = 8, \ y = x^3$

Outer radius $= 8$;

Inner radius $= x^3$.

$$V = \pi \int_{0}^{2} \left(8^2 - (x^3)^2 \right) dx$$

Step 2. Enter $\int \pi \left(8^2 - x^6, \ x, \ 0, \ 2 \right)$
and obtain $\dfrac{768\pi}{7}$.

17. (See Figure 12.9-14.)

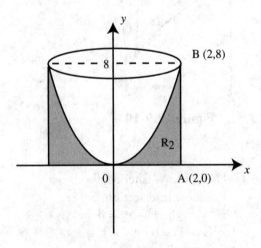

Figure 12.9-14

Using the Washer Method:
Outer radius: $x = 2$;
Inner radius: $x = y^{1/3}$.

$$V = \pi \int_0^8 \left(2^2 - \left(y^{1/3} \right)^2 \right) dy$$

Using your calculator, you obtain

$$V = \frac{64\pi}{5}.$$

18. (See Figure 12.9-15.)

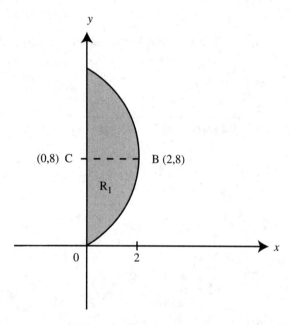

Figure 12.9-15

Step 1. Using the Disc Method:

Radius $= (8 - x^3)$.

$$V = \pi \int_0^2 \left(8 - x^3 \right)^2 dx$$

Step 2. Enter $\int \left(\pi * (8 - x^3)^2, \right.$

$\left. x, \ 0, \ 2 \right)$ and obtain $\dfrac{576\pi}{7}$.

19. (See Figure 12.9-16.)
    Using the Disc Method:

Radius $= 2 - x = \left(2 - y^{1/3} \right)$.

$$V = \pi \int_0^8 \left(2 - y^{1/3} \right)^2 dy$$

Using your calculator, you obtain

$$V = \frac{16\pi}{5}.$$

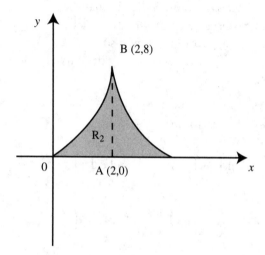

Figure 12.9-16

20. Area $= \displaystyle\sum_{i=1}^{3} f(x_i) \Delta x_i.$

x_i=midpoint of the ith interval.

Length of $\Delta x_i = \dfrac{12 - 0}{3} = 4.$

Area of $\text{Rect}_{\text{I}} = f(2)\Delta x_1 = (2.24)(4) = 8.96.$

Area of $\text{Rect}_{\text{II}} = f(6)\Delta x_2 = (3.61)(4) = 14.44.$

Area of $\text{Rect}_{\text{III}} = f(10)\Delta x_3 = (4.58)(4) = 18.32.$

Total Area $=8.96 + 14.44 + 18.32 = 41.72.$

The area under the curve is approximately 41.72.

21. The area enclosed by the curve is the upper half of an ellipse.

Find $\dfrac{dx}{dt} = -2\sin t.$

$A = \displaystyle\int_0^\pi (3\sin t)(-2\sin t)\,dt$

$= -6\displaystyle\int_0^\pi \sin^2 t\,dt$

$= -6\left[\dfrac{1}{2}t - \dfrac{1}{4}\sin 2t\right]_0^\pi = -3\pi$

The negative simply indicates that the area has been swept from right to left, rather than left to right, and so may be ignored. The area enclosed by the curve is 3π.

22. Differentiate to find

$\dfrac{dr}{d\theta} = \sin\left(\dfrac{\theta}{2}\right)\cos\left(\dfrac{\theta}{2}\right)$, and calculate

$r^2 = \sin^4\left(\dfrac{\theta}{2}\right)$ and $\left(\dfrac{dr}{d\theta}\right)^2 = \sin^2\left(\dfrac{\theta}{2}\right)$

$\cos^2\left(\dfrac{\theta}{2}\right)$. Then the length of the arc is

$L = \displaystyle\int_0^\pi \sqrt{\sin^4\left(\dfrac{\theta}{2}\right) + \sin^2\left(\dfrac{\theta}{2}\right)\cos^2\left(\dfrac{\theta}{2}\right)}\,d\theta$

$= \displaystyle\int_0^\pi \sqrt{\sin^2\left(\dfrac{\theta}{2}\right)\left(\sin^2\left(\dfrac{\theta}{2}\right) + \cos^2\left(\dfrac{\theta}{2}\right)\right)}\,d\theta$

$= \displaystyle\int_0^\pi \left|\sin\left(\dfrac{\theta}{2}\right)\right|\,d\theta = -2\cos\left(\dfrac{\theta}{2}\right)\Big|_0^\pi$

$= -2\cos\dfrac{\pi}{2} + 2\cos 0 = -2(0) + 2(1) = 2.$

23. Find $\dfrac{dx}{dt} = e^t\cos t + e^t\sin t$ and

$\dfrac{dy}{dt} = e^t\cos t - e^t\sin t.$ Square

each derivative.

$\left(\dfrac{dx}{dt}\right)^2 = (e^t\cos t + e^t\sin t)^2$

$= e^{2t}(\cos^2 t + 2\sin t\cos t + \sin^2 t)$

$= e^{2t}(1 + 2\sin t\cos t)$ and

$\left(\dfrac{dy}{dt}\right)^2 = (e^t\cos t - e^t\sin t)^2$

$= e^{2t}(\cos^2 t - 2\cos t\sin t + \sin^2 t)$

$= e^{2t}(1 - 2\cos t\sin t).$ Then

$S = 2\pi\displaystyle\int_0^{\frac{\pi}{2}} e^t\cos t$

$\times\sqrt{e^{2t}(1+2\sin t\cos t)+e^{2t}(1-2\sin t\cos t)}\,dt$

$= 2\pi\displaystyle\int_0^{\frac{\pi}{2}} e^{2t}\cos t$

$\times\sqrt{1+2\sin t\cos t+1-2\sin t\cos t}\,dt$

$= 2\pi\displaystyle\int_0^{\frac{\pi}{2}} (e^{2t}\cos t)\sqrt{2}\,dt$

$= 2\sqrt{2}\pi\dfrac{e^{2t}}{5}(\sin t + 2\cos t)\Big|_0^{\frac{\pi}{2}}$

$= 2\sqrt{2}\pi\dfrac{e^\pi - 2}{5} \approx 37.5702$

24. Square $r^2 = 4 + 8\sin\theta + 4\sin^2\theta.$ The area

$A = \dfrac{1}{2}\displaystyle\int_0^{2\pi}\left(4 + 8\sin\theta + 4\sin^2\theta\right)d\theta$

$= \dfrac{1}{2}\left[4\theta - 8\cos\theta + 4\left(\dfrac{1}{2}\theta - \dfrac{1}{4}\sin 2\theta\right)\right]_0^{2\pi}$

$= \left[3\theta - 4\cos\theta - \dfrac{1}{2}\sin 2\theta\right]_0^{2\pi}$

$= (6\pi - 4) - (-4) = 6\pi.$

25. The acceleration vector for an object moving in the plane is $\langle -e^t, e^t\rangle$. Find the position of the object at $t = 1$, if the initial velocity is $v_0 = \langle 3, 1\rangle$ and the initial position of the object is at the origin.

The acceleration of the object is known to be $a = \langle -e^t, \ e^t \rangle = -e^t i + e^t j$. Integrate to find the velocity. $v = -e^t i + e^t j + C$, and since the initial velocity is $v_0 = \langle 3, 1 \rangle$, $v_0 = -i + j + C = 3i + j$ and $C = 4i$. The velocity vector is $v = -e^t i + e^t j + 4i = (4 - e^t)i + e^t j$. Integrate again to find the position vector $s = (4t - e^t)i + e^t j + C$.

The initial position at the origin means that $s_0 = (4.0 - e^0)i + e^0 j + C = -i + j + C = 0$, and therefore, $C = i - j$. The position vector $s = (4t - e^t + 1)i + (e^t - 1)j$ can be evaluated at $t = 1$ to find the position as $(5 - e)i + (e - 1)j = \langle 5 - e, e - 1 \rangle$.

12.10 Solutions to Cumulative Review Problems

26. (See Figure 12.10-1.)

[−3,3] by [−1,7]

Figure 12.10-1

$$\int_{-a}^{a} e^{x^2} dx = \int_{-a}^{0} e^{x^2} dx + \int_{0}^{a} e^{x^2} dx$$

Since e^{x^2} is an even function, thus

$$\int_{-a}^{0} e^{x^2} dx = \int_{0}^{a} e^{x^2} dx.$$

$$k = 2 \int_{0}^{a} e^{x^2} dx \text{ and } \int_{0}^{a} e^{x^2} dx = \frac{k}{2}.$$

27. (See Figure 12.10-2.)

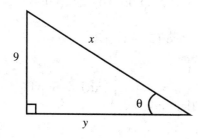

Figure 12.10-2

$$\sin \theta = \frac{9}{x}$$

Differentiate both sides:

$$\cos \theta \frac{d\theta}{dt} = (9)(-x^{-2}) \frac{dx}{dt}.$$

When $x = 15$, $9^2 + y^2 = 15^2 \Rightarrow y = 12$.

Thus, $\cos \theta = \dfrac{12}{15} = \dfrac{4}{5}; \dfrac{dx}{dt} = -2$ ft/sec.

$$\frac{4}{5} \frac{d\theta}{dt} = 9 \left(-\frac{1}{15^2} \right) (-2)$$

$$= \frac{d\theta}{dt} = \frac{18}{15^2} \frac{5}{4} = \frac{1}{10} \text{ radian/sec.}$$

28. (See Figure 12.10-3.)

[−2,5] by [−2,6]

Figure 12.10-3

Step 1. Distance Formula:

$$L = \sqrt{(x-4)^2 + (y-1)^2}$$

$$= \sqrt{(x-4)^2 + \left(\frac{x^2}{2} - 1\right)^2}$$

where the domain is all real numbers.

Step 2. Enter $y1 =$
$$\sqrt{((x-4)^\wedge 2 + (.5x^\wedge 2 - 1)^\wedge 2)}.$$
Enter $y2 = d(y1(x), x)$.

Step 3. Use the [*Zero*] function and obtain $x = 2$ for y_2.

Step 4. Use the First Derivative Test. (See Figures 12.10-4 and 12.10-5.) At $x = 2$, L has a relative minimum. Since at $x = 2$, L has the only relative extremum, it is an absolute minimum.

[−3,3] by [−15,15]

Figure 12.10-4

$y_2 = \left(\dfrac{dL}{dx}\right)$ −   0   +

L   decr.   2   incr.

rel. min.

Figure 12.10-5

Step 5. At $x = 2$, $y = \dfrac{1}{2}\left(x^2\right) =$
$\dfrac{1}{2}\left(2^2\right) = 2$. Thus, the point on
$y = \dfrac{1}{2}\left(x^2\right)$ closest to the point
(4, 1) is the point (2, 2).

29. (a) $s(0) = 0$ and

$$s(t) = \int v(t)dt = \int t\cos(t^2 + 1)dt.$$

Enter $\displaystyle\int (x * \cos(x^\wedge 2 + 1), \ x)$

and obtain $\dfrac{\sin(x^2 + 1)}{2}$.

Thus, $s(t) = \dfrac{\sin(t^2 + 1)}{2} + C$.

Since $s(0) = 0 \Rightarrow \dfrac{\sin(0^2 + 1)}{2} + C = 0$

$\Rightarrow \dfrac{.841471}{2} + C = 0$

$\Rightarrow C = -0.420735 = -0.421$

$s(t) = \dfrac{\sin(t^2 + 1)}{2} - 0.420735$

$s(2) = \dfrac{\sin(2^2 + 1)}{2} - 0.420735$

$= -0.900197 \approx -0.900.$

(b) $v(2) = 2\cos(2^2 + 1) = 2\cos(5) = 0.567324$

Since $v(2) > 0$, the particle is moving to the right at $t = 2$.

(c) $a(t) = v'(t)$

Enter $d(x * \cos(x^\wedge 2 + 1), x)|x = 2$ and obtain 7.95506.
Thus, the velocity of the particle is increasing at $t = 2$, since $a(2) > 0$.

30. (See Figure 12.10-6)

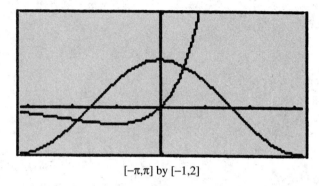

$[-\pi, \pi]$ by $[-1, 2]$

Figure 12.10-6

(a) Point of Intersection: Use the [*Intersection*] function of the calculator and obtain $(0.517757, 0.868931)$.

$$\text{Area} = \int_0^{0.51775} (\cos x - x e^x)\,dx$$

Enter $\int (\cos(x) - x * e^\wedge x,\ x,$

$0,\ 0.51775)$ and obtain 0.304261.
The area of the region is approximately 0.304.

(b) Step 1. Using the Washer Method:

Outer radius $= \cos x$;
Inner radius $= x e^x$.

$$V = \pi \int_0^{0.51775} \left[(\cos x)^2 - (x e^x)^2 \right] dx$$

Step 2. Enter $\int \left(\pi \left((\cos(x)^\wedge 2) - \right. \right.$
$\left. \left. (x * e^\wedge(x))^\wedge 2 \right), x,\ 0.51775 \right)$

and obtain 1.16678.

The volume of the solid is approximately 1.167.

31. Convert to a parametric representation with $x = r \cos\theta = 5 \cos\theta \cos 2\theta$ and $y = r \sin\theta = 5 \cos 2\theta \sin\theta$. Differentiate with respect to θ.

$$\frac{dx}{d\theta} = -5 \cos 2\theta \sin\theta - 10 \sin 2\theta \sin\theta \text{ and}$$

$$\frac{dy}{d\theta} = 5 \cos 2\theta \cos\theta - 10 \sin 2\theta \sin\theta.$$

Divide to find $\dfrac{dy}{dx}$

$$= \frac{5 \cos 2\theta \sin\theta - 10 \sin 2\theta \sin\theta}{-5 \cos 2\theta \sin\theta - 10 \sin 2\theta \sin\theta}$$

$$= \frac{-\cos 2\theta \cos\theta + 2 \sin 2\theta \sin\theta}{\cos 2\theta \sin\theta + 2 \sin 2\theta \sin\theta}. \text{ Evaluated}$$

at $\theta = \dfrac{3\pi}{2}$, $\dfrac{dy}{dx} = 0$.

The slope of the tangent line is zero, including a horizontal tangent.

32. $\displaystyle\int \frac{2}{x^2 - 4x}\,dx = \int \frac{2}{x(x-4)}\,dx$ can be

integrated with a partial fraction

decomposition. Since $\dfrac{A}{x} + \dfrac{B}{x-4} = \dfrac{2}{x(x-4)}$,

$A = \dfrac{-1}{2}$ and $B = \dfrac{1}{2}$. Therefore,

$$\int \frac{2}{x^2 - 4x} dx = \frac{-1}{2} \int \frac{dx}{x} + \frac{1}{2} \int \frac{dx}{x - 4}$$

$$= \frac{-1}{2} \ln |x| + \frac{1}{2} \ln |x - 4| + C$$

$$= \frac{1}{2} \ln \left| \frac{x - 4}{x} \right| + C.$$

33. $\displaystyle\int_e^\infty \frac{dx}{x} = \lim_{k \to \infty} \int_e^k \frac{dx}{x} = \lim_{k \to \infty} \ln |x| \Big|_e^k$

$$= \lim_{k \to \infty} [\ln |k| - 1] = \infty$$

CHAPTER 13

Big Idea 3: Integrals and the Fundamental Theorems of Calculus
More Applications of Definite Integrals

IN THIS CHAPTER

Summary: In this chapter, you will learn to solve problems using a definite integral as accumulated change. These problems include distance-traveled problems, temperature problems, and growth problems. You will also learn to work with slope fields, solve differential and logistic equations, and apply Euler's Method to approximate the value of a function at a specific value.

KEY IDEA

Key Ideas

○ Average Value of a Function
○ Mean Value Theorem for Integrals
○ Distance Traveled Problems
○ Definite Integral as Accumulated Change
○ Differential Equations
○ Slope Fields
○ Logistic Differential Equations
○ Euler's Method

13.1 Average Value of a Function

Main Concepts: Mean Value Theorem for Integrals, Average Value of a Function on $[a, b]$

Mean Value Theorem for Integrals

If f is continuous on $[a, b]$, then there exists a number c in $[a, b]$ such that $\int_a^b f(x)\, dx = f(c)(b - a)$. (See Figure 13.1-1.)

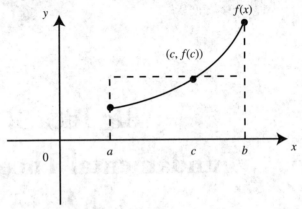

Figure 13.1-1

Example 1

Given $f(x) = \sqrt{x - 1}$, verify the hypotheses of the Mean Value Theorem for Integrals for f on $[1, 10]$ and find the value of c as indicated in the theorem.

The function f is continuous for $x \geq 1$, thus:

$$\int_1^{10} \sqrt{x - 1}\, dx = f(c)(10 - 1)$$

$$\left. \frac{2(x - 1)^{3/2}}{3} \right]_1^{10} = 9\, f(c)$$

$$\frac{2}{3}\left[(10 - 1)^{3/2} - 0 \right] = 9\, f(c)$$

$$18 = 9\, f(c);\ 2 = f(c);\ 2 = \sqrt{c - 1};\ 4 = c - 1$$

$$5 = c.$$

Example 2

Given $f(x) = x^2$, verify the hypotheses of the Mean Value Theorem for Integrals for f on $[0, 6]$ and find the value of c as indicated in the theorem.

Since f is a polynomial, it is continuous and differentiable everywhere,

$$\int_0^6 x^2 dx = f(c)(6 - 0)$$

$$\frac{x^3}{3}\bigg]_0^6 = f(c)6$$

$$72 = 6f(c); \; 12 = f(c); \; 12 = c^2$$

$$c = \pm\sqrt{12} = \pm 2\sqrt{3}\left(\pm 2\sqrt{3} \approx \pm 3.4641\right).$$

Since only $2\sqrt{3}$ is in the interval $[0, 6]$, $c = 2\sqrt{3}$.

- Remember: if f' is decreasing, then $f'' < 0$ and the graph of f is concave downward.

Average Value of a Function on [a, b]

Average Value of a Function on an Interval

If f is a continuous function on $[a, b]$, then the Average Value of f on $[a, b]$ $= \dfrac{1}{b - a} \displaystyle\int_a^b f(x)dx$.

Example 1

Find the average value of $y = \sin x$ between $x = 0$ and $x = \pi$.

$$\text{Average value} = \frac{1}{\pi - 0}\int_0^\pi \sin x \, dx$$

$$= \frac{1}{\pi}[-\cos x]_0^\pi = \frac{1}{\pi}[-\cos \pi - (-\cos(0))]$$

$$= \frac{1}{\pi}[1 + 1] = \frac{2}{\pi}.$$

Example 2

The graph of a function f is shown in Figure 13.1-2. Find the average value of f on $[0, 4]$.

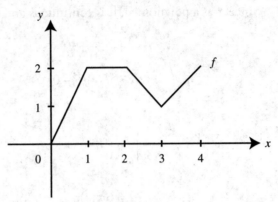

Figure 13.1-2

$$\text{Average value} = \frac{1}{4-0} \int_0^4 f(x)\, dx$$

$$= \frac{1}{4}\left(1 + 2 + \frac{3}{2} + \frac{3}{2}\right) = \frac{3}{2}.$$

Example 3

The velocity of a particle moving on a line is $v(t) = 3t^2 - 18t + 24$. Find the average velocity from $t = 1$ to $t = 3$.

$$\text{Average velocity} = \frac{1}{3-1} \int_1^3 (3t^2 - 18t + 24)\, dt$$

$$= \frac{1}{2}\left[t^3 - 9t^2 + 24t\right]_1^3$$

$$= \frac{1}{2}\left[\left(3^3 - 9(3^2) + 24(3)\right) - \left(1^3 - 9(1^2) + 24(1)\right)\right]$$

$$= \frac{1}{2}(18 - 16) = \frac{1}{2}(2) = 1.$$

Note: The average velocity for $t = 1$ to $t = 3$ is $\dfrac{s(3) - s(1)}{2}$, which is equivalent to the computations above.

13.2 Distance Traveled Problems

Summary of Formulas

Position Function: $s(t)$; $s(t) = \int v(t)\,dt$.

Velocity: $v(t) = \dfrac{ds}{dt}$; $v(t) = \int a(t)\,dt$.

Acceleration: $a(t) = \dfrac{dv}{dt}$.

Speed: $|v(t)|$.

Displacement from t_1 to $t_2 = \displaystyle\int_{t_1}^{t_2} v(t)\,dt = s(t_2) - s(t_1)$.

Total Distance Traveled from t_1 to $t_2 = \displaystyle\int_{t_1}^{t_2} \big|v(t)\big|\,dt$.

Example 1

See Figure 13.2-1.

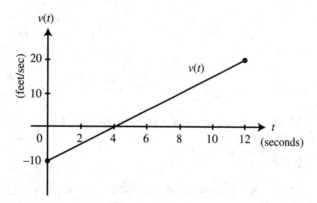

Figure 13.2-1

The graph of the velocity function of a moving particle is shown in Figure 13.2-1. What is the total distance traveled by the particle during $0 \le t \le 12$?

$$\text{Total Distance Traveled} = \left| \int_0^4 v(t)\,dt \right| + \int_4^{12} v(t)\,dt$$

$$= \frac{1}{2}(4)(10) + \frac{1}{2}(8)(20) = 20 + 80 = 100 \text{ feet.}$$

Example 2

The velocity function of a moving particle on a coordinate line is $v(t) = t^2 + 3t - 10$ for $0 \le t \le 6$. Find (a) the displacement by the particle during $0 \le t \le 6$, and (b) the total distance traveled during $0 \le t \le 6$.

(a) Displacement $= \int_{t_1}^{t_2} v(t)dt$

$$= \int_0^6 (t^2 + 3t - 10)dt = \frac{t^3}{3} + \frac{3t^2}{2} - 10t\Big]_0^6 = 66.$$

(b) Total Distance Traveled $= \int_{t_1}^{t_2} |v(t)|dt$

$$= \int_0^6 |t^2 + 3t - 10|dt.$$

Let $t^2 + 3t - 10 = 0 \Rightarrow (t + 5)(t - 2) = 0 \Rightarrow t = -5 \text{ or } t = 2$

$$|t^2 + 3t - 10| = \begin{cases} -(t^2 + 3t - 10) & \text{if } 0 \le t \le 2 \\ t^2 + 3t - 10 & \text{if } t > 2 \end{cases}$$

$$\int_0^6 |t^2 + 3t - 10|dt = \int_0^2 -(t^2 + 3t - 10)dt + \int_2^6 (t^2 + 3t - 10)dt$$

$$= \left[\frac{-t^3}{3} - \frac{3t^2}{2} + 10t \right]_0^2 + \left[\frac{t^3}{3} + \frac{3t^2}{2} - 10t \right]_2^6$$

$$= \frac{34}{3} + \frac{232}{3} = \frac{266}{3} \approx 88.667.$$

The total distance traveled by the particle is $\dfrac{266}{3}$ or approximately 88.667.

Example 3

The velocity function of a moving particle on a coordinate line is $v(t) = t^3 - 6t^2 + 11t - 6$. Using a calculator, find (a) the displacement by the particle during $1 \le t \le 4$, and (b) the total distance traveled by the particle during $1 \le t \le 4$.

(a) Displacement $= \int_{t_1}^{t_2} v(t)dt$

$$= \int_1^4 (t^3 - 6t^2 + 11t - 6)dt.$$

Enter $\int (x^3 - 6x^2 + 11x - 6, x, 1, 4)$ and obtain $\dfrac{9}{4}$.

(b) Total Distance Traveled $= \int_{t_1}^{t_2} |v(t)| dt$.

Enter $y1 = x\wedge3 - 6x\wedge2 + 11x - 6$ and use the [Zero] function to obtain x-intercepts at $x = 1, 2, 3$.

$$|v(t)| = \begin{cases} v(t) & \text{if } 1 \le t \le 2 \text{ and } 3 \le t \le 4 \\ -v(t) & \text{if } 2 < t < 3 \end{cases}$$

$$\text{Total Distance Traveled} \int_1^2 v(t)dt + \int_2^3 -v(t)dt + \int_3^4 v(t)dt.$$

Enter $\int (y1(x), x, 1, 2)$ and obtain $\dfrac{1}{4}$.

Enter $\int (-y1(x), x, 2, 3)$ and obtain $\dfrac{1}{4}$.

Enter $\int (y1(x), x, 3, 4)$ and obtain $\dfrac{9}{4}$.

Thus, total distance traveled is $\left(\dfrac{1}{4} + \dfrac{1}{4} + \dfrac{9}{4} \right) = \dfrac{11}{4}$.

Example 4

The acceleration function of a moving particle on a coordinate line is $a(t) = -4$ and $v_0 = 12$ for $0 \leq t \leq 8$. Find the total distance traveled by the particle during $0 \leq t \leq 8$.

$a(t) = -4$

$$v(t) = \int a(t)dt = \int -4dt = -4t + C$$

Since $v_0 = 12 \Rightarrow -4(0) + C = 12$ or $C = 12$.

Thus, $v(t) = -4t + 12$.

$$\text{Total Distance Traveled} = \int_0^8 \left| -4t + 12 \right| dt.$$

Let $-4t + 12 = 0 \Rightarrow t = 3$.

$$|-4t + 12| = \begin{cases} -4t + 12 & \text{if } 0 \leq t \leq 3 \\ -(-4t + 12) & \text{if } t > 3 \end{cases}$$

$$\int_0^8 \left| -4t + 12 \right| dt = \int_0^3 \left| -4t + 12 \right| dt + \int_3^8 -(-4t + 12)dt$$

$$= \left[-12t^2 + 12t \right]_0^3 + \left[2t^2 + 12t \right]_3^8$$

$$= 18 + 50 = 68.$$

Total distance traveled by the particle is 68.

Example 5

The velocity function of a moving particle on a coordinate line is $v(t) = 3\cos(2t)$ for $0 \leq t \leq 2\pi$. Using a calculator:

(a) Determine when the particle is moving to the right.

(b) Determine when the particle stops.

(c) The total distance traveled by the particle during $0 \leq t \leq 2\pi$.

Solution:

(a) The particle is moving to the right when $v(t) > 0$.

Enter $y1 = 3\cos(2x)$. Obtain $y_1 = 0$ when $t = \dfrac{\pi}{4}, \dfrac{3\pi}{4}, \dfrac{5\pi}{4},$ and $\dfrac{7\pi}{4}$.

The particle is moving to the right when:

$$0 < t < \dfrac{\pi}{4}, \dfrac{3\pi}{4} < t < \dfrac{5\pi}{4}, \dfrac{7\pi}{4} < t < 2\pi.$$

(b) The particle stops when $v(t) = 0$.

Thus, the particle stops at $t = \dfrac{\pi}{4}, \dfrac{3\pi}{4}, \dfrac{5\pi}{4},$ and $\dfrac{7\pi}{4}$.

(c) Total distance traveled $\displaystyle\int_0^{2\pi} \left|3\cos(2t)\right| dt.$

Enter $\displaystyle\int (\mathrm{abs}(3\cos(2x)), x, 0, 2\pi)$ and obtain 12.

The total distance traveled by the particle is 12.

13.3 Definite Integral as Accumulated Change

Main Concepts: Business Problems, Temperature Problem, Leakage Problem, Growth Problem

Business Problems

Profit = Revenue − Cost	$P(x) = R(x) - C(x)$
Revenue = (price)(items sold)	$R(x) = P(x)$
Marginal Profit	$P'(x)$
Marginal Revenue	$R'(x)$
Marginal Cost	$C'(x)$

$P'(x)$, $R'(x)$, and $C'(x)$ are the instantaneous rates of change of profit, revenue, and cost, respectively.

Example 1

The marginal profit of manufacturing and selling a certain drug is $P'(x) = 100 - 0.005x$. How much profit should the company expect if it sells 10,000 units of this drug?

$$P(t) = \int_0^1 P'(x)\,dx$$

$$= \int_0^{10,000} (100 - 0.005x)\,dx = 100x - \dfrac{0.005x^2}{2}\Bigg]_0^{10,000}$$

$$= \left(100(10,000) - \dfrac{0.005}{2}(10,000)^2\right) = 750,000$$

> • If $f''(a) = 0$, f may or may not have a point of inflection at $x = a$, e.g., as in the function $f(x) = x^4$, $f''(0) = 0$ *but* at $x = 0$, f has an absolute minimum.

Example 2

If the marginal cost of producing x units of a commodity is $C'(x) = 5 + 0.4x$,

find (a) the marginal cost when $x = 50$;

(b) the cost of producing the first 100 units.

Solution:

(a) Marginal cost at $x = 50$:

$$C'(50) = 5 + 0.4(50) = 5 + 20 = 25.$$

(b) Cost of producing 100 units:

$$C(t) = \int_0^1 C'(x)\,dx$$

$$= \int_0^{100} (5 + 0.4x)\,dx$$

$$= 5x + 0.2x^2 \Big]_0^{100}$$

$$= \left(5(100) + 0.2(100)^2\right) - 0 = 2500.$$

Temperature Problem
Example

On a certain day, the changes in the temperature in a greenhouse beginning at 12 noon are represented by $f(t) = \sin\left(\dfrac{t}{2}\right)$ degrees Fahrenheit, where t is the number of hours elapsed after 12 noon. If at 12 noon, the temperature is 95°F, find the temperature in the greenhouse at 5 p.m.

Let $F(t)$ represent the temperature of the greenhouse.

$$F(0) = 95°\,F$$

$$F(t) = 95 + \int_0^5 f(x)\,dx$$

$$F(5) = 95 + \int_0^5 \sin\left(\frac{x}{2}\right)\,dx$$

$$= 95 + \left[-2\cos\left(\frac{x}{2}\right)\right]_0^5 = 95 + \left[-2\cos\left(\frac{5}{2}\right) - (-2\cos(0))\right]$$

$$= 95 + 3.602 = 98.602$$

The temperature in the greenhouse at 5 p.m. is 98.602°F.

Leakage Problem

Example

Water is leaking from a faucet at the rate of $l(t) = 10e^{-0.5t}$ gallons per hour, where t is measured in hours. How many gallons of water will have leaked from the faucet after a 24 hour period?

Let $L(x)$ represent the number of gallons that have leaked after x hours.

$$L(x) = \int_0^x l(t)\, dt = \int_0^{24} 10e^{-0.5t}\, dt$$

Using your calculator, enter $\int (10e^{\wedge}(-0.5x), x, 0, 24)$ and obtain 19.9999. Thus, the number of gallons of water that have leaked after x hours is approximately 20 gallons.

- You are permitted to use the following 4 built-in capabilities of your calculator to obtain an answer; plotting the graph of a function, finding the zeros of a function, finding the numerical derivative of a function, and evaluating a definite integral. All other capabilities of your calculator can only be used to *check* your answer. For example, you may *not* use the built-in [*Inflection*] function of your calculator to find points of inflection. You must use calculus using derivatives and showing change of concavity.

Growth Problem

Example

On a farm, the animal population is increasing at a rate that can be approximately represented by $g(t) = 20 + 50\,\ln(2 + t)$, where t is measured in years. How much will the animal population increase to the nearest tens between the third and fifth years?

Let $G(x)$ be the increase in animal population after x years.

$$G(x) = \int_0^x g(t)\, dt$$

Thus, the population increase between the third and fifth years

$$= G(5) - G(3)$$

$$= \int_0^5 \left(20 + 50\ln(2 + t)\, dt\right) - \int_0^3 \left(20 + 50\,\ln(2 + t)dt\right)$$

$$= \int_3^5 [20 + 50\,\ln(2 + t)]\, dt.$$

Enter $\int (20 + 50\,\ln(2 + x), x, 3, 5)$ and obtain 218.709.

Thus, the animal population will increase by approximately 220 between the third and fifth years.

13.4 Differential Equations

Main Concepts: Exponential Growth/Decay Problems, Separable Differential Equations

Exponential Growth/Decay Problems

1. If $\dfrac{dy}{dx} = ky$, then the rate of change of y is proportional to y.

2. If y is a differentiable function of t with $y > 0$ $\dfrac{dy}{dx} = ky$, then $y(t) = y_0 e^{kt}$; where y_0 is initial value of y and k is constant. If $k > 0$, then k is a growth constant and if $k < 0$, then k is the decay constant.

Example 1—Population Growth

If the amount of bacteria in a culture at any time increases at a rate proportional to the amount of bacteria present and there are 500 bacteria after one day and 800 bacteria after the third day:

(a) approximately how many bacteria are there initially, and

(b) approximately how many bacteria are there after 4 days?

Solution:

(a) Since the rate of increase is proportional to the amount of bacteria present, then:

$\dfrac{dy}{dx} = ky$, where y is the amount of bacteria at any time.

Therefore, this is an exponential growth/decay model: $y(t) = y_0 e^{kt}$.

Step 1. $y(1) = 500$ and $y(3) = 800$
$500 = y_0 e^k$ and $800 = y_0 e^{3k}$

Step 2. $500 = y_0 e^k \Rightarrow y_0 = \dfrac{500}{e^k} = 500 e^{-k}$

Substitute $y_0 = 500 e^{-k}$ into $800 = y_0 e^{3k}$.

$800 = (500)\left(e^{-k}\right)\left(e^{3k}\right)$

$800 = 500 e^{2k} \Rightarrow \dfrac{8}{5} = e^{2k}$

Take the ln of both sides:

$\ln\left(\dfrac{8}{5}\right) = \ln\left(e^{2k}\right)$

$\ln\left(\dfrac{8}{5}\right) = 2k$

$k = \dfrac{1}{2}\ln\left(\dfrac{8}{5}\right) = \ln\sqrt{\dfrac{8}{5}}.$

Step 3. Substitute $k = \dfrac{1}{2} \ln\left(\dfrac{8}{5}\right)$ into one of the equations.

$$500 = y_0 e^k$$

$$500 = y_0 e^{\ln\left(\sqrt{\frac{8}{5}}\right)}$$

$$500 = y_0 \left(\sqrt{\dfrac{8}{5}}\right)$$

$$y_0 = \dfrac{500}{\sqrt{8/5}} = 125\sqrt{10} \approx 395.285$$

Thus, there are 395 bacteria present initially.

(b) $y_0 = 125\sqrt{10}, \ k = \ln\sqrt{\dfrac{8}{5}}$

$$y(t) = y_0 e^{kt}$$

$$y(t) = \left(125\sqrt{10}\right) e^{\left(\ln\sqrt{\frac{8}{5}}\right)t} = \left(125\sqrt{10}\right)\left(\dfrac{8}{5}\right)^{(1/2)t}$$

$$y(4) = \left(125\sqrt{10}\right)\left(\dfrac{8}{5}\right)^{(1/2)4} = \left(125\sqrt{10}\right)\left(\dfrac{8}{5}\right)^{2} = 1011.93$$

Thus, there are approximately 1011 bacteria present after 4 days.

• Get a good night's sleep the night before. Have a light breakfast before the exam.

Example 2—Radioactive Decay

Carbon-14 has a half-life of 5750 years. If initially there are 60 grams of carbon-14, how many grams are left after 3000 years?

Step 1. $y(t) = y_0 e^{kt} = 60 e^{kt}$

Since half-life is 5750 years, $30 = 60 e^{k(5750)} \Rightarrow \dfrac{1}{2} = e^{5750k}$.

$$\ln\left(\dfrac{1}{2}\right) = \ln\left(e^{5750k}\right)$$

$$-\ln 2 = 5750k$$

$$\dfrac{-\ln 2}{5750} = k$$

Step 2. $y(t) = y_0 e^{kt}$

$$y(t) = 60e^{\left[\frac{-\ln 2}{5750}\right]}$$

$$y(t) = 60e^{\left[\frac{-\ln 2}{5750}\right](3000)}$$

$$y(3000) \approx 41.7919$$

Thus, there will be approximately 41.792 grams of carbon-14 after 3000 years.

Separable Differential Equations

General Procedure

1. Separate the variables: $g(y)dy = f(x)dx$.
2. Integrate both sides: $\int g(y)dy = \int f(x)dx$.
3. Solve for y to get a general solution.
4. Substitute given conditions to get a particular solution.
5. Verify your result by differentiating.

Example 1

Given $\dfrac{dy}{dx} = 4x^3 y^2$ and $y(1) = -\dfrac{1}{2}$, solve the differential equation.

Step 1. Separate the variables: $\dfrac{1}{y^2}dy = 4x^3 dx$.

Step 2. Integrate both sides: $\displaystyle\int \dfrac{1}{y^2}dy = \int 4x^3 dx; \ -\dfrac{1}{y} = x^4 + C$.

Step 3. General solution: $y = \dfrac{-1}{x^4 + C}$.

Step 4. Particular solution: $-\dfrac{1}{2} = \dfrac{-1}{1 + C} \Rightarrow c = 1; y = \dfrac{-1}{x^4 + 1}$.

Step 5. Verify the result by differentiating.

$$y = \dfrac{-1}{x^4 + 1} = (-1)(x^4 + 1)^{-1}$$

$$\dfrac{dy}{dx} = (-1)(-1)(x^4 + 1)^{-2}(4x^3) = \dfrac{4x^3}{(x^4 + 1)^2}.$$

Note: $y = \dfrac{-1}{x^4 + 1}$ implies $y^2 = \dfrac{1}{(x^4 + 1)^2}$.

Thus, $\dfrac{dy}{dx} = \dfrac{4x^3}{(x^4 + 1)^2} = 4x^3 y^2$.

Example 2

Find a solution of the differentiation equation $\dfrac{dy}{dx} = x\sin(x^2)$; $y(0) = -1$.

Step 1.   Separate variables: $dy = x\sin(x^2)dx$.

Step 2.   Integrate both sides: $\displaystyle\int dy = \int x\sin(x^2)dx$; $\displaystyle\int dy = y$.

Let $u = x^2$; $du = 2x\,dx$ or $\dfrac{du}{2} = x\,dx$.

$$\int x\sin(x^2)dx = \int \sin u\left(\frac{du}{2}\right) = \frac{1}{2}\int \sin u\,du = -\frac{1}{2}\cos u + C$$

$$= -\frac{1}{2}\cos(x^2) + C$$

Thus, $y = -\dfrac{1}{2}\cos(x^2) + C$.

Step 3.   Substitute given condition:

$$y(0) = -1; -1 = -\frac{1}{2}\cos(0) + C; -1 = \frac{-1}{2} + C; -\frac{1}{2} = C.$$

Thus, $y = -\dfrac{1}{2}\cos(x^2) - \dfrac{1}{2}$.

Step 4.   Verify the result by differentiating:

$$\frac{dy}{dx} = \frac{1}{2}\left[\sin(x^2)\right](2x) = x\sin(x^2).$$

Example 3

If $\dfrac{d^2y}{dx^2} = 2x + 1$ and at $x = 0$, $y' = -1$, and $y = 3$, find a solution of the differential equation.

Step 1.   Rewrite $\dfrac{d^2y}{dx^2}$ as $\dfrac{dy'}{dx}$; $\dfrac{dy'}{dx} = 2x + 1$.

Step 2.   Separate variables: $dy' = (2x + 1)dx$.

Step 3.   Integrate both sides: $\displaystyle\int dy' = \int (2x + 1)dx$; $y' = x^2 + x + C_1$.

Step 4.   Substitute given condition: At $x = 0$, $y' = -1$; $-1 = 0 + 0 + C_1 \Rightarrow C_1 = -1$. Thus, $y' = x^2 + x - 1$.

Step 5.   Rewrite: $y' = \dfrac{dy}{dx}$; $\dfrac{dy}{dx} = x^2 + x - 1$.

Step 6. Separate variables: $dy = (x^2 + x - 1)dx$.

Step 7. Integrate both sides: $\int dy = \int (x^2 + x - 1)dx$

$$y = \frac{x^3}{3} + \frac{x^2}{2} - x + C_2.$$

Step 8. Substitute given condition: At $x = 0$, $y = 3$; $3 = 0 + 0 - 0 + C_2 \Rightarrow C_2 = 3$.

Therefore, $y = \dfrac{x^3}{3} + \dfrac{x^2}{2} - x + 3$.

Step 9. Verify the result by differentiating:

$$y = \frac{x^3}{3} + \frac{x^2}{2} - x + 3$$

$$\frac{dy}{dx} = x^2 + x - 1; \frac{d^2y}{dx^2} = 2x + 1.$$

Example 4

Find the general solution of the differential equation $\dfrac{dy}{dx} = \dfrac{2xy}{x^2 + 1}$.

Step 1. Separate variables:

$$\frac{dy}{y} = \frac{2x}{x^2 + 1}dx.$$

Step 2. Integrate both sides: $\int \dfrac{dy}{y} = \int \dfrac{2x}{x^2 + 1}dx$ (let $u = x^2 + 1$; $du = 2x\,dx$)

$$\ln|y| = \ln(x^2 + 1) + C_1.$$

Step 3. General Solution: solve for y.

$$e^{\ln|y|} = e^{\ln(x^2+1)+C_1}$$

$$|y| = e^{\ln(x^2+1)} \cdot e^{C_1}; |y| = e^{C_1}(x^2 + 1)$$

$$y = \pm e^{C_1}(x^2 + 1)$$

The general solution is $y = C(x^2 + 1)$.

Step 4. Verify the result by differentiating:

$$y = C(x^2 + 1)$$

$$\frac{dy}{dx} = 2Cx = 2x\frac{C(x^2 + 1)}{x^2 + 1} = \frac{2xy}{x^2 + 1}.$$

Example 5

Write an equation for the curve that passes through the point (3, 4) and has a slope at any point (x, y) as $\dfrac{dy}{dx} = \dfrac{x^2 + 1}{2y}$.

Step 1. Separate variables: $2y\, dy = (x^2 + 1)dx$.

Step 2. Integrate both sides: $\displaystyle\int 2y\, dy = \int (x^2 + 1)\, dx;\ y^2 = \dfrac{x^3}{3} + x + C.$

Step 3. Substitute given condition: $4^2 = \dfrac{3^3}{3} + 3 + C \Rightarrow C = 4.$

Thus, $y^2 = \dfrac{x^3}{3} + x + 4.$

Step 4. Verify the result by differentiating:

$$2y\dfrac{dy}{dx} = x^2 + 1$$

$$\dfrac{dy}{dx} = \dfrac{x^2 + 1}{2y}.$$

13.5 Slope Fields

Main Concepts: Slope Fields, Solution of Different Equations

A *slope field* (or a *direction field*) for first-order differential equations is a graphic representation of the slopes of a family of curves. It consists of a set of short line segments drawn on a pair of axes. These line segments are the tangents to a family of solution curves for the differential equation at various points. The tangents show the direction the solution curves will follow. Slope fields are useful in sketching solution curves without having to solve a differential equation algebraically.

Example 1

If $\dfrac{dy}{dx} = 0.5x$, draw a slope field for the given differential equation.

Step 1: Set up a table of values for $\dfrac{dy}{dx}$ for selected values of x.

x	−4	−3	−2	−1	0	1	2	3	4
$\dfrac{dy}{dx}$	−2	−1.5	−1	−0.5	0	0.5	1	1.5	2

Note that since $\dfrac{dy}{dx} = 0.5x$, the numerical value of $\dfrac{dy}{dx}$ is independent of the value of y. For example, at the points $(1, -1)$, $(1, 0)$, $(1, 1)$, $(1, 2)$, $(1, 3)$, and at all the points whose x-coordinates are 1, the numerical value of $\dfrac{dy}{dx}$ is 0.5 regardless of their y-coordinates. Similarly, for all the points whose x-coordinates are 2 (e.g., $(2, -1)$, $(2, 0)$, $(2, 3)$, etc.), $\dfrac{dy}{dx} = 1$. Also, remember that $\dfrac{dy}{dx}$ represents the slopes of the tangent lines to the curve at various points. You are now ready to draw these tangents.

Step 2: Draw short line segments with the given slopes at the various points. The slope field for the differential equation $\dfrac{dy}{dx} = 0.5x$ is shown in Figure 13.5-1.

Figure 13.5-1

Example 2

Figure 13.5-2 shows a slope field for one of the differential equations given below. Identify the equation.

Figure 13.5-2

(a) $\dfrac{dy}{dx} = 2x$ (b) $\dfrac{dy}{dx} = -2x$ (c) $\dfrac{dy}{dx} = y$

(d) $\dfrac{dy}{dx} = -y$ (e) $\dfrac{dy}{dx} = x + y$

Solution:

If you look across horizontally at any row of tangents, you'll notice that the tangents have the same slope. (Points on the same row have the same y-coordinate but different x-coordinates.) Therefore, the numerical value of $\dfrac{dy}{dx}$ (which represents the slope of the tangent) depends solely on the y-coordinate of a point and it is independent of the x-coordinate. Thus, only choice (c) and choice (d) satisfy this condition. Also notice that the tangents have a negative slope when $y > 0$ and have a positive slope when $y < 0$.

Therefore, the correct choice is (d) $\dfrac{dy}{dx} = -y$.

Example 3

A slope field for a differential equation is shown in Figure 13.5-3. Draw a possible graph for the particular solution $y = f(x)$ to the differential equation function, if (a) the initial condition is $f(0) = -2$ and (b) the initial condition is $f(0) = 0$.

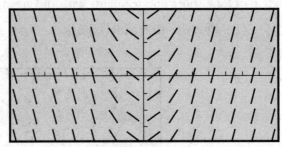

Figure 13.5-3

Solution:

Begin by locating the point $(0, -2)$ as given in the initial condition. Follow the flow of the field and sketch the graph of the function. Repeat the same procedure with the point $(0, 0)$. See the curves as shown in Figure 13.5-4.

Figure 13.5-4

Example 4

Given the differential equation $\dfrac{dy}{dx} = -xy$:

(a) Draw a slope field for the differential equation at the 15 points indicated on the provided set of axes in Figure 13.5-5.

Figure 13.5-5

(b) Sketch a possible graph for the particular solution $y = f(x)$ to the differential equation with the initial condition $f(0) = 3$.

(c) Find, algebraically, the particular solution $y = f(x)$ to the differential equation with the initial condition $f(0) = 3$.

Solution:

(a) Set up a table of values for $\dfrac{dy}{dx}$ at the 15 given points.

	$x = -2$	$x = -1$	$x = 0$	$x = 1$	$x = 2$
$y = 1$	2	1	0	-1	-2
$y = 2$	4	2	0	-2	-4
$y = 3$	6	3	0	-3	-6

Then sketch the tangents at the various points as shown in Figure 13.5-6.

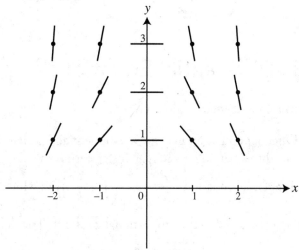

Figure 13.5-6

(b) Locate the point $(0, 3)$ as indicated in the initial condition. Follow the flow of the field and sketch the curve as shown Figure 13.5-7.

(c) Step 1: Rewrite $\dfrac{dy}{dx} = -xy$ as $\dfrac{dy}{y} = -x\,dx$.

Step 2: Integrate both sides $\displaystyle\int \dfrac{dy}{y} = \int -x\,dx$ and obtain $\ln|y| = -\dfrac{x^2}{2} + C$.

Step 3: Apply the exponential function to both sides and obtain $e^{\ln|y|} = e^{-\frac{x^2}{2}+C}$.

Step 4: Simplify the equation and get $y = \left(e^{\frac{-x^2}{2}}\right)(e^C) = \dfrac{e^C}{e^{\frac{x^2}{2}}}$.

Let $k = e^C$ and you have $y = \dfrac{k}{e^{\frac{x^2}{2}}}$.

Step 5: Substitute initial condition (0, 3) and obtain $k = 3$. Thus, you have $y = \dfrac{3}{e^{\frac{x^2}{2}}}$.

decr.

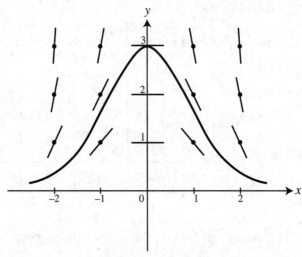

Figure 13.5-7

13.6 Logistic Differential Equations

Main Concepts: Logistic Growth

Often a population may grow exponentially at first, but eventually slows as it nears a limit, called the carrying capacity. This pattern is called logistic growth, and is represented by the differential equation $\dfrac{dP}{dt} = kP\left(1 - \dfrac{P}{K}\right)$, in which P is the population, K is the carrying capacity, and k is the proportional constant. The differential equation is separable so $\dfrac{dP}{dt} = kP\left(1 - \dfrac{P}{K}\right) \Rightarrow \dfrac{dP}{dt} = \dfrac{kP(K - P)}{K} \Rightarrow \dfrac{K\,dP}{P(K - P)} = k\,dt$. This equation can be integrated using a partial fraction decomposition.

$$\int \frac{K\,dP}{P(K - P)} = \int k\,dt$$

$$\int \left(\frac{1}{P} + \frac{-1}{K - P}\right) dP = \int k\,dt$$

$$\ln|P| - \ln|K - P| = kt + C_1$$

$$\ln\left|\frac{P}{K - P}\right| = kt + C_1$$

Exponentiation produces $\dfrac{P}{K-P} = e^{(kt+C_1)} \Rightarrow \dfrac{P}{K-P} = e^{kt} \cdot e^{C_1} \Rightarrow \dfrac{P}{K-P} = C_2 e^{kt}$. Solving for P yields $P = C_2 e^{kt}(K-P) \Rightarrow P = C_2 e^{kt} K - C_2 e^{kt} P \Rightarrow P + C_2 e^{kt} P = C_2 e^{kt} K \Rightarrow P(1 + C_2 e^{kt}) = C_2 e^{kt} K \Rightarrow P = \dfrac{C_2 e^k K}{1 + C_2 e^{kt}}$. Dividing numerator and denominator by $C_2 e^{kt}$, $P(t) = \dfrac{C_2 e^{kt} K}{1 + C_2 e^{kt}} = \dfrac{K}{\dfrac{1}{C_2 e^{kt}} + 1} = \dfrac{K}{\left(\dfrac{1}{C_2}\right) e^{-kt} + 1}$. At $t = 0$, $P_0 = \dfrac{K}{\dfrac{1}{C_2} + 1}$. Solving for C_2 yields $P_0\left(\dfrac{1}{C_2} + 1\right) = K \Rightarrow \dfrac{1 + C_2}{C_2} = \dfrac{K}{P_0} \Rightarrow$

$P_0 + P_0 C_2 = K C_2 \Rightarrow P_0 = K C_2 - P_0 C_2$ or $C_2 = \dfrac{P_0}{K - P_0}$. Let $A = \dfrac{1}{C_2}$, and the solution of this logistic differential equation with initial condition $P(0) = P_0$ is $P(t) = \dfrac{K}{A e^{-kt} + 1}$, where K is the carrying capacity and $A = \dfrac{K - P_0}{P_0}$.

Example 1

The population of the United Kingdom was 57.1 million in 2001 and 60.6 million in 2006. Find a logistic model for the growth of the population, assuming a carrying capacity of 100 million. Use the model to predict the population in 2020.

Step 1: Since the carrying capacity is $K = 100$, $\dfrac{dP}{dt} = kP\left(1 - \dfrac{P}{100}\right)$.

Step 2: The solution of the differential equation, if $A = \dfrac{k - P_0}{P_0} = \dfrac{100 - 57.1}{57.1} \approx .7513$, is

$$P(t) = \dfrac{100}{A e^{-kt} + 1} \text{ or } P(t) = \dfrac{100}{.7513 e^{-kt} + 1}.$$

Step 3: Take 2006 as $t = 5$, $P(5) = 60.6$. Then $60.6 = \dfrac{100}{.7513 e^{-k(5)} + 1}$. Solving gives $k \approx 0.0289$ so $P(t) = \dfrac{100}{.7513 e^{-0.0289t} + 1}$.

Step 4: Since the year 2020 corresponds to $t = 19$, Substitute and evaluate $P(19) = \dfrac{100}{.7513 e^{-0.0289(19)} + 1} \approx 69.742$. The population of the United Kingdom in 2020 is predicted to be approximately 69.742 million.

Example 2

The spread of an infectious disease can often be modeled by a logistic equation, with the total exposed population as the carrying capacity. In a community of 2000 individuals, the first case of a new virus is diagnosed on March 31, and by April 10, there are 500 individuals infected. Write a differential equation that models the rate at which the virus spread through the community, and determine when 98% of the population will have contracted the virus.

Step 1: The rate of spread is $\dfrac{dP}{dt} = kP\left(1 - \dfrac{P}{2000}\right)$.

Step 2: The solution of the differential equation is $P(t) = \dfrac{2000}{Ae^{-kt} + 1}$, and with one person exposed, $A = \dfrac{2000 - 1}{1} = 1999$, or $P(t) = \dfrac{2000}{1999e^{-kt} + 1}$.

Step 3: Taking April 10 as day 10, $P(10) = 500 = \dfrac{2000}{1999e^{-k(10)} + 1}$. Solving the equation gives $k \approx .6502$, so $P(t) = \dfrac{2000}{1999e^{-.6502t} + 1}$.

Step 4: 98% of the population of 2000 is 1960 people. To determine the day when 1960 people are infected, solve $1960 = \dfrac{2000}{1999e^{-.6502t} + 1}$. This gives $t \approx 17.6749$, so the 98% infection rate should be reached by April 18.

13.7 Euler's Method

Main Concepts: Approximating Solutions of Differential Equations by Euler's Method

Approximating Solutions of Differential Equations by Euler's Method

Euler's Method provides a means of estimating the numerical solution of differential equations by a series of successive linear approximations. Represent the differential equation by $y' = f'(x, y)$ and the initial condition $y_0 = f(x_0)$, and choose a small value, Δx, as the increment between estimates. Begin with the initial value y_0, and evaluate $y_1 = y_0 + \Delta x \cdot f'(x_0, y_0)$. Continue with $y_2 = y_1 + \Delta x \cdot f'(x_1, y_1)$, and in general, $y_n = y_{n-1} + \Delta x \cdot f'(x_{n-1}, y_{n-1})$.

Example 1

Given the initial value problem $\dfrac{dy}{dt} = \cos 2\pi t$ with $y(0) = 1$, approximate $y(1)$, using five steps.

Step 1: The interval $(0, 1)$ divided into five steps gives us $\Delta t = 0.2$.

Step 2: Create a table showing the iterations.

t	y	$\cos 2\pi t$	$y_n = y_{n-1} + \Delta x \cdot f'(x_{n-1}, y_{n-1})$
0	1	1	$1 + .2(1) = 1.2$
0.2	1.2	.309016	$1.2 + .2(.309016) = 1.261803$
0.4	1.261803	−.809016	$1.261803 + .2(−.809016) = 1.1$
0.6	1.1	−.809016	$1.1 + .2(−.809016) = 0.938196$
0.8	.938196	.309016	$.938196 + .2(.309016) = 1$
1	1		

$y(1) \approx 1$

Example 2

Use Euler's Method with a step size of $\Delta x = 0.1$ to compute $y(1)$ if $y(x)$ is the solution of the differential equation $\dfrac{dy}{dx} + 3x^2 y = 6x^2$ with initial condition $y(0) = 3$.

Step 1: For case of the evaluation, transform $\dfrac{dy}{dx} + 3x^2 y = 6x^2$ to $\dfrac{dy}{dx} = 3x^2(2 - y)$.

Step 2: Create a table showing the iterations. A simple problem, stored in your calculator and modified with the new differential equation and initial condition, will allow you to generate the table quickly.

x	y	$3x^2(2-y)$	$y_n = y_{n-1} + \Delta x \cdot f'(x_{n-1},\, y_{n-1})$
0	3	0	3
0.1	3	−0.03	2.997
0.2	2.997	−0.11964	2.985036
0.3	2.985036	−0.265959	2.9584400
0.4	2.958440	−0.460051	2.912434
0.5	2.912434	−0.684326	2.844002
0.6	2.844002	−0.911522	2.752850
0.7	2.752850	−1.106689	2.642181
0.8	2.642181	−1.232987	2.518882
0.9	2.518882	−1.260884	2.392793
1	2.392793		

$y(1) \approx 2.393$

Example 3

Use Euler's Method to approximate $P(4)$, given $\dfrac{dP}{dt} = .3P\left(1 - \dfrac{P}{20}\right)$ with initial condition $P(0) = 4$. Use an increment of $\Delta t = 0.5$.

t	P	$.3P\left(1-\dfrac{P}{20}\right)$	$y_n = y_{n-1} + \Delta x \cdot f'(x_{n-1}, y_{n-1})$
0	4	.96	$4 + .5(.96) = 4.48$
0.5	4.48	1.042944	$4.48 + .5(1.042944) = 5.001472$
1	5.001472	1.125220	$5.001472 + .5(1.125220) = 5.564082$
1.5	5.564082	1.204839	$5.564082 + .5(1.204839) = 6.166502$
2	6.166502	1.279564	$6.166502 + .5(1.279564) = 6.806284$
2.5	6.806284	1.347002	$6.806284 + .5(1.347002) = 7.479785$
3	7.479785	1.404727	$7.479785 + .5(1.404727) = 8.182149$
3.5	8.182149	1.450431	$8.182149 + .5(1.450431) = 8.907365$
4	8.907365		

$P(4) \approx 8.907$

13.8 Rapid Review

1. Find the average value of $y = \sin x$ on $[0, \pi]$.

   Answer: Average Value $= \dfrac{1}{\pi - 0} \displaystyle\int_0^\pi \sin x \, dx$

   $= \dfrac{1}{\pi}\left[-\cos x\right]_0^\pi = \dfrac{2}{\pi}.$

2. Find the total distance traveled by a particle during $0 \le t \le 3$ whose velocity function is shown in Figure 13.8-1.

Figure 13.8-1

   Answer: Total Distance Traveled $= \displaystyle\int_0^2 v(t)dt + \left|\int_2^3 v(t)dt\right|$

   $= 2 + 0.5 = 2.5.$

3. Oil is leaking from a tank at the rate of $f(t) = 5e^{-0.1t}$ gallons/hour, where t is measured in hours. Write an integral to find the total number of gallons of oil that will have leaked from the tank after 10 hours. Do not evaluate the integral.

Answer: Total number of gallons leaked = $\displaystyle\int_0^{10} 5e^{-0.1t}\,dt$.

4. How much money should Mary invest at 7.5% interest a year compounded continuously so that she will have $100,000 after 20 years.

   Answer: $y(t) = y_0 e^{kt}$, $k = 0.075$, and $t = 20$. $y(20) = 100{,}000 = y_0 e^{(0.075)(20)}$. Thus, using a calculator, you obtain $y_0 \approx 22313$, or $\$22{,}313$.

5. Given $\dfrac{dy}{dx} = \dfrac{x}{y}$ and $y(1) = 0$, solve the differential equation.

   Answer: $y\,dy = x\,dx \Rightarrow \displaystyle\int y\,dy = \int x\,dx \Rightarrow \dfrac{y^2}{2} = \dfrac{x^2}{2} + c \Rightarrow 0 = \dfrac{1}{2} + c \Rightarrow c = -\dfrac{1}{2}$

   Thus, $\dfrac{y^2}{2} = \dfrac{x^2}{2} - \dfrac{1}{2}$ or $y^2 = x^2 - 1$.

6. Identify the differential equation for the slope field shown.

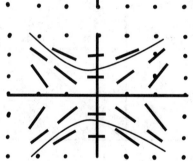

   Answer: The slope field suggests a hyperbola of the form $y^2 - x^2 = k$, so $2y\dfrac{dy}{dx} - 2x = 0$ and $\dfrac{dy}{dx} = \dfrac{x}{y}$.

7. Find the solution of the initial value problem $\dfrac{dP}{dt} = .75P\left(1 - \dfrac{P}{2500}\right)$ with $P_0 = 10$.

   Answer: $\dfrac{dP}{dt} = .75P\left(1 - \dfrac{P}{2500}\right) \Rightarrow \dfrac{2500}{P(2500 - P)}dP = .75dt$

   $\Rightarrow \displaystyle\int \dfrac{2500}{P(2500 - P)}dP = \int .75dt \Rightarrow \int \left(\dfrac{1}{P} + \dfrac{1}{2500 - P}\right)dP = \int .75dt$

   $\Rightarrow \ln|P| - \ln|2500 - P| = .75t + C_1 \Rightarrow \ln\left|\dfrac{P}{2500 - P}\right| = .75t + C_1$

   $\Rightarrow \dfrac{P}{2500 - P} = C_2 e^{.75t} \Rightarrow P(t) = \dfrac{2500C_2 e^{.75t}}{1 + C_2 e^{.75t}} \Rightarrow P(0) = \dfrac{2500C_2}{1 + C_2} = 10$

   $\Rightarrow 2500C_2 = 10 + 10C_2 \Rightarrow 2490C_2 = 10 \Rightarrow C_2 = \dfrac{1}{249}$.

   Therefore, $P(t) = \dfrac{2500(1/249)\,e^{.75t}}{1 + (1/249)\,e^{.75t}} = \dfrac{2500e^{.75t}}{249 + e^{.75t}}$ so $P(t) = \dfrac{2500}{249e^{-.75t} + 1}$.

8. Use Euler's Method with a step size of $\Delta x = 0.5$ to compute $y(2)$, if $y(x)$ is the solution of the differential equation $\dfrac{dy}{dx} = y + xy$ with initial condition $y(0) = 1$.

Answer: $y(0) = 1$; $y(0.5) = 1 + 0.5(1 + 0.1) = 1.5$;
$y(1) = 1.5 + 0.5\,[1.5 + (0.5)(1.5)] = 1.5 + 0.5[2.25] = 2.625$
$y(1.5) = 2.625 + 0.5\,[2.625 + (1)(2.625)] = 2.625 + 2.625 = 5.25$
$y(2) = 5.25 + 0.5\,[5.25 + (1.5)(5.25)] = 5.25 + 0.5[13.125] = 11.8125$

13.9 Practice Problems

Part A—The use of a calculator is not allowed.

1. Find the value of c as stated in the Mean Value Theorem for Integrals for $f(x) = x^3$ on $[2, 4]$.

2. The graph of f is shown in Figure 13.9-1. Find the average value of f on $[0, 8]$.

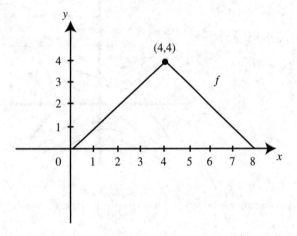

Figure 13.9-1

3. The position function of a particle moving on a coordinate line is given as $s(t) = t^2 - 6t - 7$, $0 \le t \le 10$. Find the displacement and total distance traveled by the particle from $1 \le t \le 4$.

4. The velocity function of a moving particle on a coordinate line is $v(t) = 2t + 1$ for $0 \le t \le 8$. At $t = 1$, its position is -4. Find the position of the particle at $t = 5$.

5. The rate of depreciation for a new piece of equipment at a factory is given as $p(t) = 50t - 600$ for $0 \le t \le 10$, where t is measured in years. Find the total loss of value of the equipment over the first 5 years.

6. If the acceleration of a moving particle on a coordinate line is $a(t) = -2$ for $0 \le t \le 4$, and the initial velocity $v_0 = 10$, find the total distance traveled by the particle during $0 \le t \le 4$.

7. The graph of the velocity function of a moving particle is shown in Figure 13.9-2. What is the total distance traveled by the particle during $0 \le t \le 12$?

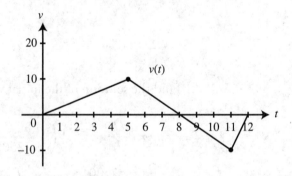

Figure 13.9-2

8. If oil is leaking from a tanker at the rate of $f(t) = 10e^{0.2t}$ gallons per hour, where t is measured in hours, how many gallons of oil will have leaked from the tanker after the first 3 hours?

9. The change of temperature of a cup of coffee measured in degrees Fahrenheit in a certain room is represented by the function $f(t) = -\cos\left(\dfrac{t}{4}\right)$ for $0 \leq t \leq 5$, where t is measured in minutes. If the temperature of the coffee is initially 92°F, find its temperature after the first 5 minutes.

10. If the *half-life* of a radioactive element is 4500 years, and initially there are 100 grams of this element, approximately how many grams are left after 5000 years?

11. Find a solution of the differential equation: $\dfrac{dy}{dx} = x\cos(x^2); \; y(0) = \pi.$

12. If $\dfrac{d^2y}{dx^2} = x - 5$ and at $x = 0$, $y' = -2$ and $y = 1$, find a solution of the differential equation.

Part B—Calculators are allowed.

13. Find the average value of $y = \tan x$ from $x = \dfrac{\pi}{4}$ to $x = \dfrac{\pi}{3}$.

14. The acceleration function of a moving particle on a straight line is given by $a(t) = 3e^{2t}$, where t is measured in seconds, and the initial velocity is $\dfrac{1}{2}$. Find the displacement and total distance traveled by the particle in the first 3 seconds.

15. The sales of an item in a company follow an exponential growth/decay model, where t is measured in months. If the sales drop from 5000 units in the first month to 4000 units in the third month, how many units should the company expect to sell during the seventh month?

16. Find an equation of the curve that has a slope of $\dfrac{2y}{x+1}$ at the point (x, y) and passes through the point $(0, 4)$.

17. The population in a city was approximately 750,000 in 1980, and grew at a rate of 3% per year. If the population growth followed an exponential growth model, find the city's population in the year 2002.

18. Find a solution of the differential equation $4e^y = y' - 3xe^y$ and $y(0) = 0$.

19. How much money should a person invest at 6.25% interest compounded continuously so that the person will have $50,000 after 10 years?

20. The velocity function of a moving particle is given as $v(t) = 2 - 6e^{-t}$, $t \geq 0$ and t is measured in seconds. Find the total distance traveled by the particle during the first 10 seconds.

21. Draw a slope field for differential equation $\dfrac{dy}{dx} = x - y$.

22. A rumor spreads through an office of 50 people at a model by $\dfrac{dP}{dt} = .65P\left(1 - \dfrac{P}{50}\right)$. On day zero, one person knows the rumor. Find the model for the population at time t, and use it to predict when more than half the people in the office will have heard the rumor.

23. A college dormitory that houses 200 students experiences an outbreak of influenza. The illness is recognized when two students are diagnosed on the same day. The residents are quarantined to restrict the infection to this one building. On the fifth day of the outbreak, 12 students are ill. Use a logistic model to describe the course of infection and predict the number of infected students on day 10.

24. Use Euler's Method with a step size of $\Delta x = 0.1$ to compute $y(.5)$ if $y(x)$ is the solution of the differential equation $\dfrac{dy}{dx} = x^2 - y^3$ with the condition $y(0) = 1$.

25. Use Euler's Method with a step size of $\Delta x = 0.5$ to compute $y(3)$ if $y(x)$ is the solution of the differential equation $\dfrac{dy}{dx} = y - 2x$ with initial condition $y(0) = 1$.

13.10 Cumulative Review Problems

(Calculator) indicates that calculators are permitted.

26. If $3e^y = x^2 y$, find $\dfrac{dy}{dx}$.

27. Evaluate $\displaystyle\int_0^1 \dfrac{x^2}{x^3 + 1}\,dx$.

28. The graph of a continuous function f that consists of three line segments on $[-2, 4]$ is shown in Figure 13.10-1. If
$$F(x) = \int_{-2}^{x} f(t)\,dt \text{ for } -2 \le x \le 4,$$

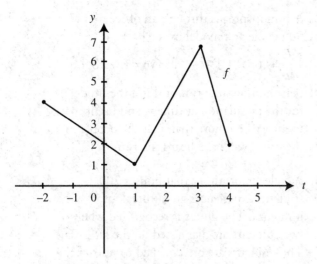

Figure 13.10-1

(a) Find $F(-2)$ and $F(0)$.

(b) Find $F'(0)$ and $F'(2)$.

(c) Find the value of x such that F has a maximum on $[-2, 4]$.

(d) On which interval is the graph of F concave upward?

29. (Calculator) The slope of a function $y = f(x)$ at any point (x, y) is $\dfrac{y}{2x + 1}$ and $f(0) = 2$.

(a) Write an equation of the line tangent to the graph of f at $x = 0$.

(b) Use the tangent in part (a) to find the approximate value of $f(0.1)$.

(c) Find a solution $y = f(x)$ for the differential equation.

(d) Using the result in part (c), find $f(0.1)$.

30. (Calculator) Let R be the region in the first quadrant bounded by $f(x) = e^x - 1$ and $g(x) = 3\sin x$.

(a) Find the area of region R.

(b) Find the volume of the solid obtained by revolving R about the x-axis.

(c) Find the volume of the solid having R as its base and semicircular cross sections perpendicular to the x-axis.

31. An object traveling on a path defined by $\langle x(\theta),\ y(\theta)\rangle$ has an acceleration vector of $\langle \sin\theta,\ -\cos\theta\rangle$. If the velocity of the object at time $\theta = \dfrac{\pi}{3}$ is $\langle -1, 0\rangle$ and the initial position of the object is the origin, find the position when $\theta = \pi$.

32. $\displaystyle\int x^2 e^{5x-2}\,dx$

33. A projectile follows a path defined by $x = t - 2$, $y = \sin^2 t$ on the interval $0 \le t \le \pi$. Find the point at which the object reaches its maximum y-value.

13.11 Solutions to Practice Problems

Part A—The use of a calculator is not allowed.

1. $\int_2^4 x^3 dx = f(c)\,(4-2)$

$\int_2^4 x^3 dx = \dfrac{x^4}{4}\bigg]_2^4 = \left(\dfrac{4^4}{4}\right) - \left(\dfrac{2^4}{4}\right) = 60$

$2\,f(c) = 60 \Rightarrow f(c) = 30$

$c^3 = 30 \Rightarrow C = 30^{(1/3)}.$

2. Average Value $= \dfrac{1}{8-0}\displaystyle\int_0^1 f(x)\,dx$

$= \dfrac{1}{8}\left(\dfrac{1}{2}(8)(4)\right) = 2.$

3. Displacement $= s(4) - s(1) = -15 - (-12) = -3.$

Distance Traveled $= \displaystyle\int_1^4 |v(t)|\,dt.$

$v(t) = s'(t) = 2t - 6$

Set $2t - 6 = 0 \Rightarrow t = 3$

$|2t - 6| = \begin{cases} -(2t-6) & \text{if } 0 \le t < 3 \\ 2t - 6 & \text{if } 3 \le t \le 10 \end{cases}$

$\int_1^4 |v(t)|dt = \int_1^3 -(2t-6)dt + \int_3^4 (2t-6)dt$

$= \left[-t^2 + 6t\right]_1^3 + \left[t^2 - 6t\right]_3^4$

$= 4 + 1 = 5.$

4. Position Function $s(t) = \displaystyle\int v(t)dt$

$= \displaystyle\int (2t + 1)dt$

$= t^2 + t + C$

$s(1) = -4 \Rightarrow (1)^2$

$+ 1 + C$

$= -4 \text{ or } C = -6$

$s(t) = t^2 + t - 6$

$s(5) = 5^2 + 5 - 6 = 24.$

5. Total Loss $= \displaystyle\int_0^5 p(t)dt$

$= \displaystyle\int_0^5 (50t - 600)dt$

$= 25t^2 - 600t\big]_0^5 = -\$2375.$

6. $v(t) = \displaystyle\int a(t)dt = \int -2\,dt = -2t + C$

$v_0 = 10 \Rightarrow -2(0) + C = 10 \text{ or } C = 10$

$v(t) = -2t + 10$

Distance Traveled $= \displaystyle\int_0^4 |v(t)|\,dt.$

Set $v(t) = 0 \Rightarrow -2t + 10 = 0 \text{ or } t = 5.$

$|-2t + 10| = -2t + 10 \text{ if } 0 \le t < 5$

$\int_0^4 |v(t)|\,dt = \int_0^4 (-2t + 10)dt$

$= -t^2 + 10t\big]_0^4 = 24$

7. Total Distance Traveled

$= \displaystyle\int_0^8 |v(t)|\,dt + \left|\int_8^{12} v(t)\right|$

$= \dfrac{1}{2}(8)(10) + \dfrac{1}{2}(4)(10)$

$= 60 \text{ meters.}$

8. Total Leakage $= \displaystyle\int_0^3 10e^{0.2t} = 50e^{0.2t}\big]_0^3$

$= 91.1059 - 50$

$= 41.1059 = 41 \text{ gallons.}$

9. Total change in temperature

$= \displaystyle\int_0^5 -\cos\left(\dfrac{t}{4}\right)dt$

$= -4\sin\left(\dfrac{t}{4}\right)\bigg]_0^5$

$= -3.79594 - 0$

$= -3.79594°\text{F.}$

Thus, the temperature of coffee after 5 minutes is $(92 - 3.79594) \approx 88.204°\text{F.}$

10. $y(t) = y_0 e^{kt}$

Half-life = 4500 years $\Rightarrow \dfrac{1}{2} = e^{4500k}$.

Take ln of both sides:

$$\ln\left(\dfrac{1}{2}\right) = \ln e^{4500k}$$

$$\Rightarrow -\ln 2 = 4500k$$

$$\text{or } k = \dfrac{-\ln 2}{4500}.$$

$$y(t) = 100 e^{\left(\frac{-\ln 2}{4500}\right)(5000)} = 25(2^{2/9})$$
$$\approx 46.293.$$

There are approximately 46.29 grams left.

11. Step 1. Separate variables:
$dy = x\cos(x^2)\,dx.$

Step 2. Integrate both sides:

$$\int dy = \int x\cos(x^2)\,dx$$

$$\int dy = y$$

$$\int x\cos(x^2)\,dx : \text{Let } u = x^2;$$

$$du = 2x\,dx, \dfrac{du}{2} = x\,dx$$

$$\int x\cos(x^2)\,dx = \int \cos u\,\dfrac{du}{2}$$

$$= \dfrac{\sin u}{2} + c = \dfrac{\sin(x^2)}{2} + C.$$

Thus, $y = \dfrac{\sin(x^2)}{2} + C.$

Step 3. Substitute given values.

$$y(0) = \dfrac{\sin(0)}{2} + C = \pi \Rightarrow C = \pi$$

$$y = \dfrac{\sin(x^2)}{2} + \pi$$

Step 4. Verify result by differentiating:

$$\dfrac{dy}{dx} = \dfrac{\cos(x^2)(2x)}{2} = x\cos(x^2).$$

12. Step 1. Rewrite $\dfrac{d^2 y}{dx^2}$ as $\dfrac{dy'}{dx}$

$$\dfrac{dy'}{dx} = x - 5.$$

Step 2. Separate variables:
$dy' = (x-5)dx.$

Step 3. Integrate both sides:

$$\int dy' = \int (x-5)\,dx$$

$$y' = \dfrac{x^2}{2} - 5x + C_1.$$

Step 4. Substitute given values:

At $x = 0$, $y' = \dfrac{0}{2} - 5(0) + C_1$

$$= -2 \Rightarrow C_1 = -2$$

$$y' = \dfrac{x^2}{2} - 5x - 2.$$

Step 5. Rewrite: $y' = \dfrac{dy}{dx}; \dfrac{dy}{dx}$

$$= \dfrac{x^2}{2} - 5x - 2.$$

Step 6. Separate variables:

$$dy = \left(\dfrac{x^2}{2} - 5x - 2\right)dx.$$

Step 7. Integrate both sides:

$$\int dy = \int \left(\dfrac{x^2}{2} - 5x - 2\right)dx.$$

$$y = \dfrac{x^3}{6} - \dfrac{5x^2}{2} - 2x + C_2$$

Step 8. Substitute given values:

At $x = 0$, $y = 0 - 0 - 0 + C_2$

$$= 1 \Rightarrow C_2 = 1$$

$$y = \dfrac{x^3}{6} - \dfrac{5x^2}{2} - 2x + 1.$$

Step 9. Verify result by differentiating:

$$\frac{dy}{dx} = \frac{x^2}{2} - 5x - 2$$

$$\frac{d^2y}{dx^2} = x - 5.$$

Part B—Calculators are allowed.

13. Average Value $= \dfrac{1}{\pi/3 - \pi/4} \displaystyle\int_{\pi/4}^{\pi/3} \tan x \, dx.$

Enter $= (1/(\pi/3 - \pi/4)) \displaystyle\int (\tan x, x, \pi/4, \pi/3)$

and obtain $\dfrac{6 \ln(2)}{\pi} = 1.32381.$

14. $v(t) = \displaystyle\int a(t)\,dt$

$= \displaystyle\int 3e^{2t} = \frac{3}{2}e^{2t} + C$

$v(0) = \dfrac{3}{2}e^0 + C = \dfrac{1}{2} \Rightarrow \dfrac{3}{2} + C = \dfrac{1}{2}$

or $C = -1$

$v(t) = \dfrac{3}{2}e^{2t} - 1$

Displacement $= \displaystyle\int_0^3 \left(\frac{3}{2}e^{2t} - 1\right) dt.$

Enter $\displaystyle\int (3/2 * e^{\wedge}(2x) - 1, x, 0, 3)$

and obtain 298.822.

Distance Traveled $= \displaystyle\int_0^3 |v(t)| \, dt.$

Since $\dfrac{3}{2}e^{2t} - 1 > 0$ for $t \geq 0$,

$\displaystyle\int_0^3 |v(t)|\,dt = \int_0^3 \left(\frac{3}{2}e^{2t} - 1\right) dt = 298.822.$

15. Step 1. $y(t) = y_0 e^{kt}$

$y(1) = 5000 \Rightarrow 5000 = y_0 e^k \Rightarrow y_0$

$= 5000e^{-k}$

$y(3) = 4000 \Rightarrow 4000 = y_0 e^{3k}$

Substituting:

$y(0) = 5000e^{-k}, \quad 4000 = (5000e^{-k})e^{3k}$

$4000 = 5000e^{2k}$

$\dfrac{4}{5} = e^{2k}$

$\ln\left(\dfrac{4}{5}\right) = \ln\left(e^{2k}\right) = 2k$

$k = \dfrac{1}{2}\ln\left(\dfrac{4}{5}\right) \approx -0.111572.$

Step 2. $5000 = y_0 e^{-0.111572}$

$y(0) = (5000)/e^{-0.111572} \approx 5590.17$

$y(t) = (5590.17)\, e^{-0.111572t}$

Step 3. $y(7) = (5590.17)e^{-0.111572(7)}$
≈ 2560
Thus, sales for the 7th month are approximately 2560 units.

16. Step 1. Separate variables:

$$\frac{dy}{dx} = \frac{2y}{x+1}$$

$$\frac{dy}{2y} = \frac{dx}{x+1}.$$

Step 2. Integrate both sides:

$$\int \frac{dy}{2y} = \int \frac{dx}{x+1}$$

$$\frac{1}{2}\ln|y| = \ln|x+1| + C.$$

Step 3. Substitute given value $(0, 4)$:

$$\frac{1}{2}\ln(4) = \ln(1) + C$$

$$\ln 2 = C$$

$$\frac{1}{2}\ln|y| - \ln|x+1| = \ln 2$$

$$\ln\left|\frac{y^{1/2}}{x+1}\right| = \ln 2$$

$$e^{\ln\left|\frac{y^{1/2}}{x+1}\right|} = e^{\ln 2}$$

$$\frac{y^{1/2}}{x+1} = 2$$

$$y^{1/2} = 2(x+1)$$

$$y = (2)^2(x+1)^2$$

$$y = 4(x+1)^2.$$

Step 4. Verify result by differentiating:

$$\frac{dy}{dx} = 4(2)(x+1) = 8(x+1).$$

Compare with $\dfrac{dy}{dx} = \dfrac{2y}{x+1}$

$$= \frac{2\left(4(x+1)^2\right)}{(x+1)}$$

$$= 8(x+1).$$

17. $y(t) = y_0 e^{kt}$

$y_0 = 750,000$

$y(22) = (750,000)\, e^{(0.03)(22)}$

$$\approx \begin{cases} 1.45109\,E6 \approx 1,451,090 \text{ using} \\ \qquad\qquad\quad \text{a TI-89,} \\ 1,451,094 \text{ using a TI-85.} \end{cases}$$

18. Step 1. Separate variables:

$$4e^y = \frac{dy}{dx} - 3xe^y$$

$$4e^y + 3xe^y = \frac{dy}{dx}$$

$$e^y(4+3x) = \frac{dy}{dx}$$

$$(4+3x)\,dx = \frac{dy}{e^y} = e^{-y}\,dy.$$

Step 2. Integrate both sides:

$$\int (4+3x)\,dx = \int e^{-y}\,dy$$

$$4x + \frac{3x^2}{2} = -e^{-y} + C$$

Switch sides: $e^{-y} = -\dfrac{3x^2}{2} - 4x + C.$

Step 3. Substitute given value: $y(0) = 0$
$\Rightarrow e^0 = 0 - 0 + c \Rightarrow c = 1.$

Step 4. Take ln of both sides:

$$e^{-y} = -\frac{3x^2}{2} - 4x + 1$$

$$\ln(e^{-y}) = \ln\left(-\frac{3x^2}{2} - 4x + 1\right)$$

$$y = -\ln\left(1 - 4x - \frac{3x^2}{2}\right).$$

Step 5. Verify result by differentiating:
Enter $d(-\ln(1 - 4x - (3x^2)/2), x)$ and obtain
$\dfrac{-2(3x+4)}{3x^2 + 8x - 2}$, which is equivalent
to $e^y(4 + 3x).$

19. $y(t) = y_0 e^{kt}$

$k = 0.0625,\ y(10) = 50,000$

$50,000 = y_0 e^{10(0.0625)}$

$$y_0 = \frac{50,000}{e^{0.625}} \begin{cases} \$26763.1 \text{ using a TI-89,} \\ \$26763.071426 \approx \$26763.07 \\ \text{using a TI-85.} \end{cases}$$

20. Set $v(t) = 2 - 6e^{-t} = 0$. Using the [*Zero*]
function on your calculator, compute
$t = 1.09861.$

Distance Traveled $= \int_0^{10} |v(t)| \, dt$

$$|2 - 6e^{-t}| = \begin{cases} -(2 - 6e^{-t}) & \text{if } 0 \le t < 1.09861 \\ 2 - 6e^{-t} & \text{if } t \ge 1.09861 \end{cases}$$

$$\int_0^{10} |2 - 6e^{-t}| \, dt = \int_0^{1.09861} -(2 - 6e^{-t}) \, dt$$
$$+ \int_{1.09861}^{10} (2 - 6e^{-t}) \, dt$$
$$= 1.80278 + 15.803 = 17.606.$$

Alternatively, use the [nInt] function on the calculator.
Enter $nInt$ (abs(2 – 6e^(–x)), x, 0, 10) and obtain the same result.

21. Build a table of value for $\frac{dy}{dx} = x - y$.

	$y = -2$	$y = -1$	$y = 0$	$y = 1$	$y = 2$	
$x = -2$	0	-1	-2	-3	-4	
$x = -1$	1	0	-1	-2	-3	
$x = 0$	2	1	0	-1	-2	
$x = 1$	3	2	1	0	-1	
$x = 2$	4	3	2	1	0	

Draw short lines at each intersection with slopes equal to the value of $\frac{dy}{dx}$ at that point.

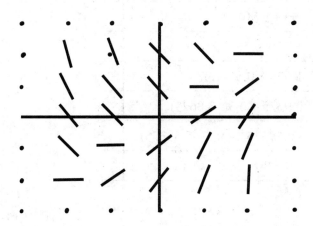

22. $\frac{dP}{dt} = .65P \left(1 - \frac{P}{50}\right)$ can be separated and integrated by partial fractions.
$$\int \frac{dP}{P} + \int \frac{dP}{(50 - P)} = \int .65 \, dt$$
produces $\ln |P| + \ln |50 - P|$
$= .65t + C_1$ and $\frac{P}{50 - P} = C_2 e^{.65t}$, so

$P = \frac{50 C_2 e^{.65t}}{1 + C_2 e^{.65t}}$. Since one person knows

the rumor on day zero, $1 = \frac{50 C_2}{1 + C_2}$ and

$C_2 = \frac{1}{49}$. The model for the population

becomes $P = \frac{50 e^{.65t} / 49}{1 + \left(e^{.65t} / 49\right)} =$

$\frac{50 e^{.65t}}{49 + e^{.65t}} = \frac{50}{49 e^{-.65t} + 1}$. Half the

population of the office would be 25

people, so solve for t in $25 = \frac{50 e^{.65t}}{49 + e^{.65t}}$.

Since t ≈ 5.987, half of the office will have heard the rumor by the sixth day.

23. The logistic model becomes
$\frac{dP}{dt} = kP \left(1 - \frac{P}{200}\right)$ since the carrying

capacity is 200. Separate the variables
$\int \frac{200 \, dP}{P(200 - P)} = \int k \, dt$ and integrate by

partial fractions $\int \frac{dP}{P} + \int \frac{dP}{200 - P} = \int k \, dt$.

You find $\ln \left| \frac{P}{200 - P} \right| = kt + C_1$. Exponentiate

to get $\frac{P}{200 - P} = e^{kt + C_1} = C_2 e^{kt}$. Solving

for P produces $P = \frac{200 C_2 e^{kt}}{1 + C_2 e^{kt}}$. On day

zero, two students are infected, so

$2 = \frac{200 C_2}{1 + C_2}$ and $C_2 = \frac{1}{99}$. On day five, 12

students are infected, so $12 = \frac{200 e^{5k} / 99}{1 + \left(e^{5k} / 99\right)}$

and $k \approx .369$.

Therefore, $P = \dfrac{200\left(\dfrac{1}{99}\right)e^{.369t}}{1+\left(\dfrac{1}{99}\right)e^{.369t}}$

$= \dfrac{200e^{.369t}}{99+e^{.369t}} = \dfrac{200}{99e^{-.369t}+1}$. On day 10,

$P = \dfrac{200}{99e^{-.369(10)}+1} = \dfrac{200}{3.472} \approx 57.600$, so

we would predict that approximately 58 students would be infected on the tenth day.

24. Apply $y_n = y_{n-1} + \Delta x \cdot f'(x_{n-1}, y_{n-1})$ with $\Delta x = 0.1$. (See table below.)

25. Apply $y_n = y_{n-1} + \Delta x \cdot f'(x_{n-1}, y_{n-1})$ with $\Delta x = 0.5$. (See table below.)

Solution to Problem 24.

x	y	dy/dx	Next y-value
0	1	−1	0.9
0.1	0.9	−0.719	0.8281
0.2	0.8281	−0.52787	0.775313075
0.3	0.775313	−0.37605	0.737708202
0.4	0.737708	−0.24147	0.713561134
0.5	0.713561		

$y(5) \approx 0.713561$

Solution to Problem 25.

x	y	dy/dx	Calculate next y-value	
0	1	1	$1 + 0.5(1)$	
0.5	1.5	.5	$1.5 + 0.5(0.5)$	
1	1.75	−0.25	$1.75 + 0.5(−0.25)$	
1.5	1.625	−1.375	$1.625 + 0.5(−1.375)$	
2	0.9375	−3.0625	$0.9375 + 0.5(−3.0625)$	
2.5	−0.59375	−5.59375	$−0.59375 + 0.5(−5.59375)$	
3	−3.390625			

$y(3) \approx -3.391$

13.12 Solutions to Cumulative Review Problems

26. $3e^y = x^2 y$

$$3e^y \frac{dy}{dx} = 2xy + \frac{dy}{dx}(x^2)$$

$$3e^y \frac{dy}{dx} - \frac{dy}{dx}x^2 = 2xy$$

$$\frac{dy}{dx}(3e^y - x^2) = 2xy$$

$$\frac{dy}{dx} = \frac{2xy}{3e^y - x^2}$$

27. Let $u = x^3 + 1$; $du = 3x^2 dx$ or $\dfrac{du}{3} = x^2 dx$.

$$\int \frac{x^2}{x^3 + 1} dx = \int \frac{1}{u}\frac{du}{3}$$

$$= \frac{1}{3}\ln|u| + C$$

$$= \frac{1}{3}\ln|x^3 + 1| + C$$

$$\int_0^3 \frac{x^2}{x^3 + 1} dx = \frac{1}{3}\ln|x^3 + 1|\Big]_0^3$$

$$= \frac{1}{3}(\ln 28 - \ln 1) = \frac{\ln 28}{3}$$

28. (a) $F(-2) = \displaystyle\int_{-2}^{-2} f(t)\,dt = 0$

$$F(0) = \int_{-2}^{0} f(t)\,dt = \frac{1}{2}(4 + 2)\,2 = 6$$

(b) $F'(x) = f(x)$; $F'(0) = 2$ and $F'(2) = 4$.

(c) Since $f > 0$ on $[-2, 4]$, F has a maximum value at $x = 4$.

(d) The function f is increasing on $(1, 3)$, which implies that $f' > 0$ on $(1, 3)$.

Thus, F is concave upward on $(1, 3)$. (Note: f' is equivalent to the 2nd derivative of F.)

29. (a) $\dfrac{dy}{dx} = \dfrac{y}{2x + 1}$; $f(0) = 2$

$$\frac{dy}{dx}\Big|_{x=0} = \frac{2}{2(0) + 1} = 2 \Rightarrow m = 2 \text{ at } x = 0.$$

$$y - y_1 = m(x - x_1)$$

$$y - 2 = 2(x - 0) \Rightarrow y = 2x + 2$$

The equation of the tangent to f at $x = 0$ is $y = 2x + 2$.

(b) $f(0.1) = 2(0.1) + 2 = 2.2$

(c) Solve the differential equation:

$$\frac{dy}{dx} = \frac{y}{2x + 1}.$$

Step 1. Separate variables:

$$\frac{dy}{y} = \frac{dx}{2x + 1}$$

Step 2. Integrate both sides:

$$\int \frac{dy}{y} = \int \frac{dx}{2x + 1}$$

$$\ln|y| = \frac{1}{2}\ln|2x + 1| + C.$$

Step 3. Substitute given values (0, 2):

$$\ln 2 = \frac{1}{2}\ln 1 + C \Rightarrow C = \ln 2$$

$$\ln|y| = \frac{1}{2}|2x + 1| + \ln 2$$

$$\ln|y| - \frac{1}{2}|2x + 1| = \ln 2$$

$$\ln\left|\frac{y}{(2x + 1)^{1/2}}\right| = \ln 2$$

$$e^{\ln\left|\frac{y}{(2x+1)^{1/2}}\right|} = e^{\ln 2}$$

$$\frac{y}{(2x + 1)^{1/2}} = 2$$

$$y = 2(2x + 1)^{1/2}.$$

Step 4. Verify result by differentiating

$$y = 2(2x + 1)^{1/2}$$

$$\frac{dy}{dx} = 2\left(\frac{1}{2}\right)(2x + 1)^{-1/2}(2)$$

$$= \frac{2}{\sqrt{2x + 1}}.$$

Compare this with:

$$\frac{dy}{dx} = \frac{y}{2x + 1} = \frac{2(2x + 1)^{1/2}}{2x + 1}$$

$$= \frac{2}{\sqrt{2x + 1}}.$$

Thus, the function is
$$y = f(x) = 2(2x + 1)^{1/2}.$$

(d) $f(x) = 2(2x + 1)^{1/2}$
$$f(0.1) = 2(2(0.1) + 1)^{1/2} = 2(1.2)^{1/2}$$
$$\approx 2.191$$

30. See Figure 13.12-1.

[−π,π] by [−4,4]

Figure 13.12-1

(a) Intersection points: Using the [*Intersection*] function on the calculator, you have $x = 0$ and $x = 1.37131$.

$$\text{Area of } R = \int_{0}^{1.37131} [3 \sin x - (e^x - 1)]dx.$$

Enter $\int (3 \sin(x)) - (e^{\wedge}(x) - 1)$, x, 0,

1.37131 and obtain 0.836303.

The area of region R is approximately 0.836.

(b) Using the Washer Method, volume of

$$R = \pi \int_{0}^{1.37131} \left[(3 \sin x)^2 - (e^x - 1)^2\right] dx.$$

Enter $\pi \int ((3 \sin(x))^{\wedge}2 - (e^{\wedge}(x) - 1)^{\wedge}2,$ x, 0, 1.37131) and obtain 2.54273π or 7.98824.

The volume of the solid is 7.988.

(c) Volume of Solid $= \pi \int_{0}^{1.37131}$ (Area of Cross Section)dx.

Area of Cross Section $= \dfrac{1}{2}\pi r^2$

$$= \frac{1}{2}\pi\left(\frac{1}{2}(3 \sin x - (e^x - 1))\right)^2.$$

Enter $\left(\dfrac{\pi}{2}\right)\dfrac{1}{4} * \int ((3 \sin(x) - (e^{\wedge}(x) - 1))^{\wedge}2, x, 0, 1.37131)$ and obtain 0.077184 π or 0.24248. The volume of the solid is approximately 0.077184 π or 0.242.

31. Integrate the acceleration vector to get the velocity vector:

$$\vec{a}(\theta) = \langle \sin\theta, -\cos\theta \rangle = \sin\theta\vec{i} - \cos\theta\vec{j}$$

$$\vec{v}(\theta) = -\cos\theta\vec{i} - \sin\theta\vec{j} + C$$

$$\vec{v}\left(\frac{\pi}{3}\right) = -\cos\left(\frac{\pi}{3}\right)\vec{i} - \sin\left(\frac{\pi}{3}\right)\vec{j} + C = -\vec{i}$$

$$-\frac{1}{2}\vec{i} - \frac{\sqrt{3}}{2}\vec{j} + C = -\vec{i}$$

$$C = -\frac{1}{2}\vec{i} + \frac{\sqrt{3}}{2}\vec{j}$$

$$\vec{v}(\theta) = \left(-\cos\theta - \frac{1}{2}\right)\vec{i} + \left(\frac{\sqrt{3}}{2} - \sin\theta\right)\vec{j}.$$

Integrate the velocity vector to get the position vector:

$$\vec{s}(\theta) = \left(-\sin\theta - \frac{1}{2}\theta\right)\vec{i}$$

$$+ \left(\frac{\sqrt{3}}{2}\theta + \cos\theta\right)\vec{j} + C$$

$\vec{s}(0) = \left(-\sin 0 - \dfrac{1}{2}(0)\right)\vec{i}$

$\qquad + \left(\dfrac{\sqrt{3}}{2}(0) + \cos 0\right)\vec{j} + C = 0$

$0\vec{i} + 1\vec{j} + C = 0$

$C = -\vec{j}$

$\vec{s}(\theta) = \left(-\sin \theta - \dfrac{1}{2}\theta\right)\vec{i}$

$\qquad + \left(\dfrac{\sqrt{3}}{2}\theta + \cos \theta - 1\right)\vec{j}.$

Substituting in $\theta = \pi$:

$\vec{s}(\pi) = \left(-\sin \pi - \dfrac{1}{2}\pi\right)\vec{i}$

$\qquad + \left(\dfrac{\sqrt{3}}{2}\pi + \cos \pi - 1\right)\vec{j}$

$\vec{s}(\pi) = \left(0 - \dfrac{1}{2}\pi\right)\vec{i} + \left(\dfrac{\sqrt{3}}{2}\pi - 1 - 1\right)\vec{j}$

$\vec{s}(\pi) = -\left(\dfrac{\pi}{2}\right)\vec{i} + \left(\dfrac{\sqrt{3}}{2}\pi - 2\right)\vec{j}$

$\vec{s}(\pi) = -\dfrac{\pi}{2}\vec{i} + \left(\dfrac{\sqrt{3}-4}{2}\pi\right)\vec{j}.$

32. Integrate $\displaystyle\int x^2 e^{5x-2}\,dx$ by parts. Let
$u = x^2,\ du = 2x\,dx,\ dv = e^{5x-2}\,dx,$ and
$v = \dfrac{e^{5x-2}}{5}.$ Then,

$\displaystyle\int x^2 e^{5x-2}\,dx = \dfrac{x^2 e^{5x-2}}{5} - \dfrac{2}{5}\int x e^{5x-2}\,dx.$

The remaining integral can be evaluated by parts, using $u = x,\ du = dx,\ dv = e^{5x-2}\,dx,$
and $v = \dfrac{e^{5x-2}}{5}.$ $\displaystyle\int x^2 e^{5x-2}\,dx$

$= \dfrac{x^2 e^{5x-2}}{5} - \dfrac{2}{5}\left[\dfrac{x e^{5x-2}}{5} - \dfrac{1}{5}\int e^{5x-2}\,dx\right]$

$= \dfrac{x^2 e^{5x-2}}{5} - \dfrac{2}{5}\left[\dfrac{x e^{5x-2}}{5} - \dfrac{1}{5}\cdot\dfrac{e^{5x-2}}{5}\right]$

$= \dfrac{x^2 e^{5x-2}}{5} - \dfrac{2x e^{5x-2}}{25} + \dfrac{2 e^{5x-2}}{125} + C.$

33. The path is defined by $x = t - 2,\ y = \sin^2 t.$
Since $\dfrac{dx}{dt} = 1$ and $\dfrac{dy}{dt} = 2\sin t \cos t,$
$\dfrac{dy}{dx} = \dfrac{2\sin t \cos t}{1}.$ This is the slope of a
tangent line to the curve, and when the
slope is zero, the curve will reach either a
maximum or a minimum. The slope
$2\sin t \cos t = 0$ when $\sin t = 0$ or when
$\cos t = 0.$ The first equation gives us $t = 0$
or $t = \pi$ and the second, $t = \dfrac{\pi}{2}.$ The
second derivative,
$\dfrac{d^2 y}{dx^2} = -2\sin^2 t + 2\cos^2 t = 2\cos 2t.$
Evaluating at each of the possible values of
$t,$ we find $2\cos 2t\big|_{t=0} = 2,\ 2\cos 2t\big|_{t=\pi} = 2,$
and $2\cos 2t|_{t=\frac{\pi}{2}} = -2.$ The maximum value
will occur when the second derivative is
negative, so the maximum y-value is
achieved when $t = \dfrac{\pi}{2},\ x = \dfrac{\pi}{2} - 2 = \dfrac{\pi - 4}{2},$
and $y = \sin^2 \dfrac{\pi}{2} = 1.$

CHAPTER 14

Big Idea 4: Series
Series

IN THIS CHAPTER

Summary: In this chapter, you will learn different types of series and the many tests for determining whether they converge or diverge. The types of series include geometric series, *p*-Series, alternating series, power, and Taylor series. The tests for convergence include the integral test, the comparison test, the limit comparison test, and the ratio test for absolute convergence. These tests involve working with algebraic expressions and lengthy computations. It is important that you carefully work through the practice problems provided in the chapter and check your solutions with the given explanations.

Key Ideas

✪ Sequences and Series
✪ Geometric Series, Harmonic Series, and *p*-Series
✪ Convergence Tests
✪ Alternating Series: Absolute and Conditional Convergence
✪ Power Series
✪ Taylor Series
✪ Operations on Series
✪ Error Bounds

14.1 Sequences and Series

Main Concepts: Sequences and Series, Convergence

A sequence is a function whose domain is the non-negative integers. It can be expressed as a list of terms $\{a_n\} = \{a_1, a_2, a_3, \ldots, a_n, \ldots\}$ or by a formula that defines the nth term of the sequence for any value of n. A series $\sum a_n = \sum_{n=1}^{\infty} a_n = a_1 + a_2 + a_3 + \cdots + a_n + \cdots$ is the sum of the terms of a sequence $\{a_n\}$. Associated with each series is a sequence of partial sums, $\{s_n\}$, where $s_1 = a_1$, $s_2 = a_1 + a_2$, $s_3 = a_1 + a_2 + a_3$, and in general, $s_n = a_1 + a_2 + a_3 + \cdots + a_n$.

Example 1

Find the first three partial sums of the series $\sum_{n=1}^{\infty} \dfrac{(-2)^n}{n^3}$.

Step 1: Generate the first three terms of the sequence $\left\{ \dfrac{(-2)^n}{n^3} \right\}$.

$$a_1 = \frac{(-2)^1}{1^3} = -2, \quad a_2 = \frac{(-2)^2}{2^3} = \frac{4}{8} = \frac{1}{2}, \quad a_3 = \frac{(-2)^3}{3^3} = \frac{-8}{27}$$

Step 2: Find the partial sums.

$$s_1 = a_1 = -2, \quad s_2 = a_1 + a_2 = -2 + \frac{1}{2} = \frac{-3}{2},$$

$$s_3 = a_1 + a_2 + a_3 = -2 + \frac{1}{2} + \frac{-8}{27} = \frac{-97}{54} \approx -1.796$$

Example 2

Find the fifth partial sum of the series $\sum_{n=1}^{\infty} \dfrac{5 + n^2}{n + 3}$.

Step 1: Generate the first five terms of the sequence $\left\{ \dfrac{5 + n^2}{n + 3} \right\}$.

$$a_1 = \frac{5 + 1^2}{1 + 3} = \frac{6}{4} = \frac{3}{2} \quad a_2 = \frac{5 + 2^2}{2 + 3} = \frac{9}{5} \quad a_3 = \frac{5 + 3^2}{3 + 3} = \frac{14}{6} = \frac{7}{3}$$

$$a_4 = \frac{5 + 4^2}{4 + 3} = \frac{21}{7} = 3 \qquad a_5 = \frac{5 + 5^2}{5 + 3} = \frac{30}{8} = \frac{15}{4}$$

Step 2: The fifth partial sum is $a_1 + a_2 + a_3 + a_4 + a_5 = \dfrac{3}{2} + \dfrac{9}{5} + \dfrac{7}{3} + 3 + \dfrac{15}{4} = \dfrac{743}{60}$.

Convergence

The series $\sum a_n$ converges if the sequence of associated partial sums, $\{s_n\}$, converges. The limit $\lim_{n \to \infty} s_n = S$, where S is a real number, and is the sum of series, $\sum_{n=1}^{\infty} a_n = S$. If $\sum_{n=1}^{\infty} a_n$ and $\sum_{n=1}^{\infty} b_n$ are convergent, then $\sum_{n=1}^{\infty} c a_n = c \sum_{n=1}^{\infty} a_n$ and $\sum_{n=1}^{\infty} (a_n \pm b_n) = \sum_{n=1}^{\infty} a_n \pm \sum_{n=1}^{\infty} b_n$.

Example 1

Determine whether the series $\sum\limits_{n=1}^{\infty} \dfrac{1}{5^n}$ converges or diverges. If it converges, find its sum.

Step 1: Find the first few partial sums.

$$s_1 = \frac{1}{5} = 0.2, \; s_2 = \frac{1}{5} + \frac{1}{25} = \frac{6}{25} = 0.24, \; s_3 = \frac{1}{5} + \frac{1}{25} + \frac{1}{125} = \frac{31}{125} = 0.248$$

$$s_4 = \frac{1}{5} + \frac{1}{25} + \frac{1}{125} + \frac{1}{625} = \frac{156}{625} = 0.2496$$

Step 2: The sequence of partial sums $\{0.2,\ 0.24,\ 0.248,\ 0.2496,\ \dots\}$ converges to 0.25, so the series converges, and its sum $\sum\limits_{n=1}^{\infty} \dfrac{1}{5^n} = 0.25$.

Example 2

Find the sum of the series $\sum\limits_{n=1}^{\infty} (5a_n - 3b_n)$, given that $\sum\limits_{n=1}^{\infty} a_n = 4$ and $\sum\limits_{n=1}^{\infty} b_n = 8$.

Step 1: $\sum\limits_{n=1}^{\infty} (5a_n - 3b_n) = \sum\limits_{n=1}^{\infty} 5a_n - \sum\limits_{n=1}^{\infty} 3b_n = 5\sum\limits_{n=1}^{\infty} a_n - 3\sum\limits_{n=1}^{\infty} b_n$

Step 2: $5\sum\limits_{n=1}^{\infty} a_n - 3\sum\limits_{n=2}^{\infty} b_n = 5(4) - 3(8) = 20 - 24 = -4$

14.2 Types of Series

Main Concepts: *p*-Series, Harmonic Series, Geometric Series, Decimal Expansion

p-Series

The *p*-series is a series of the form $1 + \dfrac{1}{2^p} + \dfrac{1}{3^p} + \dfrac{1}{4^p} + \cdots + \dfrac{1}{n^p} + \cdots = \sum\limits_{n=1}^{\infty} \dfrac{1}{n^p}$. The *p*-series converges when $p > 1$, and diverges when $0 < p \leq 1$.

Harmonic Series

The harmonic series $1 + \dfrac{1}{2} + \dfrac{1}{3} + \dfrac{1}{4} + \cdots + \dfrac{1}{n} + \cdots = \sum\limits_{n=1}^{\infty} \dfrac{1}{n}$ is a *p*-series with $p = 1$. The harmonic series diverges.

Geometric Series

A geometric series is a series of the form $\sum\limits_{n=1}^{\infty} ar^{n-1}$ where $a \neq 0$. A geometric series converges when $|r| < 1$. The sum of the first *n* terms of a geometric series is $s_n = \dfrac{a(1 - r^n)}{1 - r}$. The sum of the series $\sum\limits_{n=1}^{\infty} ar^{n-1} = \lim\limits_{n \to \infty} s_n = \lim\limits_{n \to \infty} \dfrac{a(1 - r^n)}{1 - r} = \dfrac{a}{1 - r}$.

Example 1

Determine whether the series $1 + \dfrac{3}{2} + \dfrac{9}{4} + \dfrac{27}{8} + \cdots$ converges. $1 + \dfrac{3}{2} + \dfrac{9}{4} + \dfrac{27}{8} + \cdots$ is a

geometric series with $a = 1$ and $r = \dfrac{3}{2}$. Since $r > 1$, the series diverges.

Example 2

Find the tenth partial sum of the series $12 + 9 + \dfrac{27}{4} + \dfrac{81}{16} + \cdots$.

While it is possible to extend the terms of the series and directly compute the tenth partial sum, it is quicker to recognize that this is a geometric series. The ratio of any two subsequent terms is $r = \dfrac{3}{4}$ and the first term is $a = 12$.

$$s_{10} = \frac{12\left(1 - \left(\dfrac{3}{4}\right)^{10}\right)}{1 - \dfrac{3}{4}} \approx 45.297$$

Example 3

Find the sum of the series $12 + 9 + \dfrac{27}{4} + \dfrac{81}{16} + \cdots$ Since $12 + 9 + \dfrac{27}{4} + \dfrac{81}{16} + \cdots$ is a geometric

series with $a = 12$ and $r = \dfrac{3}{4}$, $S = \dfrac{a}{1 - r} = \dfrac{12}{1 - \dfrac{3}{4}} = 48.$

Decimal Expansion

The rational number equal to the repeating decimal is the sum of the geometric series that represents the repeating decimal.

Example

Find the rational number equivalent to $3.8\overline{76}$.

Step 1: $3.8\overline{76} = 3.8 + .076 + .00076 + \cdots = \dfrac{38}{10} + \dfrac{76}{10^3} + \dfrac{76}{10^5} + \dfrac{76}{10^7} + \cdots = \dfrac{38}{10} +$

$76 \displaystyle\sum_{n=1}^{\infty} \dfrac{1}{10^{2n+1}}$

Step 2: $\displaystyle\sum_{n=1}^{\infty} \dfrac{1}{10^{2n+1}}$ is a geometric series with $a = \dfrac{1}{10^3}$ and $r = \dfrac{1}{10^2}$. The sum of the series is

$\dfrac{a}{1 - r} = \dfrac{\dfrac{1}{1000}}{1 - \dfrac{1}{100}} = \dfrac{1}{990}.$

Step 3: $3.8\overline{76} = \dfrac{38}{10} + 76 \displaystyle\sum_{n=1}^{\infty} \dfrac{1}{10^{2n+1}} = \dfrac{38}{10} + \dfrac{76}{990} = \dfrac{3838}{990} = \dfrac{1919}{495}$

14.3 Convergence Tests

Main Concepts: Divergence Test, Integral Test, Ratio Test, Comparison Test, Limit Comparison Test

Divergence Test

Given a series $\sum\limits_{n=1}^{\infty} a_n$, if $\lim\limits_{n\to\infty} a_n \neq 0$, then the series diverges.

Example

Determine whether the series $\sum\limits_{n=1}^{\infty} \dfrac{2n}{3n+1}$ converges or diverges.

The series $\sum\limits_{n=1}^{\infty} \dfrac{2n}{3n+1} = \dfrac{1}{2} + \dfrac{4}{7} + \dfrac{3}{5} + \dots$. Applying the Divergence Test, you have $\lim\limits_{n\to\infty} a_n =$

$\lim\limits_{n\to\infty} \dfrac{2n}{3n+1} = \dfrac{2}{3} \neq 0$.

Therefore, the series diverges.

Integral Test

If $a_n = f(n)$ where f is a continuous, positive, decreasing function on $[c, \infty)$, then the series $\sum\limits_{n=1}^{\infty} a_n$ is convergent if and only if the improper integral $\displaystyle\int_{c}^{\infty} f(x)\, dx$ exists.

Example 1

Determine whether the series $\sum\limits_{n=1}^{\infty} \dfrac{1}{n^2} \sin \dfrac{\pi}{n}$ converges or diverges.

Step 1: $f(x) = \dfrac{1}{x^2} \sin \dfrac{\pi}{x}$ is continuous, positive, and decreasing on the interval $[2, \infty)$.

Step 2: $\displaystyle\int_{2}^{\infty} \dfrac{1}{x^2} \sin \dfrac{\pi}{x}\, dx = \dfrac{1}{\pi} \lim_{u\to\infty} \cos\left(\dfrac{\pi}{x}\right)\Big|_{2}^{u} = \dfrac{1}{\pi} \lim_{u\to\infty} \left[\cos\left(\dfrac{\pi}{u}\right) - \cos\left(\dfrac{\pi}{2}\right)\right] =$

$\dfrac{1}{\pi} \lim\limits_{u\to\infty} \left[\cos\left(\dfrac{\pi}{u}\right)\right] = \dfrac{1}{\pi}$. The improper integral exists, so $\sum\limits_{n=1}^{\infty} \dfrac{1}{n^2} \sin \dfrac{\pi}{n}$ converges.

Example 2

Determine whether the series $1 + \dfrac{1}{4} + \dfrac{1}{9} + \dfrac{1}{16} + \dots + \dfrac{1}{n^2} + \dots = \sum\limits_{n=1}^{\infty} \dfrac{1}{n^2}$ converges or diverges.

Step 1: $f(x) = \dfrac{1}{x^2}$ is continuous, positive, and decreasing on the interval $[1, \infty)$.

Step 2: $\displaystyle\int_{1}^{\infty} \dfrac{1}{x^2} dx = \lim_{u\to\infty} \int_{1}^{u} \dfrac{1}{x^2}\, dx = \lim_{u\to\infty} (-x^{-1})\Big|_{1}^{u} = \lim_{u\to\infty} \left[\dfrac{-1}{u} - \dfrac{-1}{1}\right] =$

$\lim\limits_{u\to\infty} \left[1 - \dfrac{1}{u}\right] = 1$

Since the improper integral exists, the series $\sum\limits_{n=1}^{\infty} \dfrac{1}{n^2}$ converges.

Example 3

Determine whether the series $1 + \dfrac{1}{2} + \dfrac{1}{3} + \dfrac{1}{4} + \cdots + \dfrac{1}{n} + \cdots = \displaystyle\sum_{n=1}^{\infty} \dfrac{1}{n}$ converges or diverges.

Step 1: $f(x) = \dfrac{1}{x}$ is continuous, positive, and decreasing on $[1, \infty)$.

Step 2: $\displaystyle\int_1^{\infty} \dfrac{1}{x} dx = \lim_{u \to \infty} \int_1^{u} \dfrac{1}{x} dx = \lim_{u \to \infty} (\ln x)\Big|_1^{u} = \lim_{u \to \infty} [\ln u - \ln 1] = \infty$. Since the improper integral does not converge, the series $\displaystyle\sum_{n=1}^{\infty} \dfrac{1}{n}$ diverges.

Example 4

Determine whether the series $1 + \dfrac{1}{\sqrt{2}} + \dfrac{1}{\sqrt{3}} + \dfrac{1}{\sqrt{4}} + \cdots + \dfrac{1}{\sqrt{n}} + \cdots = \displaystyle\sum_{n=1}^{\infty} \dfrac{1}{\sqrt{n}}$ converges or diverges.

Step 1: $f(x) = \dfrac{1}{\sqrt{x}}$ is continuous, positive, and decreasing on $[1, \infty)$.

Step 2: $\displaystyle\int_1^{\infty} \dfrac{1}{\sqrt{x}} dx = \lim_{u \to \infty} \int_1^{u} \dfrac{1}{\sqrt{x}} dx = \lim_{u \to \infty} (2\sqrt{x})\Big|_1^{u} = \lim_{u \to \infty} \left[2\sqrt{u} - 2\right] = \infty$

Since the improper integral does not converge, the series $\displaystyle\sum_{n=1}^{\infty} \dfrac{1}{\sqrt{n}}$ diverges.

Ratio Test

If $\displaystyle\sum_{n=1}^{\infty} a_n$ is a series with positive terms and $\displaystyle\lim_{n \to \infty} \dfrac{a_{n+1}}{a_n} < 1$, then the series converges. If the limit is greater than 1 or is ∞, the series diverges. If the limit is 1, another test must be used.

Example 1

Determine whether the series $\displaystyle\sum_{n=1}^{\infty} \dfrac{(n + 1) \cdot 2^n}{n!}$ converges or diverges.

Step 1: For all $n \geq 1$, $\dfrac{(n + 1) \cdot 2^n}{n!}$ is positive.

Step 2: $\displaystyle\lim_{n \to \infty} \dfrac{a_{n+1}}{a_n} = \lim_{n \to \infty} \left(\dfrac{(n + 2) \cdot 2^{n+1}}{(n + 1)!} \cdot \dfrac{n!}{(n + 1) \cdot 2^n} \right) = \lim_{n \to \infty} \left(\dfrac{(n + 2) \cdot 2}{(n + 1)^2} \right) = 0$

Since this limit is less than 1, the series converges.

Example 2

Determine whether the series $\displaystyle\sum_{n=1}^{\infty} \dfrac{n^3}{(\ln 2)^n}$ converges or diverges.

Step 1: For all $n \geq 1$, $\dfrac{n^3}{(\ln 2)^n}$ is positive.

Step 2: $\displaystyle\lim_{n\to\infty}\frac{a_{n+1}}{a_n}=\lim_{n\to\infty}\left(\frac{(n+1)^3}{(\ln 2)^{n+1}}\cdot\frac{(\ln 2)^n}{n^3}\right)=\frac{1}{\ln 2}\lim_{n\to\infty}\left(\frac{n+1}{n}\right)^3=\frac{1}{\ln 2}\approx 1.443$

Since this limit is greater than 1, the series diverges.

Comparison Test

Suppose $\displaystyle\sum_{n=1}^{\infty}a_n$ and $\displaystyle\sum_{n=1}^{\infty}b_n$ are series with non-negative terms, and $\displaystyle\sum_{n=1}^{\infty}b_n$ is known to converge. If a term-by-term comparison shows that for all n, $a_n\le b_n$, then $\displaystyle\sum_{n=1}^{\infty}a_n$ converges. If $\displaystyle\sum_{n=1}^{\infty}b_n$ diverges, and if for all n, $a_n\ge b_n$, then $\displaystyle\sum_{n=1}^{\infty}a_n$ diverges. Common series that may be used for comparison include the geometric series, which converges for $r<1$ and diverges for $r\ge 1$, and the p-series, which converges for $p>1$ and diverges for $p\le 1$.

Example 1

Determine whether the series $\displaystyle\sum_{n=1}^{\infty}\frac{1}{n^2+5}$ converges or diverges.

Step 1: Choose a series for comparison. The series $\displaystyle\sum_{n=1}^{\infty}\frac{1}{n^2+5}$ can be compared to $\displaystyle\sum_{n=1}^{\infty}\frac{1}{n^2}$, the p-series with $p=2$. Both series have non-negative terms.

Step 2: A term-by-term comparison shows that $\dfrac{1}{n^2+5}<\dfrac{1}{n^2}$ for all values of n.

Step 3: $\displaystyle\sum_{n=1}^{\infty}\frac{1}{n^2}$ converges, so $\displaystyle\sum_{n=1}^{\infty}\frac{1}{n^2+5}$ converges.

Example 2

Determine whether the series $2+\dfrac{3}{5}+\dfrac{4}{10}+\dfrac{5}{17}+\cdots$ converges or diverges.

Step 1: The series $2+\dfrac{3}{5}+\dfrac{4}{10}+\dfrac{5}{17}+\cdots=\displaystyle\sum_{n=1}^{\infty}\frac{n+1}{n^2+1}$ can be compared to $\displaystyle\sum_{n=1}^{\infty}\frac{1}{n}$.

Step 2: $\dfrac{n+1}{n^2+1}=\dfrac{n^2+n}{n^3+n}\ge\dfrac{n^2+1}{n^3+n}=\dfrac{1}{n}$, so $\dfrac{n+1}{n^2+1}\ge\dfrac{1}{n}$ for all $n\ge 1$.

Step 3: Since $\displaystyle\sum_{n=1}^{\infty}\frac{1}{n}$ diverges, $2+\dfrac{3}{5}+\dfrac{4}{10}+\dfrac{5}{17}+\cdots$ also diverges.

Limit Comparison Test

If $\displaystyle\sum_{n=1}^{\infty}a_n$ and $\displaystyle\sum_{n=1}^{\infty}b_n$ are series with positive terms, and if $\displaystyle\lim_{n\to\infty}\frac{a_n}{b_n}=L$ where $0<L<\infty$, then either both series converge or both diverge. By choosing, for one of these, a series that is known to converge, or known to diverge, you can determine whether the other series converges or diverges. Choose a series of a similar form so that the limit expression can be simplified.

Informal Principle

Given a rational expression containing a polynomial in n as a factor in the numerator or denominator, often you may delete all but the highest power of n without affecting the convergence or divergence behavior of the series. For example,

$$\sum_{n=1}^{\infty} \frac{4n^3 - n + 1}{n^5 + 7n^2 - 6} \quad \text{behaves like} \quad \sum_{n=1}^{\infty} \frac{4n^3}{n^5} = 4\sum_{n=1}^{\infty} \frac{1}{n^2}$$

When choosing a series for the Limit Comparison Test, it is helpful to apply the Informal Principle.

Example 1

Determine whether the series $1 + \dfrac{1}{5} + \dfrac{1}{9} + \dfrac{1}{13} + \cdots$ converges or diverges.

The given series $1 + \dfrac{1}{5} + \dfrac{1}{9} + \dfrac{1}{13} + \cdots = \displaystyle\sum_{n=1}^{\infty} \frac{1}{4n-3}$. Choose $\displaystyle\sum_{n=1}^{\infty} \frac{1}{n}$ for comparison.

Since it has a similar structure, and we know it is a p-series with $p = 1$, it diverges. The $\displaystyle\lim_{n\to\infty} \frac{1/(4n-3)}{1/n} = \lim_{n\to\infty} \frac{n}{4n-3} = \frac{1}{4}$. The limit exists and is greater than zero; therefore, since

$\displaystyle\sum_{n=1}^{\infty} \frac{1}{n}$ diverges, $1 + \dfrac{1}{5} + \dfrac{1}{9} + \dfrac{1}{13} + \cdots = \displaystyle\sum_{n=1}^{\infty} \frac{1}{4n-3}$ also diverges.

Example 2

Determine whether the series $\displaystyle\sum_{n=1}^{\infty} \frac{n-2}{n^3}$ converges or diverges.

Compare to the known convergent p-series $\displaystyle\sum_{n=1}^{\infty} \frac{1}{n^2}$. The limit $\displaystyle\lim_{n\to\infty} \frac{(n-2)/n^3}{1/n^2} =$

$\displaystyle\lim_{n\to\infty} \frac{(n-2)(n^2)}{(n^3)} = \lim_{n\to\infty} \frac{n-2}{n} = 1$. Since $0 < \displaystyle\lim_{n\to\infty} \frac{(n-2)/n^3}{1/n^2} < \infty$ and $\displaystyle\sum_{n=1}^{\infty} \frac{1}{n^2}$ converges,

$\displaystyle\sum_{n=1}^{\infty} \frac{n-2}{n^3}$ also converges.

Example 3

Determine whether the series $\displaystyle\sum_{n=1}^{\infty} \frac{1}{\sqrt{n^3 - 3n}}$ converges or diverges. Using the informal prin-

ciple, you have $\displaystyle\sum_{n=1}^{\infty} \frac{1}{\sqrt{n^3}}$ or $\displaystyle\sum_{n=1}^{\infty} \frac{1}{n^{3/2}}$. (Note that $\displaystyle\sum_{n=1}^{\infty} \frac{1}{n^{3/2}}$ is a p-series with $p > 1$ and therefore it converges.)

Apply the limit comparison test and obtain $\displaystyle\lim_{n\to\infty} \frac{\dfrac{1}{n^{3/2}}}{\dfrac{1}{\sqrt{n^3 - 3n}}} = \lim_{n\to\infty} \frac{\sqrt{n^3 - 3n}}{n^{3/2}} =$

$\displaystyle\lim_{n\to\infty} \sqrt{\frac{n^3 - 3n}{n^3}} = \lim_{n\to\infty} \sqrt{1 - \frac{3}{n^2}} = 1$. Since $0 < \displaystyle\lim_{n\to\infty} \frac{\dfrac{1}{n^{3/2}}}{\dfrac{1}{\sqrt{n^3 - 3n}}} < \infty$, and $\displaystyle\sum_{n=1}^{\infty} \frac{1}{n^{3/2}}$

converges, the series $\displaystyle\sum_{n=1}^{\infty} \frac{1}{\sqrt{n^3 - 3n}}$ converges.

14.4 Alternating Series

Main Concepts: Alternating Series, Error Bound, Absolute and Conditional Convergence

A series whose terms alternate between positive and negative is called an alternating series. Alternating series have one of two forms: $\sum\limits_{n=1}^{\infty}(-1)^n a_n$ or $\sum\limits_{n=1}^{\infty}(-1)^{n+1} a_n$ with all a_n's > 0. An alternating series converges if $a_1 \geq a_2 \geq a_3 \geq \cdots \geq a_n \geq \cdots$ and $\lim\limits_{n\to\infty} a_n = 0$.

Example 1

Determine whether the series $\dfrac{1}{e} - \dfrac{2}{e^2} + \dfrac{3}{e^3} - \dfrac{4}{e^4} + \cdots$ converges or diverges.

Step 1: $\dfrac{1}{e} - \dfrac{2}{e^2} + \dfrac{3}{e^3} - \dfrac{4}{e^4} + \cdots = \sum\limits_{n=1}^{\infty}(-1)^{n+1}\dfrac{n}{e^n}$

Step 2: Note that $\dfrac{1}{e} > \dfrac{2}{e^2} > \dfrac{3}{e^3} > \dfrac{4}{e^4}$, and in general, $\dfrac{n}{e^n} > \dfrac{n+1}{e^{n+1}}$, since multiplying by e^{n+1} gives $en > n+1$.

Step 3: $\left\{\dfrac{1}{e}, \dfrac{2}{e^2}, \dfrac{3}{e^3}, \dfrac{4}{e^4}, \ldots\right\} \approx \{.36788, .27067, .14936, .07326, \ldots\}$, so $\lim\limits_{n\to\infty}\dfrac{n}{e^n} = 0$.

Therefore, the series converges.

Example 2

Determine whether the series $4 - 1 + \dfrac{1}{4} - \dfrac{1}{16} + \cdots$ converges or diverges. If it converges, find its sum.

Step 1: $4 - 1 + \dfrac{1}{4} - \dfrac{1}{16} + \cdots$ is a geometric series with $a = 4$ and $r = \dfrac{-1}{4}$. Since $|r| < 1$, the series converges.

Step 2: $S = \dfrac{a}{1-r} = \dfrac{4}{1 - \dfrac{-1}{4}} = \dfrac{4}{\dfrac{5}{4}} = \dfrac{16}{5} = 3.2$

Error Bound

If an alternating series converges to the sum S, then S lies between two consecutive partial sums of the series. If S is approximated by a partial sum s_n, the absolute error $|S - s_n|$ is less than the next term of the series a_{n+1}, and the sign of $S - s_n$ is the same as the coefficient of a_{n+1}.

Example 1

$4 - 1 + \dfrac{1}{4} - \dfrac{1}{16} + \cdots$ converges to 3.2. This value is greater than s_n for n odd, and less than s_n for n even. If S is approximated by the third partial sum, $s_3 = 3.25$, the absolute error

$|S - s_3| = |3.2 - 3.25| = |-0.05| = 0.05$, which is clearly less than $a_4 = \dfrac{1}{16} = 0.0625$. The coefficient of a_4 is negative, as is $S - s_3$.

Example 2

If S is the sum of the series $\displaystyle\sum_{n=1}^{\infty} \dfrac{(-1)^n}{n!}$ and s_n, its *nth* partial sum, find the maximum value of $\left| S - s_4 \right|$.

Note that $\displaystyle\sum_{n=1}^{\infty} \dfrac{(-1)^n}{n!} = -\dfrac{1}{1!} + \dfrac{1}{2!} - \dfrac{1}{3!} + \dots$ is an alternating series such that $a_1 > a_2 > a_3 \dots$,

i.e., $a_n > a_{n+1}$ and $\displaystyle\lim_{n\to\infty} a_n = \lim_{n\to\infty} \dfrac{1}{n!} = 0$. Therefore, $|S - s_n| \leq a_{n+1}$, and in this case

$|S - s_4| \leq a_5$, and $a_5 = \dfrac{1}{5!} = \dfrac{1}{120}$. Thus, $|S - s_4| \leq \dfrac{1}{120}$.

Example 3

The series $\displaystyle\sum_{n=1}^{\infty} \dfrac{(-1)^n}{\sqrt{n}}$ satisfies the hypotheses of the alternating series test, i.e., $a_n \geq a_{n+1}$ and

$\displaystyle\lim_{n\to\infty} a_n = 0$. If S is the sum of the series $\displaystyle\sum_{n=1}^{\infty} \dfrac{(-1)^n}{\sqrt{n}}$ and s_n is the *nth* partial sum, find the

minimum value of n for which the alternating series error bound guarantees that $|S - s_n| < 0.01$.

Since the series $\displaystyle\sum_{n=1}^{\infty} \dfrac{(-1)^n}{\sqrt{n}}$ satisfies the hypotheses of the alternating series test, $|S - s_n| \leq a_{n+1}$,

and in this case, $a_{n+1} = \dfrac{1}{\sqrt{n+1}}$. Set $a_{n+1} \leq 0.01$, and you have $\dfrac{1}{\sqrt{n+1}} \leq 0.01$, which

yields $10{,}000 \leq n + 1$. Therefore, $n \geq 9999$. The minimum value of n is 9999.

Absolute and Conditional Convergence

1. A series $\displaystyle\sum_{n=1}^{\infty} a_n$ is said to **converge absolutely** if the series of absolute values $\displaystyle\sum_{n=1}^{\infty} |a_n|$ converges.

2. An alternating series $\displaystyle\sum_{n=1}^{\infty} a_n$ is said to **converge conditionally** if the series $\displaystyle\sum_{n=1}^{\infty} a_n$ converges but not absolutely.

3. If a series converges absolutely, then it converges, i.e., if $\displaystyle\sum_{n=1}^{\infty} |a_n|$ converges, then $\displaystyle\sum_{n=1}^{\infty} a_n$ converges.

4. If $\displaystyle\sum_{n=1}^{\infty} |a_n|$ diverges, then $\displaystyle\sum_{n=1}^{\infty} a_n$ may or may not converge.

Example 1

Determine whether the series $-1 + \dfrac{1}{3} - \dfrac{1}{9} + \dfrac{1}{27} \cdots = \displaystyle\sum_{n=1}^{\infty} (-1)^n \dfrac{1}{3^{n-1}}$ converges.

Step 1: Consider the series $\sum_{n=1}^{\infty} \left| \dfrac{(-1)^n}{3^{n-1}} \right| = 1 + \dfrac{1}{3} + \dfrac{1}{9} + \dfrac{1}{27} + \cdots$. For this series, $s_1 = 1$,

$s_2 = 1 + \dfrac{1}{3} = \dfrac{4}{3} = 1.\bar{3}$, $s_3 = 1 + \dfrac{1}{3} + \dfrac{1}{9} = \dfrac{13}{9} = 1.\bar{4}$, $s_4 = 1 + \dfrac{1}{3} + \dfrac{1}{9} + \dfrac{1}{27} = \dfrac{40}{27} = 1.\overline{481}$. The

sequence of partial sums, $\{1, 1.\bar{3}, 1.\bar{4}, 1.\overline{481}, \ldots\}$, converges to 1.5. Or, note

that this is a geometric series with $a = 1$, $r = \dfrac{1}{3}$; thus, it converges to $\dfrac{3}{2}$.

Step 2: Since $\sum_{n=1}^{\infty} \left| (-1)^n \dfrac{1}{3^{n-1}} \right|$ converges, $\sum_{n=1}^{\infty} (-1)^n \dfrac{1}{3^{n-1}}$ converges absolutely, and thus

converges.

Example 2

Determine whether the series $\sum_{n=3}^{\infty} \dfrac{(-1)^{n+1} \ln n}{n}$ converges absolutely, converges conditionally,

or diverges. Begin by examining the series of absolute values $\sum_{n=3}^{\infty} \left| \dfrac{(-1)^{n+1} \ln n}{n} \right| = \dfrac{\ln 3}{3} + \dfrac{\ln 4}{4} +$

$\dfrac{\ln 5}{5} + \cdots$. Compare this series with the harmonic series $\sum_{n=3}^{\infty} \dfrac{1}{n} = \dfrac{1}{3} + \dfrac{1}{4} + \dfrac{1}{5} + \cdots$, which diverges.

Since the terms of the series $\dfrac{\ln 3}{3} + \dfrac{\ln 4}{4} + \dfrac{\ln 5}{5} + \cdots$ are greater than the terms of the series

$\dfrac{1}{3} + \dfrac{1}{4} + \dfrac{1}{5} + \cdots$, the series $\sum_{n=3}^{\infty} \left| \dfrac{(-1)^{n+1} \ln n}{n} \right|$ diverges and thus the series $\sum_{n=3}^{\infty} \dfrac{(-1)^{n+1} \ln n}{n}$ does

not converge absolutely. Next examine the series $\sum_{n=3}^{\infty} \dfrac{(-1)^{n+1} \ln n}{n} = \dfrac{\ln 3}{3} + \dfrac{\ln 4}{4} + \dfrac{\ln 5}{5} - \dfrac{\ln 6}{6} +$

$\cdots$, which is an alternating series. Now apply the tests for convergence for alternating series.

You must show that $a_n \geq a_{n+1}$ and $\lim_{n \to \infty} a_n = 0$ for convergence. Let $f(x) = \dfrac{\ln x}{x}$. Note

that $f'(x) = \dfrac{\left(\dfrac{1}{x} \right)(x) - (1)\ln x}{x^2} = \dfrac{1 - \ln x}{x^2}$. If $x > e$, $f'(x) < 0$. Therefore, $f(x)$ is a

strictly decreasing function for $x > e$. Thus, for the series $\sum_{n=3}^{\infty} \dfrac{(-1)^{n+1} \ln n}{n}$, $a_n \geq a_{n+1}$ for

$n \geq 3$. Also for the $\lim_{n \to \infty} a_n$, you have $\lim_{n \to \infty} a_n = \lim_{n \to \infty} \dfrac{\ln n}{n}$ with $\lim_{n \to \infty} \ln n = \infty$ and $\lim_{n \to \infty} n = \infty$.

Applying *L'Hôpital's* Rule, you have $\lim_{n \to \infty} \dfrac{1/n}{1} = 0$. The series $\sum_{n=3}^{\infty} \dfrac{(-1)^{n+1} \ln n}{n}$ satisfies the

tests for convergence for an alternating series. Therefore, the series $\sum_{n=3}^{\infty} \dfrac{(-1)^{n+1} \ln n}{n}$

converges, but not absolutely, as shown earlier, i.e., $\sum_{n=3}^{\infty} \dfrac{(-1)^{n+1} \ln n}{n}$ converges conditionally.

Example 3

Determine whether the series $\sum_{n=1}^{\infty} (-1)^n \dfrac{2k+1}{5k-1}$ converges absolutely, converges conditionally,

or diverges.

The series $\sum_{n=1}^{\infty}(-1)^n\dfrac{2k+1}{5k-1}=-\dfrac{3}{4}+\dfrac{5}{9}-\dfrac{1}{2}\ldots$. Note that $\lim\limits_{n\to\infty}a_n=\lim\limits_{n\to\infty}\dfrac{2n+1}{5n-1}=\lim\limits_{n\to\infty}\dfrac{(2n+1)/n}{(5n-1)/n}=$

$\lim\limits_{n\to\infty}\dfrac{2+\dfrac{1}{n}}{5-\dfrac{1}{n}}=\dfrac{2}{5}\neq0.$

Therefore, according to the Divergence Test, the series diverges.

14.5 Power Series

Main Concepts: Power Series, Radius and Interval of Convergence

A power series is a series of the form $\sum_{n=1}^{\infty}c_nx^n$, where c_1, c_2, c_3, $\ldots$ are constants, and x is a variable.

Radius and Interval of Convergence

A power series centered at $x=a$ converges only for $x=a$, for all real values of x, or for all x in some open interval $(a-R, a+R)$, called the interval of convergence. The radius of convergence is R. If the series converges on $(a-R, a+R)$, then it diverges if $x < a-R$ or $x > a+R$: but convergence or divergence must be investigated individually at $x = a - R$ and at $x = a + R$.

Example 1

Find the values of x for which the series $1 + x + \dfrac{x^2}{2!} + \dfrac{x^3}{3!} + \cdots + \dfrac{x^n}{n!} + \cdots$ converges.

Step 1: Use the ratio test. $\lim\limits_{n\to\infty}\left|\dfrac{a_{n+1}}{a_n}\right| = \lim\limits_{n\to\infty}\left|\dfrac{x^{n+1}}{(n+1)!}\cdot\dfrac{n!}{x^n}\right| = \lim\limits_{n\to\infty}\left|\dfrac{x}{n+1}\right| = 0$

Step 2: The series converges absolutely, so $\sum_{n=1}^{\infty}\dfrac{x^n}{n!}$ converges for all real x.

Example 2

Find the interval of convergence for the series $\sum_{n=1}^{\infty}\dfrac{(x-2)^n}{n}$.

Step 1: Use the ratio test. $\lim\limits_{n\to\infty}\left|\dfrac{a_{n+1}}{a_n}\right| = \lim\limits_{n\to\infty}\left|\dfrac{(x-2)^{n+1}}{n+1}\cdot\dfrac{n}{(x-2)^n}\right| = \lim\limits_{n\to\infty}\left|\dfrac{n(x-2)}{n+1}\right| = |x-2|$

Step 2: The series converges absolutely when $|x-2| < 1$, $-1 < x-2 < 1$, or $1 < x < 3$.

Step 3: When $x = 1$, the series becomes $\sum_{n=1}^{\infty}\dfrac{(-1)^n}{n} = -1 + \dfrac{1}{2} - \dfrac{1}{3} + \dfrac{1}{4} - \dfrac{1}{5}\cdots$. Since $1 >$

$\dfrac{1}{2} > \dfrac{1}{3} > \dfrac{1}{4} > \dfrac{1}{5} > \cdots$ and $\lim\limits_{n\to\infty}\dfrac{1}{n} = 0$, this alternating series converges. When

$x = 3$, the series becomes $\sum_{n=1}^{\infty}\dfrac{1}{n} = 1 + \dfrac{1}{2} + \dfrac{1}{3} + \dfrac{1}{4} + \dfrac{1}{5}\cdots$ which is a p-series with

$p = 1$, and therefore diverges. Therefore, the interval of convergence is $[1, 3)$.

14.6 Taylor Series

Main Concepts: Taylor Series and MacLaurin Series, Common MacLaurin Series

Taylor Series and MacLaurin Series

A Taylor polynomial approximates the value of a function $f(x)$ at the point $x = a$. If the function and all its derivatives exist at $x = a$, then on the interval of convergence, the Taylor series $\sum\limits_{n=0}^{\infty} \dfrac{f^{(n)}(a)}{n!}(x - a)^n$ converges to $f(x)$. The MacLaurin series is the name given to a Taylor series centered at $x = 0$.

Example 1

Find the Taylor polynomial of degree 3 for $f(x) = \dfrac{1}{x + 2}$ about the point $x = 3$.

Step 1: Differentiate: $f'(x) = \dfrac{-1}{(x + 2)^2}$, $f''(x) = \dfrac{2}{(x + 2)^3}$, $f'''(x) = \dfrac{-6}{(x + 2)^4}$.

Step 2: Evaluate: $f(3) = \dfrac{1}{5}$, $f'(3) = \dfrac{-1}{25}$, $f''(3) = \dfrac{2}{125}$, $f'''(x) = \dfrac{-6}{625}$.

Step 3: $\dfrac{f(3)}{0!} = \dfrac{1/5}{1} = \dfrac{1}{5}$, $\dfrac{f'(3)}{1!} = \dfrac{-1/25}{1} = \dfrac{-1}{25}$, $\dfrac{f''(3)}{2!} = \dfrac{2/125}{2} = \dfrac{1}{125}$, $\dfrac{f'''(3)}{3!} = \dfrac{6/625}{6} = \dfrac{1}{125}$

Step 4: $\sum\limits_{n=0}^{3} \dfrac{f^{(n)}(a)}{n!}(x - a)^n = \dfrac{1}{5} - \dfrac{(x - 3)}{25} + \dfrac{(x - 3)^2}{125} - \dfrac{(x - 3)^3}{625}$

Example 2

A function $f(x)$ is approximated by the third order Taylor series $1 + 2(x - 1) - (x - 1)^2 + (x - 1)^3$ centered at $x = 1$. Find $f'(1)$ and $f'''(1)$.

Step 1: Compare $\sum\limits_{n=0}^{\infty} \dfrac{f^{(n)}(a)}{n!}(x - a)^n$ to the given polynomial: $\dfrac{f(1)}{0!} = 1$, $\dfrac{f'(1)}{1!} = 2$, $\dfrac{f''(1)}{2!} = -1$, and $\dfrac{f'''(1)}{3!} = 1$.

Step 2: $f'(1) = 2 \cdot 1! = 2$ and $f'''(1) = 1 \cdot 3! = 6$.

Example 3

Find the MacLaurin polynomial of degree 4 that approximates $f(x) = \ln(1 + x)$.

Step 1: Differentiate: $f'(x) = \dfrac{1}{1 + x}$, $f''(x) = \dfrac{-1}{(1 + x)^2}$, $f'''(x) = \dfrac{2}{(1 + x)^3}$, $f^{(4)}(x) = \dfrac{-6}{(1 + x)^4}$.

Step 2: Evaluate: $f(0) = 0$, $f'(0) = 1$, $f''(0) = -1$, $f'''(0) = 2$, $f^{(4)}(0) = -6$.

Step 3: $\dfrac{f(0)}{0!}x^0 + \dfrac{f'(0)}{1!}x^1 + \dfrac{f''(0)}{2!}x^2 + \dfrac{f'''(0)}{3!}x^3 + \dfrac{f^{(4)}(0)}{4!}x^4 = \dfrac{0}{1}x^0 + \dfrac{1}{1}x^1 +$

$\dfrac{-1}{2}x^2 + \dfrac{2}{6}x^3 + \dfrac{-6}{24}x^4 = x - \dfrac{1}{2}x^2 + \dfrac{1}{3}x^3 - \dfrac{1}{4}x^4$

Example 4

Find the Taylor series for the function $f(x) = e^{-x}$ about the point $x = \ln 2$.

Step 1: $f^{(n)}(x) = e^{-x}$ when n is even and $f^{(n)}(x) = -e^{-x}$ when n is odd.

Step 2: Evaluate $f^{(n)}(\ln 2) = e^{-\ln 2} = \dfrac{1}{2}$ when n is even and $f^{(n)}(\ln 2) = \dfrac{-1}{2}$ when n is odd.

Step 3: $f(x) = e^{-x} = \dfrac{1/2}{0!}(x - \ln 2)^0 + \dfrac{-1/2}{1!}(x - \ln 2)^1 + \dfrac{1/2}{2!}(x - \ln 2)^2 + \cdots$

$= \displaystyle\sum_{n=0}^{\infty} \dfrac{(-1)^n}{2 \cdot n!}(x - \ln 2)^n$

Example 5

Find the MacLaurin series for the function $f(x) = xe^x$.

Step 1: Investigating the first few derivatives of $f(x) = xe^x$ shows that $f^{(n)}(x) = xe^x + ne^x$.

Step 2: Evaluating $f^{(n)}(x) = xe^x + ne^x$ at $x = 0$ gives $f^{(n)}(0) = n$.

Step 3: $f(x) = \displaystyle\sum_{n=0}^{\infty} \dfrac{f^{(n)}(0)}{n!}x^n = \sum_{n=0}^{\infty} \dfrac{n}{n!}x^n = \sum_{n=1}^{\infty} \dfrac{x^n}{(n-1)!}$

Common MacLaurin Series

MacLaurin Series for the Functions e^x, $\sin x$, $\cos x$, and $\dfrac{1}{1-x}$

Familiarity with these common MacLaurin series will simplify many problems.

$$f(x) = e^x = \sum_{n=0}^{\infty} \dfrac{x^n}{n!} = 1 + x + \dfrac{x^2}{2} + \dfrac{x^3}{6} + \cdots$$

$$f(x) = \sin x = \sum_{n=0}^{\infty} \dfrac{(-1)^n x^{2n+1}}{(2n+1)!} = x - \dfrac{x^3}{3!} + \dfrac{x^5}{5!} - \dfrac{x^7}{7!} + \cdots$$

$$f(x) = \cos x = \sum_{n=0}^{\infty} \dfrac{(-1)^n x^{2n}}{(2n)!} = 1 - \dfrac{x^2}{2} + \dfrac{x^4}{24} - \dfrac{x^6}{6!} + \cdots$$

$$f(x) = \dfrac{1}{1-x} = \sum_{n=0}^{\infty} x^n = 1 + x + x^2 + x^3 + \cdots$$

14.7 Operations on Series

Main Concepts: Substitution, Differentiation and Integration, Error Bounds

Substitution

New series can be generated by making an appropriate substitution in a known series.

Example 1

Find the MacLaurin series for $f(x) = \dfrac{1}{1 + x^2}$.

Step 1: Begin with the known series $f(x) = \dfrac{1}{1 - x} = \displaystyle\sum_{n=0}^{\infty} x^n$.

Step 2: Substitute $-x^2$ for x.

$$\frac{1}{1 + x^2} = \sum_{n=0}^{\infty}(-x^2)^n = \sum_{n=0}^{\infty}(-1)^n x^{2n} = 1 - x^2 + x^4 - x^6 + \cdots$$

Example 2

Find the first four non-zero terms of the MacLaurin series for $f(x) = \cos(2x)$.

Step 1: Begin with the known series $\cos x = 1 - \dfrac{x^2}{2!} + \dfrac{x^4}{4!} - \dfrac{x^6}{6!} + \cdots$

Step 2: Substitute $2x$ for x. $\cos(2x) = 1 - \dfrac{(2x)^2}{2!} + \dfrac{(2x)^4}{4!} - \dfrac{(2x)^6}{6!} + \cdots = 1 - \dfrac{4x^2}{2} + \dfrac{16x^4}{24} -$

$\dfrac{64x^6}{720} + \cdots = 1 - 2x^2 + \dfrac{2}{3}x^4 - \dfrac{4}{45}x^6$

Differentiation and Integration

If a function $f(x)$ is represented by a Taylor series with a non-zero radius of convergence, the derivative $f'(x)$ can be found by differentiating the series term by term. If the series is integrated term-by-term, the resulting series converges to $\displaystyle\int f(x)dx$. In either case, the radius of convergence is identical to that of the original series.

Example 1

Differentiate the MacLaurin series for $f(x) = \ln(x + 1)$ to find the Taylor series expansion for $f(x) = \dfrac{1}{x + 1}$.

Step 1: $f(x) = \ln(x + 1) = x - \dfrac{1}{2}x^2 + \dfrac{1}{3}x^3 - \dfrac{1}{4}x^4 + \cdots$

Step 2: $f'(x) = \dfrac{1}{x + 1} = 1 - x + x^2 - x^3 + \cdots = \displaystyle\sum_{n=0}^{\infty}(-1)^n x^n$

Example 2

Find the MacLaurin series for $f(x) = \dfrac{1}{(x + 1)^2}$.

Step 1: We know that $\dfrac{1}{x + 1} = 1 - x + x^2 - x^3 + \cdots = \displaystyle\sum_{n=0}^{\infty}(-1)^n x^n$.

Step 2: Differentiate: $\dfrac{-1}{(x+1)^2} = -1 + 2x - 3x^2 + 4x^3 - \cdots = \displaystyle\sum_{n=0}^{\infty} (-1)^{n+1}(n+1)x^n$.

Step 3: Multiply by -1.

$$\frac{1}{(x+1)^2} = 1 - 2x + 3x^2 - 4x^3 + \cdots = \sum_{n=0}^{\infty} (-1)^n (n+1)x^n$$

Example 3

Use a MacLaurin series to approximate the integral $\displaystyle\int_0^1 \sin(x^2)\,dx$ to three decimal place accuracy.

Step 1: Substitute x^2 for x in the MacLaurin series representing $\sin x$.

$$\sin(x^2) = (x^2) - \frac{(x^2)^3}{3!} + \frac{(x^2)^5}{5!} - \frac{(x^2)^7}{7!} \cdots = x^2 - \frac{x^6}{3!} + \frac{x^{10}}{5!} - \frac{x^{14}}{7!} + \cdots$$

Step 2: $\displaystyle\int_0^1 \sin(x^2)\,dx = \int_0^1 \left(x^2 - \frac{x^6}{3!} + \frac{x^{10}}{5!} - \frac{x^{14}}{7!} \cdots \right) dx = \frac{x^3}{3} - \frac{x^7}{7 \cdot 3!} + \frac{x^{11}}{11 \cdot 5!} -$

$\dfrac{x^{15}}{15 \cdot 7!} + \cdots \Big|_0^1 = \dfrac{1}{3} - \dfrac{1}{7 \cdot 3!} + \dfrac{1}{11 \cdot 5!} - \dfrac{1}{15 \cdot 7!} + \cdots = \displaystyle\sum_{n=0}^{\infty} \dfrac{1}{(4n+3)(2n+1)!}$

Step 3: For this alternating series, the absolute error for the nth partial sum is less than the

$n+1$ term so $|S - s_n| < \dfrac{1}{(4n+4)(2n+2)!}$. We want three decimal place accuracy,

so we need $|S - s_n| < \dfrac{1}{(4n+4)(2n+2)!} \leq 0.0005$ or $2000 \leq (4n+4)(2n+2)!$

This occurs for $n \geq 2$.

Step 4: Taking the sum $a_0 + a_1 + a_2 = \dfrac{1}{3} - \dfrac{1}{7.3!} + \dfrac{1}{11 \cdot 5!} = 0.3103$, $\displaystyle\int_0^1 \sin(x^2)\,dx \approx 0.3103$.

Error Bounds

The remainder, $R_n(x)$, for a Taylor series is the difference between the actual value of the function $f(x)$ and the nth partial sum that approximates the function. If the function $f(x)$ can be differentiated $n+1$ times on an interval containing x_0, and if $|f^{(n+1)}(x)| \leq M$ for all x in that interval, then $|R_n(x)| \leq \dfrac{M}{(n+1)!}|x - x_0|^{n+1}$ for all x in the interval.

Example 1

Approximate $\sqrt{e}$ accurate to three decimal places.

Step 1: Substitute $\dfrac{1}{2}$ for x in the MacLaurin series representation for e^x.

$$e^{1/2} = \sum_{n=0}^{\infty} \frac{(1/2)^n}{n!} = 1 + \frac{1}{2} + \frac{(1/2)^2}{2} + \frac{(1/2)^3}{6} + \cdots$$

$$= 1 + \frac{1}{2} + \frac{1}{8} + \frac{1}{48} + \cdots = \sum_{n=0}^{\infty} \frac{1}{2^n \cdot n!}$$

Step 2: For three decimal place accuracy, we want to find the value of n for which the remainder is less than or equal to 0.0005. Choose $x_0 = 1$ in the interval $(0, 1)$. All derivatives of e^x are equal to e^x, and therefore $|f^{(n+1)}(x)| \leq e$, so

$$M = e \cdot \left| R_n\left(\frac{1}{2}\right) \right| \leq \frac{e}{(n+1)!} \left| \frac{1}{2} - 1 \right|^{n+1} \text{ and } \frac{e}{(n+1)!} \left| \frac{1}{2} - 1 \right|^{n+1} = \frac{e}{2^{n+1} \cdot (n+1)!} \leq$$

0.0005 when $n \geq 4$.

Step 3: $\sqrt{e} = \sum_{n=0}^{4} \frac{1}{2^n \cdot n!} = 1 + \frac{1}{2} + \frac{1}{2^2 \cdot 2!} + \frac{1}{2^3 \cdot 3!} + \frac{1}{2^4 \cdot 4!} = 1.6484$

Example 2

Estimate $\sin 4°$ accurate to five decimal places.

Step 1: $4° = \dfrac{\pi}{45}$ radians. Substitute $\dfrac{\pi}{45}$ for x in the MacLaurin series that represents

$\sin x \cdot \sin \dfrac{\pi}{45} = \dfrac{\pi}{45} - \dfrac{(\pi/45)^3}{3!} + \dfrac{(\pi/45)^5}{5!} - \dfrac{(\pi/45)^7}{7!} + \cdots$

Step 2: For five decimal place accuracy, we must find the value of n for which the absolute error is less than or equal to 5×10^{-6}. For all x, $|f^{(n+1)}(x)| \leq 1$. Choose $x_0 = 0$.

$\left| R_n\left(\dfrac{\pi}{45}\right) \right| \leq \dfrac{1}{(n+1)!} \left| \dfrac{\pi}{45} - 0 \right|^{n+1} = \dfrac{(\pi/45)^{n+1}}{(n+1)!}$. The absolute error is less than or

equal to 5×10^{-6} for $n \geq 3$.

Step 3: $\sin 4° = \sin \dfrac{\pi}{45} = \dfrac{\pi}{45} - \dfrac{(\pi/45)^3}{3!} + \dfrac{(\pi/45)^5}{5!} - \dfrac{(\pi/45)^7}{7!} = 0.069756$

14.8 Rapid Review

1. Find the sum of the series $81 + 27 + 9 + 3 + 1 + \dfrac{1}{3} + \cdots$.

   Answer: This is a geometric series with first term 81 and a ratio of $\dfrac{1}{3}$,

   so $S = \dfrac{81}{1 - 1/3} = \dfrac{243}{2}$.

2. Determine whether the series $\sum_{n=1}^{\infty} \dfrac{5^n}{n!}$ converges or diverges.

   Answer: $\lim_{n \to \infty} \dfrac{5^{n+1}}{(n+1)!} \cdot \dfrac{n!}{5^n} = \lim_{n \to \infty} \dfrac{5}{n+1} = 0$ so $\sum_{n=1}^{\infty} \dfrac{5^n}{n!}$ converges by ratio test.

3. Determine whether the series $\sum_{n=1}^{\infty} \dfrac{\ln n}{\sqrt{n}}$ converges or diverges.

   Answer: $\dfrac{\ln n}{\sqrt{n}} > \dfrac{1}{\sqrt{n}}$ for $n > e$. $\sum_{n=1}^{\infty} \dfrac{1}{\sqrt{n}}$ is a p-series with $p < 1$, so it diverges.

   $\sum_{n=1}^{\infty} \dfrac{\ln n}{\sqrt{n}} = \dfrac{\ln 2}{\sqrt{2}} + \sum_{n=3}^{\infty} \dfrac{\ln n}{\sqrt{n}}$ and $\sum_{n=3}^{\infty} \dfrac{\ln n}{\sqrt{n}}$ diverges by comparison to $\sum_{n=3}^{\infty} \dfrac{1}{\sqrt{n}}$, so the

   series diverges.

4. Determine whether the series $\sum\limits_{n=1}^{\infty} \dfrac{n}{n^2 + 1}$ converges or diverges.

    Answer: $\lim\limits_{n\to\infty} \dfrac{\frac{n}{n^2+1}}{\frac{1}{n}} = \lim\limits_{n\to\infty} \dfrac{n^2}{n^2+1} = 1$ and $\sum\limits_{n=1}^{\infty} \dfrac{1}{n}$ diverges, so $\sum\limits_{n=1}^{\infty} \dfrac{n}{n^2+1}$ diverges by

    limit comparison with $\sum\limits_{n=1}^{\infty} \dfrac{1}{n}$.

5. Determine whether the series $\sum\limits_{n=1}^{\infty} \dfrac{50}{n(n+1)}$ converges or diverges.

    Answer: Since $\displaystyle\int_1^{\infty} \dfrac{50}{x(x+1)}\,dx = 50 \lim\limits_{k\to\infty} \int_1^k \left(\dfrac{1}{x} + \dfrac{-1}{x+1}\right) dx$

    $= 50 \lim\limits_{k\to\infty} [\ln x - \ln(x+1)]_1^k = 50 \lim\limits_{k\to\infty} [\ln k - \ln(k+1) + \ln 2]$

    $= 50 \lim\limits_{k\to\infty} \left[\ln \dfrac{k}{k+1} + \ln 2\right] = 50 \ln 2$, $\sum\limits_{n=1}^{\infty} \dfrac{50}{n(n+1)}$ converges by integral test.

6. Determine whether the series $\sum\limits_{n=1}^{\infty} (-1)^n \dfrac{3}{2n}$ converges absolutely, converges conditionally, or diverges.

    Examine the absolute values of $\sum\limits_{n=1}^{\infty} \left|(-1)^n \dfrac{3}{2n}\right| = \sum\limits_{n=1}^{\infty} \dfrac{3}{2n} = \dfrac{3}{2}\sum\limits_{n=1}^{\infty} \dfrac{1}{n}$. Since $\sum\limits_{n=1}^{\infty} \dfrac{1}{n}$ is a

    harmonic series that diverges, the series $\sum\limits_{n=1}^{\infty} \left|(-1)^n \dfrac{3}{2n}\right|$ diverges and $\sum\limits_{n=1}^{\infty} (-1)^n \dfrac{3}{2n}$ does

    not converge absolutely. Now examine the alternating series $\sum\limits_{n=1}^{\infty} (-1)^n \dfrac{3}{2n}$. Rewrite

    $\sum\limits_{n=1}^{\infty} (-1)^n \left(\dfrac{3}{2n}\right)$ as $\dfrac{3}{2}\sum\limits_{n=1}^{\infty} \dfrac{(-1)^n}{n}$. Since $\sum\limits_{n=1}^{\infty} \dfrac{(-1)^n}{n}$ is an alternating harmonic series that

    converges, therefore $\dfrac{3}{2}\sum\limits_{n=1}^{\infty} \dfrac{(-1)^n}{n}$ converges, and the series $\sum\limits_{n=1}^{\infty} (-1)^n \dfrac{3}{2n}$ converges

    conditionally.

7. Find the interval to convergence for the series $\sum\limits_{n=1}^{\infty} \dfrac{(x+1)^n}{\sqrt{n}}$.

    Answer: $\lim\limits_{n\to\infty} \left|\dfrac{(x+1)^{n+1}}{\sqrt{n+1}} \cdot \dfrac{\sqrt{n}}{(x+1)^n}\right| = \lim\limits_{n\to\infty} \left|\dfrac{\sqrt{n}(x+1)}{\sqrt{n+1}}\right| = |x+1|$. Since $|x+1| < 1$

    when $-1 < x+1 < 1$ or $-2 \le x < 0$, the series converges on $(-2, 0)$. When

    $x = -2$, the series becomes $\sum\limits_{n=1}^{\infty} \dfrac{(-1)^n}{\sqrt{n}}$. Since $1 > \dfrac{1}{\sqrt{2}} > \dfrac{1}{\sqrt{3}} > \dfrac{1}{2} > \cdots$ and

    $\lim\limits_{n\to\infty} \dfrac{1}{\sqrt{n}} = 0$, this alternating series converges. When $x = 0$, the series becomes

$\sum_{n=1}^{\infty} \dfrac{1}{\sqrt{n}}$, which is a p-series with $p = \dfrac{1}{2}$, and therefore diverges. Thus, the interval of convergence is $[-2, 0)$.

8. Approximate the function $f(x) = \dfrac{1}{x + 2}$ with a fourth degree Taylor polynomial centered at $x = 3$.

    Answer: $f(3) = \dfrac{1}{5}$, $f'(x) = \dfrac{-1}{(x + 2)^2} \Rightarrow f'(3) = \dfrac{-1}{25}$,

    $f''(x) = \dfrac{2}{(x + 2)^3} \Rightarrow f''(3) = \dfrac{2}{125}$, $f'''(x) = \dfrac{-6}{(x + 2)^4} \Rightarrow f'''(3) = \dfrac{-6}{625}$,

    $f^{(4)}(x) = \dfrac{24}{(x + 2)^5} \Rightarrow f^{(4)}(3) = \dfrac{24}{3125}$, so

    $$P(x) = \dfrac{1/5}{0!}(x - 3)^0 + \dfrac{-1/25}{1!}(x - 3)^1 + \dfrac{2/125}{2!}(x - 3)^2$$

    $$+ \dfrac{-6/625}{3!}(x - 3)^3 + \dfrac{24/3125}{4!}(x - 3)^4$$

    $$= \dfrac{1}{5} - \dfrac{x - 3}{25} + \dfrac{(x - 3)^2}{125} - \dfrac{(x - 3)^3}{625} + \dfrac{(x - 3)^4}{3125}.$$

9. Find the MacLaurin series for the function $f(x) = e^{-x}$ and determine its interval of convergence.

    Answer: Since $e^x = \sum \dfrac{x^n}{n!}$, substitute $-x$ to find

    $e^{-x} = \sum \dfrac{(-x)^n}{n!} = 1 - x + \dfrac{x^2}{2} - \dfrac{x^3}{6} + \cdots$. The ratio $\lim_{n \to \infty} \left| \dfrac{(-x)^{n+1}}{(n + 1)!} \dfrac{n!}{(-x)^n} \right|$

    $= \lim_{n \to \infty} \left| \dfrac{-x}{n + 1} \right| = 0$, so the series converges on the interval $(-\infty, \infty)$.

14.9 Practice Problems

For problems 1–5, determine whether each series converges or diverges.

1. $\displaystyle\sum_{n=0}^{\infty} 5^{-n}$

2. $\displaystyle\sum_{n=1}^{\infty} \dfrac{1}{n \cdot 2^n}$

3. $\displaystyle\sum_{n=0}^{\infty} \dfrac{n}{e^n}$

4. $\displaystyle\sum_{n=1}^{\infty} \dfrac{n + 1}{n(n + 2)}$

5. $\displaystyle\sum_{n=1}^{\infty} \dfrac{n}{(n + 1)^n}$

For problems 6–8, determine whether each series converges absolutely, converges conditionally, or diverges.

6. $\displaystyle\sum_{n=1}^{\infty} \frac{(-1)^{n-1}}{n!}$

7. $\displaystyle\sum_{n=1}^{\infty} (-1)^{n-1} \frac{n+1}{n}$

8. $\displaystyle\sum_{n=1}^{\infty} (-1)^n \frac{n+1}{7n^2-5}$

9. Find the sum of the geometric series

$\displaystyle\sum_{n=0}^{\infty} 4\left(\frac{1}{3}\right)^n.$

10. If the sum of the alternating series

$\displaystyle\sum_{n=1}^{\infty} \frac{(-1)^{n-1}}{2n-1}$ is approximated by s_{50}, find the maximum absolute error.

Find the interval of convergence for each series.

11. $\displaystyle\sum_{n=0}^{\infty} \frac{x^n}{1+n^2}$

12. $\displaystyle\sum_{n=1}^{\infty} \frac{3^n}{n^2} x^n$

13. The Taylor series representation of $\ln x$, centered at $x = a$.

Approximate each function with a fourth degree Taylor polynomial centered at the given value of x.

14. $f(x) = e^{x^2}$ at $x = 1$.

15. $f(x) = \cos \pi x$ at $x = \dfrac{1}{2}$.

16. $f(x) = \ln x$ at $x = e$.

Find the MacLaurin series for each function and determine its interval of convergence.

17. $f(x) = \dfrac{1}{1-x}$

18. $f(x) = \dfrac{1}{1+x^2}$

19. Estimate $\sin 9°$ accurate to three decimal places.

20. Find the rational number equivalent to $1.\overline{83}$.

14.10 Cumulative Review Problems

21. The movement of an object in the plane is defined by $x(t) = \ln t$, $y(t) = t^2$. Find the speed of the object at the moment when the acceleration is $a(t) = \langle -1, 2\rangle$.

22. Find the slope of the tangent line to the curve $r = 5\cos 3\theta$ when $\theta = \dfrac{2\pi}{3}$.

23. $\displaystyle\int_1^e x^3 \ln x \, dx$

24. $\displaystyle\int_0^1 \frac{5}{x^2 - x - 6} \, dx$

25. $\displaystyle\lim_{x \to 1} \frac{\ln x}{x^2 - 1}$

14.11 Solutions to Practice Problems

1. $\displaystyle\sum_{n=0}^{\infty} 5^{-n} = \sum \frac{1}{5^n} = 1 + \frac{1}{5} + \frac{1}{25} + \frac{1}{125}$
$+ \cdots$ is a geometric series with an initial term of one and a ratio of $\dfrac{1}{5}$. Since the

ratio is less than one, the series converges, and $\displaystyle\sum_{n=0}^{\infty} 5^{-n} = \frac{1}{1 - 1/5} = \frac{5}{4}$.

2. By the ratio test, $\lim\limits_{n\to\infty} \dfrac{1}{(n+1)\cdot 2^{n+1}} \cdot$

$\dfrac{n\cdot 2^n}{1} = \lim\limits_{n\to\infty} \dfrac{n}{2(n+1)} = \dfrac{1}{2}$; therefore,

$\sum\limits_{n=1}^{\infty} \dfrac{1}{n\cdot 2^n}$ converges.

3. Consider the integral $\int_0^\infty \dfrac{x}{e^x}dx =$

$\int_0^\infty xe^{-x}dx$. Integrate by parts, with

$u = x, du = dx, dv = e^{-x}dx$, and $v = -e^{-x}$.

$\int xe^{-x}dx = -xe^{-x}+$

$\int e^{-x}dx = -xe^{-x} - e^{-x} + C$. Therefore,

$\int_0^\infty xe^{-x}dx =$

$\lim\limits_{k\to\infty} \int_0^k xe^{-x}dx = \lim\limits_{k\to\infty}$

$\left[-xe^{-x} - e^{-x}\right]_0^k = \lim\limits_{k\to\infty}$

$-ke^{-k} - e^{-k} + 1 = 1$. Since the improper

integral converges, $\sum\limits_{n=0}^{\infty} \dfrac{n}{e^n}$ converges.

4. Use the limit comparison test, comparing

to the series $\sum\limits_{n=1}^{\infty} \dfrac{1}{n}$, which is known to

diverge. Divide $\dfrac{n+1}{n(n+2)} \div \dfrac{1}{n} =$

$\dfrac{(n+1)/n}{n/(n+2)} = \dfrac{n+1}{n+2}$. The limit

$\lim\limits_{n\to\infty} \dfrac{n+1}{n+2} = 1$, and $\sum\limits_{n=1}^{\infty} \dfrac{1}{n}$ diverges, so the

series $\sum \dfrac{n+1}{n(n+2)}$ diverges.

5. Use the ratio test.

$\lim\limits_{n\to\infty} \left[\dfrac{n+1}{(n+2)^{n+1}} \cdot \dfrac{(n+1)^n}{n}\right] =$

$\lim\limits_{n\to\infty} \left[\dfrac{(n+1)^{n+1}}{(n+2)^{n+1}} \cdot \dfrac{1}{n}\right] = 0$; therefore,

$\sum\limits_{n=1}^{\infty} \dfrac{n}{(n+1)^n}$ converges.

6. Use the ratio test,

$\lim\limits_{n\to\infty} \left|\dfrac{(-1)^n}{(n+1)!} \cdot \dfrac{n!}{(-1)^{n-1}}\right| =$

$\lim\limits_{n\to\infty} \left|\dfrac{-1}{n+1}\right| = \lim\limits_{n\to\infty} \dfrac{1}{n+1} = 0$, so the series

$\sum\limits_{n=1}^{\infty} \dfrac{(-1)^{n-1}}{n!}$ converges absolutely.

7. $\sum\limits_{n=1}^{\infty}(-1)^{n-1}\dfrac{n+1}{n}$

$= \sum\limits_{n=1}^{\infty}(-1)^{n-1}\left(1 + \dfrac{1}{n}\right)$

$= \sum\limits_{n=1}^{\infty}\left((-1)^{n-1} + \dfrac{(-1)^{n-1}}{n}\right)$

$= \sum\limits_{n=1}^{\infty}(-1)^{n-1} + \sum\limits_{n=1}^{\infty}\dfrac{(-1)^{n-1}}{n}$. Since $\sum\limits_{n=1}^{\infty}(-1)^{n-1}$

diverges, $\sum\limits_{n=1}^{\infty}(-1)^{n-1}\dfrac{n+1}{n}$ diverges.

8. Begin by inspecting the absolute values of

$\sum\limits_{n=1}^{\infty}\left|(-1)^n\dfrac{n+1}{7n^2-5}\right|$ which is equivalent to

$\sum\limits_{n=1}^{\infty}\dfrac{n+1}{7n^2-5}$. Applying the informal

principle, you have the series $7\sum\dfrac{1}{n}$.

Apply the limit comparison test and obtain

$\lim\limits_{n\to\infty}\dfrac{\frac{n+1}{7n^2-5}}{\frac{1}{n}} = \lim\limits_{n\to\infty}\dfrac{n+1}{7n^2-5}\cdot\dfrac{n}{1} =$

$\lim\limits_{n\to\infty}\dfrac{n^2+n}{7n^2-5} = \dfrac{1}{7}$. Since $\sum\limits_{n=1}^{\infty}\dfrac{1}{n}$ is a

harmonic series and it diverges, the series

$\sum\limits_{n=1}^{\infty}\dfrac{n+1}{7n^2-5}$ diverges. Therefore, the series

$\sum\limits_{n=1}^{\infty}(-1)^n\dfrac{n+1}{7n^2-5}$ does not converge

absolutely. Next examine the alternating

series $\sum\limits_{n=1}^{\infty}(-1)^n\dfrac{n+1}{7n^2-5}$. Let

$f(x) = \dfrac{x+1}{7x^2-5}$, and you have

$f'(x) = \dfrac{-(7x^2+14x+5)}{(7x^2-5)^2}, x \neq \pm\sqrt{\dfrac{5}{7}}$.

Note that $f'(x) < 0$ for $x \geq 1$ and

$x \neq \sqrt{\dfrac{5}{7}}$. Therefore, $f(x)$ is a strictly

decreasing function for $x \geq 1$ and

$x \neq \sqrt{\dfrac{5}{7}}$. Thus, for the series

$\displaystyle\sum_{n=1}^{\infty} (-1)^n \dfrac{n+1}{7n^2-5}$, $a_n \geq a_{n+1}$. Also,

note that $\displaystyle\lim_{n\to\infty} \dfrac{n+1}{7n^2-5} \lim_{n\to\infty} \dfrac{1}{14n} = 0$

(by using *L'Hôpital's* Rule).
Therefore, the alternating

series $\displaystyle\sum_{n=1}^{\infty} (-1)^n \dfrac{n+1}{7n^2-5}$ converges, and since

the series does not converge absolutely as
shown earlier, it converges conditionally.

9. The sum of the geometric series

$\displaystyle\sum_{n=0}^{\infty} 4\left(\dfrac{1}{3}\right)^n$ is $S = \dfrac{a_n}{1-r} = \dfrac{4}{1-1/3} = 6$.

10. For the alternating series $\displaystyle\sum_{n=1}^{\infty} \dfrac{(-1)^{n-1}}{2n-1}$

approximated by s_{50}, the maximum
absolute error $|R_n| < a_{n+1}$, so

$|R_{50}| < a_{51} = \dfrac{(-1)^{50}}{101} = \dfrac{1}{101} \approx 0.0099$.

11. Examine the ratio of successive terms.

$\left| \dfrac{x^{n+1}}{1+(n+1)^2} \cdot \dfrac{1+n^2}{x^n} \right| = \left| \dfrac{x(1+n^2)}{n^2+2n+2} \right|$.

Since $\displaystyle\lim_{n\to\infty} \left| \dfrac{x(1+n^2)}{n^2+2n+2} \right| = |x|$, the series

will converge when $|x| < 1$ or
$-1 < x < 1$. When $x = 1$, the series

becomes $\displaystyle\sum_{n=0}^{\infty} \dfrac{1}{1+n^2}$. This series is

term-by-term smaller than the p-series
with $p = 2$; therefore, the series converges.
When $x = -1$, the series becomes

$\displaystyle\sum_{n=0}^{\infty} \dfrac{(-1)^n}{1+n^2}$, which also converges.

Therefore, the interval of convergence
is $[-1, 1]$.

12. The ratio is $\left| \dfrac{(3x)^{n+1}}{(n+1)^2} \cdot \dfrac{n^2}{(3x)^n} \right| = \left| \dfrac{3xn^2}{(n+1)^2} \right|$

and $\displaystyle\lim_{n\to\infty} \left| \dfrac{3xn^2}{(n+1)^2} \right| = |3x|$ so the series will

converge when $|3x| < 1$. This tells you

that $-1 < 3x < 1$ and $\dfrac{-1}{3} < x < \dfrac{1}{3}$.

When $x = \dfrac{1}{3}$, the series becomes

$\displaystyle\sum_{n=1}^{\infty} \dfrac{3^n}{n^2}\left(\dfrac{1}{3}\right)^n = \sum_{n=1}^{\infty} \dfrac{1}{n^2}$, which is a

convergent p-series. When $x = -\dfrac{1}{3}$, the

series becomes $\displaystyle\sum_{n=1}^{\infty} \dfrac{3^n}{n^2}\left(-\dfrac{1}{3}\right)^n = \sum_{n=1}^{\infty} \dfrac{(-1)^n}{n^2}$,

a convergent alternating series. Therefore,

the interval of convergence is $\left[-\dfrac{1}{3}, \dfrac{1}{3}\right]$.

13. Represent $\ln x$ by a Taylor series.
Investigate the first few terms by finding
and evaluating the derivatives and
generating the first few terms.

$f(a) = \ln a$, $f'(a) = \dfrac{1}{a}$, $f''(a) = \dfrac{-1}{a^2}$,

$f'''(a) = \dfrac{2}{a^3}$, so $\ln x$ can be represented by

the series $= \dfrac{\ln a}{0!}(x-a)^0 + \dfrac{1/a}{1!}(x-a)^1$

$+ \dfrac{-1/a^2}{2!}(x-a)^2 + \dfrac{2/a^3}{3!}(x-a)^3 + \cdots$

$= \ln a + \dfrac{(x-a)}{a} - \dfrac{(x-a)^2}{2a^2} +$

$\dfrac{(x-a)^3}{3a^3} + \cdots + \dfrac{(-1)^{n-1}(x-a)^n}{na^n} + \cdots$

Using the ratio test,

$\displaystyle\lim_{n\to\infty} \left| \dfrac{(-1)^n(x-a)^{n+1}}{(n+1)a^{n+1}} \cdot \dfrac{na^n}{(-1)^{n-1}(x-a)^n} \right| =$

$\displaystyle\lim_{n\to\infty} \left| \dfrac{n}{(n+1)} \cdot \dfrac{(x-a)}{a} \right| = \left| \dfrac{x-a}{a} \right|$.

The series converges when $\left| \dfrac{x-a}{a} \right| < 1$,

that is, $-1 < \dfrac{x-a}{a} < 1$. Solving the

inequality, you find $-a < x - a < a$ or
$0 < x < 2a$. When $x = 0$, the series becomes

$\displaystyle\sum_{n=1}^{\infty} \dfrac{(-1)^{n-1}(-a)^n}{na^n} = \sum_{n=1}^{\infty} \dfrac{(-1)^{2n-1}}{n} = \sum_{n=1}^{\infty} \dfrac{-1}{n} = -\sum_{n=1}^{\infty} \dfrac{1}{n}$.

Since $\sum_{n=1}^{\infty} \dfrac{1}{n}$ diverges, this series diverges as well. When $x = 2a$, the series becomes $\sum_{n=1}^{\infty} \dfrac{(-1)^{n-1}(2a - a)^n}{na^n} = \sum_{n=1}^{\infty} \dfrac{(-1)^{n-1}}{n}$. This alternating series converges; therefore, the interval of convergence is $(0, 2a]$.

14. Calculate the derivatives and evaluate at $x = 1$. $f(x) = e^{x^2}$ and $f(1) = e$. $f'(x) = 2xe^{x^2}$ and $f'(1) = 2e$. $f''(x) = 4x^2 e^{x^2} + 2e^{x^2}$ and $f''(1) = 6e$. $f'''(x) = 8x^3 e^{x^2} + 12xe^{x^2}$ and $f'''(1) = 20e$. $f^{(4)}(x) = 16x^4 e^{x^2} + 48x^2 e^{x^2} + 12e^{x^2}$ and $f^{(4)}(1) = 76e$. Then the function $f(x) = e^{x^2}$ can be approximated by

$\dfrac{e}{0!}(x - 1)^0 + \dfrac{2e}{1!}(x - 1)^1 + \dfrac{6e}{2!}(x - 1)^2 +$

$\dfrac{20e}{3!}(x - 1)^3 + \dfrac{76e}{4!}(x - 1)^4$. Simplifying

$f(x) = e^{x^2} \approx e + 2e(x - 1) + 3e(x - 1)^2 +$

$\dfrac{10e}{3}(x - 1)^3 + \dfrac{19e}{6}(x - 1)^4$.

15. $f\left(\dfrac{1}{2}\right) = \cos\left(\dfrac{\pi}{2}\right) = 0$. Find the

derivatives and evaluate at $x = \dfrac{1}{2}$.

$f'\left(\dfrac{1}{2}\right) = -\pi \sin \pi x|_{x=1/2} = -\pi$,

$f''\left(\dfrac{1}{2}\right) = -\pi^2 \cos \pi x|_{x=1/2} = 0$,

$f'''\left(\dfrac{1}{2}\right) = \pi^3 \sin \pi x|_{x=1/2} = \pi^3$, and

$f^{(4)}\left(\dfrac{1}{2}\right) = \pi^4 \cos \pi x|_{x=1/2} = 0$. Then

$f(x) = \cos \pi x$ around $x = \dfrac{1}{2}$ can be

approximated by $\dfrac{0}{0!}\left(x - \dfrac{1}{2}\right)^0 +$

$\dfrac{-\pi}{1!}\left(x - \dfrac{1}{2}\right)^1 + \dfrac{0}{2!}\left(x - \dfrac{1}{2}\right)^2 +$

$\dfrac{\pi^3}{3!}\left(x - \dfrac{1}{2}\right)^3 + \dfrac{0}{4!}\left(x - \dfrac{1}{2}\right)^4$ or

$-\pi\left(x - \dfrac{1}{2}\right) + \dfrac{\pi^3}{6}\left(x - \dfrac{1}{2}\right)^3$.

16. At $x = e$, $f(e) = \ln e = 1$,

$f'(e) = \dfrac{1}{x}\Big|_{x=e} = \dfrac{1}{e}$, $f''(e) = \dfrac{-1}{x^2}\Big|_{x=e} = \dfrac{-1}{e^2}$,

$f'''(e) = \dfrac{2}{x^3}\Big|_{x=e} = \dfrac{2}{e^3}$, and

$f^{(4)}(e) = \dfrac{-6}{x^4}\Big|_{x=e} = \dfrac{-6}{e^4}$. $f(x) = \ln x$ can be

approximated by $\dfrac{1}{0!}(x - e)^0 +$

$\dfrac{1/e}{1!}(x - e)^1 + \dfrac{-1/e^2}{2!}(x - e)^2 + \dfrac{2/e^3}{3!}$

$(x - e)^3 + \dfrac{-6/e^4}{4!}(x - e)^4 = 1 + \dfrac{x - e}{e}$

$- \dfrac{(x - e)^2}{2e^2} + \dfrac{(x - e)^3}{3e^3} - \dfrac{(x - e)^4}{4e^4}$.

17. Calculate the derivatives and evaluate at

$x = 0$. $f(x) = \dfrac{1}{1 - x}$, $f(0) = 1$,

$f'(x) = \dfrac{1}{(1 - x)^2}$, $f'(0) = 1$,

$f''(x) = \dfrac{2}{(1 - x)^3}$, $f''(x) = 2$,

$f'''(x) = \dfrac{6}{(1 - x)^4}$, $f'''(x) = 6$,

$f^{(4)}(x) = \dfrac{24}{(1 - x)^5}$, $f^{(4)}(x) = 24$. In general,

$f^{(n)}(0) = n!$, so the MacLaurin series

$f(x) = \dfrac{1}{1 - x} = \sum_{n=0}^{\infty} \dfrac{f^{(n)}(x)}{n!}x^n =$

$\sum_{n=0}^{\infty} \dfrac{n!}{n!}x^n = \sum_{n=0}^{\infty} x^n$. The series converges to

$f(x) = \dfrac{1}{1 - x}$ when $\lim_{n \to \infty}\left|\dfrac{x^{n+1}}{x^n}\right| =$

$\lim_{n \to \infty} |x| < 1$. The series converges on

$(-1, 1)$. When $x = 1$, the series becomes

$\sum_{n=0}^{\infty} 1^n$, which diverges. When $x = -1$, the

series becomes $\sum_{n=0}^{\infty} (-1)^n$, which diverges.

Therefore, the interval of convergence
is $(-1, 1)$.

18. Begin with the known series $f(x) =$

$$\frac{1}{1-x} = \sum_{n=0}^{\infty} x^n = 1 + x + x^2 + x^3 + \cdots$$

and replace x with $-x^2$. Then $\dfrac{1}{1+x^2} =$

$$\frac{1}{1-(-x^2)} = 1 + (-x^2) + (-x^2)^2 +$$

$$(-x^2)^3 + \cdots = 1 - x^2 + x^4 - x^6 + \cdots =$$

$$\sum_{n=0}^{\infty} (-x^2)^n = \sum_{n=0}^{\infty} (-1)^n x^{2n}. \text{ The series}$$

converges to $f(x) = \dfrac{1}{1+x^2}$ when

$$\lim_{n \to \infty} \left| \frac{x^{2n+1}}{x^{2n}} \right| = \lim_{n \to \infty} |x| < 1. \text{ The series}$$

converges on $(-1, 1)$. When $x = 1$, the

series becomes $\displaystyle\sum_{n=0}^{\infty} (-1)^n$, which diverges.

When $x = -1$, the series becomes

$\displaystyle\sum_{n=0}^{\infty} (-1)^{3n}$, which diverges. Therefore, the

interval of convergence is $(-1, 1)$.

19. Use the MacLaurin series $f(x) =$

$$\sin x = \sum_{n=0}^{\infty} \frac{(-1)^n x^{2n+1}}{(2n+1)!} = x - \frac{x^3}{3!} + \frac{x^5}{5!}$$

$$-\frac{x^7}{7!} + \cdots \text{ with } 9° = \frac{\pi}{20}. \text{ Then}$$

$$\sin 9° = \sin \frac{\pi}{20} = \sum_{n=0}^{\infty} \frac{(-1)^n (\pi/20)^{2n+1}}{(2n+1)!}$$

$$= \frac{\pi}{20} - \frac{(\pi/20)^3}{3!} + \frac{(\pi/20)^5}{5!} -$$

$$\frac{(\pi/20)^7}{7!} + \cdots \approx 0.156.$$

20. $1.\overline{83} = 1 + \dfrac{83}{10^2} + \dfrac{83}{10^4} + \dfrac{83}{10^6} + \cdots$

$$= 1 + \sum_{n=1}^{\infty} \frac{83}{10^{2m}} = 1 + 83 \sum_{n=1}^{\infty} \frac{1}{10^{2m}}.$$

The geometric series $\displaystyle\sum_{n=1}^{\infty} \frac{1}{10^{2m}}$ converges

to $s = \dfrac{a}{1-r} = \dfrac{1/100}{1-1/100} = \dfrac{1}{99}.$

Therefore, $1.\overline{83} = 1 + 83 \displaystyle\sum_{n=1}^{\infty} \frac{1}{10^{2m}}$

$$= 1 + 83\left(\frac{1}{99}\right) = \frac{182}{99}.$$

14.12 Solutions to Cumulative Review Problems

21. $x'(t) = \dfrac{1}{t}$ $x''(t) = \dfrac{-1}{t^2}$ $y'(t) = 2t$

$y''(t) = 2$. The acceleration

$\left\langle \dfrac{-1}{t^2}, 2 \right\rangle = \langle -1, 2 \rangle$ when $t = 1$.

The speed of the object at time $t = 1$ is

$$\sqrt{\left(\frac{1}{t}\right)^2 + (2t)^2} = \sqrt{5}.$$

22. $x = 5\cos 3\theta \cos \theta$ and $y = 5\cos 3\theta \sin \theta$.

$\dfrac{dx}{d\theta} = -5\sin \theta \cos 3\theta - 15\cos \theta \sin 3\theta$, and

$\dfrac{dy}{d\theta} = 5\cos \theta \cos 3\theta - 15\sin \theta \sin 3\theta.$

$$\frac{dy}{dx} = \frac{5\cos \theta \cos 3\theta - 15\sin \theta \sin 3\theta}{-5\sin \theta \cos 3\theta - 15\cos \theta \sin 3\theta} =$$

$$\frac{3\sin \theta \sin 3\theta - \cos \theta \cos 3\theta}{3\cos \theta \sin 3\theta + \sin \theta \cos 3\theta}.$$

Evaluated at $\theta = \dfrac{2\pi}{3}$, $\dfrac{dy}{dx} =$

$$\frac{3\sin\left(\dfrac{2\pi}{3}\right) \sin 3\left(\dfrac{2\pi}{3}\right) - \cos\left(\dfrac{2\pi}{3}\right) \cos 3\left(\dfrac{2\pi}{3}\right)}{3\cos\left(\dfrac{2\pi}{3}\right) \sin 3\left(\dfrac{2\pi}{3}\right) + \sin\left(\dfrac{2\pi}{3}\right) \cos 3\left(\dfrac{2\pi}{3}\right)}$$

$$= \frac{1}{\sqrt{3}} = \frac{\sqrt{3}}{3}. \text{ The slope of the tangent is } \frac{\sqrt{3}}{3}.$$

23. Integrate by parts, using $u = \ln x$,

$dv = x^3 dx$, $du = \dfrac{1}{x} dx$, $v = \dfrac{x^4}{4}$. Then

$$\int x^3 \ln x\, dx = \frac{x^4}{4} \ln x - \int \frac{x^4}{4} \cdot \frac{1}{x} dx =$$

$$\frac{x^4}{4} \ln x - \frac{1}{4} \int x^3 dx = \frac{x^4}{4} \ln x - \frac{x^4}{16}.$$

Consider the limits of integration,

$$\int_1^e x^3 \ln x\, dx = \frac{x^4}{4} \ln x - \frac{x^4}{16} \bigg|_1^e =$$

$$\left(\frac{e^4}{4} \ln e - \frac{e^4}{16} \right) - \left(\frac{1^4}{4} \ln 1 - \frac{1^4}{16} \right) =$$

$$\frac{3e^4 + 1}{16} \approx 10.300.$$

24. Use partial fraction decomposition.

$$\frac{5}{x^2 - x - 6} = \frac{5}{(x-3)(x+2)} = \frac{A}{x-3} + \frac{B}{x+2}.$$

Solving the system

$$\begin{cases} A + B = 0 \\ 2A - 3B = 5 \end{cases}$$ gives $A = 1$, $B = -1$, and

$$\int_0^1 \frac{5}{x^2 - x - 6} dx = \int_0^1 \frac{1}{x-3} dx +$$

$$\int_0^1 \frac{-1}{x+2} dx. \text{ Then } \ln|x-3|\big|_0^1$$

$$-\ln|x+2|\big|_0^1 = 2\ln 2 - 2\ln 3 \approx -0.811.$$

25. $\displaystyle \lim_{x \to 1} \frac{\ln x}{x^2 - 1} = \lim_{x \to 1} \frac{1/x}{2x} = \lim_{x \to 1} \frac{1}{2x^2} = \frac{1}{2}.$

STEP 5

Build Your Test-Taking Confidence

AP Calculus BC Practice Exam 1
AP Calculus BC Practice Exam 2

AP Calculus BC Practice Exam 1

ANSWER SHEET FOR MULTIPLE-CHOICE QUESTIONS

Part A

1. (A) (B) (C) (D)
2. (A) (B) (C) (D)
3. (A) (B) (C) (D)
4. (A) (B) (C) (D)
5. (A) (B) (C) (D)
6. (A) (B) (C) (D)
7. (A) (B) (C) (D)
8. (A) (B) (C) (D)
9. (A) (B) (C) (D)
10. (A) (B) (C) (D)
11. (A) (B) (C) (D)
12. (A) (B) (C) (D)
13. (A) (B) (C) (D)
14. (A) (B) (C) (D)
15. (A) (B) (C) (D)
16. (A) (B) (C) (D)
17. (A) (B) (C) (D)
18. (A) (B) (C) (D)
19. (A) (B) (C) (D)
20. (A) (B) (C) (D)
21. (A) (B) (C) (D)
22. (A) (B) (C) (D)
23. (A) (B) (C) (D)
24. (A) (B) (C) (D)
25. (A) (B) (C) (D)
26. (A) (B) (C) (D)
27. (A) (B) (C) (D)
28. (A) (B) (C) (D)
29. (A) (B) (C) (D)
30. (A) (B) (C) (D)

Part B

76. (A) (B) (C) (D)
77. (A) (B) (C) (D)
78. (A) (B) (C) (D)
79. (A) (B) (C) (D)
80. (A) (B) (C) (D)
81. (A) (B) (C) (D)
82. (A) (B) (C) (D)
83. (A) (B) (C) (D)
84. (A) (B) (C) (D)
85. (A) (B) (C) (D)
86. (A) (B) (C) (D)
87. (A) (B) (C) (D)
88. (A) (B) (C) (D)
89. (A) (B) (C) (D)
90. (A) (B) (C) (D)

AP Calculus BC Practice Exam 1

ANSWER SHEET FOR MULTIPLE CHOICE QUESTIONS

Section I—Part A

Number of Questions	Time	Use of Calculator
30	60 Minutes	No

Directions:

Use the answer sheet provided on the previous page. All questions are given equal weight. Points are *not* deducted for incorrect answers and no points are given to unanswered questions. Unless otherwise indicated, the domain of a function f is the set of all real numbers. The use of a calculator is *not* permitted in this part of the exam.

1. What is the $\lim\limits_{x \to \ln 2} g(x)$, if

$$g(x) = \begin{cases} e^x \text{ if } x > \ln 2 \\ 4 - e^x \text{ if } x \le \ln 2 \end{cases}?$$

(A) -2 (B) $\ln 2$

(C) 2 (D) nonexistent

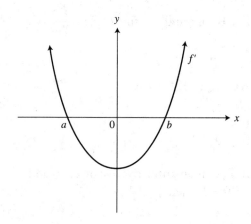

2. The graph of f' is shown above. A possible graph of f is (see below):

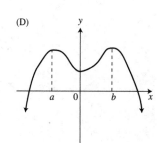

GO ON TO THE NEXT PAGE

3. What is $\lim\limits_{\Delta x \to 0} \dfrac{\sin\left(\dfrac{\pi}{3} + \Delta x\right) - \sin\left(\dfrac{\pi}{3}\right)}{\Delta x}$?

(A) $-\dfrac{1}{2}$

(B) 0

(C) $\dfrac{1}{2}$

(D) $\dfrac{\sqrt{3}}{2}$

4. If $x = \cos t$ and $y = \sin^2 t$, then $\dfrac{d^2 y}{dx^2}$ at $t = \dfrac{\pi}{4}$ is

(A) $\sqrt{2}$
(B) -2
(C) 1
(D) 0

5. If $f(x)$ is an antiderivative of xe^{-x^2} and $f(0) = 1$, then $f(1) =$

(A) $\dfrac{1}{e}$

(B) $\dfrac{1}{2e} - \dfrac{3}{2}$

(C) $\dfrac{1}{2e} - \dfrac{1}{2}$

(D) $-\dfrac{1}{2e} + \dfrac{3}{2}$

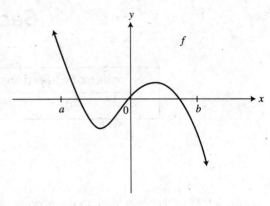

6. The graph of the function f is shown above. Which of the following statements is/are true?

I. $f'(0) = 0$
II. f has an absolute maximum value on $[a, b]$
III. $f'' < 0$ on $(0, b)$

(A) III only
(B) I and II only
(C) II and III only
(D) I, II, and III

7. $\sum\limits_{n=1}^{\infty} \dfrac{1}{(2n-1)(2n+1)} =$

(A) $\dfrac{1}{2}$

(B) 1

(C) 0

(D) 4

8. Which of the following series are convergent?

I. $12 - 8 + \dfrac{16}{3} - \dfrac{32}{9} + \cdots$

II. $5 + \dfrac{5\sqrt{2}}{2} + \dfrac{5\sqrt{3}}{3} + \dfrac{5}{2} + \sqrt{5} + \dfrac{5\sqrt{6}}{6} + \cdots$

III. $8 + 20 + 50 + 125 + \cdots$

(A) I only
(B) II only
(C) III only
(D) I and II

GO ON TO THE NEXT PAGE

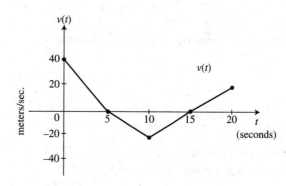

9. The graph of f is shown above and f is twice differentiable. Which of the following has the smallest value?

   I. $f(-1)$
   II. $f'(-1)$
   III. $f''(-1)$

(A) I   (B) II
(C) III   (D) II and III

10. A particle moves in the xy-plane so that its velocity vector at time t is $v(t) = \langle 2 - 3t^2, \pi \sin(\pi t) \rangle$ and the particle's position vector at time $t = 2$ is $\langle 4, 3 \rangle$. What is the position vector of the particle when $t = 3$?

(A) $\langle -25, 0 \rangle$
(B) $\langle -21, 1 \rangle$
(C) $\langle -10, 0 \rangle$
(D) $\langle -13, 5 \rangle$

11. If $\dfrac{dy}{dx} = 3e^{2x}$, and at $x = 0$, $y = \dfrac{5}{2}$, a solution to the differential equation is

(A) $3e^{2x} - \dfrac{1}{2}$

(B) $3e^{2x} + \dfrac{1}{2}$

(C) $\dfrac{3}{2}e^{2x} + 1$

(D) $\dfrac{3}{2}e^{2x} + 2$

12. The graph of the velocity function of a moving particle is shown above. What is the total displacement of the particle during $0 \le t \le 20$?

(A) 20 m   (B) 50 m
(C) 100 m   (D) 500 m

13. If $h'(x) = k(x)$ and k is a continuous function for all real values of x, then $\displaystyle\int_{-1}^{1} k(5x)\,dx$ is

(A) $h(5) - h(-5)$

(B) $5h(5) - 5h(-5)$

(C) $\dfrac{1}{5}h(5) + \dfrac{1}{5}h(-5)$

(D) $\dfrac{1}{5}h(5) - \dfrac{1}{5}h(-5)$

14. The position function of a moving particle is $s(t) = \dfrac{t^3}{6} - \dfrac{t^2}{2} + t - 3$ for $0 \le t \le 4$. What is the maximum velocity of the particle on the interval $0 \le t \le 4$?

(A) $\dfrac{1}{2}$ (B) 1   (C) $\dfrac{14}{16}$ (D) 5

15. Which of the following is an equation of the line tangent to the curve with parametric equations $x = 3t^2 - 2$, $y = 2t^3 + 2$ at the point when $t = 1$?

(A) $y = 3x^2 + 7x$
(B) $y = 6x - 2$
(C) $y = x$
(D) $y = x + 3$

GO ON TO THE NEXT PAGE

16. A function f is continuous on $[-1, 1]$ and some of the values of f are shown below:

x	-1	0	1
$f(x)$	2	b	-2

If $f(x) = 0$ has only one solution, r, and $r < 0$, then a possible value of b is

(A) -1 (B) 0 (C) 1 (D) 2

17. $\displaystyle\int_{-3}^{-2} \frac{5x}{(x+2)(x-3)}dx =$

(A) $\displaystyle\lim_{n\to 0}\int_{-3}^{n} \frac{5x}{(x+2)(x-3)}dx$

(B) $\displaystyle\lim_{n\to -3^+}\int_{n}^{-2} \frac{5x}{(x+2)(x-3)}dx$

(C) $\displaystyle\lim_{n\to -2^-}\int_{-3}^{n} \frac{5x}{(x+2)(x-3)}dx$

(D) $\displaystyle\lim_{n\to -3}\int_{-3}^{n} \frac{5x}{(x+2)(x-3)}dx$

18. $\displaystyle\int \frac{dx}{(2x-1)(x+5)} =$

(A) $\ln\left|\dfrac{2x-1}{x+5}\right| + C$

(B) $\ln\left|2x^2 + 9x - 5\right| + C$

(C) $\dfrac{1}{11}\ln\left|\dfrac{2x-1}{x+5}\right| + C$

(D) $\dfrac{1}{11}\ln\left|2x^2 + 9x - 5\right| + C$

19. What is the average value of the function $y = 2\sin(2x)$ on the interval $\left[0, \dfrac{\pi}{6}\right]$?

(A) $-\dfrac{3}{\pi}$ (B) $\dfrac{1}{2}$

(C) $\dfrac{3}{\pi}$ (D) $\dfrac{3}{2\pi}$

20. If a particle moves in the xy-plane on a path defined by $x = \sin^2 t$ and $y = \cos(2t)$ for $0 \leq t \leq \dfrac{\pi}{2}$, then the length of the arc the particle traces out is

(A) $\displaystyle\int_0^{\frac{\pi}{2}} \sqrt{\sin^2 t + \cos(2t)}\, dt$

(B) $\displaystyle\int_0^{\frac{\pi}{2}} \sqrt{\sin(2t)}\, dt$

(C) $\sqrt{5}\displaystyle\int_0^{\frac{\pi}{2}} \sin(2t)\, dt$

(D) $2\displaystyle\int_0^{\frac{\pi}{2}} \sin(2t)\, dt$

21. Given the equation $y = 3\sin^2\left(\dfrac{x}{2}\right)$, what is an equation of the tangent line to the graph at $x = \pi$?

(A) $y = 3$
(B) $y = \pi$
(C) $y = \pi + 3$
(D) $y = x - \pi + 3$

22. Which of the following statements about the series $\displaystyle\sum_{n=1}^{\infty} \frac{(-1)^n}{n+3}$ is true?

(A) The series converges absolutely.
(B) The series converges conditionally.
(C) The series diverges.
(D) None of the above.

GO ON TO THE NEXT PAGE

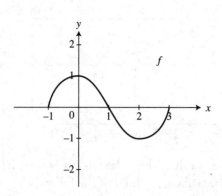

23. The graph of f for $-1 \leq x \leq 3$ consists of two semicircles, as shown above. What is the value of $\int_{-1}^{3} f(x)dx$?

(A) 0   (B) π

(C) 2π (D) 4π

24. The series expansion for $\int_{0}^{x} \cos \sqrt{t}\, dt$ is

(A) $x - \dfrac{x^2}{2 \cdot 2!} + \dfrac{x^3}{3 \cdot 4!} - \dfrac{x^4}{4 \cdot 6!} + \cdots$

$+ \dfrac{(-1)^n x^{n+1}}{(n+1)(2n)!} + \cdots$

(B) $x - \dfrac{x^2}{2!} + \dfrac{x^3}{4!} - \dfrac{x^4}{6!}$

$+ \cdots + \dfrac{(-1)^n x^{n+1}}{(2n)!} + \cdots$

(C) $x + \dfrac{x^2}{2 \cdot 2!} + \dfrac{x^3}{3 \cdot 4!} + \dfrac{x^4}{4 \cdot 6!} \cdots$

$+ \dfrac{x^{n+1}}{(n+1)(2n)!} + \cdots$

(D) $1 - \dfrac{x}{2 \cdot 2!} + \dfrac{x^2}{3 \cdot 4!} - \dfrac{x^3}{4 \cdot 6!} \cdots$

$+ \dfrac{(-1)^n x^n}{(n+1)(2n)!} + \cdots$

25. If $\displaystyle\int_{-k}^{k} f(x)dx = 2\int_{-k}^{0} f(x)dx$ for all positive values of k, then which of the following could be the graph of f?

(A)

(B)

(C)

(D)

26. Which of the following is the Taylor series for $f(x) = x^2 \sin x$ about $x = 0$?

(A) $1 - \dfrac{x^2}{2!} + \dfrac{x^4}{4!} - \dfrac{x^6}{6!} + \cdots$

(B) $x - \dfrac{x^3}{3!} + \dfrac{x^5}{5!} - \dfrac{x^7}{7!} + \cdots$

(C) $1 - \dfrac{x^4}{2!} + \dfrac{x^6}{4!} - \dfrac{x^8}{6!} + \cdots$

(D) $x^3 - \dfrac{x^5}{3!} + \dfrac{x^7}{5!} - \dfrac{x^9}{7!} + \cdots$

$[-8, 8]$ by $[-5, 4]$

27. The graph of the polar curve $r = 3 - \sin\theta$ is shown above. Which of the following expressions gives the area of the region enclosed by the curve?

(A) $\dfrac{1}{2}\displaystyle\int_{0}^{2\pi} (3 - \sin\theta)\, d\theta$

(B) $\dfrac{1}{2}\displaystyle\int_{0}^{2\pi} (3 - \sin\theta)^2\, d\theta$

(C) $\displaystyle\int_{0}^{2\pi} (3 - \sin\theta)\, d\theta$

(D) $\displaystyle\int_{0}^{2\pi} (3 - \sin\theta)^2\, d\theta$

28. What are all values of x for which the series $\displaystyle\sum_{n=0}^{\infty} \dfrac{x^n}{n!}$ converges?

(A) $-1 < x < 1$ only
(B) $-1 \le x \le 1$ only
(C) $x < -1$ and $x > 1$ only
(D) $x \in (-\infty, \infty)$

GO ON TO THE NEXT PAGE

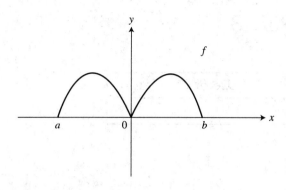

29. The graph of f is shown above, and

$$g(x) = \int_a^x f(t)dt, \ x > a.$$ Which of the

following is a possible graph of g?

30. The series $\displaystyle\sum_{n=1}^{\infty} (-1)^{n+1} \frac{1}{n}$ satisfies the hypotheses

of the alternating series test, i.e., $a_n \geq a_{n+1}$, and

$\displaystyle\lim_{n\to\infty} a_n = 0$. If S is the sum of the series

$\displaystyle\sum_{n=1}^{\infty} (-1)^{n+1} \frac{1}{n}$ and s_n is the *nth* partial sum, what

is the minimum value of n for which the
alternating series error bound guarantees that
$|S - s_n| < 0.1$?

(A) 9
(B) 10
(C) 99
(D) 100

(A)

(B)

(C)

(D)
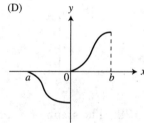

STOP. AP Calculus BC Practice Exam 1 Section I—Part A

Section I—Part B

Number of Questions	Time	Use of Calculator
15	45 Minutes	Yes

Directions:

Use the same answer sheet for Part A. *Please note that the questions begin with number 76.* This is not an error. It is done to be consistent with the numbering system of the actual AP Calculus BC Exam. All questions are given equal weight. Points are *not* deducted for incorrect answers and no points are given to unanswered questions. Unless otherwise indicated, the domain of a function f is the set of all real numbers. If the exact numerical value does not appear among the given choices, select the best approximate value. The use of a calculator is *permitted* in this part of the exam.

76. What is the acceleration vector of a particle at $t = 2$ if the particle is moving in the xy-plane and its velocity vector is $v(t) = \, < t, 4t^3 > \,$?

(A) 48

(B) $< 0, 48 >$

(C) $< 1, 48 >$

(D) $< 2, 48 >$

77. The equation of the normal line to the graph $y = e^{2x}$ at the point where $\dfrac{dy}{dx} = 2$ is

(A) $y = -\dfrac{1}{2}x - 1$

(B) $y = -\dfrac{1}{2}x + 1$

(C) $y = 2x + 1$

(D) $y = -\dfrac{1}{2}\left(x - \dfrac{\ln 2}{2}\right) + 2$

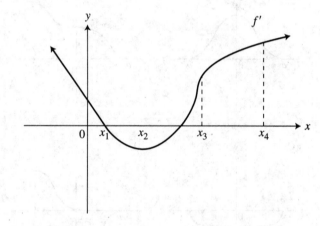

78. The graph of f', the derivative of f, is shown above. At which value of x does the graph of f have a point of inflection?

(A) x_1

(B) x_2

(C) x_3

(D) x_4

GO ON TO THE NEXT PAGE

79. The temperature of a metal is dropping at the rate of $g(t) = 10e^{-0.1t}$ for $0 \leq t \leq 10$, where g is measured in degrees in Fahrenheit and t in minutes. If the metal is initally 100°F, what is the temperature to the nearest degree Fahrenheit after 6 minutes?

(A) 37

(B) 45

(C) 55

(D) 63

80. A particle moves along the y-axis so that its position at time t is $y(t) = 5t^3 - 9t^2 + 2t - 1$. At the moment when the particle first changes direction, the (x, y) coordinates of its position are

(A) $(0, 0.124)$

(B) $(0.124, -0.881)$

(C) $(0, -0.881)$

(D) $(-0.881, 0)$

81. The interval of convergence of the series $\sum_{n=1}^{\infty} \dfrac{(x-3)^n}{n^2}$ is

(A) $(2, 4)$

(B) $(2, 4]$

(C) $[2, 4)$

(D) $[2, 4]$

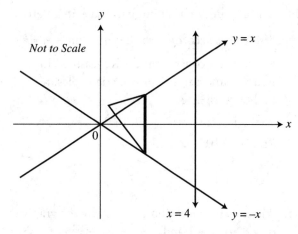

82. The base of a solid is a region bounded by the lines $y = x$, $y = -x$, and $x = 4$, as shown above. What is the volume of the solid if the cross sections perpendicular to the x-axis are equilateral triangles?

(A) $\dfrac{16\sqrt{3}}{3}$

(B) $\dfrac{32\sqrt{3}}{3}$

(C) $\dfrac{64\sqrt{3}}{3}$

(D) $\dfrac{256\pi}{3}$

83. Let f be a continuous function on $[0, 6]$ and have selected values as shown below.

x	0	2	4	6
$f(x)$	0	1	2.25	6.25

If you use the subintervals $[0, 2]$, $[2, 4]$, and $[4, 6]$, what is the trapezoidal approximation of $\int_0^6 f(x)dx$?

(A) 9.5

(B) 12.75

(C) 19

(D) 25.5

GO ON TO THE NEXT PAGE

84. The amount of a certain bacteria y in a Petri dish grows according to the equation $\frac{dy}{dt} = ky$, where k is a constant and t is measured in hours. If the amount of bacteria triples in 10 hours, then $k \approx$

(A) -1.204
(B) -0.110
(C) 0.110
(D) 1.204

85. The area of the region enclosed by the graphs of $y = \cos x + 1$ and $y = 2 + 2x - x^2$ is approximately

(A) 3.002
(B) 2.424
(C) 2.705
(D) 0.094

86. How many points of inflection does the graph of $y = \dfrac{\sin x}{x}$ have on the interval $(-\pi, \pi)$?

(A) 0
(B) 1
(C) 2
(D) 3

87. Given $f(x) = x^2 e^x$, what is an approximate value of $f(1.1)$, if you use a tangent line to the graph of f at $x = 1$?

(A) 3.534
(B) 3.635
(C) 7.055
(D) 8.155

88. The area of the region bounded by $y = -3x^2 + kx - 1$ and the x-axis, the lines $x = 1$ and $x = 2$ is approximately 5.5. Find the value of k.

(A) 9
(B) 11
(C) 5.5
(D) 16.5

89. At which of the following values of x do the graphs of $y = x^2$ and $y = -\sqrt{x}$ have perpendicular tangent lines?

(A) -1
(B) $\dfrac{1}{4}$
(C) 1
(D) None

90. Using Euler's Method, what is the approximate value of $y(1)$ if $y(0) = 4$, $\dfrac{dy}{dx} = 2x$, and a step size of 0.5 starting at $x = 0$?

(A) 3 (B) 3.5 (C) 4 (D) 4.5

STOP. AP Calculus BC Practice Exam 1 Section I—Part B

Section II—Part A

Number of Questions	Time	Use of Calculator
2	30 Minutes	Yes

Directions:

Show all work. You may *not* receive any credit for correct answers without supporting work. You may use an approved calculator to help solve a problem. However, you must clearly indicate the setup of your solution using mathematical notations and *not* calculator syntax. Calculators may be used to find the derivative of a function at a point, compute the numerical value of a definite integral, or solve an equation. Unless otherwise indicated, you may assume the following: (a) the numeric or algebraic answers need not be simplified; (b) your answer, if expressed in approximation, should be correct to 3 places after the decimal point; and (c) the domain of a function f is the set of all real numbers.

1. The temperature in a greenhouse from 7:00 p.m. to 7:00 a.m. is given by

   $f(t) = 96 - 20 \sin \left(\dfrac{t}{4} \right)$, where $f(t)$ is

   measured in Fahrenheit, and t is the number of hours since 7:00 p.m.

   (A) What is the temperature of the greenhouse at 1:00 a.m. to the nearest degree Fahrenheit?

   (B) Find the average temperature between 7:00 p.m. and 7:00 a.m. to the nearest tenth of a degree Fahrenheit.

   (C) When the temperature of the greenhouse drops below 80°F, a heating system will automatically be turned on to maintain the temperature at a minimum of 80°F. At what values of t to the nearest tenth is the heating system turned on?

   (D) The cost of heating the greenhouse is $0.25 per hour for each degree. What is the total cost to the nearest dollar to heat the greenhouse from 7:00 p.m. and 7:00 a.m.?

2. Consider the differential equation given by

   $\dfrac{dy}{dx} = \dfrac{2xy}{3}$.

   (A) On the axes provided, sketch a slope field for the given differential equation at the points indicated.

   (B) Let $y = f(x)$ be the particular solution to the given differential equation with the initial condition $f(0) = 2$. Use Euler's Method, starting at $x = 0$, with a step size of 0.1, to approximate $f(0.3)$. Show the work that leads to your answer.

   (C) Find the particular solution $y = f(x)$ to the given differential equation with the initial condition $f(0) = 2$. Use your solution to find $f(0.3)$.

STOP. AP Calculus BC Practice Exam 1 Section II—Part A

Section II—Part B

Number of Questions	Time	Use of Calculator
4	60 Minutes	No

Directions:

The use of a calculator is not permitted in this part of the exam. When you have finished this part of the exam, you may return to the problems in Part A of Section II and continue to work on them. However, you may *not* use a calculator. You should *show all work*. You may *not* receive any credit for correct answers without supporting work. Unless otherwise indicated, the numeric or algebraic answers need not be simplified, and the domain of a function f is the set of all real numbers.

3. A particle is moving on a straight line. The velocity of the particle for $0 \le t \le 30$ is shown in the table below for selected values of t.

t (sec)	0	3	6	9	12	15	18	21	24	27	30
$v(t)$ (m/sec)	0	7.5	10.1	12	13	13.5	14.1	14	13.9	13	12

(A) Using MRAM (Midpoint Rectangular Approximation Method) with five rectangles, find the approximate value of $\displaystyle\int_0^{30} v(t)\,dt$.

(B) Using the result in part (A), find the average velocity over the interval $0 \le t \le 30$.

(C) Find the average acceleration over the interval $0 \le t \le 30$.

(D) Find the approximate acceleration at $t = 6$.

(E) During what intervals of time is the acceleration negative?

4. Let R be the region enclosed by the graph of $y = x^3$, the x-axis, and the line $x = 2$.

(A) Find the area of region R.

(B) Find the volume of the solid obtained by revolving region R about the x-axis.

(C) The line $x = a$ divides region R into two regions such that when the regions are revolved about the x-axis, the resulting solids have equal volume. Find a.

(D) If region R is the base of a solid whose cross sections perpendicular to the x-axis are squares, find the volume of the solid.

5. Let f be a function that has derivatives of all orders for all real numbers. Assume $f(0) = 1$, $f'(0) = 6$, $f''(0) = -4$, and $f'''(0) = 30$.

(A) Write the third-degree Taylor polynomial for f about $x = 0$ and use it to approximate $f(0.1)$.

(B) Write the sixth-degree Taylor polynomial for g, where $g(x) = f(x^2)$, about $x = 0$.

(C) Write the seventh-degree Taylor polynomial for h, where $h(x) = \displaystyle\int_0^x g(t)\,dt$, about $x = 0$.

6. Given the parametric equations $x = 2(\theta - \sin\theta)$ and $y = 2(1 - \cos\theta)$,

(A) find $\dfrac{dy}{dx}$ in terms of θ.

(B) find an equation of the line tangent to the graph at $\theta = \pi$.

(C) find an equation of the line tangent to the graph at $\theta = 2\pi$.

(D) set up but do not evaluate an integral representing the length of the curve over the interval $0 \le \theta \le 2\pi$.

STOP. AP Calculus BC Practice Exam 1 Section II—Part B

Answers to BC Practice Exam 1—Section I

Part A
1. C
2. A
3. C
4. B
5. D
6. C
7. A
8. A
9. A
10. D
11. C

12. B
13. D
14. D
15. D
16. A
17. C
18. C
19. C
20. C
21. A
22. B
23. A

24. A
25. B
26. D
27. B
28. D
29. B
30. A

Part B
76. C
77. B
78. B

79. C
80. C
81. D
82. C
83. B
84. C
85. A
86. C
87. A
88. A
89. C
90. D

Answers to BC Practice Exam 1—Section II

Part A

1. (A) 76°   (2 pts.)
    (B) 82.7°   (2 pts.)
    (C) $3.7 < t < 8.9$ (2 pts.)
    (D) \$3   (3 pts.)

2. (A)   (2 pts.)

    (B) 2.040   (3 pts.)
    (C) $y = 2e^{\frac{x^2}{3}}$; 2.061   (4 pts.)

Part B

3. (A) 360   (3 pts.)
    (B) 12 m/sec   (1 pt.)
    (C) 0.4 m/sec^2 (2 pts.)
    (D) 0.75 m/sec^2 (1 pt.)
    (E) $18 < t < 30$ (2 pts.)

4. (A) 4   (2 pts.)
    (B) $\dfrac{128\pi}{7}$ (2 pts.)
    (C) $2^{6/7}$ (3 pts.)
    (D) $\dfrac{128}{7}$ (2 pts.)

5. (A) $f(x) \approx 1 + 6x - 2x^2 + 5x^3$;
        $f(0.1) \approx 1.585$ (5 pts.)
    (B) $g(x) \approx 1 + 6x^2 - 2x^4 + 5x^6$ (2 pts.)
    (C) $h(x) \approx x + 2x^3 - \dfrac{2}{5}x^5 + \dfrac{5}{7}x^7$ (2 pts.)

6. (A) $\dfrac{dy}{dx} = \dfrac{\sin\theta}{1 - \cos\theta}$ (2 pts.)
    (B) $y = 4$ (2 pts.)
    (C) $x = 4\pi$ (3 pts.)
    (D) $L = \displaystyle\int_0^{2\pi} \sqrt{[2(1 - \cos\theta)]^2 + [2\sin\theta]^2}\, d\theta$

        $= 2\sqrt{2} \displaystyle\int_0^{2\pi} \sqrt{1 - \cos\theta}\, d\theta$ (2 pts.)

Solutions to AP Calculus BC Practice Exam 1—Section I

Section I—Part A

1. The correct answer is (C).

$$\lim_{x \to (\ln 2)^+} (e^x) = e^{\ln 2} = 2 \text{ and } \lim_{x \to (\ln 2)^-} (4 - e^x)$$

$$= 4 - e^{\ln 2} = 4 - 2 = 2$$

Since the two one-sided limits are the same, $\lim_{x \to (\ln 2)} g(x) = 2$.

2. The correct answer is (A).

The only graph that satisfies the behavior of f is (A).

3. The correct answer is (C).

The definition of $f'(x)$ is

$$f'(x) = \lim_{\Delta x \to 0} \frac{f(x + \Delta x) - f(x)}{\Delta x}.$$

Thus, $\lim_{\Delta x \to 0} \dfrac{\sin((\pi/3) + \Delta x) - \sin(\pi/3)}{\Delta x}$

$$= \frac{d(\sin x)}{dx}\bigg|_{x=\pi/3}$$

$$= \cos\left(\frac{\pi}{3}\right) = \frac{1}{2}.$$

4. The correct answer is (B).

$$x = \cos t \Rightarrow \frac{dx}{dt} = -\sin t \text{ and}$$

$$y = \sin^2 t \Rightarrow \frac{dy}{dt} = 2 \sin t \cos t.$$

Then, $\dfrac{dy}{dx} = \left(\dfrac{dy}{dt}\right) \bigg/ \left(\dfrac{dx}{dt}\right) = \dfrac{2 \sin t \cos t}{-\sin t}$

$$= -2 \cos t.$$

Then, $\dfrac{d^2 y}{dx^2} = \left(\dfrac{dy'}{dt}\right) \bigg/ \left(\dfrac{dx}{dt}\right)$

$$= \frac{2 \sin t}{-\sin t} = -2.$$

Evaluate at $t = \dfrac{\pi}{4}$ for

$$\frac{d^2 y}{dx^2}\bigg|_{t=\frac{\pi}{4}} = -2\big|_{t=\frac{\pi}{4}} = -2.$$

5. The correct answer is (D).

Since $f(x) = \displaystyle\int x e^{-x^2} dx$, let $u = -x^2$,

$$du = -2x \, dx \text{ or } \frac{-du}{2} = x \, dx.$$

Thus, $f(x) = \displaystyle\int e^u \left(-\frac{du}{2}\right) = -\frac{1}{2} e^u + C$

$$= -\frac{1}{2} e^{-x^2} + C$$

and $f(0) = 1 \Rightarrow -\dfrac{1}{2}(e^0) + C = 1$

$$\Rightarrow -\frac{1}{2} + C = 1$$

$$\Rightarrow C = \frac{3}{2}.$$

Therefore, $f(x) = -\dfrac{1}{2} e^{-x^2} + \dfrac{3}{2}$ and

$$f(1) = -\frac{1}{2} e^{-1} + \frac{3}{2} = -\frac{1}{2e} + \frac{3}{2}.$$

6. The correct answer is (C).

 I. $f'(0) \neq 0$ since the tangent to $f(x)$ at $x = 0$ is not parallel to the x-axis.

 II. f has an absolute maximum at $x = a$.

 III. f'' is less than 0 on $(0, b)$ since f is concave downward.

Thus, only statements II and III are true.

7. The correct answer is (A).

$$\sum_{n=1}^{\infty} \frac{1}{(2n-1)(2n+1)} = \sum_{n=1}^{\infty} \frac{1}{4n^2 - 1}$$

The sequence of partial sums

$$\left\{ \frac{1}{3}, \frac{2}{5}, \frac{3}{7}, \frac{4}{9}, \cdots, \frac{n}{2n+1}, \cdots \right\} \text{ and}$$

$$= \lim_{n \to \infty} \left[\frac{n}{2n+1} \right] = \frac{1}{2}.$$

Another approach is to use partial fractions to obtain a telescoping sum.

8. The correct answer is (A).

Which of the following series are convergent?

 I. $12 - 8 + \dfrac{16}{3} - \dfrac{32}{9} + \cdots = \displaystyle\sum_{n=0}^{\infty} 12 \left(\dfrac{-2}{3} \right)^n$

 is a geometric series with $r = \dfrac{-2}{3}$. Since $|r| < 1$, the series converges.

 II. $5 + \dfrac{5\sqrt{2}}{2} + \dfrac{5\sqrt{3}}{3} + \dfrac{5}{2} + \sqrt{5} + \dfrac{5\sqrt{5}}{6} + \cdots$

 $= 5 + \dfrac{5}{\sqrt{2}} + \dfrac{5}{\sqrt{3}} + \dfrac{5}{\sqrt{4}} + \dfrac{5}{\sqrt{5}} + \dfrac{5}{\sqrt{6}} + \cdots$

 $= \displaystyle\sum_{n=1}^{\infty} \dfrac{5}{\sqrt{n}}$ is a p-series, with $p = \dfrac{1}{2}$. Since $p < 1$, the series diverges.

 III. $8 + 20 + 50 + 125 + \cdots = \displaystyle\sum_{n=0}^{\infty} 8 \left(\dfrac{5}{2} \right)^n$ is

 also a geometric series, but since $r = \dfrac{5}{2} > 1$, the series diverges.

 Therefore, only series I converges.

9. The correct answer is (A).

 I. $f(-1) = 0$

 II. Since f is increasing, $f'(-1) > 0$.

 III. Since f is concave upward, $f''(-1) > 0$.

Thus, $f(-1)$ has the smallest value.

10. The correct answer is (D).

The velocity vector $v(t) = \langle 2 - 3t^2, \pi \sin(\pi t) \rangle = (2 - 3t^2)i + (\pi \sin(\pi t))j$. Integrate to find the position.

$s(t) = (2t - t^3)i + \left(\dfrac{-\pi}{\pi} \cos(\pi t) \right) j + C.$

Evaluate at $t = 2$ to find the constant.

$s(2) = (4 - 8)i + (-1 \cos(2\pi))j + C$
 $= 4i + 3j$

$s(2) = (-4)i - j + C = 4i + 3j$

 $C = 8i + 4j$

Therefore, $s(t) = (8 + 2t - t^3) i + (4 - \cos(\pi t))j = \langle 8 + 2t - t^3, 4 - \cos(\pi t) \rangle.$

Evaluate at $t = 3$.

$s(3) = (8 + 6 - 27)i + (4 - \cos(3\pi))j$

$s(3) = -13i + 5j$

The position vector is $\langle -13, 5 \rangle$.

11. The correct answer is (C).

Since $dy = 3e^{2x} dx \Rightarrow$

$$\int 1 dy = \int 3e^{2x} dx \Rightarrow$$

$$y = \frac{3e^{2x}}{2} + C.$$

At $x = 0$, $\dfrac{5}{2} = \dfrac{3(e^0)}{2} + c \Rightarrow \dfrac{5}{2} = \dfrac{3}{2} + C$

 $\Rightarrow C = 1.$

Therefore, $y = \dfrac{3e^{2x}}{2} + 1.$

12. The correct answer is (B).

$$\int_0^{20} v(t)dt = \frac{1}{2}(40)(5) + \frac{1}{2}(10)(-20)$$

$$+ \frac{1}{2}(5)(20) = 50$$

13. The correct answer is (D).

Let $u = 5x$; $du = 5dx$ or $\dfrac{du}{5} = dx$

$$\int k(5x)dx = \frac{1}{5}\int k(u)du = \frac{1}{5}h(u) + C$$

$$= \frac{1}{5}h(5x) + C$$

$$\int_{-1}^1 k(5x)dx = \frac{1}{5}h(5x)\Big]_{-1}^1$$

$$= \frac{1}{5}h(5) - \frac{1}{5}h(-5).$$

14. The correct answer is (D).

$$v(t) = s'(t) = \frac{t^2}{2} - t + 1 \text{ and } a(t) = t - 1.$$

Set $a(t) = 0 \Rightarrow t = 1$. Thus, $v(t)$ has a relative minimum at $t = 1$ and $v(1) = \dfrac{1}{2}$. Since it is the only relative extremum, it is an absolute minimum. And, since $v(t)$ is continuous on the closed interval $[0, 4]$, $v(t)$ has an absolute maximum at the endpoints

$v(0) = 1$ and $v(4) = 8 - 4 + 1 = 5$.

Therefore, the maximum velocity of the particle on $[1, 4]$ is 5.

15. The correct answer is (D).

$$x = 3t^2 - 2 \Rightarrow \frac{dx}{dt} = 6t \text{ and}$$

$$y = 2t^3 + 2 \Rightarrow \frac{dy}{dt} = 6t^2, \text{ and since}$$

$$\frac{dy}{dx} = \left(\frac{dy}{dt}\right)\bigg/\left(\frac{dx}{dt}\right)$$

$$\frac{dy}{dx}\bigg|_{t=1} = \frac{6t^2}{6t}\bigg|_{t=1} = 1 \text{ is the slope of the tangent}$$

line. At $t = 1$, $x = 1$, $y = 4$, so the point of tangency is $(1, 4)$. Equation of tangent: $y - 4 = 1(x - 1) \Rightarrow y = x + 3$.

16. The correct answer is (A).

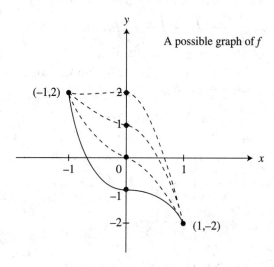

If $b = 0$, then 0 is a root and thus, $r = 0$; but $r < 0$. If $b = 1$ or 2, then the graph of f must cross the x-axis, which implies there is another root r, and that $r > 0$. Thus, $b = -1$.

17. The correct answer is (C).

$\int_{-3}^{-2} \dfrac{5x}{(x+2)(x-3)}dx$ is an improper integral

since $f(x) = \dfrac{5x}{(x+2)(x-3)}$ has an infinite

discontinuity at $x = -2$, one of the limits of integration. Therefore,

$\int_{-3}^{-2} \dfrac{5x}{(x+2)(x-3)}dx$ is equal to

$\displaystyle\lim_{n \to -2^-} \int_{-3}^{n} \dfrac{5x}{(x+2)(x-3)}dx.$

18. The correct answer is (C).

Use a partial fraction decomposition with

$\int \dfrac{A}{2x-1}dx + \int \dfrac{B}{x+5}dx.$ Then

$A(x+5) + B(2x-1) = 1 \Rightarrow$
$Ax + 2Bx = 0 \Rightarrow A = -2B.$ Substituting and
solving, $5A - B = 1 \Rightarrow 5(-2B) - B = 1,$ so

$B = -\dfrac{1}{11}$ and $A = \dfrac{2}{11}.$ Then

$\int \dfrac{dx}{(2x-1)(x+5)} = \dfrac{1}{11}\int \dfrac{2dx}{(2x-1)}$

$\qquad - \dfrac{1}{11}\int \dfrac{dx}{(x+5)}$

$\qquad = \dfrac{1}{11}\ln|2x-1| - \dfrac{1}{11}\ln|x+5|$

$\qquad = \dfrac{1}{11}\ln\left|\dfrac{2x-1}{x+5}\right| + C.$

19. The correct answer is (C).

Average value $= \dfrac{1}{(\pi/6) - 0}\displaystyle\int_{0}^{\pi/6} 2\sin(2x)dx$

$\qquad = \dfrac{6}{\pi}\left[-\cos(2x)\right]_{0}^{\pi/6}$

$\qquad = \dfrac{6}{\pi}\left[-\cos\left(\dfrac{\pi}{3}\right) - (-\cos 0)\right]$

$\qquad = \dfrac{6}{\pi}\left[-\dfrac{1}{2} + 1\right] = \dfrac{3}{\pi}.$

20. The correct answer is (C).

$x = \sin^2 t \Rightarrow \dfrac{dx}{dt} = 2\sin t \cos t = \sin(2t)$ and

$y = \cos(2t) \Rightarrow \dfrac{dy}{dt} = -2\sin(2t).$ Then

$\left(\dfrac{dx}{dt}\right)^2 = \sin^2(2t)$ and

$\left(\dfrac{dy}{dt}\right)^2 = (-2\sin(2t))^2 = 4\sin^2(2t).$ For

$0 \le t \le \dfrac{\pi}{2},$ the length of the arc the particle

traces out is

$L = \displaystyle\int_{0}^{\frac{\pi}{2}} \sqrt{\sin^2(2t) + 4\sin^2(2t)}\, dt =$

$\displaystyle\int_{0}^{\frac{\pi}{2}} \sqrt{5\sin^2(2t)}\, dt = \sqrt{5}\int_{0}^{\frac{\pi}{2}} \sin(2t)\, dt.$

Note that $\sqrt{\sin^2(2t)} = |\sin(2t)| = \sin(2t)$ for

$0 \le t \le \dfrac{\pi}{2}$

21. The correct answer is (A).

$y = 3\sin^2\left(\dfrac{x}{2}\right);$

$\dfrac{dy}{dx} = 6\sin\left(\dfrac{x}{2}\right)\left[\cos\left(\dfrac{x}{2}\right)\right]\dfrac{1}{2}$

$\qquad = 3\sin\left(\dfrac{x}{2}\right)\cos\left(\dfrac{x}{2}\right)$

$\left.\dfrac{dy}{dx}\right|_{x=\pi} = 3\sin\left(\dfrac{\pi}{2}\right)\cos\left(\dfrac{\pi}{2}\right) = 3(1)(0) = 0$

At $x = \pi,$ $y = 3\sin^2\left(\dfrac{\pi}{2}\right) = 3(1)^2 = 3.$ The

point of tangency is $(\pi, 3).$ Equation of
tangent at $x = \pi$ is $y - 3 = 0(x - \pi) \Rightarrow y = 3.$

22. The correct answer is choice B.

Examine the absolute values of

$$\sum_{n=1}^{\infty} \left| \frac{(-1)^n}{n+3} \right| = \sum_{n=1}^{\infty} \frac{1}{n+3} = \frac{1}{4} + \frac{1}{5} + \frac{1}{6} + \dots . \text{ Since}$$

$\sum_{n=1}^{\infty} \dfrac{1}{n+3}$ is a harmonic series that diverges, the

series $\sum_{n=1}^{\infty} \left| \dfrac{(-1)^n}{n+3} \right|$ diverges, which means the

series $\sum_{n=1}^{\infty} \dfrac{(-1)^n}{n+3}$ does not converge absolutely.

Now examine the alternating series

$$\sum_{n=1}^{\infty} \frac{(-1)^n}{n+3} = -\frac{1}{4} + \frac{1}{5} - \frac{1}{6} + \dots . \text{ Since } \sum_{n=1}^{\infty} \frac{(-1)^n}{n+3} \text{ is}$$

an alternating harmonic series, $\sum_{n=1}^{\infty} \dfrac{(-1)^n}{n+3}$

converges (but not absolutely as shown earlier).

Thus the series $\sum_{n=1}^{\infty} \dfrac{(-1)^n}{n+3}$ converges

conditionally.

23. The correct answer is (A).

$$\int_{-1}^{3} f(x)dx = \int_{-1}^{1} f(x)dx + \int_{1}^{3} f(x)dx$$

$$= \frac{1}{2}\pi(1)^2 - \frac{1}{2}\pi(1)^2 = 0$$

24. The correct answer is (A).

We know $f(x) = \cos x = \sum_{n=0}^{\infty} \dfrac{(-1)^n x^{2n}}{(2n)!}$

$$= 1 - \frac{x^2}{2!} + \frac{x^4}{4!} - \frac{x^6}{6!} + \dots .$$

Substitute $\sqrt{t}$ for x, and $\cos \sqrt{t}$

$$= 1 - \frac{t}{2!} + \frac{t^2}{4!} - \frac{t^3}{6!} + \dots + \frac{(-1)^n t^n}{(2n)!} + \dots . \text{ The}$$

integral, $\displaystyle\int_0^x \cos \sqrt{t}\, dt$, will be equal to

$$\int_0^x \left(1 - \frac{t}{2!} + \frac{t^2}{4!} - \frac{t^3}{6!} + \dots + \frac{(-1)^n t^n}{(2n)!} + \dots \right) dt,$$

which, when integrated term by term, is

$$t - \frac{t^2}{2 \cdot 2!} + \frac{t^3}{3 \cdot 4!} - \frac{t^4}{4 \cdot 6!} + \dots$$

$$+ \frac{(-1)^n t^{n+1}}{(n+1)(2n)!} + \dots \Bigg|_0^x$$

$$= x - \frac{x^2}{2 \cdot 2!} + \frac{x^3}{3 \cdot 4!} - \frac{x^4}{4 \cdot 6!} + \dots$$

$$+ \frac{(-1)^n x^{n+1}}{(n+1)(2n)!} + \dots .$$

The series expansion for $\displaystyle\int_0^x \cos \sqrt{t}\, dt$ is

$$x - \frac{x^2}{2 \cdot 2!} + \frac{x^3}{3 \cdot 4!} - \frac{x^4}{4 \cdot 6!} + \dots$$

$$+ \frac{(-1)^n x^{n+1}}{(n+1)(2n)!} + \dots .$$

25. The correct answer is (B).

$$\int_{-k}^{k} f(x)dx = 2\int_{-k}^{0} f(x)dx \Rightarrow f(x) \text{ is an even}$$

function, i.e., $f(x) = f(-x)$.
The graph in (B) is the only even function.

26. The correct answer is (D).

$$\sin x = x - \frac{x^3}{3!} + \frac{x^5}{5!} - \frac{x^7}{7!} + \cdots$$

$$x^2 \sin x = x^2 \left(x - \frac{x^3}{3!} + \frac{x^5}{5!} - \frac{x^7}{7!} + \cdots \right)$$

$$= x^3 - \frac{x^5}{3!} + \frac{x^7}{5!} - \frac{x^9}{7!} + \cdots$$

27. The correct answer is (B).

To enclose the area, θ must sweep through the interval from 0 to 2π. The area of the region enclosed by $r = 3 - \sin\theta$ is

$$A = \frac{1}{2} \int_0^{2\pi} (3 - \sin\theta)^2 d\theta.$$

28. The correct answer is (D). Using the Ratio Test,

$$\lim_{n\to\infty} \left| \frac{a_{n+1}}{a_n} \right| = \lim_{n\to\infty} \left| \frac{\frac{x^{n+1}}{(n+1)!}}{\frac{x^n}{n!}} \right| = \lim_{n\to\infty} \left| \frac{x^{n+1}}{(n+1)!} \cdot \frac{n!}{x^n} \right|$$

$$= \lim_{n\to\infty} \left| \frac{x}{n+1} \right| = 0$$

for all values of x.

29. The correct answer is (B).

$$g(x) = \int_a^x f(t)dt \Rightarrow g'(x) = f(x)$$

$g' = f$

a 0 b

g incr.   incr.

The graph in (B) is the only one that satisfies the behavior of g.

30. The correct answer is choice A.

Since the series $\sum_{n=1}^{\infty} (-1)^{n+1} \frac{1}{n}$ satisfies the hypotheses of the alternating series test, $|S - s_n| < a_{n+1}$, and in this case, $a_{n+1} = \frac{1}{n+1}$.

Setting $a_{n+1} \le 0.1$, you have $\frac{1}{n+1} \le 0.1$ or $n \ge 9$. The minimum value of n is 9.

Section I—Part B

76. The correct answer is (C). Since $v(t) = \; <t, 4t^3>, a(t) = \; <1, 12t^2>$ and at $t = 2, a(t) = \; <1, 48>$.

77. The correct answer is (B).

$$y = e^{2x}; \quad \frac{dy}{dx} = (e^{2x})2 = 2e^{2x}$$

Set $\frac{dy}{dx} = 2 \Rightarrow 2e^{2x} = 2 \Rightarrow e^{2x} = 1 \Rightarrow$
$$\ln(e^{2x}) = \ln 1 \Rightarrow 2x = 0 \text{ or } x = 0.$$
At $x = 0, \; y = e^{2x} = e^{2(0)} = 1;$ (0, 1) and the

normal line is $y = -\frac{1}{2}x + 1.$

78. The correct answer is (B).

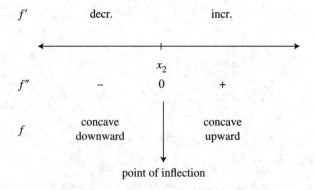

The graph of f has a point of inflection at $x = x_2$.

79. The correct answer is (C).

Temperature of metal $= 100 - \int_0^6 10e^{-0.1t}\,dt.$

Using your calculator, you obtain:

Temperature of metal $= 100 - 45.1188$
$$= 54.8812 \approx 55°\text{F}.$$

80. The correct answer is (C).

The position of the particle is $y(t) = 5t^3 - 9t^2 + 2t - 1$, and the velocity is $v(t) = y'(t) = 15t^2 - 18t + 2$. At the moment the particle changed direction, its velocity was zero, so $15t^2 - 18t + 2 = 0$. Solving tells us that the particle changes direction twice, first at $t \approx 0.124$ and later at $t = 1.076$. Taking the first of these, and evaluating the position function, $y \approx -0.881$. At the moment when the particle first changes direction, its position is $(0, -0.881)$. Remember that the particle is moving on the *y-axis* and thus the *x-coordinate* is always 0.

81. The correct answer is (D).

Use the ratio test for absolute convergence.

$$\lim_{n \to \infty} \left| \frac{(x-3)^{n+1}}{(n+1)^2} \cdot \frac{n^2}{(x-3)^n} \right|$$

$$= \lim_{n \to \infty} \left| \frac{(x-3)n^2}{(n+1)^2} \right|$$

$$= \left| x - 3 \right| \lim_{n \to \infty} \left(\frac{n}{n+1} \right)^2$$

$$= \left| x - 3 \right|$$

Set $\left| x - 3 \right| < 1 \Rightarrow -1 < (x-3) < 1$
$\Rightarrow 2 < x < 4$. At $x = 4$, the series becomes $\sum_{n=1}^{\infty} \frac{1}{n^2}$, which is a *p*-series with $p = 2$. The series converges. At $x = 2$, the series becomes $\sum_{n=1}^{\infty} \frac{(-1)^n}{n^2}$, which converges absolutely. Thus, the interval of convergence is $[2,4]$.

82. The correct answer is (C).

Area of a cross section $= \frac{\sqrt{3}}{4}(2x)^2 = \sqrt{3}x^2.$

Using your calculator, you have:

Volume of solid $= \int_0^4 \sqrt{3}(x^2)\,dx = \frac{64\sqrt{3}}{3}.$

83. The correct answer is (B).

$$\int_0^6 f(x)\,dx \approx \frac{6-0}{2(3)} \cdot [0 + 2(1) + 2(2.25) + 6.25]$$

$$\approx 12.75$$

84. The correct answer is (C).

$$\frac{dy}{dx} = ky \Rightarrow y = y_0 e^{kt}$$

Triple in 10 hours $\Rightarrow y = 3y_0$ at $t = 10$.

$$3y_0 = y_0 e^{10k} \Rightarrow 3 = e^{10k} \Rightarrow \ln 3 = \ln(e^{10k})$$

$$\Rightarrow \ln 3 = 10k \text{ or } k = \frac{\ln 3}{10}$$

$$\approx 0.109861 \approx 0.110$$

85. The correct answer is (A).

Use the intersection function to find that the points of intersection of $y = \cos x + 1$ and $y = 2 + 2x - x^2$ are $(0, 2)$ and $(2.705, 0.094)$. The area enclosed by the curves is

$$\int_0^{2.705} \left[2 + 2x - x^2 - (\cos x + 1) \right] dx$$

$$= x + x^2 - \frac{x^3}{3} - \sin x \Big|_0^{2.705} \approx 3.002.$$

Solutions to AP Calculus BC Practice Exam 1—Section II

86. The correct answer is (C).

[−1.5π,1.5π] by [−1,2]

Using the [*Inflection*] function on your calculator, you obtain $x = -2.08$ and $x = 2.08$. Thus, there are two points of inflection on $(-\pi, \pi)$.

87. The correct answer is (A).

$f(x) = x^2 e^x$ Using your calculator, you obtain $f(1) \approx 2.7183$ and $f'(1) \approx 8.15485$. Equation of tangent line at $x = 1$:
$y - 2.7183 = 8.15485(x - 1)$

$y = 8.15485(x - 1) + 2.7183$

$f(1.1) \approx 8.15485(1.1 - 1) + 2.7183$

$\approx 3.534.$

88. The correct answer is (A).

The area bounded by $y = -3x^2 + kx - 1$ and the x-axis, the lines $x = 1$ and $x = 2$ is

$$A = \int_1^2 \left(-3x^2 + kx - 1\right) dx = -x^3 + \frac{kx^2}{2} - x \Big|_1^2$$

$$= \left(-2^3 + \frac{k}{2}2^2 - 2\right) - \left(-1^3 + \frac{k}{2}1^2 - 1\right)$$

$$= (-10 + 2k) - \left(-2 + \frac{k}{2}\right).$$

Since the area is known to be 5.5,

set $A = -8 + \frac{3}{2}k = 5.5$ and solve:

$\frac{3}{2}k = 5.5 + 8 = 13.5$

$\Rightarrow \frac{3}{2}k = 13.5 \Rightarrow k = 9$. Alternatively, you could also use a TI-89 graphing calculator and solve the equation

$$\int_1^2 \left(-3x^2 + kx - 1\right) dx = 5.5$$

and obtain $k = 9$.

89. The correct answer is (C).

$y = x^2$; $\frac{dy}{dx} = 2x$

$y = -\sqrt{x} = -x^{1/2}$;

$\frac{dy}{dx} = -\frac{1}{2}x^{-1/2} = -\frac{1}{2\sqrt{x}}$

Perpendicular tangent lines ⇒ slopes are negative reciprocals.

Thus, $(2x)\left(-\frac{1}{2\sqrt{x}}\right) = -1$

$-\sqrt{x} = -1 \Rightarrow \sqrt{x} = 1$ or $x = 1$.

90. The correct answer is (D).

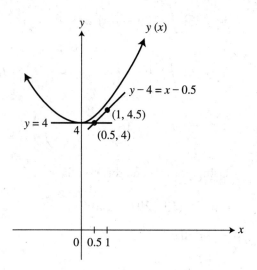

At $x = 0$, $\dfrac{dy}{dx} = 2x = 2(0) = 0$, which leads to a horizontal tangent. Since $y(0) = 4$, the point of tangency is $(0, 4)$ and the equation of the horizontal is $y = 4$. A step size of 0.5 gives the next x-value at $x = 0.5$, and you have the point $(0.5, 4)$, and $\dfrac{dy}{dx}\bigg|_{x=0.5} = 2(0.5) = 1$. Thus, the equation of the tangent at the point $(0.5, 4)$ is $y - 4 = 1(x - 0.5)$. At $x = 1$, $y - 4 = 1(1 - 0.5)$ or $y = 4.5$. Thus, $y(1) \approx 4.5$.

Section II—Part A

1. (A) At 1:00 a.m., $t = 6$.

$$f(6) = 96 - 20 \sin\left(\frac{6}{4}\right)$$

$$= 76.05° \approx 76° \text{ Fahrenheit}$$

(B) Average temperature

$$= \frac{1}{12} \int_0^{12} \left[96 - 20 \sin\left(\frac{t}{4}\right)\right] dt.$$

Using your calculator, you have:

Average temperature $= \dfrac{1}{12}(992.80)$

$$= 82.73 \approx 82.7.$$

(C) Let $y_1 = f(x) = 96 - 20 \sin\left(\dfrac{x}{4}\right)$ and

$y_2 = 80$.

Using the [*Intersection*] function of your calculator, you obtain

$x = 3.70 \approx 3.7$ or $x = 8.85 \approx 8.9$.

Thus, the heating system is turned on when $3.7 < t < 8.9$.

[−2,10] by [−10,100]

(D) Total cost

$$= (0.25) \int_{3.7}^{8.9} (80 - f(t)) dt$$

$$= (0.25) \int_{3.7}^{8.9} \left[80 - \left(96 - 20 \sin\left(\frac{t}{4}\right)\right)\right] dt$$

$$= (0.25) \int_{3.7}^{8.9} \left(-16 + 20 \sin\left(\frac{t}{4}\right)\right) dt.$$

Using your calculator, you have:

$= (0.25)(13.629) = 3.407$

≈ 3 dollars.

2. Given the differential equation $\dfrac{dy}{dx} = \dfrac{2xy}{3}$:

(A) Calculate slopes.

	$y = -2$	$y = -1$	$y = 0$	$y = 1$	$y = 2$
$x = -3$	4	2	0	-2	-4
$x = -2$	$\dfrac{8}{3}$	$\dfrac{4}{3}$	0	$-\dfrac{4}{3}$	$-\dfrac{8}{3}$
$x = -1$	$\dfrac{4}{3}$	$\dfrac{2}{3}$	0	$-\dfrac{2}{3}$	$-\dfrac{4}{3}$
$x = 0$	0	0	0	0	0
$x = 1$	$-\dfrac{4}{3}$	$-\dfrac{2}{3}$	0	$\dfrac{2}{3}$	$\dfrac{4}{3}$
$x = 2$	$-\dfrac{8}{3}$	$-\dfrac{4}{3}$	0	$\dfrac{4}{3}$	$\dfrac{8}{3}$
$x = 3$	-4	-2	0	2	4

Sketch the slope field.

(B) $f(0.1) = f(0) + 0.1 \left. \dfrac{2xy}{3} \right|_{x = 0,\, y = 2}$

$$= 2 + 0.1\,(0) = 2$$

$$f(0.2) = f(0.1) + 0.1 \left. \dfrac{dy}{dx} \right|_{x = 0.1,\, y = 2}$$

$$= 2 + 0.1\left(\dfrac{0.4}{3}\right)$$

$$= 2 + \dfrac{0.04}{3} = 2.01\overline{3}$$

$$f(0.3) = f(0.2) + 0.1 \left. \dfrac{dy}{dx} \right|_{x = 0.2,\, y = 2.01\overline{3}}$$

$$= 2.01\overline{3} + 0.02684 = 2.04017$$

$$\approx 2.040$$

(C) $\dfrac{dy}{dx} = \dfrac{2xy}{3}$

$$\dfrac{1}{y}\,dy = \dfrac{2}{3}x\,dx$$

$$\ln|y| = \dfrac{1}{3}x^2 + c_1$$

$$y = c_2 e^{x^2/3}$$

According to the initial condition, $2 = c_2 e^{0/3} \Rightarrow c_2 = 2$, so the particular solution is $y = 2e^{x^2/3}$. Evaluate at $x = 0.3$ and $y(0.3) = 2e^{0.09/3} = 2e^{0.03} \approx 2.061$.

Section II—Part B

3. (A) Midpoints of 5 subintervals of equal length are $t = 3, 9, 15, 21,$ and 27. The length of each subinterval is

$$\frac{30 - 0}{5} = 6.$$

Thus, $\displaystyle\int_0^{30} v(t)dt \approx 6[v(3) + v(9) + v(15)$

$$+ v(21) + v(27)]$$

$$= 6[7.5 + 12 + 13.5$$

$$+ 14 + 13]$$

$$= 6[60] = 360.$$

(B) Average velocity $= \displaystyle\frac{1}{30 - 0} \int_0^{30} v(t)dt$

$$\approx \frac{1}{30}(360)$$

$$\approx 12 \text{ m/sec.}$$

(C) Average acceleration $= \displaystyle\frac{12 - 0}{30 - 0}$ m/sec^2

$$= 0.4 \text{ m/sec}^2.$$

(D) Approximate acceleration at $t = 6$

$$= \frac{v(9) - v(3)}{9 - 3} = \frac{12 - 7.5}{6} = 0.75 \text{ m/sec}^2.$$

(E) Looking at the velocity in the table, you see that the velocity decreases from $t = 18$ to $t = 30$. Thus, the acceleration is negative for $18 < t < 30$.

4.

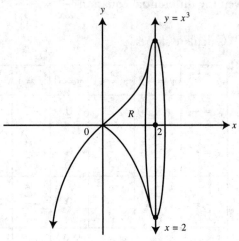

(A) Area of R $= \displaystyle\int_0^2 x^3 dx = \frac{x^4}{4}\Big]_0^2$

$$= \frac{2^4}{4} - 0 = 4$$

(B) Volume of solid $= \pi \displaystyle\int_0^2 (x^3)^2 dx$

$$= \pi \left[\frac{x^7}{7}\right]_0^2 = \frac{2^7(\pi)}{7}$$

$$= \frac{128\pi}{7}.$$

(C) $\pi \displaystyle\int_0^a (x^3)^2 dx = \frac{1}{2}\left(\frac{128\pi}{7}\right)$

$$\pi \left[\frac{x^7}{7}\right]_0^a = \frac{64\pi}{7}; \quad \frac{\pi a^7}{7} = \frac{64\pi}{7};$$

$$a^7 = 64 = 2^6; \quad a = 2^{6/7}$$

(D) Area of cross section $= (x^3)^2 = x^6.$

Volume of solid $= \displaystyle\int_0^2 x^6 dx = \frac{x^7}{7}\Big]_0^2 = \frac{128}{7}.$

5. Given $f(0) = 1$, $f'(0) = 6$, $f''(0) = -4$, and $f'''(0) = 30$.

(A) The third-degree Taylor polynomial for f about $x = 0$ is

$$f(x) \approx \frac{f(0)}{0!}x^0 + \frac{f'(0)}{1!}x^1 + \frac{f''(0)}{2!}x^2$$
$$+ \frac{f'''(0)}{3!}x^3$$

$$\approx 1 + 6x + \frac{-4}{2}x^2 + \frac{30}{6}x^3$$

$$\approx 1 + 6x - 2x^2 + 5x^3.$$

To approximate $f(0.1)$:

$$f(0.1) \approx 1 + 6(0.1) - 2(0.1)^2 + 5(0.1)^3$$

$$\approx 1 + 0.6 - 2(0.01) + 5(0.001)$$

$$\approx 1 + 0.6 - 0.02 + 0.005$$

$$\approx 1.585.$$

(B) The sixth degree Taylor polynomial for $g(x) = f(x^2)$, about $x = 0$, is

$$g(x) = f(x^2)$$

$$\approx 1 + 6(x^2) - 2(x^2)^2 + 5(x^2)^3$$

$$g(x) \approx 1 + 6x^2 - 2x^4 + 5x^6.$$

(C) The seventh degree Taylor polynomial for

$$h(x) = \int_0^x g(t)\, dt, \text{ about } x = 0, \text{ is}$$

$$h(x) \approx \int_0^x \left(1 + 6t^2 - 2t^4 + 5t^6\right) dt$$

$$h(x) \approx \left[t + \frac{6}{3}t^3 - \frac{2}{5}t^5 + \frac{5}{7}t^7\right]_0^x$$

$$h(x) \approx x + 2x^3 - \frac{2}{5}x^5 + \frac{5}{7}x^7.$$

6. Given $x = 2(\theta - \sin\theta)$ and $y = 2(1 - \cos\theta)$:

(A) $\dfrac{dx}{d\theta} = 2(1 - \cos\theta)$ and $\dfrac{dy}{d\theta} = 2\sin\theta$.

Divide to find

$$\frac{dy}{dx} = \frac{2\sin\theta}{2(1 - \cos\theta)} = \frac{\sin\theta}{1 - \cos\theta}.$$

(B) At $\theta = \pi$, $x = 2(\pi - \sin\pi) = 2\pi$,

$y = 2(1 - \cos\pi) = 4$, and

$$\left.\frac{dy}{dx}\right|_{\theta=\pi} = \frac{\sin\pi}{1 - \cos\pi} = 0.$$

The tangent line at $(2\pi, 4)$ is horizontal, so the equation of the tangent is $y = 4$.

(C) At $\theta = 2\pi$, $x = 2(2\pi - \sin 2\pi) = 4\pi$,

$y = 2(1 - \cos 2\pi) = 0$, and

$$\left.\frac{dy}{dx}\right|_{\theta=2\pi} = \frac{\sin 2\pi}{1 - \cos 2\pi} = \frac{0}{0}.$$ Since the

derivative is undefined, the tangent line at $(4\pi, 0)$ is vertical, so the equation of the tangent is $x = 4\pi$.

(D)

$$L = \int_0^{2\pi} \sqrt{[2(1 - \cos\theta)]^2 + [2\sin\theta]^2}\, d\theta$$

$$= \int_0^{2\pi} \sqrt{4(1 - 2\cos\theta + \cos^2\theta) + 4\sin^2\theta}\, d\theta$$

$$= \int_0^{2\pi} \sqrt{4 - 8\cos\theta + 4\cos^2\theta + 4\sin^2\theta}\, d\theta$$

$$= \int_0^{2\pi} \sqrt{4 - 8\cos\theta + 4}\, d\theta$$

$$= \int_0^{2\pi} \sqrt{8 - 8\cos\theta}\, d\theta$$

$$= 2\sqrt{2} \int_0^{2\pi} \sqrt{1 - \cos\theta}\, d\theta$$

Scoring Sheet for AP Calculus BC Practice Exam 1

Section I—Part A

$$\underline{\hspace{3cm}} \times 1.2 = \underline{\hspace{3cm}}$$
No. Correct   Subtotal A

Section I—Part B

$$\underline{\hspace{3cm}} \times 1.2 = \underline{\hspace{3cm}}$$
No. Correct   Subtotal B

Section II—Part A (Each question is worth 9 points.)

$$\underline{\hspace{2cm}} + \underline{\hspace{2cm}} = \underline{\hspace{2cm}}$$
Q1   Q2   Subtotal C

Section II—Part B (Each question is worth 9 points)

$$\underline{\hspace{2cm}} + \underline{\hspace{2cm}} + \underline{\hspace{2cm}} + \underline{\hspace{2cm}} = \underline{\hspace{2cm}}$$
Q1   Q2   Q3   Q4   Subtotal D

Total Raw Score (Subtotals A + B + C + D) = [　　　]

Approximate Conversion Scale:

Total Raw Score	Approximate AP Grade
80–108	5
65–79	4
50–64	3
36–49	2
0–35	1

AP Calculus BC Practice Exam 2

ANSWER SHEET FOR MULTIPLE-CHOICE QUESTIONS

Part A

1. (A) (B) (C) (D)
2. (A) (B) (C) (D)
3. (A) (B) (C) (D)
4. (A) (B) (C) (D)
5. (A) (B) (C) (D)
6. (A) (B) (C) (D)
7. (A) (B) (C) (D)
8. (A) (B) (C) (D)
9. (A) (B) (C) (D)
10. (A) (B) (C) (D)
11. (A) (B) (C) (D)
12. (A) (B) (C) (D)
13. (A) (B) (C) (D)
14. (A) (B) (C) (D)
15. (A) (B) (C) (D)
16. (A) (B) (C) (D)
17. (A) (B) (C) (D)
18. (A) (B) (C) (D)
19. (A) (B) (C) (D)
20. (A) (B) (C) (D)
21. (A) (B) (C) (D)
22. (A) (B) (C) (D)
23. (A) (B) (C) (D)
24. (A) (B) (C) (D)
25. (A) (B) (C) (D)
26. (A) (B) (C) (D)
27. (A) (B) (C) (D)
28. (A) (B) (C) (D)
29. (A) (B) (C) (D)
30. (A) (B) (C) (D)

Part B

76. (A) (B) (C) (D)
77. (A) (B) (C) (D)
78. (A) (B) (C) (D)
79. (A) (B) (C) (D)
80. (A) (B) (C) (D)
81. (A) (B) (C) (D)
82. (A) (B) (C) (D)
83. (A) (B) (C) (D)
84. (A) (B) (C) (D)
85. (A) (B) (C) (D)
86. (A) (B) (C) (D)
87. (A) (B) (C) (D)
88. (A) (B) (C) (D)
89. (A) (B) (C) (D)
90. (A) (B) (C) (D)

Section I—Part A

Number of Questions	Time	Use of Calculator
30	60 Minutes	No

Directions:

Use the answer sheet provided on the previous page. All questions are given equal weight. Points are *not* deducted for incorrect answers and no points are given to unanswered questions. Unless otherwise indicated, the domain of a function f is the set of all real numbers. The use of a calculator is *not* permitted in this part of the exam.

1. $\lim\limits_{x \to 0} \dfrac{2 \cos x - 2}{x^2} =$

   (A) -2
   (B) -1
   (C) 0
   (D) 1

(A)

(B)

2. If $f(x) = x^3 + 3x^2 + cx + 4$ has a horizontal tangent and a point of inflection at the same value of x, what is the value of c?

   (A) 0
   (B) 1
   (C) -3
   (D) 3

(C)

(D)

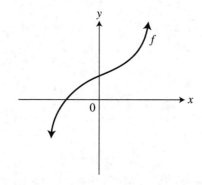

3. The graph of f is shown above. Which of the following could be the graph of f'?

GO ON TO THE NEXT PAGE

4. What are all values of x such that $\displaystyle\sum_{k=1}^{\infty} \left(\frac{x}{2}\right)^k$ converges?

(A) 0 only

(B) $-2 < x < 2$ only

(C) $-\dfrac{1}{2} < x < \dfrac{1}{2}$ only

(D) all real values

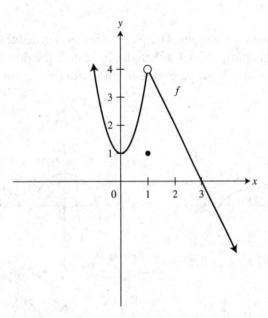

5. The graph of a function f is shown above. Which of the following statements is/are true?

   I. $\displaystyle\lim_{x \to 1} f(x)$ exists

  II. $f(1)$ exists

 III. $\displaystyle\lim_{x \to 1} f(x) = f(1)$

    (A) I only

    (B) II only

    (C) I and II only

    (D) I, II, and III

6. What is the area of the region between the graph of $y = \dfrac{1}{x^2}$ and the x-axis for $x \geq 4$?

(A) $-\dfrac{1}{4}$

(B) $-\dfrac{1}{2}$

(C) $\dfrac{1}{4}$

(D) $\dfrac{1}{2}$

7. If $g(x)$ is continuous for all real values of x, then $\displaystyle\int_{a/3}^{b/3} g(3x)\,dx =$

(A) $\dfrac{1}{3}\displaystyle\int_{a}^{b} g(x)\,dx$

(B) $3\displaystyle\int_{a}^{b} g(x)\,dx$

(C) $\dfrac{1}{3}\displaystyle\int_{3a}^{3b} g(x)\,dx$

(D) $\displaystyle\int_{a}^{b} g(x)\,dx$

8. $\displaystyle\sum_{n=0}^{\infty} \frac{3^{n+2}}{4^n} =$

(A) $\dfrac{3}{4}$

(B) 4

(C) 9

(D) 36

9. The $\displaystyle\lim_{h \to 0} \frac{\ln(x + h - 3) - \ln(x - 3)}{h}$ is

(A) $\ln(x - 3)$

(B) $\dfrac{1}{\ln(x - 3)}$

(C) $\dfrac{1}{x + 3}$

(D) $\dfrac{1}{x - 3}$

GO ON TO THE NEXT PAGE

10. Let f be a function with the following properties.

x	$f(x)$	$f'(x)$	$f''(x)$	$f'''(x)$
0	1	1	2	6
2	−1	1	−2	6

Which of the following is the third-degree Taylor polynomial for f about $x = 2$?

(A) $1 + x + x^2 + 2x^3$

(B) $x - 3 - 2(x - 2)^2 + 6(x - 2)^3$

(C) $-3 + x - (x - 2)^2 + (x - 2)^3$

(D) $-3 + x - (x - 2)^2 + 2(x - 2)^3$

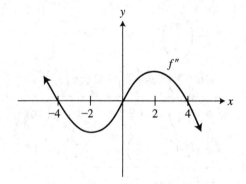

11. The graph of f'', the second derivative of f is shown above. The graph of f'' has horizontal tangents at $x = -2$ and $x = 2$. For what values of x does the graph of the function f have a point of inflection?

(A) −4, 0 and 4

(B) −2, 0 and 2

(C) −4 and 4 only

(D) 0 only

12. Given the infinite series $\sum_{k=1}^{\infty} \dfrac{\sqrt{k}}{k^n}$, what are all values of n for which the series converges?

(A) $n > \dfrac{1}{2}$

(B) $n > 1$

(C) $n > \dfrac{3}{2}$

(D) $n \geq \dfrac{3}{2}$

13. If $f(x)$ is continuous and $f(x) > 0$ on $[0, 4]$ and twice differentiable on $(0, 4)$ such that $f'(x) > 0$ and $f''(x) > 0$, which of the following has the greatest value?

(A) $\displaystyle\int_0^4 f(x)\,dx$

(B) Left Riemann sum approximation of $\displaystyle\int_0^4 f(x)\,dx$ with 4 subintervals of equal length

(C) Right Riemann sum approximation of $\displaystyle\int_0^4 f(x)\,dx$ with 4 subintervals of equal length

(D) Midpoint Riemann sum approximation of $\displaystyle\int_0^4 f(x)\,dx$ with 4 subintervals of equal length

14. Which of the following is an equation of the tangent line to the curve described by the parametric equations $x = t$ and $y = t^2$ when $t = 4$?

(A) $y = 8$

(B) $y = 2x + 8$

(C) $y = 8x - 16$

(D) $y = 8x + 16$

15. Let f and g be differentiable functions such that $g(x) = f^{-1}(x)$. If $f(2) = 4$, $f(3) = 9$, $g'(4) = \dfrac{1}{4}$ and $g'(9) = \dfrac{1}{6}$, what is the value of $f'(3)$?

(A) 3

(B) 4

(C) 6

(D) 9

16. What is the value of $\displaystyle\sum_{n=0}^{\infty} \frac{1}{(n+2)(n+3)}$?

(A) $\dfrac{1}{6}$

(B) $\dfrac{1}{3}$

(C) $\dfrac{1}{2}$

(D) 2

17. The domain of the function f is $0 \le x \le 9$ as shown above. If $g(x) = \displaystyle\int_0^x f(t)\,dt$, at what value of x is $g(x)$ the absolute maximum?

(A) 0

(B) 1

(C) 2

(D) 8

18. Which of the following represents the arc length of the curve with the parametric equations $x = \sqrt{t}$ and $y = e^t$ for $4 \le t \le 9$?

(A) $\displaystyle\int_4^9 \left(\sqrt{t} + e^t\right) dt$

(B) $\displaystyle\int_4^9 \sqrt{t + e^{2t}}\, dt$

(C) $\displaystyle\int_4^9 \left(\frac{1}{2\sqrt{t}} + e^{2t}\right) dt$

(D) $\displaystyle\int_4^9 \sqrt{\frac{1}{4t} + e^{2t}}\, dt$

19. If $f(x) = \dfrac{3x}{1 + 2^x}$, the horizontal asymptotes of the graph of f is/are

(A) $y = \dfrac{3}{2}$ only

(B) $y = 0$ only

(C) $y = 0$ and $y = \dfrac{3}{2}$

(D) nonexistent

20. Which of the following expressions gives the slope of the tangent line to the curve of the polar equation $r = 2\cos\theta$ at $\theta = \dfrac{\pi}{3}$?

(A) $-2\sin\left(\dfrac{\pi}{3}\right)$

(B) $\dfrac{-2\sin\left(\frac{\pi}{3}\right)\cos\left(\frac{\pi}{3}\right) - 2\cos\left(\frac{\pi}{3}\right)\sin\left(\frac{\pi}{3}\right)}{-2\sin\left(\frac{\pi}{3}\right)\sin\left(\frac{\pi}{3}\right) + 2\cos\left(\frac{\pi}{3}\right)\cos\left(\frac{\pi}{3}\right)}$

(C) $\dfrac{-\sin\left(\frac{\pi}{3}\right)\sin\left(\frac{\pi}{3}\right) + \cos\left(\frac{\pi}{3}\right)\cos\left(\frac{\pi}{3}\right)}{-\sin\left(\frac{\pi}{3}\right)\cos\left(\frac{\pi}{3}\right) - \cos\left(\frac{\pi}{3}\right)\sin\left(\frac{\pi}{3}\right)}$

(D) $\dfrac{-2\sin\left(\frac{\pi}{3}\right)\sin\left(\frac{\pi}{3}\right) + 2\cos\left(\frac{\pi}{3}\right)\cos\left(\frac{\pi}{3}\right)}{-2\sin\left(\frac{\pi}{3}\right)\cos\left(\frac{\pi}{3}\right) - 2\cos\left(\frac{\pi}{3}\right)\sin\left(\frac{\pi}{3}\right)}$

GO ON TO THE NEXT PAGE

[-5, 5] by [-5, 5]

21. The graph of f is shown above, and f is twice differentiable. Which of the following has the largest value?

I. $f(0)$

II. $f'(0)$

III. $f''(0)$

    (A) I

    (B) II

    (C) III

    (D) I and II

22. $\displaystyle\int x\sqrt{x+2}\,dx =$

    (A) $\dfrac{x^2}{2} + 2(x-2)^{3/2} + c$

    (B) $\dfrac{2}{3}(x+2)^{3/2} + c$

    (C) $\dfrac{2}{5}(x+2)^{5/2} - \dfrac{4}{3}(x+2)^{3/2} + c$

    (D) $\dfrac{2}{5}(x-2)^{5/2} + \dfrac{4}{3}(x-2)^{3/2} + c$

23. $\displaystyle\int \dfrac{5}{(x-3)(x+2)}\,dx =$

    (A) $\ln|x-3| + \ln|x+2| + c$

    (B) $\ln|x-3| - \ln|x+2| + c$

    (C) $2\ln|x-3| + 3\ln|x+2| + c$

    (D) $\dfrac{1}{5}\ln|(x-3)(x+2)| + c$

24. A slope field for a differential equation is shown above. Which of the following could be the differential equation?

    (A) $\dfrac{dy}{dx} = 2x$

    (B) $\dfrac{dy}{dx} = -2x$

    (C) $\dfrac{dy}{dx} = y$

    (D) $\dfrac{dy}{dx} = x - y$

25. Which of the following is a Taylor series for xe^{2x} about $x = 0$?

    (A) $x + x^2 + \dfrac{x^3}{3!} + \dfrac{x^4}{4!} + \cdots$

    (B) $1 + 2x + \dfrac{2x^2}{2!} + \dfrac{2x^3}{3!} + \cdots$

    (C) $x + 2x^2 + \dfrac{4x^3}{2!} + \dfrac{8x^4}{3!} + \cdots$

    (D) $x + 2x^2 + \dfrac{4x^3}{2} + \dfrac{8x^4}{3} + \cdots$

GO ON TO THE NEXT PAGE

26. If $\sum_{k=0}^{\infty} b_k$ converges and $0 < a_k \le b_k$ for all k, which of the following statements must be true?

(A) $\sum_{k=0}^{\infty} a_k$ diverges

(B) $\sum_{k=0}^{\infty} a_k$ converges

(C) $\sum_{k=0}^{\infty} 2a_k$ diverges

(D) $\sum_{k=0}^{\infty} (-1)^k b_k$ diverges

27. If $\displaystyle\int x \sec^2 x \, dx = f(x) + \ln|\cos x| + C$, then $f(x) =$

(A) $\tan x$

(B) $\dfrac{1}{2}x^2$

(C) $x \tan x$

(D) $x^2 \tan x$

28. A solid has a circular base of radius 1. If every plane cross section perpendicular to the x-axis is a square, then the volume of the solid is

(A) $\dfrac{16}{3}$

(B) $\dfrac{8}{3}$

(C) 4π

(D) $\dfrac{16\pi}{3}$

29. If n is a positive integer, then

$$\lim_{n\to\infty} \frac{1}{n}\left[\left(\frac{1}{n}\right)^2 + \left(\frac{2}{n}\right)^2 + \cdots + \left(\frac{n-1}{n}\right)^2\right] =$$

(A) $\displaystyle\int_0^1 \frac{1}{x^2}\, dx$

(B) $\displaystyle\int_0^1 x^2 \, dx$

(C) $\displaystyle\int_0^1 \frac{2}{x^2}\, dx$

(D) $\displaystyle\int_0^1 \frac{1}{x}\, dx$

(E) $\displaystyle\int_0^2 x^2 \, dx$

30. The area enclosed by the parabola $y = x - x^2$ and the x-axis is revolved about the x-axis. The volume of the resulting solid is

(A) $\dfrac{1}{30}$

(B) $\dfrac{1}{6}$

(C) $\dfrac{\pi}{30}$

(D) $\dfrac{\pi}{15}$

STOP. AP Calculus BC Practice Exam 2 Section I—Part A

Section I—Part B

Number of Questions	Time	Use of Calculator
15	45 Minutes	Yes

Directions:

Use the same answer sheet for Part A. *Please note that the questions begin with number 76. This is not an error. It is done to be consistent with the numbering system of the actual AP Calculus BC Exam.* All questions are given equal weight. Points are *not* deducted for incorrect answers, and no points are given to unanswered questions. Unless otherwise indicated, the domain of a function f is the set of all real numbers. If the exact numerical value does not appear among the given choices, select the best approximate value. The use of a calculator is *permitted* in this part of the exam.

76. Find the values of a and b that assure that

$$f(x) = \begin{cases} \ln(3-x) & \text{if } x < 2 \\ a - bx & \text{if } x \geq 2 \end{cases}$$

is differentiable at $x = 2$.

    (A) $a = 3, b = 1$
    (B) $a = 1, b = 2$
    (C) $a = 2, b = 1$
    (D) $a = -2, b = -1$

77. The table shows some of the values of differentiable functions f and g and their derivatives. If $h(x) = f(g(x))$, then $h'(2)$ equals

x	$f(x)$	$g(x)$	$f'(x)$	$g'(x)$
1	0	−1	−2	5
2	4	3	5	1
3	2	3	−1	0

    (A) −2
    (B) −1
    (C) 0
    (D) 1

78. Line l is tangent to the graph of a function f at the point $(0, 1)$. If f is twice differentiable with $f'(0) = 2$ and $f''(0) = 3$, what is the approximate value of $f(0.1)$ using line l?

    (A) 0.1
    (B) 0.2
    (C) 1.2
    (D) 2.1

79. Let $f(x)$ be a differentiable function on the closed interval $[1, 3]$. The average value of $f'(x)$ on $[1, 3]$ is

    (A) $2(f'(3) - f'(1))$
    (B) $\frac{1}{2}(f'(3) - f'(1))$
    (C) $f(3) - f(1)$
    (D) $\frac{1}{2}(f(3) - f(1))$

80. The position of a particle moving in the xy-plane at any time t is given as $x(t) = 2\cos(4t)$ and $y(t) = \frac{1}{2}t^2$. What is the speed of the particle at $t = 1$?

    (A) .807
    (B) 2.656
    (C) 6.136
    (D) 7.054

GO ON TO THE NEXT PAGE

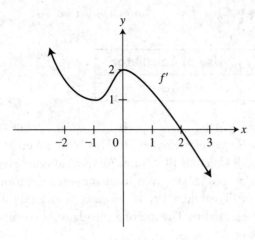

81. The graph of f' is shown above. Which of the following statements is/are true?

I. The function f is decreasing on the interval $(-\infty, -1)$.

II. The function f has an absolute maximum at $x = 2$.

III. The function f has a point of inflection at $x = -1$.

(A) II only
(B) III only
(C) II and III only
(D) I, II, and III

82. $\displaystyle\sum_{k=0}^{\infty} (-1)^k \frac{\pi^{(2k)}}{(2k)!} =$

(A) −1
(B) 0
(C) 1
(D) π

83. The slope of the normal line to $y = e^{-2x}$ when $x = 1.158$ is approximately

(A) 5.068
(B) 0.864
(C) −0.197
(D) 0.099

84. What is the approximate value of $y(1)$ using Euler's method with a step size of 0.5 and starting at $x = 0$. If $\dfrac{dy}{dx} = e^x$ and $y(0) = 1$?

(A) .135
(B) .607
(C) 2.165
(D) 2.324

85. If a function f is continuous for all values of x and k is a real number, and

$$\int_{-k}^{0} f(x)\,dx = -\int_{0}^{k} f(x)\,dx,$$ which of the following could be the graph of f?

(A)

(B)

(C)

(D)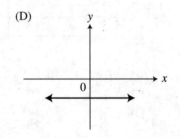

GO ON TO THE NEXT PAGE

86. Which of the following is the best approximate value of y when $x = 3.1$ if $2x \dfrac{dy}{dx} - 7 = 1$ and $y = 4.5$ when $x = 3$?

   (A) 1.290
   (B) −9.104
   (C) 4.631
   (D) 4.525

87. The velocity of a particle moving on a number line is given by $v(t) = \sin(t^2 + 1)$, $t \geq 0$. At $t = 1$, the position of the particle is 5. When the velocity of the particle is equal to 0 for the first time, what is the position of the particle?

   (A) 5.250
   (B) 4.750
   (C) 3.537
   (D) 1.463

88. $\displaystyle\sum_{n=1}^{\infty} \dfrac{n! + 2^n}{2^n \cdot n!} =$

   (A) e
   (B) $1 + e$
   (C) $2 + e$
   (D) $\dfrac{2}{3} + e$

89. At what value of x does the graph of $y = \dfrac{1}{x^2} - \dfrac{1}{x^3}$ have a point of inflection?

   (A) $x = 1$
   (B) $x = 2$
   (C) $x = 3$
   (D) $x = 4$

90. Twenty ostriches are introduced into a newly built game farm. If the rate of growth of this ostrich population is modeled by the logistic differential equation $\dfrac{dp}{dt} = .25p\left(1 - \dfrac{p}{200}\right)$ with the time t in years, and the farm can support no more than 200 ostriches, how many years, to the nearest integer, will it take for the population to reach 100?

   (A) 5
   (B) 7
   (C) 8
   (D) 9

STOP. AP Calculus BC Practice Exam 2 Section I—Part B

Section II—Part A

Number of Questions	Time	Use of Calculator
2	30 Minutes	Yes

Directions:

Show all work. You may *not* receive any credit for correct answers without supporting work. You may use an approved calculator to help solve a problem. However, you must clearly indicate the setup of your solution using mathematical notations and *not* calculator syntax. Calculators may be used to find the derivative of a function at a point, compute the numerical value of a definite integral, or solve an equation. Unless otherwise indicated, you may assume the following: (a) the numeric or algebraic answers need not be simplified; (b) your answer, if expressed in approximation, should be correct to 3 places after the decimal point; and (c) the domain of a function f is the set of all real numbers.

1. The temperature of a liquid at a chemical plant during a 20-minute period is given as

   $g(t) = 90 - 4 \tan\left(\dfrac{t}{20}\right)$, where $g(t)$ is measured

   in degrees Fahrenheit, $0 \le t \le 20$ and t is measured in minutes.

   (A) Sketch the graph of g on the provided grid. What is the temperature of the liquid to the nearest hundredth of a degree Fahrenheit when $t = 10$? (See Figure 3T-11.)

   (B) What is the instantaneous rate of change of the temperature of the liquid to the nearest hundredth of a degree Fahrenheit at $t = 10$?

   (C) At what values of t is the temperature of the liquid below 86°F?

   (D) During the time within the 20-minute period when the temperature is below 86°F, what is the average temperature to the nearest hundredth of a degree Fahrenheit?

2. The position vector of a particle moving in the xy-plane is $\langle x(t), y(t) \rangle$ with $t \ge 0$, $x(t) = 3t^2 + 4$, and $y(t) = \cos(2t - 4)$.

   (A) Find the acceleration vector of the particle at $t = 2$.

   (B) Find the speed of the particle of $t = 2$.

   (C) Write an equation of the line tangent to the path of the particle at $t = 2$.

   (D) Find the total distance traveled by the particle for $0 \le t \le 2$.

STOP. AP Calculus BC Practice Exam 2 Section II—Part A

Section II—Part B

Number of Questions	Time	Use of Calculator
4	60 Minutes	No

Directions:

The use of a calculator is *not* permitted in this part of the exam. When you have finished this part of the test, you may return to the problems in Part A of Section II and continue to work on them. However, you may not use a calculator. You should *show all work*. You may *not* receive any credit for correct answers without supporting work. Unless otherwise indicated, the numeric or algebraic answers need not be simplified, and the domain of a function f is the set of all real numbers.

3. The function f is defined as $f(x) = \displaystyle\int_0^x g(t)dt$

   where the graph of g consists of five line segments as shown in the figure below.

   (A) Find $f(-3)$ and $f(3)$.

   (B) Find all values of x on $(-3, 3)$ such that f has a relative maximum or minimum. Justify your answer.

   (C) Find all values of x on $(-3, 3)$ such that the graph f has a change of concavity. Justify your answer.

   (D) Write an equation of the line tangent to the graph to f at $x = 1$.

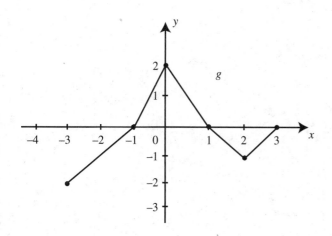

4. Let R be the region enclosed by the graph of $y = x^2$ and the line $y = 4$.

   (A) Find the area of region R.

   (B) If the line $x = a$ divides region R into two regions of equal area, find a.

   (C) If the line $y = b$ divides the region R into two regions of equal area, find b.

   (D) If region R is revolved about the x-axis, find the volume of the resulting solid.

5. The slope of a function f at any point (x, y) is $\dfrac{y}{2x^2}$. The point $(2, 1)$ is on the graph of f.

   (A) Write an equation of the tangent line to the graph of f at $x = 2$.

   (B) Use the tangent line in part (A) to approximate $f(2.5)$.

   (C) Solve the differential equation $\dfrac{dy}{dx} = \dfrac{y}{2x^2}$ with the initial condition $f(2) = 1$.

   (D) Use the solution in part (C) and find $f(2.5)$.

GO ON TO THE NEXT PAGE

6. The Maclaurin series given below for the function $f(x) = \tan^{-1} x$ is
$$\tan^{-1} x = x - \frac{x^3}{3} + \frac{x^5}{5} - \cdots + (-1)^{n+1} \frac{x^{2n-1}}{2n-1}.$$

(A) If $g(x) = f'(x)$, write the first four non-zero terms of the Maclaurin series for $g(x)$.

(B) If $h(x) = f(2x)$, write the first four non-zero terms and the general term of the Maclaurin series for $h(x)$.

(C) Find the interval of convergence for the Maclaurin series for $h(x)$.

(D) The approximate value of $h\left(\frac{1}{4}\right)$ is $\frac{11}{24}$ using the first two non-zero terms of the Maclaurin series. Show that $\left| h\left(\frac{1}{4}\right) - \frac{11}{24} \right|$ is less than $\frac{1}{150}$.

STOP. AP Calculus BC Practice Exam 2 Section II—Part B

Answers to BC Practice Exam 2—Section I

Part A
1. B
2. D
3. C
4. B
5. C
6. C
7. A
8. D
9. D
10. C
11. A

12. C
13. C
14. C
15. C
16. C
17. C
18. D
19. B
20. D
21. C
22. C
23. B

24. B
25. C
26. B
27. C
28. A
29. B
30. C

Part B
76. C
77. B
78. C

79. D
80. C
81. C
82. A
83. A
84. D
85. B
86. C
87. A
88. A
89. B
90. D

Answers to BC Practice Exam 2—Section II

Part A

1. (A) See graph, and $g(10) = 87.82°$ or $87.81°$.

(3 pts.)

(B) $-0.26°/\min$ (2 pts.)

(C) $15.708 < t \leq 20$ (2 pts.)

(D) $84.99°$ (2 pts.)

2. (A) $\langle 6, -4 \rangle$ (2 pts.)

(B) 12 (2 pts.)

(C) $y = 1$ (3 pts.)

(D) 12.407 (2 pts.)

Part B

3. (A) $f(-3) = 1$ and $f(3) = 0$ (2 pts.)

(B) $x = -1, 1$ (3 pts.)

(C) $x = 0$ and $x = 2$ (2 pts.)

(D) $y = 1$ (2 pts.)

4. (A) $\dfrac{32}{3}$ (3 pts.)

(B) $a = 0$ (1 pt.)

(C) $b = 4^{2/3}$ (2 pts.)

(D) $\dfrac{256\pi}{5}$ (3 pts.)

5. (A) $y = \dfrac{1}{8}(x - 2) + 1$ (3 pts.)

(B) 1.063 or $\dfrac{17}{16}$ (1 pt.)

(C) $y = e^{\left(-\frac{1}{2x} + \frac{1}{4}\right)}$ (4 pts.)

(D) $e^{1/20}$ (1 pt.)

6. (A) $1 - x^2 + x^4 - x^6$ (2 pts.)

(B) $(2x) - \dfrac{8x^3}{3} + \dfrac{32x^5}{5} - \dfrac{128x^7}{7}$ (1 pt.)

General term is $(-1)^{n+1} \dfrac{(2x)^{2n-1}}{2n - 1}$ (1 pt.)

(C) $-\dfrac{1}{2} \leq x \leq \dfrac{1}{2}$ (3 pts.)

(D) $\left| h\left(\dfrac{1}{4}\right) - \dfrac{11}{24} \right| < \dfrac{\left(2\left(\frac{1}{4}\right)\right)^5}{5} = \dfrac{1}{160} < \dfrac{1}{150}$

(2 pts.)

Solutions to AP Calculus BC Practice Exam 2—Section I

Section I—Part A

1. The correct answer is (B).

Substituting 0 into the numerator and denominator leads to $\dfrac{0}{0}$.

Apply *L'Hopital's* Rule and obtain

$\displaystyle\lim_{x\to 0}\frac{-2\sin x}{2x}=\lim_{x\to 0}-\frac{\sin x}{x}$. Since $\displaystyle\lim_{x\to 0}\frac{\sin x}{x}=1$,

$\displaystyle\lim_{x\to 0}-\frac{2\cos x-2}{x^2}=-1$. Note that you could

also apply *L'Hopital's* Rule again to $\displaystyle\lim_{x\to 0}-\frac{\sin x}{x}$

and obtain $\displaystyle\lim_{x\to 0}-\cos x=-1$.

2. The correct answer is (D).

$f(x)=x^3+3x^2+cx+4$
$\Rightarrow f'(x)=3x^2+6x+c \Rightarrow f''(x)=6x+6$.
Set $6x+6=0$ so $x=-1$. $f''>0$ if
$x>-1$ and $f''<0$ if $x<-1$. Thus, f has a
point of inflection at $x=-1$, and $f'(-1)$
$=3(-1)^2+6(-1)+c=0 \Rightarrow 3-6+c=0$
$\Rightarrow -3+c=0 \Rightarrow c=3$.

3. The correct answer is (C).

Since f is an increasing function, $f'>0$.
The only graph that is greater than 0 is
choice (C).

4. The correct answer is (B).

$\displaystyle\sum_{k=1}^{\infty}\left(\frac{x}{2}\right)^k=\frac{x}{2}+\left(\frac{x}{2}\right)^2+\left(\frac{x}{2}\right)^3$. This is a

geometric series with a ratio of $\dfrac{x}{2}$. Thus,

$\left|\dfrac{x}{2}\right|<1$ or $-1<\dfrac{x}{2}<1$ or $-2<x<2$.

5. The correct answer is (C).

Since $\displaystyle\lim_{x\to 1^+}f(x)=\lim_{x\to 1^-}f(x)=4$, $\displaystyle\lim_{x\to 1}f(x)$
exists. The graph shows that at $x=1$, $f(x)=1$
and thus $f(1)$ exists. Lastly, $\displaystyle\lim_{x\to 1}f(x)\neq f(1)$.

6. The correct answer is (C).

The area of the region can be obtained as
follows:

$$Area=\lim_{b\to\infty}\int_4^b\frac{1}{x^2}dx=\lim_{b\to\infty}\int_4^b x^{-2}dx$$

$$=\lim_{b\to\infty}\left[-\frac{1}{x}\right]_4^b=\lim_{b\to\infty}\left[-\frac{1}{b}-\left(-\frac{1}{4}\right)\right]$$

$$=\lim_{b\to\infty}\left[-\frac{1}{b}+\frac{1}{4}\right]=0+\frac{1}{4}=\frac{1}{4}.$$

7. The correct answer is (A).

Let $u=3x$, $du=3dx \Rightarrow dx=\dfrac{1}{3}du$,

$x=\dfrac{a}{3}\Rightarrow u=a$, and $x=\dfrac{b}{3}\Rightarrow u=b$. Then

$$\int_{a/3}^{b/3}g(3x)dx=\int_a^b\frac{1}{3}g(u)du$$

$$=\frac{1}{3}\int_a^b g(u)du$$

$$=\frac{1}{3}[G(b)-G(a)]$$

$$=\frac{1}{3}\int_a^b g(x)dx.$$

Note that $G(x)$ is the antiderivative of $g(x)$.

8. The correct answer is (D).

Rewrite

$$\sum_{n=1}^{\infty} \frac{3^{n+2}}{4^n} \text{ as } \sum_{n=0}^{\infty} (3)^2 \left(\frac{3^n}{4^n}\right) = 9 \sum_{n=0}^{\infty} \left(\frac{3}{4}\right)^n$$

$$= 9 \left(1 + \frac{3}{4} + \left(\frac{3}{4}\right)^2 + \left(\frac{3}{4}\right)^3 + \cdots\right). \text{ Note}$$

that $1 + \frac{3}{4} + \left(\frac{3}{4}\right)^2 + \left(\frac{3}{4}\right)^3$ is a geometric

series with a ratio of $\frac{3}{4}$. Thus the infinite series

is $\frac{a_1}{1-r} = \frac{1}{1 - \frac{3}{4}} = 4$ and $9 \sum_{n=0}^{\infty} \left(\frac{3}{4}\right)^n = 36.$

9. The correct answer is (D).

The $\lim_{h \to 0} \frac{\ln(x+h-3) - \ln(x-3)}{h}$ is the

definition of the derivative for the function
$y = \ln(x-3)$; therefore, the limit is equal to

$y' = \frac{1}{x-3}.$

10. The correct answer is (C).

The Taylor polynomial of third degree about
$x = a$ is $f(a) + f'(a)(x-a) + \frac{f''(a)}{2!}(x-a)^2 +$

$\frac{f'''(a)}{3!}(x-a)^3$. In this case, the third-degree

polynomial about $x = 2$ is $-1 + (1)(x-2) -$
$\frac{2}{2!}(x-2)^2 + \frac{6}{3!}(x-2)^3$ or $-3 + x - (x-2)^2 +$
$(x-2)^3$.

11. The correct answer is (A).

Note that $f'' > 0$ on the intervals $(-\infty, -4)$
and $(0, 4)$. Thus, the graph of the function f is
concave up on these intervals. Similarly,
$f'' < 0$ and concave down on the intervals
$(-4, 0)$ and $(4, \infty)$. Therefore, f has a point of
inflection at $x = -4, 0,$ and 4.

12. The correct answer is (C).

Rewrite $\frac{\sqrt{k}}{k^n}$ as $\frac{k^{\frac{1}{2}}}{k^n}$ or $\frac{1}{k^{n-\frac{1}{2}}}$, which is a p-series.

In order for the series to converge, $\left(n - \frac{1}{2}\right)$

must be greater than 1. Thus, $n - \frac{1}{2} > 1$

or $n > \frac{3}{2}.$

13. The correct answer is (C).

Since $f'(x) > 0$, $f(x)$ is increasing, and since
$f'' > 0$, $f(x)$ is concave up. The graph of
$f(x)$ may look like the one below. The right
Riemann sum contains the largest rectangles.

Right Riemann Sum

14. The correct answer is (C).
When $t = 4$, you have $x = 4$ and $y = 16$, and thus the point $(4, 16)$ is on the curve. The slope of the tangent line is $\dfrac{dy}{dx} = \dfrac{\frac{dy}{dt}}{\frac{dx}{dt}} = \dfrac{2t}{1} = 2t$

and when $t = 4$, $\dfrac{dy}{dx} = 8$. The equation of the tangent line is $y - 16 = 8(x - 4)$ or $y = 8x - 16$.

15. The correct answer is (C).
Since $f(x)$ and $g(x)$ are inverse functions, $f(3) = 9$ implies that $g(9) = 3$. Also for inverse functions, $f'(a) = \dfrac{1}{g'(f(a))}$. Thus,

$$f'(3) = \dfrac{1}{g'(9)} = \dfrac{1}{(1/6)} = 6.$$

16. The correct answer is (C).
Write $\dfrac{1}{(n+2)(n+3)}$ as partial fractions

$\dfrac{A}{n+2} - \dfrac{B}{n+3} = \dfrac{A(n+3) + B(n+2)}{(n+2)(n+3)}$. Set

$A(n+3) + B(n+2) = 1$. Let $n = -2$ and obtain $A = 1$. Similarly, let $n = -3$ and obtain $B = -1$.
Thus, $\dfrac{1}{(n+2)(n+3)} = \dfrac{1}{n+2} - \dfrac{1}{n-3}$ and

$$\sum_{n=0}^{\infty} \dfrac{1}{(n+2)(n+3)} = \sum_{n=0}^{\infty} \left(\dfrac{1}{n+2} - \dfrac{1}{n-3}\right) =$$

$\left(\dfrac{1}{2} - \dfrac{1}{3}\right) + \left(\dfrac{1}{3} - \dfrac{1}{4}\right) + \left(\dfrac{1}{4} - \dfrac{1}{5}\right) + \cdots$

$\left(\dfrac{1}{n+2} - \dfrac{1}{n+3}\right) + \cdots$

Note that $\displaystyle\lim_{n\to\infty} \left(\dfrac{1}{2} - \dfrac{1}{n+3}\right) = \dfrac{1}{2}$. Therefore,

$$\sum_{n=0}^{\infty} \dfrac{1}{(n+2)(n+3)} = \dfrac{1}{2}.$$

17. The correct answer is (C).

First, the graph of $f(x)$ is above the x-axis on the interval $[0, 2]$ thus $f(x) \geq 0$, and

$\displaystyle\int_0^x f(t)dt > 0$ on the interval $[0, 2]$.

Secondly, $f(x) \leq 0$ on the interval $[2, 8]$ and

$\displaystyle\int_2^8 f(x)dx < 0$, and thus $\displaystyle\int_0^2 f(t)dt$ is a

relative maximum. Note that the area of the region bounded by $f(x)$ and the x-axis on $[2, 8]$ is greater than the sum of the areas of the two regions above the x-axis. Therefore,

$$\int_0^2 f(x)dx + \int_2^8 f(x)dx +$$

$\displaystyle\int_8^9 f(x)dx < 0$ and thus $\displaystyle\int_0^9 f(x) < 0$.

Consequently, $\displaystyle\int_0^2 f(x)dx$ is the absolute

maximum value. Alternatively, you could also use the first derivative test noting that $g'(x) = f(x)$.

18. The correct answer is (D).

The arc length of a curve from $t = a$ to $t = b$ is

$L = \displaystyle\int_a^b \sqrt{\left[x'(t)^2 + y'(t)^2\right]}\, dt$ and in this case

$x'(t) = \dfrac{1}{2}t^{-\frac{1}{2}}$ and $y'(t) = e^t$, and thus,

$$L = \int_a^b \sqrt{\left[\left[\dfrac{1}{2}t^{-\frac{1}{2}}\right]^2 + (e^t)^2\right]}\, dt =$$

$\displaystyle\int_4^9 \sqrt{\dfrac{1}{4t} + e^{2t}}\, dt$.

19. The correct answer is (B).

As $x \to \infty$ the denominator $1 + 2^x$ increases much faster than the numerator $3x$. Thus,

$\displaystyle\lim_{x\to\infty} \dfrac{3x}{1 + 2^x} = 0$, and $y = 0$ is a horizontal

asymptote. Secondly, as $x \to -\infty$, $3x$ approaches $-\infty$, and $(1 + 2^x)$ approaches 1.

Thus, $\displaystyle\lim_{x\to\infty} \dfrac{3x}{1 + 2^x} = -\infty$. Therefore, $y = 0$ is

the only horizontal asymptote. Note that you could also apply *L'Hôpital's* Rule.

20. The correct answer is (D).

The slope of a tangent line to a polar curve

$r = f(\theta)$ is $\dfrac{dy}{dx} = \dfrac{\frac{dy}{d\theta}}{\frac{dx}{d\theta}}$. Since $x = r\cos\theta$ and

$y = r\sin\theta$, you have

$\dfrac{dx}{d\theta} = f'(\theta)\cos\theta - f(\theta)\sin\theta$ and

$\dfrac{dy}{d\theta} = f'(\theta)\sin\theta + f(\theta)\cos\theta$, and thus

$\dfrac{dy}{dx} = \dfrac{f'(\theta)\sin\theta + f(\theta)\cos\theta}{f'(\theta)\cos\theta - f(\theta)\sin\theta}$. Note that

$r = f(\theta) = 2\cos\theta$ and $f'(\theta) = -2\sin\theta$. At

$\theta = \dfrac{\pi}{3}, \dfrac{dy}{dx} =$

$$\frac{-2\sin\left(\dfrac{\pi}{3}\right)\sin\left(\dfrac{\pi}{3}\right) + 2\cos\left(\dfrac{\pi}{3}\right)\cos\left(\dfrac{\pi}{3}\right)}{-2\sin\left(\dfrac{\pi}{3}\right)\cos\left(\dfrac{\pi}{3}\right) - 2\cos\left(\dfrac{\pi}{3}\right)\sin\left(\dfrac{\pi}{3}\right)}.$$

21. The correct answer is (C).

Since f is decreasing, $f' < 0$ and since f is concave up, $f'' > 0$. The graph also shows that $f(0) < 0$. Thus $f''(0)$ has the largest value.

22. The correct answer is (C).

Let $u = x + 2$ and thus $\dfrac{du}{dx} = 1$ or $du = dx$.

Since $u = x + 2$, $u - 2 = x$ and therefore

$\int x\sqrt{x-2}\,dx$ becomes $\int (u-2)\sqrt{u}\,du$ or

$\int (u-2)(u^{\frac{1}{2}})\,du$ or $\int (u^{\frac{3}{2}} - 2u^{\frac{1}{2}})\,du$.

Integrating, you have $\dfrac{u^{5/2}}{5/2} - \dfrac{2u^{\frac{3}{2}}}{\frac{3}{2}} + c$ or

$\dfrac{2}{5}(u)^{5/2} - \dfrac{4}{3}(u)^{3/2} + c$ or

$\dfrac{2}{5}(x+2)^{5/2} - \dfrac{4}{3}(x+2)^{3/2} + c$.

23. The correct answer is (B).

Apply partial fraction decomposition

$\dfrac{5}{(x-3)(x+2)} = \dfrac{A}{x-3} + \dfrac{B}{x+2} =$

$\dfrac{A(x+2) + B(x-3)}{(x-3)(x+2)}$. Thus

$A(x+2) + B(x-3) = 5$ and by letting $x = 3$, you have $A = 1$ and letting $x = -2$, you have

$B = -1$. Therefore, $\displaystyle\int \dfrac{5}{(x-3)(x+2)}\,dx$

$= \displaystyle\int \left(\dfrac{1}{x-3} - \dfrac{1}{x+2}\right)dx = \int \dfrac{1}{x-3}\,dx$

$- \displaystyle\int \dfrac{1}{x+2}\,dx = \ln|x-3| - \ln|x+2| + c$.

24. The correct answer is (B).

Note that for each column, all the tangents have the same slope. For example, when $x = 0$ all tangents are horizontal, which is to say their slopes are all zero. This implies that the slope of the tangents depends solely on the x-coordinate of the point and is independent of the y-coordinate. Also note that when $x > 0$ slopes are negative, and when $x < 0$ slopes are positive. Thus, the only differential equation that satisfies these conditions is $\dfrac{dy}{dx} = -2x$.

25. The correct answer is (C).

The Taylor series for e^x about $x = 0$ is

$e^x = 1 + x + \dfrac{x^2}{2!} + \dfrac{x^3}{3!} + \cdots$, and thus, for e^{2x} is

$e^{2x} = 1 + 2x + \dfrac{(2x)^2}{2!} + \dfrac{(2x)^3}{3!} + \cdots = 1 + 2x$

$+ \dfrac{(2^2)x^2}{2!} + \dfrac{(2^3)x^3}{3!} + \cdots$. Therefore

$xe^{2x} = x + 2x^2 + \dfrac{(2^2)x^3}{2!} + \dfrac{(2^3)x^4}{3!} + \cdots =$

$x + 2x^2 + \dfrac{4x^3}{2!} + \dfrac{8x^4}{3!} + \cdots$

26. The correct answer is (B).

Since $0 < a_k \leq b_k$ for all k, $\sum_{k=0}^{\infty} a_k \leq \sum_{k=0}^{\infty} b_k$,

and since $\sum_{k=0}^{\infty} b_k$ converges, by the comparison

test, $\sum_{k=0}^{\infty} a_k$ converges.

27. The correct answer is (C).

Integrate $\int x \sec^2 x \, dx$ by parts. Let $u = x$,

$du = dx$, $dv = \sec^2 x \, dx$, and $v = \tan x$. Then

$$\int x \sec^2 x \, dx = x \tan x - \int \tan x \, dx$$

$$= x \tan x + \ln | \cos x | + C.$$

Comparing to the given information,

$$\int x \sec^2 x \, dx = f(x) + \ln | \cos x | + C \text{ tells us}$$

that $f(x) = x \tan x$.

28. The correct answer is (A) as shown below.

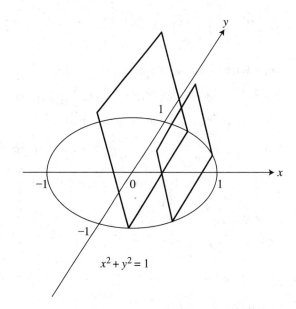

$$x^2 + y^2 = 1$$

Place the solid on the xy-plane as illustrated in the accompanying diagram.

Since $x^2 + y^2 = 1$, $y = \pm\sqrt{1 - x^2}$. Volume

$$V = \int_{-1}^{1} \left(\sqrt{1 - x^2} - (\sqrt{1 - x^2})\right)^2 dx =$$

$$\int_{-1}^{1} \left(2\sqrt{1 - x^2}\right)^2 dx = 4 \int_{-1}^{1} (1 - x^2) dx$$

$$= 4 \left(\left[x - \frac{x^3}{3} \right]_{-1}^{1} \right) =$$

$$4 \left(\left(1 - \frac{1}{3}\right) - \left(-1 + \frac{1}{3}\right) \right) = 4 \left(\frac{4}{3}\right) = \frac{16}{3}.$$

29. The correct answer is (B).

$$\frac{1}{n}\left[\left(\frac{1}{n}\right)^2 + \left(\frac{2}{n}\right)^2 + \cdots \left(\frac{n-1}{n}\right)^2\right]$$

represents the sum of the areas of n rectangles using LRAM each of width $\frac{1}{n}$. The heights of the rectangles are the squares of the division points, $0, \frac{1}{n}, \frac{2}{n}, \frac{3}{n}, \ldots, \frac{n-1}{n}$, all of which are between 0 and 1. Note that the first point from the left is $x = 0$. Thus,

$$\lim_{n\to\infty} \frac{1}{n}\left[\left(\frac{1}{n}\right)^2 + \left(\frac{2}{n}\right)^2 + \cdots \left(\frac{n-1}{n}\right)^2\right]$$

represents the area under the $y = x^2$ from 0 to 1, or $\int_0^1 x^2 dx$.

30. The correct answer is (C).

$$V = \pi \int_0^1 (x - x^2)^2 dx$$

$$= \pi \int_0^1 (x^4 - 2x^3 + x^2)dx$$

$$= \pi\left[\frac{x^5}{5} - \frac{x^4}{2} + \frac{x^3}{3}\right]_0^1$$

$$= \frac{\pi}{30}$$

Section I—Part B

76. The correct answer is (C).

To assure that $f(x) = \begin{cases} \ln(3-x) & \text{if } x < 2 \\ a - bx & \text{if } x \geq 2 \end{cases}$

is differentiable at $x = 2$, we must first be certain that the function is continuous. As $x \to 2$, $\ln(3 - x) \to 0$, so we want $a - 2b = 0$ $\Rightarrow a = 2b$. Continuity does not guarantee differentiability, however; we must assure that $\lim_{h\to 0} \frac{f(2+h) - f(2)}{h}$ exists. We must be certain that $\lim_{h\to 0^-} \frac{\ln(3 - (2+h)) - \ln(3-2)}{h}$ is equal to $\lim_{h\to 0^+} \frac{(a - b(x+h)) - (a - bx)}{h}$.

$$\lim_{h\to 0^-} \frac{\ln(3 - (2+h)) - \ln(3-2)}{h}$$
$$= \lim_{h\to 0^-} \frac{\ln(1-h)}{h} = \frac{0}{0}. \text{ Thus, } \lim_{h\to 0^-} \left(\frac{1}{1-h}\right)(-1)$$
$$= -1. \lim_{h\to 0^+} \frac{(a - b(2+h)) - (a - 2b)}{h} =$$
$$-b \Rightarrow -b = -1 \Rightarrow b = 1 \Rightarrow a = 2.$$

77. The correct answer is (B).
Since $h(x) = f(g(x))$, $h'(x) = f'(g(x))g'(x)$ and $h'(2) = f'(g(2))g'(2) = f'(3)(1) = -1$.

78. The correct answer is (C) as shown below.

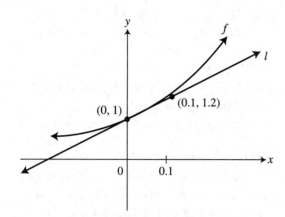

Since $f''(0) = 3$, the graph of f is concave upward at $x = 0$. Since $f'(0) = 2$ the slope of line l is 2. The equation of line l using $y - y_1 = m(x - x_1)$ is $y - 1 = 2(x - 0)$ or $y = 2x + 1$. At $x = 0.1$, $y = 2(0.1) + 1 = 1.2$. Thus, $f(0.1) \approx 1.2$.

79. The correct answer is (D).

The average value of $f'(x)$ on $[1, 3]$ is

$$f'_{average} = \frac{1}{3-1} \int_1^3 f'(x)\, dx$$

$$= \frac{1}{2}\left(f(3) - f(1)\right).$$

80. The correct answer is (C).

The velocity of the particle is $x'(t) = -8\sin(4t)$ and $y'(t) = t$. The speed of the particle is

$$|v(t)| = \sqrt{\left(-8\sin(4t)\right)^2 + (t)^2},$$ and at $t = 1$ the speed of the particle is

$$\sqrt{\left(-8\sin(4(1))\right)^2 + (1)^2} \approx 6.136.$$

81. The correct answer is (C).

Since $f' > 0$ on the interval $(-\infty, -1)$, f is increasing on $(-\infty, -1)$. Thus, statement I is false. Also $f' > 0$ on $(-\infty, 2)$ and $f' < 0$ on $(2, \infty)$, which implies that f is increasing on $(-\infty, 2)$ and decreasing on $(2, \infty)$, respectively. Therefore, f has an absolute maximum at $x = 2$. Statement II is true. Finally, f' is decreasing on $(-\infty, -1)$ and increasing on $(-1, 0)$, which means $f'' < 0$ on $(-\infty, -1)$ and $f'' > 0$ on $(-1, 0)$. Thus, f is concave down on $(-\infty, -1)$ and concave up on $(-1, 0)$ producing a point of inflection at $x = -1$. Statement III is true.

82. The correct answer is (A).

$$\sum_{k=0}^{\infty} (-1)^k \frac{\pi^{(2k)}}{(2k)!} = 1 - \frac{\pi^2}{2!} + \frac{\pi^4}{4!} - \frac{\pi^6}{6!} + \cdots$$

Note that $\cos x = 1 - \dfrac{x^2}{2!} + \dfrac{x^4}{4!} - \dfrac{x^6}{6!} + \cdots$.

Thus, $\displaystyle\sum_{k=0}^{\infty} (-1)^k \frac{\pi^{(2k)}}{(2k)!} = \cos \pi = -1$.

83. The correct answer is (A).

The slope of the *tangent* line to $y = e^{-2x}$ is $\dfrac{dy}{dx} = -2e^{-2x}$. The slope of the *normal* is the negative reciprocal, $m = \dfrac{1}{2e^{-2x}} = \dfrac{e^{2x}}{2}$.

When $x = 1.158$, $m = \dfrac{e^{2(1.158)}}{2} \approx 5.068$.

The slope of the normal line is approximately 5.068.

84. The correct answer is (D).

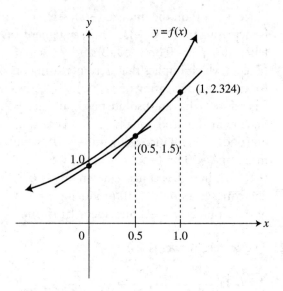

Since $y(0) = 1$, the graph of y passes through the point $(0, 1)$. The slope of the tangent line at $(0, 1)$ is $\dfrac{dy}{dx}\bigg|_{x=0} = e^0 = 1$. The equation of the tangent is $y - 1 = 1(x - 0)$ or $y = x + 1$. At $x = 0.5$, $y = 0.5 + 1 = 1.5$. Thus, the point $(0.5, 1.5)$ is your next starting point, and $\dfrac{dy}{dx}\bigg|_{x=0.5} = e^{0.5} = \sqrt{e}$. The equation of the next line is $y - 1.5 = \sqrt{e}(x - 0.5)$ or $y = \sqrt{e}(x - 0.5) + 1.5$. At $x = 1$, $y = \sqrt{e}(1 - 0.5) + 1.5 \approx 2.324$.

85. The correct answer is (B).

The property $\displaystyle\int_{-k}^{0} f(x)dx = -\int_{0}^{k} f(x)dx$ implies that the regions bounded by the graph of f and the x-axis are such that one region is above the x-axis and the other region is below. The property also implies that f is an odd function, which means that $f(-x) = -f(x)$ or that the graph of f is symmetrical with respect to the origin. The only graph that satisfies those conditions is choice (B).

86. The correct answer is (C).

If $2x\dfrac{dy}{dx} - 7 = 1 \Rightarrow \dfrac{dy}{dx} = \dfrac{8}{2x} = \dfrac{4}{x}$.

Integrate $dy = \dfrac{4\,dx}{x}$ to get $y = 4\ln|x| + C$. Since $y = 4.5$ when $x = 3$, $4.5 = 4\ln 3 + C \Rightarrow 0.10555 = C$. Thus, $y = 4\ln|x| + 0.10555$. At $x = 3.1$, $y = 4.631$.

87. The correct answer is (A)

Step 1. Begin by finding the first non-negative value of t such that $v(t) = 0$. To accomplish this, use your graphing calculator, set $y_1 = \sin(x^2 + 1)$, and graph.

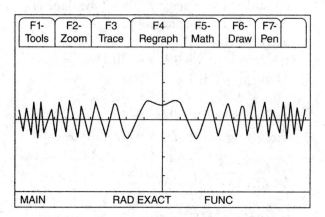

Use the [*Zero*] function and find the first non-negative value of x such that $y_1 = 0$. Note that $x = 1.46342$.

Step 2. The position function of the particle is $s(t) = \displaystyle\int v(t)dt$. Since $s(1) = 5$, we have

$\displaystyle\int_{1}^{1.46342} v(t) = s(1.46342) - s(1)$. Using your

calculator, evaluate $\displaystyle\int_{1}^{1.46342} \sin(x^2 + 1)dx$ and

obtain 0.250325. Therefore, $.250325 = s(1.46342) - s(1)$ or $.250325 = s(1.46342) - 5$. Thus, $s(1.46342) = 5.250325 \approx 5.250$.

88. The correct answer is (A).

$$\sum_{n=1}^{\infty} \frac{n! + 2^n}{2^n \cdot n!} = \sum_{n=1}^{\infty} \frac{n!}{2^n \cdot n!} + \sum_{n=1}^{\infty} \frac{2^n}{2^n \cdot n!}$$

$$= \sum_{n=1}^{\infty} \frac{1}{2^n} + \sum_{n=1}^{\infty} \frac{1}{n!}$$

The series $\sum_{n=1}^{\infty} \frac{1}{2^n}$ is a geometric series, so

$$\sum_{n=1}^{\infty} \frac{1}{2^n} = \frac{1/2}{1 - 1/2} = 1.$$

Compare the series $\sum_{n=1}^{\infty} \frac{1}{n!}$ to the known

MacLaurin series

$$\sum_{n=0}^{\infty} \frac{x^n}{n!} = 1 + x + \frac{x^2}{2!} + \frac{x^3}{3!} \cdots = e^x, \text{ and}$$

at $x = 1$, $\sum_{n=0}^{\infty} \frac{x^n}{n!} = \sum_{n=0}^{\infty} \frac{1}{n!}$

$= 1 + 1 + \frac{1}{2!} + \frac{1}{3!} \cdots = e^1$. Thus, $\sum_{n=1}^{\infty} \frac{1}{n!} = e^1 - 1$.

(Note that the summation index changes from $n = 0$ to $n = 1$.) Therefore,

$$\sum_{n=1}^{\infty} \frac{1}{2^n} + \sum_{n=1}^{\infty} \frac{1}{n!} = 1 + e - 1 = e. \text{ (Also, you}$$

could have evaluated $\sum_{n=1}^{\infty} \frac{1}{n!}$ using your T1-89

calculator.)

89. The correct answer is (B).

$$y = \frac{1}{x^2} - \frac{1}{x^3} = x^{-2} - x^{-3}$$

$\Rightarrow y' = -2x^{-3} + 3x^{-4} \Rightarrow y'' = 6x^{-4} - 12x^{-5}$. Set the second derivative equal to zero and solve.

$$\frac{6}{x^4} - \frac{12}{x^5} = \frac{6x - 12}{x^5} = 0$$

$\Rightarrow 6x - 12 = 0 \Rightarrow x = 2$. Also $y'' < 0$ for $x < 2$ and $y'' > 0$ for $x > 2$.

90. The correct answer is (D).

The logistic growth model to the logistic differential equation $\frac{dp}{dt} = kp\left(1 - \frac{p}{M}\right)$ with M equal to the maximum value is

$p = \dfrac{M}{1 + Ae^{-kt}}$. In this case, $p = \dfrac{200}{1 + Ae^{-.25t}}$ and $t = 0$, you have $p = 20$. Thus,

$$20 = \frac{200}{1 + Ae^{(-.25)(0)}} \text{ or } 20 = \frac{200}{1 + A} \text{ or } A = 9,$$

Thus, at $p = 100$, $100 = \dfrac{200}{1 + 9e^{-.25t}}$ and entering the equation into your calculator, you have $t \approx 8.789 \approx 9$ years.

Solutions to AP Calculus BC Practice Exam 2—Section II

Section II—Part A

1. The correct answer is (A).

$$g(10) = 90 - 4 \tan\left(\frac{10}{20}\right) = 90 - 4 \tan\left(\frac{1}{2}\right)$$

$$\approx 90 - 4(0.5463) \approx 90 - 2.1852$$

$$\approx 87.81° \text{ or } 87.82° \text{ F}$$

(B) $g'(t) = -4 \sec^2\left(\frac{t}{20}\right)\left(\frac{1}{20}\right)$

$$g'(10) = -\frac{1}{5} \sec^2\left(\frac{10}{20}\right) \approx -0.26°/\text{min}.$$

(C) Set the temperature of the liquid equal to 86°F. Using your calculator, let

$$y1 = 90 - 4 \tan\left(\frac{x}{20}\right); \text{ and } y2 = 86.$$

To find the intersection point of y_1 and y_2, let $y3 = y1 - y2$ and find the zeros of y_3.

Using the [*Zero*] function of your calculator, you obtain $x = 15.708$. Since $y_1 < y_2$ on the interval $15.708 < x \le 20$, the temperature of the liquid is below 86°F when $15.708 < t \le 20$. Alternatively, you could use the Intersection Function of your calculator and find the intersection of the graphs of y_1, and y_2.

(D) Average temperature below 86°

$$= \frac{1}{20 - 15.708} \int_{15.708}^{20} \left(90 - 4 \tan\left(\frac{x}{20}\right)\right) dx.$$

Using your calculator, you obtain:

Average temperature $= \dfrac{1}{4.292}(364.756)$

$$\approx 84.9851$$

$$\approx 84.99° \text{ F.}$$

2. (A) Velocity vector
$\langle x'(t), y'(t) \rangle = \langle 6t, -2 \sin(2t - 4) \rangle$ and the acceleration vector
$\langle x''(t), y''(t) \rangle = \langle 6, -4 \cos(2t - 4) \rangle$, and at $t = 2$, the acceleration vector is $\langle 6, -4 \rangle$.

(B) The speed of the particle at $t = 2$ equals
$$\sqrt{(x'(2))^2 + (y'(2))^2} = \sqrt{(12)^2 + (0)^2} = 12.$$

(C) At $t = 2$ the position vector is $\langle 16, 1 \rangle$. The slope of the line tangent to the path of the particle at $t = 2$ is $\dfrac{y'(2)}{x'(2)} = \dfrac{0}{12} = 0$, which means you have a horizontal tangent. Thus, the equation is $y = 1$.

(D) The total distance traveled by the particle for $0 \le t \le 2$ is the length of the path,

which is $\int_0^2 \sqrt{\left(\dfrac{dx}{dt}\right)^2 + \left(\dfrac{dy}{dt}\right)^2}\, dt =$

$$\int_0^2 \sqrt{(6t)^2 + (-2 \sin(2t - 4))^2}\, dt = 12.407.$$

Section II—Part B

3. (A) $f(-3) = \int_0^{-3} g(t)dt = -\int_{-3}^0 g(t)dt$

$= -\int_{-3}^{-1} g(t)dt - \int_{-1}^0 g(t)dt$

$= -\left(-\frac{1}{2}(2)(2)\right) - \left(\frac{1}{2}(1)(2)\right)$

$= 2 - 1 = 1$

$f(3) = \int_0^3 g(t)dt$

$= \int_0^1 g(t)dt + \int_1^3 g(t)dt$

$= \frac{1}{2}(1)(2) + \left(-\frac{1}{2}(1)(2)\right)$

$= 1 - 1 = 0$

(B) Think in terms of area above and below the curve. The function f increases on $(0, 1)$ and decreases on $(1, 3)$. Thus, f has a relative maximum at $x = 1$. Also, f decreases on $(-3, -1)$ and increases on $(-1, 0)$. Thus, f has a relative minimum at $x = -1$. Another approach is as follows: Note that $f'(x) = g(x)$ and the behavior of the graph of $f(x)$ on $[-3, 3]$ is summarized below.

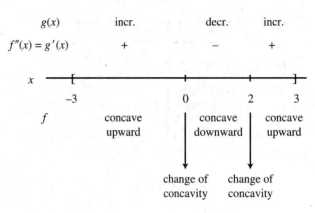

(C) $f'(x) = g(x)$ and $f''(x) = g'(x)$

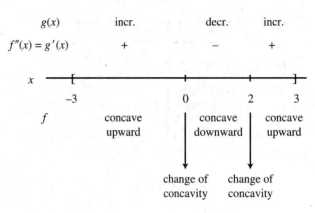

The function f has a change of concavity at $x = 0$ and $x = 2$.

(D) $f(1) = \int_0^1 g(t)dt = \frac{1}{2}(1)(2) = 1$

$f'(1) = g(1) = 0$

Thus, $m = 0$, point $(1, 1)$; at $x = 1$, the equation of the tangent line to $f(x)$ is $y = 1$.

4. The correct answer is shown below.

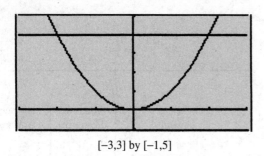

[−3,3] by [−1,5]

(A) Set $x^2 = 4 \Rightarrow x = \pm 2$.

$$\text{Area of } R = \int_{-2}^{2} (4 - x^2)dx = 4x - \frac{x^3}{3}\bigg]_{-2}^{2}$$

$$= \left(4(2) - \frac{2^3}{3}\right) - \left(4(-2) - \frac{(-2)^3}{3}\right)$$

$$= \frac{16}{3} - \left(-\frac{16}{3}\right) = \frac{32}{3}.$$

(B) Since $y = x^2$ is an even function, $x = 0$ divides R into two regions of equal area. Thus, $a = 0$.

(C) Area R_1 = Area R_2 = $\frac{16}{3}$.

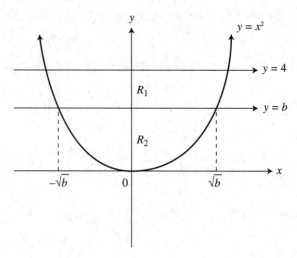

$$\text{Area } R_2 = \int_{-\sqrt{b}}^{\sqrt{b}} (b - x^2)dx$$

$$= 2\int_{0}^{\sqrt{b}} (b - x^2)dx$$

$$= 2\left[bx - \frac{x^3}{3}\right]_{0}^{\sqrt{b}}$$

$$= 2\left[b\left(\sqrt{b}\right) - \frac{\left(\sqrt{b}^3\right)}{3}\right]$$

$$= 2\left(b^{3/2} - \frac{b^{3/2}}{3}\right) = 2\left(\frac{2b^{3/2}}{3}\right)$$

$$= \frac{4b^{3/2}}{3}.$$

Set $\frac{4b^{3/2}}{3} = \frac{16}{3} \Rightarrow b^{3/2} = 4$ or $b = 4^{2/3}$.

(D) Washer Method

$$V = \pi \int_{-2}^{2} (4^2 - (x^2)^2)dx$$

$$= \pi \int_{-2}^{2} (16 - x^4)dx$$

$$= \pi \left[16x - \frac{x^5}{5}\right]_{-2}^{2} = \frac{256\pi}{5}$$

5. (A) $\dfrac{dy}{dx} = \dfrac{y}{2x^2}$; $(2,1)$

$\left.\dfrac{dy}{dx}\right|_{x=2,\,y=1} = \dfrac{1}{2(2)^2} = \dfrac{1}{8}$

Equation of tangent:

$y - 1 = \dfrac{1}{8}(x - 2)$ or

$y = \dfrac{1}{8}(x - 2) + 1$.

(B) $f(2.5) \approx \dfrac{1}{8}(2.5 - 2) + 1 = 1.0625$

≈ 1.063 or $\dfrac{17}{16}$.

(C) $\dfrac{dy}{dx} = \dfrac{y}{2x^2}$

$\dfrac{dy}{y} = \dfrac{dx}{2x^2}$ and $\displaystyle\int \dfrac{dy}{y} = \int \dfrac{dx}{2x^2}$

$\ln|y| = \displaystyle\int \dfrac{1}{2}x^{-2}dx = \dfrac{1}{2}\dfrac{(x^{-1})}{(-1)} + C$

$= -\dfrac{1}{2x} + C$

$e^{\ln|y|} = e^{\left(-\frac{1}{2x} + C\right)}$

$y = e^{-\frac{1}{2x}+C}$; $f(2) = 1$

$1 = e^{-\frac{1}{2(2)}+C} \Rightarrow 1 = e^{-\frac{1}{4} + C}$

Since $e^0 = 1$, $-\dfrac{1}{4} + C = 0 \Rightarrow C = \dfrac{1}{4}$.

Thus, $y = e^{\left(-\frac{1}{2x} + \frac{1}{4}\right)}$.

(D) $f(2.5) = e^{\left(-\frac{1}{2(2.5)} + \frac{1}{4}\right)}$

$= e^{\left(-\frac{1}{5} + \frac{1}{4}\right)} = e^{\frac{1}{20}}$.

6. (A) The first four non-zero terms of the Maclaurin series for $f(x)$ are

$x - \dfrac{x^3}{3} + \dfrac{x^5}{5} - \dfrac{x^7}{7}$. Since $g(x) = f'(x)$, the

first four non-zero of $g(x)$ are
$1 - x^2 + x^4 - x^6$.

(B) The Maclaurin series for

$h(x) = (2x) - \dfrac{(2x)^3}{3} + \dfrac{(2x)^5}{5} - \dfrac{(2x)^7}{7} \cdots$

$= (2x) - \dfrac{8x^3}{3} + \dfrac{32x^5}{5} - \dfrac{128x^7}{7} \cdots$ and the

general term is $(-1)^{n+1}\dfrac{(2x)^{2n-1}}{2n-1}$.

(C) The ratio test tells you that $\displaystyle\lim_{n\to\infty} \dfrac{|a_{n+1}|}{|a_n|} < 1$

for a series to converge. Thus, you have

$\displaystyle\lim_{n\to\infty}\left(\left|\dfrac{(2x)^{2(n+1)-1}}{2(n+1)-1}\right| \cdot \left|\dfrac{2n-1}{(2x)^{2n-1}}\right|\right) < 1$

or $\displaystyle\lim_{n\to\infty}\left|\dfrac{(2x)^{2n+1}}{2n+1} \cdot \dfrac{2n-1}{(2x)^{2n-1}}\right| < 1$ or

$\displaystyle\lim_{n\to\infty}\left(\dfrac{2n-1}{2n+1}\right)(2x)^2 < 1$. Since

$\displaystyle\lim_{n\to\infty}\left(\dfrac{2n-1}{2n+1}\right) = 1$, $(2x)^2 < 1$, which

implies $-1 < 4x^2 < 1$ or $-\dfrac{1}{4} < x^2 < \dfrac{1}{4}$.

And since $x^2 \geq 0$, $0 < x^2 < \dfrac{1}{4}$ and

$-\dfrac{1}{2} < x < \dfrac{1}{2}$.

At $x = \dfrac{1}{2}$ the series is $1 - \dfrac{1}{3} + \dfrac{1}{5} - \dfrac{1}{7} + \cdots$,

which is also a convergent alternating series with $\displaystyle\lim_{n\to\infty} a_n = 0$ and

$a_1 \geq a_2 \geq a_3 \geq \cdots$ and thus the series converges. At $x = -\dfrac{1}{2}$, the series is

$-1 + \dfrac{1}{3} - \dfrac{1}{5} + \dfrac{1}{7} - \cdots$, which is also a

convergent alternating series. Thus, the interval of convergences is $-\dfrac{1}{2} \leq x \leq \dfrac{1}{2}$.

(D) Since the series is a convergent alternating series,

$\left|h\left(\dfrac{1}{4}\right) - \dfrac{11}{24}\right| < \dfrac{\left(32\left(\frac{1}{4}\right)\right)^5}{5} = \dfrac{1}{160}$,

which is less than $\dfrac{1}{150}$.

Scoring Sheet for AP Calculus BC Practice Exam 2

Section I—Part A

$$\underline{\hspace{3cm}} \times 1.2 = \underline{\hspace{3cm}}$$
No. Correct   Subtotal A

Section I—Part B

$$\underline{\hspace{3cm}} \times 1.2 = \underline{\hspace{3cm}}$$
No. Correct   Subtotal B

Section II—Part A (Each question is worth 9 points.)

$$\underline{\hspace{2cm}} + \underline{\hspace{2cm}} = \underline{\hspace{2cm}}$$
Q1   Q2   Subtotal C

Section II—Part B (Each question is worth 9 points.)

$$\underline{\hspace{1.5cm}} + \underline{\hspace{1.5cm}} + \underline{\hspace{1.5cm}} + \underline{\hspace{1.5cm}} = \underline{\hspace{1.5cm}}$$
Q1   Q2   Q3   Q4   Subtotal D

Total Raw Score (Subtotals A + B + C + D) = ☐

Approximate Conversion Scale:

Total Raw Score	Approximate AP Grade
80–108	5
65–79	4
50–64	3
36–49	2
0–35	1

5 Minutes to a 5

180 Activities and Questions in

5 Minutes a Day

INTRODUCTION

Welcome to *5 Minutes to a 5: 180 Questions and Activities*! This bonus section is another tool for you to use as you work toward your goal of achieving a 5 on the AP exam in May. It includes 180 AP questions and activities that cover the most essential course materials and are meant to be completed in conjunction with the *5 Steps* book.

One of the secrets to excelling in your AP class is spending a bit of time *each day* studying the subject(s). The questions and activities offered here are designed to be done one per day, and each should take 5 minutes or so to complete. (Although there might be exceptions depending on the exam—some exercises may take a little longer, some a little less.) You will encounter stimulating questions to make you think about a topic in a big way and some very subject-specific activities that cover the main book's chapters; some science subjects will offer at-home labs, and some humanities subjects will offer ample chunks of text to be read on one day, with questions and activities for follow-up on the following day(s). There will also be suggestions for relevant videos for you to watch, websites to visit, or both. Most questions and activities are linked to the specific chapters of your book so that you are constantly fortifying your knowledge.

Remember—approaching this section for 5 minutes a day is much more effective than binging a week's worth in one sitting! So if you practice all the extra exercises in this section and reinforce the main content of this book, we are certain you will build the skills and confidence needed to succeed on your exam. Good luck!

—Editors of McGraw Hill

Check off each activity as it is completed.

1. ❏		46. ❏		91. ❏		136. ❏	
2. ❏		47. ❏		92. ❏		137. ❏	
3. ❏		48. ❏		93. ❏		138. ❏	
4. ❏		49. ❏		94. ❏		139. ❏	
5. ❏		50. ❏		95. ❏		140. ❏	
6. ❏		51. ❏		96. ❏		141. ❏	
7. ❏		52. ❏		97. ❏		142. ❏	
8. ❏		53. ❏		98. ❏		143. ❏	
9. ❏		54. ❏		99. ❏		144. ❏	
10. ❏		55. ❏		100. ❏		145. ❏	
11. ❏		56. ❏		101. ❏		146. ❏	
12. ❏		57. ❏		102. ❏		147. ❏	
13. ❏		58. ❏		103. ❏		148. ❏	
14. ❏		59. ❏		104. ❏		149. ❏	
15. ❏		60. ❏		105. ❏		150. ❏	
16. ❏		61. ❏		106. ❏		151. ❏	
17. ❏		62. ❏		107. ❏		152. ❏	
18. ❏		63. ❏		108. ❏		153. ❏	
19. ❏		64. ❏		109. ❏		154. ❏	
20. ❏		65. ❏		110. ❏		155. ❏	
21. ❏		66. ❏		111. ❏		156. ❏	
22. ❏		67. ❏		112. ❏		157. ❏	
23. ❏		68. ❏		113. ❏		158. ❏	
24. ❏		69. ❏		114. ❏		159. ❏	
25. ❏		70. ❏		115. ❏		160. ❏	
26. ❏		71. ❏		116. ❏		161. ❏	
27. ❏		72. ❏		117. ❏		162. ❏	
28. ❏		73. ❏		118. ❏		163. ❏	
29. ❏		74. ❏		119. ❏		164. ❏	
30. ❏		75. ❏		120. ❏		165. ❏	
31. ❏		76. ❏		121. ❏		166. ❏	
32. ❏		77. ❏		122. ❏		167. ❏	
33. ❏		78. ❏		123. ❏		168. ❏	
34. ❏		79. ❏		124. ❏		169. ❏	
35. ❏		80. ❏		125. ❏		170. ❏	
36. ❏		81. ❏		126. ❏		171. ❏	
37. ❏		82. ❏		127. ❏		172. ❏	
38. ❏		83. ❏		128. ❏		173. ❏	
39. ❏		84. ❏		129. ❏		174. ❏	
40. ❏		85. ❏		130. ❏		175. ❏	
41. ❏		86. ❏		131. ❏		176. ❏	
42. ❏		87. ❏		132. ❏		177. ❏	
43. ❏		88. ❏		133. ❏		178. ❏	
44. ❏		89. ❏		134. ❏		179. ❏	
45. ❏		90. ❏		135. ❏		180. ❏	

Day 1

There are a few key strategies to deal with situations when you can't just evaluate a limit directly, and the most common of these is factoring and cancelling. Use this strategy to find the following limits.

1. $\lim\limits_{x \to 1} \left(\dfrac{4x^2 - 3x - 1}{x^2 - 3x + 2} \right)$

2. $\lim\limits_{x \to 2} \dfrac{x^2 - 4}{x^3 - 8}$

3. $\lim\limits_{x \to 2} \dfrac{x^3 - 8}{x^2 + 3x - 10}$

Rationalizing denominators is common throughout algebra, but when working on limits, you'll sometimes want to rationalize a numerator instead. Multiply both the denominator and the numerator by the conjugate of the expression you want to rationalize.

Use rationalization to find the limits.

1. $\displaystyle\lim_{x \to 0} \frac{x}{\sqrt{x+9}-3}$

2. $\displaystyle\lim_{x \to 4} \frac{\sqrt{x}-2}{x-4}$

3. $\displaystyle\lim_{x \to -3} \frac{\sqrt{x+3}}{\sqrt{x+3}-\sqrt{3}}$

The Squeeze Theorem says that if you are able to find two functions $g(x)$ and $h(x)$ such that $g(x) \le f(x) \le h(x)$ and $\lim\limits_{x \to a} g(x) = \lim\limits_{x \to a} h(x) = L$, then $\lim\limits_{x \to a} f(x)$ will also $= L$. It's common to use the Squeeze Theorem on expressions involving $\sin x$ or $\cos x$ because both can be squeezed between -1 and 1.

Use the Squeeze Theorem to find:

1. $\lim\limits_{x \to \infty} \dfrac{\cos(\pi x)}{x - 1}$

2. $\lim\limits_{x \to -\infty} \dfrac{2 - \sin\left(x - \dfrac{\pi}{2}\right)}{e^{-x}}$

One of the most powerful results obtained by using the Squeeze Theorem is that $\lim\limits_{x\to 0}\dfrac{\sin x}{x}=1$.

It can be applied to similar problems as long as the denominator matches the argument of the sine function. Use $\lim\limits_{x\to 0}\dfrac{\sin x}{x}=1$ with appropriate adjustments to find the following limits.

1. $\lim\limits_{x\to 0}\dfrac{\sin(2x)}{2x}$

2. $\lim\limits_{x\to 0}\dfrac{\sin x}{2x}$

3. $\lim\limits_{x\to 0}\dfrac{\sin(3x)}{x}$

Day 5

The notation $\lim\limits_{x \to a^-} f(x)$ or $\lim\limits_{x \to a^+} f(x)$ denotes a one-sided limit, the limit as x approaches a "from the left" or "from the right," respectively. If $\lim\limits_{x \to a^-} f(x) = \lim\limits_{x \to a^+} f(x)$, then $\lim\limits_{x \to a} f(x)$ exists and is equal to the one-sided limits.

Find each of the following limits:

1. $\lim\limits_{x \to 0^-} \dfrac{|x|}{x}$

2. $\lim\limits_{x \to 0^+} \dfrac{|x|}{x}$

3. $\lim\limits_{x \to 0} \dfrac{|x|}{x}$

Given $f(x) = \begin{cases} -2x - 7 & \text{if } x \le -2 \\ 4 - x^2 & \text{if } -2 < x \le 3 \\ -5 & \text{if } x > 3 \end{cases}$

4. $\lim\limits_{x \to -2^+} f(x)$

5. $\lim\limits_{x \to 3^-} f(x)$

6. $\lim\limits_{x \to 3} f(x)$

If a function f increases without bound as x approaches a, $\lim_{x \to a} f(x) = \infty$. If, as x approaches a, the function decreases without bound, $\lim_{x \to a} f(x) = -\infty$. Those limits only exist if the limit from the left and the limit from the right both exist and are equal.

Use the graph of $f(x)$ shown to find each of these limits.

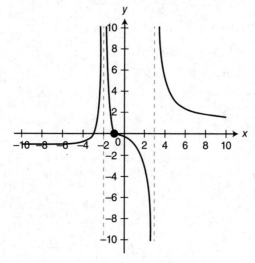

1. $\lim_{x \to 3^-} f(x)$

2. $\lim_{x \to 3^+} f(x)$

3. $\lim_{x \to 3} f(x)$

4. $\lim_{x \to -2^-} f(x)$

5. $\lim_{x \to -2^+} f(x)$

6. $\lim_{x \to -2} f(x)$

7. $\lim_{x \to -1} f(x)$

Finding that $\lim_{x \to a} f(x) = \infty$ or $-\infty$ makes it clear that the function has a vertical asymptote $x = a$. It's also possible to consider what happens to the function as x increases without bound or decreases without bound. There may be a horizontal or an oblique asymptote or the function may increase or decrease without bound.

Find each limit.

1. $\lim_{x \to \infty} \dfrac{2x - 3}{x + 4}$

2. $\lim_{x \to -\infty} \left(4 - 3x + 2x^2 \right)$

3. $\lim_{x \to \infty} \dfrac{2x - 3}{x^2 - 3x + 1}$

4. $\lim_{x \to -\infty} \dfrac{4}{x^2}$

5. $\lim_{x \to -\infty} \dfrac{3x^5}{2x^2}$

Because $\lim\limits_{x \to 0}\left(\dfrac{x}{\sin x}\right) \cdot \lim\limits_{x \to 0}\left(\dfrac{\sin x}{x}\right) = \lim\limits_{x \to 0}\left(\dfrac{x}{\sin x} \cdot \dfrac{\sin x}{x}\right) = \lim\limits_{x \to 0} 1 = 1$, it's possible to show

that $\lim\limits_{x \to 0}\dfrac{x}{\sin x} = 1$. Use $\lim\limits_{x \to 0}\left(\dfrac{x}{\sin x}\right)$ and $\lim\limits_{x \to 0}\dfrac{\sin x}{x}$ to find the following limits.

1. $\lim\limits_{x \to 0}\dfrac{x \cos x}{\sin 2x}$

2. $\lim\limits_{x \to 0}\left(\dfrac{-\pi \sin(-x)}{\sin(\pi x)}\right)$

3. $\lim\limits_{x \to 0}\dfrac{\sin(2x)}{\sin(3x)}$

Day 9

Each of the functions below has at least one discontinuity. Locate each discontinuity and classify it as Essential, Removable or Jump.

1. $f(x) = \dfrac{|x|}{x}$

2. $f(x) = \dfrac{x^2 - 4}{x^2 - 5x + 6}$

3. $f(x) = \begin{cases} x^2 + 10x + 21 & \text{if } x \le -2 \\ 6 - x & \text{if } -2 < x < 3 \\ -x^2 + 8x - 12 & \text{if } x \ge 3 \end{cases}$

Find a value for the constant k, if possible, that will make the function continuous.

1. $f(x) = \begin{cases} 1 - 4x & x \leq 0 \\ x^2 + k & x > 0 \end{cases}$

2. $f(x) = \begin{cases} kx^2 & x \leq -1 \\ 3x - k & x > -1 \end{cases}$

3. $f(x) = \begin{cases} \dfrac{\sin 2x}{x} & x \neq 0 \\ k - 2x & x = 0 \end{cases}$

Day 11

If f is continuous on a closed interval $[a, b]$, and c is any number between $f(a)$ and $f(b)$ inclusive, then there is at least one number x in the closed interval such that $f(x) = c$.

The Intermediate Value Theorem above is often used to assert that a continuous function has a zero in a closed interval, if the conditions of the theorem are met, and $f(a)$ and $f(b)$ have opposite signs. For each of the following functions, determine if the function has a zero in the given interval.

1. $f(x) = \dfrac{7 - 2x}{x}$ on $[3, 4]$

2. $f(x) = \dfrac{7 - 2x}{x}$ on $[-1, 1]$

3. $f(x) = \dfrac{2x^2 - 3}{x^2 + 1}$ on $[-2, -1]$

4. $f(x) = \dfrac{2x^2 - 3}{x^2 + 1}$ on $[-1, 1]$

The derivative f' of a function f is defined as $f'(x) = \lim\limits_{h \to 0} \dfrac{f(x+h) - f(x)}{h}$. Use the definition to find the derivative of each function.

1. $f(x) = x^3 + 8$

2. $f(x) = \dfrac{2x}{x-3}$

3. $f(x) = \sqrt{x-2}$

5 Minutes to a 5

The derivative of a constant is zero. The derivative of a sum (or difference) is the sum (or difference) of the derivative of the individual terms. The Power Rule asserts that the derivative of x^n is nx^{n-1}. Use these fundamental rules to find the derivative of each of the polynomial functions.

1. $f(x) = 3x^7 - 4x^5 + x^2 - 1$

2. $f(x) = 12 - 8x^9 + 5x^6$

3. $f(x) = \frac{2}{3}x^{12} + \frac{1}{5}x^{10} - \frac{3}{4}x^8 - \frac{1}{3}x^6$

4. $f(x) = x^7 - x^5 + x^3 - x$

5. $f(x) = 2 - x^4 + 4x^6 - 3x^8$

The Product Rule says that the derivative of a product of two functions, u and v is $uv' + vu'$, and the Quotient Rule ensures that the derivative of $\dfrac{u}{v}$ is $\dfrac{vu' - uv'}{v^2}$.

Use the Product and Quotient Rules to find the derivative of each function.

1. $f(x) = (3x - 7)(x^2 - 4)$

2. $f(x) = 2x^4 \sqrt{x}$

3. $f(x) = (x^2 + 1)(2x^3 + 5)$

4. $f(x) = \dfrac{4 - 3x^2}{2x + 5}$

Day 15

The Chain Rule provides a method of differentiating a function that is formed by composing two (or more) simpler functions. Use the Chain Rule to find the derivative of each of the following functions.

1. $f(x) = \left(x^2 - 3x + 2\right)^2$

2. $f(x) = \sqrt{4 + 5x^2}$

3. $f(x) = \dfrac{1}{x^3 - 2x + 5}$

4. $f(x) = (3x - 1)^2 (2x + 3)^3$

5. $f(x) = \dfrac{x^2 - 4}{(2x + 1)^2}$

Given functions f and g continuous and differentiable on $[-1, 2]$. Let $u(x) = f(g(x))$, $v(x) = g(f(x))$ and $w(x) = f(f(x))$. Use the information in the table to evaluate each derivative.

x	−1	0	1	2
f	0	−2	2	−1
g	3	1	0	2
f'	−1	4	−3	1
g'	−2	−1	2	3

1. $\dfrac{d}{dx}(f + g)\Big|_{x=2}$

2. $\dfrac{d}{dx}\left(\dfrac{g}{f}\right)\Big|_{x=1}$

3. $\dfrac{d}{dx}u\Big|_{x=0}$

4. $\dfrac{d}{dx}v\Big|_{x=-1}$

5. $\dfrac{d}{dx}w\Big|_{x=2}$

Use the derivatives of the six trig functions and the Product, Quotient, and Chain Rules to find the derivatives.

1. $\dfrac{d}{dx}(4 - \cos(2x))$

2. $\dfrac{d}{dx}\left(\tan^2\left(\dfrac{\pi}{2}x\right)\right)$

3. $\dfrac{d}{dx}\left(3x^2\left(\sin^2 x\right)\right)$

4. $\dfrac{d}{dx}\left(\dfrac{\csc x}{1 - 1\cot x}\right)$

5. $\dfrac{d}{dx}\left(\sin(3x)\cos(2x)\right)$

Day 18

Don't let the simplicity of the derivative of e^x lead you into errors. Apply the Chain Rule as appropriate and remember that for bases other than e, $\dfrac{d\left(b^x\right)}{dx} = b^x \ln b,\, b > 0$.

Find each derivative.

1. $\dfrac{d}{dx}\left(e^{x^2}\right)$

2. $\dfrac{d}{dx}\left(e^{x^2}\sqrt{x}\right)$

3. $\dfrac{d}{dx}\left(e^{\cos(2x)}\right)$

4. $\dfrac{d}{dx}\left(2^x \cdot \sin^2 x\right)$

5. $\dfrac{d}{dx}\left(\dfrac{e^{2x+1}}{2^{1-3x}}\right)$

As is the case with derivatives of exponential functions, the derivative of $\ln x$ is simple: $\frac{1}{x}$. For other bases, the derivative involves the log of the base: $\frac{d}{dx}\log_b x = \frac{1}{x \ln b}, x > 0, b > 0,$ and $b \neq 1$. The Chain Rule may be necessary as well, depending on the argument of the log.

For each logarithmic function in column A, choose the correct derivative from column B. Derivatives may be used more than once.

COLUMN A

1. $f(x) = \ln(x + 3)$

2. $f(x) = \ln(x^2 + 3)$

3. $f(x) = \ln(2x + 3)$

4. $f(x) = \ln(x^2 + 3x)$

5. $f(x) = 2\ln(x) + 3$

6. $f(x) = 2\log_3(x)$

7. $f(x) = \log_3(x^2)$

8. $f(x) = \log_2(x^3)$

9. $f(x) = \log_3(x^2 + 3x)$

10. $f(x) = \log_3(2x + 3)$

COLUMN B

(A) $f'(x) = \dfrac{2}{2x + 3}$

(B) $f'(x) = \dfrac{1}{x + 3}$

(C) $f'(x) = \dfrac{2}{x}$

(D) $f'(x) = \dfrac{2}{x \ln 3}$

(E) $f'(x) = \dfrac{3}{x \ln 2}$

(F) $f'(x) = \dfrac{2x}{x^2 + 3}$

(G) $f'(x) = \dfrac{2x + 3}{x^2 + 3x}$

(H) $f'(x) = \dfrac{2}{(\ln 3)(2x + 3)}$

(I) $f'(x) = \dfrac{2x + 3}{(\ln 3)(x)(x + 3)}$

Day 20

In many cases, it's a simple matter to solve an equation to express y explicitly as a function of x. The equation $4x^2 - 2y = 12$ can be transformed to $y = 2x^2 - 6$. When that is not possible, or when the explicit form is difficult to differentiate, implicit differentiation may be the better choice. In each of the following, assume y is a function of x and find the derivative of y with respect to x.

1. $y^3 - x^2 = 4$
2. $2x - 3y + 1 = (x + y)^2$
3. $x^2y + xy^2 = x$
4. $e^{x+y} = e^x + e^y$

Implicit differentiation can be useful when functions involve trigonometric expressions, exponentials, or logs. Find the derivative of y with respect to x for each of the following.

1. $x \sin y - y \cos x = x^2$

2. $\sin(x + y) + \cos(x - y) = 1$

3. $e^{x+y} = x^2 - 3y$

4. $\ln\left(\dfrac{x}{y}\right) = x + y$

Day 22

The rule for the derivative of an inverse is a valuable tool in those situations for which it is difficult or impossible to find the derivative of the inverse function directly. If f is a function that has an inverse $f^{-1}(x)$, and if f is differentiable at $f^{-1}(x)$, and if $f'\left(f^{-1}(x)\right) \neq 0$, then $\dfrac{d}{dx} f^{-1}(x) = \dfrac{1}{f'\left(f^{-1}(x)\right)}$.

Let $f(x)$ and $g(x)$ be inverse functions. Values of $f(x)$ and $f'(x)$ are given in the table below. Find the values of $g'(x)$ requested below.

x	−3	−2	−1	0	1	2	3
$f(x)$	9	4	1	−1	−2	−3	−10
$f'(x)$	−6	−4	−2	−1	−1	−3	−14

1. $g'(1)$

2. $g'(-1)$

3. $g'(-3)$

Day 23

The derivative of a function, depending on context, may give information about instantaneous rate of change, velocity, or the increasing or decreasing behavior of the function graph. The second derivative, taken in context, may talk about acceleration or concavity. Finding higher-order derivatives uses the techniques of differentiation repetitively.

Find the requested derivatives.

1. $f(x) = x^5 - 2x^2 + 3$, $f'''(x)$

2. $f(x) = \dfrac{3x - 1}{x + 2}$, $f''(x)$

3. $f(x) = e^{x^2 - 4}$, $f'''(x)$

4. $f(x) = 3\sin^2 x$, $f'''(x)$

5. $f(x) = \cos x$, $f^{(4)}(x)$

Rolle's Theorem states: If $f(x)$ is continuous on the closed interval $[a, b]$ and differentiable on the open interval (a, b), and if $f(a) = f(b)$, then there is a number c such that $a < c < b$ and $f'(c) = 0$.

Check if Rolle's Theorem applies in each of the following situations, and if so, find the value of c.

1. $f(x) = x^3 - 3x^2 + 1$ on $[-1, 2]$

2. $f(x) = 2 - 5\cos\left(\dfrac{x}{4}\right)$ on $[-\pi, \pi]$

Day 25

The Mean Value Theorem states that if $f(x)$ is continuous on the closed interval $[a, b]$, and differentiable on the open interval (a, b), then there is a number c such that $a < c < b$ and $f'(c) = \dfrac{f(b) - f(a)}{b - a}$.

For each of the following functions, verify that the conditions of the Mean Value Theorem are met, and find a value, c, at which a tangent line is parallel to the line containing $\big(a, f(a)\big)$ and $\big(b, f(b)\big)$.

1. $f(x) = x^3 - 2x^2 - x + 2$ on $[-2, 2]$

2. $f(x) = \sin^2 x + 2\cos x$ on $[0, 2\pi]$

3. $f(x) = 1 + e^{-x}$ on $[0, 1]$

The Extreme Value Theorem guarantees that if a function $f(x)$ is continuous on a closed interval $[a, b]$, it has both a maximum and minimum value on $[a, b]$. Note that the extrema will occur on the closed interval, so it is important to remember to examine the endpoints.

Locate the maximum and minimum values of the function on the given interval.

1. $f(x) = \dfrac{3 - x^2}{x^2 + 3}$ on $[-1, 2]$

2. $f(x) = x^3 - 5x^2 + 3x - 4$ on $[-2, 5]$

3. $f(x) = x^4 - 2x^2$ on $\left[-\dfrac{3}{2}, \dfrac{1}{2}\right]$

Day 27

The first derivative is positive when the function is increasing, negative when the function is decreasing, and zero at critical points. Use the first derivative test to determine where each function is increasing and where it is decreasing.

1. $f(x) = 7 + 6x - x^3$

2. $f(x) = x^3 - 6x^2 + 12x + 5$

3. $f(x) = -x^3 + 6x - 1$

4. $f(x) = x^3 - 4x^2 + 4x + 6$

Day 28

A critical point is a relative maximum if at that point the function changes from increasing to decreasing, and a relative minimum if the function changes from decreasing to increasing. Use the first derivative test to determine whether the given critical point is a relative maximum or a relative minimum.

1. $f(x) = x^4 - 8x^2 + 3$, critical point: $x = -2$

2. $f(x) = e^{-x^2/2}$, critical point: $x = 0$

3. $f(x) = x^2 \ln x$, critical point: $x = \dfrac{1}{\sqrt{e}} \approx 0.607$

4. $f(x) = \cos^2 x - 2\sin x$, critical point: $x = \dfrac{\pi}{2}$

5. $f(x) = \cos^2 x - 2\sin x$, critical point: $x = \dfrac{3\pi}{2}$

The sign of the first derivative indicates whether the function is increasing or decreasing. In a similar fashion, the sign of the second derivative communicates the concavity of the graph, whether it holds water or spills water. For the second derivative, a positive value indicates the graph is concave upward, holding water, while a negative result occurs when the graph is concave downward, spilling water. At a point of inflection, a change in concavity must occur, and the graph of the function has a tangent line.

Find any inflection points for the function, and then determine where the function is concave upward and where it is concave downward.

1. $f(x) = (x-1)^3$
2. $f(x) = \ln\left(4 + x^2\right)$

Day 30

Testing the sign of the first derivative to the left and right of a critical point can identify the point as a relative maximum or relative minimum. The same information can be obtained by letting the second derivative tell whether the graph is concave upward, indicating a minimum, or concave downward, at a relative maximum.

Find the critical points and use the second derivative test to identify each as a relative maximum or a relative minimum.

1. $f(x) = \sin^2 x$, $0 < x < 2\pi$

2. $f(x) = \dfrac{2}{3}x^3 - \dfrac{1}{2}x^2 - 3x + 4$

3. $f(x) = \dfrac{2x-1}{x^2}$, $x > 0$

The first and second derivatives combine to provide quite a bit of information about the graph of a function: relative extrema, points of inflection, increasing, decreasing, constant, concavity. Add domain and range, nature of discontinuities, behavior near asymptotes, end behavior, and intercepts, and you have a good image of the graph (without the help of technology).

Use the graph of $f(x)$ shown above to complete each of the statements.

1. On the interval from A to B, $f'(x)$ is _____.

2. On $[-1,1]$, $f''(x)$ is _____.

3. At point C, $f'(x)$ is _____ and $f''(x)$ is_____.

4. $\lim\limits_{x \to -3^-} f(x) =$ _____ and $\lim\limits_{x \to -3^+} f(x) =$ _____ , therefore,

  $\lim\limits_{x \to -3} f(x) =$ _____.

5. $\lim\limits_{x \to -\infty} f(x) =$ _____ and $\lim\limits_{x \to \infty} f(x) =$ _____.

The graph of the function $f(x)$ is shown. Sketch a graph of $f'(x)$.

Day 33

The graph shown is the first derivative, $f'(x)$, of a function $f(x)$. Use information derived from the first derivative to sketch a graph of the function $f(x)$.

Day 34

Every Related Rates problem has a defining equation or formula. One of the most common is the Pythagorean Theorem, when lengths of the sides of the triangle created by objects moving at right angles are all seen as functions of time. For each of the following problems, establish the Pythagorean relationship, differentiate with respect to time, plug in known quantities, and solve for the unknown.

1. Tony and Tim leave their office at the same time. Tony drives to his home, 30 miles due east of the office, and stops. Tim continues to drive due north at 40 mph toward his home. How fast is the distance between Tony and Tim changing at the moment that Tim is 80 miles north of the office?

2. Ship A leaves the dock in San Clemente, sailing due south at 20 mph, at the same moment that ship B leaves Santa Catalina Island, 46 miles due west of San Clemente, sailing east at 15 mph. How fast is the distance between the two ships changing when Ship A is 50 miles south of San Clemente?

Day 35

Related Rates problems about filling or draining containers are structured by volume formulas. For each of the following problems, set up the appropriate volume formula, differentiate assuming each dimension is a function of time, plug in known quantities, and solve for the unknown.

A water container in the shape of an inverted cone is 12 feet in diameter and 16 feet deep at its deepest point. Water leaks out of the container at a constant rate of 2 cubic feet per minute. How fast is the water level dropping when the depth of water remaining in the tank is 4 feet?

Day 36

For any Related Rates problem, even one that doesn't fit the common patterns, there's a formula or rule to tie the situation together. Look for that equation and solve the Related Rates problems below.

A photographer covering the launch of a new satellite sets up a camera 2,000 feet from the base of the launch pad across level ground. When the rocket carrying the satellite is 3,000 feet off the ground, it rises vertically at 1,200 feet per second. At what rate must the angle of elevation of the camera change to keep the rocket in view?

Day 37

To solve problems that ask for the maximum or the minimum value of a function, use the first derivative to identify the critical values of the function, and then either the first derivative test or the second derivative test to determine at which x values will the maxima (or minima) occur.

1. $f(x) = x^{1/2}(x-3)^2$
2. $f(x) = \sin 2x - 2\cos x, \ 0 < x < 2\pi$
3. $f(x) = -2x + (x+1)^{3/2}$

1. Find the dimensions of the rectangular garden of largest area that can be enclosed with 100 feet of fencing.

2. Find the dimensions of the rectangular garden of largest area that can be enclosed with 100 feet of fencing if one side of the garden is the wall of a barn and so only three sides need to be fenced.

3. Find the shortest distance from the point $(3, -1)$ to the line $y = 2x - 1$.

Day 39

Sketch a graph of a function $f(x)$ that has all of these characteristics.

Domain: $[-5, 5]$, Range: $[-5, 5]$

5 x-intercepts

y-intercept: $(0, -2)$

x	−4	−3	−2	1	3.5
$f'(x)$	0	DNE	0	0	0
$f''(x)$	−		−	+	−

L'Hôpital's Rule provides another tool for finding limits. When $\lim\limits_{x \to a} \dfrac{f(x)}{g(x)}$ is an indeterminate form $\dfrac{0}{0}$ or $\dfrac{\pm\infty}{\pm\infty}$, *L'Hôpital's* Rule says $\lim\limits_{x \to a} \dfrac{f(x)}{g(x)} = \lim\limits_{x \to a} \dfrac{f'(x)}{g'(x)}$. It doesn't solve every problem but it can help. Use *L'Hôpital's* Rule to find these limits, if possible.

1. $\lim\limits_{x \to 0} \dfrac{\sin x}{2x}$

2. $\lim\limits_{x \to 3} \dfrac{\ln(x - 2)}{x^2 - 9}$

3. $\lim\limits_{x \to \infty} \dfrac{e^{2x}}{2x^2}$

Day 41

The derivative of a function gives a formula for the slope of a tangent line to the graph at any point. When evaluated for a particular value of x, it gives the slope of a tangent drawn to that point. With the slope and a point, it's possible to find the equation of the tangent line. Match each function with the tangent to the curve at the point $(-1, -2)$.

COLUMN A

1. $f(x) = x^3 - 2x^2 + 1$
2. $f(x) = \dfrac{1-x}{x}$
3. $f(x) = -1 - e^{-x^2 - 2x - 1}$
4. $x^2 + 2y^2 = 9$
5. $f(x) = 2\sin\left(\dfrac{\pi x}{2}\right)$

COLUMN B

(A) $y = -x - 3$

(B) $y = -2$

(C) $y = -2x - 1$

(D) $y = 7x + 5$

(E) $y = -\dfrac{1}{2}x - \dfrac{5}{2}$

A normal line is one that is perpendicular to a tangent line at the point of tangency. For a circle, any normal line is a line that contains a radius, because a radius drawn to the point of tangency is perpendicular to the tangent. For other curves, however, the normal lines are not so predictable. For each curve, find an equation of the normal line at the given point.

1. $f(x) = 2x^4 - 5x^3 + 2$ at $(1, -1)$

2. $f(x) = \sin(2x) + \cos x$ at $(-\pi, -1)$

Day 43

A tangent line to the graph of a function runs so close to the curve that it can be used to approximate values of the function close to the point of tangency. It is also possible to tell if the estimate is larger or smaller than the actual value by examining the concavity of the function graph. For each function below, use the equation of a tangent line to estimate the requested function value and tell whether it is an underestimate or an overestimate.

1. $f(x) = 5 + 2x - x^3$; $f(1.01)$
2. $f(x) = 3 - \ln(2x + 1)$; $f(0.9)$

Use tangent line to estimate indicated function value and tell whether it is an underestimate or an overestimate.

$f(x) = 2 + 3e^{-x}; \ f(-0.01)$

Day 45

Finding approximate values for roots of integers is one case in which linear approximation can be helpful. Of course, how close to the actual value your estimate is will depend on how far you are from the point of tangency. Use linear approximation to estimate each of the following roots, and calculate the difference from the actual value.

Desired root	$\sqrt{17}$	$\sqrt{20}$	$\sqrt[3]{-26}$	$\sqrt[3]{-25}$	$\sqrt[5]{33}$
Linear Approximation					
Actual Value (to nearest thousandth)	4.123	4.472	−2.962	−2.924	2.012
Actual minus Approximate					

Day 46

Estimating the values of trig functions for angles near those commonly memorized is another application of linear approximation. Measures should be in radians, but conversion is simple if you remember that one degree is $\dfrac{\pi}{180}$ radians. Complete the chart for these approximations.

Desired	cos 58°	sin 50°	tan 170°
Function	$y = \cos x$		
Point of tangency		$\left(\dfrac{\pi}{4}, \dfrac{\sqrt{2}}{2} \right)$	
Derivative			
Derivative Evaluated			
Distance from point of tangency			$-10° = -\dfrac{\pi}{18}$
(Derivative)(distance) + y-value of point of tangency			
Approximate Value	cos 58° ≈	sin 50° ≈	tan 170° ≈
Actual (to nearest thousandth)	0.530	0.766	−0.176

The phrase "vertical motion" refers to the movement of an object that has been dropped from a height or thrown upward (and ultimately comes down). The position of the object is usually modeled by the equation $s(t) = -\frac{1}{2} gt^2 + v_0 t + s_0$, where g is the acceleration due to gravity (32 ft/sec^2 in customary units or 9.8 m/sec^2 in metric), v_0 is the initial velocity, and s_0 is the initial position. The graph shows the position of an object launched upward from a height of 3 feet, with an initial velocity of 100 ft/sec.

1. Approximate the velocity of the object 1.5 seconds after launch.

2. Approximate the velocity of the object 5 seconds after launch.

3. Use the derivative of the position function to calculate those velocities.

4. At what time does the object reach maximum height?

5. What is the average velocity of the object from $t = 2$ to $t = 5.5$?

6. At what time is the instantaneous velocity equal to this average velocity?

7. True or False: The acceleration is greater at $t = 1$ than at $t = 2$.

8. When is the object slowing down?

Day 48

Horizontal motion examines movement to the left and to the right along a line. Imagine a particle moving along the x-axis, with its position at any time $t \geq 0$ given by the function $s(t) = 1 - \cos\left(\dfrac{\pi t}{2}\right)$.

1. Chart the position of the particle each second from $t = 0$ to $t = 4$.

time (seconds)	0	1	2	3	4
position	(,0)	(,0)	(,0)	(,0)	(,0)

2. When does the particle change direction?

3. When is the particle speeding up? When is it slowing down?

4. Find the total distance traveled by the particle.

A water container in the shape of an inverted cone is 6 feet in diameter and 8 feet deep at its deepest point. Water leaks out of the container at a constant rate of 2 cubic feet per minute.

The water leaking from the cone drips into a tank that is 4 feet high and has a square base 3 feet on a side. How fast is the depth of water in this tank changing?

Find the maximum and minimum values of the functions.

1. $f(x) = x^3 + \dfrac{2}{x^2}$

2. $f(x) = x^4 - 3x^3 + 3x^2 + 1$

Day 51

The long-running television game show *Jeopardy* is based on giving contestants the answer and asking them to come up with the correct question. Antiderivatives are a lot like *Jeopardy*. You're given the derivative, and asked for the function it came from. The derivative of a constant is zero, so remember there may have been a constant in the original function. Find a function that could have each of these derivatives.

1. $f'(x) = 5$
2. $f'(x) = 3x^2 + 8x + 3$
3. $f'(x) = \dfrac{5}{x}$
4. $f'(x) = \sin x$
5. $f'(x) = \sec^2 x$

Day 52

Evaluate each of the following summations, using the properties of summations to simplify the calculation.

1. $\displaystyle\sum_{i=1}^{5} i$

2. $\displaystyle\sum_{i=1}^{10} \left(\frac{i}{5}\right)$

3. $\displaystyle\sum_{i=2}^{4} \left(i^2\right)(i+3)$

4. $\displaystyle\sum_{i=-3}^{1} \left(i^3 + 2i^2 - 5i + 4\right)$

Day 53

Use geometric reasoning to estimate the area between the x-axis and the graph on the interval [a, b]. Then find the antiderivative $F(x)$ and evaluate $F(b) - F(a)$.

1. $f(x) = 4$ on [0, 4]

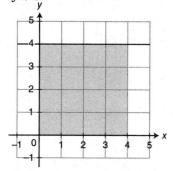

2. $f(x) = 4 - 2x$ on [0, 2]

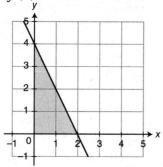

3. $f(x) = 3x$ on [0, 1]

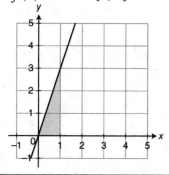

4. $f(x) = 3x + 1$ on [0, 1]

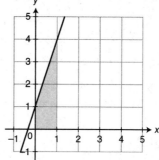

5. $f(x) = |x - 1|$ on [0, 4]

5 Minutes to a 5

Given $\int\limits_{5}^{9} f(x)\ dx = 12$, $\int\limits_{2}^{5} f(x)\ dx = -3$, $\int\limits_{5}^{9} g(x)\ dx = 12$, and $\int\limits_{2}^{5} g(x)\ dx = -1$, find:

1. $\int\limits_{8}^{8} g(x)\ dx$

2. $\int\limits_{9}^{5} f(x)\ dx$

3. $\int\limits_{2}^{5} 7g(x)\ dx$

4. $\int\limits_{2}^{9} f(x)\ dx$

5. $\int\limits_{2}^{5} \left[f(x) + g(x) \right]\ dx$

Evaluate each of the definite integrals.

1. $\displaystyle\int_{-3}^{1}\left(6x^2-5x+2\right)dx$

2. $\displaystyle\int_{1}^{2}\frac{x^5+x^2+x}{x}\,dx$

3. $\displaystyle\int_{1}^{3}\frac{dx}{x^3}$

4. $\displaystyle\int_{1}^{4}\sqrt{x}\,\,dx$

5. $\displaystyle\int_{1}^{32}\sqrt[5]{x^2}\,\,dx$

Day 56

Sum, Difference, and Power Rules are not always enough to find the integrals of exponential, logarithmic, or trigonometric functions. Thoughtful application of memorized forms will help with finding these definite integrals.

1. $\displaystyle\int_{0}^{\pi/3} \left(2\sin\theta - 5\cos\theta\right) d\theta$

2. $\displaystyle\int_{\pi/4}^{\pi/3} 5\sec^2 x \; dx$

3. $\displaystyle\int_{1}^{e} \left(\frac{3}{z}\right) dz$

4. $\displaystyle\int_{-\pi}^{\pi/2} \left(2\sin\theta\cos\theta\right) d\theta$

5. $\displaystyle\int_{0}^{\ln(1+\pi)} \left(-e^x \cos\left(1 - e^x\right)\right) dx$

Recognizing ways to rewrite functions is a key skill for integration. Match each integral with an equivalent form that is easier to integrate.

COLUMN A

1. $\int x\sqrt{x}\,dx$

2. $\int \dfrac{x^3 + x}{x}\,dx$

3. $\int \left(\sqrt{x}\,(x-2)\right)dx$

4. $\int \left(\dfrac{2x^5 - x + 3}{x^2}\right)dx$

5. $\int \sqrt[4]{x^3}\,dx$

COLUMN B

(A) $\int \sqrt{x^2 - 2x}\,dx$

(B) $\int x^{3/2}\,dx$

(C) $\int \dfrac{1}{x}\left(x^3 + x\right)dx$

(D) $\int x^{3/4}\,dx$

(E) $\int \sqrt{x^3}\,dx$

(F) $\int \left(2x^3 - x^{-1} + 3x^{-2}\right)dx$

(G) $\int x^{4/3}\,dx$

(H) $\int \left(x^2 + 1\right)dx$

(I) $\int \left(x^{3/2} - 2x^{1/2}\right)dx$

(J) $\int \left(2x^3 - x + 3x^2\right)dw$

Each of these integrals has the form $\int u \cdot du$ (give or take a constant multiplier). For each, identify u and du, then evaluate the integral.

1. $\displaystyle\int_{-\pi}^{\pi/2} \left(\cos\theta \cos(\sin\theta) \right) d\theta$

2. $\displaystyle\int_{0}^{\ln(1+\pi)} \left(e^x \cos\left(1 - e^x\right) \right) dx$

3. $\displaystyle\int_{0}^{1/4} \left(\frac{2t}{1 - 4t^2} \right) dt$

Let f be continuous and differentiable on $(-\infty, \infty)$.

1. For which values of k does $\displaystyle\int_{-2}^{k} x^2\, dx = 24$?

    a) 1   **b)** 2   **c)** 3   **d)** 4

2. Which of the following is an expression for $f'(x)$ when $f(x) = \displaystyle\int_{0}^{x} \left(3t^2 - t\right) dt$?

    a) $x^3 - \dfrac{x^2}{2}$ **b)** $t^3 - \dfrac{t^2}{2}$ **c)** $3x^2 - x$ **d)** $3t^2 - t$

3. $\displaystyle\int_{\pi}^{\pi} \frac{\sin^2(3x)}{\cos(2x)}\, dx =$

    a) 0   **b)** $\dfrac{1}{2}$ **c)** 1   **d)** $\dfrac{3}{2}$

4. If $\displaystyle\int_{2}^{5} f(x)\, dx = 8$, then $\displaystyle\int_{5}^{2} f(x)\, dx =$

    a) -8 **b)** 0   **c)** $\dfrac{1}{8}$ **d)** 8

5. $\displaystyle\int_{1}^{5} 2\, dx =$

    a) 4   **b)** 5   **c)** 8   **d)** 10

Whenever you find an antiderivative, you must contend with the invisible constant term, but if you have the right bit of information, you can actually find that constant. Once the constant is identified, you can apply antiderivatives again.

Find $y = f(x)$ if $f''(x) = 6x - 4$, $f'(0) = 1$, and $f(1) = -3$

For each integral, identify u and du, make any necessary adjustments, and integrate.

1. $\int \dfrac{x}{2x^2 - 3}\, dx$

2. $\int \dfrac{x^2}{x^3 - 5}\, dx$

3. $\int \dfrac{x}{4 - x^2}\, dx$

4. $\int e^{3x}\, dx$

5. $\int x^2 e^{x^3}\, dx$

Recognizing an integrand as the derivative of an inverse trig function can be challenging, so be sure you've done the necessary memory work, and practice recognizing the forms as you work problems.

1. $\displaystyle\int \frac{-2dx}{1+4x^2}$

2. $\displaystyle\int \frac{-3dx}{\sqrt{1-9x^2}}$

3. $\displaystyle\int \frac{1}{\sqrt{4-x^2}} = \int \frac{\dfrac{1}{2}}{\sqrt{1-\dfrac{x^2}{4}}}$

4. $\displaystyle\int \frac{\cos x}{1+\sin^2 x}\,dx$

Find the dimensions of the rectangle of greatest area that can be inscribed in a semi-circle with the radius of 10 centimeters.

The graph of a piecewise linear function *f*, on [–4, 3], is shown.

What is the value of

1. $\int\limits_{0}^{2} f(x)\,dx$

2. $\int\limits_{0}^{-2} f(x)\,dx$

3. $\int\limits_{-4}^{-2} f(x)\,dx$

4. $\int\limits_{-4}^{3} f(x)\,dx$

The graph shows the rate of flow of water, in gallons per hour, through a pipe over the course of 24 hours.

Estimate the number of gallons of water that flowed through the pipe

1. in the first 4 hours

2. between hour 8 and hour 16

3. over the 24-hour period

$f(x)$ is a twice differentiable function defined on the interval $[-3, 2]$. The graph below is the graph of $f'(x)$.

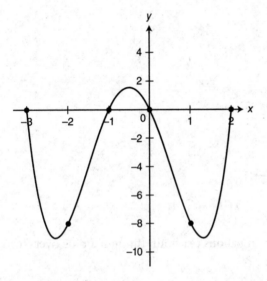

Label each of the following statements True or False.

1. $f'(-2) < f''(-2)$

2. $f(0) < f'(0) < f''(0)$

3. $f'(-1) < f''(-1)$

4. $f(-2) < f(-1)$

5. $f(-1) < f(0)$

A function f is continuous and twice differentiable on the interval (a, b). The graph of the derivative $f'(x)$ is shown below. Sketch the graphs of $f(x)$ and $f''(x)$ on [a, b].

The function f is continuous on the closed interval [2, 8] and has values as shown in the table. Using four subintervals, find the trapezoidal approximation of $\int_{2}^{8} f(x)\, dx$.

x	2	3	5	6	8
f(x)	1	4	7	3	2

Set up and evaluate Riemann sums for the area under the graph of $f(x)$ shown, on the interval $[-3, 2]$, using the partitions given.

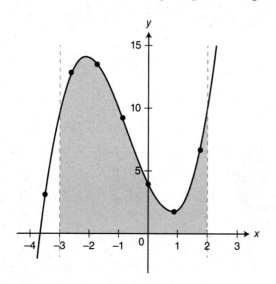

1. Use $\Delta x = 1$ and LRAM (Left Rectangular Approximation Method).

2. Use $\Delta x = 1$ and RRAM (Right Rectangular Approximation Method).

Evaluate each definite integral.

1. $\int\limits_{-2}^{2} \left(4 - x^2 \right) dx$

2. $\int\limits_{-1}^{7} \sqrt{x+2}\ dx$

3. $\int\limits_{-3}^{2} \left(x^3 + 2x^2 - 5x + 4 \right) dx$

Day 71

Use the second part of the Fundamental Theorem of Calculus to complete the chart.

1.	$F(x) = \int_{5}^{x}\left(2t\sqrt{t}\right)dt$	$F'(x) =$	$F'(9) =$
2.	$F(x) = \int_{0}^{4x} t\left(1+t^3\right)dt$	$F'(x) =$	$F'(1) =$
3.	$F(x) = \int_{4}^{2x}\left(\dfrac{t-3}{t}\right)dt$	$F'(x) =$	$F'(10) =$
4.	$F(x) = \int_{-1}^{x} t\left(t^2-4\right)dt$	$F'(x) =$	$F'(2) =$
5.	$F(x) = \int_{0}^{x} e^{t^2}\, dt$	$F'(x) =$	$F'(1) =$

Day 72

The second part of the Fundamental Theorem of Calculus says that if $f(x)$ is continuous on an open interval and a is any value in that interval, and $F(x) = \int_a^x f(t)\,dt$, then at every point in that interval, $F'(x) = f(x)$. State $F'(x)$ if:

1. $F(x) = \int_0^x \left(t^3 - 7t + 1\right) dt$

2. $F(x) = \int_{-3}^x \sqrt{t+5}\ dt$

3. $F(x) = \int_1^{2x} \left(t^2 - 2t + 5\right) dt$

Each graph shows the same function $f(x)$. Use the rectangles provided to estimate the area under the curve from $x = -4$ to $x = 4$.

1.

3.

2.

x	−4	−3.5	−3	−2.5	−2	−1.5	−1	−0.5	0	0.5	1	1.5	2	2.5	3
$f(x)$	0	4.5	6	5.5	4	2	0	−1.5	−2.5	−2.5	−2	−1	0	0.5	0

Let $f(x)$ be a continuous function on [−4, 3] that takes the values shown in the table. Write and evaluate an approximation of the area under the curve using the conditions described.

1. From $x = -4$ to $x = -1$ using 6 subintervals of equal width and left-hand approximation

2. From $x = -1$ to $x = 2$ using 6 subintervals of equal width and right-hand approximation

3. From $x = -4$ to $x = -1$ using 3 subintervals of equal width and midpoint approximation

x	−4	−3.5	−3	−2.5	−2	−1.5	−1	−0.5	0	0.5	1	1.5	2	2.5	3
f(x)	0	4.5	6	5.5	4	2	0	−1.5	−2.5	−2.5	−2	−1	0	0.5	0

Let $f(x)$ be a continuous function on $[-4, 3]$ that takes the values shown in the table.

Use a trapezoidal approximation to estimate the area under the curve from $x = -1$ to $x = 2$, using 3 subintervals of equal width.

Find the area of the region(s) bounded by:

1. $f(x) = x^3 + 3x^2$ and the x-axis.

2. $f(x) = 2x^3 + 3x^2 + 4$, the x-axis, and the vertical lines $x = -3$ and $x = -1$.

Evaluate each of the definite integrals.

1. $\int\limits_{0}^{\pi}(1+\cos x)\,dx$

2. $\int\limits_{\pi/6}^{\pi/3}(-\sin x)\,dx$

3. $\int\limits_{-\pi/2}^{\pi/2}(x+\sin x)\,dx$

The definite integrals below involve exponential functions and log functions. Find each definite integral.

1. $\displaystyle\int_{-2}^{2}\left(xe^{-x^2}\right)dx$

2. $\displaystyle\int_{1}^{4}\frac{x+2}{x^2+4x}dx$

When evaluating a definite integral that involves an absolute value, rewrite the integrand as a piecewise function. Then rewrite the integral as a sum of two integrals, or as a single integral that does not include an absolute value if the limits of integration are both in the same portion of the domain.

1. $\displaystyle\int_{1}^{5} |x-3|\, dx$

2. $\displaystyle\int_{-1}^{3} |2x+1|\, dx$

3. $\displaystyle\int_{-2}^{2} |x^3|\, dx$

Let $f(x) = 3 + 2x - x^2$, $g(x) = x^2 - 2x - 3$, $h(x) = 9 + 9x - x^2 - x^3$, and $s(x) = \sin\left(\dfrac{\pi x}{3}\right)$. Find the area between the curves on the specified interval.

1. $f(x)$ and $g(x)$ between $x = -1$ and $x = 3$.

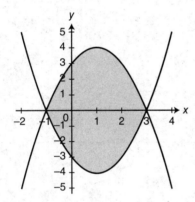

3. $f(x)$ and $s(x)$ between $x = 0$ and $x = 3$.

2. $f(x)$ and $h(x)$ between $x = -1$ and $x = 3$.

Match each solid of revolution with the integral that will produce its volume, and then find the volume.

COLUMN A

1.

2.

3.

4.

COLUMN B

(A) $\pi \int_0^2 \left(4 - x^2\right)^2 dx$

(B) $\pi \int_0^2 \left(\sqrt{4-y}\right)^2 dy$

(C) $\pi \int_0^2 \left(4 - x\right)^2 dx$

(D) $\pi \int_0^4 \left(4 - x\right)^2 dx$

(E) $\pi \int_0^4 \left(\sqrt{4-y}\right)^2 dy$

(F) $\pi \int_0^2 \left(4 - y^2\right)^2 dy$

(G) $\pi \int_0^4 \left(4 - y\right)^2 dy$

5 Minutes to a 5

Let R be the region in the first quadrant enclosed by the graphs of $y = x^2$ and $y = 2x$, as shown. Use the Method of Washers to find the volume of each solid of revolution formed when the region R is revolved about the given line.

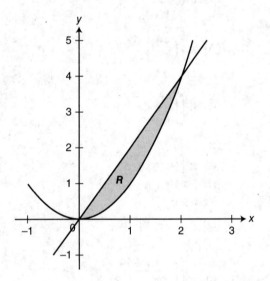

1. About the y-axis

2. About the x-axis

3. About the line $y = 4$

4. About the line $x = 2$

Let R be the region in the first quadrant enclosed by the graphs of $y = x^2$, $y = 4$, and $x = 0$. Let A be the region enclosed by the graphs of $y = -x$, $y = 3$, and $x = 1$. Find the volume of each solid of revolution described.

1. Region R revolved around the line $y = 4$

2. Region A revolved around the line $y = 3$

3. Region A revolved around the line $x = 1$

Let R be the region enclosed by the graphs of $y = x^2$, $y = 1$, and $x = 3$. Find the volume of each solid generated when region R is revolved about the given line.

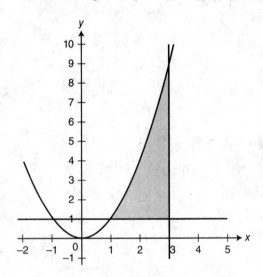

1. R revolved about $x = 4$

2. R revolved about $y = -1$

3. R revolved about $y = 10$

4. R revolved about $x = -1$

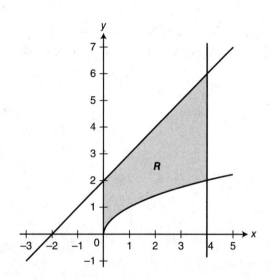

Let R be the region enclosed by the graphs of $y = x + 2$, $y = \sqrt{x}$, $x = 4$, and the y-axis.

1. Find the area of region R.

2. Find the volume of a solid with R as its base and square cross sections perpendicular to the x-axis.

3. Find the volume of a solid with R as its base and cross sections that are isosceles right triangles with hypotenuse perpendicular to the x-axis.

Let A be the region enclosed by the graphs of $y = \sin(x)$, $y = \cos(x)$, and the y-axis, as shown. Let B be the region under the graphs of $y = \sin(x)$ and $y = \cos(x)$ and above the x-axis, as marked.

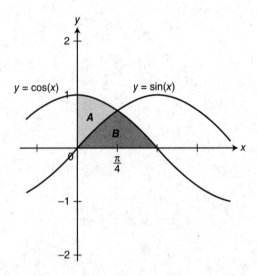

1. Write, but do not integrate, an expression for the volume of the solid created when region B is revolved about the y-axis.

2. Write, but do not integrate, an expression for the volume of the solid created when region A is revolved about the y-axis.

3. Find the volume of the solid created when region A is revolved about the x-axis.

Find the dimensions of a right - circular cylindrical container with minimum surface area if it must have a volume of 1,000 cubic centimeters.

If your pastry has a circular base with a radius of 3 inches and has parallel cross sections that are semicircles, what is the volume of the pastry?

Slope Fields allow you to visualize what the antiderivative might look like. Create a Slope Field for each of the differential equations on the axes provided. Then sketch the graph of the antiderivative that meets the given initial condition.

1. $\dfrac{dy}{dx} = 3x^2 + 2x$, $y(0) = 1$

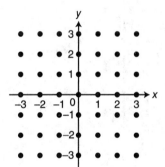

3. $\dfrac{dy}{dx} = x \cos x + \sin x$, $y(0) = -2$

2. $\dfrac{dy}{dx} = \dfrac{1}{x + 2}$, $y(-1) = 0$

Create a Slope Field for each of the given differential equations.

1. $\dfrac{dy}{dx} = 3x^2 - 1$

3. $\dfrac{dy}{dx} = 2x + y$

2. $\dfrac{dy}{dx} = \dfrac{1}{(x-1)^2}$

Day 91

A differential equation, one containing derivatives, may be simple or quite complex. If the differential equation can be rearranged so that one variable is on the left side and the other is on the right, finding the antiderivative of each side can lead to a solution. Solve each of the following separable differential equations.

1. $\dfrac{dy}{dx} = \dfrac{2\cos x}{y^2}$

2. $\dfrac{dy}{dx} = x(1+2y)$

Day 92

For a discrete function, finding the average value of the function on an interval is a simple task: add the values the function takes on that interval and divide by the number of values. For a continuous function, however, an integral is necessary to find the sum of the function values. The divisor is the length of the interval. Find the average value of each function on the specified interval.

1. $f(x) = \sqrt{x - 2}$ on $[2, 6]$

2. $g(x) = e^{1-x}$ on $[0, 1]$

3. $f(x) = x^3 - 2x + 1$ on $[-1, 2]$

5 Minutes to a 5

Day 93

Mean Value Theorem for integrals says that if $f(x)$ is a continuous function on $[a, b]$, then there is a number c in $[a, b]$ such that $\int_a^b f(x)\,dx = f(c)(b - a)$. Find the value of c that satisfies the Mean Value Theorem for each of the following functions on the interval $[0, 2]$.

1. $f(x) = 4 - x^2$

2. $f(x) = x^2 - x - 2$

3. $f(x) = 5\sin\left(\dfrac{x-1}{2}\right)$

The graph shows the velocity of a car traveling on a straight road.

1. Over what period of time is the acceleration of the car negative?

2. What is the average velocity of the car over the 5-hour period?

3. What is the total distance traveled by the car over the 5-hour period.

A furniture company produces a line of chairs that has cost function given by the function $C(x) = 17x + 0.025x^2$.

1. Find the marginal cost function.

2. If 5,000 chairs are produced, what is the average cost per chair?

3. If each chair is sold for $250, what is the total profit on a run of 5,000 chairs?

Find the maximum and minimum values of the function on the given interval.

1. $f(x) = \dfrac{x-1}{2x+1}$ on $[0,3]$

2. $f(x) = x + 4x^{-2}$ on $[1,4]$

Day 97

Oil is pumped into a tank at a constant rate of 1 gallon per minute but leaks out at $3\sqrt{t}$ gallons per minute, $t \geq 0$. At time $t = 0$, the tank contains 50 gallons of oil.

1. How many gallons of oil leak out of the tank from time $t = 0$ until $t = 9$ minutes?

2. How many gallons of oil are in the tank at time $t = 9$ minutes?

A colony of a certain bacterium initially has a population of 5 million bacteria. Suppose that the colony grows at a rate of $f(t) = e^{(t+1)/2}$ million bacteria per hour.

1. Find the total change in the bacteria population during the time from $t = 0$ to $t = 3$.

2. Find the bacteria population at time $t = 3$.

Day 99

At time $t = 0$, a cup of coffee at 200°F is put into a 72°F room. The coffee is left to cool, with its temperature changing at a rate of $r(t) = -12e^{-t/6}$ degrees per minute.

1. Estimate the temperature of the coffee when $t = 5$.

2. At what time will the temperature of the coffee drop to 140°F, which some say is the perfect drinking temperature?

The same types of plants are planted in two comparable garden plots to investigate the effects of different methods of watering. The rates of growth for the two plots are shown in the following figure.

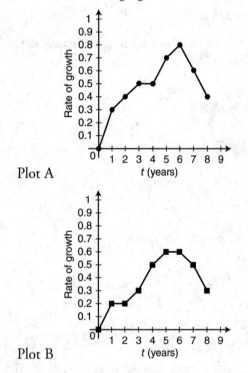

Plot A

Plot B

Assume that the populations of the two plots are equal at time $t = 0$. Using RRAM (Right Rectangular Approximation Method):

1. Estimate the change in the population of plot A during the first 3 years.

2. Estimate the change in the population of plot B during years 4 to 8.

3. Which population is larger after 8 years?

Day 101

At time $t = 0$, a cup of coffee at 200°F is put into a 72°F room. The temperature of the coffee is measured every 3 minutes and recorded in the table below.

time (min)	0	3	6	9	12	15	18	21	24
temp (°F)	200	153	124	107	96	90	86	84	82

1. Estimate the average temperature of the coffee over the first 15 minutes.

2. Estimate the rate of change of the temperature at $t = 15$.

A cylindrical container with a diameter of 12 inches contains 900 in^3 of water when a leak forms. Let $t = 0$ represent the moment the leak forms. Water leaks out of the container at a rate modeled by $r(t) = -45e^{-t/20}$.

1. How many in^3 of water leak out of the container in the first 10 minutes?

2. How many in^3 of water remain in the container after 30 minutes?

3. Write an equation that relates the change in volume over time to the change in the height of the water in the container over time.

A woman 168 cm tall is walking at a rate of 90 cm per second toward a streetlight 610 cm tall. How fast is the length of her shadow changing?

A particle moves along the y-axis so that its velocity at any time $t \geq 0$ is given by $v(t) = t^2 - \sin t$. At time $t = 0$, the position of the particle is $y = 1$.

1. Write an expression for the acceleration of the particle in terms of t.

2. Write an expression for the position $y(t)$ of the particle.

3. Find the position of the particle the first time, $t > 0$, when the velocity of the particle is zero.

5 Minutes to a 5

Consider the curve defined by $2y^2 - xy + x^3 = 16$.

1. Find $\dfrac{dy}{dx}$.

2. Write an equation for the line tangent to the curve at the point $(-2, 3)$.

3. There is a number k such that the point $(-2.2, k)$ is on the curve. Use the tangent line to approximate the value of k.

The graphs of $f(x) = x^3 + 1$ and $g(x) = 4x - x^3$ enclose two regions, labeled *R1* and *R2*, as shown. The graphs intersect at $x = a$, $x = b$, and $x = c$ with $a < b < c$.

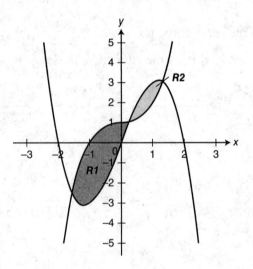

1. Without using absolute value, set up an expression involving one or more integrals that gives the area enclosed by the graphs of f and g.

2. Assume $b = 0.3$ and $c = 1.3$. Set up an expression involving one or more integrals that gives the volume of the solid generated by revolving the region *R2* about the x-axis. Find the volume of this solid.

Water is draining from a conical tank, completely filled with water, with a height of 8 feet and a diameter of 6 feet into a cylindrical tank that has a base with an area of 100π square feet. The depth, h, in feet, of the water in the conical tank is changing at the rate of $(h - 1)$ feet per minute.

1. Write an expression for the volume of water in the conical tank as a function of h.

2. At what rate is the volume of water in the conical tank changing with $h = 6$?

3. Let y be the depth, in feet, of the water in the cylindrical tank. At what rate is y changing when $h = 6$?

The graph of a differentiable function $f(t) = 1 + \dfrac{2t}{t^2+1}$ f on the closed interval $[-1, 5]$ is shown. Let $h(x) = \displaystyle\int_0^x f(t)\,dt$ for $-1 \leq x \leq 5$.

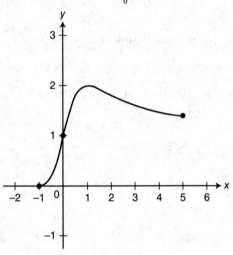

1. Find $h(0)$ and $h'(1)$.

2. On what interval(s) is the graph of h concave upward?

3. Find any inflection points of h on the interval $-1 < x < 5$.

Consider the graph of the function $h(x) = 8 - \dfrac{x^4}{2}$ for $x \geq 0$. Let R be the region in the first quadrant below the graph of h, and let $A(w)$ be the area of a rectangle in the first quadrant with sides along the x- and y-axis and diagonally opposite vertices at the origin and the point $(w, h(w))$.

1. Find the maximum value of $A(w)$.

2. Find the area included in R but not included in the rectangle with maximum value as described in Question 1.

The cost of a single dose of a particular drug in the United States is approximately given by $S(t) = Ce^{kt}$, where S is measured in dollars and t is measured in years from the beginning of 2007. The single-dose price at the beginning of 2007 was $57, and in 2015, $375.

1. Find C and k.

2. Find the average price of a single dose of the drug over the 8-year time period beginning January 1, 2011.

A family of functions has the form $f(x) = \cos(x) - bx$, where b is a positive constant and $-2\pi \le x \le 2\pi$.

Find the x-coordinates of all points, $-2\pi \le x \le 2\pi$, where the line $y = 1 - bx$ is tangent to the graph of $f(x) = \cos(x) - bx$.

A storage tank has the shape shown, obtained by revolving the curve $y = \dfrac{x^6}{64}$ from $x = 0$ to $x = 3$ about the y-axis. Both x and y are measured in feet. A lubricant weighing 35 pounds per cubic foot flowed into an initially empty tank at a constant rate of 5 cubic feet per minute. When the depth of the oil reached 8 feet, the flow stopped.

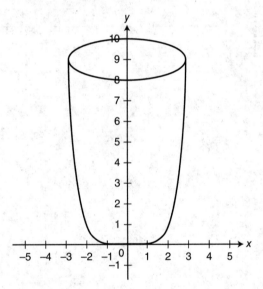

1. Find the volume of the lubricant in the tank, and the total weight of that volume of lubricant.

2. To the nearest minute, how long would it take to fill the tank to a depth of 8 feet?

3. How fast is the depth of lubricant in the tank, h, measured in feet, increasing when $h = 1$ ft?

Distance (cm)	x	0	2	6	10	15
Temperature (°C)	$f(x)$	80	73	65	62	60

A metal wire 15 cm long is heated at one end. The table gives selected values of the temperature $f(x)$ in degrees Celsius of the wire x centimeters from the end where heat was applied. The temperature $f(x)$ is decreasing and twice differentiable.

1. Approximate $f'(4)$.

2. Estimate the average temperature of the wire, using a trapezoidal approximation.

3. Find $\int_0^{15} f'(x)\,dx$ and explain its significance.

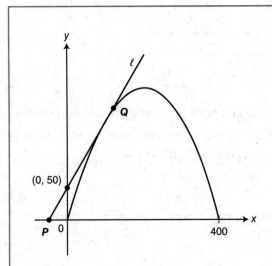

Line ℓ is tangent to the graph of $y = \dfrac{400x - x^2}{200}$ at point Q as shown.

Find the x-coordinate of point Q.

5 Minutes to a 5

Consider the curve given by $x^3 y^2 + 3x^2 y^2 + xy^2 = 2$.

1. Show that $\dfrac{dy}{dx} = -\dfrac{y\left(3x^2 + 6x + 1\right)}{2x\left(x^2 + 3x + 1\right)}$.

2. Find all points on the curve whose x-coordinate is -1, and write an equation for the tangent line at each of these points.

A particle moves along the y-axis with velocity $v(t) = 3 + 5t - t^2$ for $0 \leq t \leq 10$.

1. In which direction is the particle moving at time $t = 5$? Why?

2. Find the acceleration of the particle at time $t = 5$. Is the particle speeding up or slowing down at $t = 5$? Explain.

3. Find the position function $s(t)$ if $s(0) = 1$, and determine the position of the particle at $t = 6$.

The shaded region, R, is bounded by the graph of $y = \dfrac{x^3}{9}$ and the y-axis and the line $y = 3$, as shown in the figure.

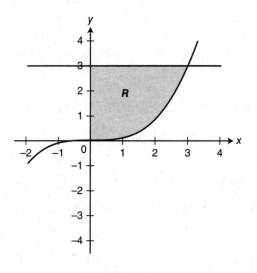

1. Find the area of R.

2. Find the volume of the solid generated by revolving R about the x-axis.

3. There exists a number k, $k > 3$, such that when R is revolved about the line $y = k$, the resulting solid has the same volume as that in question 2. Set up an equation containing an integral such that the solution to the equation will yield the value of k. Do not solve the equation.

t (hours)	0	2	4	6	8	10	12
R(t) (gallons/ hour)	16.67	17.67	18	17.67	16.67	15	12.67

The rate at which water flows out of a pipe, in gallons per hour, is given by a differentiable function R of time t. The table above shows the rate as measured every 2 hours for a 12-hour period.

1. Use a midpoint Riemann sum with 3 subdivisions of equal length to approximate $\int_0^{12} R(t)\,dt$. Explain the meaning of your answer, using correct units.

2. The rate of water flow $R(t)$ can be approximated by $Q(t) = \dfrac{200 + 8t - t^2}{12}$. Use $Q(t)$ to approximate the average rate of water flow during the 12-hour period and indicate units of measure.

Suppose that the function f is at least three times differentiable for all x, and that $f(0)=1$, $f'(0)=2$, and $f''(0)=-1$. Let g be a function whose derivative is given by $g'(x)=6xf(x)+\left(3x^2+2\right)f'(x)+2xf''(x)$ for all x.

1. Write an equation of the line tangent to the graph of f at the point where $x=0$.

2. If $g(0)=-3$, write an equation of the line tangent to the graph of g at the point where $x=0$.

3. Show that $g''(x)=6f(x)+12xf'(x)+\left(3x^2+4\right)f''(x)+2xf'''(x)$.

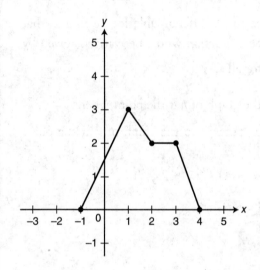

The graph of the function f, consisting of four line segments, is shown. Let $g(x) = \int\limits_0^x f(t)\,dt$.

1. Compute $g(1)$ and $g(-1)$.

2. Find the instantaneous rate of change of g, with respect to x, at $x = 3$.

3. Find the absolute minimum value of g on the closed interval $[-1, 4]$.

Line ℓ is tangent to the graph of $y = \dfrac{5}{x}$ at point $\left(w, \dfrac{5}{w} \right)$. This point of tangency is point P. Point Q is the point $(w, 0)$ and point R is the x-intercept of line ℓ, which has coordinates $(k, 0)$.

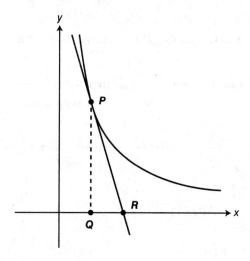

1. Find the value of k when $w = 1$.

2. Express k in terms of w, for all $w > 0$.

3. Suppose that w is increasing at a constant rate of 2 units per second. When $w = 1$, what is the rate of change of k with respect to time?

Let R be the region bounded by the x-axis, the graph of $y = x^2$, and the line $x = 3$.

1. Find the area of the region R.

2. Find the value of k for which the vertical line $x = k$ divides the region R into two regions of equal area.

3. Find the volume of the solid generated when the region R is revolved about the x-axis.

4. The vertical line $x = c$ divides the region R into two regions, such that the volumes of the solids formed when these two regions are revolved about the x-axis are equal. Find the value of c.

Day 123

Let f be the function given by $f(x) = \dfrac{\ln(x)}{x^2}$

1. Find $\lim\limits_{x \to \infty} f(x)$ and $\lim\limits_{x \to 0^+} f(x)$.

2. Find the absolute maximum value of f. Justify your answer.

t	0	5	10	15	20	25	30
$v(t)$	0	10	25	40	60	50	45

The velocity $v(t)$ in ft/sec of a car traveling on a straight road for $0 \leq t \leq 30$ is shown.

1. During what intervals of time is the acceleration of the car negative?

2. Use a trapezoidal sum of 6 subintervals of equal width to approximate the total distance traveled by the car over the interval $0 \leq t \leq 30$.

3. Find the average velocity of the car in ft/sec, over the interval $0 \leq t \leq 30$.

For a certain equation, the slope of the graph at every point (x, y) is given by $\dfrac{dy}{dx} = \dfrac{x - 3x^2}{y}$, and the point (2, 2) is on the graph.

1. Write an equation of the line tangent to the graph at $x = 2$, and use it to approximate y when $x = 2.1$.

2. Solve the differential equation $\dfrac{dy}{dx} = \dfrac{x - 3x^2}{y}$ with initial condition $y = 2$ when $x = 2$.

3. Use the result of question 2 to find y when $x = 2.1$.

The temperature outside a house during a 24-hour period is given by $F(t) = 65 + 8\sin\left(\dfrac{\pi t}{12}\right)$, $0 \le t \le 24$, where $F(t)$ is measured in degrees Fahrenheit and t is measured in hours.

1. At what time, t, does the highest temperature of the day occur? At what time does the lowest temperature occur?

2. Find the average temperature, to the nearest degree Fahrenheit, between the two values of t found in question 1.

Day 127

t	0	2	4	6	8	10	12	14	16	18	20
v(t)	0	22	48	73	98	112	120	117	106	86	62

A sled moves on a straight track with positive velocity $v(t)$, in feet per minute at time t minutes, where v is a differentiable function of t. Selected values of $v(t)$ for $0 \leq t \leq 20$ are shown in the table.

1. Use a midpoint Riemann sum with five subintervals of equal length and values from the table to approximate $\int_0^{20} v(t)\,dt$ and explain its meaning.

2. The function $v(t) = 20 + 80\sin\left(\dfrac{t}{8}\right) - 20\cos\left(\dfrac{t}{4}\right)$ is used to model the velocity of the sled, in feet per minute, for $0 \leq t \leq 20$. According to this model, what is the acceleration of the sled at $t = 16$?

3. According to the model, what is the average velocity of the sled, in feet per minute, over the interval $0 \leq t \leq 20$?

The figure shows the graph of $f'(x)$, the derivative of the function $f(x)$, on the closed interval $[-3, 7]$. The graph of $f'(x)$ has horizontal tangent lines at $x = -1$ and $x = 5$. The function $f(x)$ is twice differentiable with $f(2) = \dfrac{13}{3}$.

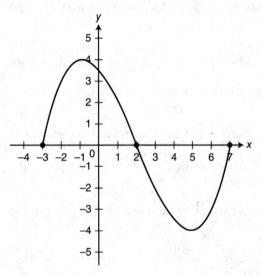

1. Find the coordinates of any relative maxima or minima of the graph of f.

2. Write an equation of the line tangent to the graph of f at $x = 2$.

3. Let g be the function defined by $g(x) = x^3 f(x)$. Find an equation for the line tangent to the graph of g at $x = 2$.

Let g be the function given by $g(x) = 1 + \sin\left(\dfrac{\pi x}{2}\right)$.

1. Find the area of the region R, in the first quadrant, enclosed by the graph of $y = g(x)$ and the x-axis and y-axis.

2. Find the average value of g on the closed interval $[0, 3]$.

3. Let S by the solid generated when the region R is revolved about the x-axis. Set up an integral that could be used to find the volume of S. Do not evaluate the integral.

Let R be the region in the first quadrant bounded by the y-axis, the graph of $f(x) = 5 - x^2$, and the line $y = \dfrac{x}{2}$.

1. Find the area of the region R.

2. Find the volume of the solid generated when R is revolved about the y-axis.

Day 131

Given the curve $x = t^2$ and $y = \dfrac{1}{3}t^3$, what is $\dfrac{d^2 y}{dx^2}$ at $t = 1$?

(A) $\dfrac{1}{4}$

(B) $\dfrac{1}{2}$

(C) 1

(D) 4

Using your calculator, determine which of the following is the area of the region in first quadrant enclosed by the cardioid $r = 2 + 2\cos\theta$?

(A) $\dfrac{3\pi + 8}{2}$

(B) 3π

(C) $3\pi + 8$

(D) 6π

Day 133

The values of a differentiable function $f(x)$ and its derivatives $f'(x)$ at $x = 1$ and $x = 3$ are shown in the table below.

x	1	3
f(x)	1	9
f'(x)	2	6

If $\int_1^3 f(x)\,dx = \dfrac{26}{3}$, what is the value of $\int_1^3 xf'(x)\,dx$?

(A) $\dfrac{52}{3}$

(B) $\dfrac{55}{3}$

(C) 26

(D) $\dfrac{104}{3}$

Given the series $\displaystyle\sum_{k=1}^{\infty}\left(\frac{3}{5}\right)^{k+1}$, if it converges, which of the following is its sum?

(A) $\dfrac{3}{5}$

(B) $\dfrac{9}{10}$

(C) 1

(D) *The series diverges.*

Which of the following is the interval of convergence for the series $\sum_{k=0}^{\infty} \dfrac{x^k}{k+2}$?

(A) $(-1,1)$

(B) $(-1,1]$

(C) $[-1,1)$

(D) $[-1,1]$

$$\int \frac{-5}{(2x+1)(x-2)}dx =$$

(A) $\frac{1}{2}\ln|2x+1| - \ln|x-2| + C$

(B) $\ln|2x+1| - \ln|x-2| + C$

(C) $\ln|2x+1| - \frac{1}{2}|x-2| + C$

(D) $-\ln|2x+1| + \ln|x-2| + C$

5 Minutes to a 5

$$\int 5xe^x dx =$$

(A) $5xe^x + C$

(B) $xe^x - e^x + C$

(C) $5xe^x - e^x + C$

(D) $5xe^x - 5e^x + C$

A moving particle in the *xy-plane* with the velocity vector $v(t) = \langle 2t^3, 7t \rangle$, $t \geq 0$. What is the acceleration vector of the particle at time $t = 2$?

(A) $\langle 16,14 \rangle$

(B) $\langle 24,0 \rangle$

(C) $\langle 24,7 \rangle$

(D) $\langle 24,14 \rangle$

$$\int_0^4 \frac{dx}{\sqrt{4-x}} =$$

(A) −4

(B) 0

(C) 4

(D) 8

A parametric curve is given as $x(t) = 5t + 2$ and $y(t) = 12t - 1$. What is the arc length of the curve for $0 \le t \le 3$?

(A) 13

(B) 39

(C) 169

(D) 507

Which of the following is the Taylor series for $f(x) = x^2 \cos(2x)$ about $x = 0$?

(A) $x^2 - \dfrac{x^4}{2!} + \dfrac{x^6}{4!} - \dfrac{x^8}{6!} + \ldots$

(B) $1 - \dfrac{4x^2}{2!} + \dfrac{16x^4}{4!} - \dfrac{64x^6}{6!} + \ldots$

(C) $x^2 - \dfrac{4x^2}{2!} + \dfrac{16x^4}{4!} - \dfrac{64x^6}{6!} + \ldots$

(D) $x^2 - \dfrac{4x^4}{2!} + \dfrac{16x^6}{4!} - \dfrac{64x^8}{6!} + \ldots$

Given $\sum_{n=1}^{\infty} a_n$ and $\sum_{n=1}^{\infty} b_n$, and that $\sum_{n=1}^{\infty} b_n$ converges and $0 \le a_n \le b_n$ for all n, which of the following statements must be true?

(A) $\sum_{n=1}^{\infty} 5b_n \ diverges$

(B) $\sum_{n=1}^{\infty} a_n \ diverges$

(C) $\sum_{n=1}^{\infty} a_n \ converges$

(D) $\sum_{n=1}^{\infty} (-1)^n b_n \ diverges$

If $\int_1^\infty \dfrac{1}{x^{(2p+3)}}\,dx$ converges, what are all values of p?

(A) $p < -\dfrac{3}{2}$

(B) $p < -1$

(C) $p > -1$

(D) *There are no values of p for which the integral converges.*

If $p(x) = 1 + 2x + 4x^2 + 8x^3 + 16x^4$ is the fourth degree Taylor polynomial for a function f about $x = 0$, what is the value of $f''(0)$?

(A) 2

(B) 4

(C) 8

(D) 16

What is the value of $\displaystyle\sum_{n=1}^{\infty}\frac{3^{n+2}}{5^n} = ?$

(A) $\dfrac{1}{6}$

(B) $\dfrac{3}{2}$

(C) $\dfrac{27}{50}$

(D) $\dfrac{27}{2}$

What is the arc length of the curve $y = \frac{2}{3}x^{\frac{3}{2}}$ from $x = 0$ to $x = 1$.

(A) $\dfrac{4\sqrt{2}}{3} - \dfrac{2}{3}$

(B) $\dfrac{4\sqrt{2}}{3}$

(C) $\dfrac{4\sqrt{2}}{3} + 1$

(D) $\dfrac{4\sqrt{2}}{3} + \dfrac{2}{3}$

Which of the following is an equation of the tangent line to the curve represented by the parametric equations $x = 2t + 1$ and $y = 4t^2 - 2t + 3$ at the point where $t = 2$?

(A) $y = 7x$

(B) $y = 4x - 1$

(C) $y = 7x - 20$

(D) $y = 7x + 20$

Which of the following series converge?

I. $\displaystyle\sum_{k=0}^{\infty} \frac{k+2}{k+4}$

II. $\displaystyle\sum_{k=1}^{\infty} \frac{1}{\sqrt{k^2+1}}$

III. $\displaystyle\sum_{k=1}^{\infty} \left(1+\frac{1}{k}\right)^k$

(A) *I only*

(B) *II only*

(C) *III only*

(D) *None*

Day 149

Given that $y = f(x)$, $\dfrac{dy}{dx} = 2x + y$, $f(2) = 4$, using *Euler's Method*, what is the approximate value for $f(3)$, starting at $x = 2$ with a step size of $\triangle x = 0.5$.

(A) 6.5

(B) 14.5

(C) 24.5

(D) 71.5

The position of a particle moving on *xy-plane* at any time t, is given by $x(t) = 2t^2$ and $y(t) = \cos(2t)$. Which of the following is the closest to the particle's speed when $t = 1$?

(A) 4.394

(B) 5.514

(C) 16.827

(D) 19.307

Day 151

What is the value of $\displaystyle\sum_{x=0}^{\infty}\frac{(\ln 3)^x}{x!}$?

(A) $\dfrac{1}{1-\ln 3}$

(B) $\ln 3$

(C) 3

(D) *series diverges*

Given $\displaystyle\sum_{n=1}^{\infty}\left(\frac{5}{\sqrt{x}+1}\right)^{n}$, what are all values of x for which the series converges?

(A) $x = 2$

(B) $x = 4$

(C) $x < 9$

(D) $x > 16$

The parametric equations $x(t) = \dfrac{t^3}{3} - 2t^2 + 3t + 1$ and $y(t) = \dfrac{t^3}{3} - \dfrac{3t^2}{2}$ describe the position of a moving particle in the *xy-plane*. For what values of t is the particle at rest?

(A) 0 *only*

(B) 1 *only*

(C) 3 *only*

(D) 0,1 *and* 3

Using a calculator, determine which of the following is the area of the region enclosed by the cardioid $r = 1 + \sin\theta$

(A) $\dfrac{3\pi}{2}$

(B) 2π

(C) 3π

(D) 6π

Using a calculator, determine which of the following is the area of the region inside the circle $r = 2$ and outside of the cardioid $r = 2 - 2\sin\theta$?

(A) $8 - \pi$

(B) $16 - 2\pi$

(C) $5\pi - 8$

(D) $10\pi - 16$

What is the value of $\displaystyle\sum_{n=1}^{100}\frac{1}{n^2+n}$?

(A) $\dfrac{1}{10{,}100}$

(B) $\dfrac{100}{101}$

(C) 1

(D) $\dfrac{102}{101}$

Given, the alternating series $\sum_{k=1}^{\infty} \dfrac{(-1)^{k+1}}{k!}$, if the *nth* partial sum has an error $< .01$, what is the smallest value of *n*?

(A) 3

(B) 4

(C) 5

(D) 6

Which of the following is the interval of convergence of $\displaystyle\sum_{k=1}^{\infty} \frac{(3x)^k}{5k}$?

(A) $[-3,3)$

(B) $(-3,3]$

(C) $\left(-\dfrac{1}{3}, \dfrac{1}{3}\right]$

(D) $\left[-\dfrac{1}{3}, \dfrac{1}{3}\right)$

The fourth *Maclaurin* polynomial for $\cos(2x)$ is:

(A) $1 - \dfrac{1}{2}x^2 + \dfrac{1}{24}x^4$

(B) $1 - 2x^2 + \dfrac{2}{3}x^4$

(C) $x - x^3$

(D) $2x - 8x^3$

Which of the following series diverge?

I. $\sum_{k=1}^{\infty} \dfrac{k}{3^k}$

II. $\sum_{k=1}^{\infty} \dfrac{1}{4k-1}$

III. $\sum_{k=1}^{\infty} \dfrac{k!}{k^3}$

    (A) *I only*

    (B) *II only*

    (C) *III only*

    (D) *II and III only*

Which of the following series behaves like the *series* $\displaystyle\sum_{k=1}^{\infty} \frac{5k^3 - 2k + 1}{k^4 + k^2 - 3k}$ as k approaches $\pm\infty$?

(A) $\displaystyle\sum_{k=1}^{\infty} \left(5k^3 - 2k + 1\right)$

(B) $\displaystyle\sum_{k=1}^{\infty} \left(k^4 + k^2 - 3k\right)$

(C) $\displaystyle\sum_{k=1}^{\infty} \frac{5}{k^4 + k^2 - 3k}$

(D) $\displaystyle\sum_{k=1}^{\infty} \frac{5}{k}$

What is the slope of the tangent line to the polar curve $r = \sin\theta + 1$ at $\theta = \dfrac{\pi}{4}$?

(A) $-4 + \sqrt{2}$

(B) $-4 - \sqrt{2}$

(C) $-1 - 2\sqrt{2}$

(D) $-1 - \sqrt{2}$

The logistic differential equation $\dfrac{dP}{dt} = 0.02P - 0.0002P^2$ represents the relative growth rate of a population P, and $P = \dfrac{M}{1 + Ae^{-kt}}$ with M being the carrying capacity for the population. What are the values of M and k?

(A) $M = 200 \ and \ k = 20$

(B) $M = 200 \ and \ k = 10$

(C) $M = 200 \ and \ k = 2$

(D) $M = 100 \ and \ k = 0.02$

Given that $\sin x \approx x - \dfrac{x^3}{3!}$ and using *Lagrange's* form of the remainder, how many decimal places of accuracy can be guaranteed for $\sin x$ for $-0.1 < x < 0.1$?

(A) 4

(B) 6

(C) 7

(D) 8

If $\dfrac{dr}{dt} = \left(3t^2 + 1\right)\boldsymbol{i} + 2t\,\boldsymbol{j}$, $t \geq 0$ is the velocity vector of a moving particle in the plane, which of the following is the particle's position function $r(t)$, with $r(0) = 2\boldsymbol{i} + \boldsymbol{j}$?

(A) $6t\boldsymbol{i} + 2\boldsymbol{j}$

(B) $12t\boldsymbol{i} + 2\boldsymbol{j}$

(C) $\left(t^3 + t\right)\boldsymbol{i} + t^2\boldsymbol{j}$

(D) $\left(t^3 + t + 2\right)\boldsymbol{i} + \left(t^2 + 1\right)\boldsymbol{j}$

Day 166

Given that $y = f(x)$, $\dfrac{dy}{dx} = 2xy$ and the point $(0,1)$ is on the curve of $f(x)$, using *Euler's Method* and a step size of $\triangle x = 0.5$, what is the approximate value of y at $x = 1$?

(A) 0.5

(B) 1

(C) 1.5

(D) 2

$$\int \frac{1}{x^2 - 4x}\, dx =$$

(A) $\dfrac{1}{x^3 - 2x^2} + C$

(B) $-4\ln|x| + 4\ln|x - 4| + C$

(C) $\dfrac{1}{4}\ln|x| - \dfrac{1}{4}\ln|x - 4| + C$

(D) $-\dfrac{1}{4}\ln|x| + \dfrac{1}{4}\ln|x - 4| + C$

Which of the following *series* converges absolutely?

I. $\displaystyle\sum_{k=1}^{\infty} \frac{(-1)^{k+1}}{k}$

II. $\displaystyle\sum_{k=1}^{\infty} \frac{(-1)^{k}\, 3^{k}}{k!}$

III. $\displaystyle\sum_{k=3}^{\infty} \frac{(-1)^{k} \ln k}{k}$

(A) *I only*

(B) *II only*

(C) *III only*

(D) *II and III only*

$\int_0^3 \dfrac{1}{(x-1)^2}\, dx =$

(A) $-\dfrac{3}{2}$

(B) $\dfrac{1}{2}$

(C) $\dfrac{3}{2}$

(D) *divergent*

Day 170

Given that $\dfrac{20}{P}\cdot\dfrac{dP}{dt}=1-\dfrac{P}{200}$ and that $\dfrac{dP}{dt}$ represents the relative growth rate of a population P, and $P=\dfrac{M}{1+Ae^{-kt}}$ with M being the carrying capacity for the population, what are the values of M and k?

(A) $M=2000$ *and* $k=5$

(B) $M=2000$ *and* $k=0.5$

(C) $M=200$ *and* $k=0.5$

(D) $M=200$ *and* $k=0.05$

Let $y = x^2$. Which of the following integrals represents the length of the curve from $x = 0$ to $x = 3$?

(A) $\int_0^3 \sqrt{1 + 2x^2}\, dx$

(B) $\int_0^9 \sqrt{1 + 4x^2}\, dx$

(C) $\int_0^9 \sqrt{1 + \dfrac{1}{4y}}\, dy$

(D) $\int_0^3 \sqrt{1 + \dfrac{1}{4y^2}}\, dy$

Given $r = 2\cos\theta$, what is the slope of the tangent line to the polar curve r at the point $\theta = \dfrac{\pi}{4}$?

(A) -2

(B) -1

(C) 0

(D) 2

Day 173

What is the radius of convergence for the series $\displaystyle\sum_{k=0}^{\infty} \frac{(x-1)^k}{4^k(3k+1)}$?

(A) $\dfrac{1}{4}$

(B) $\dfrac{1}{3}$

(C) 3

(D) 4

231

Given the parametric equations $x = \sin t$ and $y = \cos t$, what is the value of $\dfrac{d^2 y}{dx^2}$ at $t = \dfrac{\pi}{4}$?

(A) -4

(B) $-2\sqrt{2}$

(C) $2\sqrt{2}$

(D) 4

Given the parametric equations $x = \cos t$ and $y = \sin t$, what is the arc length of the curve from $t = 0$ to $\frac{\pi}{2}$?

(A) $\dfrac{\pi}{4}$

(B) $\dfrac{\pi}{2}$

(C) π

(D) 2π

Using the *Maclaurine series* and the *Lagrange's* form of the remainder, determine which of the following could be the approximate value of $\cos\left(\dfrac{\pi}{6}\right)$ with two decimal place accuracy.

(A) 0.452

(B) 0.502

(C) 0.863

(D) 0.896

Which of the following is the interval of convergence for the series $\sum_{k=3}^{\infty} \dfrac{(-1)^{k+1}}{k(\ln k)^2}(x-2)^k$?

(A) $[-1,1]$

(B) $[-1,3)$

(C) $(1,3)$

(D) $[1,3]$

Using your calculator, determine which of the following is the area of the region inside the cardioid $r = 1 + \sin\theta$ and outside the circle $r = 1$?

(A) $\dfrac{\pi}{4} + 2$

(B) $\dfrac{\pi}{4} + 8$

(C) $\dfrac{5\pi}{4} + 2$

(E) $\dfrac{5\pi}{4} + 8$

Given that $\dfrac{dr}{dt} = \left(t^2 + 6t\right)\boldsymbol{i} + (2t)\boldsymbol{j}$ and $r(0) = 2\boldsymbol{i} + \boldsymbol{j}$, which of the following is $r(t)$, a vector function of t?

(A) $r(t) = 16\boldsymbol{i} + 2\boldsymbol{j}$

(B) $r(t) = (t^2 + 6t + 2)\boldsymbol{i} + (2t + 1)\boldsymbol{j}$

(C) $\left(\dfrac{t^3}{3} + 3t\right)\boldsymbol{i} + \left(t^2\right)\boldsymbol{j}$

(D) $\left(\dfrac{t^3}{3} + 3t + 2\right)\boldsymbol{i} + (t^2 = 1)\boldsymbol{j}$

For $x > 0$, the power series $\displaystyle\sum_{k=0}^{\infty}(-1)^k \frac{x^{2k+2}}{(2k+1)!} = x^2 - \frac{x^4}{3!} + \frac{x^6}{5!} - \frac{x^8}{7!} + \ldots$ converges to which of the following?

(A) $\cos x$

(B) $\cos x - 1$

(C) $\sin x - x$

(D) $x \sin x$

Answers

Day 1

1. $\lim\limits_{x\to 1}\left(\dfrac{4x^2-3x-1}{x^2-3x+2}\right)=\lim\limits_{x\to 1}\left[\dfrac{(4x+1)\,(x-1)}{(x-2)\,(x-1)}\right]=\lim\limits_{x\to 1}\left[\dfrac{4x+1}{x-2}\right]=\dfrac{4(1)+1}{1-2}=-5$

2. $\lim\limits_{x\to 2}\dfrac{x^2-4}{x^3-8}=\lim\limits_{x\to 2}\dfrac{(x-2)(x+2)}{(x-2)\left(x^2+2x+4\right)}=\lim\limits_{x\to 2}\dfrac{x+2}{x^2+2x+4}=\dfrac{2+2}{4+4+4}=\dfrac{4}{12}=\dfrac{1}{3}$

3. $\lim\limits_{x\to 2}\dfrac{x^3-8}{x^2+3x-10}=\lim\limits_{x\to 2}\dfrac{(x-2)\left(x^2+2x+4\right)}{(x-2)\,(x+5)}=\lim\limits_{x\to 2}\dfrac{x^2+2x+4}{x+5}=\dfrac{4+4+4}{2+5}=\dfrac{12}{7}$

Day 2

1. $\lim\limits_{x\to 0}\dfrac{x}{\sqrt{x+9}-3}=\lim\limits_{x\to 0}\dfrac{x}{\sqrt{x+9}-3}\cdot\dfrac{\sqrt{x+9}+3}{\sqrt{x+9}+3}=\lim\limits_{x\to 0}\dfrac{x\left(\sqrt{x+9}+3\right)}{x}=\lim\limits_{x\to 0}\sqrt{x+9}+3=6$

2. $\lim\limits_{x\to 4}\dfrac{\sqrt{x}-2}{x-4}=\lim\limits_{x\to 4}\dfrac{\sqrt{x}-2}{x-4}\cdot\dfrac{\sqrt{x}+2}{\sqrt{x}+2}=\lim\limits_{x\to 4}\dfrac{x-4}{(x-4)\left(\sqrt{x}+2\right)}=\lim\limits_{x\to 4}\dfrac{1}{\sqrt{x}+2}=\dfrac{1}{4}$

3. $\lim\limits_{x\to -3}\dfrac{\sqrt{x+3}}{\sqrt{x+3}-\sqrt{3}}=\lim\limits_{x\to -3}\dfrac{\sqrt{x+3}}{\sqrt{x+3}-\sqrt{3}}\cdot\dfrac{\sqrt{x+3}+\sqrt{3}}{\sqrt{x+3}+\sqrt{3}}=\lim\limits_{x\to -3}\dfrac{\sqrt{x+3}\cdot\left(\sqrt{x+3}+\sqrt{3}\right)}{x+3-3}$

$=\lim\limits_{x\to -3}\dfrac{\sqrt{x+3}\cdot\left(\sqrt{x+3}+\sqrt{3}\right)}{x}=\lim\limits_{x\to -3}\dfrac{x+3+\sqrt{3x+9}}{x}=\dfrac{-3+3+0}{-3}=0$

Day 3

1. $-1 \leq \cos(\pi x) \leq 1$. Because x approaches $+\infty$, so it's safe to consider $x-1$ positive.

Divide through by $x-1$. $\dfrac{-1}{x-1} \leq \dfrac{\cos(\pi x)}{x-1} \leq \dfrac{1}{x-1}$. Then $\displaystyle\lim_{x \to \infty} \dfrac{-1}{x-1} = 0$ and

$\displaystyle\lim_{x \to \infty} \dfrac{1}{x-1} = 0$, so $\displaystyle\lim_{x \to \infty} \dfrac{\cos(\pi x)}{x-1} = 0$.

2. $-1 \leq \sin\left(x - \dfrac{\pi}{2}\right) \leq 1$. Multiply by -1. $1 \geq -\sin\left(x - \dfrac{\pi}{2}\right) \geq -1$ or

$-1 \leq -\sin\left(x - \dfrac{\pi}{2}\right) \leq 1$. Add 2. $1 \leq 2 - \sin\left(x - \dfrac{\pi}{2}\right) \leq 3$. As $x \to -\infty$,

and e^{-x} can be assumed to be positive. $\dfrac{1}{e^{-x}} \leq \dfrac{2 - \sin\left(x - \dfrac{\pi}{2}\right)}{e^{-x}} \leq \dfrac{3}{e^{-x}}$. Because

$\displaystyle\lim_{x \to -\infty} \dfrac{1}{e^{-x}} = \lim_{x \to -\infty} \dfrac{3}{e^{-x}} = 0$ $\displaystyle\lim_{x \to -\infty} \dfrac{2 - \sin\left(x - \dfrac{\pi}{2}\right)}{e^{-x}} = 0$.

Day 4

1. $\displaystyle\lim_{x \to 0} \dfrac{\sin(2x)}{2x} = 1$

2. $\displaystyle\lim_{x \to 0} \dfrac{\sin x}{2x} = \lim_{x \to 0}\left(\dfrac{1}{2} \cdot \dfrac{\sin x}{x}\right) = \lim_{x \to 0}\left(\dfrac{1}{2}\right) \cdot \lim_{x \to 0}\left(\dfrac{\sin x}{x}\right) = \dfrac{1}{2} \cdot 1 = \dfrac{1}{2}$

3. $\displaystyle\lim_{x \to 0} \dfrac{\sin(3x)}{x} = \lim_{x \to 0}\left[\dfrac{\sin(3x)}{x} \cdot \dfrac{3}{3}\right] = \lim_{x \to 0}\left[3\left(\dfrac{\sin(3x)}{3x}\right)\right] = 3$

Day 5

1. -1 **2.** 1 **3.** DNE

4. 0 **5.** -5 **6.** -5

Day 6

1. $-\infty$

2. ∞

3. DNE

4. ∞

5. ∞

6. ∞

7. 0

Day 7

1. $\lim\limits_{x\to\infty}\dfrac{2x-3}{x+4}=\lim\limits_{x\to\infty}\dfrac{2-\frac{3}{x}}{1+\frac{4}{x}}=2$

2. $\lim\limits_{x\to-\infty}\left(4-3x+2x^2\right)=\infty$

3. $\lim\limits_{x\to\infty}\dfrac{2x-3}{x^2-3x+1}=0$

4. $\lim\limits_{x\to-\infty}\dfrac{4}{x^2}=0$

5. $\lim\limits_{x\to-\infty}\dfrac{3x^5}{2x^2}=\lim\limits_{x\to-\infty}\dfrac{3}{2}x^3=-\infty$

Day 8

1. $\lim\limits_{x\to0}\dfrac{x\cos x}{\sin 2x}=\lim\limits_{x\to0}\left(\dfrac{x}{\sin 2x}\cdot\dfrac{\cos x}{1}\right)=\lim\limits_{x\to0}\left(\dfrac{2x}{\sin 2x}\cdot\dfrac{\cos x}{2}\right)$

$=\lim\limits_{x\to0}\dfrac{2x}{\sin 2x}\cdot\lim\limits_{x\to0}\dfrac{\cos x}{2}=1\cdot\dfrac{1}{2}=\dfrac{1}{2}$

2. $\lim\limits_{x\to0}\left(\dfrac{-\pi\sin(-x)}{\sin(\pi x)}\right)=\lim\limits_{x\to0}\left(\dfrac{\sin(-x)}{-1}\cdot\dfrac{\pi}{\sin(\pi x)}\right)=\lim\limits_{x\to0}\left(\dfrac{\sin(-x)}{-1x}\cdot\dfrac{\pi x}{\sin(\pi x)}\right)=1$

3. $\lim\limits_{x\to0}\dfrac{\sin(2x)}{\sin(3x)}=\lim\limits_{x\to0}\left[\dfrac{\sin(2x)}{1}\cdot\dfrac{1}{\sin(3x)}\right]=\lim\limits_{x\to0}\left[\dfrac{\sin(2x)}{1}\cdot\dfrac{1}{\sin(3x)}\cdot\dfrac{2x}{2x}\cdot\dfrac{3x}{3x}\right]$

$=\lim\limits_{x\to0}\left[\dfrac{\sin(2x)}{2x}\cdot\dfrac{3x}{\sin(3x)}\cdot\dfrac{2x}{1}\cdot\dfrac{1}{3x}\right]=\dfrac{2}{3}$

Day 9

1. Jump discontinuity at $x=0$.

2. Essential discontinuity at $x=3$, removable discontinuity at $x=2$.

3. Jump discontinuity at $x=-2$.

Day 10

1. $\lim\limits_{x \to 0^-} 1 - 4x = 1$, $\lim\limits_{x \to 0^+} x^2 + k = k$, $k = 1$

2. $\lim\limits_{x \to -1^-} kx^2 = k$, $\lim\limits_{x \to -1^+} 3x - k = -3 - k$, $k = -3 - k$, $2k = -3$, $k = -1.5$

3. $\lim\limits_{x \to 0^-} \dfrac{\sin 2x}{x} = \lim\limits_{x \to 0^-} \left[2\left(\dfrac{\sin 2x}{2x} \right) \right] = 2$, $\lim\limits_{x \to 0^+} \dfrac{\sin 2x}{x} = \lim\limits_{x \to 0^+} \left[2\left(\dfrac{\sin 2x}{2x} \right) \right] = 2$,
$f(0) = k - 2(0) = k$, $k = 2$

Day 11

1. There is a zero on $[3,4]$. $f(x) = \dfrac{7 - 2x}{x}$ is continuous on $[3,4]$, $f(3) = \dfrac{7 - (2 \cdot 3)}{3} = \dfrac{1}{3}$,
$f(4) = \dfrac{7 - (2 \cdot 4)}{4} = -\dfrac{1}{4}$

2. $f(x) = \dfrac{7 - 2x}{x}$ is not continuous on $[-1,1]$. Cannot apply the Intermediate Value Theorem.

3. There is a zero on $[-2,-1]$. $f(x) = \dfrac{2x^2 - 3}{x^2 + 1}$ is continuous on $[-2,-1]$.

$f(-2) = \dfrac{2(-2)^2 - 3}{(-2)^2 + 1} = \dfrac{8 - 3}{4 + 1} = 1$, $f(-1) = \dfrac{2(-1)^2 - 3}{(-1)^2 + 1} = \dfrac{-1}{2}$

4. $f(x) = \dfrac{2x^2 - 3}{x^2 + 1}$ is continuous on $[-1,1]$. However, $f(-1) = \dfrac{2(-1)^2 - 3}{(-1)^2 + 1} = -\dfrac{1}{2}$ and

$f(1) = \dfrac{2(1)^2 - 3}{(1)^2 + 1} = -\dfrac{1}{2}$. Because $f(-1)$ and $f(1)$ are not opposite in sign, it is

not possible to apply the Intermediate Value Theorem to conclude that there is a zero on $[-1,1]$.

Day 12

1. $f'(x) = \lim_{h \to 0} \dfrac{\left[(x+h)^3 + 8\right] - \left[x^3 + 8\right]}{h} = \lim_{h \to 0} \dfrac{\left[x^3 + 3hx^2 + 3h^2x + h^3 + 8\right] - \left[x^3 + 8\right]}{h}$

$= \lim_{h \to 0} \dfrac{3hx^2 + 3h^2x + h^3}{h} = \lim_{h \to 0}\left(3x^2 + 3hx + h^2\right) = 3x^2$

2. $f'(x) = \lim_{h \to 0} \dfrac{\dfrac{2(x+h)}{(x+h-3)} - \dfrac{2x}{x-3}}{h} = \lim_{h \to 0} \dfrac{1}{h} \cdot \dfrac{2(x+h)(x-3) - 2x(x+h-3)}{(x+h-3)(x-3)}$

$= \lim_{h \to 0} \dfrac{1}{h} \cdot \dfrac{2x^2 + 2hx - 6x - 6h - 2x^2 - 2hx + 6x}{(x+h-3)(x-3)} = \lim_{h \to 0} \dfrac{1}{h} \cdot \dfrac{-6h}{(x+h-3)(x-3)}$

$= \lim_{h \to 0} \dfrac{-6}{(x+h-3)(x-3)} = \dfrac{-6}{(x-3)^2}$

3. $f'(x) = \lim_{h \to 0} \dfrac{\sqrt{x+h-2} - \sqrt{x-2}}{h} = \lim_{h \to 0} \dfrac{\sqrt{x+h-2} - \sqrt{x-2}}{h} \cdot \dfrac{\sqrt{x+h-2} + \sqrt{x-2}}{\sqrt{x+h-2} + \sqrt{x-2}}$

$= \lim_{h \to 0} \dfrac{x+h-2 - (x-2)}{h\left(\sqrt{x+h-2} + \sqrt{x-2}\right)} = \lim_{h \to 0} \dfrac{h}{h\left(\sqrt{x+h-2} + \sqrt{x-2}\right)}$

$= \lim_{h \to 0} \dfrac{1}{\sqrt{x+h-2} + \sqrt{x-2}} = \dfrac{1}{2\sqrt{x-2}}$

Day 13

1. $f'(x) = 21x^6 - 20x^4 + 2x$

2. $f'(x) = -72x^8 + 30x^5$

3. $f'(x) = 8x^{11} + 2x^9 - 6x^7 - 2x^5$

4. $f'(x) = 7x^6 - 5x^4 + 3x^2 - 1$

5. $f'(x) = -4x^3 + 24x^5 - 24x^7$

Day 14

1. $f'(x) = (3x-7)(2x) + \left(x^2 - 4\right)(3) = 9x^2 - 14x - 12$

2. $f'(x) = 2x^4\left(\tfrac{1}{2}x^{-\frac{1}{2}}\right) + x^{\frac{1}{2}}\left(8x^3\right) = x^{\frac{7}{2}} + 8x^{\frac{7}{2}} = 9x^{\frac{7}{2}}.$

3. $f'(x) = \left(x^2 + 1\right)\left(6x^2\right) + \left(2x^3 + 5\right)(2x) = 10x^4 + 6x^2 + 10x$

4. $f'(x) = \dfrac{(2x+5)(-6x) - \left(4 - 3x^2\right)(2)}{(2x+5)^2} = \dfrac{-6x^2 - 30x - 8}{(2x+5)^2}$

Day 15

1. $f'(x) = 2(x^2 - 3x + 2)(2x - 3)$

2. $f'(x) = \dfrac{1}{2}(4 + 5x^2)^{-\frac{1}{2}}(10x)$

3. $f'(x) = -1(x^3 - 2x + 5)^{-2}(3x^2 - 2)$

4. $f'(x) = \left[(3x - 1)^2 \cdot 3(2x + 3)^2 \cdot 2\right] + \left[(2x + 3)^3 \cdot 2(3x - 1) \cdot 3\right]$

5. $f'(x) = \dfrac{\left[(2x + 1)^2 \cdot 2x\right] - \left[(x^2 - 4) \cdot 2(2x + 1) \cdot 2\right]}{(2x + 1)^4}$

Day 16

1. $f'(2) + g'(2) = 1 + 3 = 4$

2. $\dfrac{f(1) \cdot g'(1) - g(1) \cdot f'(1)}{(f(1))^2} = \dfrac{2 \cdot 2 - 0 \cdot (-3)}{2^2} = 1$

3. $f'(g(0)) \cdot g'(0) = f'(1) \cdot g'(0) = (-3)(-1) = 3$

4. $g'(f(-1)) \cdot f'(-1) = g'(0) \cdot f'(-1) = (-1)(-1) = 1$

5. $f'(f(2)) \cdot f'(2) = f'(-1) \cdot f'(2) = (-1)(1) = -1$

Day 17

1. $\dfrac{d}{dx}(4 - \cos(2x)) = 0 - (-\sin(2x))(2) = 2\sin(2x)$

2. $\dfrac{d}{dx}\left(\tan^2\left(\dfrac{\pi}{2}x\right)\right) = 2\tan\left(\dfrac{\pi}{2}x\right)\sec^2\left(\dfrac{\pi}{2}x\right)\left(\dfrac{\pi}{2}\right) = \pi\tan\left(\dfrac{\pi}{2}x\right)\sec^2\left(\dfrac{\pi}{2}x\right)$

3. $\dfrac{d}{dx}\left(3x^2\left(\sin^2 x\right)\right) = 3x^2(2\sin x \cos x) + 6x\sin^2 x = 6x\sin x(x\cos x + \sin x)$

4. $\dfrac{d}{dx}\left(\dfrac{\csc x}{1 - \cot x}\right) = \dfrac{(1 - \cot x)(-\csc x \cot x) - \csc x\left(\csc^2 x\right)}{(1 - \cot x)^2}$

$$= \dfrac{-\csc x\left(\cot x - \cot^2 x + \csc^2 x\right)}{(1 - \cot x)^2} = \dfrac{-\csc x(\cot x + 1)}{(1 - \cot x)^2}.$$

Note that $\cot^2 x + 1 = \csc^2 x$ and thus $1 = \csc^2 x - \cot^2 x$.

5. $\dfrac{d}{dx}(\sin(3x)\cos(2x)) = \sin(3x)(-2\sin(2x)) + \cos(2x)(3\cos(3x))$

$$= -2\sin(3x)\sin(2x) + 3\cos(2x)\cos(3x)$$

Day 18

1. $\dfrac{d}{dx}\left(e^{x^2}\right)=e^{x^2}(2x)=2xe^{x^2}$

2. $\dfrac{d}{dx}\left(e^{x^2}\sqrt{x}\right)=e^{x^2}\left(\dfrac{1}{2\sqrt{x}}\right)+\sqrt{x}\left(2xe^{x^2}\right)=\dfrac{e^{x^2}\sqrt{x}}{2x}+\dfrac{4x^2e^{x^2}\sqrt{x}}{2x}=\dfrac{e^{x^2}\sqrt{x}}{2x}\left(1+4x^2\right)$

3. $\dfrac{d}{dx}\left(e^{\cos(2x)}\right)=\left(e^{\cos(2x)}\right)\left(-2\sin(2x)\right)=-2\sin(2x)e^{\cos(2x)}$

4. $\dfrac{d}{dx}\left(2^x\cdot\sin^2 x\right)=2^x\left(2\sin x\cos x\right)+\left(\sin^2 x\right)\left(2^x\ln 2\right)=2^x\sin x\left[2\cos x+(\ln 2)\sin x\right]$

5. $\dfrac{d}{dx}\left(\dfrac{e^{2x+1}}{2^{1-3x}}\right)=\dfrac{2^{1-3x}\left(2e^{2x+1}\right)-e^{2x+1}\left(2^{1-3x}\right)(\ln 2)(-3)}{\left(2^{1-3x}\right)^2}$

$$=\dfrac{\left(2^{1-3x}\right)e^{2x+1}\left[2+3\ln 2\right]}{\left(2^{1-3x}\right)^2}=\dfrac{e^{2x+1}\left[2+3\ln 2\right]}{2^{1-3x}}$$

Day 19

1. B   2. F   3. A   4. G   5. C

6. D   7. D   8. E   9. I   10. H

Day 20

1. $3y^2\dfrac{dy}{dx}-2x=0,\ \dfrac{dy}{dx}=\dfrac{2x}{3y^2}$

2. $2-3\dfrac{dy}{dx}=2(x+y)\left(1+\dfrac{dy}{dx}\right),\ \dfrac{2-2x-2y}{3+2x+3y}=\dfrac{dy}{dx}$

3. $x^2\dfrac{dy}{dx}+2xy+x\cdot 2y\dfrac{dy}{dx}+y^2=1,\ \dfrac{dy}{dx}=\dfrac{1-2xy-y^2}{x^2+2xy}$

4. $e^{x+y}\left(1+\dfrac{dy}{dx}\right)=e^x+e^y\dfrac{dy}{dx},\ \dfrac{dy}{dx}=\dfrac{e^x-e^{x+y}}{e^{x+y}-e^y}$

Day 21

1. $x\cos y\dfrac{dy}{dx}+\sin y-\left(-y\sin x+\cos x\dfrac{dy}{dx}\right)=2x,\ \dfrac{dy}{dx}=\dfrac{2x-\sin y-y\sin x}{x\cos y-\cos x}$

2. $\cos(x+y)\left(1+\dfrac{dy}{dx}\right)-\sin(x-y)\left(1-\dfrac{dy}{dx}\right)=0,\ \dfrac{dy}{dx}=\dfrac{\sin(x-y)-\cos(x+y)}{\cos(x+y)+\sin(x-y)}$

3. $e^{x+y}\left(1+\dfrac{dy}{dx}\right)=2x-3\dfrac{dy}{dx},\ \dfrac{dy}{dx}=\dfrac{2x-e^{x+y}}{e^{x+y}+3}$

4. $\dfrac{y}{x}\cdot\dfrac{y-x\dfrac{dy}{dx}}{y^2}=1+\dfrac{dy}{dx},\ \dfrac{y-xy}{x+xy}=\dfrac{dy}{dx}$

Day 22

1. $g'(1) = \dfrac{1}{f'(f^{-1}(1))} = \dfrac{1}{f'(-1)} = \dfrac{1}{-2} = -\dfrac{1}{2}$

2. $g'(-1) = \dfrac{1}{f'(f^{-1}(-1))} = \dfrac{1}{f'(0)} = \dfrac{1}{-1} = -1$

3. $g'(-3) = \dfrac{1}{f'(f^{-1}(-3))} = \dfrac{1}{f'(2)} = \dfrac{1}{-3} = -\dfrac{1}{3}$

Day 23

1. $f'(x) = 5x^4 - 4x,\ f''(x) = 20x^3 - 4,\ f'''(x) = 60x^2$

2. $f'(x) = \dfrac{7}{(x+2)^2},\ f''(x) = \dfrac{-14(x+2)}{(x+2)^4} = \dfrac{-14}{(x+2)^3}$

3. $f'(x) = 2xe^{x^2-4},\ f''(x) = \left(4x^2 + 2\right)e^{x^2-4},\ f'''(x) = \left(8x^3 + 12x\right)e^{x^2-4}$

4. $f'(x) = 6\sin x \cos x,\ f''(x) = 6\cos^2 x - 6\sin^2 x,\ f'''(x) = -24\sin x \cos x$

5. $f'(x) = -\sin x,\ f''(x) = -\cos x,\ f'''(x) = \sin x,\ f^{(4)}(x) = \cos x$

Day 24

1. $f(x) = x^3 - 3x^2 + 1$ is a polynomial function, and so continuous everywhere and differentiable on $(-1,\ 2)$. $f(-1) = -1 - 3 + 1 = -3$ and $f(2) = 8 - 12 + 1 = -3$. Rolle's Theorem applies. $f'(x) = 3x^2 - 6x = 3x(x - 2)$ is equal to zero at $x = 0$ and $x = 2$. $-1 < 0 < 2$, so $c = 0$. The critical point is $(0, 1)$.

2. $f(x) = 2 - 5\cos\left(\dfrac{x}{4}\right)$ is continuous everywhere and differentiable on $(-\pi,\ \pi)$.

$f(-\pi) = 2 - 5\cos\left(\dfrac{-\pi}{4}\right) = \dfrac{4 - 5\sqrt{2}}{2}$, $\quad f(\pi) = 2 - 5\cos\left(\dfrac{\pi}{4}\right) = \dfrac{4 - 5\sqrt{2}}{2}$. Rolle's

Theorem applies. The derivative $f'(x) = \dfrac{5}{4}\sin\left(\dfrac{x}{4}\right) = 0$, when $\sin\left(\dfrac{x}{4}\right) = 0$, or

when $x = 0$, and $-\pi < 0 < \pi$. The critical point is $(0, -3)$.

Day 25

1. $\dfrac{f(2) - f(-2)}{2 + 2} = \dfrac{0 + 12}{4} = 3$, $\quad f'(c) = 3c^2 - 4c - 1 = 3$ $\quad c = -\dfrac{2}{3}$ or 2. But only

$c = -\dfrac{2}{3}$ satisfies $-2 < -\dfrac{2}{3} < 2$.

2. $\dfrac{f(b) - f(a)}{b - a} = \dfrac{2 - 2}{2\pi - 0} = 0$, $\ f'(c) = 2\sin c \cos c - 2\sin c$, $\ c = \pi$

3. $\dfrac{f(b) - f(a)}{b - a} = \dfrac{\left(1 + e^{-1}\right) - 2}{1 - 0} = e^{-1} - 1$, $\ f'(x) = -e^{-x} = e^{-1} - 1$, $\ c = 1 - \ln(e - 1)$

Day 26

1. $f(x) = \dfrac{3 - x^2}{x^2 + 3}$ on $[-1,\ 2]$

$f'(x) = \dfrac{-12x}{(x^2 + 3)^2}$; set $f'(x) = 0$ and obtain $x = 0$.

x	$f(x)$
-1	$1/2$
0	1
2	$-1/7$

Maximum point: $(0,\ 1)$, and Minimum point: $\left(2, -\dfrac{1}{7}\right)$

2. Maximum point: $(5,\ 11)$, Minimum point: $(-2,\ -38)$

3. Maximum point: $\left(-\dfrac{3}{2}, \dfrac{9}{16}\right)$, Minimum point: $(-1,\ -1)$

Day 27

1. $f'(x) = 6 - 3x^2$, Critical values: $x = \pm\sqrt{2}$, Increasing: $\left(-\sqrt{2}, \sqrt{2}\right)$, Decreasing: $\left(-\infty, -\sqrt{2}\right)$ and $\left(\sqrt{2}, \infty\right)$

2. $f'(x) = 3x^2 - 12x + 12$, Critical values: $x = 2$, Increasing: $(-\infty, 2) \cup (2, \infty)$

3. $f'(x) = -3x^2 + 6$, Critical values: $x = \pm\sqrt{2}$, Increasing: $\left(-\sqrt{2}, \sqrt{2}\right)$, Decreasing: $\left(-\infty, -\sqrt{2}\right)$ and $\left(\sqrt{2}, \infty\right)$

4. $f'(x) = 3x^2 - 8x + 4$, Critical values: $x = \dfrac{2}{3}, x = 2$, Increasing: $\left(-\infty, \dfrac{2}{3}\right)$ and $(2, \infty)$, Decreasing: $\left(\dfrac{2}{3}, 2\right)$

Day 28

1. $f'(x) = 4x^3 - 16x$, $f'(-3) = -60$, $f'(-1) = 12$, minimum

2. $f'(x) = -xe^{-x^2/2}$, $f'(-1) = e^{-1/2}$, $f'(1) = -e^{-1/2}$, maximum

3. $f'(x) = x + 2x\ln x$, $f'(0.1) = 0.1 + 0.2\ln 0.1 \approx -0.36$, $f'(1) = 1$, minimum

4. $f'(x) = -2\sin x \cos x - 2\cos x$, $f'\left(\dfrac{\pi}{4}\right) = -1 - \sqrt{2}$, $f'\left(\dfrac{3\pi}{4}\right) = 1 + \sqrt{2}$, minimum

5. $f'(x) = -2\sin x \cos x - 2\cos x$, $f'\left(\dfrac{5\pi}{4}\right) = -1 + \sqrt{2}$, $f'\left(\dfrac{7\pi}{4}\right) = 1 - \sqrt{2}$, maximum

Day 29

1. $f''(x) = 6(x-1)$, $f''(1) = 0$, and $f''(x) < 0$ for $x < 1$, concave downward on $(-\infty, 1)$, and $f''(x) > 0$, for $x > 1$, concave upward on $(1, \infty)$, point of inflection at $x = 1$.

2. $f''(x) = \dfrac{8 - 2x^2}{(4 + x^2)^2}$, $f''(-2) = 0$ and $f''(2) = 0$, $f''(x) > 0$ for $-2 < x < 2$, concave upward on $(-2, 2)$, and $f''(x) < 0$ for $x < -2$ or $x > 2$, concave downward on $(-\infty, -2)$ and $(2, \infty)$, point of inflection at $x = -2$ and $x = 2$.

Day 30

1. $f'(x) = 2\sin x \cos x, 0 < x < 2\pi$ critical values: $x = \dfrac{\pi}{2}$, $x = \pi$, $x = \dfrac{3\pi}{2}$,

   $f''(x) = 2\cos^2 x - 2\sin^2 x$, $f''\left(\dfrac{\pi}{2}\right) = -2$, maximum, $f''(\pi) = 2$, minimum,

   $f''\left(\dfrac{3\pi}{2}\right) = -2$, maximum

2. $f'(x) = 2x^2 - x - 3$, critical values: $x = -1$, $x = \dfrac{3}{2}$, $f''(x) = 4x - 1$, $f''(-1) = -5$,
   maximum, $f''\left(\dfrac{3}{2}\right) = 5$, minimum

3. $f'(x) = \dfrac{2 - 2x}{x^3}$, critical value: $x = 1$, $f''(x) = \dfrac{4x - 6}{x^4}$, $f''(1) = -2$, maximum

Day 31

1. negative

2. positive

3. zero, negative

4. $-\infty$, ∞, does not exist

5. 1.5, $-\infty$

Day 32

The function is decreasing for all values $x < 1.5$, so $f'(x) < 0$ for $x < 1.5$. The graph has a horizontal tangent at $x = 1.5$, so $f'(x) = 0$ at $x = 1.5$. The function is increasing for $x > 1.5$, so $f'(x) > 0$. Since the graph of $f(x)$ is concave up, $f''(x) > 0$ and $f'(x)$ is increasing. Therefore, the graph of $f'(x)$ could look like the graph in the accompanying diagram.

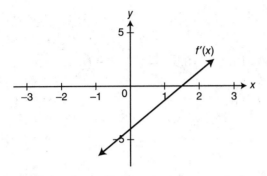

Day 33

The derivative is negative $-5 < x < -3$, so the function is decreasing, and turns at $x = -3$, where the derivative is zero. From -3 to -1, the derivative is positive and the function increases. Undefined at -1, the function continues to increase until just below 0, reaches a max and begins to decrease. There is a point of inflection just past 1, a minimum just below 3, after which the function increases.

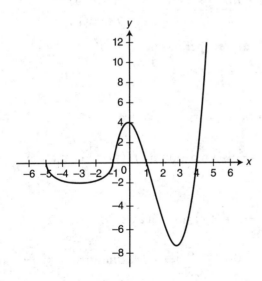

Day 34

Assuming a, b, and c are all functions of time, and differentiating $a^2 + b^2 = c^2$ with respect to time produces $2a\dfrac{da}{dt} + 2b\dfrac{db}{dt} = 2c\dfrac{dc}{dt}$, or $a\dfrac{da}{dt} + b\dfrac{db}{dt} = c\dfrac{dc}{dt}$

1. $a = 30$, $\dfrac{da}{dt} = 0$, $b = 80$, $\dfrac{db}{dt} = 40$, $c = \sqrt{30^2 + 80^2} \approx 85.4$, $30(0) + 80(40) = 85.4\dfrac{dc}{dt}$,

$\dfrac{dc}{dt} \approx 37.5$ mph

2. $a = 50$, $\dfrac{da}{dt} = 20$, $t = 2.5$, $\dfrac{db}{dt} = -15$, $b = 46 - 15(2.5) = 8.5$, $c = \sqrt{(50)^2 + (8.5)^2} \approx 50.7$,

$50(20) + 8.5(-15) = 50.7\dfrac{dc}{dt}$, $\dfrac{dc}{dt} \approx 17.2$ mph

Day 35

$\dfrac{r}{h} = \dfrac{6}{16}$, $r = \dfrac{3h}{8}$, $V = \dfrac{1}{3}\pi r^2 h = \dfrac{1}{3}\pi\left(\dfrac{3h}{8}\right)^2 h = \dfrac{3\pi h^3}{64}$, $\dfrac{dV}{dt} = \dfrac{9\pi h^2}{64}\dfrac{dh}{dt}$, $-2 = \dfrac{9\pi(4)^2}{64}\dfrac{dh}{dt}$,

$\dfrac{dh}{dt} = \dfrac{-8}{9\pi} \approx -0.283$ ft/min

Day 36

$\tan\theta = \dfrac{h}{2,000}$, $\sec^2\theta\dfrac{d\theta}{dt} = \dfrac{1}{2,000}\dfrac{dh}{dt}$, $\left(\dfrac{\sqrt{13}}{2}\right)^2\dfrac{d\theta}{dt} = \dfrac{1,200}{2,000}$, $\dfrac{d\theta}{dt} = \dfrac{1,200(4)}{2,000(13)} \approx 0.185$

radians per second or approximately 10.578 degrees per second.

Day 37

1. $f'(x) = x^{-\frac{1}{2}}(x-3)\left(\dfrac{5x-3}{2}\right)$ and the critical points are $x = \dfrac{3}{5}$ or $x = 3$.

$f'\left(\dfrac{1}{2}\right) = \dfrac{5\sqrt{2}}{8} > 0$, $f'(1) = -2 < 0$, at $x = \dfrac{3}{5}$ is a maximum, $f'(4) = \dfrac{17}{4}$, at $x = 3$

is a minimum.

2. $f'(x) = 2\cos 2x + 2\sin x$, $x = \dfrac{\pi}{2}, \dfrac{7\pi}{6}, \dfrac{11\pi}{6}$, $f''(x) = -4\sin 2x + 2\cos x$,

$f''\left(\dfrac{7\pi}{6}\right) = -3\sqrt{3} < 0$, $f''\left(\dfrac{11\pi}{6}\right) = 3\sqrt{3} > 0$, $f''\left(\dfrac{\pi}{2}\right) = 0$. Maximum at $x = \dfrac{7\pi}{6}$,

minimum at $x = \dfrac{11\pi}{6}$. (at $x = \dfrac{\pi}{2}$ is an Inflection Point.)

3. $f'(x) = -2 + \dfrac{3}{2}(x+1)^{\frac{1}{2}} = 0$ at $x = \dfrac{7}{9}$. $f''(x) = \dfrac{3}{4}(x+1)^{-\frac{1}{2}}$ and $f''\left(\dfrac{7}{9}\right) = \dfrac{9}{16} > 0$.

at $x = \dfrac{7}{9}$ is a minimum.

Day 38

1. $A = x(50 - x)$, $A' = 50 - 2x = 0$, $x = 25$, $50 - x = 25$. $A'' = -2$.
   Maximum area with a square 25 ft on a side.

2. $A = x(100 - 2x)$, $A' = 100 - 4x = 0$, $x = 25$, $100 - 2x = 50$. $A'' = -4$.
   Maximum area with a 25-by-50-foot rectangle.

3. $d = \sqrt{(x-3)^2 + (2x-1+1)^2}$, $d' = \frac{1}{2}\left[5x^2 - 6x + 9\right]^{-\frac{1}{2}}(10x - 6) = 0$, $x = \frac{3}{5}$,
   $d \approx 2.683$. $d''\left(\frac{3}{5}\right) > 0$. The shortest distance, which is the perpendicular distance,
   is approximately 2.683 units.

Day 39

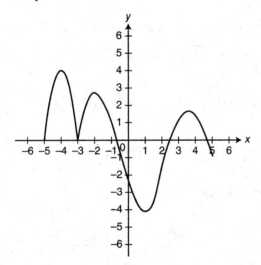

Day 40

1. $\displaystyle\lim_{x \to 0} \frac{\sin x}{2x} = \lim_{x \to 0} \frac{\cos x}{2} = \frac{1}{2}$

2. $\displaystyle\lim_{x \to 3} \frac{\ln(x - 2)}{x^2 - 9} = \lim_{x \to 3} \frac{1/(x-2)}{2x} = \lim_{x \to 3} \frac{1}{2x(x - 2)} = \frac{1}{6}$

3. $\displaystyle\lim_{x \to \infty} \frac{e^{2x}}{2x^2} = \lim_{x \to \infty} \frac{2e^{2x}}{4x} = \lim_{x \to \infty} \frac{4e^{2x}}{4} = \lim_{x \to \infty} e^{2x} = \infty$

Day 41

1. D $\quad f'(x)=3x^2-4x,\ f'(-1)=7,\ y+2=7(x+1),\ y=7x+5$

2. A $\quad f'(x)=-\dfrac{1}{x^2},\ f'(-1)=-1,\ y+2=-1(x+1),\ y=-x-3$

3. B $\quad f'(x)=(2x+2)e^{-x^2-2x-1},\ f'(-1)=0,\ y=-2$

4. E $\quad 2x+2y\dfrac{dy}{dx}=0,\ \dfrac{dy}{dx}=-\dfrac{x}{y}\bigg|_{(-1,-2)}=-\dfrac{1}{2},\ y+2=-\dfrac{1}{2}(x+1),\ y=-\dfrac{1}{2}x-\dfrac{5}{2}$

5. B $\quad f'(x)=\pi\cos\left(\dfrac{\pi x}{2}\right),\ f'(-1)=\pi\cos\left(-\dfrac{\pi}{2}\right)=0,\ y=-2$

Day 42

1. $f'(x)=8x^3-15x^2,\ f'(1)=-7,\ y+1=\dfrac{1}{7}(x-1),\ y=\dfrac{1}{7}x-\dfrac{8}{7}$

2. $f'(x)=2\cos(2x)-\sin x,\ f'(-\pi)=2,\ y+1=-\dfrac{1}{2}(x+\pi),\ y=-\dfrac{x}{2}-\dfrac{\pi+2}{2}$

Day 43

1. $f'(x)=2-3x^2,\ f'(1)=-1,\ y=7-x;\ f(1.01)\approx 5.99.\ f''(x)=-6x,\ f''(1)<0,$ overestimate.

2. $f'(x)=\dfrac{-2}{2x+1},\ f'(1)=-\dfrac{2}{3},\ y=-\dfrac{2}{3}x+\dfrac{11}{3}-\ln 3,\ f(0.9)\approx 1.968.$

   $f''(x)=\dfrac{4}{(2x+1)^2}$ and $f''(1)=\dfrac{4}{9}>0,$ underestimate.

Day 44

$f'(x)=-3e^{-x},\ f'(0)=-3,\ y=5-3x,\ f(-0.01)\approx 5.03.\ f''(x)=3e^{-x}$ and $f''(0)=3>0,$ underestimate.

Day 45

$f(x)=\sqrt{x},\ f'(x)=\dfrac{1}{2\sqrt{x}},\ f'(16)=\dfrac{1}{8},\ y-4=\dfrac{1}{8}(x-16).$ At $x=17,\ y=4.125$

$\sqrt{17}\approx 4.125,$ difference: 0.002

At $x=20,\ y=4.5;\ \sqrt{20}\approx 4.5;$ difference: 0.028

$f(x)=\sqrt[3]{x},\ f'(x)=\dfrac{x^{-\frac{2}{3}}}{3},\ f'(-27)=\dfrac{1}{27},\ y+3=\dfrac{1}{27}(x+27)$

$\sqrt[3]{-26}\approx -2.963,$ difference: 0.001

$\sqrt[3]{-25}\approx -2.926,$ difference: 0.002

$f(x)=\sqrt[5]{x},\ f'(x)=\dfrac{1}{5x^{4/5}}$ and $f'(32)=\dfrac{1}{80},\ y-2=\dfrac{1}{80}(x-32)$

$\sqrt[5]{33}\approx 2.0125,$ difference: -0.0005

Day 46

Desired	cos 58°	sin 50°	tan 170°
Function	$y = \cos x$	$y = \sin x$	$y = \tan x$
Point of tangency	$\left(\dfrac{\pi}{3}, \dfrac{1}{2}\right)$	$\left(\dfrac{\pi}{4}, \dfrac{\sqrt{2}}{2}\right)$	$(\pi, 0)$
Derivative	$y' = -\sin x$	$y' = \cos x$	$y' = \sec^2 x$
Derivative Evaluated	$-\dfrac{\sqrt{3}}{2}$	$\dfrac{\sqrt{2}}{2}$	1
Distance from point of tangency	$-2° = -\dfrac{\pi}{90}$	$5° = \dfrac{\pi}{36}$	$-10° = -\dfrac{\pi}{18}$
(Derivative)(distance) + y-value of point of tangency	$\left(-\dfrac{\sqrt{3}}{2} \cdot -\dfrac{\pi}{90}\right) + \dfrac{1}{2}$	$\left(\dfrac{\sqrt{2}}{2} \cdot \dfrac{\pi}{36}\right) + \dfrac{\sqrt{2}}{2}$	$1\left(-\dfrac{\pi}{18}\right) + 0$
Approximate Value	$\cos 58° \approx 0.530$	$\sin 50° \approx 0.769$	$\tan 170° \approx -0.175$
Actual (to nearest thousandth)	0.530	0.766	-0.176

Day 47

1. $v \approx \dfrac{139 - 87}{2 - 1} = 52\,{}^{ft}\!/_{sec}$

2. $v \approx \dfrac{69 - 129}{5.5 - 4.5} = -60\,{}^{ft}\!/_{sec}$

3. $s(t) = -16t^2 + 100t + 3$, $v(t) = -32t + 100$, $v(1.5) = -48 + 100 = 52$,
   $v(5) = -160 + 100 = -60$

4. $v(t) = -32t + 100 = 0$, $t = 3.125$. It reaches a maximum height of 159.25 feet after 3.125 seconds.

5. $v_{average} = \dfrac{69 - 139}{5.5 - 2} = \dfrac{-70}{3.5} = -20$

6. $v(t) = -32t + 100 = -20$, $t = 3.75$ seconds

7. False. The acceleration is constant at -32 feet per second per second.

8. The object slows when velocity and acceleration have opposite signs. Acceleration is constant (-32 feet per second per second), so the object is slowing when velocity is positive: $0 < t < 3.125$. It is slowing down as it rises and speeding up as it falls.

Answers

Day 48

1.

time (seconds)	0	1	2	3	4
position	(0, 0)	(1, 0)	(2, 0)	(1, 0)	(0, 0)

2. $v(t) = s'(t) = \dfrac{\pi}{2} \sin\left(\dfrac{\pi t}{2}\right) = 0,\ t = 2$

time	0	0.5	1	1.5	2	2.5	3	3.5	4
velocity	0	+	+	+	0	−	−	−	0
acceleration	+	+	0	−	−	−	0	+	+

3. $a(t) = \left(\dfrac{\pi}{2}\right)^2 \cos\left(\dfrac{\pi t}{2}\right)$ Speeding up: $0 < t < 1$ and $2 < t < 3$. Slowing down: $1 < t < 2$ and $3 < t < 4$.

4. Particle travels from (0, 0) to (2, 0), then reverses direction and returns to (0, 0). It travels a total of 4 units.

Day 49

$V = 9h,\ \dfrac{dV}{dt} = 9\dfrac{dh}{dt},\ 2 = 9\dfrac{dh}{dt},\ \dfrac{dh}{dt} = \dfrac{2}{9} \approx 0.222$ ft/min

Day 50

1. $f'(x) = 3x^2 - 4x^{-3} = 0$ at $x = \left(\dfrac{4}{3}\right)^{1/5} \approx 1.059$. $f''(x) = 6x + 12x^{-4}$ and

$f''\left(\dfrac{4}{3}\right)^{1/5} = 6\left(\dfrac{4}{3}\right)^{1/5} + 12\left(\dfrac{4}{3}\right)^{-4/5} > 0$. Relative minimum at $x = \left(\dfrac{4}{3}\right)^{1/5} \approx 1.059$

and $f(1.059) \approx 2.971$, relative minimum value of f.

2. $f'(x) = 4x^3 - 9x^2 + 6x = 0$ at $x = 0$. $f''(x) = 12x^2 - 18x + 6$ and $f''(0) = 6 > 0$. Minimum at $x = 0$ and $f(0) = 1$, minimum value of f.

Day 51

1. $f(x) = 5x + C$

2. $f(x) = x^3 + 4x^2 + 3x + C$

3. $f(x) = 5\ln|x| + C$

4. $f(x) = -\cos x + C$

5. $f(x) = \tan x + C$

Day 52

1. $\displaystyle\sum_{i=1}^{5} i = 1+2+3+4+5 = 15$

2. $\displaystyle\sum_{i=1}^{10}\left(\frac{i}{5}\right) = \frac{1}{5}\sum_{i=1}^{10} i = \frac{1}{5}(1+2+3+4+5+6+7+8+9+10) = \frac{55}{5} = 11$

3. $\displaystyle\sum_{i=2}^{4}\left(i^2\right)(i+3) = (4)(5)+(9)(6)+(16)(7) = 20+54+112 = 186$

4. $\displaystyle\sum_{i=-3}^{1}\left(i^3+2i^2-5i+4\right) = \sum_{i=-3}^{1}\left(i^3\right)+2\sum_{i=-3}^{1}\left(i^2\right)-5\sum_{i=-3}^{1}(i)+\sum_{i=-3}^{1}(4)$

$$= -35+2(15)-5(-5)+20 = 40$$

Day 53

1. $A = 16,\ F(x) = 4x+C,\ F(4)-F(0) = 16-0 = 16$

2. $A = 4,\ F(x) = 4x-x^2+C,\ F(2)-F(0) = 4-0 = 4$

3. $A = 1.5,\ F(x) = \frac{3}{2}x^2+C,\ F(1)-F(0) = \frac{3}{2}-0 = 1.5$

4. $A = 2.5,\ F(x) = \frac{3}{2}x^2+x+C,\ F(1)-F(0) = \frac{3}{2}+1-0 = 2.5$

5. $A = 5,\ F(x) = \begin{cases} -\dfrac{1}{2}x^2+x+C_1, & x<1 \\[2mm] \dfrac{1}{2}x^2-x+C_2, & x\geq 1 \end{cases}$

$$F(4)-F(0) = (8-4)-\left(\frac{1}{2}-1\right)+\left(-\frac{1}{2}+1\right)-0 = 5$$

Alternatively, using your TI-89 calculator, you obtain

$F(x) = \int |x-1|\,dx = \dfrac{(x-1)\,|x-1|}{2}+c.$ And

$F(4)-F(0) = \dfrac{9}{2}-\left(-\dfrac{1}{2}\right) = 5.$

Day 54

1. $\displaystyle\int_8^8 g(x)\ dx = 0$

2. $\displaystyle\int_9^5 f(x)\ dx = -\int_5^9 f(x)\ dx = -12$

3. $\displaystyle\int_2^5 7g(x)\ dx = 7\int_2^5 g(x)\ dx = 7(-1) = -7$

4. $\displaystyle\int_2^9 f(x)\ dx = \int_2^5 f(x)\ dx + \int_5^9 f(x)\ dx = -3 + 12 = 9$

5. $\displaystyle\int_2^5 [f(x)+g(x)]\ dx = \int_2^5 f(x)\ dx + \int_2^5 g(x)\ dx = -3 - 1 = -4$

Day 55

1. $\displaystyle\int_{-3}^1 \left(6x^2 - 5x + 2\right) dx = 2x^3 - \frac{5}{2}x^2 + 2x\,\Big|_{-3}^1 = \left(2 - \frac{5}{2} + 2\right) - \left(-54 - \frac{45}{2} - 6\right) = 84$

2. $\displaystyle\int_1^2 \frac{x^5 + x^2 + x}{x}\, dx = \int_1^2 \left(x^4 + x + 1\right) dx = \frac{x^5}{5} + \frac{x^2}{2} + x\,\Big|_1^2$

$$= \left(\frac{32}{5} + \frac{4}{2} + 2\right) - \left(\frac{1}{5} + \frac{1}{2} + 1\right) = 8.7$$

3. $\displaystyle\int_1^3 \frac{dx}{x^3} = \int_1^3 x^{-3} dx = \frac{x^{-2}}{-2}\,\Big|_1^3 = \frac{1}{-2(9)} - \frac{1}{-2(1)} = \frac{-8}{-18} = \frac{4}{9}$

4. $\displaystyle\int_1^4 \sqrt{x}\ dx = \int_1^4 x^{1/2}\ dx = \frac{2}{3}x^{3/2}\,\Big|_1^4 = \frac{2}{3}(8) - \frac{2}{3}(1) = \frac{14}{3}$

5. $\displaystyle\int_1^{32} \sqrt[5]{x^2}\ dx = \int_1^{32} x^{2/5}\ dx = \frac{5}{7}x^{7/5}\,\Big|_1^{32} = \frac{5}{7}(128) - \frac{5}{7}(1) = \frac{635}{7}$

Day 56

1. $\displaystyle\int_{0}^{\pi/3}\left(2\sin\theta-5\cos\theta\right)d\theta=\left(-2\cos\theta-5\sin\theta\right)\Big|_{0}^{\pi/3}=1-5\left(\frac{\sqrt{3}}{2}\right)=\frac{2-5\sqrt{3}}{2}$

2. $\displaystyle\int_{\pi/4}^{\pi/3}5\sec^{2}x\ dx=\left(5\tan x\right)\Big|_{\pi/4}^{\pi/3}=5\sqrt{3}-5=5\left(\sqrt{3}-1\right)$

3. $\displaystyle\int_{1}^{e}\left(\frac{3}{z}\right)dz=\left(3\ln z\right)\Big|_{1}^{e}=3-0=3$

4. $\displaystyle\int_{-\pi}^{\pi/2}\left(2\sin\theta\cos\theta\right)d\theta=\sin^{2}\theta\Big|_{-\pi}^{\pi/2}=\sin^{2}\left(\frac{\pi}{2}\right)-\sin^{2}\left(-\pi\right)=1-0=1$

5. $\displaystyle\int_{0}^{\ln(1+\pi)}\left(-e^{x}\cos\left(1-e^{x}\right)\right)dx=\sin\left(1-e^{x}\right)\Big|_{0}^{\ln(1+\pi)}=\sin\left(1-e^{\ln(1+\pi)}\right)-\sin\left(1-e^{0}\right)$

$$=\sin(1-1-\pi)-\sin(0)=\sin(-\pi)-\sin(0)=0$$

Day 57

1. B

2. H

3. I

4. F

5. D

Day 58

1. Let $u=\sin\theta,\ \dfrac{du}{d\theta}=\cos\theta$

$$\int_{-\pi}^{\pi/2}\left(\cos\theta\cos(\sin\theta)\right)d\theta=\int_{\sin(-\pi)}^{\sin\left(\pi/2\right)}\cos(u)\frac{du}{d\theta}d\theta=\sin(u)\Big|_{0}^{1}=\sin(1)-\sin(0)\approx0.841$$

2. Let $u=1-e^{x},\ \dfrac{du}{dx}=-e^{x}$

$$\int_{0}^{\ln(1+\pi)}\left(e^{x}\cos\left(1-e^{x}\right)\right)dx=-\int_{1-e^{0}}^{1-e^{\ln(1+\pi)}}\cos(u)\frac{du}{dx}dx=-\sin(u)\Big|_{0}^{-\pi}=0$$

3. Let $u=1-4t^{2},\ \dfrac{du}{dt}=-8t$

$$\int_{0}^{1/4}\left(\frac{2t}{1-4t^{2}}\right)dt=\int_{1-4\cdot0^{2}}^{1-4\left(1/4\right)^{2}}\frac{1}{u}\left(-\frac{1}{4}\cdot\frac{du}{dt}\right)dt=-\frac{1}{4}\ln u\Big|_{1}^{3/4}=-\frac{1}{4}\ln\left(\frac{3}{4}\right)+\frac{1}{4}\ln1=\frac{\ln4-\ln3}{4}\approx0.072$$

Day 59

1. d $\quad \int_{-2}^{k} x^2\, dx = \dfrac{x^3}{3}\Big|_{-2}^{k} = \dfrac{k^3}{3} + \dfrac{8}{3} = 24,\ k = 4$

2. c $\quad$ Fundamental Theorem of Calculus

3. a $\quad$ Limits of integration are equal.

4. a $\quad$ Reversing the limits of integration changes the sign.

5. c $\quad \int_{1}^{5} 2\, dx = 2x\Big|_{1}^{5} = 10 - 2 = 8$

Day 60

If $f''(x) = 6x - 4$, then $f'(x) = 3x^2 - 4x + C$. The value of the first derivative at $x = 0$ is known. $f'(0) = 3(0)^2 - 4(0) + C = 1$ indicates $C = 1$, so $f'(x) = 3x^2 - 4x + 1$. Find the antiderivative of $f'(x) = 3x^2 - 4x + 1$ to get $f(x) = x^3 - 2x^2 + x + C$. Use $f(1) = -3$ to find the constant. $f(1) = (1)^3 - 2(1)^2 + 1 + C = -3$, so $C = -3$. Conclude $f(x) = x^3 - 2x^2 + x - 3$.

Day 61

1. $u = 2x^2 - 3,\ du = 4x,\ \displaystyle\int \dfrac{x}{2x^2 - 3}\, dx = \dfrac{1}{4}\int \dfrac{4x}{2x^2 - 3}\, dx = \dfrac{1}{4}\int \dfrac{du}{u} = \dfrac{1}{4}\ln\left|2x^2 - 3\right| + C$

2. $u = x^3 - 5,\ du = 3x^2,\ \displaystyle\int \dfrac{x^2}{x^3 - 5}\, dx = \dfrac{1}{3}\int \dfrac{3x^2}{x^3 - 5}\, dx = \dfrac{1}{3}\int \dfrac{du}{u} = \dfrac{1}{3}\ln\left|x^3 - 5\right| + C$

3. $u = 4 - x^2,\ du = -2x,\ \displaystyle\int \dfrac{x}{4 - x^2}\, dx = -\dfrac{1}{2}\int \dfrac{-2x}{4 - x^2}\, dx = -\dfrac{1}{2}\int \dfrac{du}{u} = -\dfrac{1}{2}\ln\left|4 - x^2\right| + C$

4. $u = 3x,\ du = 3,\ \displaystyle\int e^{3x}\, dx = \dfrac{1}{3}\int 3e^{3x}\, dx = \dfrac{1}{3}\int e^{u}\, du = \dfrac{1}{3}e^{3x} + C$

5. $u = x^3,\ du = 3x^2,\ \displaystyle\int x^2 e^{x^3}\, dx = \dfrac{1}{3}\int 3x^2 e^{x^3}\, dx = \dfrac{1}{3}\int e^{u}\, du = \dfrac{1}{3}e^{x^3} + C$

Day 62

1. $\displaystyle\int \frac{-2\,dx}{1+4x^2} = \cot^{-1}(2x) + C$

2. $\displaystyle\int \frac{-3\,dx}{\sqrt{1-9x^2}} = \cos^{-1}(3x) + C$

3. $\displaystyle\int \frac{1}{\sqrt{4-x^2}} = \int \frac{\frac{1}{2}}{\sqrt{1-\frac{x^2}{4}}} = \sin^{-1}\left(\frac{x}{2}\right) + C$

4. $\displaystyle\int \frac{\cos x}{1+\sin^2 x}\,dx = \tan^{-1}(\sin x) + C$

Day 63

$A = 2x\left(\sqrt{100-x^2}\right)$, $A' = \dfrac{200-4x^2}{\sqrt{100-x^2}} = 0$, $x = 5\sqrt{2} \approx 7.071$; $A''(5\sqrt{2}) < 0$. The rect-

angle of greatest area is 14.142 by 7.071 units.

Day 64

1. $\displaystyle\int_0^2 f(x)\,dx = \frac{1}{2}(1+3)(2) = 4$

2. $\displaystyle\int_0^{-2} f(x)\,dx = -2$

3. $\displaystyle\int_{-4}^{-2} f(x)\,dx = \frac{-3(1.5)}{2} + \frac{1(0.5)}{2} = \frac{-4}{2} = -2$

4. $\displaystyle\int_{-4}^{3} f(x)\,dx = \int_{-4}^{-2} f(x)\,dx + \int_{-2}^{0} f(x)\,dx + \int_{0}^{2} f(x)\,dx + \int_{2}^{3} f(x)\,dx$
$$= -2 + 2 + 4 + 1.5 = 5.5$$

Day 65

1. Using (0, 240), and (4, 400) and a trapezoidal approximation, the total number of gallons $\approx \frac{1}{2}(4)(240+400) = 1{,}280$ gallons.

2. Using (8, 650), (10, 700), (12, 720), (14, 700), and (16, 650), the total number of gallons $\approx 2\left[\frac{1}{2}(2)(650+700)+\frac{1}{2}(2)(700+720)\right] = 2[2{,}770] = 5{,}540$.

3. Using previous calculations and the symmetry of the graph, the total number of gallons over 24 hours $\approx 2[1{,}280 + \frac{1}{2}(2)(400+550)+\frac{1}{2}(2)(550+650) + 2{,}770]$

$= 2[1{,}280 + 950 + 1{,}200 + 2{,}770] = 2[6{,}240] = 12{,}400$ gallons.

Day 66

1. True

2. False

3. False

4. False

5. True

Day 67

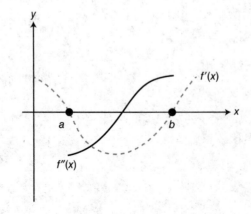

Day 68

$$\int_{2}^{8} f(x)\,dx \approx \frac{1}{2}(3-2)(1+4)+\frac{1}{2}(5-3)(4+7)+\frac{1}{2}(6-5)(7+3)+\frac{1}{2}(8-6)(3+2)$$

$$\approx \frac{1}{2}(1)(5)+\frac{1}{2}(2)(11)+\frac{1}{2}(1)(10)+\frac{1}{2}(2)(5)$$

$$\approx \frac{1}{2}(5+22+10+10)$$

$$\approx 23.5$$

Day 69

1. $1\big[f(-3)+f(-2)+f(-1)+f(0)+f(1)\big]=10+14+10+4+2=40$

2. $1\big[f(2)+f(1)+f(0)+f(-1)+f(-2)\big]=(1)\big[10+2+4+10+14\big]=40$

Day 70

1. $\displaystyle\int_{-2}^{2}\left(4-x^2\right)dx = 4x-\frac{x^3}{3}\Big|_{x=-2}^{x=2} = \left(8-\frac{8}{3}\right)-\left(-8+\frac{8}{3}\right)=16-\frac{16}{3}=\frac{32}{3}$

2. $\displaystyle\int_{-1}^{7}\sqrt{x+2}\;dx = \frac{2}{3}(x+2)^{3/2}\Big|_{x=-1}^{x=7} = \frac{2}{3}\left[\left(9^{3/2}\right)-\left(1^{3/2}\right)\right]=\frac{2}{3}[27-1]=\frac{52}{3}$

3. $\displaystyle\int_{-3}^{2}\left(x^3+2x^2-5x+4\right)dx = \left(\frac{x^4}{4}+\frac{2x^3}{3}-\frac{5x^2}{2}+4x\right)\Big|_{x=-3}^{x=2}$

$$=\left(\frac{16}{4}+\frac{16}{3}-\frac{20}{2}+8\right)-\left(\frac{81}{4}-\frac{54}{3}-\frac{45}{2}-12\right)=\frac{475}{12}$$

Day 71

1.	$F(x)=\displaystyle\int_{5}^{x}\left(2t\sqrt{t}\right)dt$	$F'(x)=2x\sqrt{x}$	$F'(9)=18\cdot3=54$
2.	$F(x)=\displaystyle\int_{0}^{4x}t(1+t^3)\,dt$	$F'(x)=16x(1+64x^3)$	$F'(1)=16(65)=1{,}040$
3.	$F(x)=\displaystyle\int_{4}^{2x}\left(\frac{t-3}{t}\right)dt$	$F'(x)=\dfrac{2x-3}{x}$	$F'(10)=\dfrac{20-3}{10}=1.7$
4.	$F(x)=\displaystyle\int_{-1}^{x}t(t^2-4)\,dt$	$F'(x)=x^3-4x$	$F'(2)=8-8=0$
5.	$F(x)=\displaystyle\int_{0}^{x}e^{t^2}\,dt$	$F'(x)=e^{x^2}$	$F'(1)=e^{1^2}=e$

Day 72

1. $\dfrac{d}{dx}\displaystyle\int_0^x \left(t^3 - 7t + 1\right)dt = x^3 - 7x + 1$

2. $\dfrac{d}{dx}\displaystyle\int_{-3}^x \sqrt{t+5}\ dt = \sqrt{x+5}$

3. $\dfrac{d}{dx}\displaystyle\int_1^{2x}\left(t^2 - 2t + 5\right)dt = \dfrac{d}{dx}\displaystyle\int_1^u\left(t^2 - 2t + 5\right)dt = \dfrac{d}{du}\left[\displaystyle\int_1^u\left(t^2 - 2t + 5\right)dt\right]\dfrac{du}{dx}$

$$= \left(u^2 - 2u + 5\right)(2) = 2\left(4x^2 - 4x + 5\right) = 8x^2 - 8x + 10$$

Day 73

1. $\displaystyle\sum_{k=-4}^3 1\cdot\left(f(k)\right) = 2 + 5.5 + 7 + 6.8 + 5.5 + 4 + 2.5 + 2 = 35.3$

2. $\displaystyle\sum_{k=-3}^4 1\cdot\left(f(k)\right) = 5.5 + 7 + 6.8 + 5.5 + 4 + 2.5 + 2 + 2.5 = 35.8$

3. $\displaystyle\sum_{k=-2}^1 2\cdot\left(f(2k+1)\right) = 2(5.5 + 6.8 + 4 + 2) = 2(18.3) = 36.6$

Day 74

1. $\displaystyle\sum_{k=1}^6 0.5f\left(\dfrac{k-9}{2}\right) = 0.5\left(f(-4) + f(-3.5) + f(-3) + f(-2.5) + f(-2) + f(-1.5)\right)$

$$= 0.5(0 + 4.5 + 6 + 5.5 + 4 + 2) = 0.5(22) = 11$$

2. $\displaystyle\sum_{k=1}^6 0.5f\left(\dfrac{k}{2}-1\right) = 0.5\left(f(-0.5) + f(0) + f(0.5) + f(1) + f(1.5) + f(2)\right)$

$$= 0.5(-1.5 - 2.5 - 2.5 - 2 - 1 + 0) = 0.5(-9.5) = -4.75;\ \text{Area} = 4.75$$

3. $\displaystyle\sum_{k=1}^3 1f(k-4.5) = 1\left(f(-3.5) + f(-2.5) + f(-1.5)\right)$

$$= 1(4.5 + 5.5 + 2) = 12$$

Day 75

$$A = \sum_{k=-1}^1 \dfrac{1}{2}\left(f(k) + f(k+1)\right)\Delta x$$

$$= \dfrac{1}{2}\left[f(-1) + 2f(0) + 2f(1) + f(2)\right]$$

$$= \dfrac{1}{2}\left[0 + 2(-2.5) + 2(-2) + 0\right] = \dfrac{1}{2}(-9) = -4.5;\ \text{Area} = 4.5$$

Day 76

1. $\displaystyle\int_{-3}^{0}\left(x^3+3x^2\right)dx=\frac{x^4}{4}+x^3\Big|_{-3}^{0}=0-\left[\frac{81}{4}-27\right]=\frac{27}{4}$

2. $\displaystyle\int_{-3}^{-2}\left(2x^3+3x^2+4\right)dx=\frac{x^4}{2}+x^3+4x\Big|_{-3}^{-2}=-9.5$

$\displaystyle\int_{-2}^{-1}\left(2x^3+3x^2+4\right)dx=\frac{x^4}{2}+x^3+4x\Big|_{-2}^{-1}=\left(\frac{1}{2}-1-4\right)-\left(\frac{16}{2}-8-8\right)=-4.5+8=3.5$

Total Area = |−9.5| + 3.5 = 13.

Day 77

1. $\displaystyle\int_{0}^{\pi}\left(1+\cos x\right)dx=x+\sin x\Big|_{0}^{\pi}=\left(\pi+0\right)-\left(0\right)=\pi$

2. $\displaystyle\int_{\pi/6}^{\pi/3}\left(-\sin x\right)dx=\cos x\Big|_{\pi/6}^{\pi/3}=\frac{1}{2}-\frac{\sqrt{3}}{2}\approx-0.366$

3. $\displaystyle\int_{-\pi/2}^{\pi/2}\left(x+\sin x\right)dx=\left(\frac{x^2}{2}-\cos x\right)\Big|_{-\pi/2}^{\pi/2}=\left(\frac{\pi^2}{8}-0\right)-\left(\frac{\pi^2}{8}-0\right)=0$

Day 78

1. $u=e^{-x^2},\ du=-2xdx,\ \displaystyle\int_{-2}^{2}\left(xe^{-x^2}\right)dx=-\frac{1}{2}\int_{-2}^{2}\left(e^{-x^2}\right)(-2x)dx=-\frac{1}{2}\left[e^{-x^2}\right]_{-2}^{2}=0$

2. $u=\left(x^2+4x\right),\ du=(2x+4)dx,$

$\displaystyle\frac{1}{2}\int\frac{2x+4}{x^2+4x}dx=\frac{1}{2}\ln\left|x^2+4x\right|\Big]_{1}^{4}=\frac{1}{2}(\ln32-\ln5)=\frac{\ln\left(\frac{32}{5}\right)}{2}\approx.928$

Day 79

1. $\displaystyle\int_{1}^{5}|x-3|\,dx = \int_{1}^{3}(3-x)\,dx + \int_{3}^{5}(x-3)\,dx = \left(3x - \frac{x^2}{2}\right)\Big|_{1}^{3} + \left(\frac{x^2}{2} - 3x\right)\Big|_{3}^{5}$

$\qquad = \left[\left(9 - \frac{9}{2}\right) - \left(3 - \frac{1}{2}\right)\right] + \left[\left(\frac{25}{2} - 15\right) - \left(\frac{9}{2} - 9\right)\right]$

$\qquad = [6-4] + [8-6] = 4$

2. $\displaystyle\int_{-1}^{3}|2x+1|\,dx = \int_{-1}^{-\frac{1}{2}}(-2x-1)\,dx + \int_{-\frac{1}{2}}^{3}(2x+1)\,dx = \left(-x^2 - x\right)\Big|_{-1}^{-\frac{1}{2}} + \left(x^2 + x\right)\Big|_{-\frac{1}{2}}^{3}$

$\qquad = \left[\left(-\frac{1}{4} + \frac{1}{2}\right) - (-1+1)\right] + \left[(9+3) - \left(\frac{1}{4} - \frac{1}{2}\right)\right] = \left[\frac{1}{4}\right] + \left[12 + \frac{1}{4}\right] = 12\frac{1}{2}$

3. $\displaystyle\int_{-2}^{2}|x^3|\,dx = \int_{-2}^{0}(-x^3)\,dx + \int_{0}^{2}x^3\,dx = \left(-\frac{x^4}{4}\right)\Big|_{-2}^{0} + \left(\frac{x^4}{4}\right)\Big|_{0}^{2} = [0+4] + [4-0] = 8$

Day 80

1. $\displaystyle\int_{-1}^{3}\left[(3+2x-x^2) - (x^2-2x-3)\right]dx = -2\int_{-1}^{3}(x^2-2x-3)\,dx = 2\left[\frac{x^3}{3} - x^2 - 3x\right]_{-1}^{3}$

$\qquad = -2\left[(9-9-9) - \left(-\frac{1}{3} - 1 + 3\right)\right]$

$\qquad = -2\left[-9 - \frac{5}{3}\right] = -2\left[-\frac{32}{3}\right] = \frac{64}{3}$

2. $\displaystyle\int_{-1}^{3}\left[(9+9x-x^2-x^3) - (3+2x-x^2)\right]dx = \int_{-1}^{3}(6+7x-x^3)\,dx$

$\qquad = 6x + \frac{7}{2}x^2 - \frac{x^4}{4}\Big|_{-1}^{3}$

$\qquad = \left[\left(18 + \frac{63}{2} - \frac{81}{4}\right) - \left(-6 + \frac{7}{2} - \frac{1}{4}\right)\right]$

$\qquad = 24 + 28 - 20 = 32$

3. $\displaystyle\int_{0}^{3}\left[(3+2x-x^2) - \sin\left(\frac{\pi x}{3}\right)\right]dx = 3x + x^2 - \frac{x^3}{3} + \frac{3}{\pi}\cos\left(\frac{\pi x}{3}\right)\Big|_{0}^{3}$

$\qquad = \left(9 + 9 - 9 + \frac{3}{\pi}\cos(\pi)\right) - \frac{3}{\pi}\cos(0)$

$\qquad = 9 + \frac{3}{\pi}(-1) - \frac{3}{\pi}(1) = \frac{9\pi - 6}{\pi}$

Day 81

1. D $\pi \int_0^4 (4-x)^2 \, dx = \pi \int_0^4 (16 - 8x + x^2) \, dx = \pi \left[16x - 4x^2 + \frac{x^3}{3} \right]_0^4 = \frac{64\pi}{3} \approx 67.021$

2. E $\pi \int_0^4 \left(\sqrt{4-y} \right)^2 \, dy = \pi \int_0^4 (4-y) \, dy = \pi \left[4y - \frac{y^2}{2} \right]_0^4 = \pi \left[(16-8) - (0) \right] = 8\pi \approx 25.133$

3. A $\pi \int_0^2 (4-x^2)^2 \, dx = \pi \int_0^2 (16 - 8x^2 + x^4) \, dx = \pi \left[16x - \frac{8x^3}{3} + \frac{x^5}{5} \right]_0^2$

$$= \pi \left[\left(32 - \frac{64}{3} + \frac{32}{5} \right) - (0) \right] = \frac{256\pi}{15} \approx 53.617$$

4. G $\pi \int_0^4 (4-y)^2 \, dy = \pi \int_0^4 (16 - 8y + y^2) \, dy = \pi \left[16y - 4y^2 + \frac{y^3}{3} \right]_0^4$

$$= \pi \left[\left(64 - 64 + \frac{64}{3} \right) - (0) \right] = \frac{64\pi}{3} \approx 67.021$$

Day 82

1. Outer: $R = \sqrt{y}$, Inner: $r = \frac{y}{2}$.

$$V = \pi \int_0^4 \left[\sqrt{y}^2 - \left(\frac{y}{2} \right)^2 \right] dy = \pi \int_0^4 \left[y - \frac{y^2}{4} \right] dy = \pi \left[\frac{y^2}{2} - \frac{y^3}{12} \right]_0^4 = \pi \left(8 - \frac{16}{3} \right) = \frac{8\pi}{3}$$

2. Outer: $R = 2x$, Inner: $r = x^2$.

$$V = \pi \int_0^2 \left[(2x)^2 - (x^2)^2 \right] dx = \pi \int_0^2 \left[4x^2 - x^4 \right] dx = \pi \left[\frac{4x^3}{3} - \frac{x^5}{5} \right]_0^2$$

$$= \pi \left(\frac{32}{3} - \frac{32}{5} \right) = \frac{64\pi}{15}$$

3. Outer: $R = 4 - x^2$, Inner: $r = 4 - 2x$.

$$V = \pi \int_0^2 \left[(4-x^2)^2 - (4-2x)^2 \right] dx = \pi \int_0^2 \left[(16 - 8x^2 + x^4) - (16 - 16x + 4x^2) \right] dx$$

$$= \pi \int_0^2 (16x - 12x^2 + x^4) \, dx = \pi \left[8x^2 - 4x^3 + \frac{x^5}{5} \right]_0^2 = \pi \left(32 - 32 + \frac{32}{5} \right) = \frac{32\pi}{5}$$

4. Outer: $R = 2 - \frac{y}{2}$, Inner: $r = 2 - \sqrt{y}$.

$$V = \pi \int_0^4 \left[\left(2 - \frac{y}{2} \right)^2 - \left(2 - \sqrt{y} \right)^2 \right] dy = \pi \int_0^4 \left[\left(4 - 2y + \frac{y^2}{4} \right) - \left(4 - 4y^{1/2} + y \right) \right] dy$$

$$= \pi \int_0^4 \left(-3y + \frac{y^2}{4} + 4y^{1/2} \right) dy = \pi \left[-\frac{3y^2}{2} + \frac{y^3}{12} + \frac{8y^{3/2}}{3} \right]_0^4 = \pi \left(-24 + \frac{16}{3} + \frac{64}{3} \right) = \frac{8\pi}{3}$$

Day 83

1. $\pi \int\limits_{0}^{2} \left(4 - x^2\right)^2 dx = \pi \left[16x - \dfrac{8x^3}{3} + \dfrac{x^5}{5}\right]_{0}^{2} = \pi \left[32 - \dfrac{64}{3} + \dfrac{32}{5}\right] = \dfrac{256\pi}{15} \approx 53.617$

2. $\pi \int\limits_{-3}^{1} \left(3 + x\right)^2 dx = \pi \left[9x + 3x^2 + \dfrac{x^3}{3}\right]_{-3}^{1} = \pi \left[\left(9 + 3 + \dfrac{1}{3}\right) - \left(-27 + 27 - 9\right)\right]$

   $= \dfrac{64\pi}{3} \approx 67.021$

3. $\pi \int\limits_{-1}^{3} \left(1 + y\right)^2 dy = \pi \left[y + y^2 + \dfrac{y^3}{3}\right]_{-1}^{3} = \pi \left[\left(3 + 9 + 9\right) - \left(-1 + 1 - \dfrac{1}{3}\right)\right]$

   $= \dfrac{64\pi}{3} \approx 67.021$

Day 84

1. $\pi\int_{1}^{9}\left[\left(4-\sqrt{y}\right)^2-(4-3)^2\right]dy = \pi\int_{1}^{9}\left[15-8y^{1/2}+y\right]dy = \pi\left[15y-\dfrac{16y^{3/2}}{3}+\dfrac{y^2}{2}\right]_{1}^{9}$

$$= \pi\left[(135-144+40.5)-\left(15-\dfrac{16}{3}+\dfrac{1}{2}\right)\right]$$

$$= \dfrac{64\pi}{3} \approx 67.021$$

2. $\pi\int_{1}^{3}\left[\left(-1-x^2\right)^2-(-1-1)^2\right]dx = \pi\int_{1}^{3}\left[-3+2x^2+x^4\right]dx = \pi\left[-3x+\dfrac{2x^3}{3}+\dfrac{x^5}{5}\right]_{1}^{3}$

$$= \pi\left[(-9+18+48.6)-\left(-3+\dfrac{2}{3}+\dfrac{1}{5}\right)\right]$$

$$= \dfrac{896\pi}{15} \approx 187.658$$

3. $\pi\int_{1}^{3}\left[(10-1)^2-\left(10-x^2\right)^2\right]dx = \pi\int_{1}^{3}\left(-19+20x^2-x^4\right)dx = \left[-19x+\dfrac{20x^3}{3}-\dfrac{x^5}{5}\right]_{1}^{3}$

$$= \left[(-57+180-48.6)-\left(-19+\dfrac{20}{3}-\dfrac{1}{5}\right)\right]$$

$$= \pi\left[74.4-\left(\dfrac{-188}{15}\right)\right]$$

$$= \dfrac{1304\pi}{15} \approx 273.109$$

4. $\pi\int_{1}^{9}\left[(-1-3)^2-\left(-1-\sqrt{y}\right)^2\right]dy = \pi\int_{1}^{9}\left(15-2y^{1/2}-y\right)dy = \pi\left[15y-\dfrac{4y^{3/2}}{3}-\dfrac{y^2}{2}\right]_{1}^{9}$

$$= \pi\left[(135-36-40.5)-\left(15-\dfrac{4}{3}-\dfrac{1}{2}\right)\right]$$

$$= \dfrac{272\pi}{6} = \dfrac{136\pi}{3} \approx 142.419$$

Day 85

1. $A = \int\limits_0^4 \left(x + 2 - \sqrt{x}\right) dx = \dfrac{x^2}{2} + 2x - \dfrac{2x^{3/2}}{3}\bigg|_0^4 = 8 + 8 + \dfrac{16}{3} = \dfrac{32}{3}$

2. $V = \int\limits_0^4 \left(x + 2 - \sqrt{x}\right)^2 dx = \int\limits_0^4 \left(x^2 + 5x + 4 - 2x^{3/2} - 4x^{1/2}\right) dx$

$= \dfrac{x^3}{3} + \dfrac{5x^2}{2} + 4x - \dfrac{4x^{5/2}}{5} - \dfrac{8x^{3/2}}{3}\bigg|_0^4 = \dfrac{64}{3} + \dfrac{80}{2} + 16 - \dfrac{128}{5} - \dfrac{64}{3} = 56 - 25.6 = 30.4$

3. $c = x + 2 - \sqrt{x}$, $a = b = \dfrac{x + 2 - \sqrt{x}}{\sqrt{2}}$, $A = \dfrac{1}{2}ab = \dfrac{1}{2}\left(\dfrac{x + 2 - \sqrt{x}}{\sqrt{2}}\right)^2$

$= \dfrac{x^2 + 5x + 4 - 2x^{3/2} - 4x^{1/2}}{4}$, $V = \int\limits_0^4 \dfrac{x^2 + 5x + 4 - 2x^{3/2} - 4x^{1/2}}{4} dx$

$= \dfrac{1}{4}\left[\dfrac{x^3}{3} + \dfrac{5x^2}{2} + 4x - \dfrac{4x^{5/2}}{5} - \dfrac{8x^{3/2}}{3}\right]_0^4 = \dfrac{1}{4}(30.4) = 7.6$

Day 86

1. $V = \pi \int\limits_0^{\sqrt{2}/2} \left(\arccos y\right)^2 - \left(\arcsin y\right)^2 dy$

2. $V = \pi \int\limits_0^{\sqrt{2}/2} \left(\arcsin y\right)^2 dy + \int\limits_{\sqrt{2}/2}^1 \left(\arccos y\right)^2 dy$

3. $V = \pi \int\limits_0^{\pi/4} \left(\cos^2 x - \sin^2 x\right) dx = \dfrac{\pi}{2} \int\limits_0^{\pi/4} \cos(2x) \cdot 2 \, dx = \dfrac{\pi}{2}\sin(2x)\big|_0^{\pi/4} = \dfrac{\pi}{2}(1 - 0) = \dfrac{\pi}{2}$

Day 87

$V = \pi r^2 h$, $\quad h = \dfrac{1{,}000}{\pi r^2}$, $\quad S = 2\pi r^2 + 2\pi r h = 2\pi r^2 + 2\pi r\left(\dfrac{1{,}000}{\pi r^2}\right) = 2\pi r^2 + \dfrac{2{,}000}{r}$,

$S' = 4\pi r - 2{,}000 r^{-2} = 0$, $r = \sqrt[3]{\dfrac{500}{\pi}} \approx 5.419$, $h \approx 10.839$; $S''(5.419) > 0$, minimum.

Day 88

Each slice is a semicircle with a radius $r = \sqrt{9-x^2}$.

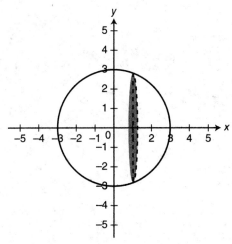

$$V = \int_{-3}^{3} \frac{1}{2}\pi\left(\sqrt{9-x^2}\right)^2 dx = 2\int_{0}^{3} \frac{1}{2}\pi\left(\sqrt{9-x^2}\right)^2 dx$$

$$= \pi\int_{0}^{3}\left(9-x^2\right)dx = \pi\left[9x - \frac{x^3}{3}\right]_{0}^{3}$$

$$= \pi\left[(27-9)-0\right] = 18\pi$$

Day 89

1.

2.

3.

Day 90

1.

2.

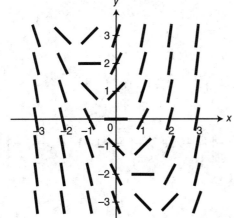

3.

Day 91

1. $\dfrac{dy}{dx} = \dfrac{2\cos x}{y^2} \implies y^2\,dy = 2\cos x\,dx$

$\displaystyle\int y^2\,dy = 2\int \cos x\,dx$

$\dfrac{y^3}{3} = 2\sin x + C_1$

$y^3 = 6\sin x + 3C_1$

$y = \sqrt[3]{6\sin x + 3C_1} = \sqrt[3]{6\sin x + C}.$

Note that C_1 and C are arbitrary constants.

2. $\dfrac{dy}{dx} = x(1+2y) \implies \dfrac{dy}{1+2y} = x\,dx$

$\dfrac{1}{2}\displaystyle\int \dfrac{2\,dy}{1+2y} = \int x\,dx$

$\dfrac{1}{2}\ln|1+2y| = \dfrac{x^2}{2} + C_1$

$\ln|1+2y| = x^2 + 2C_1$

$|1+2y| = e^{\left(x^2+2C_1\right)} = C_2 e^{x^2}$

$1 + 2y = \pm C_2 e^{x^2}$

$y = \dfrac{\pm C_2 e^{x^2} - 1}{2} = \dfrac{Ce^{x^2} - 1}{2}.$

Note that C_1, C_2, and C are arbitrary constants.

Day 92

1. $\dfrac{1}{4}\displaystyle\int_2^6 (x-2)^{1/2}\,dx = \dfrac{1}{4}\cdot\dfrac{2}{3}(x-2)^{3/2}\Big|_2^6 = \dfrac{1}{6}(8-0) = \dfrac{4}{3}$

2. $\dfrac{1}{1}\displaystyle\int_0^1 e^{1-x}\,dx = -\int_0^1 e^{1-x}(-1)\,dx = -e^{1-x}\Big|_0^1 = -(1-e) = e-1 \approx 1.718$

3. $\dfrac{1}{3}\displaystyle\int_{-1}^2 (x^3 - 2x + 1)\,dx = \dfrac{1}{3}\left(\dfrac{x^4}{4} - x^2 + x\right)\Big|_{-1}^2 = \dfrac{1}{3}\left[(4-4+2) - \left(\dfrac{1}{4}-1-1\right)\right] = \dfrac{1}{3}\left(\dfrac{15}{4}\right) = \dfrac{5}{4}$

Day 93

1. $\int_0^2 (4-x^2)\,dx = \left[4x - \dfrac{x^3}{3}\right]_0^2 = 8 - \dfrac{8}{3} = \dfrac{16}{3} = f(c)(2-0)$

$4 - c^2 = \dfrac{8}{3} \Rightarrow c^2 = \dfrac{4}{3} \Rightarrow c = \pm\dfrac{2\sqrt{3}}{3}; c = \dfrac{2\sqrt{3}}{3}$ on the interval $[0,2]$

2. $\int_0^2 (x^2 - x - 2)\,dx = \left[\dfrac{x^3}{3} - \dfrac{x^2}{2} - 2x\right]_0^2 = \dfrac{8}{3} - 2 - 4 = -\dfrac{10}{3} = f(c)(2-0)$

$f(c) = \dfrac{1}{2}\left(-\dfrac{10}{3}\right) = -\dfrac{5}{3}$

$x^2 - x - 2 = -\dfrac{5}{3} \Rightarrow 3x^2 - 3x - 1 = 0 \Rightarrow x = \dfrac{3 \pm \sqrt{9 - 4(3)(-1)}}{2(3)} = \dfrac{3 \pm \sqrt{21}}{6};$

$c = \dfrac{3 + \sqrt{21}}{6} \approx 1.264$ on $[0,2]$.

3. $\int_0^2 \left(5\sin\left(\dfrac{x-1}{2}\right)\right)dx = 10\int_0^2 \sin\left(\dfrac{x-1}{2}\right)\cdot\dfrac{1}{2}\,dx = -10\cos\left(\dfrac{x-1}{2}\right)\Big|_0^2$

$= -10\left[\cos\left(\dfrac{1}{2}\right) - \cos\left(-\dfrac{1}{2}\right)\right] = 0$

$\dfrac{5}{2}\sin\left(\dfrac{c-1}{2}\right) = 0 \Rightarrow \sin\left(\dfrac{c-1}{2}\right) = 0 \Rightarrow \dfrac{c-1}{2} = 0 \Rightarrow c = 1$

Day 94

1. Acceleration is the derivative of velocity and will be negative from $t = 3$ to $t = 5$.

2. Average velocity

$\dfrac{1}{5}\left[\dfrac{(1)(20)}{2} + \dfrac{(20+50)(1)}{2} + \dfrac{(50+65)(1)}{2} + \dfrac{(50+65)(1)}{2} + \dfrac{(50+10)(1)}{2}\right] = 38$ mph.

3. Total distance is the area under the curve which is 190 miles.

Day 95

1. $C'(x) = 17 + 0.05x$.

2. Average cost $= \dfrac{\text{total cost}}{\text{quantity}} = \dfrac{17(5{,}000) + 0.025(5{,}000)^2}{5{,}000}$

$= 17 + 0.025(5{,}000) = 17 + 125 = \$142$

3. Total profit $=$ total revenue $-$ total cost

$= 250(5{,}000) - \left(17(5{,}000) + 0.025(5{,}000)^2\right)$

$= 1{,}250{,}000 - 710{,}000 = \$540{,}000$

Day 96

1. $f(x) = \dfrac{x-1}{2x+1}$ on $[0,3]$

$f'(x) = \dfrac{3}{(2x+1)^2}$; note that $f'(x) > 0$ on $[0,3]$.

Thus, $f(x)$ is increasing on $[0,3]$.

x	$f(x)$
0	-1
3	$2/7$

Maximum value is $\dfrac{2}{7}$ occurring at point $\left(3, \dfrac{2}{7}\right)$.

Minimum value is -1 occurring at point $(0, -1)$.

2. Maximum value is 5 occurring at point $(1, 5)$.

Minimum value is 3 occurring at point $(2, 3)$.

Day 97

1. $\displaystyle\int_0^9 3\sqrt{t}\, dt = 2t^{3/2}\Big|_0^9 = 2(27) = 54$ gallons

2. $50 + \displaystyle\int_0^9 \left(1 - 3\sqrt{t}\right) dt = 50 + \left[t - 2t^{3/2}\right]_0^9 = 50 + 9 - 54 = 5$ gallons

Day 98

1. $2\displaystyle\int_0^3 \left(e^{(t+1)/2}\right)\left(\dfrac{1}{2} dt\right) = 2e^{(t+1)/2}\Big|_0^3 = 2\left(e^2 - e^{1/2}\right) \approx 11.481$ million bacteria

2. $5 + \displaystyle\int_0^3 f(t)\, dt \approx 5 + 11.481 \approx 16.481$ million bacteria

Day 99

1. $200 - 12\displaystyle\int_0^5 \left(e^{-t/6}\right) dt = 200 + 72\int_0^5 \left(e^{-t/6}\right)\left(-\dfrac{1}{6} dt\right) = 200 + 72\left[e^{-t/6}\right]_0^5$

$= 200 + 72\left[e^{-5/6} - 1\right] \approx 200 + 72\left[e^{-5/6} - 1\right] \approx 159.291°$

2. $-12\displaystyle\int_0^T \left(e^{-t/6}\right) dt = -60 \Rightarrow -6\int_0^T \left(e^{-t/6}\right)\left(-\dfrac{1}{6} dt\right) = 5 \Rightarrow -6\left(e^{-T/6} - 1\right) = 5$

$\Rightarrow e^{-T/6} - 1 = -\dfrac{5}{6} \Rightarrow e^{-T/6} = \dfrac{1}{6} \Rightarrow -\dfrac{T}{6} = \ln\left(\dfrac{1}{6}\right) \Rightarrow T = -6\ln\left(\dfrac{1}{6}\right) \approx 10.751$ min

Day 100

1. $1(0.3 + 0.4 + 0.5) = 1.2$

2. $1(0.6 + 0.6 + 0.5 + 0.3) = 2.0$

3. Plot A: $1(0.3 + 0.4 + 0.5 + 0.5 + 0.7 + 0.8 + 0.6 + 0.4) = 4.2$

Plot B: $1(0.2 + 0.2 + 0.3 + 0.5 + 0.6 + 0.6 + 0.5 + 0.3) = 3.0$

Assuming populations were equal at $t = 0$, Plot A is larger after 8 years.

Day 101

1. Using RRAM $\frac{1}{15}\left[3(153) + 3(124) + 3(107) + 3(96) + 3(90)\right] = \frac{1}{5}(570) = 114°F$ or

Using LRAM $\frac{1}{15}\left[3(200) + 3(153) + 3(124) + 3(107) + 3(96)\right] = \frac{1}{5}(680) = 136°F$

You could also use MRAM or Trapezoidal approximation.

2. $\dfrac{90 - 96}{15 - 12} = -2$ or $\dfrac{86 - 90}{18 - 15} = -\dfrac{4}{3}$ or $\dfrac{86 - 96}{18 - 12} = -\dfrac{5}{3}$ degree F/min

Day 102

1. $\displaystyle\int_0^{10} r(t)\,dt = -45\int_0^{10} e^{-t/20}\,dt = 900\int_0^{10} e^{-t/20}\left(-\frac{1}{20}\right)dt$

$\qquad = 900\,e^{-t/20}\Big|_0^{10} = 900e^{-1/2} - 900 \approx -354.122 \text{ in}^3.$

2. $900 - 45\displaystyle\int_0^{30} e^{-t/20}\,dt = 900 + 900\int_0^{30} e^{-t/20}\left(\frac{-1}{20}\right)dt = 900 + 900\left[e^{-t/20}\right]\Big|_0^{30}$

$\qquad = 900 + 900\left[e^{-3/2} - 1\right] \approx 200.817$

3. Volume of a cylinder is $V = \pi r^2 h$, and the radius is constant at $r = 6$, so $V = 36\pi h$.

Differentiate with respect to time. $\dfrac{dV}{dt} = 36\pi\dfrac{dh}{dt}$.

Day 103

Let x be her distance from the lamp, and s the length of her shadow. $\dfrac{s}{s+x} = \dfrac{168}{610}$.

$84x = 221s$, $84\dfrac{dx}{dt} = 221\dfrac{ds}{dt}$, $84(-90) = 221\dfrac{ds}{dt}$, $\dfrac{ds}{dt} \approx -34.21$ cm per second.

Day 104

1. $a(t) = v'(t) = 2t - \cos t$

2. $y(t) = \int v(t)\,dt = \int \left(t^2 - \sin t\right)dt = \dfrac{t^3}{3} + \cos t + C$. At $t = 0$, $0 + \cos 0 + C = 1 + C$, so

$C = 0$, and $y(t) = \dfrac{t^3}{3} + \cos t$.

3. $v(t) = t^2 - \sin t = 0$ when $t^2 = \sin t$, which is when $t = 0$ or $t \approx .8767$. When $t \approx .8767$,

$y \approx \dfrac{(.8767)^3}{3} + \cos(.8767) \approx .864$.

Day 105

1. $4y\dfrac{dy}{dx} - x\dfrac{dy}{dx} - y + 3x^2 = 0$, $\dfrac{dy}{dx}\left(4y - x\right) = y - 3x^2$, $\dfrac{dy}{dx} = \dfrac{y - 3x^2}{4y - x}$

2. At $(-2, 3)$, $\dfrac{dy}{dx} = \dfrac{y - 3x^2}{4y - x} = \dfrac{3 - 12}{12 + 2} = \dfrac{-9}{14}$, so the equation of the tangent line is

$y - 3 = -\dfrac{9}{14}(x + 2)$ or $9x + 14y = 24$.

3. $9(-2.2) + 14k = 24$

$\qquad -19.8 + 14k = 24$

$\qquad\qquad 14k = 43.8$

$\qquad\qquad\quad k \approx 3.129$

Day 106

1. $\int_a^b \left[\left(x^3 + 1 \right) - \left(4x - x^3 \right) \right] dx + \int_b^c \left[\left(4x - x^3 \right) - \left(x^3 + 1 \right) \right] dx$

2. $\pi \int_b^c \left[\left(4x - x^3 \right)^2 - \left(x^3 + 1 \right)^2 \right] dx$

$\approx \pi \int_{0.3}^{1.3} \left[16x^2 - 8x^4 + x^6 - \left(x^6 + 2x^3 + 1 \right) \right] dx$

$\approx \pi \int_{0.3}^{1.3} \left[-8x^4 - 2x^3 + 16x^2 - 1 \right] dx$

$\approx \pi \left[-\frac{8}{5} x^5 - \frac{1}{2} x^4 + \frac{16}{3} x^3 - x \right]_{0.3}^{1.3}$

$\approx \pi \left[3.048595 - (-0.163938) \right] \approx 3.213\pi$

Day 107

1. $V = \frac{1}{3} \pi \cdot r^2 h, \frac{h}{r} = \frac{8}{3}$ thus $r = \frac{3h}{8}$ and

$V = \frac{\pi}{3} \left(\frac{3h}{8} \right)^2 h = \frac{3\pi}{64} h^3.$

2. $V = \frac{3\pi}{64} h^3, \quad \frac{dv}{dt} = \frac{9\pi}{64} (h^2) \frac{dh}{dt}.$

At $h = 6, \quad \frac{dv}{dt} = \frac{9\pi}{64} (36)(5) \approx 79.522$ ft^3/min

3. $V = 100\pi y$, so $\frac{dV}{dt} = 100\pi \frac{dy}{dt}$. $79.523 = 100\pi \frac{dy}{dt}$, so $\frac{dy}{dt} = 0.253$ ft/min

Day 108

1. $h(0) = \int_0^0 f(t) dt = 0, \ h'(1) = f(1) = 2$

2. The function h will be concave upward when $f'(t) > 0$ or when $f(t)$ is increasing. This occurs when $-1 < x < 1$.

3. The point of inflection will occur when the second derivative of h, $f'(t)$, is equal to zero, and h changes from concave upward to concave downward. The point of inflection occurs at $x = 1$. $h(1) = \int_0^1 f(t) dt = \int_0^1 \left(1 + \frac{2t}{t^2 + 1} \right) dt = t + \ln\left(t^2 + 1 \right) \Big|_0^1 = (1 + \ln 2) - \ln 1 = 1 + \ln 2$. The point of inflection is $(1, 1 + \ln 2) \approx (1, 1.693)$.

Day 109

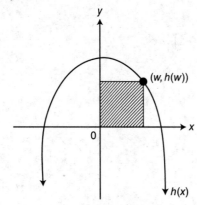

1. $A(w) = w\left(8 - \dfrac{w^4}{2}\right) = 8w - \dfrac{w^5}{2}$

$A'(w) = 8 - \dfrac{5}{2}w^4 = 0 \Rightarrow \dfrac{5}{2}w^4 = 8 \Rightarrow w^4 = \dfrac{16}{5} \Rightarrow w = \dfrac{2}{\sqrt[4]{5}} \approx 1.337.$

$A''(w) = -10w^3$ and $A''(1.337) < 0 \Rightarrow$ maximum.

$h(1.337) = 8 - \dfrac{(1.337)^4}{2} = 8 - \dfrac{16/5}{2} = \dfrac{40 - 8}{5} = \dfrac{32}{5} = 6.4$

$A(1.337) \approx 1.337(6.4) = 8.560$

2. $\displaystyle\int_0^2 \left(8 - \dfrac{x^4}{2}\right)dx = \left[8x - \dfrac{x^5}{10}\right]_0^2 = \left[(16 - 3.2) - (0)\right] = 12.8,\ 12.8 - 8.560 = 4.240$

Day 110

1. $S(t) = Ce^{kt} \Rightarrow 57 = Ce^{k0} \Rightarrow C = 57$

$375 = 57e^{8k} \Rightarrow 6.57895 \approx e^{8k} \Rightarrow \ln(6.57895) = 8k$

$k = \dfrac{\ln(6.57895)}{8} \approx 0.235$

2. Average Price $= \dfrac{1}{8}\displaystyle\int_4^{12} 57e^{0.235t}\, dt$

$= \dfrac{3448.34701}{8} = \$431.04$

Day 111

1. If $y = 1 - bx$ is tangent to the graph of $f(x) = \cos(x) - bx$, $\cos(x) - bx = 1 - bx$, and $f'(x) = -\sin(x) - b = -b$. This occurs when $\cos(x) = 1$ and $\sin(x) = 0$, or when $\cos(x) = 1$, $x = -2\pi, 0, 2\pi$ and when $\sin(x) = 0$, $x = -2\pi, -\pi, 0, \pi, 2\pi$.

Thus, when $\cos(x) = 1$ and $\sin(x) = 0$, $x = -2\pi, 0, 2\pi$.

Day 112

1. $V = \pi \int_0^8 \left(\sqrt[6]{64y} \right)^2 dy = 4\pi \int_0^8 y^{\frac{1}{3}} dy = 4\pi \left[\frac{3}{4} y^{\frac{4}{3}} \right]_0^8 = 3\pi \cdot \left(8^{\frac{4}{3}} \right) = 48\pi \approx 150.796 \text{ ft}^3.$

$W = 35(150.796) \approx 5,277.876 \text{ lb.}$

2. 30 min

3. $V(h) = 4\pi \int_0^h y^{\frac{1}{3}} dy = 3\pi h^{\frac{4}{3}}$

$\dfrac{dV}{dt} = 4\pi h^{\frac{1}{3}} \dfrac{dh}{dt}$

$5 = 4\pi \left(1^{\frac{1}{3}} \right) \dfrac{dh}{dt}$

$\dfrac{dh}{dt} = \dfrac{5}{4\pi} \approx 0.398$

Day 113

1. $f'(4) \approx \dfrac{65 - 73}{6 - 2} \approx \dfrac{-8}{4} \approx -2$

2. $\dfrac{1}{15} \int_0^{15} f(x)\, dx \approx \dfrac{1}{15} \left[\dfrac{1}{2} \big((80+73) \cdot 2 \big) + \dfrac{1}{2} \big((73+65) \cdot 4 \big) + \dfrac{1}{2} \big((65+62) \cdot 4 \big) + \dfrac{1}{2} \big((62+60) \cdot 5 \big) \right]$

$\approx \dfrac{1}{30} \left[\big((153) \cdot 2 \big) + \big((138) \cdot 4 \big) + \big((127) \cdot 4 \big) + \big((122) \cdot 5 \big) \right]$

$\approx \dfrac{1}{30} [306 + 552 + 508 + 610]$

$\approx \dfrac{1}{30} [1976] \approx 65.867$

3. $\int_0^{15} f'(x)\, dx = f(15) - f(0) = 60 - 80 = -20.$ There is a total change of $-20\,°C$ from one end of the wire to the other.

Day 114

The derivative of $y = \dfrac{400x - x^2}{200} = 2x - \dfrac{x^2}{200}$ is $y' = 2 - \dfrac{x}{100}$. The equation of the line

takes the form $y = \left(2 - \dfrac{x}{100} \right) x + 50.$ The intersection of the line and the parabola can

be found by solving $2x - \dfrac{x^2}{200} = \left(2 - \dfrac{x}{100} \right) x + 50.$ $400x - x^2 = 400x - 2x^2 + 10,000,$

gives $x^2 = 10,000$, so $x = 100$ is the x-coordinate of point Q.

Day 115

1. $2x^3 y \dfrac{dy}{dx} + 3x^2 y^2 + 6x^2 y \dfrac{dy}{dx} + 6xy^2 + 2xy \dfrac{dy}{dx} + y^2 = 0$

$2x^3 y \dfrac{dy}{dx} + 6x^2 y \dfrac{dy}{dx} + 2xy \dfrac{dy}{dx} = -\left(3x^2 y^2 + 6xy^2 + y^2\right)$

$\dfrac{dy}{dx} = -\dfrac{3x^2 y^2 + 6xy^2 + y^2}{2x^3 y + 6x^2 y + 2xy} = -\dfrac{y^2\left(3x^2 + 6x + 1\right)}{2xy\left(x^2 + 3x + 1\right)} = -\dfrac{y\left(3x^2 + 6x + 1\right)}{2x\left(x^2 + 3x + 1\right)}$

2. $-y^2 + 3y^2 - y^2 = 2$, $y^2 = 2$, $y = \pm\sqrt{2}$, At $\left(-1, \sqrt{2}\right)$, $\dfrac{dy}{dx} = -\dfrac{\sqrt{2}(3-6+1)}{-2(1-3+1)} = \sqrt{2}$ and

the tangent line is $y - \sqrt{2} = \sqrt{2}(x+1)$. At $\left(-1, -\sqrt{2}\right)$, $\dfrac{dy}{dx} = -\dfrac{-\sqrt{2}(3-6+1)}{-2(1-3+1)} = -\sqrt{2}$

and the tangent line is $y + \sqrt{2} = -\sqrt{2}(x+1)$.

Day 116

1. $v(5) = 3 + 5(5) - (5)^2 = 3 > 0$. At $t = 5$, the particle is moving upward.

2. $v(t) = 3 + 5t - t^2 \Rightarrow a(t) = 5 - 2t \Rightarrow a(5) = 5 - 2(5) = -5 < 0$. The velocity and acceleration have opposite signs at $t = 5$, so the particle is slowing down.

3. $v(t) = 3 + 5t - t^2 \Rightarrow s(t) = 3t + \dfrac{5t^2}{2} - \dfrac{t^3}{3} + C$. If $s(0) = 1$, $s(t) = 3t + \dfrac{5t^2}{2} - \dfrac{t^3}{3} + 1$.

At $t = 6$, $s(6) = 3(6) + \dfrac{5(6)^2}{2} - \dfrac{(6)^3}{3} + 1 = 18 + 90 - 72 + 1 = 37$.

Day 117

1. $\displaystyle\int_0^3 \left(3 - \dfrac{x^3}{9}\right) dx = \left[3x - \dfrac{x^4}{36}\right]_0^3 = 9 - \dfrac{9}{4} = \dfrac{27}{4} = 6.75$

2. $\displaystyle\pi\int_0^3 \left(3^2 - \left(\dfrac{x^3}{9}\right)^2\right) dx = \pi\int_0^3 \left(9 - \dfrac{x^6}{81}\right) dx = \pi\left[9x - \dfrac{x^7}{567}\right]_0^3$

$= \pi\left[27 - \dfrac{27}{7}\right] = \dfrac{162\pi}{7} \approx 72.705$

3. $\displaystyle\pi\int_0^3 \left[\left(k - \dfrac{x^3}{9}\right)^2 - (k-3)^2\right] dx = \dfrac{162\pi}{7}$

Day 118

1. $\int_0^{12} R(t)\,dt \approx 4(17.67 + 17.67 + 15) \approx 4(50.34) \approx 201.36$ Over the 12-hour period, approximately 201.36 gallons of water flowed through the pipe.

2. $\dfrac{1}{12}\displaystyle\int_0^{12}\left(\dfrac{200 + 8t - t^2}{12}\right)dt = \dfrac{1}{144}\left[200t + 4t^2 - \dfrac{t^3}{3}\right]_0^{12}$

$$= \dfrac{1}{144}(2,400 + 576 - 576) = \dfrac{2,400}{144} = 16\dfrac{2}{3} \text{ gallons/hour.}$$

Day 119

1. $y - 1 = 2(x - 0)$

2. $g'(0) = 2f'(0) = 2(2) = 4$, $\ y + 3 = 4(x - 0)$

3. $g'(x) = 6xf(x) + (3x^2 + 2)f'(x) + 2xf''(x)$

$g''(x) = \left[6xf'(x) + 6f(x)\right] + \left[(3x^2 + 2)f''(x) + 6xf'(x)\right] + \left[2xf'''(x) + 2f''(x)\right]$

$g''(x) = 6f(x) + 6xf'(x) + 6xf'(x) + (3x^2 + 2)f''(x) + 2f''(x) + 2xf'''(x)$

$g''(x) = 6f(x) + 12xf'(x) + (3x^2 + 4)f''(x) + 2xf'''(x)$

Day 120

1. $g(1) = \displaystyle\int_0^1 f(t)\,dt = \dfrac{1}{2}(1.5 + 3)(1) = 2.25$, $\ g(-1) = \displaystyle\int_0^{-1} f(t)\,dt = -\dfrac{1}{2}(1.5)(1) = -0.75$

2. Instantaneous rate of change of g, with respect to x, at $x = 3$ is $g'(3) = f(3) = 2$

3. The derivative of g is equal to 0 only at the endpoints of the closed interval $[-1, 4]$. The function g has no turning points on the interval. $g(-1) = -0.75$,

$$g(4) = \int_0^4 f(t)\,dt = \int_0^1 f(t)\,dt + \int_1^4 f(t)\,dt$$

$$= 2.25 + \dfrac{1}{2}(3 + 2)(1) + \dfrac{1}{2}(2 + 2)(1) + \dfrac{1}{2}(2)(1)$$

$$= 2.25 + \dfrac{1}{2}(5 + 4 + 2) = 2.25 + 5.5 = 7.75$$

The minimum value of g is $g(-1) = -0.75$.

Alternatively, $g'(x) = f(x) > 0$ on the open interval $(-1, 4)$. Thus, $g(x)$ is strictly increasing on the interval $[-1, 4]$ and the minimum value of g is $g(-1) = -0.75$.

Day 121

1. If $w = 1$, $P = (1,5)$, $y' = -\dfrac{5}{x^2}\Big|_{x=1} = -5$. The tangent line is $y - 5 = -5(x-1)$ or $y = 10 - 5x$. The x-intercept is $x = 2$.

2. For all w, $P = \left(w, \dfrac{5}{w}\right)$, $y' = -\dfrac{5}{x^2}\Big|_{x=w} = -\dfrac{5}{w^2}$. The tangent line is $y - \dfrac{5}{w} = -\dfrac{5}{w^2}(x - w)$ or $y = \dfrac{10}{w} - \dfrac{5}{w^2}x$. When $y = 0$, $0 = \dfrac{10}{w} - \dfrac{5}{w^2}k$, so $k = \dfrac{10}{w} \cdot \dfrac{w^2}{5} = 2w$.

3. If $k = 2w$, $\dfrac{dk}{dt} = 2\dfrac{dw}{dt} = 2(2) = 4$. Note that k is increasing at a constant rate of 4 units per second for all values of w in the domain.

Day 122

1. $\displaystyle\int_0^3 x^2\,dx = \left[\dfrac{x^3}{3}\right]_0^3 = 9$

2. If $\displaystyle\int_0^k x^2\,dx = \int_k^3 x^2\,dx$, then $\left[\dfrac{x^3}{3}\right]_0^k = \left[\dfrac{x^3}{3}\right]_k^3$ or $\dfrac{k^3}{3} = 9 - \dfrac{k^3}{3}$. Solving $\dfrac{2k^3}{3} = 9$ gives $k^3 = \dfrac{27}{2}$ or $k = \dfrac{3}{\sqrt[3]{2}} \approx 2.381$.

3. $\pi\displaystyle\int_0^3 \left(x^2\right)^2\,dx = \pi\int_0^3 x^4\,dx = \pi\left[\dfrac{x^5}{5}\right]_0^3 = \dfrac{243\pi}{5} = 48.6\pi \approx 152.681$

4. If $\pi\displaystyle\int_0^c x^4\,dx = \pi\int_c^3 x^4\,dx$, then $\dfrac{\pi x^5}{5}\Big|_0^c = \dfrac{\pi x^5}{5}\Big|_c^3$ or $\dfrac{\pi c^5}{5} = \dfrac{243\pi}{5} - \dfrac{\pi c^5}{5}$. Solving $\dfrac{2\pi c^5}{5} = \dfrac{243\pi}{5}$ gives $2c^5 = 243$ or $c = \sqrt[5]{121.5} \approx 2.612$.

Day 123

1. $\displaystyle\lim_{x\to\infty} f(x) = \lim_{x\to\infty}\dfrac{\ln(x)}{x^2} = \lim_{x\to\infty}\dfrac{(1/x)}{2x} = \lim_{x\to\infty}\dfrac{1}{2x^2} = 0$, $\displaystyle\lim_{x\to 0^+} f(x) = \lim_{x\to 0^+}\dfrac{\ln(x)}{x^2} = -\infty$

2. $f'(x) = \dfrac{x^2\left(\frac{1}{x}\right) - 2x\ln(x)}{x^4} = \dfrac{x - 2x\ln(x)}{x^4} = \dfrac{1 - 2\ln(x)}{x^3}$

$\dfrac{1 - 2\ln(x)}{x^3} = 0$

$1 - 2\ln(x) = 0$

$\ln(x) = \dfrac{1}{2}$

$x = \sqrt{e} \approx 1.649$, $f''(x) = \dfrac{6\ln(x) - 5}{x^4}$ and $f''(\sqrt{e}) = -\dfrac{2}{e^2} < 0$.

$f(\sqrt{e}) = \dfrac{\ln(\sqrt{e})}{\sqrt{e}^2} = \dfrac{1/2}{e} = \dfrac{1}{2e} \approx 0.184$, maximum value.

Day 124

1. $a(t) = v'(t) < 0$ when $20 < t < 30$.

2. $\displaystyle\int_0^{30} v(t)\,dt \approx \frac{5}{2}[0 + (2\cdot 10) + (2\cdot 25) + (2\cdot 40) + (2\cdot 60) + (2\cdot 50) + 45]$

$\qquad\qquad \approx \dfrac{5}{2}(20 + 50 + 80 + 120 + 100 + 45)$

$\qquad\qquad \approx \dfrac{5}{2}(415) \approx 1{,}037.5$ feet.

3. $\displaystyle\frac{1}{30-0}\int_0^{30} v(t)\,dt = \frac{1{,}037.5}{30} \approx 34.583$ feet/second.

Day 125

1. At $x = 2$, $\dfrac{dy}{dx} = \dfrac{x - 3x^2}{y} = \dfrac{2 - 12}{2} = -5$. The tangent line is $y - 2 = -5(x - 2)$ or

$y = -5x + 12$. $f(2.1) \approx -5(2.1) + 12 \approx -10.5 + 12 \approx 1.5$

2. $\dfrac{dy}{dx} = \dfrac{x - 3x^2}{y}$ becomes $\displaystyle\int y\,dy = \int (x - 3x^2)\,dx$ or $\dfrac{y^2}{2} = \dfrac{x^2}{2} - x^3 + C$. If $x = 2$

and $y = 2$, $\dfrac{4}{2} = \dfrac{4}{2} - 8 + C$ gives $C = 8$. The equation is $\dfrac{y^2}{2} = \dfrac{x^2}{2} - x^3 + 8$ or

$y^2 = x^2 - 2x^3 + 16$. Or $y = \sqrt{x^2 - 2x^3 + 16}$. Note that $y \neq -\sqrt{x^2 - 2x^3 + 16}$ since the point $(2,2)$ is on the graph.

3. Evaluating $y^2 = x^2 - 2x^3 + 16$ at $x = 2.1$ gives $y^2 = 4.41 - 2(9.261) + 16 = 1.888$ and $y \approx 1.374$.

Day 126

1. Setting the first derivative $F'(t) = \dfrac{2\pi}{3}\cos\left(\dfrac{\pi t}{12}\right) = 0$ and solving gives $t = 6$ and $t = 18$.

Using a second derivative test, $F''(x) = \dfrac{-\pi^2 \sin\left(\frac{\pi x}{12}\right)}{18}$, $F''(6) = -\dfrac{\pi^2}{18}\sin\left(\dfrac{\pi}{2}\right) < 0$,

indicates that at $t = 6$, a maximum, and $F''(18) = -\dfrac{\pi^2}{18}\sin\left(\dfrac{3\pi}{2}\right) > 0$, indicates a minimum at $t = 18$.

2. $\dfrac{1}{18-6}\displaystyle\int_6^{18} 65 + 8\sin\left(\dfrac{\pi t}{12}\right)dt = \dfrac{1}{12}\int_6^{18} 65\,dt + \dfrac{8}{12}\cdot\dfrac{12}{\pi}\int_6^{18} \sin\left(\dfrac{\pi t}{12}\right)\left(\dfrac{\pi}{12}dt\right)$

$\qquad\qquad = \left[\dfrac{65}{12}t - \dfrac{8}{\pi}\cos\left(\dfrac{\pi t}{12}\right)\right]_6^{18}$

$\qquad\qquad = \left(\dfrac{195}{2} - \dfrac{8}{\pi}\cos\left(\dfrac{3\pi}{2}\right)\right) - \left(\dfrac{65}{2} - \dfrac{8}{\pi}\cos\left(\dfrac{\pi}{2}\right)\right)$

$\qquad\qquad = \dfrac{195}{2} - \dfrac{65}{2} = 65$

Day 127

1. $\int_0^{20} v(t)\,dt \approx 4(22+73+112+117+86) \approx 4(410) \approx 1{,}640$. The sled travels a total of 1,640 feet in 20 minutes.

2. $a(t) = v'(t) = 10\cos\left(\dfrac{t}{8}\right) + 5\sin\left(\dfrac{t}{4}\right)$ and $a(16) = 10\cos(2) + 5\sin(4) \approx -7.945$ ft/min^2.

3. $\dfrac{1}{20}\int_0^{20}\left[20 + 80\sin\left(\dfrac{t}{8}\right) - 20\cos\left(\dfrac{t}{4}\right)\right]dt$

$= \dfrac{1}{20}\int_0^{20} 20\,dt + \dfrac{640}{20}\int_0^{20}\left[\sin\left(\dfrac{t}{8}\right)\right]\left(\dfrac{1}{8}dt\right) - \dfrac{80}{20}\int_0^{20}\left[\cos\left(\dfrac{t}{4}\right)\right]\left(\dfrac{1}{4}dt\right)$

$= t\Big|_0^{20} - 32\cos\left(\dfrac{t}{8}\right)\Big|_0^{20} - 4\sin\left(\dfrac{t}{4}\right)\Big|_0^{20}$

$\approx 20 - 32(-1.80114) - 4(-.95892) \approx 81.477$ ft/min

Day 128

1. Relative extrema, or turning points, occur when $f'(x) = 0$. From the graph, $f'(x) = 0$ at the endpoints of the closed interval $[-3, 7]$ and at $x = 2$. At $x = 2$, the derivative changes from positive to negative, so $f(x)$ changes from increasing to decreasing. The graph of f has a relative maximum at $\left(2, \dfrac{13}{3}\right)$.

2. Because the first derivative is equal to zero at $x = 2$, the tangent line is a horizontal line $y = \dfrac{13}{3}$.

3. If $g(x) = x^3 f(x)$, then $g(2) = 8f(2) = 8 \cdot \dfrac{13}{3} = \dfrac{104}{3}$. $g'(x) = x^3 f'(x) + 3x^2 f(x)$, so $g'(2) = 8f'(2) + 3(4)f(2) = 8(0) + 12\left(\dfrac{13}{3}\right) = 52$. The equation of the tangent line is $y - \dfrac{104}{3} = 52(x - 2)$.

Day 129

1. $A(R) = \int_0^3 \left[1 + \sin\left(\frac{\pi x}{2}\right) \right] dx = \int_0^3 [1]\, dx + \frac{2}{\pi} \int_0^3 \left[\sin\left(\frac{\pi x}{2}\right) \right]\left(\frac{\pi}{2}\, dx\right)$

$= x\Big|_0^3 - \frac{2}{\pi} \cos\left(\frac{\pi x}{2}\right)\Big|_0^3 = 3 - \frac{2}{\pi}\left[\cos\left(\frac{3\pi}{2}\right) - \cos(0) \right] = 3 + \frac{2}{\pi} \approx 3.637$

2. Average value $= \frac{1}{3} \int_0^3 \left[1 + \sin\left(\frac{\pi x}{2}\right) \right] dx \approx \frac{1}{3}(3.637) \approx 1.212 \left(\text{Or } 1 + \frac{2}{3\pi} \right)$

3. Volume $= \pi \int_0^3 \left[1 + \sin\left(\frac{\pi x}{2}\right) \right]^2 dx$ or $\pi \int_0^3 \left[1 + 2\sin\left(\frac{\pi x}{2}\right) + \sin^2\left(\frac{\pi x}{2}\right) \right] dx$

Day 130

1. $A = \int_0^2 \left(5 - x^2 - \frac{x}{2} \right) dx = \left[5x - \frac{x^3}{3} - \frac{x^2}{4} \right]\Big|_0^2 = 10 - \frac{8}{3} - 1 = \frac{19}{3}$

2. $y = 5 - x^2 \Rightarrow x = \sqrt{5 - y}$, $y = \frac{x}{2} \Rightarrow x = 2y$.

$V = \pi \int_0^1 (2y)^2\, dy + \pi \int_1^5 \left(\sqrt{5 - y} \right)^2 dy$

$= 4\pi \int_0^1 y^2\, dy + \pi \int_1^5 (5 - y)\, dy = 4\pi \cdot \frac{y^3}{3}\Big|_0^1 + \pi \left(5y - \frac{y^2}{2} \right)\Big|_1^5$

$= \frac{4\pi}{3} + \pi \left[\left(25 - \frac{25}{2} \right) - \left(5 - \frac{1}{2} \right) \right] = \frac{4\pi}{3} + 8\pi = \frac{28\pi}{3} \approx 29.322$

Day 131

Given $x = t^2$ and $y = \frac{1}{3}t^3$, therefore $\frac{dx}{dt} = 2t$ and $\frac{dy}{dt} = t^2$.

And $\frac{dy}{dx} = \dfrac{\frac{dy}{dt}}{\frac{dx}{dt}} = \frac{t^2}{2t} = \frac{t}{2}$ and $\frac{d^2 y}{dx^2} = \dfrac{\frac{dy'}{dt}}{\frac{dx}{dt}} = \frac{\frac{1}{2}}{2t} = \frac{1}{4t}$.

Thus $\left.\dfrac{d^2 y}{dx^2}\right|_{t=1} = \frac{1}{4(1)} = \frac{1}{4}$. Choice (A).

Day 132

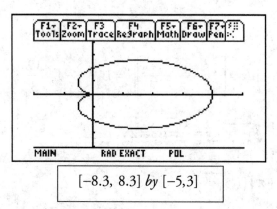

[−8.3, 8.3] *by* [−5,3]

Using the formula $Area = \frac{1}{2}\int_{\alpha}^{\beta} r^2 d\theta$, we have the area of the region in the first quadrant

enclosed by the cardioid $r = 2 + 2\cos\theta$ equals to $Area = \frac{1}{2}\int_{0}^{\frac{\pi}{2}}(2 + 2\cos\theta)^2 d\theta = \frac{3\pi + 8}{2}$.

Choice (A).

Day 133

Using integration by parts, let $u = x$ and $dv = f'(x)dx$. Therefore $du = dx$ and $v = f(x)$.

Applying the formula $\int u\,dv = uv - \int v\,du$, we have $\int x f'(x)dx = xf(x) - \int f(x)dx$.

Substituting the upper and lower limits of x, we have $x f(x)\Big]_1^3 - \int_1^3 f(x)dx$ and that

$\left[(3)f(3) - (1)f(1)\right] - \frac{26}{3}$. Or $\left[(3)(9) - (1)(1)\right] - \frac{26}{3} = \frac{52}{3}$. Choice (A).

Day 134

Write out the first few terms of the series and we have

$$\left(\frac{3}{5}\right)^2 + \left(\frac{3}{5}\right)^3 + \left(\frac{3}{5}\right)^4 + \dots$$

We see that it is a geometric series with $a_1 = \left(\frac{3}{5}\right)^2$ and the ratio $r = \frac{3}{5}$,

and thus $|r| < 1$. Therefore the $sum = \dfrac{a_1}{1-r} = \dfrac{\left(\frac{3}{5}\right)^2}{1-\frac{3}{5}} = \dfrac{9}{10}$. Choice (B).

Day 135

Using the Ratio Test, we have

$$p = \lim_{k \to 0} \left| \frac{x^{(k+1)}}{(k+1)+2} \cdot \frac{k+2}{x^k} \right| = \lim_{k \to 0} \left(\frac{k+2}{k+3} \right) \cdot |x| = |x| \cdot$$

If the series converges, $|x| < 1$, we have $-1 < x < 1$. If $x = 1$, the series becomes

$\displaystyle\sum_{k=0}^{\infty} \frac{1^k}{k+2}$, which is harmonic and it diverges. If $x = -1$, the series is $\displaystyle\sum_{k=0}^{\infty} \frac{(-1)^k}{k+2}$, which

is an alternating harmonic series, and thus converges. Therefore the interval of convergence is $[-1,1)$. Choice (C).

Day 136

Using Integration by Partial Fractions, we have

$$\frac{A}{2x+1} + \frac{B}{x-2} = \frac{-5}{(2x+1)(x-2)} \text{ and } A(x-2) + B(2x+1) = -5. \text{ Set } x = 2$$

and obtain $5B = -5$ or $B = -1$. Set $x = -\dfrac{1}{2}$ and obtain $-\dfrac{5}{2}A = -5$

or A = 2.

$$\int \left(\frac{2}{2x+1} - \frac{1}{x-2} \right) dx = \frac{2\ln|2x+1|}{2} - \ln|x-2| + C = \ln|2x+1| - \ln|x-2| + C.$$

Choice (B).

Day 137

Rewrite $\int 5xe^x\,dx$ as $5\int xe^x\,dx$. Using Integration by Parts, and following

LIPET, we set $u = x$ and $dv = e^x\,dx$ and obtain $du = dx$ and $v = e^x$.

Following $\int u\,dv = uv - \int v\,du$, we have $\int xe^x\,dx = xe^x - \int e^x\,dx = xe^x - e^x + C_1$.

Thus $5\int xe^x\,dx = 5xe^x - 5e^x + C$. Note that if C_1 is an arbitrary constant,

then $5C_1$ is also an arbitrary constant. And in this case, we represented $5C_1$ by C. Choice (D).

Day 138

Differentiating $V(t) = \langle 2t^3, 7t \rangle$, we have $A(t) = \langle 6t^2, 7 \rangle$. At $t = 2$,

$A(2) = \langle 6(2)^2, 7 \rangle = \langle 24, 7 \rangle$. Choice (C).

Day 139

The integral is improper because as $x \to 4^-$, $\dfrac{1}{\sqrt{4-x}} \to \infty$. Rewrite the

integral as $\displaystyle\lim_{l \to 4^-} \int_0^l \frac{dx}{\sqrt{4-x}}$, which is $\displaystyle\lim_{l \to 4^-} \int_0^l (4-x)^{-\frac{1}{2}}\,dx$. Integrating, we have

$\displaystyle\lim_{l \to 4^-}\left[-2(4-x)^{\frac{1}{2}} \right]_0^l$ and thus $\displaystyle\lim_{l \to 4^-}\left[-2(4-l)^{\frac{1}{2}} - \left(-2(4-0)^{\frac{1}{2}} \right) \right]$, which is

$0 + (2(2)) = 4$. Choice (C).

Day 140

The formula for arc length of a parametric curve is $L = \int_a^b \sqrt{\left(\dfrac{dx}{dt}\right)^2 + \left(\dfrac{dy}{dt}\right)^2}\,dt$.

Given $x(t) = 5t + 2$ and $y(t) = 12t - 1$, we

have $\dfrac{dx}{dt} = 5$ and $\dfrac{dy}{dt} = 12$. Therefore

$L = \int_0^3 \sqrt{5^2 + 12^2}\,dt = \int_0^3 13\,dt = 13t \Big]_0^3 = 39$. Choice (B).

Day 141

The Taylor series for $f(x) = x^2 \cos(2x)$ is given as

$$p(x) = f(0) + f'(0)x + \frac{f''(0)}{2!}x^2 + \frac{f'''(0)}{3!}x^3 + \ldots$$

Note that $\cos(x) = 1 - \frac{x^2}{2!} + \frac{x^4}{4!} - \frac{x^6}{6!} + \ldots$ and substituting $2x$ for x,

we have $\cos(2x) = 1 - \frac{(2x)^2}{2!} + \frac{(2x)^4}{4!} - \frac{(2x)^6}{6!} + \ldots$

Multiplying each term of the series by x^2, we have

$$x^2 \cos(2x) = x^2 - \frac{x^2(2x)^2}{2!} + \frac{x^2(2x)^4}{4!} - \frac{x^2(2x)^6}{6!} + \ldots \text{ Simplifying, we have}$$

$$x^2 \cos(2x) = x^2 - \frac{4x^4}{2!} + \frac{16x^6}{4!} - \frac{64x^8}{6!} + \ldots \text{ Choice (D)}.$$

Day 142

Given that $0 \le a_n \le b_n$ for all n, we have $\sum_{n=1}^{\infty} a_n \le \sum_{n=1}^{\infty} b_n$. Therefore

$\sum_{n=1}^{\infty} b_n$ is the "bigger series" and $\sum_{n=1}^{\infty} a_n$ is the "smaller series". Since

the bigger series $\sum_{n=1}^{\infty} b_n$ converges, the smaller series $\sum_{n=1}^{\infty} a_n$ converges.

Choice (C).

Day 143

The *p-series* $\sum_{k=1}^{\infty} \frac{1}{k^p}$ converges if $p > 1$ and diverges if $0 < p \le 1$. Therefore,

the integral $\int_1^{\infty} \frac{1}{x^p} dx$ converges if $p > 1$ and diverges if $0 < p \le 1$. Thus

$\int_1^{\infty} \frac{1}{x^{(2p+3)}} dx$ converges if $2p + 3 > 1$ and diverges if

$0 < (2p+3) \le 1$. Solving for p inequality the in $2p + 3 > 1$, we have

$p > -1$. The integral $\int_1^{\infty} \frac{1}{x^{(2p+3)}} dx$ converges if $p > -1$. Choice (C).

Day 144

Given a function f that is differentiable $n + 1$ times, the nth degree

Taylor polynomial about $x = 0$ for the function is

$$p_n(x) = f(0) + f'(0) + \frac{f''(0)x^2}{2!} + \frac{f'''(0)x^3}{3!} + \ldots + \frac{f^n(0)}{n!}x^n.$$

The coefficient of the x^2 term is $\dfrac{f''(0)}{2!}$ and in this case, the coefficient of

x^2 term is 4. Therefore $\dfrac{f''(0)}{2!} = 4$ or $f''(0) = 8$. Choice (C).

Day 145

Rewrite $\displaystyle\sum_{n=1}^{\infty} \frac{3^{n+2}}{5^n}$ as $\displaystyle\sum_{n=1}^{\infty} \frac{3^2(3^n)}{5^n}$ or $9\displaystyle\sum_{n=1}^{\infty}\left(\frac{3}{5}\right)^n$. Note that $\displaystyle\sum_{n=1}^{\infty}\left(\frac{3}{5}\right)^n$ is an

infinite geometric series with $a_1 = \dfrac{3}{5}$, $r = \dfrac{3}{5}$ and it's $sum = \dfrac{a_1}{1-r}$ or

$sum = \dfrac{\frac{3}{5}}{1-\frac{3}{5}} = \dfrac{3}{2}$. Don't forget the 9. Therefore $\displaystyle\sum_{n=1}^{\infty} \frac{3^{n+2}}{5^n} = 9\left(\frac{3}{2}\right) = \frac{27}{2}$.

Choice (D).

Day 146

The formula for finding the arc length of a curve is $L = \displaystyle\int_a^b \sqrt{1 + \left(\frac{dy}{dx}\right)^2}\, dx$.

Given $y = \dfrac{2}{3}x^{\frac{3}{2}}$, $\dfrac{dy}{dx} = x^{\frac{1}{2}}$ and $\left(\dfrac{dy}{dx}\right)^2 = x$ and $L = \displaystyle\int_0^1 \sqrt{1+x}\, dx$.

Integrating, we have $L = \left[\dfrac{2}{3}(1+x)^{\frac{3}{2}}\right]_0^1 = \dfrac{2}{3}(2)^{\frac{3}{2}} - \dfrac{2}{3} = \dfrac{4\sqrt{2}}{3} - \dfrac{2}{3}$.

Choice (A).

Day 147

The slope of the tangent line is $\dfrac{dy}{dx} = \dfrac{\frac{dy}{dt}}{\frac{dx}{dt}} = \dfrac{8t-2}{2} = 4t-1$, and

at $t = 2$, $\dfrac{dy}{dx} = 7$. Also, at $t = 2$, we have $x = 2(2) + 1 = 5$ and

$y = 4(2)^2 - 2(2) + 3 = 15$. The point of tangency is $(5, 15)$.

Using $y = mx + b$, we have $15 = 7(5) + b$, or $b = -20$ and the equation of

the tangent line is $y = 7x - 20$. Choice (C).

Day 148

By the Divergence Test, $\lim\limits_{k\to\infty} \dfrac{k+2}{k+4} = 1 \neq 0$ and therefore *Series I* diverges.

Using the Limit Comparison, note that $\lim\limits_{k\to\infty} \dfrac{\frac{1}{\sqrt{k^2+1}}}{\frac{1}{\sqrt{k^2}}} = 1$ and that

$\sum\limits_{k=1}^{\infty} \dfrac{1}{\sqrt{k^2}} = \sum\limits_{k=1}^{\infty} \dfrac{1}{k}$ is harmonic and therefore diverges. Thus *Series II*

diverges. For *Series III*, $\lim\limits_{k\to\infty}\left(1+\dfrac{1}{k}\right)^k = e \neq 0$, and by the Divergence Test,

Series III diverges. Choice (D).

Day 149

Starting at point (2,4), $\dfrac{dy}{dx}\bigg|_{(2,4)} = 8$. The equation of the tangent to f

at (2,4) is $y - 4 = 8(x-2)$ or $y = 8x - 12$. Using tangent line

approximation, at $x = 2.5$, we have $y = 8(2.5) - 12 = 8$. and

$\dfrac{dy}{dx}\bigg|_{(2.5,8)} = 2(2.5) + 8 = 13$. The equation of the line passing through the

point (2.5,8) with the slope of 13 is $y - 8 = 13(x - 2.5)$ or $y = 13x - 24.5$.

Using this line, at $x = 3$, $y = 13(3) - 24.5.5 = 14.5$. Choice (B).

Day 150

The position of the moving particle is $x(t) = 2t^2$ and $y(t) = \cos(2t)$.

Differentiating, we have the velocity of the particle as $x'(t) = 4t$ and

$y'(t) = -2\sin(2t)$. Note that *speed* $= |velocity|$, which is the magnitude of

velocity. Therefore, the speed of the particle is $\sqrt{\left(x'(t)\right)^2 + \left(y'(t)\right)^2}$.

Thus the speed at $t = 1$ is $\sqrt{\left(4t\right)^2 + \left(-2\sin(2t)\right)^2}\bigg|_{t=1}$

or 4.394. Choice (A).

Day 151

The *Maclaurin Series* for e^x is $e^x = \sum_{k=0}^{\infty} \frac{x^k}{k!} = 1 + x + \frac{x^2}{2!} + \frac{x^3}{3!} + \frac{x^4}{4!} + \ldots$ Note

that the series $\sum_{x=0}^{\infty} \frac{(\ln 3)^x}{x!} = 1 + \ln 3 + \frac{(\ln 3)^2}{2!} + \frac{(\ln 3)^3}{3!} + \frac{(\ln 3)^4}{4!} + \ldots$

can be obtained by substituting $\ln 3$ for x in the *Maclaurin Series* for e^x.

Thus $e^{(\ln 3)} = 3$. Choice (C).

Day 152

Note that $\sum_{n=1}^{\infty} \left(\frac{5}{\sqrt{x}+1} \right)^n$ is a geometric series with the ratio of $r = \frac{5}{\sqrt{x}+1}$,

$x > 0$. For a geometric series to converge, we must have $|r| < 1$ and in this

case, $\left| \frac{5}{\sqrt{x}+1} \right| < 1$. Since $x > 0$, then $\frac{5}{\sqrt{x}+1}$ is positive, and

$\left| \frac{5}{\sqrt{x}+1} \right| = \frac{5}{\sqrt{x}+1}$. We have $\frac{5}{\sqrt{x}+1} < 1$. Solving the inequality, we have

$5 < \sqrt{x}+1$ and $x > 16$. Choice (D).

Day 153

The velocity of the moving particle is $x'(t) = t^2 - 4t + 3$ and

$y'(t) = t^2 - 3t$. The particle is at rest when $x'(t)$ and $y'(t)$ are both 0.

Setting $x'(t) = 0$, we have $t^2 - 4t + 3 = 0$ or $(t-3)(t-1) = 0$,

and thus $t = 1$ or $t = 3$. Setting $y'(t) = 0$, we have $t^2 - 3t = 0$ or

$t(t-3) = 0$ and thus $t = 0$ or $t = 3$. Note that at $t = 3$, both $x'(t)$ and

$y'(t)$ are zero. Therefore at $t = 3$, the particle is at rest. Choice (C).

Day 154

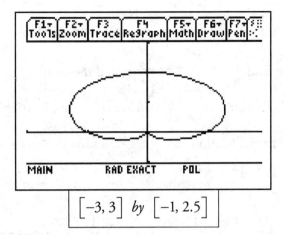

$$\left[-3, 3\right] \ by \ \left[-1, 2.5\right]$$

Given a polar curve $r = f(\theta)$ and $f(\theta)$ is continuous and nonnegative for $\alpha \le \theta \le \beta$, then the area of the region enclosed by the curve $r = f(\theta)$ and the lines $\theta = \alpha$ and $\theta = \beta$ is $A = \dfrac{1}{2}\displaystyle\int_{\alpha}^{\beta} r^2 \, d\theta$. In this case, the area of the region enclosed by the cardioid is $Area = \dfrac{1}{2}\displaystyle\int_{0}^{2\pi} (1 + \sin\theta)^2 d\theta$. Using a calculator, we have the $area = \dfrac{3\pi}{2}$. Choice (A).

Day 155

$$\left[-8.3, 8.3\right] \ by \ \left[-5, 3\right]$$

Area between two Polar Curves: Given $r_1 = f(\theta)$ and $r_2 = g(\theta)$, $0 \le r_1 \le r_2$ and $\alpha \le \theta \le \beta$, the area between r_1 and r_2: $A = \displaystyle\int_{\alpha}^{\beta} \dfrac{1}{2}(r_2)^2 \, d\theta - \displaystyle\int_{\alpha}^{\beta} \dfrac{1}{2}(r_1)^2 \, d\theta$ or $A = \displaystyle\int_{\alpha}^{\beta} \dfrac{1}{2}(r_2)^2 - (r_1)^2 \, d\theta$. In this case, we begin by finding the intersection points of the circle and the cardioid by setting $2 = 2 - 2\sin\theta$ and obtaining $\sin\theta = 0$. Therefore $\theta = 0$, π, and 2π. Using symmetry, the area of the region inside the circle and outside the cardioid is

$area = (2)\left(\dfrac{1}{2}\right)\displaystyle\int_{2}^{\frac{\pi}{2}}\left((2)^2 - (2 - 2\cos\theta)^2\right) d\theta$ or $(8 - \pi)$. Choice (A).

Day 156

Rewrite $\dfrac{1}{n^2+n}$ by using partial fraction decomposition. We have

$\dfrac{1}{n^2+n}=\dfrac{1}{n(n+1)}$ and $\dfrac{A}{n}+\dfrac{B}{n+1}=\dfrac{1}{n(n+1)}$, and therefore

$A(n+1)+B(n)=1$. Letting $n=-1$, we have $B=-1$ and letting $n=0$, we

have $A=1$. The partial fractions are $\dfrac{1}{n}-\dfrac{1}{n+1}$ and

$\displaystyle\sum_{n=1}^{100}\dfrac{1}{n^2+n}=\sum_{n=1}^{100}\left(\dfrac{1}{n}-\dfrac{1}{n+1}\right)$. Note that $\displaystyle\sum_{n=1}^{100}\dfrac{1}{n}=\dfrac{1}{1}+\dfrac{1}{2}+\dfrac{1}{3}+\dfrac{1}{4}...+\dfrac{1}{100}$

and $\displaystyle\sum_{n=1}^{100}\dfrac{1}{n+1}=\dfrac{1}{2}+\dfrac{1}{3}+\dfrac{1}{4}...+\dfrac{1}{100}+\dfrac{1}{101}$, and $\displaystyle\sum_{n=1}^{100}\dfrac{1}{n}-\sum_{n=1}^{100}\dfrac{1}{n+1}=\dfrac{1}{1}-\dfrac{1}{101}=\dfrac{100}{101}$.

Choice (B).

Day 157

The alternating series $\displaystyle\sum_{k=1}^{\infty}\dfrac{(-1)^{k+1}}{k!}=\dfrac{1}{1!}-\dfrac{1}{2!}+\dfrac{1}{3!}-\dfrac{1}{4!}+...$ satisfies the

conditions $a_1\geq a_2\geq a_3\geq...$ and $\displaystyle\lim_{k\to\infty}a_k=0$. Therefore the series converges

and the error for the *nth* partial sum is less than or equal to a_{n+1}. In this

case, $\dfrac{1}{(n+1)!}\leq.01$ or $(n+1)!\geq100$. Note that $4!=24$ and $5!=120$.

Therefore $n+1=5$ or the smallest integer value is $n=4$. Choice (B).

Day 158

Using the Ratio Test, we have $\displaystyle\lim_{k\to\infty}\left|\dfrac{(3x)^{k+1}}{5(k+1)}\cdot\dfrac{5k}{(3x)^k}\right|<1$ which is

$\displaystyle\lim_{k\to\infty}\left|\dfrac{k}{k+1}\cdot3x\right|<1$. Since $\displaystyle\lim_{k\to\infty}\dfrac{k}{k+1}=1$, we have $|3x|<1$ or $-\dfrac{1}{3}<x<\dfrac{1}{3}$

At $x=-\dfrac{1}{3}$, we have $\dfrac{1}{5}\displaystyle\sum_{k=1}^{\infty}\dfrac{(-1)^k}{5k}=\sum_{k=1}^{\infty}\dfrac{(-1)^k}{k}$ and $\displaystyle\sum_{k=1}^{\infty}\dfrac{(-1)^k}{k}$ is an

alternating Harmonic series; it converges. At $x=\dfrac{1}{3}$, we have $\displaystyle\sum_{k=1}^{\infty}\dfrac{1}{5k}$

which is $\dfrac{1}{5}\displaystyle\sum_{k=1}^{\infty}\dfrac{1}{k}$ and $\displaystyle\sum_{k=1}^{\infty}\dfrac{1}{k}$ is the Harmonic series; it diverges.

Thus the interval of convergence of $\displaystyle\sum_{k=1}^{\infty}\dfrac{(3k)^k}{5k}$ is $\left[-\dfrac{1}{3},\dfrac{1}{3}\right)$. Choice (D).

Day 159

The fourth *Maclaurin* polynomial is

$$p_4(x) = f(0) + f'(0)x + \frac{f''(0)}{2!}x^2 + \frac{f'''(0)}{3!}x^3 + \frac{f^4(0)}{4!}x^4. \text{ Begin with } \cos x$$

and that

$$f(0) = \cos(0) = 1$$
$$f'(0) = \sin(0) = 0$$
$$f''(0) = -\cos(0) = -1$$
$$f'''(0) = \sin(0) = 0$$
$$f^4(0) = \cos(0) = 1$$

We have $\cos x \approx 1 - \frac{1}{2}x^2 + \frac{1}{24}x^4$ and thus $\cos(2x) \approx 1 - \frac{1}{2}(2x)^2 + \frac{1}{24}(2x)^4$

or $\cos(2x) \approx 1 - 2x^2 + \frac{2}{3}x^4$. Choice (B).

Day 160

Using the Ratio test for $\sum_{k=1}^{\infty} \frac{k}{3^k}$, we have

$\lim_{k \to \infty} \left(\frac{k+1}{3^{k+1}} \cdot \frac{3^k}{k} \right) = \lim_{k \to \infty} \left(\frac{k+1}{k} \cdot \frac{1}{3} \right) = \frac{1}{3} < 1$. Therefore *series I* converges. For

series II, note that $\sum_{k=1}^{\infty} \frac{1}{k}$ is the Harmonic series and therefore diverges, and

$\sum_{k=1}^{\infty} \frac{1}{4k} = \frac{1}{4}\sum_{k=1}^{\infty} \frac{1}{k}$ also diverges. In addition, $\frac{1}{4k-1} > \frac{1}{4k}$ and $\sum_{k=1}^{\infty} \frac{1}{4k-1}$ is

a bigger series than $\sum_{k=1}^{\infty} \frac{1}{4k}$. Therefore $\sum_{k=1}^{\infty} \frac{1}{4k-1}$, series II, diverges. We

could have also used either the Integral Test or the Limit Comparison Test

for *series II*. Lastly, for *series III*, using the Ratio Test, we have

$\lim_{k \to 0} \frac{(k+1)!}{(k+1)^3} \cdot \frac{k^3}{k!} = \lim_{k \to \infty} \frac{k^3}{(k+1)^2} = \infty$. Thus *series III* diverges. Choice (A).

Day 161

Using the Informal Principle, we delete all terms except the highest powers

in the numerator, and also in the denominator. We have $\displaystyle\sum_{k=1}^{\infty}\frac{5k^3}{k^4}$

or $\displaystyle\sum_{k=1}^{\infty}\frac{5}{k}$. Thus the series $\displaystyle\sum_{k=1}^{\infty}\frac{5}{k}$ behaves like the series $\displaystyle\sum_{k=1}^{\infty}\frac{5k^3-2k+1}{k^4+k^2-3k}$

as k approaches $\pm\infty$. Choice (D).

Day 162

Slope of the tangent line is $\displaystyle\frac{dy}{dx}=\frac{\dfrac{dr}{d\theta}\sin\theta+r\cos\theta}{\dfrac{dr}{d\theta}\cos\theta-r\sin\theta}$.

Given $r=\sin\theta+1$, at $\theta=\dfrac{\pi}{4}$, we have $\dfrac{dr}{d\theta}=\cos\theta\big|_{\theta=\frac{\pi}{4}}=\cos\left(\dfrac{\pi}{4}\right)=\dfrac{\sqrt{2}}{2}$.

Also, note that $\sin\left(\dfrac{\pi}{4}\right)=\dfrac{\sqrt{2}}{2}$ and $r=\sin\left(\dfrac{\pi}{4}\right)+1=\dfrac{\sqrt{2}+2}{2}$.

$$\frac{dy}{dx}\bigg|_{\theta=\frac{\pi}{4}}=\frac{\dfrac{\sqrt{2}}{2}\left(\dfrac{\sqrt{2}}{2}\right)+\left(\dfrac{\sqrt{2}+2}{2}\left(\dfrac{\sqrt{2}}{2}\right)\right)}{\dfrac{\sqrt{2}}{2}\left(\dfrac{\sqrt{2}}{2}\right)-\left(\dfrac{\sqrt{2}+2}{2}\left(\dfrac{\sqrt{2}}{2}\right)\right)}=\frac{2+2+2\sqrt{2}}{2-\left(2-2\sqrt{2}\right)}=\frac{4+2\sqrt{2}}{-2\sqrt{2}}=-1-\sqrt{2}.$$

Alternatively, we could also use the formula $\displaystyle\frac{dy}{dx}=\frac{r+\tan\theta\dfrac{dr}{d\theta}}{-r\tan\theta+\dfrac{dr}{d\theta}}$.

Choice (D).

Day 163

The relative growth rate of P is $\displaystyle\frac{dP}{dt}=\frac{k}{m}(P)(M-P)$. In this case

$\displaystyle\frac{dP}{dt}=0.02P-0.0002P^2$. Factoring out $0.0002P$, $\displaystyle\frac{dP}{dt}=0.0002P(100-P)$.

Rewriting $.0002$ as $\dfrac{0.02}{100}$, we have $\displaystyle\frac{dP}{dt}=\frac{0.02}{100}(P)(100-P)$. Thus

$M=100$ and $k=0.02$. Choice (D).

Day 164

Note That:

Decimal Place Accuracy	Magnitude of the Error is less than
1 decimal place accuracy	$0.05 = 0.5 x 10^{-1}$
2 decimal place accuracy	$0.005 = 0.5 x 10^{-2}$
3 decimal place accuracy	$0.0005 = 0.5 x 10^{-3}$
n decimal place accuracy	$0.5 x 10^{-n}$

Lagrange's form of the remainder is $R_n(x) = \dfrac{f^{(n+1)}(c)}{(n+1)!} x^{(n+1)}$.

Therefore $\sin x = x - \dfrac{x^3}{3!} + 0x^4 + R_4(x)$ and

$|R_4(x)| \le \dfrac{|x|^5}{5!} < \dfrac{(0.1)^5}{5!} = 0.833 x 10^{-7} < 0.5 x 10^{-6}$. Thus 6 decimal place

accuracy is guaranteed. Choice (B).

Day 165

The particle's position function $r(t) = \left(\int (3t^2 + 1) dt \right) i + \left(\int (2t) dt \right) j$

$= (t^3 + t + C_1) i + (t^2 + C_2) j$ and $r(0) = 2i + j = C_1 i + C_2 j$,

obtaining $C_1 = 2$ and $C_2 = 1$. Therefore $r(t) = (t^3 + t + 2) i + (t^2 + 1) j$

is the particle's position function. Choice (D).

Day 166

At the point $(0,1)$, $\dfrac{dy}{dx} = 2(0)(1) = 0$. The equation of the tangent line

at $(0,1)$ is $y - 1 = 0(x - 0)$ or $y = 1$. Using a step size of $\triangle x = 0.5$, we have

the point $(0.5,1)$ and $\dfrac{dy}{dx}\Big|_{(0.5,1)} = 1$. The equation of the line passing through

$(0.5,1)$ with the slope of $m = 1$ is $y - 1 = 1(x - 0.5)$ or $y = x + 0.5$. Using

this line, at $x = 1$, the *y-coordinate* is $y = 1 + 0.5$ or $y = 1.5$.

Choice (C)

Answers

Day 167

Using *Integraton by Partial Fractions*, we have

$$\frac{1}{x^2-4x}=\frac{1}{x(x-4)}=\frac{A}{x}+\frac{B}{x-4}, \text{ which is equivalent to } \frac{A(x-4)+B(x)}{x(x-4)}.$$

Set $A(x-4)+B(x)=1$. At $x=4$, $4B=1$ or $B=\dfrac{1}{4}$,

and at $x=0$, $-4A=1$ or $A=-\dfrac{1}{4}$. Therefore

$$\frac{A}{x}+\frac{B}{x-4}=\frac{-\dfrac{1}{4}}{x}+\frac{\dfrac{1}{4}}{x-4}=-\frac{1}{4}\left(\frac{1}{x}\right)+\frac{1}{4}\left(\frac{1}{x-4}\right) \text{ and}$$

$$\int\frac{1}{x^2-4x}\,dx=\int\left(-\frac{1}{4}\left(\frac{1}{x}\right)+\frac{1}{4}\left(\frac{1}{x-4}\right)\right)dx=-\frac{1}{4}\ln|x|+\frac{1}{4}\ln|x-4|+C.$$

Choice (D).

Day 168

Series I is the alternating harmonic series, $\dfrac{1}{1}-\dfrac{1}{2}+\dfrac{1}{3}-\dfrac{1}{4}+...$, thus

converges. However $\displaystyle\sum_{k=1}^{\infty}\left|\frac{(-1)^{k+1}}{k}\right|=\frac{1}{1}+\frac{1}{2}+\frac{1}{3}+\frac{1}{4}+...$ is the harmonic

series, therefore diverges. *Series I* converges conditionally. *Series II*,
using *Ratio Test* for absolute convergence, and noting that both

$$\left|(-1)^{k+1}\right|=1 \text{ and } \left|(-1)^k\right|=1, \text{ we have } \lim_{k\to\infty}\left|\frac{3^{k+1}}{(k+1)!}\cdot\frac{k!}{3^k}\right|=\lim_{k\to\infty}\left|\frac{3}{k+1}\right|=0<1.$$

Thus *Series II* converges absolutely. *Series III* is an alternating series,

$$-\frac{\ln 3}{3}+\frac{\ln 4}{4}-\frac{\ln 5}{5}+... \text{ with } a_1\geq a_2\geq a_3\geq ... \text{ and } \lim_{k\to\infty}a_k=0. \text{ Therefore}$$

Series III converges by the *Alternating series* test. However

$$\sum_{k=3}^{\infty}\left|\frac{(-1)^k\ln k}{k}\right|=\sum_{k=3}^{\infty}\frac{\ln k}{k} \text{ diverges by the } Integral\ Test, \int_3^{\infty}\frac{\ln x}{x}\,dx \text{ diverges.}$$

Therefore *Series III* converges conditionally. Thus only *Series II*
converges absolutely. Choice (B).

Day 169

Note that $x \neq 1$, because if $x = 1$, $\dfrac{1}{(x-1)^2}$ is undefined.

Rewrite $\displaystyle\int_0^3 \dfrac{1}{(x-1)^2}\,dx$ as $\displaystyle\int_0^1 \dfrac{1}{(x-1)^2}\,dx$ and $\displaystyle\int_1^3 \dfrac{1}{(x-1)^2}\,dx$.

In order for $\displaystyle\int_0^3 \dfrac{1}{(x-1)^2}\,dx$ to converge, both $\displaystyle\int_0^1 \dfrac{1}{(x-1)^2}\,dx$ and $\displaystyle\int_1^3 \dfrac{1}{(x-1)^2}\,dx$

have to converge. We begin with $\displaystyle\int_0^1 \dfrac{1}{(x-1)^2}\,dx$. Integrating, we have

$$\int_0^1 \frac{1}{(x-1)^2}\,dx = \lim_{l \to 1^-} \int_0^l \frac{1}{(x-1)^2}\,dx = \lim_{l \to 1^-}\left[-\frac{1}{(x-1)}\right]_0^l$$

$\displaystyle\lim_{l \to 1^-}\left[-\dfrac{1}{(l-1)} - \left(\dfrac{1}{0-1}\right)\right] = \infty$. Since $\displaystyle\int_0^1 \dfrac{1}{(x-1)^2}\,dx$ is divergent,

$\displaystyle\int_0^3 \dfrac{1}{(x-1)^2}\,dx$ is also divergent. Alternatively, we could examine

$\displaystyle\int_1^3 \dfrac{1}{(x-1)^2}\,dx$ which is also divergent. Choice (D).

Day 170

The relative growth rate of the population P is $\dfrac{dP}{dt} = \dfrac{k}{M}(P)(M-P)$.

Rewrite $\dfrac{20}{P} \cdot \dfrac{dP}{dt} = 1 - \dfrac{P}{200}$ as $\dfrac{dP}{dt} = \dfrac{P}{20}\left(1 - \dfrac{P}{200}\right)$. Factor out $\dfrac{1}{200}$ and

we have $\dfrac{dP}{dt} = \dfrac{P}{20} \cdot \dfrac{1}{200}(200 - P)x$ or $\dfrac{dP}{dt} = \dfrac{0.05}{200}(P)(200 - P)$.

Therefore $M = 200$ *and* $k = 0.05$. Alternatively, we could also use the

formula $\dfrac{dP}{dt} = kP\left(1 - \dfrac{P}{M}\right)$. Choice (D).

Day 171

The length of the curve from $(0,0)$ to $(3,9)$ is either $L = \int_0^3 \sqrt{1 + \left(\dfrac{dy}{dx}\right)^2}\, dx$

or $L = \int_0^9 \sqrt{1 + \left(\dfrac{dx}{dy}\right)^2}\, dy$. Using $L = \int_0^3 \sqrt{1 + \left(\dfrac{dy}{dx}\right)^2}\, dx$, we have $y = x^2$,

$\dfrac{dy}{dx} = 2x$ and $\left(\dfrac{dy}{dx}\right)^2 = 4x^2$ and therefore $L = \int_0^3 \sqrt{1 + 4x^2}\, dx$. Using

$L = \int_0^9 \sqrt{1 + \left(\dfrac{dx}{dy}\right)^2}\, dy$, we solve for x and have $x = \sqrt{y}$, $\dfrac{dx}{dy} = \dfrac{1}{2\sqrt{y}}$

and $\left(\dfrac{dx}{dy}\right)^2 = \dfrac{1}{4y}$ and thus $\int_0^9 \sqrt{1 + \dfrac{1}{4y}}\, dy$. Choice (C).

Day 172

The slope of the tangent line to a polar curve is $\dfrac{dy}{dx} = \dfrac{\dfrac{dr}{d\theta}\sin\theta + r\cos\theta}{\dfrac{dr}{d\theta}\cos\theta - r\sin\theta}$.

In this case, $r = 2\cos\theta$, $\dfrac{dr}{d\theta} = -2\sin\theta$ and

at $\theta = \dfrac{\pi}{4}$, $r = \sqrt{2}$ and $\dfrac{dr}{d\theta} = -\sqrt{2}$. Therefore

$\dfrac{dy}{dx} = \dfrac{(-\sqrt{2})\left(\dfrac{\sqrt{2}}{2}\right) + (\sqrt{2})\left(\dfrac{\sqrt{2}}{2}\right)}{(-\sqrt{2})\left(\dfrac{\sqrt{2}}{2}\right) - (\sqrt{2})\left(\dfrac{\sqrt{2}}{2}\right)} = \dfrac{0}{-2} = 0$. The slope of the tangent line at

$\theta = \dfrac{\pi}{4}$ is 0. Alternatively, we could also use the formula

$\dfrac{dy}{dx} = \dfrac{r + \tan\theta \dfrac{dr}{d\theta}}{-r\tan\theta + \dfrac{dr}{d\theta}}$. Choice (C).

Day 173

Using the *Ratio Test*, we have $\lim\limits_{k \to \infty} \left| \dfrac{a_{k+1}}{a_k} \right| < 1$. In this case, we have

$$\lim_{k \to \infty} \left| \frac{(x-1)^{k+1}}{4^{k+1}\left(3(k+1)+1\right)} \cdot \frac{4^k 3(k+1)}{(x-1)^k} \right| = \lim_{k \to \infty} \left| \frac{(x-1)(3k+1)}{4(3k+4)} \right| = \left| \frac{x-1}{4} \right| < 1.$$

Therefore $|x - 1| < 4$, $-4 < (x - 1) < 4$, or $-3 < x < 5$ and the radius of convergence is 4. Choice (D).

Day 174

Note that $\dfrac{dy}{dx} = \dfrac{\dfrac{dy}{dt}}{\dfrac{dx}{dt}}$. Given $x = \sin t$ and $y = \cos t$,

we have $\dfrac{dx}{dt} = \cos t$, $\dfrac{dy}{dt} = -\sin t$, $\dfrac{dy}{dx} = \dfrac{-\sin t}{\cos t} = -\tan t$. Also

$\dfrac{d^2 y}{dx^2} = \dfrac{dy'}{dx} = \dfrac{\dfrac{dy'}{dt}}{\dfrac{dx}{dt}}$. Note that $\dfrac{dy'}{dt} = -\sec^2 t$. Thus $\dfrac{d^2 y}{dx^2} = \dfrac{\dfrac{dy'}{dt}}{\dfrac{dx}{dt}} = \dfrac{-\sec^2 t}{\cos t}$,

and at $t = \dfrac{\pi}{4}$, we have $\dfrac{-\left(\sqrt{2}\right)^2}{\dfrac{\sqrt{2}}{2}} = \dfrac{-2}{\dfrac{\sqrt{2}}{2}} = \dfrac{-4}{\sqrt{2}} = -2\sqrt{2}$. Choice (B).

Day 175

The arc length of a curve given by parametric equations is

$L = \displaystyle\int_a^b \sqrt{\left(\dfrac{dx}{dt}\right)^2 + \left(\dfrac{dy}{dt}\right)^2}\, dt$. Given $x = \cos t$ and $y = \sin t$, we have

$\dfrac{dx}{dt} = -\sin t$, $\dfrac{dy}{dt} = \cos t$ and

$L = \displaystyle\int_0^{\frac{\pi}{2}} \sqrt{\left(-\sin t\right)^2 + \left(\cos t\right)^2}\, dt = \int_0^{\frac{\pi}{2}} 1\, dt = t\Big]_0^{\frac{\pi}{2}} = \dfrac{\pi}{2}$. Alternatively, the curve

represented by $x = \cos t$ and $y = \sin t$ is a circle with a radius of 1.

Therefore, if $0 \leq t \leq \dfrac{\pi}{2}$, the arc length is $\dfrac{1}{4}$ of the *circumference* $= \dfrac{2\pi}{4} = \dfrac{\pi}{2}$.

Choice (B).

Day 176

Note that:

Decimal Place Accuracy	Magnitude of the Error is less than
1 decimal place accuracy	$0.05 = 0.5x10^{-1}$
2 decimal place accuracy	$0.05 = 0.5x10^{-2}$
3 decimal place accuracy	$0.0005 = 0.5x10^{-3}$
n decimal place accuracy	$0.5x10^{-n}$

The *Maclaurine series* for $\cos x$ is $\cos x = 1 - \dfrac{x^2}{2!} + \dfrac{x^4}{4!} - \dfrac{x^6}{6!} + ...$ and the

Lagrange's form of the remainder is $R_n(x) = \dfrac{f^{(n+1)}(c)}{(n+1)!} \cdot x^{n+1}$. Note that

$-1 \le \cos x \le 1$ and $-1 \le \sin x \le 1$, and therefore $-1 \le f^{(n+1)}(c) \le 1$.

We have $\dfrac{\left(\dfrac{\pi}{6}\right)^{n+1}}{(n+1)!} < 0.5x10^{-2}$. Using trial and error, we have $n = 3$.

Thus $\cos\left(\dfrac{\pi}{6}\right) \approx 1 - \dfrac{x^2}{2!}\bigg|_{x=\frac{\pi}{6}} \approx 0.862922 \approx 0.863$. Choice (C).

Day 177

Note that both $\left|(-1)^{k+1}\right|$ and $\left|(-1)^{k+2}\right|$ are 1.

Using the *Ratio Test* for absolute convergence, we have

$$P = \lim_{k \to \infty} \left| \frac{(x-2)^{k+1}}{(k+1)\left(\ln(k+1)\right)^2} \cdot \frac{k(\ln k)^2}{(x-2)^k} \right| = \lim_{k \to \infty} \left| (x-2)\left(\frac{k}{k+1}\right)\left(\frac{\ln(k)}{\ln(k+1)}\right)^2 \right|.$$

Note that $\lim_{k \to \infty}\left(\dfrac{k}{k+1}\right) = 1$ and $\lim_{k \to \infty} \dfrac{\ln(k)}{\ln(k+1)} = 1$. Therefore

$P = |x-2| < 1$, which yields $-1 < (x-2) < 1$ or $1 < x < 3$.

Therefore the series converges absolutely for $1 < x < 3$. Now testing the endpoints, at $x = 1$, the series becomes

$$\sum_{k=3}^{\infty} \frac{(-1)^{k+1}(-1)^k}{k(\ln k)^2} = \sum_{k=3}^{\infty} \frac{(-1)}{k(\ln k)^2} = -\sum_{k=3}^{\infty} \frac{1}{k(\ln k)^2} \quad \text{which}$$

converges using the *Integral Test*, with $\displaystyle\int_3^{\infty} \frac{-1}{x(\ln x)^2}\, dx$

and by letting $u = \ln x$. At $x = 3$, we have $\displaystyle\sum_{k=3}^{\infty} \frac{(-1)^{k+1}}{k(\ln k)^2}$

which also converges using the *Alternating Series Test*. Thus the interval of convergence is $[1,3]$. Choice (D).

Day 178

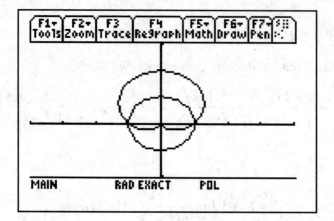

Begin by finding the intersection points of the two curves. Setting $1 + \sin\theta = 1$, we have $\sin\theta = 0$ and $\theta = 0$, π or 2π. The area of the region inside the cardiod and outside the circle is

$\frac{1}{2}\int_0^\pi \left((1+\sin\theta)^2 - (1)^2\right)d\theta$. Enter the integral into a calculator and

obtain $\frac{\pi+8}{4}$ or $\frac{\pi}{4} + 2$. Alternatively, using symmetry, we could find the

area of the region as $(2)\left(\frac{1}{2}\right)\int_0^{\frac{\pi}{2}}(1+\sin\theta)^2 - (1)^2\, d\theta = \frac{\pi}{4} + 2$. Choice (A).

Day 179

Since $\frac{dr}{dt} = \left(t^2 + 6t\right)\boldsymbol{i} + (2t)\boldsymbol{j}$, we have $r(t) = \left(\int \left(t^2 + 6t\right)dt\right)\boldsymbol{i} + \left(\int (2t)\,dt\right)\boldsymbol{j}$

$= \left(\frac{t^3}{3} + 3t + C_1\right)\boldsymbol{i} + \left(t^2 + C_2\right)\boldsymbol{j}$. Also, $r(0) = 2\boldsymbol{i} + \boldsymbol{j}$, we have

$0 + 0 + C_1 = 2$ and $0 + C_2 = 1$. Therefore,

$r(t) = \left(\frac{t^3}{3} + 3t + 2\right)\boldsymbol{i} + \left(t^2 + 1\right)\boldsymbol{j}$. Choice (D).

Day 180

The given series is $x^2 - \dfrac{x^4}{3!} + \dfrac{x^6}{5!} - \dfrac{x^8}{7!} + \ldots$

In Choice (A), $\cos x = 1 - \dfrac{x^2}{2!} + \dfrac{x^4}{4!} - \dfrac{x^6}{6!} + \ldots$ which is not the same.

In Choice (B) $\cos - 1 = -\dfrac{x^2}{2!} + \dfrac{x^4}{4!} - \dfrac{x^6}{6!} + \ldots$ which is also not the same.

In Choice (C) $\sin x = x - \dfrac{x^3}{3!} + \dfrac{x^5}{5!} - \dfrac{x^7}{7!} + \ldots$ and $(\sin x - x) = -\dfrac{x^3}{3!} + \dfrac{x^5}{5!} - \dfrac{x^7}{7!} + \ldots$

which is again not the same.

Lastly, Choice (D), $x \sin x = x\left(x - \dfrac{x^3}{3!} + \dfrac{x^5}{5!} - \dfrac{x^7}{7!} + \ldots \right) = x^2 - \dfrac{x^4}{3!} + \dfrac{x^6}{5!} - \dfrac{x^8}{7!} + \ldots$

which is identical to the given series. Choice (D).

FORMULAS AND THEOREMS

1. Quadratic Formula:

   $ax^2 + bx + c = 0 \ (a \neq 0)$

   $x = \dfrac{-b \pm \sqrt{b^2 - 4ac}}{2a}$

2. Distance Formula:

   $d = \sqrt{(x_2 - x_1)^2 + (y_2 - y_1)^2}$

3. Equation of a Circle:

   $x^2 + y^2 = r^2$ center at $(0, 0)$ and radius $= r$.

4. Equation of an Ellipse:

   $\dfrac{x^2}{a^2} + \dfrac{y^2}{b^2} = 1$ center at $(0, 0)$.

   $\dfrac{(x - h)^2}{a^2} + \dfrac{(y - k)^2}{b^2} = 1$ center at (h, k).

5. Area and Volume Formulas:

FIGURE	AREA FORMULA
Trapezoid	$\dfrac{1}{2}[\text{base}_1 + \text{base}_2]\,(\text{height})$
Parallelogram	(base)(height)
Equilateral triangle	$\dfrac{s^2\sqrt{3}}{4}$
Circle	πr^2 (circumference $= 2\pi r$)

SOLID	VOLUME	SURFACE AREA
Sphere	$\dfrac{4}{3}\pi r^3$	$4\pi r^2$
Right circular cylinder	$\pi r^2 h$	Lateral S.A.: $2\pi r h$ Total S.A.: $2\pi r h + 2\pi r^2$
Right circular cone	$\dfrac{1}{3}\pi r^2 h$	Lateral S.A.: $\pi r \sqrt{r^2 + h^2}$ Total S.A.: $\pi r^2 + \pi r \sqrt{r^2 + h^2}$

6. Special Angles:

ANGLE FUNCTION	0°	$\pi/6$ 30°	$\pi/4$ 45°	$\pi/3$ 60°	$\pi/2$ 90°	π 180°	$3\pi/2$ 270°	2π 360°
Sin	0	1/2	$\sqrt{2}/2$	$\sqrt{3}/2$	1	0	−1	0
Cos	1	$\sqrt{3}/2$	$\sqrt{2}/2$	1/2	0	−1	0	1
Tan	0	$\sqrt{3}/3$	1	$\sqrt{3}$	Undefined	0	Undefined	0

7. Double Angles:

- $\sin 2\theta = 2\sin\theta\cos\theta$
- $\cos 2\theta = \cos^2\theta - \sin^2\theta$ or $1 - 2\sin^2\theta$ or $2\cos^2\theta - 1$.
- $\cos^2\theta = \dfrac{1 + \cos 2\theta}{2}$
- $\sin^2\theta = \dfrac{1 - \cos 2\theta}{2}$

8. Pythagorean Identities:

- $\sin^2\theta + \cos^2\theta = 1$
- $1 + \tan^2\theta = \sec^2\theta$
- $1 + \cot^2\theta = \csc^2\theta$

9. Limits:

$$\lim_{x\to\infty}\frac{1}{x} = 0 \qquad \lim_{x\to 0}\frac{\cos x - 1}{x} = 0$$

$$\lim_{x\to 0}\frac{\sin x}{x} = 1 \qquad \lim_{h\to\infty}\left(1 + \frac{1}{h}\right)^h = e$$

$$\lim_{h\to 0}\frac{e^h - 1}{h} = 1 \qquad \lim_{x\to 0}(1 + x)^{\frac{1}{x}} = e$$

10. *L'Hôpital's* Rule for Indeterminate Forms
Let *lim* represent one of the limits:
$\lim_{x\to c}, \lim_{x\to c^+}, \lim_{x\to c^-}, \lim_{x\to\infty}, \text{ or } \lim_{x\to -\infty}$. Suppose
$f(x)$ and $g(x)$ are differentiable, and $g'(x) \neq 0$
near c, except possibly at c, and suppose
$\lim f(x) = 0$ and $\lim g(x) = 0$, then the
$\lim \dfrac{f(x)}{g(x)}$ is an indeterminate form of the type
$\dfrac{0}{0}$. Also, if $\lim f(x) = \pm\infty$ and
$\lim g(x) = \pm\infty$, then the $\lim \dfrac{f(x)}{g(x)}$ is an
indeterminate form of the type $\dfrac{\infty}{\infty}$. In both
cases, $\dfrac{0}{0}$ and $\dfrac{\infty}{\infty}$, *L'Hôpital's* Rule states that
$\lim \dfrac{f(x)}{g(x)} = \lim \dfrac{f'(x)}{g'(x)}$.

11. Rules of Differentiation:

a. Definition of the Derivative of a Function:

$$f'(x) = \lim_{h\to 0}\frac{f(x+h) - f(x)}{h}$$

b. Power Rule: $\dfrac{d}{dx}(x^n) = nx^{n-1}$

c. Sum & Difference Rules:

$$\frac{d}{dx}(u \pm v) = \frac{du}{dx} \pm \frac{dv}{dx}$$

d. Product Rule:

$$\frac{d}{dx}(uv) = v\frac{du}{dx} + u\frac{dv}{dx}$$

e. Quotient Rule:

$$\frac{d}{dx}\left(\frac{u}{v}\right) = \frac{v\dfrac{du}{dx} - u\dfrac{dv}{dx}}{v^2}, \quad v \neq 0$$

Summary of Sum, Difference, Product, and Quotient Rules:

$$(u \pm v)' = u' \pm v' \qquad (uv)' = u'v + v'u$$

$$\left(\frac{u}{v}\right)' = \frac{u'v - v'u}{v^2}$$

f. Chain Rule:

$$\frac{d}{dx}[f(g(x))] = f'(g(x)) \cdot g'(x)$$

or $\dfrac{dy}{dx} = \dfrac{dy}{du} \cdot \dfrac{du}{dx}$

12. Inverse Function and Derivatives:

$$\left(f^{-1}\right)'(x) = \frac{1}{f'(f^{-1}(x))} \text{ or } \frac{dy}{dx} = \frac{1}{dx/dy}$$

13. Differentiation and Integration Formulas: Integration Rules:

a. $\displaystyle\int f(x)dx = F(x) + C \Rightarrow F'(x) = f(x)$

b. $\displaystyle\int a f(x)dx = a\int f(x)dx$

c. $\displaystyle\int -f(x)dx = -\int f(x)dx$

d. $\int [f(x) \pm g(x)]\, dx$

$\quad = \int f(x)dx \pm \int g(x)dx$

Differentiation Formulas:

a. $\dfrac{d}{dx}(x) = 1$

b. $\dfrac{d}{dx}(ax) = a$

c. $\dfrac{d}{dx}(x^n) = nx^{n-1}$

d. $\dfrac{d}{dx}(\cos x) = -\sin x$

e. $\dfrac{d}{dx}(\sin x) = \cos x$

f. $\dfrac{d}{dx}(\tan x) = \sec^2 x$

g. $\dfrac{d}{dx}(\cot x) = -\csc^2 x$

h. $\dfrac{d}{dx}(\sec x) = \sec x \tan x$

i. $\dfrac{d}{dx}(\csc x) = -\csc x \cot x$

j. $\dfrac{d}{dx}(\ln x) = \dfrac{1}{x}$

k. $\dfrac{d}{dx}(e^x) = e^x$

l. $\dfrac{d}{dx}(a^x) = (\ln a)\, a^x$

m. $\dfrac{d}{dx}\left(\sin^{-1} x\right) = \dfrac{1}{\sqrt{1-x^2}}$

n. $\dfrac{d}{dx}\left(\tan^{-1} x\right) = \dfrac{1}{1+x^2}$

o. $\dfrac{d}{dx}\left(\sec^{-1} x\right) = \dfrac{1}{|x|\sqrt{x^2-1}}$

Integration Formulas:

a. $\int 1\, dx = x + C$

b. $\int a\, dx = ax + C$

c. $\int x^n dx = \dfrac{x^{n+1}}{n+1} + C,\ n \neq -1$

d. $\int \sin x\, dx = -\cos x + C$

e. $\int \cos x\, dx = \sin x + C$

f. $\int \sec^2 x\, dx = \tan x + C$

g. $\int \csc^2 x\, dx = -\cot x + C$

h. $\int \sec x\,(\tan x)\, dx = \sec x + C$

i. $\int \csc x\,(\cot x)\, dx = -\csc x + C$

j. $\int \dfrac{1}{x}\, dx = \ln |x| + C$

k. $\int e^x dx = e^x + C$

l. $\int a^x dx = \dfrac{a^x}{\ln a} + C\ \ a > 0,\ a \neq 1$

m. $\int \dfrac{1}{\sqrt{1-x^2}}\, dx = \sin^{-1} x + C$

n. $\int \dfrac{1}{1+x^2}\, dx = \tan^{-1} x + C$

o. $\int \dfrac{1}{|x|\sqrt{x^2-1}}\, dx = \sec^{-1} x + C$

More Integration Formulas:

a. $\int \tan x\, dx = \ln \left|\sec x\right| + C$ or

$\quad -\ln \left|\cos x\right| + C$

b. $\int \cot x\, dx = \ln \left|\sin x\right| + C$ or

$\quad -\ln \left|\csc x\right| + C$

c. $\int \sec x\, dx = \ln \left|\sec x + \tan x\right| + C$

d. $\int \csc x\, dx = \ln \left|\csc x - \cot x\right| + C$

e. $\int \ln x\, dx = x \ln |x| - x + C$

f. $\int \dfrac{1}{\sqrt{a^2 - x^2}} \, dx = \sin^{-1}\left(\dfrac{x}{a}\right) + C$

g. $\int \dfrac{1}{a^2 + x^2} \, dx = \dfrac{1}{a} \tan^{-1}\left(\dfrac{x}{a}\right) + C$

h. $\int \dfrac{1}{x\sqrt{x^2 - a^2}} \, dx = \dfrac{1}{a}\sec^{-1}\left|\dfrac{x}{a}\right| + C$ or

$\dfrac{1}{a}\cos^{-1}\left|\dfrac{a}{x}\right| + C$

i. $\int \sin^2 x \, dx = \dfrac{x}{2} - \dfrac{\sin(2x)}{4} + C$

Note: $\sin^2 x = \dfrac{1 - \cos 2x}{2}$ and

$\cos^2 x = \dfrac{1 + \cos(2x)}{2}$

Note: After evaluating an integral, always check the result by taking the derivative of the answer (i.e., taking the derivative of the antiderivative).

14. The Fundamental Theorems of Calculus:

$$\int_a^b f(x)dx = F(b) - F(a),$$

where $F'(x) = f(x)$.

If $F(x) = \int_a^x f(t)dt$, then $F'(x) = f(x)$.

15. Trapezoidal Approximation:

$$\int_a^b f(x)dx$$

$$= \dfrac{b-a}{2n}\left[\begin{array}{l} f(x_0) + 2f(x_1) + 2f(x_2)\dots \\ +2f(x_{n-1}) + f(x_n) \end{array}\right]$$

16. Average Value of a Function:

$$f(c) = \dfrac{1}{b-a}\int_a^b f(x)dx$$

17. Mean Value Theorem:

$$f'(c) = \dfrac{f(b) - f(a)}{b - a} \text{ for some } c \text{ in } (a, b).$$

Mean Value Theorem for Integrals:

$$\int_a^b f(x)\,dx = f(c)(b - a) \text{ for some } c$$

in (a, b).

18. Area Bounded by 2 Curves:

$$\text{Area} = \int_{x_1}^{x_2} (f(x) - g(x))dx,$$

where $f(x) \geq g(x)$.

19. Volume of a Solid with Known Cross Section:

$$V = \int_a^b A(x)dx,$$

where $A(x)$ is the cross section.

20. Disc Method:

$$V = \pi \int_a^b (f(x))^2\,dx, \text{ where } f(x) = \text{radius}.$$

21. Using the Washer Method:

$$V = \pi \int_a^b \left((f(x))^2 - (g(x))^2\right)dx,$$

where $f(x) = $ outer radius and

$g(x) = $ inner radius.

22. Distance Traveled Formulas:

• Position Function: $s(t); s(t) = \int v(t)dt$

• Velocity: $v(t) = \dfrac{ds}{dt}; v(t) = \int a(t)dt$

• Acceleration: $a(t) = \dfrac{dv}{dt}$

• Speed: $|v(t)|$

- Displacement from t_1 to $t_2 = \displaystyle\int_{t_1}^{t_2} v\,(t)$

  $= s\,(t_2) - s\,(t_1)$.
- Total Distance Traveled from t_1 to

$$t_2 = \int_{t_1}^{t_2} |v(t)|\,dt.$$

23. **Business Formulas:**

Profit = Revenue – Cost	$P(x) = R(x) - C(x)$
Revenue = (price)(items sold)	$R(x) = px$
Marginal Profit	$P'(x)$
Marginal Revenue	$R'(x)$
Marginal Cost	$C'(x)$

$P'(x)$, $R'(x)$, $C'(x)$ are the instantaneous rates of change of profit, revenue, and cost respectively.

24. **Exponential Growth/Decay Formulas:**

$$\frac{dy}{dt} = ky,\ y > 0 \text{ and } y\,(t) = y_0 e^{kt}.$$

25. **Logistic Growth Models:**

$$\frac{dP}{dt} = kP\left(1 - \frac{P}{M}\right) \quad \text{or}$$

$$\frac{dP}{dt} = \left(\frac{k}{M}\right)(P)(M - P).$$

$$P = \frac{M}{1 + Ae^{-kt}}$$

26. **Integration by Parts:**

$$\int u\,dv = uv - \int v\,du \text{ also written as}$$

$$\int f(x)g'(x)\,dx = f(x)g(x) - \int f'(x)g(x)\,dx$$

Note: When matching u and dv, begin with u and follow the order of the acronym LIPET (Logarithmic, Inverse Trigonometric, Polynomial, Exponential, and Trigonometric functions).

27. **Derivatives of Parametric Functions:**

$$\frac{dy}{dx} = \frac{\dfrac{dy}{dt}}{\dfrac{dx}{dt}},\ \frac{dx}{dt} \neq 0,$$

and

$$\frac{d^2y}{dx^2} = \frac{\dfrac{dy'}{dt}}{\dfrac{dx}{dt}},\ \frac{dx}{dt} \neq 0.$$

28. **Vector Functions:**

Given $\mathbf{r}\,(t) = f\,(t)\,\mathbf{i} + g\,(t)\,\mathbf{j}$:

(a) $\dfrac{d\mathbf{r}}{dt} = \dfrac{df}{dt}\mathbf{i} + \dfrac{dg}{dt}\mathbf{j}$

(b) $\displaystyle\int_a^b \mathbf{r}\,(t)\,dt = \left(\int_a^b f\,(t)\,dt\right)\mathbf{i}$

$$+ \left(\int_a^b g\,(t)\,dt\right)\mathbf{j}$$

29. **Arc Length of a Curve:**

(a) $L = \displaystyle\int_a^b \sqrt{1 + \left(\dfrac{dy}{dx}\right)^2}\,dx,\ y = f(x)$

(b) Parametric Equations:

$$L = \int_a^b \sqrt{\left(\frac{dx}{dt}\right)^2 + \left(\frac{dy}{dt}\right)^2}\,dt,$$

$$x = f\,(t) \text{ and } y = g\,(t)$$

(c) Polar Equations:

$$L = \int_a^b \sqrt{r^2 + \left(\frac{dr}{d\theta}\right)^2}\,d\theta, \quad r = f\,(\theta)$$

30. **Polar Curves:**

(a) Slope of $r = f\,(\theta)$ at (r,θ)

$$\frac{dy}{dx} = \frac{\dfrac{dy}{d\theta}}{\dfrac{dx}{d\theta}} = \frac{f'\,(\theta)\sin\theta + f\,(\theta)\cos\theta}{f'\,(\theta)\cos\theta - f\,(\theta)\sin\theta},$$

$$\frac{dx}{d\theta} \neq 0,$$

or written as $m = \dfrac{r + \tan\theta\,\dfrac{dr}{d\theta}}{-r\tan\theta + \dfrac{dr}{d\theta}}$.

(b) Given $r = f(\theta)$ and $\alpha \le \theta \le \beta$, the area of the region between the curve, the origin, $\theta = \alpha$ and $\theta = \beta$:

$$A = \int_{\alpha}^{\beta} \frac{1}{2} r^2 d\theta \quad \text{or} \quad A = \frac{1}{2} \int_{\alpha}^{\beta} [f(\theta)]^2 d\theta.$$

(c) Area between two Polar Curves:

Given $r_1 = f(\theta)$ and $r_2 = g(\theta)$, $0 \le r_1 \le r_2$ and $\alpha \le \theta \le \beta$, the area between r_1 and r_2:

$$A = \int_{\alpha}^{\beta} \frac{1}{2} (r_2)^2 d\theta - \int_{\alpha}^{\beta} \frac{1}{2} (r_1)^2 d\theta$$

$$= \int_{\alpha}^{\beta} \frac{1}{2} \left((r_2)^2 - (r_1)^2 \right) d\theta.$$

31. Series and Convergence:

(a) Geometric Series:

$$\sum_{k=0}^{\infty} ar^k = a + ar + ar^2 + ar^3 + \cdots$$
$$+ ar^{k-1} \cdots \quad (a \ne 0)$$

if $|r| \ge 1$, series diverges;

if $|r| < 1$, series converges and the

sum $= \dfrac{a}{1-r}$.

(Partial sum of the first n terms:

$S_n = \dfrac{a - ar^n}{1 - r}$ for all geometric series.)

(b) p-Series: $\displaystyle\sum_{k=1}^{\infty} \frac{1}{k^p} = 1 + \frac{1}{2^p} + \frac{1}{3^p} + \frac{1}{4^p} \cdots$

$$+ \frac{1}{k^p} + \cdots$$

if $p > 1$, series converges;

if $0 < p \le 1$, series diverges.

(c) Alternating Series: $\displaystyle\sum_{k=1}^{\infty} (-1)^{k+1} a_k = a_1 -$

$a_2 + a_3 - a_4 + \cdots + (-1)^{k+1} a_k + \cdots$ or

$$\sum_{k=1}^{\infty} (-1)^k a_k = -a_1 + a_2 - a_3 + a_4 -$$

$\cdots + (-1)^k a_k + \cdots$, where $a_k > 0$ for all ks.

Series converges if

(1) $a_1 \ge a_2 \ge a_3 \cdots \ge a_k \ge \cdots$ and

(2) $\displaystyle\lim_{k \to \infty} a_k = 0.$

(Note: Both conditions must be satisfied before the series converges.)

Error Approximation:

If $S = $ *sum of an alternating series*, and $S_n = $ *partial sum of n terms*, then

$$\left| error \right| = |S - S_n| \le a_{n+1}.$$

(d) Harmonic Series:

$$\sum_{k=1}^{\infty} \frac{1}{k} = 1 + \frac{1}{2} + \frac{1}{3} + \frac{1}{4} + \cdots \text{ diverges.}$$

Alternating Harmonic Series:

$$\sum_{k=1}^{\infty} (-1)^{k+1} \frac{1}{k} = 1 - \frac{1}{2} + \frac{1}{3} - \frac{1}{4} + \cdots +$$

$(-1)^{k+1} \dfrac{1}{k} + \cdots$ converges.

$(\displaystyle\sum_{k=1}^{\infty} (-1)^k \frac{1}{k} = -1 + \frac{1}{2} - \frac{1}{3} + \frac{1}{4} -$

$\cdots + (-1)^k \dfrac{1}{k} + \cdots$ also converges.)

32. Convergence Tests for Series:

(a) Divergence Test:

Given a series $\displaystyle\sum_{k=1}^{\infty} a_k$, if $\displaystyle\lim_{k \to \infty} a_k \ne 0$, then the series diverges.

(b) Ratio Test for Absolute Convergence:

Given $\displaystyle\sum_{k=1}^{\infty} a_k$ where $a_k \ne 0$ for all ks and let

$$p = \lim_{k \to \infty} \frac{|a_{k+1}|}{|a_k|}, \text{ then the series } \sum_{k=1}^{\infty} a_k$$

(1) converges absolutely if $p < 1$;

(2) diverges if $p > 1$;

(3) needs more testing if $p = 1$.

(c) Comparison Test:

Given $\displaystyle\sum_{k=1}^{\infty} a_k$ and $\displaystyle\sum_{k=1}^{\infty} b_k$ with

$a_k > 0, b_k > 0$ for all ks, and

$a_1 \le b_1, a_2 \le b_2, \ldots a_k \le b_k$ for all ks:

(1) If $\displaystyle\sum_{k=1}^{\infty} b_k$ converges, then $\displaystyle\sum_{k=1}^{\infty} a_k$ converges.

(Note that if the bigger series converges, then the smaller series converges.)

(2) If $\displaystyle\sum_{k=1}^{\infty} a_k$ diverges, then $\displaystyle\sum_{k=1}^{\infty} b_k$ diverges.

(Note that if the smaller series diverges, then the bigger series diverges.)

(d) Limit Comparison Test:

Given $\displaystyle\sum_{k=1}^{\infty} a_k$ and $\displaystyle\sum_{k=1}^{\infty} b_k$ with

$a_k > 0$, $b_k > 0$ for all ks, and

let $p = \displaystyle\lim_{k \to \infty} \frac{a_k}{b_k}$, if $0 < p < \infty$, then both

series converge or both series diverge.

(e) Integral Test:

Given $\displaystyle\sum_{k=1}^{\infty} a_k$, $a_k > 0$ for all ks, and

$a_k = f(k)$ for some function $f(x)$,

if the function f is positive, continuous,

and decreasing for all $x \geq 1$, then $\displaystyle\sum_{k=1}^{\infty} a_k$

and $\displaystyle\int_{1}^{\infty} f(x)dx$, either both converge or

both diverge.

33. Maclaurin Series:

$$f(x) = \sum_{k=0}^{\infty} \frac{f^{(k)}(0)}{k!} x^k$$

$$= f(0) + f'(0)x + \frac{f''(0)}{2!}x^2$$

$$+ \cdots + \frac{f^{(k)}(0)}{k!}x^k + \cdots$$

$$\sin x = \sum_{k=0}^{\infty} (-1)^k \frac{x^{2k+1}}{(2k+1)!}$$

$$= x - \frac{x^3}{3!} + \frac{x^5}{5!} - \frac{x^7}{7!} + \cdots \quad x \in \mathrm{R}$$

$$\cos x = \sum_{k=0}^{\infty} (-1)^k \frac{x^{2k}}{(2k)!}$$

$$= 1 - \frac{x^2}{2!} + \frac{x^4}{4!} - \frac{x^6}{6!} + \cdots \quad x \in \mathrm{R}$$

$$e^x = \sum_{k=0}^{\infty} \frac{x^k}{k!}$$

$$= 1 + x + \frac{x^2}{2!} + \frac{x^3}{3!} + \frac{x^4}{4!} + \cdots \quad x \in \mathrm{R}$$

$$\frac{1}{1-x} = \sum_{k=0}^{\infty} x^k$$

$$= 1 + x + x^2 + x^3 + \cdots \quad x \in (-1, 1)$$

$$\frac{1}{1+x} = \sum_{k=0}^{\infty} (-1)^k x^k$$

$$= 1 - x + x^2 - x^3 + \cdots + (-1)^k x^k + \cdots$$

$$x \in (-1, 1)$$

$$\ln(1+x) = \sum_{k=0}^{\infty} (-1)^k \frac{x^{k+1}}{k+1}$$

$$= x - \frac{x^2}{2} + \frac{x^3}{3} - \frac{x^4}{4} + \cdots$$

$$x \in (-1, 1]$$

$$\tan^{-1} x = \sum_{k=0}^{\infty} (-1)^k \frac{x^{2k+1}}{2k+1}$$

$$= x - \frac{x^3}{3} + \frac{x^5}{5} - \frac{x^7}{7} + \cdots$$

$$x \in [-1, 1]$$

34. Taylor Series:

$$f(x) = \sum_{k=0}^{\infty} \frac{f^{(k)}(a)}{k!} (x-a)^k$$

$$= f(a) + f'(a)(x-a)$$

$$+ \frac{f''(a)}{2!}(x-a)^2 + \cdots$$

$$+ \frac{f^{(k)}(a)}{k!}(x-a)^k + \cdots$$

Partial Sum:

$$P_n(x) = \sum_{k=0}^{n} \frac{f^{(k)}(a)}{k!}(x-a)^k$$

$$= f(a) + f'(a)(x-a)$$

$$+ \frac{f''(a)}{2!}(x-a)^2 + \cdots$$

$$+ \frac{f^{(n)}(a)}{n!}(x-a)^n$$

$$R_n \,(error\,for\,P_n(x)) = \frac{f^{(n+1)}(c)}{(n+1)!}(x-a)^{n+1} \,, if$$

$x > a, c \in (a, x)$, or if $x < a, c \in (x, a)$, or if $x = a, c = a$.

35. Testing a Power Series for Convergence
Given:

$$\sum_{k=0}^{\infty} c_k(x-a)^k = c_0 + c_1(x-a) + c_2(x-a)^2$$

$$+ \cdots + c_k(x-a)^k + \cdots$$

(1) Use Ratio Test to find values of x for absolute convergence.

(2) Exactly one of the following cases will occur:

  (a) Series converges only at $x = a$.

  (b) Series converges absolutely for all $x \in \mathrm{R}$.

  (c) Series converges on all $x \in (a - R, a + R)$ and diverges for $x < a - R$ or $x > a + R$. At the endpoints $x = a - R$ and $x = a + R$, use an Integral Test, an Alternating Series Test, or a Comparison Test to test for convergence.

Anton, H., Bivens, I., Davis, S. *Calculus*, 7th edition. New York: John Wiley & Sons, 2001.

Apostol, Tom M. *Calculus*. Waltham, MA: Blaisdell Publishing Company, 1967.

Berlinski, David. *A Tour of the Calculus*. Colorado Springs: Vintage, 1997.

Boyer, Carl B. *The History of the Calculus and Its Conceptual Development*. New York: Dover, 1959.

Finney, R., Demana, F. D., Waits, B. K., Kennedy, D. *Calculus Graphical, Numerical, Algebraic*, 3rd edition. Boston: Pearson Prentice Hall, 2002.

Larson, R. E., Hostetler, R. P., Edwards, B. H. *Calculus*, 8th edition. New York: Brooks Cole, 2005.

Leithold, Louis. *The Calculus with Analytic Geometry*, 5th edition. New York: Longman Higher Education, 1986.

Sawyer, W. W. *What Is Calculus About?* Washington, DC: Mathematical Association of America, 1961.

Spivak, Michael. *Calculus*, 4th edition. New York: Publish or Perish, 2008.

Stewart, James. *Calculus*, 4th edition. New York: Brooks/Cole Publishing Company, 1999.

5 Steps to Teaching
AP Calculus BC

TEACHER'S MANUAL

Emily Pillar

AP Calculus Teacher
Schreiber High School, Port Washington, New York

Thanks to Greg Jacobs, an AP Physics teacher at Woodberry Forest School in Virginia, for developing the 5-step approach used in this teaching guide. Thanks also to Courtney Mayer, an AP Environmental Science teacher, for creating a sample teacher's manual that AP teachers could use to create their own guide.

Introduction to the Teacher's Manual

Nowadays, teachers have no shortage of resources for the AP Calculus BC class. No longer limited to just the teacher and the textbook, today's teachers can utilize online simulations, apps, computer-based homework, video lectures, etc. Even the College Board itself provides so much material related to the AP Calculus BC exam that the typical teacher—and student—can easily become overwhelmed by an excess of teaching materials and resources.

One vital resource for you and your class is this book. It explains in straightforward language exactly what a student needs to know for the AP Calculus BC exam. It also provides a complete review for the test including explanatory materials, questions to check student understanding, and test-like practice exams.

This teacher's manual will take you through the 5 steps of teaching AP Calculus BC. These 5 steps are:

1. **Prepare a strategic plan for the course**

2. **Hold an interesting class every day**

3. **Evaluate your students' progress**

4. **Get students ready to take the AP exam**

5. **Become a better teacher every year**

I'll discuss each of these steps, providing suggestions and ideas of things that I use in my class. I present them here because, over the years, I found that *they work*. There are many different course strategies, teaching activities, and evaluation techniques that help students succeed; each teacher must find what works in his/her classroom. But I hope you find in this teacher's manual something that will be useful to you.

STEP 1

Prepare a Strategic Plan for the Course

The Course and Exam Description (CED) from the College Board, which can be found at **https://apcentral.collegeboard.org/courses/ ap-calculus-bc/course**, lays out a suggested scope and sequence for the AP Calculus BC class. The College Board has set it up in a way that topics and skills build as the year goes on. Especially if you are new to the course, I recommend that you follow that scope and sequence.

The chart below shows the units and the time suggested for each unit. The number of class periods is based on a typical 45-minute class. If your school is on a form of block schedule or other atypical schedule, you will need to adjust the pacing to fit your class needs.

TOPICS	PACING	5 STEPS TO A 5
Unit 1: Limits and Continuity	13–14 Class Periods	Chapter 5, pp. 49–74
Unit 2: Differentiation: Definition and Fundamental Basic Derivative Rules	9–10 Class Periods	Chapter 6, pp. 75–80
Unit 3: Differentiation: Composite, Implicit, and Inverse Functions	8–9 Class Periods	Chapter 6, pp. 81–102
Unit 4: Contextual Applications of Differentiation	6–7 Class Periods	Chapter 8, pp. 149–154, Chapter 9, pp. 174–189
Unit 5: Analytical Applications of Differentiation	10–11 Class Periods	Chapter 7, pp. 103–127, Chapter 8, pp. 155–173
Unit 6: Integration and Accumulation of Change	15–16 Class Periods	Chapter 10–12, pp. 207–266
Unit 7: Differential Equations	9–10 Class Periods	Chapter 13, pp. 319–345
Unit 8: Applications of Integration	13–14 Class Periods	Chapter 12–13, pp. 267–318
Unit 9: Parametric Equations, Polar Coordinates, and Vector-Valued Functions	10–11 Class Periods	Chapter 7, pp. 128–148, Chapter 9, pp. 190–206
Unit 10: Infinite Sequences and Series	17–18 Class Periods	Chapter 14, pp. 346–370

After you have taught the course a few times and feel comfortable with the material, you may want to move topics and units around to better meet your classroom needs. While the overall units should be primarily taught in the sequence outlined by the College Board, there is some flexibility with Units 6–10, as well as some sub-topics in Units 4, 5, 8, and 10.

For example, there is flexibility in the order in which you teach derivative rules; below is the order that I have found works for me. It allows me to have students derive derivative rules based on prior knowledge from this sequence. The order is as follows:

Derivatives:

▶ Power Rule

▶ Constant, Sum, Difference, Constant Multiple

▶ Product Rule

▶ Quotient Rule

▶ High-Order Derivatives

▶ Trigonometry Derivatives

▶ Chain Rule

▶ Exponential and Logarithmic Derivatives

▶ Implicit Differentiation

▶ Differentiating Inverse Functions

▶ Differentiating Inverse Trigonometry Functions

After derivative rules, I teach applications of derivatives, including particle motion and related rates. I suggest waiting to teach linearization until after Unit 5, so students can also analyze if the approximation is an over or underestimate.

There is also flexibility in integrals. Unit 7 is a shorter, stand-alone unit, so you can choose to teach it after Unit 8. I have found that within Unit 8 (especially 8.2 and 8.3) there are some great areas for AP review and practice. There are plenty of past free-response questions that can serve as a mid-year cumulative review.

The topic of evaluating improper integrals, while listed in Unit 6, is better taught with Taylor Series to start off the Infinite Sequences and Series unit. Furthermore, Units 9 and 10 can be taught in the reverse order. There is some flexibility with the order of Unit 10.

As you plan your year, make sure to leave plenty of time for review. It is important to give students practice with actual AP exam questions and call upon them to synthesize material from the entire year. I like to leave 2–3 weeks of dedicated review time just before the test.

STEP 2

Hold an Interesting Class Every Day

AP Calculus students should love coming to your class. Why? Because you should offer many opportunities and strategies to help students understand the material and internalize what they learn. I follow the same schedule daily but with different activities to keep it interesting.

▶ **Challenge Question.** Each day in class, students walk in to a "Challenge Question" on the board. They are each given a very small slip of paper, on which they must write their solution. I collect this paper and take a quick look at each to get a fast assessment of where students stand on a particular topic that will feed into that day's lesson. While this activity only takes five minutes, it allows me the opportunity to focus on either a pre-calculus, algebra, or calculus skill required for that lesson. If you have the Elite Edition of the *5 Steps to a 5: AP Calculus BC*, the "5 Minutes to a 5" section at the end provides great questions for these challenge questions.

The breakdown of the questions by units is provided in a chart in this guide.

▶ **Homework Presentation.** I assign homework each night to students, which includes a short problem set focusing on material from that lesson; it can include a worksheet, problems from the *5 Steps to a 5*, or free-response questions from the AP Classroom. I pick three of the most important or challenging problems and assign them to three different students. The next day in class, these students are asked to present their solutions to the class. They are responsible for answering questions from their peers regarding their work. I have found that this affords students the opportunity to get another level of understanding of the material when asked to present and explain to their peers.

▶ **Flipped Classroom.** A flipped classroom can be a great way to change things up. There are many excellent videos available online, including those from Khan Academy and AP Classroom. You can assign a video that teaches the topic and then have students work on practice problems in class. This allows you to spend class time correcting any misconceptions and assisting students with the more challenging AP problems.

▶ **Creative Problem Sets.** There are various ways to shake up problem sets for class time. You can try these different ways of presenting and completing problems, including:

▶ **Calculus maze:** Students answer a question and must search for the answer to find which problem to complete next.

Ans: $-3\sin 3x$ # ____1____ Find $f''(x) \cdot f(x) = 3x^3 + 2x^2 + x$	Ans: $-\dfrac{\sin x + y}{x}$ # _____ Find $f'(x) \cdot f(x) = \dfrac{4}{x^3}$
Ans: $-\dfrac{12}{x^4}$ # _____ Find $\dfrac{dy}{dx} \cdot y = \cos 3x$	Ans: $18x + 4$ # _____ Find $\dfrac{dy}{dx} \cdot xy = \cos x$

▶ **I Have, Who Has? game:** A class activity in which each student has a function and a derivative, for example. The first person reads his/her function out loud and the person with that function's derivative says the derivative out loud and then asks for the derivative of their function; this continues until you return to the first person.

Student A Example: I have: $\dfrac{2x}{x^2 + 7}$ Who has? $\dfrac{d}{dx}(e^{x^2})$	Student B Example: I have: $2xe^{x^2}$ Who has? $\dfrac{d}{dx}(\cos(3x^2 - 4))$

▶ **Pair and share activity:** Students are grouped in pairs. Within the pair, one student completes column A and one student column B of a worksheet. Each column, while providing different questions, has the same answers for corresponding questions. After completing the problems, pairs work together to discuss and check answers.

Column A	Column B
Evaluate the definite integral. $\int_{-1}^{3} (-x^3 + 3x^2 + 1)\,dx$	Evaluate the definite integral. $\int_{-1}^{0} 12x^2(3x^3 + 3)^2\,dx$

The rigor of the AP exam can be of a different level than prior math classes. Having students work together, whether in groups or partners, will help them capitalize on their strengths. I have found that at this level students really can find their strengths, be it algebra skills, applying the rules of calculus, or understanding modeling/applied problems. Thoughtfully grouping students and having them work together allows each student to bring something to the table as this course is a synthesis of material from their entire high school career.

If you have a classroom set of the *5 Steps to a 5: AP Calculus BC*, you can assign your students homework of reading a few pages of the book that correlates to the topics you are teaching next. You can also assign them the review questions at the end of each chapter as homework. The book covers each unit and topic in the CED and all the review questions are aligned to the math practices. This book is also available online; follow the instructions on the back cover of this book to access the Cross-Platform Edition.

Additionally, *5 Steps to a 5: AP Calculus BC* provides Cumulative Review problems at the end of each section. You can assign these problems for homework occasionally to spiral prior material. This book provides solutions to these problems, so you can efficiently have students check homework prior to class and come in only with questions.

---

5 Steps to a 5 AP Calculus BC: Elite Edition

The Elite Edition provides additional questions that can be used in your class. It contains 180 activities and questions that require five minutes a day. While they are primarily intended to be used by students studying for the test, you can use these as daily warm-ups in your course. To do this, you will need the table below that organizes these questions and activities by unit since they do not follow the course in chronological order.

UNIT	Questions/Activities in the Elite Edition
Unit 1: Limits and Continuity	1–11
Unit 2: Differentiation: Definition and Basic Derivative Rules	12–14, 111, 114
Unit 3: Differentiation: Composite, Implicit, and Inverse Functions	15–23, 41–42, 105, 115, 119
Unit 4: Contextual Applications of Differentiation	34–36, 40, 43–49, 103, 107, 121, 123
Unit 5: Analytical Applications of Differentiation	24–33, 37–39, 50, 63, 95–96, 109, 128
Unit 6: Integration and Accumulation of Change	51–62, 64, 66–75, 77–79, 100, 108, 118, 120, 133, 136–137, 139, 167, 169
Unit 7: Differential Equations	89–91, 125, 149, 163, 166, 170
Unit 8: Applications of Integration	65, 76, 80–88, 92–94, 97–99, 101–102, 104, 106, 110, 112–113, 116–117, 122, 124, 126–127, 129–130, 146, 171
Unit 9: Parametric Equations, Polar Coordinates, and Vector-Valued Functions	131–132, 138, 140, 147, 150, 153–155, 162, 165, 172, 174–175, 178–179
Unit 10: Infinite Sequences and Series	134–135, 141–145, 148, 151–152, 156–161, 164, 168, 173, 176–177, 180

STEP 3

Evaluate Your Students' Progress

I assess progress on the majority of the AP topics with larger unit exams. I recommend incorporating released questions from the College Board (found on AP Classroom) on these exams. While you may incorporate questions from other sources such as your textbook or from *5 Steps to a 5: AP Calculus BC*, it is important to expose students to the rigor and style of AP questions throughout the year. You may select questions on AP Classroom by filtering by unit, subtopic, questions-type (multiple choice or free response), and calculator/non-calculator.

I use a variety of multiple-choice AP questions on my exam and adapt some free-response questions (FRQs) to include as well. FRQs may be difficult to include in the fall semester, as many questions include topics from various units, but once I get to derivative applications I have found these questions to be appropriate. Whether they are AP level or not, I make sure that each exam has both multiple-choice and free-response questions.

If I include a free-response question on my exam, I allow students to leave their answers in non-simplified form to practice for the AP exam. When students do calculator-active free-response questions, they must have the answer correct to three decimal places, like the AP exam. I encourage students to truncate answers at four decimal places so they don't make a rounding error. Let students focus on the calculus and eliminate any chance for an algebra mistake!

On the first two units, students are not allowed to use a calculator. Remember, the AP exam is two-thirds non-calculator, so it is important for students to limit dependency on their calculators. Once I introduce calculator-active topics and questions, in Unit 4: Contextual Applications of Differentiation, I give both calculator and non-calculator sections for exams. Students are given both sections at the beginning of the exam and are only able to take out their calculators once they hand in the non-calculator section. Printing one of the sections on colored paper allows for an easier monitoring process.

AP Classroom is a valuable resource, allowing to students to practice with released AP questions from previous exams. Just before the unit exam, I give an AP Classroom assignment of multiple-choice questions that covers all the topics for that exam. These assignments are due the day of the test and graded on a curve, as the AP will be. The assignments give students a chance to practice with the AP-style questions and rigor, as well as review for the upcoming exam.

#FlashBackFriday. On select Fridays I give students a #FBF quiz. This is a short quiz focused on algebra and pre-calculus material that is essential for success on the AP exam. I review the topic for 5–10 minutes in a previous class or give students notes and/or example problems on the topic. Each quiz is no more than 10 minutes and forces students to refresh these imperative skills.

Some topics for the quiz include:

- Factoring
- Simplifying rational functions
- Domain and range
- Graphs of natural log and exponential functions
- The unit circle and exact trig values
- Reciprocal trigonometric functions
- Inverse trigonometric functions
- Evaluating and manipulating functions with fractional and negative exponents
- Long division with polynomials

STEP 4

Get Students Ready to Take the AP Exam

I leave two or three weeks to dedicate to review for the exam in class. By this point, we have covered all units in the curriculum, and take time just to synthesize the material and practice with exam questions. The best way for students to succeed on the AP exam is exposure to real AP questions and *practice, practice, practice*. I consider this to be the most important unit of the year. I love to get students to buy in at the end of their senior year with a team challenge I call it "Review-O-Mania."

For my review unit, I place students in heterogeneous groups of three (or four) students.

The teams cooperatively compete against one another. Each team earns points each class, as delineated below. Each member of the first-place team wins all the pride and glory that comes with being the review-o-mania champion, points on their final, and lunch with me! The challenge is outlined in an introduction sheet I give my students; this handout is attached at the end of this teacher's manual.

I give students a schedule in advance with all assignments and due dates listed. Each assignment is typically 15–25 multiple-choice questions or 3–4 free response questions.

Schedule

Assign. #	Assignment	Due Date	Completed?	Questions?

I have found that offering students the opportunity to grade their own work, or their peer's work on free-response questions is very valuable. I have done this in various ways, but one way is to give a group quiz of one AP free-response question in class. I then have groups exchange papers and have them grade their peer's based on the AP rubric provided by the College

Board. Having students work with the rubric allows them to become familiar with how they can earn points on the exam.

I provide my students a list of tips for succeeding on the AP exam during the review unit. A sample of this list is also provided at the end of this teacher's manual.

STEP 5

Become a Better Teacher Every Year

A good AP teacher tries to do better, regardless of how they measure success. If there is anything that didn't work as well as you had hoped this year, there's always next year to try something different. The message is the same whether you are a novice AP teacher or a veteran: Your goal is to become a better teacher every year.

My advice for a teacher new to AP Calculus would be to focus on the content and let go of the nuances of the test. It is challenging to teach a rigorous course for the first time, sprinkle in interesting activities, and prepare for the "tricks" of the AP. There are a ton of resources out there, but focus on two or three. After you have conquered the first year, start adding activities, maybe one unit at a time. Finally, the most important task for a teacher new to AP Calculus is practice AP problems yourself! My first year, in preparation for my review unit, I did about a decade's worth of free-response questions. You will start to notice patterns.

Be reflective. After a unit is complete, assess what your students understood and what you need to change. Each year I typically change sequence a bit, or focus on different aspects of each unit. For example, following the 2020–2021 school year, I found students had weak pre-calculus skills, so I integrated more limits and pre-calculus topics throughout my lessons and units.

It is difficult to judge your success as a teacher solely based on AP scores. Each year, your group of students comes to class with different backgrounds. Their math courses prior to AP Calculus offered different areas of focus and, with the ever-changing curriculum, their strengths and weaknesses will vary from year to year.

Prior to reviewing for the AP exam, I ask students to be honest about their goals for the exam. You can use these goals to help motivate students when they need it, as well as to assess your success in helping students achieve their goals once scores are in. My goal each year is a combination of affording every student the opportunity to "pass" the exam, aiding students in obtaining their goals, and pushing students to aim high and work hard to achieve what they set out for themselves.

A "passing" score on the AP exam is considered a 3 or better. This means students have understood the material at a college level. Most colleges and universities will accept this score and give college credit for Calculus 2, depending on the student's score breakdown. Students may then choose to place into Calculus 3 or simply not have to take Calculus 2 again. Students who score a 2 on the exam, while not earning credit for the course, will be very prepared to take Calculus 2 in college and can use this background knowledge to succeed. As teachers, all we can do is offer our students the best chance to earn what they are capable of achieving and then celebrate in that achievement with them, be it a 2 or a 5! Remember, all students who take the BC exam receive a sub-score for the AB exam as well, so while students may not earn credit for AP Calculus BC (Calculus II), they may receive credit for AP Calculus AB (Calculus I) with their AB sub-score.

For all AP teachers, both new and experienced, the best thing you can do to improve is to use the Instructional Planning Report that you receive after student scores are calculated. You can access this document in the AP Classroom. You will get a breakdown of scores by unit, by question type, etc. With this information, you can to adjust your course for the next school year. If you notice that students as a whole struggled with a particular unit, this is where you make changes. Perhaps you spend a little extra time on this unit or maybe you spiral questions from that unit into later units throughout the year. Maybe you review this unit in class before next year's AP exam. If students did better on either multiple choice or free response, you can choose to focus more on the question type they found challenging. With reflection and analysis of the Instructional Planning Report, you can adjust your class effectively.

Another great way to learn new teaching tips and tactics is to attend an AP Summer Institute. Both new and experienced teachers can gain ideas and insights into the course and the AP exam. If you take more than one institute over the course of your career, make sure to attend courses from different instructors. Check with peers on some of the respected instructors in your area.

Additionally, you can see if a local school hosts a symposium after the exam. In my area, a local high school holds a short meeting following the exam each year to discuss the free-response questions. Different teachers present each one of the six free-response questions. It is a great way to converse with other teachers about their experience teaching the course that year, chat about their assessment of the questions from the exam, and discuss how the exam informs any changes to their focus in class for the next year.

Finally, another great way to gain insight into the exam is to become an AP reader for the exam. After three years of teaching the course, you may apply. Grading the exam is one of the best ways to truly understand student errors, misconceptions, and how the exam is graded. You can apply online through the College Board website.

Additional Resources for Teachers

COLLEGE BOARD

Make sure to always use the College Board's CED for the course that is found at https://apcentral.collegeboard.org/courses/ap-calculus-bc/course. If the topic is in the CED, it will be on the AP test. If the topic is not in the CED, it is out of the scope for the course and will not be tested.

In addition, the College Board has created AP Curriculum Modules. These include: Volumes of Solid of Revolution, Extrema, Motion, Reasoning from Tabular Data, Fundamental Theorem of Calculus, and Functions Defined by Integrals. The College Board also has available some "Special Focus Material" on the following topics: Approximation, The Fundamental Theorem of Calculus, and Differential Equations.

https://apcentral.collegeboard.org/courses/ap-calculus-ab/classroom-resources?course=ap-calculus-bc

WEBSITES

Some of these might be good to use with students and others are good for you as the teacher as a reference.

Khan Academy: AP Calculus BC
Provides videos and practice problems
https://www.khanacademy.org/math/ap-calculus-bc

PATRICK JMT

Provides videos for calculus topics (and beyond)

▶ First-Semester Videos: Limits, Continuity, and Derivatives:
https://www.youtube.com/playlist?list=PL58C7BA6C14FD8F48

- ▸ Second-Semester Videos: Integration
  https://www.youtube.com/
  playlist?list=PLD371506BCA23A437

- ▸ Third-Semester Videos: Multivariable
  Calculus
  https://www.youtube.com/
  watch?v=odhAVmAahb4&list=PLF83D74
  BA4DE75897

MATHISPOWER4U VIDEOS

Provides videos for various topics
http://www.mathispower4u.com/calculus.php

CALCULUS MAXIMUS

Provides notes, worksheets, and solutions broken
down by topic
http://www.korpisworld.com/Mathematics/
Calculus%20Maximus/Calculus%20
Maximus%20Splash.htm

PAUL'S ONLINE NOTES

Includes notes (very helpful for a first-time
teacher), practice problems with solutions, and
problems for assignments
https://tutorial.math.lamar.edu/Classes/CalcII/
CalcII.aspx

FLIPPED MATH CALCULUS

Provides video lessons, including practice
problems and answers
https://calculus.flippedmath.com/

Review-O-Mania

How Do I Earn Points?

Homework:

▸ Multiple Choice (complete and on time) 4 points

▸ Free Response (complete and on time) 4 points

Classwork

▸ Presentations of a problem/explanation to the class: 2 points

Attendance

▸ Class attendance (all members of group present) 1 point/group

▸ Attendance of a review session 4 points/person

Quizzes

▸ Points vary depending on quiz (group and individual quizzes)

Further Explanation

Homework: Each multiple-choice homework assignment is worth four points for your team. *You are expected to come in with work corrected and highlight questions you still need clarification on.* All assignments must be completed on time to receive credit.

Classwork: If you are on a team where a teammate got a question wrong and you got it right, it is your duty to explain that question thoroughly. Each member should be able to explain a question they once got wrong after a teammate explains it to him/her, unless all team members got it wrong.

Participation: Any problems that an entire team needs clarification on will be put up on the board by a representative from another team.

This representative must rotate each time that team takes a turn and we will make sure all teams are given an equal chance of putting up a problem. The entire team will earn two team points for their board work and possible explanation.

Attendance: Each group will receive one point per class if every member of the group is in attendance. Missing class for another AP exam is excused.

Quizzes: There will be a few short quizzes that students will complete in groups and individually.

How is the winning team decided upon?

The winning team is the team with the greatest number of points. You will get a group grade that counts towards your quarter average.

How will this affect my average?

You will also get an individual score based on homework completion/participation.

Can I really pass the AP exam?!

Yes! You have been practicing all year with AP-style questions on your exams, without a curve! The AP exam is curved and, with effort, your goals are attainable. Practice, practice practice. Want to estimate your score on a practice exam?… go to **http://appass.com/calculators/calculusab** to calculate your score out of 5.

This is the final stretch. Work hard and cooperatively with your team! Let's get ready to derive…and integrate! (crowd goes wild)

Tips for Success on the AP Calculus Exam

Multiple Choice

1. Answer EVERY question—there is no penalty for a wrong answer. If you are running out of time and have some questions blank, just guess! Points are not deducted for incorrect answers.

2. Some multiple-choice questions can be answered by working backwards. Plug the answer choices into the problem and see which answer works out.

3. If you do not find your solution as one of the choices, plug in a number to your answer and to all choices to see if it appears in a different form.

4. Don't rush through the test, but be mindful of timing. Work slowly enough so that you don't make careless mistakes on the easier questions. Easy questions count the same as difficult ones. Yet don't take too much time on very difficult questions. Skip them and come back.

5. Know your trig value of special angles, especially sin and cos of 0, 30, 45, 60, 90, 180, and 270 (and in radians) and $\text{Tan}^{-1}(1) = 45°$.

Free Response

1. Free-response questions must be correct to three decimal places. Show four places to ensure you don't make a rounding error! And don't round until the end of the problem. Don't forget units.

2. Show ALL WORK on free-response questions, even if you are using your calculator. You must show the integral or derivative you are taking.

3. Don't waste time simplifying answers. It's OK to leave $\dfrac{93}{6}$, cos 30, ln 1, or $e^{\ln 2}$.

4. When questions say justify your answer, you must explain with a sentence or two. A graph or picture or arrows on a number line are not counted as a justification.

5. Don't use words like "it"; specifically refer to the function, e.g., $f(x)$, $f'(x)$, $f''(x)$, $g(x)$, etc.

6. If you change your mind about an answer, cross it our lightly. *Do not waste time erasing*.

7. Never let the beginning of a problem keep you from the points at the end. You can often answer (b) or (c) parts of a problem without even doing part (a).